HUMAN INTIMACY:
MARRIAGE, THE FAMILY, AND ITS MEANING

HUMAN INTIMACY:
MARRIAGE, THE FAMILY, AND ITS MEANING

THIRD EDITION

Frank D. Cox
Santa Barbara City College

WEST PUBLISHING COMPANY
St. Paul   New York   Los Angeles   San Francisco

Copy editing: Jerilyn Emori
Design: Janet Bollow
Illustrations: Brenda Booth, John Foster, Sue Sellars
Production Coordination: Janet Bollow Associates
Composition: Hansen & Associates Graphics
Cover photo: B. Carter, © 1980 The Image Bank West

Library of Congress Cataloging in Publication Data

Cox, Frank D.
  Human intimacy.

  Bibliography: p.
  Includes index.
  1. Family—United States.   2. Marriage—United
States.   3. Sex customs—United States.   I. Title.
HQ536.C759 1984   306.8'0973   83–21822
ISBN 0–314–77872–1

Acknowledgements

Page 19 From *Marriage and Alternatives: Exploring Intimate Relationships* by Roger W. Libby and Robert N. Whitehurst. Copyright © 1977 by Scott, Foresman & Co. Reprinted by permission.

Pages 33–35 Ruth Sidel, *Families of Fensheng: Urban Life in China*. (New York: Penguin Books, 1974). Copyright © Ruth Sidel, 1974. Reprinted by permission of Penguin Books.

Page 39 From *Marriage: East & West* by David and Vera Mace. Copyright © 1959, 1960 by David and Vera Mace. Reprinted by permission of Doubleday & Co. Inc.

Page 42 "Love Birds" by Cynthia Moorman. Reprinted by permission of Cynthia Moorman, Santa Monica, California.

Page 47 © 1983 Ann Landers and Field Newspaper Syndicate.

Page 50 © 1975 United Features Syndicate, Inc.

Page 59 Dennis the Menace® used by permission of Hank Ketchum and © Field Enterprises Inc.

Page 64 © 1975 by Jules Feiffer. Reprinted by permission.

Pages 64–71 "The Love Research." Copyright © 1977 Human Behavior Magazine. Reprinted by permission.

Pages 52–55 Adaptation of Chapter 5, "The Six Basic Styles of Loving" by Marcia Lasswell and Norman Lobsenz. Copyright © 1980. Reprinted by permission of Doubleday and Co. Inc.

Page 87 © 1977 United Press Syndicate.

Pages 142–143 © 1969 Claude Steiner.

Page 150 From Richard Hunt and Edward Rydman, *Creative Marriage*. (Boston: Holbrook Press, 1976) pp. 50–51.

Page 158 Reproduced by permission from *Beyond Sex Roles*, edited by Alice G. Sargent, from *Man/Woman Dynamics: Some Typical Communication Patterns* by Carol Pierce and Janice Sanfaco. Copyright © 1977, West Publishing Co. All rights reserved.

Pages 155–156 Reprinted by permission of William Morrow and Co., Inc. From *The Intimate Enemy* by Dr. George R. Bach and Peter Wyden. Copyright © 1968 by George R. Bach and Peter Wyden. Also reprinted by permission of Dr. George Bach, Distinguished Professor of Psychology, Professional School of Humanities, San Diego, California.

Pages 174–175 Disguised case history from the files of CALM as written by Enid L. Pike, first executive director.

Page 178 Copyright © 1948 by Cole Porter. Copyright renewed, assigned to John F. Wharton, trustee of the Cole Porter Musical and Literary Property Trusts, Chappell & Co., Inc., owner of publication and allied rights. International copyright secured. *All Rights Reserved.* Used by permission.

Page 178 Copyright © 1956 by Alan Jay Lerner and Frederick Loewe, Chappell & Co., Inc., publisher and owner of allied rights throughout the world. International copyright secured. *All rights reserved.* Used by permission.

Pages 184–185 From *Human Sexuality*, a title in the Human Behavior Series by John Gagon and Bruce Henderson and the editors of Time-Life Books, 1975.

Page 191 Reprinted by permission of *The Village Voice.* Copyright © The Village Voice, Inc., 1971.

Page 196 Reprinted by permission of *People Weekly*, copyright Time Inc., July, 1982.

Page 204 Copyright 1979 by *Newsweek*, Inc. All rights reserved. Reprinted by permission.

Page 205 Reprinted by permission from *Time*, The Weekly Newsmagazine. Copyright Time Inc., August, 1982.

Page 212 © 1983 United Press Syndicate.

Page 218–221 Reprinted with permission from *Newsweek*, May, 1981.

Page 239 Reprinted with permission from the September

(continued following Subject Index)

CONTENTS IN BRIEF

CONTENTS

Chapter 3   American Dating and Mate Selection   73

Chapter 4   Marriage, Intimacy, Expectations, and the Fully Functioning Person

Chapter 5   Communication in Intimate Relationships   145

Chapter 6   People Liberation:
Changing Masculine and Feminine Roles   177

Chapter 7   The Family as an Economic System   223

Chapter 10   Family Planning   333

Chapter 13   Family Life Stages: Midlife Crises to Surviving Spouses   447

Chapter 14   The Dissolution of Marriage   475

Chapter 15   Remarriage: A Growing Way of American Life   509

Chapter 16   Actively Seeking Marital Growth and Fulfillment   527

PREFACE

Continuing editions of a textbook are always exciting for an author. First, they mean that the book has been well enough received that new editions are warranted. Second, they mean that the author has a great deal of new input coming from the many people who have used the book. With such input a new edition cannot help but be improved. Third, in a field as complex and rapidly changing as marriage and the family, the need to update is perhaps more pressing than in many other fields. And last, the writer can rethink his or her basic assumptions and the writing that has gone before. It is hoped that such rethinking leads to a better textbook—more up to date, thorough, interesting, readable, and above all more exciting.

Human Intimacy: Marriage, the Family and Its Meaning was written to stimulate thinking about the meaning and function of marriage and family in American life and, in particular, in the reader's own personal life. Criticizing marriage and the family has always been popular and easy. Yet despite this, marriage and the family remain a prominent and important part of the American scene. Most of us grow up in families, and 95 percent of us will be a marriage partner at some time in our lives. This high percentage places America among the most marrying nations in the world. I believe that the family is functioning better than doomsday critics would have us believe and that intimacy is still most often found within the family setting.

It is difficult for the newly married to concentrate on improving the marital relationship. Yet a marriage does not naturally take care of itself, nor will "love" alone make a marriage successful. After all, most people who have divorced married their former spouse out of "love." What happened? Why didn't their relationship work?

Human Intimacy stresses the point that every person does have the ability to improve his or her intimate relationships. Marriages tend to get into trouble because people believe that they cannot do much about their marriage and because many of us are unwilling to take time to nourish and enrich our intimate relationships.

In *Human Intimacy* I take a positive view of the potentials inherent in the marital relationship and throughout the book emphasize how those potentials may be actualized. In addition the book examines and discusses the entire field of family life in a positive and constructive manner.

One advantage of American society is the wide spectrum of choice it offers individuals in most aspects of life. Although family patterns have been somewhat limited in the past, a wider variety of intimate lifestyles is becoming acceptable. For example, the loosening of traditional sex roles allows individuals greater freedom to adapt marriage to their own liking, to make their intimate relationships more unique and vital. Marriage is now seen to involve personal satisfaction rather than just the proper fulfillment of duties and specific roles. However, greater freedom of choice also means the freedom to err; hence becoming knowledgeable about marriage and the family is even more important today if faulty decisions are to be avoided.

It is my hope that *Human Intimacy* will contribute to your ability to make intelligent, satisfying choices about intimate relationships. Individuals who are able to make satisfying choices in their lives are most apt to be fulfilled persons. And fulfilled persons have the best chance of making their marital relationships exciting and growth producing.

Human Intimacy remains a positive statement about marriage and the family. It realistically reflects the place of marriage and the family in today's American society. More important, it tries to offer hope for tomorrow's family by emphasizing what the family ideally can become as well as what it currently is. The beauty of the institution called family is that it is adaptable and flexible. Those persons with knowledge of themselves, the family, and their culture have the opportunity in America to build a marriage and a family that will suit their own liking. Families can change for the better; intimate relationships can become more deeply satisfying and fulfilling. It is with these ends in mind that *Human Intimacy* was written.

This book has several features designed to aid your reading. First, each chapter is preceded by a comprehensive outline that gives an overview of the material to follow. The outline also serves as a excellent study guide and tool of review.

Second, "Insets" supply interesting detail, allow hypothesizing, and present controversy. They also add variety to the reading much as an aside adds variety to a lecture.

Because the field of marriage and family is fraught with controversy and divergent opinions, "Scenes from Marriage" appear at the end of each chapter. These are essentially condensed excerpts and discussions from other sources that add new dimensions and/or conflicting viewpoints to each chapter.

To add life and realism, many case studies are scattered throughout the book. They highlight the principles being discussed and help one to see how a principle might be applied in everyday life. Most of the cases are composites, built on real life experiences shared by my students over the years.

Several major changes have been made in this third edition. First, the chapter on alternatives to marriage has been deleted as a separate chapter because some of the much-publicized alternatives of the past decade have faded from view. Communes and group marriage, for example, have mostly disappeared from the popular press and interest among Americans has wanned. On the other hand, some of the alternatives, such as cohabitation, have become so much more accepted, for better and worse, among Americans that they no longer seem as much an alternative as part of the ongoing process. Thus, where appropriate, the material in the old chapter on alternatives has been deleted or placed in other, more appropriate chapters.

The chapter on sex roles, "People Liberation," has been moved back in the book next to the chapters on working and family economics. This was done because the changes in sex roles seem to be making the greatest impact in this area of family life.

A series of appendixes have been added for reader reference. Some of this material has appeared within the appropriate chapter in earlier editions, although much of it is new to this edition. The rationale for placing it in an appendix can best be seen in the tables that list marriage and divorce requirements by state. Each table covers all fifty states; yet a given reader is usually interested only in one state, the state in which he or she resides. Thus all of the material in the table is important; yet only a fraction of the material will be used by any one reader. The information, by being placed in appendix form, does not clutter up a chapter; yet each reader has quick access to material of interest.

It goes without saying that the whole book has been updated, and much new material has been added throughout.

As with all such undertakings, many more people than myself have contributed to *Human Intimacy*. The most important contributors are the many family members with whom I have interacted all my life. Grandparents, parents, aunts, uncles, cousins, siblings, and, of course, my immediate family—Pamela, Randy, and Michelle. In addition are the many fine researchers and writers who have influenced and contributed to my thoughts. And then there are the important contributions of the direct reviewers of the previous edition, without whom *Human Intimacy* could not exist. To them I wish to extend a special thanks.

Marilyn T. Hagans, Champlain College

Wilma Beavers, Cameron University

James M. Henslin, Southern Illinois University at Edwardsville

Arlene Chandler, Cuesta College

Dixie Dickinson, Tidewater Community College

Barbara Lindemann, Santa Barbara City College

Henry Bagish, Santa Barbara City College

John Bowman, Santa Barbara City College

Although *Human Intimacy* has my name on it, the actual production of the book rests with Janet Bollow, the designer, the wonderful editorial staff at West Publishing, and above all those oft-forgotten production people at West Publishing who turn the final copy into a beautiful book and place it in the hands of the many teachers and students who use it. Please know that I always am grateful for your fine work and consider *Human Intimacy* to be *our* book, not my book.

Frank D. Cox

THE ELOQUENT STORY OF LIFE IN ANCIENT SYMBOLS

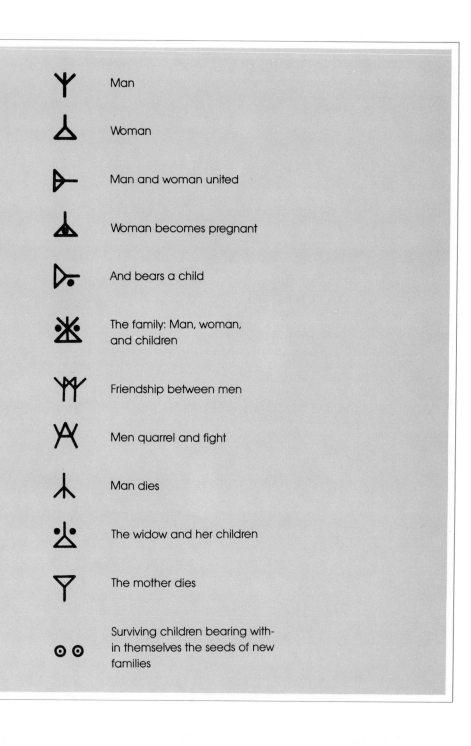

Man

Woman

Man and woman united

Woman becomes pregnant

And bears a child

The family: Man, woman, and children

Friendship between men

Men quarrel and fight

Man dies

The widow and her children

The mother dies

Surviving children bearing within themselves the seeds of new families

CHAPTER 1

HUMAN INTIMACY: THE FAMILY AND ITS MEANING

CONTENTS

1

What an exciting — and essential — field of study: intimate relationships. Communicating and caring. Boyfriend/girlfriend. Husband/wife.
Parent/child. Grandmother/grandfather. Grandparent/grandchild. Family,
friends. The relationships that give meaning to life; the relationships that
give us a sense of identity, of well-being, of security, of being needed. The
relationships that ward off loneliness and insecurity. The relationships
that allow us to love and be loved. Without human intimacy where would
the human being be? Perhaps the *human* part of ''human being'' would
disappear and we'd all simply ''be'' — automatons similar to our home
computers, able to solve problems but lacking in those markedly human
qualities of loving, caring, and feeling compassion. In a word, those
characteristics that allow human beings to become intimate.

Can we study ''intimacy''? We can, if we study relationships that can
and often should be intimate. Within marriage and the family is where
we most often find intimacy. Thus to study the family is also to study
intimacy.

The study of the family deals with many topics, as the table of contents
of this book reflects. It is clear that such study cuts across many disciplines: psychology, sociology, anthropology, and so on (see Figure 1-1). To
identify the study of marriage and family more clearly, we will use the
term *famology* suggested by Wesley Burr (Burr & Leigh, 1982).

FIGURE 1-1 Famology in-
volves the study of many
disciplines.

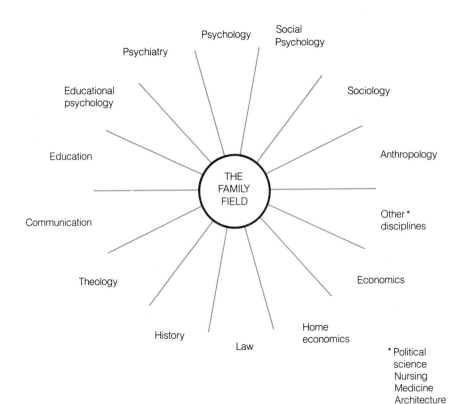

Because each of us is born into a family (the family of orientation) and 95 percent (U.S. Bureau of the Census, May 1982) of us establish a family (the family of procreation) at some time in our lives, we usually have strong feelings about marriage, families, love, and intimacy. Such feelings are natural. Yet we must examine our feelings about such an intimate topic in order to understand just how the American family might affect us personally. Thus to study the research data on marriage and the family is also to study one's own feelings about the institutions. A piece of data may appear simple and clear (one in two American marriages will break up), yet its meaning will vary with the individual according to his or her own feelings. This is why there appears to be so little agreement about how marriages and families are changing and what the changes mean. We each interpret the data in a personal manner based on our own experience.

Lest one take this to mean that there are *only* personal opinions about the family institution, let me hasten to add that there is, indeed, a broad and rich foundation of scientific information about this most personal and intimate of relationships. Persons who acquaint themselves with this information are in a better position to understand their own feelings about marriage and family. Those who understand both the scientific information and their own feelings are in the best position to build intimate relationships that are successful and satisfying. It is towards this end that this book has been written.

The Basic Assumptions

As we mentioned, all people, lay and professional alike, hold certain beliefs about marriage and the family, and this includes authors. Because these beliefs color an author's writing, it is important to recognize and make clear just what they are. Let me state clearly the major assumptions on which this book is based; the remainder of Chapter 1 will be organized around them. The discussion of each assumption in this first chapter is of necessity short and cursory. Therefore when appropriate, I have listed the chapter or chapters within the text where additional information can be found.

Each assumption is supported with some facts that also serve to introduce many of the basic statistics about American families. Remember, an assumption is a belief that may or may not be well supported by facts. Although the various assumptions are supported with some facts, acceptance is left to the reader's discretion.

The American Family: Many Structures and Much Change

Assumption 1:   *A free and creative society is one that offers many structural forms by which family functions, such as childrearing, may be fulfilled (Chapters 4, 8, and 15).*

Nuclear family
A married couple and their children living by themselves

Mom and Dad, Sissy and Junior, a dog, and maybe a cat represent the stereotypical American **nuclear family**. Yet to talk of the American family perpetuates the myth that one family structure represents *the* American family. If we examine the structural form of the family, we find that there are, in fact, many kinds of American families.

For example, the single-parent family, usually a mother and her children, has been one of the fastest-growing family structures during the past decade. In 1981 single-parent families accounted for 21 percent of the 31.6 million families with children, in contrast to 1970 when they accounted for only 11 percent. During this period the number of families that included children under eighteen years of age increased by 2.7 million. During the same time span, however, the number of two-parent families declined by 606,000, while the number of one-parent families increased by 3.4 million (U.S. Bureau of the Census, May 1982).

It is true that single-parent families tend to be temporary, but the fact is that this family structure accounts for a significant number of American families. The large increase can be accounted for by the greatly increased divorce rate in America. To a lesser extent the greater social acceptance of the unwed mother who keeps her child has also contributed to the increasing number of single-parent families.

Reconstituted family
A husband and wife, at least one of whom has been married before, and one or more children from previous marriage(s)

Divorce is a good example of changing family structure within a single family. The family begins as a nuclear family, becomes a single-parent family, and then, in most cases, becomes a **reconstituted family** when

FIGURE 1-2 Types of households in the United States. (Source: U.S. Bureau of the Census. *Current Population Reports*, Series P-20, No. 381. Household and family characteristics: March 1982. U.S. Government Printing Office, Washington, D.C., May 1983, p. 3.)

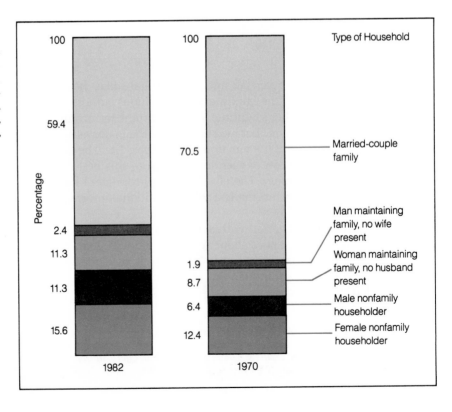

the single parent remarries. These kinds of changes signal the end of the initial relationship, at least as an intimate love relationship.

However, a relationship that remains intimate also changes structure over time. Such a relationship usually begins as a couple relationship, then broadens to include children and finally sons- and daughters-in-law and grandchildren. And when the children leave home, the couple returns to a two-person household once more. Table 1-1, Different Family Structures, gives an idea of the many structural forms that families take.

The 1970s were a period when Americans experimented widely with different family structures. In fact, a popular cliché was that marriage, as we had known it, was dead. Communal living (Scenes from Marriage, p. 31), multiple sex partners, cohabitation, childlessness, and other family experiments blossomed and were quickly reported and dramatized in the mass media. Some experiments, such as cohabitation, have become for some Americans a relatively permanent family structure. Other experiments, such as **swinging**, have withered and lost much of their appeal.

The criticism of the family and the experimentation of the 1970s were thought by many Americans to be new. Yet throughout the twentieth century there have been continued criticisms of marriage and the family. Suggestions for "new" family forms have always been made by critics of the status quo. For example, in 1936 Bertrand Russell saw marriage collapsing as a social institution unless drastic changes were made:

Swinging
Agreement by married couples to swap mates sexually

> In the meantime, if marriage and paternity are to survive as social institutions, some compromise is necessary between complete promiscuity and lifelong monogamy. Although it is difficult to decide the best compromise at a given time, certain points seem clear:
>
> Young unmarried people should have considerable freedom as long as children are avoided so that they may better distinguish between mere physical attraction and the sort of congeniality that is necessary to make marriage a success.
>
> Divorce should be possible without blame to either party and should not be regarded as in any way disgraceful.
>
> Everything possible should be done to free sexual relations from economic taint. At present, wives, just as much as prostitutes, live by the sale of their sexual charms: and even in temporary free relations the man is usually expected to bear all the joint expenses. The result is that there is a sordid entanglement of money with sex, and that a woman's motives not infrequently have a mercenary element. A woman, like a man, should have to work for a living, and an idle wife is no more intrinsically worthy of respect than a gigolo. (Reprinted in 1957, pp. 171 – 72)

Perhaps the major contribution of the turmoil of the 1960s and 1970s for the family was broadening the available alternatives for intimacy. If a couple decides not to have children, that is all right; divorce doesn't mean the end of the world; a cohabitation experience does not make one unmarriable.

Modern America is remarkably permissive toward and accepting of multiple forms of intimate relationships. Other cultures have had different marital systems, but they have usually disallowed deviance from the system chosen at a given historical time. A free and creative society,

TABLE 1-1 Different Family Structures

KIND	COMPOSITION	FUNCTIONS
TYPES OF MARRIAGE		
Monogamy	One spouse and children	Procreative, affectional, economic consumption
Serial monogamy	One spouse at a time but several different spouses over time. Married, divorced, re-married	Same
Common-law	One spouse. Live together as husband and wife for long enough period that state recognizes couple as married without formal or legal marriage ceremony. Recognized by only a few states	Same
Polygamy	Multiple spouses	Same
Polygyny	One husband, multiple wives	Any, power vested in male
Polyandry	One wife, multiple husbands	Any
Group	Two or more men collectively married to two or more women at the same time	Any. Very rare
TYPES OF FAMILIES		
Nuclear family	Husband, wife, children	Procreative, affectional, economic consumption
Extended family	One or more nuclear families plus other family positions such as grandparents, uncles, etc.	Historically might serve all social, educational, economic, reproductive, affectional, and religious functions as in precommunist China
Composite family	Two or more nuclear families sharing a common spouse	Normally those of the nuclear family
Tribal family	Many families living together as a larger clan or tribe	Usually those of the extended family
Consensual family (cohabitation)	Man, woman, and children living together in legally unrecognized relationship	Any
Commune	Group of people living together sharing a common purpose with assigned roles and responsibilities normally associated with the nuclear family	Can provide all functions with leadership vested in an individual, council, or some other organized form to which all families are beholden
Single-parent family	Usually a mother and child. Father/child combination less common (about 10% of American single-parent families)	Same as monogamy without a legally recognized reproductive function
Concubine	Extra female sexual partner recognized as a member of the household but without full status	Usually limited to sex and reproduction
Reconstituted (blended)	Husband and wife, at least one of whom has been previously married, plus one or more children from previous marriage or marriages	Any
AUTHORITY PATTERNS		
Paternalistic	Any power vested in male	Any
Maternalistic	Any power vested in female	Any
Egalitarian	Powers divided in some fair manner between spouses	Any

however, will offer many structural forms of the family by which its functions, such as childrearing and meeting sexual needs, may be fulfilled. The reasons for America's permissiveness are partly philosophic but mainly economic. For example, as Russell pointed out, "Wives, just as much as prostitutes, live by the sale of their sexual charms." Marriage forms historically have been limited because women have been economically tied to the men who support them and the family.

With industrialization and affluence it becomes more possible to consider alternate lifestyles and marital forms. For example, affluence allows more people to further their education and thus be exposed to new ideas and knowledge. Affluence also brings mobility and mobility brings contact with new people and new lifestyles, often without the constraint of immediate supervision by parents. If a person discovers greater personal satisfaction in some alternate lifestyle, affluence makes it possible to seek out others who have the same interests. Affluence often enables people to postpone assuming adult responsibility (earning one's own living), thus allowing wider experimentation and lessening the consequences of failure. Affluence has also given rise to the mass media — magazines, radio, television, and movies — which have spread news about various lifestyles and experimental relationships into all parts of the country. In addition the media have taken part in creating new lifestyles by portraying them as desirable or exciting or "in."

In part then because of America's affluence, the young have a broader choice of acceptable relationships (family structures) than their grandparents did. Perhaps couples, by choosing wisely the roles that best fit them as individuals, will be able to create growing intimate relationships that are more fulfilling than those in the past. On the other hand there are

> some . . . risks involved in the new life-styles. The major risk in opening up choice is error in choice. When choices open up, one must carefully consider priorities. The older restricted system exacted a price; it placed a person in a mold which did not enable him [her] to choose a life-style that would allow maximum self-growth and social contribution. In a more open system people run the risk of acting impulsively. Such precipitate action might destroy long-range life prospects and opportunities. For example, one may impulsively get involved in a sexual encounter, and thereby cause a break in a meaningful relationship; or one may hastily get involved in divorce proceedings, and thereby avoid facing up to faults in oneself. Thus, the price of a more open system is the greater need for a rational examination of the alternatives.
>
> The old system had many people trapped in a rut; the new one may have many people constantly running from one style of life to another, unable to choose wisely. (Reiss, 1972, p. 246)

It may be that freedom will encourage people to run from one lifestyle to another as Ira Reiss suggests. On the other hand, it is also possible that freedom will encourage experimentation, which can lead to better decisions. Free inquiry leading to reasoned decisions with opportunities to test one's decisions is the way of science. There is no reason why this method should not improve the intimate life of people just as it has improved their material life. Too, having freely chosen a lifestyle can counteract feelings of entrapment that are often expressed by long-married couples.

Change within Continuity and Uniqueness within Commonality

Assumption 2:   *There is continuity to the changes that take place in the families.*

Assumption 3:   *Each family is unique but also shares characteristics in common with all other families in a given culture.*

As you try to understand the family and what is happening to it, remember that the American family, like social change, covers a vast territory and at the same time is far from uniform in design. Everyone is conscious how family life has changed, and yet the central core of family life continues much the same as it has existed for many generations (Glick, 1977, p. 13). Grasping the two ideas — *change within continuity* and *uniqueness within commonality* — will help you cope with the seeming riddles of the American family.

Some examples of diverse data will help clarify what we mean by these two principles. For example, the divorce rate has risen steadily throughout this century. In 1900 there was about one divorce for every twelve marriages. Today there is about one divorce for every two marriages, although the recent dramatic upsurge in divorce (starting about 1965) has slowed in the past five years. Many use these statistics to support their contention that the family in America is in real trouble, the institution is on the rocks, and the family will soon be dead and buried. Yet many others see these statistics as positive. Americans will have better marriages and more fulfilling family lives because they must no longer put up with the dissatisfactions and empty-shell marriages that previous generations accepted. Indeed, remarriage statistics indicate that divorced persons have even higher marriage rates than single, never-married persons. Most divorced persons leave a particular mate but not the institution of marriage.

A second example also illustrates the conflict that statistics about changing family characteristics evoke. America's birthrate has generally been falling for the past 200 years with the major exception of the baby boom between about 1945 and 1956, which was related to dislocations and the prosperity caused by World War II. However, the birthrate has fallen more dramatically since 1957, reaching a low of about 14.5 births per 1000 population in 1975. In 1982 that figure had risen to 16.0 per 1000 population ("Vital Statistics, Living Longer and Better," October 19, 1983), still relatively low compared with earlier levels. Many suggest that the decreased birthrate resulted because many young women decided not to have children: "Having children is no longer an important part of marriage." "Careers are more important and children are only troublesome to the pursuit of one's own goals." Yet although the proportion of women who state they expect to remain childless went up slightly from 1967 to 1974, decreasing again in 1975 (Bane, 1976), if as few women remain childless as say they will, the childless proportion among women born between 1940 and 1955 will be the lowest ever recorded. The birthrate is decreasing not because more women are remaining childless, but because there has been a large decrease in the number of children each mother has. The average mother born between 1846 and 1855 had 5.7 children. Women born between 1931 and 1935 had an average of 3.4 children.

INSET 1-1

The Family Riddle

Marriage, children, forever together, mom, dad, apple pie, love, Sunday softball in the park, grandmother's for Sunday dinner — The American Family.

Cohabitation, childlessness, divorce and remarriage, stepdad, stepmom, junk food, child abuse and wife beating, spectator sports in front of the TV, Pizza Hut for Sunday dinner — The American Family.

Student: "But these two descriptions can't both be of the American family."

Friend: "Oh, but they are, and, indeed, there are infinite other descriptions that also would fit. American families, each and every one, are unique and representative of the individuals and their interactions within the family."

Student: "But how then can we study the American family if each is unique?"

Friend: "Because they all have certain things in common. They are all alike in some ways."

Student: "But they can't be. You just said they were all different and unique."

Friend: "They are and they are also always changing."

Student: "But how can you study something that is unique and also always changing?"

Friend: "Because change occurs in the midst of continuity and continuity can remain despite change."

Student: "You are saying then that each family is unique but has things in common with all other families and, besides, families are always changing but have continuity."

Friend: "Yes."

Student: "It sounds like a riddle."

Friend: "It is a riddle because in order to understand the family one must be able to live with and understand two abstract principles:

1. Change can occur within continuity, and
2. Uniqueness can exist within commonality."

Women born between 1940 and 1945 have not quite reached the end of their childbearing years, but it appears they will average less than 3 children.

Thus the decreasing birthrate may not mean that families are abandoning having children at all. Rather, it seems to mean that families are having fewer children, which is probably positive for the children. Evidence suggests that children do better in smaller families where they receive more adult time and attention. Mary Jo Bane, after reviewing much demographic data about the family and children, concluded:

> In short, the major demographic changes affecting parents and children in the course of this century have not much altered the basic picture of children living with and being cared for by their parents. The patterns of structural change so often cited as evidence of family decline do not seem to be weakening the bonds between parents and children. (1976, p. 23)

These two examples help point out just how confusing and controversial interpretation of marriage and family data can be. Further, they demonstrate both principles that our two friends were discussing. First, both examples show change within continuity. The divorce rate has increased dramatically in the past few years, which is indicative of change. Yet those divorcing return to marriage rather quickly (close to 50 percent are remarried within three years), indicating continuity of the marriage institution. Families are having fewer children, a change from the past. But they are indeed having and rearing children as families have always done (continuity).

Both examples can also demonstrate uniqueness within commonality. Two married couples share the commonality of being married. Each partner of one marriage is in his or her first marriage. One partner of the other marriage is in his or her second marriage. Thus each couple, although sharing the characteristic of being married, is also unique insofar as their previous marriage experience is concerned.

Some couples opt for no children, others for one or two or three. All couples share the opportunity to have children in their marriage but are individual in the way they utilize the opportunity.

Many changes are occurring in the American family. As we discuss these changes, keep in mind the continuity. The year 1982 was the seventh consecutive year that the total number of marriages grew, and that total was the largest ever — 2.5 million, or nearly double the 1.2 million divorces recorded. The number of marriages exceeded by about 200,000 the earlier all-time peak of 2.29 million marriages in 1946. So we see that marriage remains popular and that most Americans still spend the greater share of their lives in family units.

Table 1-2 points out some of the changes in the American family. For example, we noted earlier the rapid rise of single-parent families (up 212 percent between 1970 and 1980). Yet America has always had single-parent families. In fact, the proportion of such families remained about one in ten for the 100 years between 1870 and 1970. Early single-parent families resulted largely because of the premature death of the husband/father rather than because of divorce as is true today. Although the 1970s saw a large increase in the single-parent family structure, the structure itself is not new to American society.

An examination of other items in Table 1-2 demonstrates clearly the principle of change within continuity. Ostensibly the table shows the great

TABLE 1-2   Changes in the American Family: 1970 to 1980

	1970	1980	PERCENT CHANGE	
Marriages performed	2,159,000	2,413,000	Up	8.9%
Divorces granted	708,000	1,182,000	Up	66.9%
Married couples	44,728,000	48,643,000	Up	8.8%
Unmarried couples	523,000	1,600,000	Up	305.9%
Persons living alone	10,851,000	17,800,000	Up	64.0%
Married couples with children	25,541,000	24,501,000	Down	4.1%
Unmarried couples with children	196,000	424,000	Up	216.0%
Children living with two parents	58,926,000	48,295,000	Down	18.0%
Children living with one parent	8,230,000	12,200,000	Up	48.2%
Single-parent families	3,100,000	6,600,000	Up	212.0%
Births	3,731,000	3,598,000	Down	3.6%
Births to unmarried women	398,000	600,000	Up	150.7%

changes taking place in the American family. Yet how great are the changes? Unmarried couple cohabitation increased 305.9 percent from 1970 to 1980, yet in actual numbers these couples still account for only 3.2 percent of the total number of married couples (1,600,000 cohabiting couples compared with 48,643,000 married couples). Change (an increase in unmarried cohabitation) yet continuity (most couples living together are married) is clearly demonstrated in these statistics. And how new is cohabitation to the American society? Not so new. During the 1920s common-law cohabitation involved about one in five couples (Ramey, 1981).

Another example — children living with only one parent — increased by 48.2 percent; yet if we look at the numbers, we find that 79 percent of all children still live with two parents. Change (more children live with one parent than before), yet continuity (most children still live with two parents) is again shown.

Perhaps the biggest change of all is the increasing acceptance of various forms of intimate relationships. We are, after all, a pluralistic society, a society made up of diverse groups. Thus it seems natural that different family structures may become accepted.

Family: The Basic Unit of Human Organization

Assumption 4:   The family is the basic unit of human organization. If defined functionally, the family is essentially universal. However, families' structural form and strength vary greatly across cultures and time.

The term *family* is used here in the broadest possible sense; it is defined as whatever system a society uses to support and control reproduction and human sexual interaction. This broad definition solves many apparent conflicts over the meaning of changes presently taking place in family functions and structure. For example, in this usage Israeli kibbutzim are families, even though major childrearing responsibilities are assumed by persons other than parents.

Most authors give a narrower definition. For example, Robert Winch (1971, pp. 10–11) defines family as: "A set of persons related to each other by blood, marriage, or adoption, and constituting a social system whose structure is specified by familial positions and whose basic societal function is replacement." Lucille Duberman (1977, p. 10) says the family is "an institution found in several variant forms, that provides children with a legitimate position in society and with the nurturance that will enable them to function as fully developed members of society." Narrow definitions like these seem to limit family functions to childrearing.

Part of the reason for the debate over the health of the American family is confusion between the functions of the family institution and the structure by which these functions are fulfilled. There are many structures that can fulfill the responsibilities of the family. In modern America the duties and thus the functions of the family have been reduced. And new structures, or alternative family forms, are being tried to fulfill some functions. Let us take a closer look at these functions.

Family Functions   The family serves both the society and the individual. Sometimes, of course, there is a conflict between social and individual needs, as with recent mandatory sterilization laws in India. Although having more children may benefit a particular family, the Indian government believes that too many children harm the larger society. For the family to remain a viable social institution, it must meet the needs of society and society's individual members and must hold conflict between these two levels to a minimum.

The family has handled a broad range of functions in different times and societies. In some primitive societies the family is synonymous with the society itself, bearing all the powers and responsibilities for societal survival. As societies become more complex and elaborate, social institutions form to take over many responsibilities that formerly belonged to the family.

Let us look at the functions that must be carried out for a society to remain intact. Robert F. Winch (1971) identifies the following as necessary for the maintenance of society:

1. Replacements for dying members of the society must be produced.
2. Goods and services must be produced and distributed.

Three generations: Close family ties lend stability to people's lives.

3. Provision must be made for accommodating conflicts and maintaining order internally and externally.
4. Newborn human replacements must be socialized to become participating members of the society.
5. Individual goals must be harmonized with the values of the society, and there must be procedures for dealing with emotional crises and maintaining a sense of purpose.

Although the American family is still involved with all five of these functions, other social institutions have assumed the primary responsibility for some of them. For example, the family is no longer a production unit per se. Individuals within the family may work to produce goods and services, but this is usually done outside the family setting in a more formalized job situation. The family is still an economic unit, however, in that it demands goods and services and is the major consumption unit in the United States (Assumption 8). The courts and police maintain external order, although the family is still primarily responsible for maintaining order within its own boundaries. Formal education now trains children to become participating members of society, although the family begins and maintains the socialization process.

Thus we find that the contemporary American family is left with two of Winch's primary functions: (1) providing a continuing replacement of individuals so that society continues to exist, (2) providing emotional gratification and intimacy to members, helping them deal with emotional crises so they grow in the most fulfilling manner possible.

Despite sperm banks and surrogate mothers, human beings are still being conceived and born in the age-old, time-honored fashion. Thus the family's importance as the means of replenishing the population remains. Too, the family is the most efficient way of nurturing the human newborn, who is physically dependent during the first years of life. Without some kind of stable adult unit to provide child care during this long period of dependence, the human species would have disappeared long ago.

Sexual Regulation   Each family structure, then, has reproduction as its primary function. Along with this is the regulation of sexual behavior.

In the animal world sex and reproduction are, for the most part, handled automatically and instinctively. When the female is in estrus (ready to conceive), the male responds and impregnates her. Most of the mechanisms and behaviors of sex and reproduction are built into the biology of the animal. There are fixed periods of sexual readiness, and the animal has little choice in its sexual behavior.

Human beings, as we all know, are different. Sexual behavior may be sought and enjoyed at any time, regardless of the stage of the female reproductive cycle. Humans are free to use sex not only for reproduction but also for pleasure. But, as in so many other aspects of human life, freedom of choice is a mixed blessing. Humans must balance their continual sexual receptivity and desire with the needs of other individuals and with the needs of society as a whole. They must find a system that will provide physical and mental satisfaction in a socially acceptable context of time, place, and partner.

No matter what system is worked out to handle sexuality, humans seem to be comfortable only when they can convince themselves that the system is proper, just, and virtuous. When each culture has established a satisfactory and "correct" system, it bolsters this system with a complex set of rules accompanied by prescribed punishments for transgressions.

However, our society has evolved to a point where the old rules no longer work well, so we are faced with trying to create new ethics to control sexuality. Western literature on marriage and the family is filled with arguments about the proper sexual system for humans. Were men and women originally promiscuous, **polygamous**, or **monogamous**? We have even applied Darwin's theory of evolution to the male/female relationship in an effort to demonstrate that the monogamy of Western cultures is the highest and therefore the only proper form of relationship. Yet close and objective study of the multiple methods devised by humans to work out their sexual and family life tends to destroy most of the historical arguments for any straight-line evolutionary theory of family development. In their book *The Family in Various Cultures* (1974, pp. 3–5), Stuart A. Queen and Robert W. Habenstein conclude that because there is such variance among family patterns and the way sexuality is controlled, "no single form need be regarded as inevitable nor more 'natural' than any other." They futher state: "We assume that all forms of the domestic institution are in process, having grown out of something different and tending to become something still different. But there is no acceptable evidence of a single, uniform series of stages through which the developing family must pass."

Polygamy
Having multiple spouses

Monogamy
Having one spouse in a sexually exclusive relationship

New Family Functions   Although consensus has it that the modern family has lost some functions, it may also be true that it has gained new ones. For example, F. I. Nye (1974) suggests that three new roles are present in the middle-class American family:

1. *The recreational role*: Family members spend their leisure time, especially vacation time, together.
2. *The therapeutic role*: Each family member assists the others in solving individual problems that may either originate in the family or be external to it. As we become more isolated from the larger ongoing society, such support becomes more crucial.
3. *Changed sexual roles*: Traditionally it was the woman's role to meet her husband's sexual needs. Now the feminist movement has emphasized the equal importance of the husband's meeting his wife's sexual needs, thereby placing a new responsibility on the man, and changing the female role also.

We have seen the family's functions changing over time. And we can certainly assume that its functions will continue to change. Do changing functions mean that the family as we know it will disappear? Not necessarily. Clark Vincent (1966) has pointed out an additional and overriding family function — the family's high adaptive capability. The family is a system in process rather than a rigid unchanging system. As John F. Crosby has pointed out:

No one can yet foresee what the structure of the future family will look like because no one can know with certainty what the functions and needs of the future family will be. It is likely, however, that the needs for primary affection bonds, intimacy, economic subsistence, socialization of the young, and reproduction will not yield to obsolescence. To the extent that human needs do not change drastically, the family structure will not change drastically. (1975, p. 40)

Family: A Buffer against Mental and Physical Illness

Assumption 5:   *The family becomes increasingly important to its members as social stability decreases and/or people feel more isolated and alienated. Indeed, the fully functioning family can act as a buffer against mental and physical illness.*

In general as the pace of life quickens and as people become increasingly alienated from their larger society, the family can become more important as a refuge and source of emotional gratification for its members. The family has been called the "shock absorber" of society — the place where bruised and battered individuals can return after doing battle with the world, the one stable point in an ever-changing environment. If you do not belong to a family, where do you turn for warmth and affection? Who cares for you when you are sick? What other group tolerates your failures the way a devoted wife, husband, mother, or father does?

The family can serve as "portable roots," anchoring one against the storm of change. Furthermore, the family can provide the security and acceptance that lead to inner strength, the strength to behave individually rather than always in conformity with one's peers. In one husband's words,

> The power, strength, the refuge of our marriage has given us a kind of core to operate from, which has allowed both of us to be very much mavericks in most social terms. My hunch would be, for instance, that if you see a man who is very conventional, very frightened, you know, very unsure of what direction to move and always looking at how his peers evaluate him — my bet is you can predict he doesn't have a very good marriage because if he did, he wouldn't have to do that. He'd find his core, his identity, and his being somewhere else [in his marriage]. And these things would be secondary as they ought to be. (Rogers, 1972, p. 192)

That is, the family can be a source of security, a protective shield against environmental pressures.

To the degree that environmental stress on individual family members can be reduced, the family *can* act as a buffer against mental and physical illness of its members. It is important that we emphasize the word "can." The family can act as a buffer if it is well integrated, fully functioning, and successful. This status is an ideal and we realize that few families probably will approach it. Yet ideals are important. They can give us direction, goals toward which to move. In many ways pointing out ideals, what families could be, how families can optimally function, is an important purpose of this book.

As families have become smaller and more isolated from societal sup-

Love and intimacy are important parts of growing up.

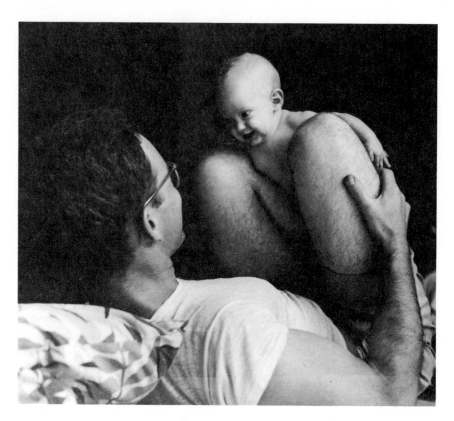

ports because of industrialization and alienation processes, intimate relations within the family have become more intense, more emotional, and more fragile. For example, if a child has no other significant adults to interact intimately with besides his or her parents, then this emotional interaction becomes crucial to the child's development. If this interaction is positive and healthy, the child develops in a healthy manner. On the other hand, if it is not, then the child is apt to develop in an unhealthy manner. The family, in a sense, is a hothouse of intimacy and emotionality because of its close interaction and intensity of relationships. It has the potential to do either great good or great harm for its members. Because of the potential for harm, it becomes even more important to understand how the family can help its members toward health.

As we pointed out earlier, we all will spend a good part, if not all, of our lives in a family unit. It is within this setting that most of us will achieve our closest intimacy with other persons — the shared human intimacy that promotes security, feelings of self-esteem, and openness and sharing. Such feelings lead to improved communication, and good communication both within oneself and with others tends to be therapeutic. According to Carl Rogers (1951, p. 1), "the emotionally maladjusted person is in difficulty first, because communication within himself has broken down, and second, because, as a result of this, his communication with others has become damaged." To the degree that our family can help us become good communicators, it can help us toward better life adjustment.

When one compares health statistics on married, single, divorced, separated, and widowed people, it is clear that married people are the healthiest. Lois Verbrugge (1979) surveyed a great deal of data on the following six general health indicators: (1) incidence of acute health conditions, (2) percentage of people limited in activity by a chronic condition, (3) percentage of people with a work disability, (4) rates of restricted activity, bed disability, and work loss, (5) average number of physician (or dental) visits per year, and (6) percentage of people with a hospital stay in the past year, average length of stay, and hospital discharge rates.

She adjusted rates for age and found that significant differences existed between the various groups. Divorced and separated people clearly appeared least healthy, while married people appeared overall to be the most healthy. A single dramatic example shows the differences between the groups: commitments to mental hospitals in 1970, expressed as rate per 10,000 population:

	Single	Married	Widowed	Divorced	Separated
Men	213	10	47	101	115
Women	116	11	26	48	77

You can see dramatic differences between the groups and between men and women. In this particular case single men and women had the highest institutionalization rates, and men's rates were generally higher than women's rates.

Examining rates for other specific health problems is equally interesting. For example, the American Council of Life Insurance reports that divorced white American males under 65 — compared with married men — had a death rate from strokes and lung cancer that was double, seven times greater for cirrhosis of the liver, double for stomach cancer and heart disease, and five times higher for suicide.

Interpretation of such data is complex and controversial. The differences between various marital groups, however, are substantial enough to suggest that they are real rather than simply chance. The fact that married persons generally appear most healthy and divorced and separated persons least healthy suggests that the family may have a strong influence on health. The successful family operates to improve its members' health, while the unsuccessful family may do the opposite. If this is true, it becomes a matter of health to work toward improved family functioning and increased levels of intimacy.

The Need for Intimacy   Seeking closeness with others, whether the closeness is physical, intellectual, or emotional, seems to be a basic need of most people (Fromm, 1956; Maslow, 1971; Morris, 1971; Murstein, 1974). To feel close to another, to love and feel loved, to experience comradeship, to care and be cared about are all feelings that most of us wish and need to experience. Such feelings can be found in many human relationships. It is within the family, though, that such feelings ideally are most easily found and shared. I say "ideally" because it is apparent that in many families such feelings are not found. Families that do not supply intimacy are usually families in trouble, and often these families disintegrate because members are frustrated in their needs for meaningful intimate relationships. A successful family, then, supplies intimate relationships to its members and through this intimacy contributes to their health.

Intimacy
Experiencing the essence of oneself in intense intellectual, physical, and/or emotional relationships with others

The term **intimacy** generally covers all of the feelings mentioned in the preceding paragraph as well as being a commonly used euphemism for sexual intercourse. Because of the many meanings, a clear and concise definition is difficult to make. For our purposes we will use Carolynne Kieffer's (1977) definition: "Intimacy is the experiencing of the essence of one's self in intense intellectual, physical and/or emotional communion with another human being" (p. 267).

The primary components of intimacy are choice, mutuality, reciprocity, trust, and delight (Calderone, 1972). Two people like one another and make overtures toward establishing a closer relationship. They have made a *choice*. Their act, of course, must be *mutual* for an intimate relationship to develop. As confidence in each other grows, each reveals more and more thoughts and feelings. *Reciprocity* means that each partner gives to the relationship and to each other: sharing, confidences, caring, and feelings expressed. With this sharing acceptance and trust grow, which in turn increase the sharing. This growing open sharing eventually leads to the experience of *delight* in one another that true intimates always share.

B. J. Biddle (1976) has shed light on the concept of intimacy. Biddle suggests that intimacy must be considered on each of three dimensions — breadth, openness, and depth. *Breadth* describes the range of activities shared by two people. Do they spend a great deal of time together? Do they share occupational activities, home activities, leisure time, and so on? *Openness* implies that a pair share meaningful self-disclosures with one another. They feel secure enough and close enough to share intellectually, physically, and emotionally. They trust each other enough that they can be honest most of the time and this encourages further trust in one another. *Depth* means that partners share really true, central, and meaningful aspects of themselves. Self-disclosure leads to deeper levels of interaction. In the ultimate sense both are able to transcend their own egos and fuse in a spiritual way with the essence or central being of their partner. Such an experience is difficult to attain, yet many believe that it is in the deepest intimate experiences that love and potential for individual growth are found. Abraham Maslow (1968), for example, holds that each individual must find deep intimacy to become a self-actualizing and fulfilled person.

Kieffer (1977) adds to Biddle's three dimensions the age-old idea of intellectual, physical, and emotional *realms of action*. A totally intimate relationship would have breadth, openness, and depth in each activity realm. Table 1-3 describes a highly intimate relationship. Of course, as Kieffer cautions, such a description is simplistic and does not include the numerous psychological processes that characterize the interaction of the partners or that brought them to their level of involvement. In addition, she reminds us that intimacy is a process, not a state of being. Thus this

TABLE 1-3   Intensity Matrix for the Analysis of an Intimate Relationship*

	INTELLECTUAL	PHYSICAL	EMOTIONAL
BREADTH (RANGE OF SHARED ACTIVITIES)	Telling of the meaningful events in one's day Participating in a political rally Years of interaction resulting in the sharing of meanings (phrases, gestures, etc.) understood only by the partners Decision making regarding management of household	Dancing Caressing Swimming Doing laundry Tennis Shopping Gardening Sexual intercourse Other sensual/sexual activities	Phone calls providing emotional support when separated Experiencing grief in a family tragedy Witnessing with pride a daughter's graduation from college Resolving conflict in occasional arguments
OPENNESS (DISCLOSURE OF SELF)	Disclosing one's values and goals Discussing controversial aspects of politics, ethics, etc. Using familiar language Not feeling a need to lie to the partner Sharing of secrets with the partner and using discretion regarding the secrets of the partner	Feeling free to wear old clothes Grooming in presence of the other Bathroom behavior (elimination, etc.) in presence of the other Nudity Few limitations placed on exploration of one's body by the partner Sharing of physical space (area, possessions, etc.) with few signs of territoriality	Describing one's dreams and daydreams Feeling free to call for "time out" or for togetherness Maintaining openness (disclosure) regarding one's emotional involvement with other intimates Telling of daily joys and frustrations Emotional honesty in resolving conflict Expressing anger, resentment, and other positive and negative emotions
DEPTH (SHARING OF CORE ASPECTS OF SELF)	"Knowing" of the partner Having faith in the partner's reliability and love Occasional experiencing of the essence of one's self in transcendental union Working collectively to change certain core characteristics of the self and of the partner	Physical relaxation, sense of contentment and well-being in the presence of the other	Committing oneself without guarantee, in the hope that one's love will be returned Caring as much about the partner as about oneself Nonjealous supportiveness toward the other intimate relationships of the partner

Source: From *Marriage and Alternatives: Exploring Intimate Relationships* by Roger W. Libby and Robert N. Whitehurst. Copyright © 1977 by Scott, Foresman and Company. Reprinted by permission.
*You can use this matrix to analyze your own intimate relationships or to compare levels of involvement or discern patterns among your various relationships.

description only indicates where this particular couple is at a moment in time.

In the past intimacy was built into one's life by the social acceptance and support of the family. However, as the economic pattern changed in this country, and as increasing geographical mobility separated people from their families, social emphasis shifted from family closeness to individual self-fulfillment. Many people have found the achievement of intimacy more difficult because of this shift.

Why Do We Avoid Intimacy?

To seek and find intimacy with another is highly rewarding. Yet people often avoid intimacy — and for many reasons. To open ourselves to another invites intimacy but also risks hurt. What if we open ourselves to others, trust them to reciprocate, and they do not? Each of us has probably had such an experience. Who hasn't liked someone and been rejected by that person? We may now be able to laugh at some of our early failures with intimacy (label them "puppy love," and so forth), yet each time we fail at intimacy, we become more guarded and apprehensive.

Fear of rejection is one of the strongest barriers to intimacy. Each time we are hurt by another, it becomes more difficult to be open, trusting and caring in a new relationship. To be the first to share our innermost feelings, to say "I like you" or "I love you" leaves one open to rejection. The first steps toward an intimate relationship are especially hard for the insecure person who lacks self-confidence. To build an intimate relationship, one must first be intimate, accepting, and comfortable with oneself. To the degree that we are not these things with ourselves, we will probably be fearful to enter an intimate relationship.

Intimacy demands active involvement with another. Often passive spectator roles seem more comfortable — let the other person supply the intimacy. Our society teaches us to be spectators via television. Society often conditions us to play roles, to always please others, to deny our feelings. We shall see how intimacy is avoided when we play our stereotypical masculine and feminine roles (macho males don't cry or show caring emotions, for example).

Anger can be another barrier to intimacy if it is not dealt with openly. When we suppress, deny, and disguise anger, we do not rid ourselves of it. Rather the anger lingers as growing hostility. Of course, we all become angry on occasion with our most intimate loved ones. Anger does not destroy intimacy. Suppressed anger, though, leads to hostility and will, over time, tend to destroy intimacy. Remember that intimacy implies openness between intimates. Suppressed anger is unexpressed, thus keeping us closed rather than open. Suppressing anger also implies lack of trust in the partner. Without trust there cannot be intimacy.

Fear of rejection, nonacceptance of ourselves, spectator roles, and unexpressed anger are four of the strongest barriers to intimacy.

What Do You Think?

With which people in your life do you find it easiest to be intimate?

Why is it easier with each of these persons than with others?

Is it easier for you to be intimate with men or women? If there is a difference, what do you think that difference is?

Is your family of orientation generally close and intimate?

Do your friends generally consider you to be a person with whom they can be intimate?

If so, why? If not, why not?

But life today offers many different opportunities for fulfilling intimacy needs. Marriage is no longer seen as the *only* avenue to intimacy. If we examine our lives, we will probably find we have a "patchwork intimacy." By this Kieffer means that most people are involved in a multitude of intimate relationships of varying intensity.

We can see this idea more clearly if we examine the concept of "open marriage" (O'Neill & O'Neill, 1972). Nena and George O'Neill propose that the old idea of marriage expected both partners to fill *all* of their intimacy needs within the marriage. In an "open marriage," on the other hand, a partner can limit physical intimacy to the marriage relationship but share intellectual intimacy with, perhaps, some work colleagues. Also, the partners are free to spend time away from each other, with other companions.

If one is secure in a marital relationship of deep intimacy, enough trust may develop so that each partner can say to the other, "I love and care for you so much that I encourage you to seek fulfillment through finding intimacy wherever it might exist for you." Such trust must be earned and respected; it is not easy to come by.

If intimacy is as rewarding as we have suggested and if American society is allowing each person to seek it in ways other than marriage, we need to develop an ethic for intimates. For example, how do we keep the quest for individual intimacy and fulfillment within acceptable boundaries to our spouse? How do we keep the quest from lapsing into the selfish pursuit of always "doing one's own thing"? Questions such as these must be considered by all couples seeking intimacy.

The Family as Interpreter of Society

Assumption 6:   *The attitudes and reactions of family members toward environmental influences are more important to the socialization of family members than are the environmental influences themselves (Chapters 4 and 5).*

We have seen that the family supplies the society's population, through reproducing children. It not only produces offspring but physically and psychologically nurtures the offspring into adulthood. Because humans have such a long period of dependence before becoming independent adults, the family is the main source for **socialization** of the children to their culture. Formal education takes over part of the job of socializing the young when they reach school age. The family, though, retains the greatest overall influence on preschool children. Indeed the family's continuing formal and informal socialization of its children may supply the most deeply lasting lessons. However, with increasing numbers of mothers joining the workforce when their children are young, formal preschool child-care programs and television are decreasing the family's influence even with preschoolers.

Social learning theory has long pointed out the importance of modeling in learning, especially for young children (Bandura, 1969). **Modeling** is learning vicariously through observation of other people's behavior. Par-

What Do You Think?

Is intimacy a goal for you?

If it is, why is it difficult for you to be intimate?

In what action realm (intellectual, physical, emotional) do you share intimacy most easily? Why?

Which realm is most difficult? Why?

In what ways is your relationship with your parents intimate? Why?

In what ways can you not be intimate with your parents? Why?

Socialization
Acquiring skills necessary to survive as an individual and as a member of society

Modeling
Learning vicariously by observing others' behavior

ents and other family members are the most significant models for young children. How they react to their society is often more important than what they might formally teach their children about it. For instance, the father who teaches his children the importance of obeying rules and then asks them to watch for policemen when he exceeds the speed limit is teaching a different lesson about rules than obeying them.

Social problems—depression, inflation, unemployment, poverty—also greatly influence families. General social upheaval such as America went through during the Vietnam War in the 1960s and the continuing furor over minority rights affect the family drastically. For example, if my child is to be bused twenty miles into a new neighborhood and school so that racial equality can be achieved, there will certainly be consequences within the family. I, as a parent, will lose some control over my child. The distance to school may mean that I cannot participate in school activities such as PTA and class parties. I will not know the families of my child's playmates. My child will be exposed to different social mores and expectations, which I may or may not find acceptable.

Yet more important than the political fact of busing will be the family's reaction to it. Will the family accept and support it? Will it picket, riot, and protest? Will it transfer children from public into private school? Each family's reaction to busing teaches its children values about minority groups, racial prejudice and/or tolerance, law, and authority. That is, how the family reacts is as important to its members as the social stimulus.

An additional function of the family, then, is to help family members interpret social influences. This function also brings the possibility that an individual family may teach an interpretation unacceptable to others in the society as a whole.

Unique Characteristics of the American Family

Assumption 7:   *The American family, especially the middle-class family, has certain characteristics that make it unique. Among these, the following four stand out (Chapters 3, 7, and 8):*

a. *Relative freedom of choice in mate and vocational selection.* Most cultures, historically at least, believed that mate and vocational selection were too important to be left to inexperienced people. The decisions that would influence one's entire life were best made by adults and often were made long before a child reached puberty. To this day in many countries children enter the labor market early. Whether tending the family's goats in Morocco or tying the thousands of knots that go into the creation of an Iranian carpet, children contribute to their family's economic well-being and learn early their lifetime vocation.

Western society, especially the United States, long ago rejected child labor as inappropriate. As America became increasingly child centered and affluent, childhood (an historically recent concept) became a protected period of freedom from adult responsibility. Today children whose parents believe in the value of education and have the means to supply it are encouraged to educate themselves and to seek out vocations for which they are best suited. Families may make suggestions about possible vocations, but the final decision is usually left to the child. This freedom is even more evident in mate selection. As we shall see in Chapter 3, unstructured dating as a method of mate selection is a relatively new American contribution to the mate selection process.

b. *Relative freedom within the family, fostered by a high standard of living, physical mobility, lack of broader familial responsibilities, and the pluralistic nature of American society.* Freedom of vocational choice and mate selection stem from the general freedom that exists for the young within the American family and society. We have already examined the role that societal affluence plays in allowing broader choice of family structure. This affluence leads to

c. *The high economic standard and abundant personal possessions that also characterize the American middle-class family.* As we saw, affluence, increased education, and mass media proliferation all combine to allow America's young wider experiences. Such experiences weaken the ties to one's family, thereby increasing youth's freedom both within the family and later in the life choices that all youth must make. Of course, such freedom also incurs the liability of decision making and the responsibility for those decisions. Freedom also means freedom to make mistakes. Thus the freedom that American youth enjoys tends to increase anxiety and insecurity among the young. This increased anxiety and insecurity may partially explain the interest of some young Americans in cults, most of which ask their members to give up freedom and to live by strict rules. Compare your own freedom within your family with the description of the traditional Chinese family found in Scenes from Marriage on p. 32.

d. *The extremely private character of the American family.* This characteristic of the American family also results from the general affluence of our society. In most of the world housing is in short supply. Many families are fortunate if they have more than one room. Living quarters often house not only the nuclear family but many other relatives as well.

The average size of American families living together has decreased over the years. In 1790 the average American household living together was 5.6 persons. In 1970 the size had dropped to 3.14 persons and in 1981 had further dropped to just 2.73 persons (U.S. Bureau of the Census, May 1982b). This decrease is accounted for mainly by the loss of the additional relatives that used to live with families.

The number of single persons living alone has also increased, especially in the past decade, as Table 1-2 showed. Both the shrinking household size and the increased number of persons living alone are possible only in a society affluent enough to supply abundant housing. An American family living in a 1400-square-foot, three-bedroom, bath-and-a-half house uses enough space to house approximately twenty persons in a country such as Afghanistan or Upper Volta.

It is this ability of the American nuclear family to live separately from relatives and neighbors that has allowed it to become private. Such

Privacy is a unique characteristic of the affluent American family.

privacy is a luxury of economic affluence. Our society's privacy brings
both advantages and disadvantages. Living with fewer people increases individual freedom, but living privately also increases the opportunity for spouse or child abuse because others aren't around to
observe such abuse. And although living alone certainly is private, the
chances of experiencing loneliness also increase.

Family: The Consuming Unit of the American Economy

Assumption 8:   *The family in modern America is the basic economic unit for the
society because it is the primary consuming unit (Chapters 7
and 8).*

As Scenes from Marriage (p. 32) shows, the traditional Chinese family
supplied its members with work because production centered in the family. The early American farm family also exemplified this arrangement in
which family members were also production workers. The industrial revolution removed much of the economic production from the American
family. Family members remained production workers, but the production
was moved from the home into factories and did not necessarily include
all family members. The money earned by outside work served to support
the family. Thus the family's economic well-being became more subject to
the whim of the anonymous marketplace than to the industry of individual family members. Rather than each family producing what it needed
to survive, each had to go to the marketplace and buy what it needed.
Thereby, the family became the consuming unit of society's agricultural
and industrial output.

The family, of course, still provides services to its members. Such services as meal preparation and keeping the house in repair require productive work from family members. However, such production is largely unpaid and unrecognized by the larger society. Some feminists suggest that these services, which are provided mainly by women, be paid for. Payment for such family services would probably have a significant impact on husband/wife relationships, as family power, in part, relates to who earns the money. Estimates based on current wage scales of cooks, baby sitters, and so forth place the value of services provided by the nonemployed, full-time mother/housewife at approximately $25,000 to $35,000 per year. Feminists suggest that such productive work be recognized not only by the woman's husband but also by the government for the granting of social security benefits.

Family consuming—consumer spending—is important to the health of the economy. When consumer spending drops as it did during the recession of 1981–83, the economy suffers. Thus economically the family also acts as a foundation block to American society.

Family Myths: "The One and Only"

Assumption 9: *Each individual can marry any one of a number of persons within the broad limits set by social norms and can build a satisfying and stable relationship if both partners' expectations and attitudes are realistic (Chapters 2 and 3).*

When Americans are asked why they marry, invariably they list "love" as their most important reason. To marry for romantic love is another American contribution to the mate selection process. Although romantic love has always been recognized historically, it has almost never served as a basis for marriage. Marriages were contracted by parents for their children. The contracts were made for economic, political, power, and prestige reasons, not for love. If love were to appear in the contracted relationship, generally it would have to grow as time passed. The lyrics to the song "Do You Love Me?" from *Fiddler on the Roof* exemplify a contracted marriage.

Tevye to his wife Golde

Do you love me?
Do I what?
Do you love me?
Do I love you? With our daughters getting married and this trouble in town, you're upset, you're worn out. Go inside, go lie down. Maybe it's indigestion.
Golde, I'm asking you a question: Do you love me?
You're a fool!
I know, but do you love me?
Do I love you? Well, for twenty-five years I've washed your clothes, cooked your meals, cleaned your house, given you children, milked the cow. After twenty-five years why talk about love right now?
Golde, the first time I met you was on our wedding day. I was scared, I was shy, I was nervous.

So was I.

But my father and mother said we'd learn to love each other, and now I am asking, Golde, do you love me?

I'm your wife.

I know, but do you love me?

Do I love him? For twenty-five years I've lived with him, fought with him, starved with him. Twenty-five years my bed is his; if that's not love, what is?

Then you love me.

I suppose I do.

And I suppose I love you too.

It doesn't change a thing, but even so, after twenty-five years it's nice to know.

The fact that Americans marry "for love" is also one of the reasons that American marriages are less stable than marriages in many other cultures. "Love" is hard to define; staying "in love" for a long time is difficult. Thus as a major reason for marrying, love is a fragile foundation for the relationship.

When we examine the underlying reasons that lead to attraction and love, we find that such mundane factors as **propinquity** (nearness in time or place), years of schooling, social class, and religion often direct our attractions. Living in the same neighborhood, going to the same school, working at the same place of employment are all important factors directing us toward the person we ultimately fall in love with. Such factors aren't very romantic.

Propinquity
Nearness in time or place

Although romantic love dictates that there is a perfect "one and only" for each of us, practical considerations dictate otherwise. Each society will set certain rules about whom their members can and cannot marry. American society sets comparatively fewer rules and leaves mate selection mostly up to its youth, as we have seen. Human beings can be attracted to numerous others. The high divorce and remarriage rates yield perhaps the best evidence that there is more than one "one and only" for each of us.

Once we have located a mate, it is up to us as a couple to build a satisfying and stable relationship. Failure to recognize this dooms a "love" marriage to failure. A basic theme throughout this book is the need to nurture, to build, and continually to work toward improving one's intimate relationships. Romantic love can help us find a "one and only," but only realistic recognition that a relationship must be cultivated and tended can lead to long-term love and intimacy.

Some Words about Marriage and Family Data

Hard and fast data in such an intimate field of study as the family are difficult to produce. Most of the data come from surveys and from clinicians who work in the field.

Survey data are often problematic for three reasons. The first problem is that the sample may not be representative of the population in which you are interested. For example, if you are interested in the cohabiting behavior of college students, which college students do you survey? Certainly state university students will give answers different from students at a small denominational college where dormitory residence is required. You must always ask whether the sample surveyed accurately represents the population about which you want to draw conclusions.

A second problem with survey data is who *actually* responded. The researcher will, in most cases, set up a representative sample. However, responding to surveys is not mandatory but depends on voluntary cooperation. Although 100 percent of the sample may indeed be representative of the population about which you want to generalize, you will be fortunate if 50 to 80 percent of those in the sample cooperate. Thus you need to know if those who cooperated with the survey are the same as those who didn't. For example, Alfred Kinsey and his associates worked hard to draw a representative sample of Americans to interview about sexual behavior. They took people from all geographic areas and from various social classes. But can we be sure that the people who volunteered to discuss their most intimate sexual behavior with the interviewers behaved the same sexually as those who did not volunteer? Of course we can't, and thus there will always be a question about how representative of Americans the two monumental Kinsey studies really are.

The third problem with surveys is the difficulty of validating the respondents' answers. Are they telling the truth? The more intimate the questions, such as those about marriage or sex habits, the more likely the respondents are to hedge their answers or perhaps not even to answer at all. Researchers try to overcome this problem by making surveys anonymous, but, again, we can never really be sure that an answer is true. Also, while respondents might not actually lie, sometimes memories are inadequate, or what we think we'd do in a hypothetical situation is not at all what we would actually do in real life. Thus always be careful about uncritically accepting all data that surveys yield.

Clinicians such as marriage counselors, clergy, psychologists, psychiatrists, and others who work with families also supply data to the research field. These data are usually anecdotal (storytelling), and unfortunately the clinicians' conclusions may be overgeneralized. Too, because they work with those seeking help, they may only see troubled families. After working eight hours a day over long periods with people who have problems, clinicians may come to hold an overly pessimistic view of the family.

Data on individual cases are usually valid for those cases, but can such data be generalized to the entire population? In most cases probably not. Also, group data does not accurately predict what an individual will do. For example, data from large group studies indicate that the chances of divorce go up if one's parents are divorced. Yet we all know persons who are long married and indeed have worked harder to make their marriage succeed because their parents were divorced. Does this mean that the group data are incorrect? Not at all. The statistics are correct for the group but cannot predict the behavior of any specific individual within the group. As Sherlock Holmes (in *The Sign of the Four*) said, ''While the individual man is an insoluble puzzle, in the aggregate he becomes a mathematical certainty. You can never foretell what any one man will do, but you can say with precision what an average number will be up to. Individuals vary but percentages remain constant."

In general, then, remember to be cautious about immediately accepting all supposed facts in the field of marriage and family research.

Conclusion: Marriage, A Resilient Institution

It is easy and popular to attack marriage and suggest alternatives to current practices. But such attacks tend to imply that marriage is a rigid relationship that has passed relatively unchanged into our modern culture. In reality "marriage has undergone dramatic change, and is still steadily changing, as it adapts itself to today's world" (Mace & Mace, 1977, p. 391).

In fact, changes in the family because of modernization have led some critics of marriage to long for "the good old days." This suggests that there was some lost golden age of the family. Study of family history, however, fails to uncover any such golden age. Jerome and Arlene Skolnick (1980, p. 16) point out that those condemning modernization may have forgotten the problems of the past. Our current problems inside and outside of the family are genuine, but we should remember that many of these issues derive from the very benefits of modernization—benefits too easily taken for granted or forgotten in the lately fashionable denunciation of modern times. In the past there was no problem of the aged because most people never aged; they died before they got old. Nor was adolescence a difficult stage of the life cycle when children worked and education was a privilege of the rich. And when most people were hungry illiterates, only aristocrats could worry about sexual satisfaction and self-fulfillment. Modernization surely brings its troubles, yet how many of us would trade the troubles of our era for the ills of earlier times?

David and Vera Mace note that the family has changed from an institution characterized as "formal," "authoritarian," "rigidly disciplined," and as maintaining "rigid sex roles" to a companionship pattern described as an "interpersonal relationship," with "mutual affection," "sympathetic understanding," and "comradeship":

> Surely the first group of terms represents precisely the values in marriage which the counterculture has deplored, and the second group the very values which it has extolled.
>
> What we are saying is that the monogamous marriage and nuclear family function far better in the companionship mode than they ever did in the institutional pattern; and that they can adapt very easily . . . to the new emphasis on personal and relational growth and development. (Mace & Mace, 1977, pp. 393–94)

Our discussion has been about family life in general. Yet for most Americans it is within a creative and changing marriage that they will find intimacy and satisfaction. Despite the popularity of attacking marriage as an institution, most Americans spend the bulk of their lives within a marriage and family relationship. This indicates that we need to expend more energy on making marriage viable and fulfilling than we spend on suggesting alternatives to it. As the Maces point out:

> The possibilities for better marriage are exciting. In what we now call the marriage enrichment movement, we are experimenting with new tools and getting encouraging results. In skillfully led couple groups, we are seeing significant and lasting changes taking place in dull, superficial marriages as they break loose and embark on new growth. We are becoming aware that the majority of marriages in North America are functioning far below their potential. But we now realize that couples need no longer accept this miserable yield. With proper help and guidance they can appropriate the locked-up capacity for depth within the relationship that has been there all the time, but that no one helped them to actualize.
>
> In short, we are at last beginning to provide the services to marriages which should have been available a generation ago, when the new alternative companionship style was emerging to replace traditional marriage. (Mace & Mace, 1977, p. 392)

The family remains because it is a flexible institution with great resilience. It is able to be pressed and stretched and bent but always seems able to recover its strength and spirit and buoyancy. Despite the many criticisms of it, the family remains the basic unit of society. When functioning well, the family is the individual's greatest source of love and intimacy.

Summary

Human intimacy is based on nine major assumptions about marriage and the family in America.

1. A free and creative society is one that offers many structural forms by which family functions, such as childrearing, may be fulfilled.
2. There is continuity to the changes that take place in families.
3. Each family is unique but also shares characteristics in common with all other families in a given culture.
4. The family is the basic unit of human organization. If defined functionally, the family is essentially universal. However, families' structural form and strength vary greatly across cultures and time.
5. The family becomes increasingly important to its members as social stability decreases and/or people feel more isolated and alienated. Indeed, the fully functioning family *can* act as a buffer against mental and physical illness.
6. The attitudes and reactions of family members toward environmental influences are more important to the socialization of family members than are the environmental influences themselves.
7. The American family, especially the middle-class family, has certain characteristics that make it unique. Among these, the following stand out:

    a. Relative freedom in mate and vocational selection.

    b. Relative freedom within the family, fostered by a high standard of living, physical mobility, lack of broader familial responsibilities, and the pluralistic nature of American society.

    c. A high economic standard and abundant personal possessions.

    d. The extremely private character of the American family.

8. The family in modern America is the basic economic unit for the society since it is the primary consuming unit.

9. An individual can marry any one of a number of persons within the broad limits set by social norms and can build a satisfying and stable relationship if both partners' expectations and attitudes are realistic.

SCENES FROM MARRIAGE

A. Communes

Communes, or group living arrangements, represent an alternate family pattern that some find attractive. Communes themselves are markedly diverse: Some are agrarian, some urban; some limit sexual contact, drugs, and alcohol, some have no limits; some are based on religious ideals, some on utopian ideals; some have no rules, some have rigid rules, and so on.

Reports suggest that there were approximately 3000 intentional communes scattered throughout America in 1970, although the movement has greatly declined since then (Zablocki, 1971). In general people join communes to escape from an increasing sense of alienation and isolation. Alienation may lead them to join rural communes where they can see—and eat—the results of their labor. Communes often sanction ideas or behavior that differ from those of the ongoing society at large.

In actuality most communes last less than a year. Only those that are authoritarian or have strong ideals seem to last, though, as one contributor to the *Whole Earth Catalog* ironically noted, "If the intentional community hopes to survive, it must be authoritarian, and if it is authoritarian, it offers no more freedom than the conventional society" ("The American Family . . .," 1970).

Living in a Commune

Jerry and Ann have been married for a year. He works downtown in a large city and she works part-time at the local university. During their vacation last summer, they visited friends who lived in a rural commune in northern California. Jerry and Ann only stayed overnight, but life in the commune seemed pastoral and simple compared with theirs and they began to think about joining it. Finally, they decided to quit their jobs and move to the commune.

The commune operates on a laissez-faire basis inasmuch as most of the members believe that leadership is synonymous with oppression. Most members live in couples, though sexual experimentation is tolerated. Drugs, however, are not. Members live in cabins they have built themselves.

When Ann and Jerry arrive, Jerry immediately begins to build a cabin. He and Ann spend time working in the communal garden. Ann, who is a good organizer, also begins finding methods to make handling the chores and daily work more efficient. However, after they have been living in the commune for three months, they become aware that the more work they do, the less others seem to do. They also become aware that freeloaders seem to wander in and out constantly. And, although the membership seems to stay around twenty-four, only about half are the same as when Ann and Jerry arrived three months earlier. The new people seem to share the food but do not remain long enough to share the work.

About this time the older members decide that the commune does need rules after all. At a group meeting job hierarchies, time tables, and work responsibilities are agreed on. The group decides that penalties for not working will be denial of communal goods (fruits and vegetables as well as tools and materials) at first, and then if the person still shirks duties, he or she will be asked to leave. The group also decides to discourage visitors for a while.

Ann has begun to notice that though the men talk about female equality and about being nonsexist, it is the women who do the housework, washing, and cooking. When she mentions this at a meeting, she is told that this division is more efficient, and doesn't she believe in efficiency, and anyway none of the women are strong enough to do the heavy work of building cabins or felling trees. Since the men do the heavy labor, it isn't fair for them to have to do cooking and cleaning too. She finds herself stunned at the hostility in some of the men's voices and notes that the other women seem embarrassed by her bringing up the point.

Several weeks later while Jerry is away visiting his parents, Ann spends the night with one of the members she has thought warm and loving. But in the morning he announces to the group at breakfast, "You know, Ann has the potential of becoming a good sexual technician." She feels humiliated and degraded. When Jerry returns, he is told about her infidelity, and he threatens to leave her.

About this time the health department sends an inspector to the commune, and the commune is cited for unsatisfactory bathroom and kitchen facilities. A county building inspector also cites them for not building to code and for not having building permits. All the structures built without permits will have to come down.

Jerry and Ann decide to return to the city. They still believe in the ideal of communal living but feel that this group just wasn't suited for them. They think they might try the experience again, perhaps with a commune that has been in existence for several years.

What Do You Think?

What are some of the major ways in which this commune failed?

How would you have solved the problems of this commune?

Why do some urban youth want to return to farming as a way of life?

What are some advantages of living communally? What are some disadvantages?

The major reasons for the failure of most communes appear to be: (1) inability to handle interpersonal conflicts, (2) lack of an economic base, (3) jealousy, (4) lack of a secure one-to-one relationship compounded by the insecurity of relating to an amorphous group, (5) the difficulty of maintaining multiple relationships, (6) lack of privacy, and (7) difficulty of living anarchistically with individuals who are not mature and responsible (Rogers, 1972).

Children within the commune setting also present some unique problems. Basically, unless special arrangements are made for children, they face multiple rule makers and rule enforcers. Inconsistency, ambiguity, and contradictions often arise because each adult communal member has a different set of expectations for children. Infractions of the rules are likely to bring several reprimands in addition to those from the parents (for a fuller discussion of children in a communal setting, see Kanter et al., 1975). Parents experience a dilution of control and influence over their children. In some cases multiple control and responsibility for children turns out to be almost no control and responsibility. In fact, rather badly neglected children come from some communes (especially those with heavy drug usage). Because everyone is supposed to be responsible for the children, each thinks other adults will be doing the job when, in reality, no one is. Yet being able to turn to more adults can also be an advantage for children, as they are exposed to many role models and as they find solace and approval elsewhere when they are in trouble with their parents.

B.   The Chinese Family

To help you better understand the characteristics of the American family, it is worthwhile to compare families from other cultures. The structure of both historical and modern Chinese families is different from the American family, yet family functions are successfully fulfilled.

The Pre-Communist Chinese Extended Family

The dominant family structure in pre-Communist China was a broad *extended family* (two or three generations living together). It was, in many ways, the essential unit of society.

Most economic production within the society was carried out by the Chinese family. The husband/father was the employer and the wife/mother and the children were the workers. The home often also served as a shop or factory. Because the family was the source of most employment and because family ties were closely adhered to, one could not leave the family and have much chance of finding work. In a sense one inherited a job. Families limited employment to kin, little land was available for sale; therefore the young had to remain within the family to survive. There was no government charity, because the family was expected to care for its own. Although such a system was restrictive, it offered security in that all had a place and knew that other family members would help them survive. This system of family loyalty is found among Chinese families no matter where in the world they have migrated.

The system has actually maintained itself here in America. There are still clan lofts that act as activity centers for the extended family clan. In a new city, a clan member is always welcome at the clan loft and given help if necessary. A Chinese mother and father worked long hours in their laundry, in part to help their eldest son through medical school. When the son finally was ready to enter practice, he was int'oduced at a clan gathering and immediately acquired a large practice. Since he was the only doctor in the clan, all of the clan members were obligated to go to him for their medical needs.[1]

The Chinese family was also the major *political* or control unit. All family members were responsible to the entire family for their actions: "Doing one's own thing" simply was not contemplated. The oldest male held ultimate authority and responsibility. If one member of the family did wrong,

[1]This quote is from C. K. Yang's Sociology of the Family classes. University of Hawaii, 1970.

the whole family was held responsible.

In today's era of giant government bureaucracies it is hard to believe that late in the nineteenth century the central Chinese government governed 400 million people spread over 4.5 million square miles with only about 40,000 officials. Los Angeles city and county governments have more employees than this. It was possible to govern with so few officials only because of the strong family authority.

In America one still finds evidence of this powerful controlling function of the Chinese family. Very few Chinese children are delinquent. When they are, the family assumes responsibility. For example, a Chinese boy was caught shoplifting. During his trial, his grandfather was helped to the stand and stated that he was responsible for the theft. When questioned by the judge, the grandfather explained that he had fathered and raised the father who had failed to properly rear the boy, thus he was ultimately responsible for the breakdown in family morality.

Chinese families also educated their own children. Such education was mainly vocational, teaching the children to farm, to work in the family business, and otherwise to contribute to family well-being.

Religion was a family function. Worship was mainly within the home, which contained an altar. The male head of the household led the prayers. The major Chinese religion, Confucianism, emphasized ancestor worship; devotion to parents, family, and friends; and the maintenance of justice and peace. Thus the religion reinforced the family functions.

Concubinage (the taking of secondary wives) existed among most groups except the peasants, whose rural mores and poverty prohibited it. In those families that did practice concubinage, the secondary wife (or wives) resided in the family but was considered the first wife's inferior and was dominated by the first wife. The concubine could never assume the status of first wife. Her main function was to produce sons. When she did produce sons, they were considered the offspring of the principal wife. If affection did not develop between the primary wife and husband, concubinage often made divorce unnecessary and so preserved the social unity of the family.

It should be noted that concubinage and the large successful extended family structure were limited to the middle and upper classes. Many of the peasants were forced to sell their children in order to survive the poverty and famine of nineteenth-century China, thus weakening the family unity for that class. However, for a period of nearly 2500 years, until the beginning of the present century, a remarkable social and cultural continuity characterized the Chinese family (for a fuller discussion of the Chinese family, see Queen and Habenstein, 1974, pp. 96–126).

The Communist Chinese Family[2]

After many years of fighting first the Japanese and then an extended civil war, China finally came under Communist rule in 1949. Because so much power

[2]Adapted from Ruth Sidel, *Families of Fengsheng* (Baltimore: Penguin, 1974, pp. 73, 74, 147–58). Reprinted by permission of Penguin Books, Inc.

historically had been vested in the family, especially in the eldest male, it was necessary for the Communists to change this power structure if they were to control the people.

The Communists emphasized collectivism and community good rather than the individual. But the Chinese family was a private entity and emphasized the family good, feeling no allegiance to others. Family allegiances had to be turned from the family to the state if people were to be changed. It appears, from what little information is available since the easing of tension between China and America, that the Communists have been successful in making the family an agency of the state rather than a private refuge for the individual. Little is said in official publications about private man/woman relationships. Rather, publications emphasize the community, political work, and devotion to the state as the ends to be sought by the family.

The major structural change is the breakup of the extended family and its replacement by the smaller nuclear unit. As will be seen, however, although the extended family of relations is to a large extent gone, the nuclear group is still part of a larger group, only now the larger group is the neighborhood. The state has also taken over the political and educational functions that were carried out by the pre-Communist Chinese family.

Life in Communist China

The organization of life in China's neighborhoods can perhaps best be viewed as a total community support system, one fostered and maintained by the residents of the neighborhoods themselves. As life in the Fengsheng neighborhood demon-

strates, the people of China's cities have a myriad of ways in which they can interact: within their courtyard, where residents talk informally, communally clean the courtyard, plant and prune the greenery, admire one another's children, and discuss the latest political events; within their study group, where people read together, discuss politics, evaluate their own and others' attitudes and contributions, and are in turn evaluated; within the residents' committee, in which members are encouraged to help one another and to come together in large numbers for common purposes such as the Great Patriotic Sanitation Movement; within the neighborhood, where people work cooperatively to provide preschool care, to provide work for the unemployed in local factories, and to provide health care; and finally within the place of work, which provides not only study groups but a larger central focus, an avenue to contributing to the society, a parallel system of providing human services, and a setting for warm social relationships. This total structure is characterized first by intimacy. People live and work together very closely and know each other well. The concept of privacy seems to be quite different in China, where an individual's personal life, his health, and his work performance are all viewed as being in the public domain, since they all affect the role he plays and the contribution he makes to society. The very structure of work and of residential communities, even the physical structure of the courtyards built within walls, serve to enhance this intimacy. (Sidel, 1974, pp. 147–48)

It is clear from this description of modern Chinese society that the family and the society blend into one another. The Chinese husband, wife, and children are part of an immediate family, but in addition each participates in the larger community in meaningful and personal ways. Their obligation is not only to themselves and their immediate family but to the larger community in which and by which their individual family exists.

Also, the family has many ties

to the community from which to draw support. For example:

If a couple is quarreling, a member of the residents' committee will go to the home and advise the couple to unite. Sometimes even children of eight or nine will come to the residents' committee to ask for help. Whoever is available will go. [They] will talk separately with the husband and with the wife and then all [will] talk together. If the children are at home, they will attend, and if older people live in the home, they may attend, too.

If the marital problems persist and the couple wish to request a divorce, they must go to see a "cadre of basic state power" in the Administrative Office of the Ching Nian commune. This cadre is a man about forty years old without any special training but one who has a "good knowledge of the Chinese Marriage Law and of party policy." According to members of the committee, this cadre has "more experience with this kind of work" and "is good with other people's problems." He will first ask the couple their reason for wanting a divorce; he will then "try his best to advise them to unite, not to separate." He will talk with members of their working units and consult with members of their residents' committee. He will then meet with the marital partners separately, then together—often three to five times and sometimes even as many as ten times.

If the couple still wish a divorce, they will then simply obtain a certificate from this same cadre. Out of 9,100 families in the Ching Nian commune from January to September, 1972, seventeen couples requested divorces. Six couples were "united," and the remaining eleven, whose "characters and feelings were different," received divorces. . . .

Thus the functioning of the entire person is seen as the concern of the community in which he lives and works, and that community is responsible for helping him, through criticism, support, and if necessary, through modifying his environment. This amount of peer or societal control would, no doubt, be intolerable to many in the West, but it seems to be accepted, by and large, by the Chinese, and indeed it seems to stem at least in part from their past. The individual's right to self-determination, to personal growth, or even to self-destruction has never been revered in China as it is in the West. (Sidel, 1974, pp. 73, 149)

Thus family structures that bear little relation to the American nuclear family structure can manage to control sexual activity, reproduce societal members, and supply emotional support and gratification.

What Do You Think?

What are the gains for the society in investing political power in the family rather than in the state?

What are the losses to the individual if the family controls both economic and political power?

Would you rather live in a pre-Communist Chinese extended family, a modern Chinese Communist family, or an American nuclear family? Why?

C. Government and Family Policy

In recent years people have started to study the effect that government policies and laws have on the family. The family, after all, exists within a society and that society is governed by laws. The family is therefore affected by those laws.

Formerly, little direct effort was made by the government to understand what effect, if any, a given law might have on the family institution. For example, until

recently women with children on welfare received more support if their husbands left them. Social workers had to check on welfare families to be sure that there was no husband present. In essence the welfare system worked to break up families.

More recently, various *income maintenance* (guaranteeing all families a minimum income) experiments that ensure support to all members of a family even if the marriage is terminated have been tried. One rationale for these experiments was that a family that survives economically is less apt to break up than one that does not. Yet in actuality another effect was also discovered—the independence effect (Steiner, 1979). For some women who are guaranteed an income for themselves and their dependent children, divorce is the outcome because the guaranteed income allows them to be independent of their husbands. In surveying these experiments, Suzanne M. Bianchi and Reynolds Farley (1979, p. 548) conclude:

The net outcome of the opposing effects (increased stability vs. increased independence) depends upon the magnitude of the support level and the income of the family in the absence of support. Most discussions of the negative income tax or other income maintenance programs envision modest levels of support which would be focused upon families near the poverty level. The experiments conducted thus far suggest that, in such circumstances, the independence effect will far outweigh the income effect and rates of family dissolution will increase.

Family policy research is aimed at uncovering these kinds of practical relationships between governmental actions and the family.

The White House Conference on Families, as well as the family conferences held by most states

during 1979 and 1980, also signal growing governmental concern for the family. The following paraphrased excerpt from the report on the White House Conference on Families (1981) will give you an idea of the kinds of issues raised at these conferences.

The number one concern cited at the hearings was the sensitivity, or insensitivity, of federal, state, and local government toward families. Policies covering tax, welfare, and foster care were among the policies critics claimed ignored or undermined families.

Economic pressure was the number two concern, with the impact of inflation, poverty, and unemployment the most frequently cited problems. Support for specific family structures, such as traditional families, single parent families, and extended families was the third major concern.

Participants mentioned child care — its cost and availability — as their fourth concern, while education followed as number five. Among issues raised that related to education were its quality and availability, home/school relations, moral concerns, and the responsiveness of educational systems to diverse needs.

Concern six covered health care issues, while the seventh focused on work and families, i.e., the conflict between work and family responsibilities, the need for flexible employment practices, discrimination in the workplace, increased participation in the work force, and redefinition of the relationship between business and families.

Americans have mixed feelings about government formally declaring interest in the family. Many fear it will lead to more governmental interference in their lives. On the other hand, intentionally or not, the government is a part of every family.

CHAPTER 2

AMERICAN WAYS OF LOVE

CONTENTS

To most Americans, love and marriage are like hand and glove, apple pie and ice cream, bacon and eggs — they belong together. Where there is one, there should be the other. Of course, we all know of marriages without love, and romantic literature is full of examples of love without marriage. But the traditional ideal, the ultimate in human relationships for most Americans, is the steady, time-honored, and sought-after combination of love and marriage.

Love and Marriage

When Americans are asked "Why do you want to marry?" they often reply "Because I love. . . ." So we Americans marry for love. But, doesn't everyone? What other reasons could there be?

Indeed, there are other reasons. Historically, not everyone has married for love. Even today many cultures do not accept love as a reasonable basis for marriage. Love as a basis for marriage may be a unique American contribution to the world. As Ralph Linton pointed out many years ago, "All societies recognize that there are occasional violent emotional attachments between persons of the opposite sex, but our present American culture is the only one which has attempted to capitalize on these and make them the basis for marriage." (Linton, 1936, p. 175)

Love in most societies historically has been an amusing pastime, a distraction, or, in some cases, a godsent affliction. For example, courtly love began as a sport among the feudal aristocracy. It exalted both chastity and adultery. Courtly love glorified love from afar and made a fetish of suffering over love affairs. It made a great game of love where men proved their manliness on the jousting field in the name of love and a woman's honor. Adultery was an integral part of courtly love. The intrigue and excitement of adultery added to the sport and made the love even more sweet. Marriage was not considered the proper place for courtly love. Married love was too mundane and unexciting.

The story of the knight Ulrich von Lichtenstein highlights courtly love which seldom found consummation in marriage. At an early age Ulrich pledged his love and admiration to an unnamed lady. He accepted every challenge in an effort to prove himself worthy of serving his love. He was filled with melancholy and painful longings for his lady, a condition which he claimed gave him joy.

The heartless lady, however, rejected his admiration even after his ten years of silent devotion and his many feats of valor. Undaunted, perhaps even inspired by her rebuffs, he undertook a stupendous journey in 1227 from Venice north to Bohemia during which he claimed to have broken the incredible total of three hundred and seven lances fighting his way to Vienna and his lady love.

It comes as something of a shock when by his own statement he stopped off for three days to visit his wife and children. For the fact is that this lovesick Galahad, this kissless wonder, this dauntless knight-errant had long had a wife to lie with when he had the urge, and a family to live with when he felt lonely. He even speaks of his affection for his wife, but, of course, not his love; to love

---

I Certainly Don't Want the Responsibility of Picking My Own Mate

David Mace, a marriage scholar, reports the following conversation with a group of coeds in India:

"Wouldn't you like to be free to choose your own partners, like the young people in the West?"

"Oh no!" several voices replied in chorus.

"Why not?"

"For one thing," said one of them, "Doesn't it put the girl in a very humiliating position?"

"Humiliating? In what way?"

"Well, doesn't it mean that she has to try to look pretty and call attention to herself, and attract a boy, to be sure she'll get married?"

"Well, perhaps so."

"And if she doesn't want to do that, or if she feels it's undignified, wouldn't that mean she mightn't get a husband?"

"Yes, that's possible."

"So a girl who is shy and doesn't push herself forward might not be able to get married. Does that happen?"

"Sometimes it does."

"Well, surely that's humiliating. It makes getting married a sort of competition in which the girls are fighting each other for the boys. And it encourages a girl to pretend she's better than she really is. She can't relax and be herself. She has to make a good impression to get a boy, and then she has to go on making a good impression to get him to marry her."

Before we could think of an answer to this unexpected line of argument, another girl broke in.

"In our system, you see," she explained, "we girls don't have to worry at all. We know we'll get married. When we are old enough, our parents will find a suitable boy, and everything will be arranged. We don't have to enter into competition with each other."

"Besides," said a third girl, "how would we be able to judge the character of a boy we met and got friendly with?

We are young and inexperienced. Our parents are older and wiser, and they aren't as easily deceived as we would be. I'd far rather have my parents choose for me. It's so important that the man I marry should be the right one. I could so easily make a mistake if I had to find him for myself."

Another girl had her hand stretched out eagerly.

"But does the girl really have any choice in the West?" she said. "From what I've read, it seems that the boy does all the choosing. All the girl can do is say yes or no. She can't go up to a boy and say 'I like you. Will you marry me?' Can she?"

We admitted that this was not done.

"So," she went on eagerly, "when you talk about men and women being equal in the West, it isn't true. When our parents are looking for a husband for us, they don't have to wait until some boy takes it into his head to ask for us. They just find out what families are looking for wives for their sons, and see whether one of the boys would be suitable. Then, if his family agrees that it would be a good match, they arrange it together."

her would have been improper and unthinkable to the ethic of courtly love. (Hunt, 1959, pp. 132–39)

On the other hand, ancient Japan felt love to be a grave offense if not properly sanctioned, for it interfered with proper marriage arrangements. Etsu Sugimoto describes this in *A Daughter of the Samurai*:

When she was employed in our house, she was very young, and because she was the sister of father's faithful Jiya, she was allowed much freedom. A youthful servant, also of our house, fell in love with her. For young people to become lovers without the sanction of the proper formalities was a grave offense in any class, but in a samurai household it was a black disgrace to the house. The penalty was exile through the water gate — a gate of brush built over a stream and never used except by one of the Eta, or outcast class. The departure was public and the culprits were everafter shunned by everyone. The penalty was unspeakably cruel, but in the old days severe measures were used as a preventative of law-breaking. (Sugimoto, 1935, pp. 115–16)

As surprising as it may be, such attitudes are still widespread. Marriage in many cultures has been and still is based on considerations other than love. In India, as Inset 2-1 demonstrates, the Hindu place responsibility for finding a suitable mate on the parents or older relatives. The potential mate is judged by his or her economic status, caste, family, and physical appearance. These criteria are not by any means simple snobbery; they reflect the couple's prospects for rapport, financial stability, and social acceptance, all valid concerns in marriage. Even in the United States such considerations are often found hidden in the ephemeral concept of love, as we shall see in Chapter 3.

Defining Love

Trying to define love is a task that has kept poets, philosophers, and sages busy since the beginning of history. Americans, as we have discussed, generally marry for love, or think they do — but what is this phenomenon that causes two people to react to one another so strongly? Is it physical? Spiritual? A mixture of the two? Why does it only occur with some people and not others? Is it the same as infatuation? The questions are endless, yet each person speaks of love, recognizes love, and seeks love whether or not he or she can define just what this vivid and strong emotion is.

The Greek poet Sappho twenty-five centuries ago described the physical state of love:

What Do You Think?

What do you personally mean when you say, "I love you"?

What do your parents mean when they say "I love you" to each other? To you?

Does saying "I love you" carry a commitment to marriage? To sexual intercourse?

How do you recognize if a person is sincere in saying that he or she loves you?

How does love make you feel physically?

> For should I but see thee a little moment,
>   Straight is my voice hushed;
> Yea, my tongue is broken, and through and through me
> 'Neath the flesh impalpable fire runs tingling;
> Nothing see mine eyes, and a noise of roaring
>   Waves in my ear sounds;
> Sweat runs in rivers, a tremor seizes
> All my limbs, and paler than grass in Autumn,
> Caught by pains of menacing death, I falter,
>   Lost in the love-trance.

Sappho, trans. by J. Addington Symonds

The Greeks divided love into three elements: *eros* (carnal or physical love), *agape* (spiritual love), and *philos* (brotherly or friendly love).

Eros is the physical, sexual side of love. It is needing, desiring, and wanting the other person physically. Sappho's poem describes the effect of eros. The Romans called eros Cupid, and, as we know, Cupid shoots the arrow of love into our hearts. Eros is that aspect of love that makes our knees shake, upsets our routines, and causes us to be obsessed with thoughts of our lover.

Eros
The physical, sexual side of love; termed "Cupid" by the Romans

Agape is the altruistic, giving, nondemanding side of love. It is an active concern for the life and growth of those whom we love. It is most clearly demonstrated by the love of a parent for his or her child. Agape is an unconditional affirmation of another person. It is the desire to do things for the beloved, to care, to help, and to give to the loved one.

Agape
Greek term for spiritual love

Theologian Paul Tillich sees the highest form of love as a merging of eros and agape: "No love is real without a unity of eros and agape. Agape without eros is obedience to moral law, without warmth, without longing, without reunion. Eros without agape is a chaotic desire, denying the validity of the claim of the other one to be acknowledged as an independent self, able to love and to be loved" (1957, pp. 114 – 15).

Philos is the love found in deep and enduring friendships. It is also the kind of love described in the Bible as: "Love thy neighbor as thyself." It can be deep friendship for specific people, or it can be a love that generalizes to all people. Philos is often nonexclusive, whereas eros and agape are often exclusive. It is this element of love that is most important to the overall society — to a society's humanity. A loving person creates loving relationships, and enough loving relationships make a loving society. The philos element of love is perhaps what is needed most in modern American society as well as many others. Lack of this kind of love creates a society of alienated and isolated individuals. When people are alienated and isolated from one another, the chance of dehumanized conflict between them escalates. Crime statistics in the United States make it clear that the Christian doctrine "Love thy neighbor" (philos) is too often lacking in our society. It is this kind of love that turns strangers into friends; certainly it is more difficult to perpetrate a crime against a friend than against a stranger. Also, a society that has a high level of philos among its members is a society that fosters the other elements of love.

Philos
Greek term for the love found in deep, enduring friendships; a general love of mankind

Theories of Love

Probably there are as many theories of love as there are persons in love (although it should be noted that such theories do not enjoy much empirical support). However, it is worthwhile to examine a few of them, even if only superficially. To understand how other thoughtful people have theorized about love will help us understand our own feelings and thoughts. And, as we shall see, the better we know our own attitudes and definitions of love, the better we will become in making long-lasting intimate relationships.

In his classic book *The Art of Loving*, Erich Fromm defines love as an active power in man (people), a power that breaks through the walls that separate man from his fellow man. In love we find the paradox of two beings becoming one yet remaining two (Fromm, 1956). Like the Greeks,

INSET 2-2

Love Is . . .

How do I love thee? Let me count the ways.
I love thee to the depth and breadth and height
My soul can reach, when feeling out of sight
For the ends of Being and ideal Grace.
I love thee to the level of everyday's
Most quiet need, by sun and candle-light.
I love thee freely, as men strive for Right;
I love thee purely, as they turn from Praise.
I love thee with the passion put to use
In my old griefs, and with my childhood's faith.
I love thee with a love I seemed to lose
With my lost saints — I love thee with the breath,
Smiles, tears, of all my life! — and, if God choose,
I shall but love thee better after death.

Elizabeth Barrett Browning

When God would invent a thing
apart from eating or drink or
game or sport, and yet a world —
restful while in which our
minds can melt and smile. He
made of Adam's rib an Eve
creating thus the game of
love.

Piet Hein

Love is such a tissue of
paradoxes, and exists in
such an endless variety of
forms and shades that you
may say almost anything
about it that you please,
and it is likely to be correct.

Henry Fink
Romantic Love and Personal Beauty

Love is patient and kind;
love is not jealous or boastful;
it is not arrogant or rude.
Love does not insist on its own
way; it is not irritable and
resentful; it does not rejoice
at wrong, but rejoices in the right.
Love bears all things,
believes all things, hopes all
things, endures all things.

I Corinthians 13:4 – 7

Let me not to the marriage of true minds
Admit impediments. Love is not love
Which alters when it alteration finds,
Or bends with the remover to remove.
O, no! It is an ever-fixed mark
That looks on tempests and is never shaken.
It is the star to every wandering bark,
Whose worth's unknown, although his height be taken.
Love's not Time's fool, though rosy lips and cheeks
Within his bending sickle's compass come.
Love alters not with his brief hours and weeks,
But bears it out even to the edge of doom.
If this be error and upon me proved,
I never writ, nor no man ever loved.

William Shakespeare
Sonnet 116

Love birds burn in the sky,
The Flame of Passion carries them high.
Beaks touching as one,
Wings beginning to melt, as they ride the crest of the flames.
With nothing to hold them in their flight
They fall
Into the inferno
Of their own passion.

Cynthia Moorman

Fromm discusses several kinds of love, including brotherly and maternal love. Brotherly love is characterized by friendship and companionship with affection. Maternal love is characterized by an unselfish interest in your partner and a placing of yourself second to your partner's needs. For Fromm mature love includes attachment plus sexual response. More importantly it includes the four basic elements necessary to any intimate relationship: care, responsibility, respect, and knowledge. People who share all of the elements of mature love are *pair-bonded*. The relationship is reciprocal. Fromm goes on to suggest that a person's need to love and be loved in this full sense arises from the feelings of separateness and aloneness we all experience to some extent. Love helps us escape these feelings and gain a feeling of unitedness.

Taking off from this idea, Lawrence Casler (1969) considers that love develops in part because of our human needs for acceptance and confirmation. These needs are heightened in a society as competitive and individualized as ours. Thus it is a relief to meet someone whose choices coincide with our own, who doesn't try to undermine us in some way. We tend to attach ourselves to such a person because he or she offers us validation, and such validation is an important basis for love (see Rubin, 1973, Chapter 7).

Casler points out that American dating may serve to provoke love feelings in the partners more as a by-product than from some innate attraction. For example, a person, for any number of reasons including simple politeness, may pretend to like his date more than he really does. The date, also seeking validation, responds favorably. This favorable response makes the first person feel good and feel fondness for the one who has made him feel good. As one person's feelings increase, the other's are likely to also. Obviously, it is easier to love someone who loves you than someone who is indifferent.

Of course, falling in love is more complex than in this example because of our many needs besides validation. Sex is another of these needs:

> Society emphasizes the necessity for love to precede sex. Although many disregard this restriction, others remain frightened or disturbed by the idea of a purely sexual relationship. The only way for many sexually aroused individuals to avoid frustration or anxiety is to fall in love — as quickly as possible. More declarations of love have probably been uttered in parked cars than in any other location; some of these are surely nothing more than seduction ploys, but it is likely that self-seduction is involved in most cases. (Casler, 1969, p. 33)

Because our society is marriage-oriented, most of us learn early that not only love but marriage as well is a prerequisite to sex. Thus for most Americans, love, sex, and marriage go together, ideally at least if not always in practice.

In more general terms Casler's sources of love are: (1) the need for security, (2) sexual satisfaction, and (3) social conformity. If these are the causes of love, what are the consequences of love?

First, in this culture Casler says, "Being in love makes it easier to have guilt-free sex, to marry, and to view oneself as a normal healthy citizen." Being in love also creates the error of overevaluation (romanticized ideal images; see Chapter 4) of the love object. Love will foster dependency on the love object insofar as the love object is relied on for much need gratification.

If maturity is, in part, establishing independence, then love, as viewed by Casler, acts as a deterrent to maturity. Although the individual who is unable to love is viewed as pathological in American culture, Casler's interpretation of love can lead to an opposite conclusion. The individual who is not loving may be in excellent mental health. If, as Casler suggests, the need for love is based largely on insecurity, conformity, and sexual frustration, then the person who is secure, independent, and leading a satisfactory sex life may not need love. Such a person will

> be a person who does not find his own company boring, a person whose inner resources are such that other persons, although they supply pleasure and stimulation, are not absolutely necessary. We have long been enjoined to love others as we love ourselves, but perhaps we seek love relationships with others only because we do not love ourselves sufficiently. (p. 36)

Ira Reiss (1960) suggests the wheel as a model of love. In the rapport, or first, stage the partners are struck by feelings that they have known each other before, that they are comfortable with one another, and that they both want to deepen the relationship. These feelings lead to the second stage — self-revelation — during which more and more intimate thoughts and feelings are shared. This sharing deepens the relationship because such sharing is only done with special people — that is, we are special to one another. As the sharing becomes more and more intimate, a feeling of mutual dependency develops (stage three). With it comes a feeling of loss when the partner is not present. More and more personal needs are being met (stage four) as the couple deepens their relationship. Reiss suggests that it was perhaps the hope of having these deeper needs met that caused the initial rapport.

> These four processes are in a sense really one process for when one feels rapport, he/she reveals him/herself and becomes dependent, thereby fulfilling his/her personality needs. The circularity is most clearly seen in that the needs being fulfilled were the original reason for feeling rapport. (1960, p. 143)

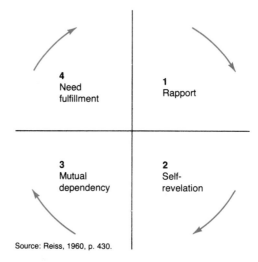

Source: Reiss, 1960, p. 430.

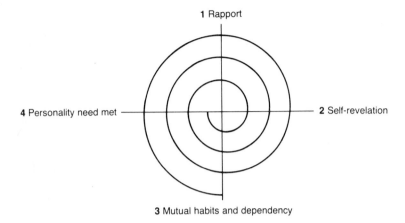

1 Rapport

4 Personality need met — — **2** Self-revelation

3 Mutual habits and dependency

Borland (1975) changes the model slightly, likening it to a clock spring rather than a circle.

> As these four processes occur and lead one into the other, they wind themselves toward a closer and more intimate relationship with an understanding of the real inner self of the other person. As this occurs, the individuals form an increasingly tighter bond to one another in much the same way as a clock spring tightens as it is wound. (Borland, 1975, p. 291)

Romantic Love

For many Americans the idea of **romantic love** most influences their thoughts about attraction and intimacy. This concept of love encompasses such ideas as "love at first sight," "the one and only love mate," "life-long commitment to the one and only," "the continuing excitement of the 'eros' kind of love," "I can't live without him/her," "the perfect mate," and so forth.

In essence the concept of romantic love supplies a set of idealized images by which we can judge the object of our love as well as the quality of the relationship. Unfortunately, such romanticized images usually bear little relationship to the real world. Often we project our beliefs onto another person, exaggerating the characteristics that match the qualities we are looking for and masking those that do not. That is, we transform the other person into an unreal hero or heroine to fit our personal concept of a romantic marital partner. Thus we often fall in love with our own romantic ideas rather than with a real human being.

For example, the traditional romantic ideals dictate a strong, confident, protective role for a man and a charming, loving, dependent role for a woman. A woman holding this stereotype will tend to overlook and deny dependent needs of her mate. She will tend to repress independent qualities she discovers in herself. Love for her means each correctly fulfilling the proper role. The same holds true for a man who has traditional romantic ideals.

Those who "fall in love with love" in this way will suffer disappoint-

Romantic love
Love at first sight, based on the ideas that there is only one true love and that love is the most important criterion for marriage

ment when their partner's "real person" begins to emerge. Rather than meet this emerging person with joy and enthusiasm, partners who hold romanticized ideals may reject reality in favor of their stereotypic images. They may again begin to search for a love object, rejecting the real-life partner as unworthy or changed (see Chapter 4 for a more complete discussion of the problems of idealized expectations). Dating and broad premarital experience with the opposite sex can help correct much of this romantic idealism.

And so we see how people often fall in love with their romanticized expectations rather than with their partner. This tends to lead to one of two actions: Either they reject the partner or they attempt to change the partner into the romantic ideals. John Robert Clark (1961, p. 18) has a pithy description of the first action:

> In learning how to love a plain human being today, as during the romantic movement, what we usually want unconsciously is a fancy human being with no flaws. When the mental picture we have of someone we love is colored by wishes of childhood, we may love the picture rather than the real person behind it. Naturally, we are disappointed in the person we love if he does not conform to our picture. Since this kind of disappointment has no doubt happened to us before, one might suppose we would tear up the picture and start all over. On the contrary, we keep the picture and tear up the person. Small wonder that divorce courts are full of couples who never gave themselves a chance to know the real person behind the pictures in their lives.

The second action, attempting to change one's spouse, also leads to trouble. Making changes is difficult, and the person being asked to do so may resent the demand or may not wish to change.

Generally, romantic love's rose-colored glasses tend to distort the real world, especially the mate, thereby creating a barrier to happiness. This is not to deny that romantic love can add to an intimate relationship. Romance will bring excitement, emotional highs, and color to one's relationship. From there we can move toward a more mature love relationship. As intimacy develops in many ways — emotionally, intellectually, socially, and physically — romance then takes its place as one of several aspects of the relationship, not the only one.

Romantic Love and Infatuation

Romantic love and infatuation are often confused. Some (Hatfield and Walster, 1978) say that they are actually the same thing. Lovers use the term "romantic love" to describe an ongoing love relationship. The couple's feelings, bodily reactions, and interactions when they are romantically in love are the same as with infatuation. The difference may be only semantic. The term *infatuation* is used to negate one's past feelings of love that have now changed. Love is supposed to last forever, so falling out of love means that the feeling for the other person was not really love; it must have been something less — namely, infatuation (Udry, 1974). According to this line of thinking, perhaps it is only possible to tell infatuation from romantic love in retrospect.

Still others suggest that infatuation may be the first step toward love. The feelings of physical attraction, the chemical arousal, the intense preoccupation with your partner, all characteristics of infatuation, are also the precursors to "real" love. Other persons may use the word infatuation to describe your state: "You were infatuated with him before you met me." "Our daughter is infatuated with someone we don't approve of." From the many ways the term is used, it is apparent that we probably cannot agree completely on the difference between romantic love and infatuation. Ann Landers periodically reprints a suggested list of differences between the two terms:

Love or Infatuation?

Infatuation is instant desire. It is one set of glands calling to another.

Love is friendship that has caught fire. It takes root and grows — one day at a time.

Infatuation is marked by a feeling of insecurity. You are excited and eager, but not genuinely happy. There are nagging doubts, unanswered questions, little bits and pieces about your beloved that you would just as soon not examine too closely. It might spoil the dream.

Love is the quiet understanding and mature acceptance of imperfection. It is real. It gives you strength and grows beyond you — to bolster your beloved. You are warmed by their presence, even when they are far away.

Infatuation says "We must get married right away. I can't risk losing you."

Love says, "Be patient. Don't panic. Plan your future with confidence."

Infatuation has an element of sexual excitement. If you are honest, you will admit it is difficult to be in one another's company unless you are sure it will end in intimacy.

Love is the maturation of friendship. You must be friends before you can be lovers.

Infatuation lacks confidence. When they are away you wonder if they are being true.

Love means trust. You are calm, secure, and unthreatened. Your partner feels that trust and it makes him/her even more trustworthy.

Infatuation might lead you to do things you'll regret later, but love never will.

Love lifts you up. It makes you look up. It makes you think up. It makes you a better person than you were before.

Such a list makes love sound grown-up and infatuation childish. Yet playfulness and childishness are also acceptable and are important parts of any intimate relationship.

How can we avoid the pitfalls of romantic love and infatuation? How can we be sure that we love someone just as they are and are not dazzled by our own romantic image of them? Perhaps we can't. Love is learned and part of the learning to move toward a mature, realistic love may be simply trial and error.

Furthermore, the most important prerequisite for true love may be knowing and accepting ourselves, complete with faults and virtues. If we cannot deal with our own imperfections, how can we be tolerant of someone else's? As Erich Fromm . . . puts it,

Love of others and love of ourselves are not alternatives. On the contrary, an attitude of love toward themselves will be found in all those who are capable of loving others. *Love, in principle, is indivisible as far as the connection between "objects" and one's own self is concerned.* Genuine love is an expression of productiveness and implies care, respect, responsibility, and knowledge. (1956, p. 59)

Love Is What You Make It

The more one investigates the idea of love, the harder it becomes to pin down. Everyone is quick to describe it, most have experienced it, and all know the mythology of the romantic ideal even though many disclaim their belief in it. Although there does seem to be some agreement on at least a few of the aspects of love, much of what love is appears to be unique to each person. That is to say, we each define love for ourselves. This may lead to problems for a couple if each member defines love somewhat differently from the other. It is important to examine your concept of love in order to understand it and thereby recognize differences between what you and your partner may mean by love. For example, A. Lynn Scoresby (1977, p. 168) suggests that "since love is the word symbol we are accustomed to use in explaining great varieties of marital events, if actual feelings of love are not determinant of happy marriages, then mutual agreement about what love means is. Love is, after all, the most often given reason for getting married, and loss of love is the most often given reason for dissolving a marriage." So, if a couple can agree on what love is, on what loving acts are, and, most of the time, can act on this agreement, then their chances are great of maintaining love in their relationship.

So, let us begin by examining those aspects of love where there seems to be at least some agreement. Most people agree that there is a strong physical attraction between lovers at least during the early stages of their relationship. This attraction is often accompanied by a variety of physiological reactions such as more rapid breathing, increased pulse rate, and muscular tension. In other words, the person "in love" experiences general emotional arousal when thinking of the loved one or when in his or her presence.

Of course, such a reaction could be just sexual attraction and infatuation rather than love. But if the physical attraction is accompanied by a strong and growing emotional attachment, and if there is a marked tendency to idealize and be preoccupied with the person, then the reactions are more indicative of love.

Generally there is a feeling of openness between lovers. Both feel they can confide in the other. Both believe the other likes them as they really are, so they can be more open, more honest, more communicative — in a word, more intimate — than in nonlove relationships. One way of viewing love may be as "intimate self-disclosure" (Schultz & Rodgers, 1975, p. 2).

Such open sharing of your true feelings can be risky. A person in love is easily hurt, as all lovers, past and present, will attest. Thus to love is always an adventure because danger is involved. Indifference is the opposite of love. A lover cares, a lover reveals more of himself or herself and

INSET 2-3

Adrenaline Makes the Heart Grow Fonder

A frightened man is a potentially romantic man. So is an angry man, a jealous man, a rejected man, or a euphoric man. Anyone, in fact, who experiences the physical arousal that accompanies strong human emotion is a potentially romantic person in that he has already fulfilled one of the two essential conditions for love and is a step ahead of the person whose emotions are in a quiescent stage. If he should meet an unusually desirable woman while he is in this state, he is likely to be more intensely drawn to her than he would be in normal circumstances.

To love passionately, a person must be physically aroused, a condition manifested by palpitations of the heart, nervous tremor, flushing, and accelerated breathing. Once he is so aroused, all that remains is for him to identify this complex of feelings as passionate love, and he will have experienced authentic love (Walster and Berscheid, 1971, p. 46).

This is a highly simplified account of some fascinating research on emotion and love. Based on the idea that both physiological arousal and the intellectual interpretation or labeling of the arousal are necessary to produce an emotional experience (Schachter, 1964), researchers have found that both positive and negative physiological arousal can lead one to love if the labeling process is strong enough.

For example, in one study men were led to believe they would soon receive three "pretty stiff" electrical shocks. Later the experimenters told half of them that there had been an error and they would not receive the shocks. A third group used as a control was not told about any electrical shocks. The experimenters introduced each of the men to a young woman and asked later how much each liked her. Those who were still expecting the electrical shock and those who had been told to expect one initially, but later told that they wouldn't be shocked, exhibited more liking for the woman than did the control group. The experimenters concluded that the fear, though irrelevant to the emotion of liking, facilitated the attraction. Likewise, the relief from fear, which is also emotional, seemed to facilitate attraction.

Another example might be the fact that many American women of traditional upbringing label their sexual experiences as love. They have been taught that sex without love is taboo. If they feel highly aroused sexually, then social pressure leads them to label their feelings as "love." This then justifies their sexual feelings and thereby reduces their guilt if they act on their sexual feelings.

a lover is therefore vulnerable to being hurt. When hurt occurs, a lover may react to the pain with hostility and anger, and, at times, with hate. Indifference is the reaction of someone who doesn't care, who isn't hurt — who isn't in love. It is interesting to note that the indifferent person, the person who cares least in a relationship, is the one who exercises more control over the relationship. The caring person, the most loving person in the relationship, is more vulnerable to being hurt. Therefore the caring persons often go out of their way to placate and please their mates. The fact that the mate who cares least in a relationship has more power and control over the relationship is termed "the principle of least interest."

Another way of thinking of love is to ask whether the love experience is leading to personal growth. Most people in love experience an expansion of self. Being loved by another leads to feelings of confidence and

security. Many people are encouraged to venture into new and perhaps unknown areas of themselves. "I feel more emotions than I've ever felt before." "I used to feel awkward meeting new people, but when I'm with Mary, I have no trouble at all." "Bill makes me feel like I can do anything I want."

Probably most Americans will agree on the characteristics of love thus far discussed: physical attraction, emotional attachment, self-disclosure and openness, and feelings of personal growth. Yet how these characteristics are expressed by individuals will vary greatly, and such variance can lead to communication breakdowns. To say and mean "I love you" is one thing. We all recognize the word, but it has become so worn by its indiscriminate passage through time that we no longer can identify it with certainty or clearly tell what it represents (Lasswell & Lobsenz, 1980, p. xii).

Two people very much "in love" may have quite different ideas about what this means and how to express it. For example, it is not uncommon for one partner to feel loving toward the other while at the same time the other feels unloved. It is as if they are on different emotional wavelengths. "But you never tell me that you love me," she may say. "I shouldn't have to tell you. I do loving things for you," he replies. Those "loving things" may in his eyes include such actions as bringing home the pay check, fixing broken appliances, avoiding arguments. In her eyes they are merely things any good man routinely does. She defines evidence of love as words of endearment, gifts, touching, tenderness — the kinds of behavior that he is perhaps uncomfortable with. And yet he knows he loves her. But she is not getting the message. In other words love is more than emotion. Love is also an intellectual concept. It is what you think it is. It is how you define it, which will probably differ to some extent from how your partner defines it (Lasswell & Lobsenz, 1980).

Because we usually assume that our meaning of love is the same as our partner's, we may often feel unloved when, in fact, our partner's expression of love is simply unrecognized. The emotional script in this case is:

> I, like every man and woman, want to be loved. But I have my own idea, grounded in my personality and attitudes and experience, of what loving and being loved means. Moreover, locked in the prison of my own ways of thinking and feeling, I assume that my definition of love is the only correct one. As a result, I want and expect to be loved in the same way that I love others, with the same responses that I interpret as the evidence of lovingness.
>
>   But I am not loved in that way. Instead (and quite logically, if one could be logical about love), I am loved the way my partner thinks and feels about love, the way he or she understands and expresses it. In my own distress, I do not recognize that my partner is experiencing the same incongruity in reverse. Puzzled, hurt, unable to communicate our confusion to each other, we both unreasonably feel unloved. (Lasswell & Lobsenz, 1980, p. 15)

In a truly loving relationship, each partner tries to learn the meaning of love as defined by the other person and to incorporate the differences into one's own concept of love. Ideally, in a successful love relationship, each partner's concept of love grows to include the other's concept. As our personal definitions of love move closer together, our chances of feeling loved increase.

Jill and Bob are much in love. When Bob is alone with her and feeling particularily loving, he often grabs her and wrestles her down to the floor or couch, makes karatelike yells, and unfortunately, often hurts her slightly but only unintentionally. She hates this behavior and tells him, "If you really loved me, you wouldn't act like this and you wouldn't hurt me. People who love one another don't wrestle." His feelings are hurt by her rejection of his wrestling, although he always feels badly if he hurts her. Jill feels most loved when Bob approaches her slowly and gently; she feels unloved when he is rough with her. He feels that she doesn't love him because she is never enthusiastically physically attacking him.

In Jill and Bob's case it is clear that each person demonstrates love of the other in a different way. Bob's physically wrestling with Jill is perhaps his most comfortable way of touching her. Certainly it is the way American men are taught to display affection toward other men, especially on the sports field, as one can easily observe during a football game. On the other hand Jill has been taught that the more you love someone or something, the gentler you are. Again this is a message from our society: "Don't roughhouse; ladies don't act like that!" Both Jill and Bob are expressing their love, yet their differences of expression cause each to think that they are loved less than they really are. Love, it seems, is what *you* make it through your attitudes and behaviors.

Styles of Loving*

Marcia Lasswell and Norman Lobsenz agree with our thesis that love is defined by each person in a unique manner based on one's life experiences. They believe that these definitions of love and one's attitudes towards love, although individual, can be classified into six general styles. Most people will be a mixture of styles, with one or two predominating. To understand various styles of loving is valuable because they are basic to all of us and will characterize our intimate loving relationships.

Best-Friends Love

When Jennifer and Gary told their families they were going to be married, the news was a pleasant surprise to everyone. "We knew they were close," said Jennifer's mother. "After all, our families have lived on the same block for years and the children went through school together. But we never dreamed they would fall in love." Neither did Jennifer and Gary. "Actually it's not as if we fell in love at all. It's more that we're comfortable with each other. We have a really warm and easy relationship, so why bother to search for anyone else?"

In this case a comfortable intimacy has developed out of close association over a substantial period of time. For persons in whom this style predominates, love grows through companionship, rapport, mutual sharing and dependency, and gradual self-revelation. There is seldom any assumption at the outset of the relationship that it will flower into love or marriage. Friendly lovers find it hard to conceive of becoming emotionally involved with someone they do not know well. They rarely fantasize about other potential lovers. Even if this thought should occur to them, they would probably want to share it with their partners. After all, isn't that what a best friend is for? Such persons tend to speak of their love as "mature" compared with other styles of love, which they are likely to see as infatuation.

Typically, a person with the best-friends love style is the product of an

*This material has been taken from *Styles of Loving* by Marcia Lasswell and Norman Lobsenz. Garden City, New York: Doubleday & Co., 1980.

emotionally secure and close-knit family. He or she has usually been able to count on parents and siblings for companionship, warmth, and support. In many respects this style of love resembles a good sibling relationship. The divorce rate is low for best-friend couples, but if such a relationship does break up, the lover will most likely want to remain close to his/her former partner. After all, two people who had once loved one another could not become enemies simply because they ceased to be lovers.

Game-Playing Love

To the game-playing lover an emotional relationship is a challenge to be enjoyed, a contest to be won. The more experienced one grows at the game, the more skilled one's moves can be, and often a wide range of strategies is developed to keep the game interesting. Commitment is virtually anathema to this style of lover. The object of the game is to play amiably at love, to encourage intimacy, yet to hold it at arm's length. The other person is usually kept emotionally off balance, and the game player's affections are never to be taken for granted.

Game-playing lovers have many artifices. For example, they avoid making long-range plans with partners. Dates are usually arranged on a spur-of-the-moment basis. They are careful not to go out with the same person too often; this might lead him or her to believe there was some prospect of stability. Much of this kind of love style is found before marriage when a one-to-one commitment is not required or expected. Obviously, men and women who play at love have both charming and infuriating qualities. They are usually self-sufficient, making few demands on the other person and preferring not to have demands made on them. They tend to be amusing, quick-witted, self-confident. On the other hand, they tend to be self-centered. The charge often is made that game-playing love is not truly love at all, that it is hedonism at best and promiscuity at worst. But the true game player believes in playing fair and tries not to hurt the other person.

Logical Love

The logical lover concentrates on the practical values that may be found in a relationship. This style has been called "love with a shopping list." "I could never love anyone who didn't meet my requirements for a husband and father (or wife and mother)." Moreover, logical lovers are quite realistic. They usually know exactly what kind of partner they want and are willing to wait for the person who comes closest to meeting their specifications.

It is not uncommon for a lover of this pragmatic bent to avoid any relationship that he or she does not think has a good chance of becoming permanent. "Why should I waste my time?" In one sense logical love is an updated version of the traditional "arranged" matchmaking of earlier times. The modern logical lover may think that romance does have some place in love, but he or she believes more strongly that love should be an outgrowth of a couple's practical compatibility.

Pragmatic lovers consider themselves in love so long as the relationship is perceived as a fair exchange. If matters turn out to be not what they seemed, logical love calls for a two-step response. First, an effort is made to help the partner fulfill his or her original potential. If such efforts fail, then the relationship is ended. Not surprisingly, logical love requires patience: patience to find the proper partner; patience to work out problems; and if the relationship should break up, patience to wait to end it until a reasonable and logical time.

Possessive Love

The possessive lover presents perhaps the most unfulfilling and disturbing love style. Alternating between peaks of excitement and depths of despair, capable of shifting in an eyeblink from intense devotion to intense jealousy, he or she is consumed by the need to possess the beloved totally, and simultaneously to be possessed by the other person. The fear of loss or rejection is omnipresent. Despite this bleak picture, the pattern is usually considered one of the most common definitions of being in love.

At the root of possessive love are two seemingly contradictory emotional factors. On the one hand, such lovers are enormously dependent. At the outset of the love affair they may be too excited to sleep, eat, or think clearly. Unable to control their intense reactions, they often feel helplessly at the mercy of the beloved. Yet at the same time such lovers are demanding, often placing great emotional burdens on the other person. Supersensitive, the possessive lover is constantly on the alert for the slightest sign that the partner's affection may be slackening. If such a sign is detected, or even imagined, the anxiety-ridden lover demands immediate reassurance.

When affairs with possessive lovers break up, the ending is usually bitter and angry. The possessive lover finds it almost impossible to see his or her former partner again or to retain any concern or affection for him or her. It is easy to give possessive love a bad name and to concentrate on its unpleasant characteristics. Nevertheless, it has been our experience that many perfectly adequate and emotionally healthy people evidence this style of love to some degree. They prefer intense togetherness. They see jealousy as a natural part of being in love.

Romantic Love

Cupid's arrow piercing the heart and instantaneously awakening passionate devotion — no other image so accurately delineates this style. The romantic lover is often as much in love with love itself as with the beloved. Love at first sight is not only possible but almost a necessity. The typical romantic lover seeks a total emotional relationship with the partner. Moreover, he or she expects it to provide a constant series of emotional peaks. The fires of this love style are fueled in large part by a powerful sense of physical attraction.

Once they have found each other, two romantic lovers are likely to be in each other's arms quickly. There is a great urgency to merge physically as well as emotionally. Obviously the intensity of this initial attraction and passion cannot be maintained indefinitely at the same high level. When it begins to taper off, the romantic lover must either substitute fantasies for realities or confront the growing evidence that the other person is not perfect.

One must be willing and able to reveal oneself completely, to commit oneself totally, to risk emotional lows as well as highs, and, finally, to survive without despair if one's love is rejected. A romantic does not demand love but is confidently ready to grasp it when it appears.

Unselfish Love

Unselfish love is unconditionally caring and nurturing, giving and forgiving, and at its highest level, self-sacrificing. A characteristic of this love style is that one has no sense of martyrdom, no feeling of being put upon. Rather, the style rests on the genuine belief that true love is better expressed in giving than in receiving. This style of love is sometimes called *agape*. In a sense men and women with this style of love never actually "fall in love." Rather, they seem to have a reservoir of loving kindness that is always available. They are ruled less by their own needs than by the needs of others. Unselfish love occurs less often in real life than imagined. Not many people have the emotional fortitude to be so giving. And even if they have, their altruism is not necessarily devoid of all personal rewards. An unselfish lover experiences in return feelings of satisfaction, recognition, even gratitude.

Learning to Love

If there really are such styles of loving as set forth by Lasswell and Lobsenz, where do they come from and how do we learn them? Essentially we learn the meaning of love and how to demonstrate it from those around us — our parents, siblings, peers — and from the general culture in which we are raised. For example, such a simple thing as birth order will influence our definition of love. An only child becomes accustomed to a great deal of adult attention. Such a child may later feel unloved if the spouse (who is the third of four children and received relatively little adult attention) does not attend to him or her all of the time.

Our personal experiences mold our attitudes and behaviors. Thus the way we express love and what we define as love are the results of our past experiences.

Actions and Attitudes

The attitudes a person brings to love, to dating, and later to marriage have developed over many years. Because no two people experience the same upbringing, it is not surprising to find great attitudinal differences between people, even when they are "in love." Many of the difficulties we experience in our interpersonal relationships stem from conflicting attitudes and unrealistic expectations rather than from specific behavior. For example, a few socks on the floor is not as upsetting to a new wife as is her husband's general attitude toward neatness — does he expect her to wait on him? Often it is necessary to change underlying attitudes if behavior is to change, but this is difficult to do. We take our attitudes for granted without being aware of them. For example, a young man roundly criticized the double standard. But a day later, when discussing spouses' freedom to be apart occasionally, he stated that he certainly deserved time out with "the boys," but girls probably shouldn't go out with their girl-friends after marriage because this might be misunderstood as an attempt to meet other men.

Attitudes generally consist of three components: affective, cognitive, and behavioral. The *affective* aspect is one's emotional response resulting from an attitude, such as "I like blondes." The *cognitive* component consists of a person's beliefs and/or factual knowledge supporting the particular attitude, such as "blondes have more fun." The *behavioral* component involves the person's overt behavior resulting from the attitude, "I date blondes."

Unfortunately, these components are not necessarily consistent. For example, my attitudes may not be founded on fact. I may not act on my attitudes. Or I may voice attitudes that are not really a part of me. The young man above is an example of someone who voices one attitude, support for women, although he favors another, the double standard.

Where do such attitudes come from? We are not born with them. We learn our most basic attitudes as we grow up, generally from our parents, siblings, and peers. The values of a society are passed on to new members, beginning at birth. This is why we must trace our attitudes toward sex, love, and marriage from early childhood in order to understand adult behavior.

Developmental Stages in Learning to Love

As we shall see in Chapter 12, children pass through varying stages of development as they grow to adulthood. Such stages are actually arbitrary classifications set up by theorists in their effort to understand development, yet the stages are useful to that understanding. Sigmund Freud early delineated four psychosexual stages leading to adult sexual and love expression. Eric Erikson expanded on these to suggest eight general stages of development across a person's life span (see pp. 429–433). The following overview of Freud's four psychosexual stages will help us understand how we learn to love.

Self-Love Stage: Infancy and Early Childhood   During early years young children are so busy learning about their environment that almost all of their energy is focused on themselves and exploring the environment. Many believe that this early period of self-involvement sets the foundation for subsequent attitudes toward the self. It is important during these early years for the child to receive stimulation, including physical fondling. "By being stroked, and caressed, and carried, and cuddled, and cooed to, by being loved, the child learns to stroke, and caress, and cuddle, and coo to, and love others" (Montagu, 1972, p. 194). Ashley Montagu concludes that involvement, concern, tenderness, and awareness of others' needs are communicated to the infant through physical contact in the early months of life. It is here that the child begins to learn the meaning of love and to develop attitudes about intimacy, although the infant cannot intellectually understand these concepts. Thus the child deprived of early physical contact may later be unable to make relationships based on love and caring because he or she has not experienced loving relationships. Breastfeeding is particularly important because the infant is thereby assured of holding, cuddling, and fondling. Feeding becomes a time of psychological as well as physical nourishment for the child (see p. 400, Chapter 11).

If children are given love and security and are generally successful in learning to master the environment during this first stage, the chances are that their attitude toward themselves will be accepting and positive. These positive self-attitudes are necessary for us to relate lovingly to others: "The affirmation of one's own life, happiness, growth, and freedom is rooted in one's capacity to love, i.e., in care, respect, responsibility, and knowledge. If an individual is able to love productively, *he loves himself* too; if he can only love others, he cannot love at all" (Fromm, 1956, pp. 59–60).

By loving oneself Fromm means a coming to terms with oneself, a realistic acceptance of both shortcomings and assets, and a feeling of ease with oneself. People who hate or despise themselves have great difficulty loving others. Thus even as small children, we learn about love from the way in which we are loved.

Parental Identification Stage: Early and Middle Childhood   During this stage children learn the role, masculine or feminine, that goes with their biological gender. In many respects children act in a neuter way until they are about five or six years old, even though they start learning their gender roles much earlier. Many parents start guiding their children toward the appropriate gender role at birth. However, children are usually five or six before they make a commitment to the gender role by identifying with the like-sexed parent.

Although the parental identification stage is quite short, usually lasting a few months to a year, it is a crucial period, especially in a culture that has highly defined and differentiated sex roles. For although sex roles are moving closer together in the United States, there is still fairly strong sentiment in favor of the traditional roles: a strong, protective male and a more dependent and passive female.

During this stage it is important for children to have close contact with an adult of their own sex. Under normal circumstances this is the father or mother. However, with the increasing number of single-parent families, this person may be a grandfather or grandmother or a male or female companion of the parent. One can usually recognize when children have made this transition because they become more certain of their gender.

The boy will probably not want to do things that he labels for girls and vice versa. Girls and boys will want to take the proper gender roles when playing house. Children usually talk a lot during this time about what is proper for a girl and for a boy. The importance of this stage to the child's development suggests that parents who can maintain a comfortable relationship even if apart and who can work together to help the child make the proper identification will make the child's transition smoother. If identification does not occur during this stage, it may occur later, but it will be more difficult for the child to achieve.

Masculine and feminine roles dictate, in part, the way in which an individual demonstrates love. If it is unmasculine for a male to show tenderness, then tenderness may not be a part of his style of love. The sex role that we learn will be an important determinant of our definition of love and an even more important influence on how we display love.

Gang Stage: Late Childhood and Preadolescence

This stage coincides fairly well with the usual elementary school years in our society. It is called the gang stage because of the tendency of each gender to avoid the other, preferring to spend time with groups of friends of the same sex. Freud called this the "latency" period because it appeared to be a relatively calm time sexually. Recent research has indicated that there is more sexual experimentation during this period than was first thought. There is some sex play, such as "I'll show you mine if I can see yours."

The main tasks of this stage are consolidation of the socially appropriate gender role and adjustment to cooperative endeavor and formal learning. The gang, or peer group of his or her own sex, helps the child to learn cooperative behavior and the give and take of social organization. In addition masculine and feminine roles are strengthened by the gang members' approval and disapproval as well as by adult models the gang admires.

During this period the average boy or girl is often openly hostile toward the opposite sex. But the onset of puberty usually signals the end of this stage. The age that puberty begins is so varied in our culture that each child will probably enter it at a slightly different time. Thus the primary importance of the gang only gradually diminishes as the members one by one begin to turn their attention toward the opposite sex. The girls' groups dissolve first, because on the average they reach puberty two years ahead of boys. They have been ahead biologically all along, but the distance is greatest at the onset of puberty.

Entering the Heterosexual Adult Stage

Children who arrive at puberty earlier or later than average have additional problems during the transition into the fourth stage, adult heterosexuality. Those who are early often face ridicule and disdain from the gang when they begin showing interest in the opposite sex. The first boy in the gang who suddenly finds himself attracted to one of his sixth-grade female classmates will have to be careful to keep the gang from finding out, or he will be teased and perhaps ostracized. An early-developing girl faces different problems. She may want to date and do things she sees older girls doing, but her family

"I DON'T PLAY WITH GIRLS, MARGARET...."   "...WHERE PEOPLE CAN *SEE ME!*"

will most likely set limits, paving the way for arguments and conflict. Her peer group, on the other hand, may be titillated by her daring and she may "show off" to keep their approval. This may involve her seeing older, more sophisticated boys who may try to take advantage of her and who may succeed inasmuch as she is entering a game whose rules she does not yet know.

Children, especially males, who develop late usually suffer through a period of exclusion. They are deserted by friends who are no longer interested in their old activities, and they do not share the new interest in the opposite sex. Late developers often feel rejected and inferior. They may turn to the company of younger children. For a boy this solution may be reasonably satisfying, as his age may bring him a position of leadership in the younger group, thus helping to offset his feelings of inferiority. Some boys may not have to go through a period of exclusion because male gangs usually retain their interest in sports and cars, which the late-developing boy can still share with them. He can also pretend an interest in girls to go along with his friends and thereby avoid ridicule.

The slow-developing girl finds herself left out more completely, for girls become almost exclusively interested in boys during the transition to early puberty. With her confidence undermined, and lacking compensating support from the group, she faces a difficult time. She may withdraw from social activities and may suffer from depression that may be masked behind future plans to enter a self-sacrificing vocation. If she remains biologically behind the group for an extended period, say, more than a year or two, she can develop such a strong inferiority complex that she may need additional help and guidance when at last she does catch up biologically.

Young persons who enter adulthood at the same time as most of their peers avoid these problems. They begin to turn their attention toward the opposite sex and soon begin dating.

Each stage of development becomes the foundation for the next stage. And we must assimilate the lessons of all stages to become mature, loving individuals.

People who have passed successfully through the first three stages of development reach the heterosexual stage with a positive attitude toward themselves, a fairly clear idea of their roles as men or women, and a heightened interest in the opposite sex. They have learned several different kinds of love in their relationships with their parents and their peers. Their definitions of and attitudes about love are fairly well set and so is their own personal style of loving.

Love Over Time: From Passionate to Companionate Love

Many of the characteristics of love thus far described can be labeled passionate love and are most apparent early in a love relationship. With time the wild emotional excitement of passionate love tends to fade into a lower-key emotional state of friendly affection and deep attachment. Being in love at age twenty with your new mate will probably be quite different from the love experienced with your mate after twenty years of marriage.

David Orlinsky (1972) postulates varying kinds of love relationships over the life cycle, starting in infancy and moving through eight stages into parenthood. Let us briefly examine his ideas about love and then consider what further changes in love might occur in the later years of a love relationship.

He suggests that each stage of the life cycle is marked by the emergence of a new form of love experience that is not only exciting but also necessary to the full development of the person. Each love relationship is a medium or vehicle of personal growth.

> One grows as a person through loving, though not only in this way. As one becomes a new and different self through this experience, one also becomes ready to engage in a new and different mode of relatedness to others. Love relationships are not merely pleasant or edifying but essential experiences in life, "growthful" in the same generous sense in which travel is "broadening." They are in fact necessary links in the process of personal growth. (p. 144)

Love and intimacy know no age boundaries.

What Orlinsky is saying, as many others have also noted, is that children become loving adults through interacting in loving relationships as they grow up. This preparation is necessary to experience mature love relationships. We have looked more closely at these early stages and their contributions to mature love in the last section. At this point we will quickly review the early stages to help us understand how love might change over time. Orlinsky's first four stages are *infancy*, and *early*, *middle*, and *late childhood*. Each stage involves dependency on others. For example, infants must be nursed and children taught. If they are nursed and taught in a loving environment, the chances are good that they will have a positive self-image, a prerequisite for mature adult love. By the fifth stage, *preadolescence*, relations with peers are becoming more important, and the love experience changes to one between equals rather than unequals. In the sixth stage, *youth*, the exciting, passionate, romantic love we have discussed becomes dominant. If a partnership is formed during the seventh stage, *adulthood*, the couple will grow together and find the emotional attachment becoming stronger, and some of the passion may give way to a more enduring, caring, and comfortable relationship. The last stage, *parenthood*, is when a couple's love broadens to include children. There will then be a greater proportion of agape or selfless love. This selfless love is seen by many philosophers and prophets as a more mature, higher order love than just eros alone.

Where might love go from here? Hopefully, it will become more and more a mixture of eros, agape, and philos. Rollo May (1970) calls this mixture "authentic love." Erich Fromm (1956) uses the phrase "mature love" to describe healthy adult love. Mature love preserves the integrity and individuality of both persons. It is an action, not just a passive emotion. Giving takes precedence over taking. Yet this giving is not felt as deprivation but as a positive experience (Miller & Siegel, 1972).

Besides giving, one must be able to receive love if a relationship is to remain loving. Loving is a reciprocal relationship. By the act of accepting your partner's love, you affirm that person as an accepted and valued companion (Scoresby, 1977).

It is hoped that a couple can maintain an interplay of all three kinds of love throughout most of their relationship. Stated another way, there are social, physical, intellectual, and emotional sides to love expression. Different periods in one's life may find one or another of these aspects dominant, and thus the way in which love is shown will vary from time to time. Such changes do not necessarily mean an end of love but may only signal a changing interplay of all of its factors.

So the route love might take in a relationship that lasts a lifetime is basically the pattern of dependency, mutuality, passion, caring, and respect, and then perhaps dependency again in old age. Of course, there are other courses that love can take when couples find their love has diminished or died.

American culture presents some obstacles to an enduring love relationship. Our culture, especially through mass media, exalts passionate love which is usually linked closely to sexual expression. For those who equate *only* passionate love with true love, intimate relationships are doomed to end in disappointment. It is impossible to maintain a constant state of highly passionate love with its concomitant elation and pain, anxiety and relief, altruism and jealousy, and constant sexual preoccupation. Certainly no one newly in love wants to hear that the flame will burn lower in time. Who, newly in love, preoccupied from morning till night with thoughts of their love, can think, much less believe, that the feelings they are experiencing so strongly will ever fade? On the other hand, who could tolerate being in this highly charged emotional state forever? The fact that love changes over time makes it no less important, no less intimate, no less meaningful when some of the passion is replaced by a warm, deeply abiding and caring, quieter love.

Mass media's exaltation of passionate love and sex has led many Americans to equate sex with love. Unfortunately this concentration on the sexual element in love brings neglect of other important personal and interpersonal capacities and may diminish the overall quality of love in a relationship. Luther Baker (1983, p. 299) points out "that sex is not the 'pièce de résistance' of the good life, and our present concentration upon it often prevents people from developing other aspects of personal functioning which will produce a good life." The best sex, he says, flows "spontaneously out of a life and a relationship filled with love, joy, struggle, growth and intimacy. Good sex is a by-product and, like happiness, is most likely to occur when one is not worried about having it. We may find that when we come to know one another better in non-sexual ways, the expression of sexual intimacy will take on a new and more fulfilling dimension."

Following Baker's suggestion to deemphasize the "sex is love" philosophy would make it easier for two people passionately in love to accept the changes that slowly bring their love feelings toward a subtler, more relaxed companionate love style.

Another obstacle to an enduring love relationship is our culture's emphasis on the individual, which leads to a preoccupation with oneself, self-improvement, self-actualization, and so forth. As Amitai Etzioni (1983) suggests, in this age of the individual ego, marriage (love) is often less an emotional bonding than a breakable alliance between two self-seeking individuals. Love must involve a strong feeling of community, the caring and loving of mate, children, and other intimates within one's environment. Passionate love tends to preclude all but oneself and the object of one's love. Indeed, if all Americans remained passionately in love, there would never be a sense of community. Passionate love ultimately is selfish love. As it transforms into companionate love, there will be room again for community caring. As the selfish element is reduced, once more one can have time for other aspects of the loving relationship than just the passionate and sexual. As the preoccupation with the loved one subsides, one can again attend to the broader community.

It should be remembered that companionate love does not preclude passionate love. Ideally there will always be times of high passion in a loving relationship, no matter how long the relationship has lasted. These times are to be savored and enjoyed. Because such times will become less frequent with the passage of time in a successfully loving relationship, one need not, must not, value the "loving" less.

Loving and Liking

In the play *Who's Afraid of Virginia Woolf*, the author depicts a couple who are in love but who also dislike, and at times hate, one another. Can you really be in love with someone whom you dislike? The answer is that you can be passionately in love with someone you don't like, but your love probably will not evolve into companionate love over time. Rather, it will diminish as the dislike grows and ultimately will lead to the breakup of the relationship. In *Virginia Woolf* the dislike leads to hate and horrendous fighting instead of breakup.

Elaine Hatfield and William Walster (1978, p. 9) suggest that "liking and companionate love have much in common. Liking is simply the affection we feel for a casual acquaintance. Companionate love is the affection we feel for those with whom our lives are deeply intertwined. The only real difference between liking and loving is the depth of our feelings and the degree of our involvement with the other person." It is probably more important to like someone than it is to love them if you are to live together over an extended period of time. Roommate situations clearly demonstrate this. To live closely together on a day-to-day basis is difficult. Sharing cooking, eating, cleaning, and the many mundane chores that make daily living successful is next to impossible if you dislike your roommate. On the other hand, you don't have to love your roommate to live successfully together.

© 1975 Jules Feiffer

Positive reinforcement and positive associations are important to the maintenance of a liking relationship. It is obvious that someone you feel good being with is easier to like than someone with whom you feel rotten. It is also important that the liked person be associated with positive experiences.

> You must associate your mate with pleasure if you're going to keep on loving [and liking]. Romantic dinners, trips to the theater, evenings at home together, and vacations never stop being important. It's critical that you don't come to associate your partner with wet towels thoughtlessly dropped on the floor, barked out orders, crying and nagging, or guilt ("You never say you love me"). If your relationship is to survive, it's important that you both continue to associate your partner with good things. And this requires some thought and effort. (Hatfield and Walster, 1978, p. 12)

From our discussions it is clear that it takes little effort to fall passionately in love even if we don't exactly understand what such love is or just why we fall into it. It is equally clear that thought and work are required to remain in love. Love neglected will not survive in most cases. To fall passionately in love is not the "end all." It must be a beginning that when nurtured and cared for will endure, albeit in a changed form to some degree. To love long and well, to like and care for another over a lasting period of time is a unique gift that humans can give one another. To believe that enduring love will simply occur because one is passionately "in love" is a false belief that may destroy a relationship. Enduring love, if it is to evolve from passionate love, must be worked at and tended so that it will not wilt and die with the passage of time.

Love's Oft-Found Companion: Jealousy

Jealousy, the green-eyed monster, is an unwelcome acquaintance of nearly everyone who has ever been in love. Because it is a personal acquaintance, it is described in many different ways, almost as many as there are descriptions of love.

Jealousy relates to one's own feelings of confidence and security as much if not more than it relates to the actions of the loved one. As Margaret Mead (1968) has said: "Jealousy is not a barometer by which the depth of love can be read. It merely records the degree of the lover's insecurity. . . . It is a negative miserable state of feeling having its origin in the sense of insecurity and inferiority." Further, jealousy usually involves feelings of lost pride and threat to self-esteem and/or feelings that one's property rights have been violated. The threat or violation may be real, potential, or entirely imaginary, yet the jealous feelings aroused are real and strong.

Jealousy is also related to what one's culture teaches about love and possession inasmuch as the culture prescribes the cues that trigger jealousy (Hatfield & Walster, 1978).

> On her return trip from the local watering well, a married woman is asked for a cup of water by a male resident of the village. Her husband, resting on the porch of their dwelling, observes his wife giving the man a cup of water. Subsequently, they approach the husband and the three of them enjoy a lively and friendly conversation into the late evening hours. Eventually the husband puts out the lamp, and the guest has sexual intercourse with the wife. The next morning the husband leaves the house early in order to catch fishes for breakfast. Upon his return he finds his wife having sex again with the guest. The husband becomes violently enraged and mortally stabs the guest. (Hupka, 1977, p. 8)

This story seems unintelligible to an American. How can the husband condone his wife having sexual intercourse with another man on one occasion and be enraged by it a short time later? The answer lies in the cultural ways of the Ammassalik Eskimo. In this culture the husband would be considered inconsiderate if he did not share his wife sexually with his overnight guest. "Putting out the lamp" is a culturally sanctioned game that acts as an invitation for the guest to have sex with the host's wife. Yet it is not unusual for an Ammassalik Eskimo husband to become so enraged as to try to kill a man he catches having sex with his wife outside of the prescribed game rules.

So too in American society we are taught the rules of love. In the past love has meant exclusivity, monogamy, and life-long devotion and faithfulness. Lovers were also possessions of one another. Historically, adultery was grounds for divorce in every state. Thus jealousy was usually nearby when a young American fell in love.

And for most who experience it, what an unpleasant experience jealousy is. Suspicious feelings that seem to manufacture their own evidence to support the jealousy at every turn; compulsive preoccupation with the perceived infidelity, anger, sorrow, self-pity, and depression all wrapped into one continual emotional upheaval, eating and sleeping problems along with an assortment of physical ills evolving out of the continual emotional turmoil — all of these seem to characterize the jealous person.

Researchers lately have begun to shed some light on the manifestation of jealousy among Americans. The following characteristics have emerged from various studies (Adams, 1980):

Jealousy
The state of being resentfully suspicious of a loved one's behavior toward a suspected rival

- Jealousy goes with feelings of insecurity and an unflattering self-image.
- People who feel jealous because of a mate's real or imagined infidelity are often themselves faithless.
- People who report the greatest overall dissatisfaction with their lives are those who feel jealous most often.
- Happy or not, jealous people feel strongly bound to their mates.
- Younger people report jealousy more often than older people.
- It is difficult to conceal jealousy from others.
- Jealousy seems to cause women greater suffering than men.
- Women tend more often to try to repair the damaged relationship, whereas men try to repair their damaged egos (self-esteem).
- Men are more apt to give up a relationship in which jealousy is triggered by the woman's infidelity than are women in the reverse situation.
- Women are more apt to induce jealousy in their partner to test the relationship, to bolster their own self-esteem, to gain increased attention, to get revenge, and/or to punish the mate for some perceived offense.

One last point: To the degree that one's culture teaches the cues that trigger jealousy, changes in the culture may change the characteristics and incidence of jealousy. As American sexual mores have loosened, as long-lived monogamy has eroded through increased divorce, as cohabitation and premarital sexual intimacy have become more acceptable, so too has the need for jealousy changed. Although it is unclear at this time, greater

Feelings of rejection usually accompany jealousy.

sexual freedom may be leading to decreased sexual jealousy for some people. Gary Hansen (1982) found that nontraditional sex role subjects were less jealous in their reactions to hypothetical jealousy-producing events than were traditional sex role subjects.

Is there anything that one can do to manage and control irrational jealous feelings? This question is difficult to answer, especially when one is in the midst of a jealous emotional reaction. Naturally, anything we can do toward becoming confident, secure individuals will help us cope with our own jealousy. We can try to learn what is making us jealous. What exactly are we feeling and why are we feeling that way? We can try to keep our jealous feelings in perspective. We can also negotiate with our partner to change certain behaviors that seem to trigger our jealousy. Negotiation assumes that we too are working to reduce our own unwarranted jealousy. Choosing partners who are reassuring and loving will also help reduce our irrational jealousies. Unfortunately, following such advice is difficult because jealousy is so often irrational and unreasonable, and, for the jealous partner, at the moment of jealousy, all too often uncontrollable. It remains one of the puzzling components of love relationships.

Summary

American youths are given relative freedom to choose a mate. Unlike other societies where mate choice is directed by rigid prescriptions and parental and social guidance, ours permits young people to seek their own mates with a minimum of social interference or parental participation. American mate choice is usually based on the nebulous concept of romantic love: "I will marry the person I fall in love with."

"Love" is a difficult word to define. One helpful approach is the view of the ancient Greeks who classified three possible kinds of love: *eros*, sexual love; *agape*, spiritual love; and *philos*, brotherly or friendly love. Mature love includes all three aspects.

Our attitudes about and personal definition of love guide mate selection and lead each of us to form a set of idealized expectations as to the kind of mate we desire. These expectations, if highly unrealistic, often cause disappointment because the partner cannot live up to them. Overromanticized expectations of what a mate and a marriage should be almost ensure disappointment in, and subsequent failure of, a relationship.

Attitudes about love and marriage develop through a number of stages as one grows from infancy to adulthood. Each stage presents problems that the developing person must successfully overcome if, as an adult, mature love relationships are to be sustained. The first stage is the *self-love* stage. During this early period children begin to come to terms with themselves, establishing security, trust, and self-respect. In the *parental identification* stage, children identify with their like-sexed parent and begin to incorporate the masculine or feminine roles of their culture. In the *gang* stage further consolidation of appropriate roles is accomplished in addition to learning interpersonal relations and communication skills. Finally, the *heterosexual adult* stage is reached, which is the stage of adult sexuality and eventual marital fulfillment.

Such stages, of course, are only theoretical and will vary with cultures and individuals. Yet the idea that we develop our attitudes toward love and marriage as we grow up is important. Childrearing practices, the immediate family, and the general subcultures in which one is reared will all influence one's attitudes toward intimacy. Conflicting experiences during childhood may lead to confusion as an individual strives for intimacy. And differing childhood experiences may later lead to conflicts between lovers as they try to relate to one another. Awareness of these differences and concern for the other individual will make the transition to mature love more likely. And, finally, knowing and accepting ourselves is a necessary first step on the path to a successful love relationship.

It is important that we like as well as love our mate if our relationship is to endure. Passionate love can withstand dislike of the loved one for a short time, but unless the dislike can be changed into liking, passionate love can never evolve into a more permanent companionate love.

Jealousy is an oft found, yet unwanted companion of love. The reasons for it are many; it is closely related to one's own security and self-confidence. Although we are starting to understand some of its characteristics, thus far we have had little success in helping people control and manage jealousy. There is some evidence that sexual jealousy may be declining as sexual freedom has increased in the United States.

SCENES FROM MARRIAGE

The Love Research

Love has always been one thing, maybe the only thing, that seemed safely beyond the research scientist's ever-extending grasp. With an assist from Masters and Johnson, behavioral scientists have, to be sure, dug rather heavily into the topic of human sexual behavior. But whereas sex might now be explored scientifically, love remained sacrosanct.

Or so we thought.

Love was a taboo topic for researchers as recently as 1958, when the president of the American Psychological Association, Dr. Harry F. Harlow, declared in faintly mournful tones, "So far as love or affection is concerned, psychologists have failed in their mission. The little we know about love does not transcend simple observation, and the little we write about it has been written better by poets and novelists." Since the poets and novelists had always been notoriously contradictory about love, defining it as everything from "a spirit all compact of fire" to "a state of perceptual anesthesia," this was a pretty severe indictment.

But the psychologists did not take this charge lying down. Instead, they rallied to the call and started a quiet revolution. Over the past dozen years, and at a positively accelerating pace, behavioral scientists have begun to study love. They have done so on their own terms, with the help of such tools of the trade as laboratory experiments, questionnaires, interviews and systematic behavioral observation. And although the new love research is still in its early stages, it has already made substantial progress. The research has proceeded on several fronts, including explorations of the psychological origins of love, its links to social and cultural factors and the ways in which it deepens — or dies — over time.

Recent studies of falling in love have indicated that there is a sense in which love is like a Brooks Brothers suit or a Bonwit dress. For one person's feelings toward another to be experienced as "love," they must not only feel good and fit well, they must also have the appropriate label. Sometimes a sexual experience contributes to such labeling. One college student told an interviewer that she was surprised to discover that she enjoyed having sex with her boyfriend, because until that time she had not been sure that she loved him. The pleasant surprise helped to convince her that she was actually "in love."

Paradoxically, however, people sometimes label as "love," experiences that seem to be negative rather than positive. Consider the rather interesting case of fear. Ovid noted in *The Art of Love*, written in first-century Rome, that an excellent time for a man to arouse passion in a woman is while watching gladiators disembowel one another in the arena. Presumably the emotions of fear and repulsion stirred up by the grisly scene would somehow be converted into romantic interest.

Ovid himself did not conduct any controlled experiments to check the validity of the fear-breeds-love principle, but two psychologists at the University of British Columbia, Drs. Donald L. Dutton and Arthur P. Aron, recently did so. They conducted their experiment on two footbridges that cross the Capilano river in North Vancouver. One of the bridges is a narrow, rickety structure that sways in the wind 230 feet above the rocky canyon;

the other is a solid structure upriver, only 10 feet above a shallow stream. An attractive female experimenter approached men who were crossing one or the other bridge and asked if they would take part in her study of "the effects of exposure to scenic attractions on creative expression." All they had to do was to write down their associations to a picture she showed them. The researchers found that the men accosted on the fear-arousing bridge were more sexually aroused than the men on the solid bridge, as measured by the amount of sexual imagery in the stories they wrote. The men on the high-fear bridge were also much more likely to telephone the young woman afterward, ostensibly to get more information about the study.

The best available explanation for these results comes from a general theory of emotion put forth by Dr. Stanley Schachter of Columbia University. Schachter's experiments suggested that the experience of emotion has two necessary elements. The first is physiological arousal — a racing heart, heightened breathing, sweating and the like. These symptoms tend to be more or less identical for any intense emotion, whether it be anger, fear or love. The second necessary element, therefore, is the person's subjective labeling of his or her arousal. In order to determine which emotion he or she is experiencing, the person must look around and determine what external stimulus is causing the inner upheaval.

This labeling is a complicated process, and (as Ovid apparently knew some 2,000 years ago) mistakes can happen. In the Capi-

lano Canyon study, subjects apparently relabeled their inner stirrings of fear, at least in part, as sexual arousal and romantic attraction. This sort of relabeling is undoubtedly encouraged by the fact that the popular stereotype of falling in love — a pounding heart, shortness of breath, trembling hands — all bear an uncanny resemblance to the physical symptoms of fear. With such traumatic expectations of what love should feel like, it is no wonder that it is sometimes confused with other emotions. As the Supremes put it in a song of the 1960s, "Love is like an itching in my heart."

. . .

The pressure to label a promising relationship as "love" seems especially strong for women. Sociologist William Kephart of the University of Pennsylvania asked over a thousand Philadelphia college students the following question: "If a boy (girl) had all the other qualities you desired, would you marry this person even if you were not in love with him (her)?" Very few of the respondents (4 percent of the women and 12 percent of the men) were so unromantic as to say yes. But fully 72 percent of the women (compared with only 24 percent of the men) were too practical to answer with a flat no and, instead, pleaded uncertainty.

One of Dr. Kephart's female respondents put her finger on the dilemma, and also on the resolution of it. She wrote in on her questionnaire, "If a boy had all the other qualities I desired, and I was not in love with him — well, I think I could talk myself into falling in love."

Whereas women may be more

highly motivated than men to fall in love with a potential spouse, men tend to fall in love more quickly and less deliberately than women. In a study of couples who had been computer-matched for a dance at Iowa State University, men were more satisfied than women with their dates, reported feeling more "romantic attraction" toward them and even were more optimistic about the possibility of a happy marriage with their machine-matched partners. In a study of dating couples at the University of Michigan, I found that among couples who had been dating briefly — up to three months — boyfriends scored significantly higher than their girlfriends did on a self-report "love scale." These men were more likely than their partners to agree with such statements as "It would be hard for me to get along without _____ ," "One of my primary concerns is _____ 's welfare" and "I would do almost anything for _____ ." Among couples who had been together for longer periods of time the male-female difference disappeared.

. . .

Skeptics may point out, of course, that a paper-and-pencil love scale does not really measure how much people love each other, but simply how much they *say* they love each other. But there is some corroborating behavioral evidence for the scale's validity. For example, scores on the scale checked out with the well-known folk wisdom that lovers spend a great deal of their time gazing into each other's eyes. Surreptitious laboratory observation through a one-way mirror confirmed that "strong lovers" (couples whose members received above-average scores on the love scale) made significantly more eye contact than "weak lovers" (couples whose scores on the love scale were below average). Or, as the popular song puts it, "I only have eyes for you."

Whereas men seem to fall in love more quickly and easily than women, women seem to fall out of love more quickly and with less difficulty than men, at least in the premarital stages. For the past several years, my co-workers and I have been conducting an extensive study of student dating couples in the Boston area. We found, to our initial surprise, that women were somewhat more likely to be "breaker-uppers" than men were, that they saw more problems in the relationship and that they were better able to disengage themselves emotionally when a breakup was coming. Men, on the other hand, tended to react to breakups with greater grief and despair.

These tendencies run counter to the popular stereotypes of women as star-struck romantics and men as aloof exploiters. In fact, women may learn to be more practical and discriminating about love than men for simple economic reasons. In most marriages, the wife's status, income and life chances are far more dependent on the husband's than vice versa. As a result, the woman must be discriminating. She cannot allow herself to fall in love too quickly, nor can she afford to stay in love too long with "the wrong person." The fact that a woman's years of marriageability tend to be more limited than a man's may also contribute to her need to be selective. Men, on the other hand, can better afford the luxury of being "romantic."

Sociologist Willard Waller put the matter most bluntly when he wrote 40 years ago, "There is this difference between the man and the woman in the pattern of bourgeois family life: a man, when he marries, chooses a companion and perhaps a helpmate, but a woman chooses a companion and at the same time a standard of living. It is necessary for a woman to be mercenary." As more women enter business and professional careers, and as more men make major commitments to home-making and childrearing, it is likely that this difference will diminish.

From *Human Behavior*, February 1977. Copyright © 1977 *Human Behavior* Magazine. Reprinted by permission.

CHAPTER 3

AMERICAN DATING AND MATE SELECTION

CONTENTS

3

Every society has a system, formal or informal, by which mates are selected and new families are started. In the United States mate selection is carried out by relatively unrestricted dating among young persons. That is, the selection process is fairly informal. However, once the couple decides that each is indeed his or her choice for a future mate, the system becomes more structured and engagement and marriage usually follow.

Puberty and Sexual Stress

Puberty signals the beginning of adult sexuality. Children are now biologically able to reproduce, and the male/female relationship takes on an overtly sexual nature.

Adolescent years in most Western cultures are a time of sexual stress because although biology has prepared the individual for sexual intercourse and reproduction, society has traditionally denied and tried to restrain these biological impulses by placing restrictive rules and taboos on adolescent sexual behavior. For most, stress lasts until the individual marries, for it is primarily in marriage that our culture allows its members to freely engage in sexual activities. If, in round figures puberty begins for males at age fourteen and they marry at age twenty-four on the average, there is a ten-year period of stress after biology prepares the male for adult sexuality before society condones sexual intercourse (that is, in marriage). There is a comparable ten-year period for females, assuming that puberty begins at approximately age twelve and that females marry on the average at about age twenty-two.

There are instances when the stress period is less evident, such as when the average age of marriage is low. Some societies practice child marriage, which eliminates this period of sexual stress. Some cultures, such as the Polynesian, are also highly permissive in allowing sexual activities among the young. In fact, an anthropological study by George Murdock (1950) found that of 250 societies throughout the world, 70 percent permit nonincestuous sexual relations before marriage. In the last twenty years the American culture has also become much more permissive about sexual relations before marriage.

The stress period can also be reduced by prolonging the gang stage. The middle and upper classes of most European countries keep girls and boys more segregated than they are in the United States. Many European schools are segregated according to sex. Early adult behavior, such as dating, using makeup, and heterosexual school activities such as dances, is discouraged. The middle-class European girl of fifteen or sixteen is, on the average, similar to the American girl of eleven or twelve. She still spends most of her free time with her group of girlfriends bike riding, attending movies and cultural events, and going to youth hostels in the summer. Contact with boys is limited and usually confined to teasing and flirtation. American culture is influencing European youth, however, and this description is quickly changing.

Our society encourages early contact between the sexes. Even elementary schools promote coeducational dances and parties. Some parents, worried that their children will not become popular, pressure them into developing an early interest in the opposite sex. Makeup, adult fashions, and bras for preteens are advertised as ways of increasing popularity. The teenage market is large, and business creates and caters to the tastes of adolescents (see Stone & Church, 1973, pp. 447 – 48). Much advertising is based on sex appeal, thus heightening the tensions of this period.

The stress of emerging sexuality is compounded by the extended opportunities a young American couple have to be alone together. The automobile not only has revolutionized transportation and contributed to the highly mobile American way of life, it has also revolutionized early sexual experimentation. Vans have literally become mobile bedrooms. A boy and girl can be alone at almost any time in almost any place. The feeling of anonymity and distance from the social system is increased. Group control and influence are lessened, and there is no one who might comment or report on their behavior.

Thus what we find in America is a society that supposedly prohibits premarital sexual relations, yet through the mass media and the support of early boy/girl relations actually encourages them. In essence a young couple is often thrown completely on their own resources to determine what their sexual behavior will be. In the end they will make the decision about the extent of their sexual relationship based on their attitudes, peer influences, and the pressures of the moment.

American Dating

Mate selection through **dating** is an American invention and is relatively new, having developed largely after World War I, mainly because of the emancipation of women and the new mobility afforded by the car. In place of the church meeting, the application to the girl's father, the chaperoned evenings, modern youth meet at parties, make dates via telephone, and go off alone in cars to spend evenings together.

Dating
Social interaction and activity with a person of the opposite sex

Modern youth are so accustomed to having almost free access to one another that it is difficult to appreciate just how hard it was for a young man to meet a young woman at the turn of the century. Secondary schools were not often coeducational then, so that after elementary school years boys and girls were not surrounded by students of the opposite sex. An introduction of the young man to the young woman's parents had to be arranged, and this was not always easy. If the parents approved of the young man, there was little leisure time that the couple could spend together, as most young people's time was occupied with work in addition to studies. What little time they had together was usually spent doing things with other family members.

Why Do We Date?

We date for many reasons in addition to mate seeking. Dating serves to fill in time between puberty and marriage. It is often simply recreation,

Casual recreational dating
of numerous persons

Multiple dates
with fewer persons

Going steady

Informal commitment
to marriage such as
"pinning" in fraternities
and sororities

Cohabitation and/or
engagement

Final commitment

Marriage

FIGURE 3-1　A continuum of
dating.

fun, an end in itself. It is a way to gain social status by whom one dates and how often one dates (see Winch, 1971, pp. 530–31).

Dating is an opportunity for the sexes to interact and learn about one another. Because Americans live in small nuclear families, they may have had little opportunity to learn about the opposite sex if they had no opposite-sex siblings near their own age. Dating is also an avenue to self-knowledge. Interacting with others gives one a chance to learn about one's own personality as well as the personalities of others. Dating allows one to try out a succession of relationships. And one learns something about marital and familial roles by relating with the opposite sex.

In early adolescence dating is mostly considered fun and recreation and learning about oneself. But the older one gets the more serious dating becomes, and the more concerned one becomes with mate selection. Thus dating patterns can be placed on a continuum leading from casual dating to marriage (see Figure 3-1).

In general mate selection in America may be viewed as movement down two paths (see Broderick, 1967). One is the path of commitment and the other is the path of physical intimacy. At first commitments are superficial: "Let's get together for an evening." Finally, at the end of the path there is the deep-seated commitment: "Let's spend our lives together." The intimacy road runs from casual hand holding to a full and continuing sexual relationship.

In recent years the intimacy road has been traveled much faster than the commitment road. In fact, a complaint of today's young, especially young women, is the inability of others in whom they are romantically interested to make a commitment. For some the emphasis in America today on sexual intimacy seems to lead to the neglect of other important aspects of the relationship that help support commitment. Social compatibility, development of shared interests, and increased knowledge of one another as well as of oneself are all important, especially if the relationship is to become permanent.

Patterns of Dating

Adolescent boy/girl interactions have become increasingly more individualized in the past few years. This great variation makes it difficult to describe a common American dating pattern. In general, formal dating, where a boy approaches a girl beforehand and arranges a meeting time, place, and activity for them, has declined (Murstein, 1980), especially in the larger urban areas such as Los Angeles and New York City. Formal "going steady," where class rings and lettermen's jackets are given by the boy to the girl, has also declined in these areas. However, one still finds more traditional, formalized dating in small cities and towns and among those past college age. In small towns Main Street is cruised on Friday and Saturday nights, dates are prearranged, and afterward everyone meets at a drive-in restaurant or couples head into the countryside to neck and pet. Many go steady for a good portion of their high school years.

There is another generalization we can make. The first date used to be the first time a couple would become acquainted. It usually involved a function or activity, such as going to the movies. By concentrating on the activity, some of the difficulties and embarrassments of getting to know one another were avoided. After all, you can't talk if you are at a movie theater. Today young people generally know one another better before actually dating. They have chatted with each other and perhaps done things together in the context of a larger group. Their first date comes more casually; they may decide on the spur of the moment to go to the beach together. Couples still go steady, but again, the relationship seems less formal, more relaxed and casual. Also, once they are past a period of almost total preoccupation with one another, there seems to be more group activity, going out with other couples or with friends. It seems, then, that dates of the 1950s were more task-oriented (what will we do on our date), whereas today dates have become more person/relationship oriented (what will the relationship be on our date).

David Knox and Kenneth Wilson (1981) report that "our relationship" is the most frequent topic of conversation for their university student sample. The largest percentage of students meet their date through a friend. Although we have stressed how free young Americans are to choose dating partners and activities, Knox reports that 60 percent of the women and 40 percent of the men in his sample indicated that some parental influence was involved in their dating patterns. Women are much more likely than men to say that it is important to date the "kind of people their parents would approve of" (p. 257).

Because there is a diversity of dating patterns, let's take a look at the two ends of the spectrum. First we'll follow a young couple through an extended period of dating and observe how the traditional, more formal game is played. Then we'll jump to the other end of the spectrum and look at dating as "hanging around" or "getting together," where few formal guidelines exist.

Traditional Dating and Going Steady   Let's start when our hypothetical couple is first beginning to date. Age at first dating varies greatly with each family and with social class, but in general people are dating earlier so that dating at twelve and thirteen, especially for a girl, is not unusual. Let us further assume that the boy has just reached the legal driving age (fifteen or sixteen).

The two will probably have known each other superficially for some time. They attend the same school and have met at various school functions. Although it requires courage, the boy asks the girl to a movie on the coming Saturday night. A movie is usually a safe first date for a young adolescent because it requires little interaction. Neither has to worry about being boring or having nothing to say because the movie will occupy their time. At the appointed time the boy proudly arrives to pick up the girl. Although she has been ready for some time, she is discreetly "not ready." This serves a twofold purpose: She does not appear overeager (her mother has told her to play hard to get), and it gives her parents a few moments to look him over and discuss the evening's rules with him, mainly at what

Dating can take a variety
of forms.

Ready for marriage?

time to return. If the girl is particularly independent, she may make a special effort to be ready when her date arrives so she can leave quickly to avoid interaction between her parents and her date.

In the darkened theater the boy strongly feels the pressure of his friends and the anonymous larger group of peers loosely defined as "the boys" to approach her physically. He is also under pressure from himself, wanting to prove to himself that the girl likes him, thus boosting his self-esteem. The intimacy road leading to sexual contact enters dating immediately. The boy generally pays for the date, at least at first, and this pressures the girl into paying him back, usually with some kind of physical response. The double standard, where sexual advances are expected of the boy but are inappropriate for the girl, still operates in traditional dating. To feel masculine and proud among his peers, the boy wants to at least try to have some type of physical contact with the girl. Thus as he sits watching the movie, the first of many conflicts concerning sexuality arises. He notices that her hands are lying one inch in his direction on her lap. Perhaps this is a cue. Should he attempt to hold her hand? If she vigorously rejects this advance, someone in the row might notice and he'll be embarrassed. If, however, she accepts, how will he be able to withdraw his hand when it becomes sweaty and begins to cramp? Will she take it personally as some kind of rejection if he withdraws it?

The fascinating characteristic of traditional American dating is what one may call "escalation." In other words, resolution of this first minor intimacy conflict does not end the problem. If the girl accepts his first advance, then the pressure he feels to prove his masculinity will actually increase because the whole procedure is designed to test just how far he can go toward overt sexuality. Granted, much of this pressure may be unconscious for the boy, yet he feels the need to prove himself. Naturally, the further the boy moves, the more pride he will feel when bragging to his friends of his success. Thus once he has taken her hand, he must now look to the slightly greater problem of attempting to place his arm around her. The reward of increased intimacy is obviously greater, but so are the risks. If she vigorously rejects his attempt, the entire audience will notice (at least, it will seem this way to him). If she accepts, there is always the cramped shoulder to look forward to as well as the necessity of facing the new escalation level with its ensuing conflicts and insecurities.

The girl is having conflicts too because she does not want to lose her reputation and yet at the same time she does not want him to think her a prude and not ask for another date. Of course, she may just have gone out with him to have a date and doesn't really want to date him again. In that case total rejection of his physical advances will let him know further dates are not desired. If she does like him, she wants to encourage him but not too much. How much physical contact can she allow without leading the boy to think she will eventually go all the way?

If the relationship continues, the couple will gradually limit their dating to each other. They enjoy the security of knowing they always have a date. They find being together comfortable, and it's a relief to them not to have to face the insecurity of a new date. Going together requires a higher degree of commitment than casual dating; this ability to commit oneself becomes the foundation of later marriage. Going together helps the couple understand what kind of commitments are necessary to marriage.

Going together, though, does create problems. It tends to add pressure to the sexual conflicts experienced by the young couple. They see each other more frequently, and it may become harder for the girl to retain her virginity and still encourage the boy. Also, an American boy tends to be possessive. He tends to regard any attention or compliments paid to his girlfriend as insulting, and he tries to restrict her social interaction to himself. She may resent this, and fights may result.

On the whole starting early and remaining in a steady relationship throughout adolescence is probably disadvantageous to later adult relations. The young person who has always gone steady is unlikely to have had enough experience with a broad cross section of the opposite sex to have developed his or her interpersonal abilities to the fullest. Going steady early usually leads to earlier marriage, which tends to be less stable than later marriage. If dating is to work as a method of mate selection, then it is important to date enough to ensure a good mate choice.

On the other hand, dating so many people that only brief relationships are formed during the dating period is also dysfunctional. The young person never gets any practice in the give and take of long-term relationships. Thus ideally, one must date enough people to understand the many individual differences that are to be found and at the same time experience some longer-term relationships in order to gain knowledge of the commitments and compromises necessary to maintain a relationship over time.

Getting Together   At the other end of the spectrum is much less formal dating, "getting together" or "hanging out" together. Even the term "date" seems old fashioned to describe this more casual interaction. In "getting together" there is no orderly progression from the first parent-approved date to going steady to eventual marriage. Here meetings and even dates tend to "just happen," are spur-of-the-moment affairs. One of these casual "dates" can end with the couple having sex, or they may never even think of sex. They may decide to "hang out" together, or they may just drift away and not see each other again — it all seems to depend on the "vibes" of the moment.

For example, the boy may notice the girl at a local snack bar or other neighborhood hangout. When he comes back with a fresh cup of coffee, he moves his chair nearer to hers. He notices that she laughs at some of his jokes. A day or two later he bumps into her on the street and asks if she wants to go along to the beach. On the way they find they both like the same rock groups and that both were hitchhiking in Europe last summer. Sex depends on how they feel at the moment, and neither considers it a "big thing."

The problems of this type of dating are, as you might expect, almost the opposite of those of going steady. Rather than too limited experience with the opposite sex, there tends to be too much experience and too little commitment. Neither the boy nor the girl is likely to feel chosen or special when he or she knows the partner is likely to have sex with anyone who turns up. Since both have learned to avoid conflicts or "scenes" by moving on, neither has learned to work things through or to compromise. Because marriage involves commitment and compromise, both persons are poor marriage prospects if this type of dating is their only experience.

Probably our own personal dating experiences will fall somewhere between traditional dating and "getting together," depending on where we live, our upbringing and values, and what our peers are doing. Regardless of our dating style, each of us has the problems of finding dating partners, coping with "bad" dates, and avoiding exploitation. The fact that American dating today is so informal and without rules compared with mate selection processes historically and in other countries means that each young person has to make his or her own decisions about what is best. Of course, when we say "make his or her own decisions" we realize that there will be many social and cultural pressures guiding such decisions, but these pressures are not always clear-cut nor is there just one set of pressures, as we have sometimes experienced.

These two descriptions of American dating probably don't describe many American young people accurately. Most persons have dating experiences that fall between the two extremes. Sometimes a couple may just "hang around" together; at other times they may date more formally. Much will depend on the circle of friends the couple has. Even within a small high school there will be different dating patterns. The important thing to remember is that any dating pattern, if it is to contribute to the courtship process, must give each person sufficient experience with the opposite sex to make good decisions about intimate relationships. Knowledge about the opposite sex comes largely through interacting with the opposite sex. Knowledge about intimate relationships in general comes through being in such relationships. The courting process, whatever its exact pattern, should give people these kinds of experiences.

Dating and Extended Singleness

Our discussion to this point has examined the dating patterns of young Americans with the implicit assumption that dating is, in part, a form of courtship that leads to marriage. Not all dating Americans want to marry, though, and not all dating Americans are young. These statements refer to the fact that the period of singleness before marriage is longer today than it has been in the recent past. Also, the greatly increased divorce rate has increased the number of single persons, many of whom are older.

Table 3-1 gives you some idea of the increase in singleness between 1970 and 1981. Note that the increase is age specific and does not imply fewer marriages. Indeed if we look at the single rate for those over forty

TABLE 3-1   Marital Status of Persons Living Alone

MARITAL STATUS, AGE AND SEX	PERCENT INCREASE 1970 – 1981	
Total living alone	74.5	
Marital status:		
married, spouse absent	67.5	
widowed	36.1	
divorced	150.8	
never married	115.0	
Age:		
Under 25 years	196.9	
25 to 34 years	290.4	
35 to 44 years	132.3	
45 to 64 years	28.7	
65 years and over	47.6	
Percent never married by age and sex:	women	men
Total 15 years and over	1.8	4.6
Under 40 years	1	2.1
40 years and over	−21	−27
20 to 24 years	45	27.1
25 to 29 years	107.6	77.0
30 to 34 years	67.7	74.5

Source: U.S. Bureau of the Census, June 1982.

years of age, in 1981 there are 21 percent fewer single women and 27 percent fewer single men than in 1970. The large increases in singleness occur mainly from ages twenty to twenty-nine for both men and women. This increase has resulted, in part, from the postponement of marriage by today's Americans. The median age of marriage rose by 1.5 years for both men and women from 1970 to 1981. By March 1981 the median age had reached 22.3 years for women and 24.8 years for men. During this same period the divorce ratio (number of divorced persons per 1000 persons who are married and living with their spouse) more than doubled, 109 to 47. Overall then, the number of persons living alone who were under twenty-five tripled and those between twenty-five and thirty-four quadrupled.

Postponing marriage means that the dating period of one's life will often be longer. And for those who divorce, there may be a return to dating later in life. Despite the increase in singleness, it is still a transitory state for most Americans and usually ends with marriage or remarriage. Dating then is more than just the young learning about and courting one another. Dating will vary greatly in its purposes and patterns according to the kind of single person — whether young and starting to date, divorced, and so on.

Encouragement to marry undoubtedly will remain strong in America, yet several factors are acting to make prolonged single life more acceptable. The increasing emphasis on self-fulfillment as a major life goal and society's greater tolerance of differing lifestyles both reduce the pressure to marry. Growth and change are becoming popular goals, and they conflict directly with the traditional goals of long-range commitment to stability that marriage requires. The women's movement has also contributed to singleness in that it says to all women, "There are other roles you can fulfill that do not necessarily include being a wife and mother." Greater educational opportunity also acts, in some cases, to postpone marriage because going to school usually postpones economic independence (Stein, 1981).

What effect will remaining single longer have on marriage? Obviously, both partners will be older. Older persons, used to a long period of singleness, may well become more set in their ways and thus find the compromises of the marriage relationship more difficult. Also, couples will be older when they have children, thus increasing the age difference between themselves and their children. Risks during pregnancy and childbirth are greater for older women. And older persons will probably have fewer children, with a resultant effect on schools, the baby food and clothing industries, and so on.

On the other hand, later marriage should mean better economic circumstances for the couple. Too, the maturity of older couples may make them more willing to work toward making marriage a positive experience.

But what of the single life itself? What are its advantages? Freedom is probably the major advantage. You need only worry about yourself. Obligations are made by voluntary decision rather than dictated by tradition, role, or law. You have the time to do what you want when you want. Expenses are lower than for a family, and you can change jobs or even cities more easily. Independence can be maintained, and the conflicts about activities and lifestyle that can arise in a marriage don't occur.

Possible loneliness, failure to relate intimately, and a sense of meaninglessness are potential disadvantages of singleness. It is interesting and contrary to popular belief, but research shows that old people are less prone to loneliness than young people. Loneliness is particularly prevalent and intense during adolescence (Rubin, 1979). In addition single people have a higher incidence of mental illness (see Figure 3-2). It is difficult to

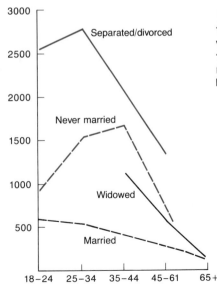

FIGURE 3-2 Admission rates to outpatient psychiatric services per 100,000 population 18 years of age and over (National Institute of Mental Health, 1973).

Sex and the Singles Apartment Complex

In the midsixties apartment complexes began to be built to cater to the singles group. The complexes usually include elaborate recreation facilities such as swimming pools and hot tubs, game rooms and party facilities, saunas and tennis courts. Such facilities are designed to bring the residents together and create a full social life within the complex itself. According to Cynthia Proulx:

Of all the high-tension areas in a singles complex, by far the highest is the social center. Woodway's (a well-known singles complex in Houston, Texas) social center is informally referred to as the Meat Rack, Body Works, Pig Place, or any number of other standard nicknames signifying a sexual marketplace. Besides accommodating all of Woodway's communal indoor social activities, the Meat Rack is the scene of a phenomenon called Ladies' Night. This takes place every Tuesday, rain or shine, and has nothing to do with baseball. Unescorted women get free drinks and on a typical Tuesday the bartender will hand out as many as 1,500 drinks between 7 p.m. and midnight. . . .

The King Ranch of the singles-complex social centers, the Meat Rack, is 10,000 square feet of shag-carpeted, bead-curtained conviviality, complete with a roaring fire of gas flames and eternal logs. The place is divided into a huge lounge, where couples make contact, and a discotheque, where prospective partners are mutually interrogated and either given the go-ahead to make the next move or dropped cold. . . .

As couples weave and bob in a self-conscious version of rock dancing, a revolving, multimirrored chandelier right out of the Avalon ballroom era turns the Meat Rack's discotheque into a deep red fish bowl of undulating bodies and unblinking eyes tirelessly in search of bait. Meanwhile, out in the lounge, wrought-iron, pseudo-Moorish chandeliers cast an amber glow over clusters of girls wearing skin-tight pant suits.

By 1 a.m., most of the prettiest girls have disappeared. (Proulx, 1973)

Popular accounts like this continue to exaggerate the glamour and sexual preoccupation of the singles lifestyle.

say just why the incidence of mental illness is higher for single persons than for married. Perhaps those with a proclivity toward mental illness are bypassed by those seeking mates and are thus forced to remain single. Living closely with another person does serve a corrective function because the other person validates or invalidates many of one's thoughts and actions, thus serving to keep one closer to reality. In addition the social stigma placed on the single person may act to increase mental stress. General health is also not as good in single persons as in married persons (Verbrugge, 1979).

Cohabitation: Unmarried Couple Households

The increasing incidence of unmarried heterosexual **cohabitation** is, in part, directly related to the increase in the single lifestyle. The number of such couples has grown from 523,000 in 1970 to 1,808,000 in 1981, an increase of 246 percent (U.S. Bureau of Census, June 1982). Although the increase is dramatic, such households make up only 3 percent of all households in the United States. In addition not all such households involve sexually intimate relationships. Although seldom reported in the mass media, these figures include a variety of living arrangements, such as that of an elderly woman who rents a room to a male college student or that of an elderly man who employs a live-in female nurse or housekeeper. One other change in this statistic is noteworthy. In 1970 a sizable majority (73 percent) of the cohabiting couples without children were over forty-five years of age. By 1981 the number had dropped to 24 percent. This probably reflects the later age of marriage that we earlier discussed plus more acceptance by society of cohabitation by the young.

Paul Glick and Graham Spanier (1980) characterize this data by stating: "Rarely does social change occur with such rapidity. Indeed there have been few developments relating to marriage and family life which have been as dramatic as the rapid increase in unmarried cohabitation."

It is possible that some of the increase is accounted for by a greater willingness to reveal the fact of living together outside of marriage. On the other hand, there are an unknown number of couples living together who pass themselves off as married or, at least, do not divulge their living arrangement. They, of course, would not be included in the total figures. However, enough couples are openly living together in intimate

Cohabitation
A man and woman living together in an intimate relationship without being legally married

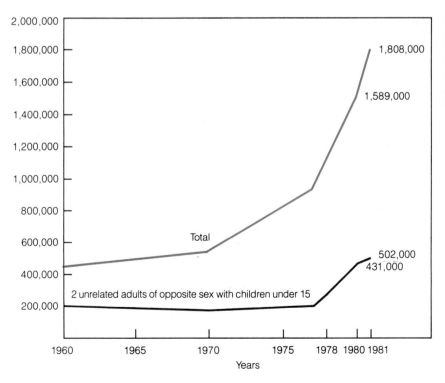

FIGURE 3-3 Unmarried couples living together in the United States. (Source: Glick and Norton, 1977; U.S. Bureau of the Census, June 1975; U.S. Bureau of the Census, June 1982.)

relationships that some theorists now consider living together to be an ongoing part of the mate selection process for a growing minority of couples (Macklin, 1983).

The Nature of Cohabiting Relationships

People choose to live together for many reasons, some of which may not be true for every cohabiting couple. First, it is clear that many consider these experiences to be no more than *short-lived sexual flings*. For example, among male cohabiting students in a large research study (Peterman et al., 1974), 82 percent of those twenty years of age or younger reported that their longest cohabitation was three months or less. Sixty-three percent of the males aged twenty-one and twenty-two reported the same average. Among females in the twenty and under age group, 67 percent reported three-months or briefer cohabitations, and 48 percent of those aged twenty-one and twenty-two reported the same (Peterman et al., 1974). These couples had no firm future plans. The authors conclude that:

1. The opportunity to cohabit has increased in recent years, especially as college housing arrangements have become less restrictive and the fear of pregnancy has been reduced by improved contraception.
2. There is limited commitment, although commitment increases with age and class standing.
3. Most cohabitation experience is probably not in the nature of a "trial marriage" because of its short duration and the living situation in which there are often other persons.
4. A minority of parents are told of the cohabiting experience.
5. Marriage is still the popular choice for cohabitors, although cohabitation on a more permanent basis ranks higher than for noncohabitors.

Generally, living together does not seem to portend a new experiment leading to a happier life. To date, living together seldom survives long as a permanent form of relationship. Most couples either break up or eventually marry in time (Kapecky, 1972; Bower & Christopherson, 1977; Risman, 1981; Watson, 1983).

Second, there are those couples who live together for practical reasons. They are essentially no more than *opposite-sex roommates*. In this case the couple live together without necessarily having a deep or intimate relationship. Living with a member of the opposite sex as a roommate affords certain advantages. A woman may feel safer living with a man if she lives in a high-crime-rate area. They can learn to share skills; for example, she might teach him to cook while he teaches her automobile maintenance. Generally, the couple simply lives together as would two same-sex roommates. They each date others, generally keep their love lives out of their living quarters, and react to one another as friends, each gaining something from living together in partnership rather than separately. The reason given most often for such an arrangement is "to save money." This is especially true of elderly cohabitants.

Third, there are couples who see cohabiting as a *true trial marriage*. As one young woman explained, "We are thinking of marriage in the future, and we want to find out if we really are what each other wants. If everything works out, we will get married." Some of these couples go so far as to set a specific time period.

Fourth, there are couples who view cohabiting as a *permanent alternative to marriage*. They often express a philosophical rejection of the marital institution as being unfavorable to healthy and growing relationships. They are especially critical of the constraints imposed by laws on partners' rights in marriage. Many of the couples who see consensual union as a permanent alternative to legal marriage write their own contracts in an effort to form a more egalitarian union even though such contracts cannot invalidate state marriage laws.

Many who live together state their desire to avoid what they perceive to be the constraining, love-draining formalities associated with legal marriage. They say, "If I stay with my mate out of my own free desire rather than because I legally must remain, our relationship will be more honest and caring. The stability of our relationship is its very instability."

©1977 Universal Press Syndicate

**"If you keep bugging me about getting married,
I'm gonna break off our engagement."**

Is the Woman Exploited in Cohabitation Relationships?

Obviously the answer to this question will depend on the individual relationship. However, some interesting statistics bear on this question in a general way. A number of studies indicate that males seem less committed to their live-together relationships than do their female partners (Budd, 1976; Johnson, 1973; Kieffer, 1972; Lewis et al., 1975; Lyness et al., 1972; Risman, 1981; Macklin, 1983).

In the Lyness study couples living together were compared with couples going together. No significant differences were found between the groups in level of trust and reported happiness, both of which were high. A difference was found, however, in the reported degree of commitment to marriage. The couples who were going together, both males and females, were committed to future marriage. But males in the living-together couples were the least committed, far less so than the women with whom they were living. The researchers' tentative conclusions were, in part:

> To a striking degree, living-together couples did *not* reciprocate the kinds of feelings (of need, respect, involvement, or commitment to marriage) that one would expect to be the basis of a good heterosexual relationship. The question of whether such a lack of reciprocity is typical of such relationships and thus reflects the difficulties of bringing off a successful nonnormative relationship or whether it is merely typical of those who volunteered for our research cannot be answered. (Lyness et al., 1972, p. 309)

We have already seen that many of the cohabitation relationships are short-lived and seem to revolve around the sexual part of the relationship. If the man tends to be less committed than the woman, it appears to be a reasonable assumption that he is often the one to end the relationship, if not directly then indirectly by refusing equal commitment.

Glick and Spanier (1980) also point out that cohabiting men are much *less* likely to be employed than married men, but cohabiting women were much *more* likely to be employed than married women. This might suggest that the men are using the women economically to help themselves get through school or pursue their own interests, which at the time may not produce much, if any, monetary return.

It is also of interest to note that although cohabitation appears to be avant-garde, suggesting that those who are involved are liberated, the division of labor in the household tends to be traditional (Macklin, 1983; Whitehurst, 1974; Risman, 1981). That is, the woman does the cooking, cleaning, and household work. This, combined with the findings that she is much more apt to be in the workforce than her married counterpart, makes it clear that she is often overburdened in the cohabitation relationship.

Perhaps the woman considering cohabitation should examine carefully the nature of the intended relationship before entering it. One way that she can do this is to answer the questions posed in Appendix D p. 557.

The Relationship between Cohabitation and Marriage

Many young people argue persuasively that living together provides a good test for future marriage. Living together, they say, is like a test marriage without the legal framework required to end the relationship if it doesn't work. Cohabitors espouse a variety of other arguments in support of premarital cohabitation:

1. It provides an opportunity to try to establish a meaningful relationship.
2. It can be a source of financial, social and emotional security.
3. It provides a steady sexual partner and companionship, thus providing some of the central pleasures of marriage without commitment.
4. It provides a chance for personal growth, a chance to increase self-understanding vis-à-vis relating to another person on an intimate basis.
5. Cohabitors would have a more realistic notion of their partner and should generally have less romanticized ideas about the relationship.
6. Cohabitors have a chance to get beyond typical courtship game-playing.
7. Long periods of intimate contact provide an opportunity for self-disclosure and concomitant modification and/or realization of personal goals. (Jacques & Chason, 1979, p. 37)

Although these arguments are logical and reasonable, research to date on the quality of marriage after cohabitation experiences finds little if any relationship between cohabitation and the degree of satisfaction, conflict, emotional closeness, or egalitarianism in later marriage (Macklin, 1983). Clatworthy and Scheid (1977) report that while all couples in their sample who had premaritally cohabited considered the experience to be beneficial to their marriage, there was no evidence that they actually had better marriages or that they had selected more compatible mates than noncohabiting couples.

The one study that has found cohabitation before marriage to be positively related to marital quality was done on remarriage families, forty of whom had cohabited before remarriage and forty of whom had not (Hanna & Knaub, 1981). Remarried couples who lived together before marriage reported significantly higher degrees of happiness, closeness, concern for partner's welfare, and positive communication, and they perceived more environmental support than remarried couples who had not cohabited.

Perhaps the dissimilarities between cohabitation and marriage negate the apparent advantages of cohabitation insofar as future marriage success is concerned. Gerald Leslie (1979) lists the following dissimilarities between cohabitation and marriage:

1. In marriage one partner doesn't keep an address elsewhere to which he or she can retreat when the going gets rough.
2. Couples who live together know that they are not legally bound to one another. They can get out of the relationship with few sanctions.

INSET 3-2

Couple Wed So They Know What to Call Each Other

This piece will use names of two people, Pietro and Tess.

For three years Pietro and Tess lived together without marrying. Such an arrangement had ceased to be scandalous when they took it up, had even become fashionable. It expressed the partners' reevaluation of the culture, or their liberation from tired old values, or something. It doesn't matter what. Pietro and Tess did it.

They were married a few weeks ago.

The canker in the love nest was the English language. Though English is the world's most commodious tongue, it provided no words to define their relationship satisfactor-

ily to strangers. When Tess took Pietro to meet her parents the problem became troublesome. Presenting Pietro, she said, "Mommy and daddy, this is my lover, Pietro."

Pietro was not amused. "It made me sound like a sex object," he said.

A few weeks later they were invited to meet the president. Entering the reception line, Pietro was asked by the protocol officer for their names. "Pietro," he said. "And this is my mate."

As they came abreast of the president, the officer turned to Mr. Reagan and said, "Pietro and his mate."

"I felt like the supporting actress in a Tarzan movie," said Tess. It took Pietro three nights of sleeping at the YMCA to repair the relationship.

Back to the drawing board, on which they kept the dictionary.

For a while they tried "my friend." One night at a glamorous party Pietro introduced Tess to a marrying millionaire with the words, "This is my friend, Tess." To which the marrying million-

aire replied, "Let's jet down to the Caribbean, Tess, and tie the knot."

"You don't understand," said Pietro. "Tess is my *friend*."

"So don't you like seeing your friends headed for big alimony?" asked the marrying millionaire.

"She's not that kind of friend," said Pietro.

"I'm his *friend*," said Tess.

"Ah," said the matrimonialist, upon whom the dawn was slowly breaking, "Ah — your — *friend*."

As Tess explained at the wedding, they couldn't spend the rest of their lives rolling their eyeballs suggestively every time they said "friend." There was only one way out. "The simple thing," Pietro suggested, "would be for me to introduce you as 'my wife.'"

"And for me," said Tess, "to say, 'This is my husband, Pietro.'"

And so they were wed, victims of a failure in language.

Russell Baker
New York Times

3. Most living-together couples retain a degree of financial independence uncommon in most marriages.
4. Unwed couples have to worry about possible contraceptive failure, but they don't have to plan for children.
5. Cohabiting couples don't necessarily have to make plans for the future.

In discussing the high breakup rate of cohabiting couples, Leslie finds that cohabitors may unknowingly be creating a self-fulfilling prophecy.

They enter a relationship partly to see if it will last, and, by keeping the possibility of discontinuing the relationship in mind, they actually help cause the breakup. It is possible that some relationships might turn out differently if the partners enter them with an unshakable determination to succeed. Leslie suggests that living together can be a way for young people to avoid responsibility. It is easier to play house than to be married. If this is true, the attitude may be carried into a subsequent marriage, thus contributing to the marriage's instability.

Despite such criticisms, cohabitation, especially among college students, seems to be finding more acceptance in our society. However, deciding to cohabit is not a decision to be taken lightly. One needs to consider carefully the ramifications of such a decision. Legal ramifications, which we will discuss in a coming section, must also be considered, now more than ever.

Breaking Up

Society, including the cohabiting couples themselves, has largely ignored one of the philosophical foundations of cohabitation: that it is easy to break up if the relationship fails. Yet for those partners who are highly committed to the relationship, a breakup can be as emotionally uncomfortable as a divorce. At least with divorce society has support systems (see Chapter 14). However, no such support systems exist for the person leaving a cohabitation relationship. As the preceding statistics showed, the breakup rate is high, and thus the number of people who must cope with the trauma of breakup by themselves or perhaps with only a friend's shoulder to cry on will increase as the number of cohabiting couples increases. This problem requires study (Hill, Rubin & Peplau, 1976).

Living Together and the Law

Many readers may be surprised to know that as of July 1980 cohabitation was a crime in fifteen states (Weitzman, 1981).* Indeed, sexual intercourse between unmarried persons is still a crime in sixteen states and in Washington, D.C. It is true that such laws are seldom enforced, but if they are, the penalties are stringent. Many states set a maximum fine of $500 and six months in jail. Macklin (1978a) suggests that such laws may be unconstitutional and may violate one's right to privacy. At this time, however, they are still law.

In the states where such laws are in effect, there are numerous ramifications for the cohabiting couple. For example, living together can be grounds for losing one's job. Because membership in professional associations and licensing may be conditional on demonstration of moral fitness, such privileges could be denied to someone cohabiting outside of marriage (Macklin, 1978a).

Laws making cohabitation a crime, however, are so seldom enforced

*Alabama, Arizona, Florida, Georgia, Idaho, Illinois, Kansas, Michigan, Mississippi, North Carolina, Rhode Island, South Carolina, Utah, Virginia, and Wisconsin.

that they are not nearly so meaningful to the cohabiting couple as are several recent court decisions concerning property distribution and the obligation of support.* Perhaps the best known case involved actor Lee Marvin and his live-in friend, Michelle Triola. Out of this case came the coined term "palimony" to describe settlements made to a nonmarried live-in partner. The term has no legal significance but is descriptive of what Michelle Triola was finally awarded.

Michelle Triola and Lee Marvin lived together for seven years. During this period she acted as a companion and homemaker. There was no pooling of earnings, no property purchased in joint names, and no joint income tax returns were filed. They often spoke proudly of their freedom as unmarried cohabitors and went to some length to keep property separate. Eventually, Lee Marvin asked Michelle Triola to leave the household. He continued to support her for two years after the separation and then refused further support. Michelle Triola then brought suit and asked the court to determine her contract and property rights and to award her half of the property acquired during the period of their relationship.

The trial court dismissed the action as inappropriate; it was then appealed to the California Supreme Court, which ruled:

> The fact that a man and woman live together without marriage and engage in a sexual relationship, does not in itself invalidate agreements between them relating to their earnings, property, or expenses. . . . Agreements between nonmarital partners fail only to the extent that they rest upon a consideration of meretricious sexual services. (*Marvin* v. *Marvin*, 1976, as reported in Myricks, 1980, p. 210)

A meretricious relationship is essentially that of a prostitute to her customer; that is, sexual services are being paid for. This ruling enabled Michelle Triola to pursue her claim for support payments and established a precedent for unwed couples in that it granted such persons the right to sue for property settlements. Michelle Triola became the first unmarried person to win compensation from a former lover in a U.S. court (*Marvin* v. *Marvin*, 1979). She was awarded $104,000 for "rehabilitation purposes so that she may have economic means to re-educate herself and to learn new, employable skills or to refurbish those utilized . . . during her most recent employment, and so that she may return from her status as companion of a motion picture star to a separate, independent but perhaps more prosaic existence" (*Marvin* v. *Marvin*, 1979, as reported in Myricks, 1980, p. 211). The award was primarily for retraining, yet some of the funds could be used for living expenses. Such equitable relief is similar to rehabilitative alimony, hence the term palimony. In effect the judge gave her disguised alimony. However, this award was later thrown out by the California appellate court, and the California Supreme Court has refused to reinstate it (*Marvin* v. *Marvin*, 1981).

Numerous other cases have been litigated both before and after the Marvin case. In those cases where the courts see the union as meretri-

*This section has been adapted from Noel Myricks, 1980, 1983.

cious, any implied contracts are illegal. However, to 1979 seventeen states had followed the Marvin rationale.

The bottom line is that a given court will have the final word as to a cohabiting couple's obligations to one another if they break up. After a review of many palimony cases, Noel Myricks (1980) draws the following conclusions:

1. Distribution of property acquired during cohabitation remains subject solely to judicial decision.
2. Courts should enforce express contracts between cohabitors except where the contract is explicitly founded on payment for sexual services.
3. Without an express contract courts should inquire into the nature of the relationship to determine if there is an implied contract.
4. Courts may compensate a person for the reasonable value of services regardless of any agreement as to the value of such services.
5. Generally sexual services must be separated from other domestic services to make a valid argument. However, the state of Oregon has ruled more liberally and is willing to disregard the lifestyle of the parties (*Latham* v. *Latham*, 1976).
6. An implied contract may be inferred entitling a cohabitant to one-half of the accumulated property where parties have held themselves out as husband and wife (*Carlson* v. *Olson*, 1977).
7. Palimony may be provided to a cohabitant for rehabilitation purposes.
8. Lawsuits may be kept to a minimum if cohabitants have written agreements concerning the nature of their relationship, although the court may change or invalidate such agreements.

Despite the fact that courts are slowly giving unwed cohabitants some legal rights, to date cohabitation has few legal safeguards for either partner. As Lenore Weitzman summarizes (1981), a sanctioned marriage has legal rules and forums that provide otherwise unprepared married couples with an efficient system for dealing with the unexpected; the married couple is thus helped to minimize hardships resulting from unforeseen events. For example, if a spouse is killed, the state has rules for allocating that person's property in the absence of a will and for guaranteeing a share of it to the surviving spouse. By contrast, if one member of a cohabiting relationship dies without a will, the surviving partner has no legal rights at all. Legally, cohabiting couples are at a distinct disadvantage compared with married couples. This is especially true for the woman and is yet another reason to answer yes to the earlier question: Is the woman exploited in the cohabitation relationship?

Premarital Sexuality

As we have seen, movement down the path of intimacy is a part of American dating. For most it is a gradual movement characterized by escalating sexual intimacy. Traditional American dating often evolves into a sexual game of offense versus defense. With each step the couple moves closer to sexual intercourse. In traditional dating, because it is the male who pressures the female for greater physical intimacy, it is she who is on the defense. Because her value system may be vague or may become confused by the swiftly changing and pragmatic character of American society, the continuing pressure for more intimacy will often cause her confusion and insecurity.

Continuing escalation of physical intimacy moves from the first cautious hand holding at the movies to necking, petting, and, in some cases, intercourse. How rapidly the couple proceeds depends on the inner security of each member, the length of time and exclusiveness with which they date each other, and the dating patterns of their friends. The more insecure the persons are, the more they will seek security in conforming to what they believe the peer group is doing. Time is an important factor, too. To place vigorous young adults who like one another together for long periods of time without supervision in a culture that promotes sexuality is likely to lead to sexual activity.

But it is up to the individual couple to decide how far they will go. This strategy can be called "sex — not sex," and it is usually the female who makes the rules. Because she must control how sexual the male becomes, she must have a personal definition of what sexual behavior is. She knows that intercourse is sex, but she may be unsure how to categorize other behavior: kissing, necking, and various degrees of petting. If she can categorize kissing as "nonsex," she can kiss as much as she likes and feel no guilt. If, on the other hand because of upbringing she categorizes kissing as "sex," she will feel guilty when she engages in such behavior. Premarital sex in America is largely a matter of learning how to handle guilt.

When one asks a cross section of young American women what they define as sexual behavior, there is no single answer. One girl may become upset at any action beyond kissing. Another may participate in mutual masturbation with little if any conflict because she has defined as nonsex all but actual intercourse. In reality, in the broadest sense intimate physical contact of any kind between male and female is sexual behavior.

The boy feels he cannot judge where any one girl will draw the line, and he will be insecure in a new girl's presence until he knows the rules whereby she plays the game. He also may be timid and afraid of overt sexuality, although he is obliged to hide any fears by the masculine stereotype that demands he be a sexual initiator.

The escalation toward physical intimacy may cause young persons to become centered on sex to the exclusion of most other things. And even the final "solution" to escalation problems, sexual intercourse, does not end the preoccupation with sex. Instead, it often serves to exaggerate it.

Although premarital sex is against our societal standards, it is not uncommon. The classical sexuality studies of the past forty years have indicated that some 85 percent of unmarried American males and about 50 percent of unmarried females have engaged in sexual intercourse (Kinsey et al., 1948, 1953). Age, social class, education, and strength of religious ties are all important determinants of such behavior.

The Sexual Revolution

The preceding description of movement down the path of intimacy will seem old-fashioned to many young Americans. The sexual revolution of the past twenty years has greatly affected the mores surrounding premarital sexual interaction. Essentially the sexual revolution has been a revolution for women. The double standard that tacitly allowed males premarital sexual relations but forbade them to females is gradually disappearing since it was first studied by Alfred Kinsey and coresearchers around 1950. A look at the results of just one or two of the many studies of the incidence of premarital sexual experience makes it clear that young women have become more like young men in their sexual behavior. (See R. L. Clayton and Janet Bakemeier, 1980, for an overview of the many studies done on premarital sexual behavior during the 1970s.)

Ira Robinson and Davor Jedlicka (1982) compared the percentage of college students having premarital intercourse in 1965, 1970, 1975, and 1980 (Table 3-2) and found little increase for college men (12.3 percent) but a large increase for college women (34.8 percent). In addition they found that college students' rejection of premarital sexual intercourse as immoral had dropped dramatically. The number of students strongly agreeing with the statement, "I feel that premarital intercourse is immoral," showed a continual decline over the fifteen years studied except for a reversal of the decline for women in 1980, the last year studied (Table 3-3).

Robinson and Jedlicka did find, however, that there was a similar reversal in 1980 for both men and women on the question of whether it is immoral to have sexual intercourse with many partners. More men and women agreed in 1980 that this was immoral than had agreed in 1975. Robinson and Jedlicka suggest that there may be a "sexual contradiction" in today's college students: Sexual intercourse is reported at higher levels than earlier while at the same time there is increasing disapproval.

TABLE 3-2   Percentage of College Students Having Premarital Intercourse

	MALES	FEMALES
1965	65.1	28.7
1970	65.0	37.3
1975	73.9	57.1
1980	77.4	63.5

TABLE 3-3   Percentage of Students Strongly Agreeing with the Statement, "I feel that premarital sexual intercourse is immoral."

	MALES	FEMALES
1965	33.0	70.0
1970	14.0	34.0
1975	19.5	20.7
1980	17.4	25.3

John DeLamater and Patricia MacCorquodale (1979) found a similar incidence of premarital sexual relations in both college student and nonstudent samples. This similarity would seem to indicate that the sexual revolution encompasses all youth, not just college students. These researchers also discovered that the average age of onset of various sexual behaviors is lower for nonstudent men, whereas the reverse is true for nonstudent women. For example, the age of first intercourse for male nonstudents was 17.2 years, whereas it was 17.5 years for male students. For female students it was 17.9 years, whereas for female nonstudents it was 18.3 years.

Many of these studies may be biased in the direction of showing a high percentage of premarital sexual activity because the respondents are volunteers. Generally, volunteers in sexuality studies tend to be more liberal. For example, in Morton Hunt's (1973) study only one in five persons contacted agreed to participate in the study. Those who refused may have had quite different experiences from those who did participate. Be that as it may, the more recent figures for premarital sexual experience are so much higher than in previous studies that, at the very least, they show continued movement in the direction of increasing premarital sexual experience for young women.

Although the sexual mores of American youth are becoming more permissive, adults tend to react negatively to these changes. Most adults still support a position against premarital intercourse. The most common reasons they list for this position are:

1. Religious attitudes prohibit such behavior.
2. My own upbringing and personal moral code prohibit such behavior.
3. Sexual relations before marriage lead to serious problems — illegitimate children, damaged reputation, psychological problems.
4. Premarital sex contributes to the breakdown of morals in this country.
5. Sex is sacred and belongs only in marriage.
6. Premarital sex leads to extramarital sex and casual marital commitment.

It is easy for middle-aged individuals to urge young people to suppress their sex drive, but the fact remains that sexual needs are among the most basic human needs. It is extremely difficult for young adults to accept admonitions against premarital sex. Instead of discussing stan-

TABLE 3-4   Percentage of Females Having Intercourse

	JEW			PROTESTANT			CATHOLIC			TOTAL		
	1958	1968	1978	1958	1968	1978	1958	1968	1978	1958	1968	1978
Dating	11	20	45	10	35	56	8	15	46	10	23	50
Going steady	14	26	64	20	41	79	14	17	63	15	28	67
Engaged	20	40	69	38	67	88	18	56	69	31	39	76

Source: Bell & Coughey, 1980.

dards of behavior that have not been adhered to for some time, parents need to discuss openly and honestly the problems youth face. Any ultimate decision about premarital intercourse will be made by the young couples themselves. Surely, rather than lectures about morality, it is better to supply young persons with as much good information as possible so that their decision will be sound and based on a firm foundation of knowledge rather than ignorance.

Deciding for Yourself

There are four major areas for the couple contemplating premarital sexual intercourse to consider: (1) personal principles, (2) social principles, (3) religious principles, and (4) psychological principles.

Every person has a set of personal principles by which to guide his or her life. The following are some personal questions young adults should ask themselves when they are contemplating premarital intercourse:

1. Is my behavior going to harm the other person or myself, either physically or psychologically? Will I still like myself? What problems might arise? Am I protecting my partner and myself against sexually transmitted diseases and pregnancy?
2. Will my behavior help me become a good future spouse or parent? Do I believe sex belongs only in marriage?
3. Is my sexual behavior acceptable to my principles and upbringing? If not, what conflicts might arise?

Of course, there are no general answers to questions such as these. Each individual has personal principles and a personal manner of applying these principles in a particular situation, but the fact remains that most young adults should answer such questions if they engage in premarital sexual experimentation.

Again, questions arise when one considers general social principles. Our society has long supported certain rules about premarital sex. If enough people break these rules, pressure is placed on the society to change them. Thus each person who decides to act against the established code adds his or her weight to the pressure for change. Before you make such a decision, you should ask yourself:

1. What kind of behavior do I wish to have prevail in my society? Is

premarital sex immoral? Will premarital sex contribute to a break-down of morals? Is this desirable?

2. What kind of sexual behavior do I believe would make the best kind of society? Would I want my friends to follow in my footsteps?
3. Am I willing to support the social rules? What will happen if I don't?

Questions concerning religious principles also need answering. Most of us have had religious training, and we have learned attitudes toward sexual behavior from that training. In a study of several hundred junior college students' attitudes toward premarital sex (Cox, 1978), 90 percent of those who were against it gave religion as their primary reason. The following are some questions you should ask yourself:

1. What does my religion say about sexual conduct? Do I agree?
2. Am I willing or able to follow the principles of my religion?
3. Do I believe there is a conflict between the sexual attitudes of my church and of society? My church and my friends?

Psychological principles may be the hardest to uncover. Because the socialization process begins at birth and continues throughout one's lifetime, it is difficult, if not impossible, to remain completely unaffected by society and family. Many of our attitudes are so deeply ingrained that we are unaware of them. When our behavior is in conflict with these attitudes, there will usually be stress and guilt. Some of the psychological questions we must grapple with are:

1. Can I handle the guilt feelings that may arise when I engage in premarital sex?
2. How will premarital sex influence my attitudes and the quality of sex after marriage?
3. What will I do if I (or my partner) get pregnant? Can I handle an abortion? A child? Marriage?

Possible Problems Associated with Premarital Sexual Relations

As American mores have relaxed, the differentiation between premarital and marital sex activities has lessened. However, there are a number of problems that are clearly related to premarital sex.

Sexually transmitted disease is more prevalent among unmarried participants in sexual activities, whose chances of having more than one sexual partner are greater than married persons'. The chances are also greater of having short-duration sexual encounters where communication is less open. Such encounters may lead, especially for women, to later discovery of sexually transmitted disease. (Sexually transmitted disease is discussed fully in Chapter 9.)

Unwanted pregnancies are also a problem. Despite improved birth control methods, especially birth control pills, premarital pregnancies have continued to increase. It is estimated that the number of illegitimate births per 1000 unmarried women ages fifteen to forty-four has increased from 14.1 in 1950 to 29.4 in 1981 (National Center for Health Statistics, 1982). Illegitimacy rates do not give the complete picture, though, because many babies conceived outside of marriage are legitimized by subsequent marriage. Perhaps as many as one-third of all first-born babies are conceived outside of marriage. "CBS Reports" (1980) has noted that over half of all teenage births resulted from pregnancies outside marriage.

Recent increases in the number of births to unmarried women have been due to a combination of two factors: a higher rate of childbearing by unmarried women and the growth in the number of unmarried women of childbearing age. It is difficult to determine precisely the weight of each factor because each varies substantially by race and age. It is clear, however, that the growth in the number of unmarried women age twenty-five and over continues to be a significant factor in the recent large increases in births to these women. By contrast, the number of unmarried teenagers has leveled off and begun to decline in recent years; the continued rise in births to these women is thus due to the increased rate of childbearing among unmarried teens.

An unmarried pregnant woman has limited alternatives. She may marry. She may seek an abortion. She may give birth to the baby and then give it up for adoption. She may simply desert the infant. She may keep the child and go on welfare. Or she may let her parents care for the child while she works or continues with school. Regardless of how one handles a premarital pregnancy, the problems are many and stay with one for years.

TABLE 3-5   Illegitimate Live Births by Race and Age of Mother

RACE AND AGE	1950	1960	1965	1970	1974	1981
Total numbers (1000s)	141,600	224,300	291,200	398,700	418,100	665,747
Percent of all births	3.9	5.3	7.7	10.7	13.2	17.8
Rate per 1000 unmarried women	14.1	21.6	23.5	26.4	24.1	29.4
White women	6.1	9.2	11.6	13.8	11.8	17.9
Negro and other women	71.2	98.3	97.6	89.9	81.5	67.2
AGE OF MOTHER (1000s)						
under 15	3,200		6,100		10,600	9,024
15 – 19	56,000		123,100		210,800	262,777
20 – 24	43,100		90,700		122,700	237,265
25 – 29	20,900		36,800		44,900	99,583
30 – 34	10,800		19,600		18,600	40,984
35 – 39	6,000		11,400		8,200	13,187
40 and over	1,700		3,700		2,300	2,927

Dawn and Jim:
But I Want to Keep the Baby Even If We Aren't Married

Dawn is twenty years old and a college junior, majoring in business administration. She has gone with Jim for two years. He is a senior in premed and has been accepted for medical school. She has recently discovered that she is pregnant. In the past both she and Jim have agreed to postpone marriage until they are finished with school and Jim has established himself.

Jim is angry with her for becoming pregnant. "How stupid of you to forget to take your pill, especially in the middle of the cycle when you knew your chances of pregnancy were higher. Are you sure you didn't do it on purpose? You could have told me and I could have used something although I don't like to. It isn't natural. It is really up to the girl to protect herself, and you were plain dumb to forget after all this time."

Dawn doesn't quite agree. "You're having sex with me, too. I don't see why birth control is always just *my* responsibility. You know as well as I do that I didn't want to get pregnant. It wasn't my fault that I forgot. After all, you didn't have to make love to me. You were the one that was hard up and pushing, not me. But now that I'm pregnant, I'm going to keep the baby. A lot of my friends are doing it. Having a baby before you are married isn't half as bad as it used to be. I really don't care what you or our folks think; it's the modern thing to do."

Jim objects strongly. "Well, I'm not going to marry you under these conditions. We agreed to wait until I was finished with medical school and you blew it. The only thing you can do is get an abortion. They're easy to get now. There is nothing to them physically, and I'm willing to pay for it. Keeping the baby will just foul up our lives and tie us down. We'll have plenty of time to have children after we're finished with school."

"No abortion for me," replies Dawn. "I don't think they're right. Besides, I don't expect you to marry me. I wouldn't want you to feel forced into anything. I've only a year of school left and I'm sure my folks would watch out for the baby until I'm working and independent. Then, with child care, I'll be able to take care of it just fine, without you."

"Well, if you're that stupid, I'm glad to find out now," retorts Jim. "I won't be a part of such a dumb plan. Unless you do the smart thing and get an abortion, I'm through with you, pregnant or not."

What Do You Think?

How will they resolve their conflict? What would you advise?

What would you do if you were Jim? Dawn?

What kind of attitudes show through Jim's statements? Dawn's?

How would your parents react to such a situation?

What are the alternatives open to the couple?

How do you feel about illegitimacy? How do you think society feels today?

Whose responsibility is birth control? Why?

Early commitment and isolation are frequent partners of premarital sexual involvement. Sex is such a powerful force in young people's lives that it often overrides other aspects of a relationship. Sexual involvement often excludes growth in other areas such as social or intellectual. Also, sexual relationships can make for exclusivity, thus narrowing a young person's interpersonal experiences. Such relationships may lead to commitment on a sexual basis alone rather than to a total relationship. An early commitment based on only one aspect of a relationship (sexual) is usually an unstable basis for any long-term relationship.

The *quality of sex may be impaired* by premarital sexual experience. William Masters and Virginia Johnson (1966) point out that fear, hostility, and conflict are the three mental states that most often cripple the sex life of both men and women. Through education, Masters and Johnson assert, these three can be defeated. In their treatment conferences with couples they examine the couple's past sexual history and slowly guide them toward overcoming the negative emotional reactions that may be attached to early unhappy sexual experiences. Assuming that the couple's sexual problems are mental rather than physiological in nature, they help the couple through actual practice and desensitization to become more satisfactory sexual partners to one another. They find that early unsatisfactory sexual experiences often have negatively influenced an individual's whole attitude toward sexuality. Unfortunately, as long as society holds taboos against early sexual experience, indulging in premarital intercourse may be, for some, a factor working against later sexual fulfillment.

Premarital sexual intercourse is becoming more prevalent, as Tables 3-3 and 3-4 have shown. Thus an increasing number of American youth may be initiated into sexual intercourse under the often adverse circumstances that surround much premarital sexual activity. It is my hypothesis that early sexual experiences largely set the attitudes that an individual will hold toward sexual intercourse throughout his or her life. If one's early sexual experiences occur premaritally, the chances are that the quality of such experiences will be under less than optimum conditions. As a result large numbers of youth may begin their adult sexual life with negative attitudes toward sex. Premarital sex in our culture is often of relatively poor quality for two major reasons.

First, the environment in which these early clandestine experiences take place is usually negative and is seldom, if ever, conducive to relaxed, uninhibited sexual activities. Many of these activities take place in a car — having to duck each time another car passes doesn't help the couple relax and feel secure. Both relaxation and security are important psychological attributes to having satisfying sex. The general environment is especially important to the girl's ability to find satisfaction. The boy's response is much more direct; he can feel satisfied, through ejaculation, almost regardless of the environment. The girl's response is more diffused psychologically and depends more on her state of mind than does the boy's. The girl who is highly afraid of being caught, who is suffering from intense guilt over her action, and who may be feeling used and manipulated by the boy seldom will find great satisfaction in sexual intercourse. For example, the girl's home is now reported to be the place where first intercourse most often occurs. This environment can heighten her guilt, especially if her parents do not approve of premarital sex.

Indeed, most girls report that their first intercourse experience was not very enjoyable. Only 18 percent in a large recent study reported their first experience to be "thrilling," and only 10 percent reported having had an orgasm (Wolfe, 1980). This is not to deny that first intercourse is pleasurable and exciting. In light of what it could be, though, the girl may find herself disappointed. Such disappointment may breed later problems in her attitude toward sex. Because much modern literature, as well as movies and television, depict sexual satisfaction for the female as a wild and violent complete climax, she may interpret her ensuing disappointment as personal shortcomings. She may begin to think that something is wrong with her sexually, a belief that will in turn increase anxiety and make her more incapable of finding satisfaction. Thus the early sexual experience of an individual, if negative, may start a "vicious circle" pattern of behavior.

In most cases there is nothing wrong with the girl. If the environment is one of security and romance, if the boy appeals to the girl on a total basis — that is, psychologically as well as physically, offering her intellectual rapport, warmth, and a feeling of self-respect — and if her conception of the experience is realistic, in all likelihood she will experience a great deal of satisfaction. Although we have discussed the problems of the disappointed girl, it should be noted that when the girl shows disappointment, this threatens the boy, who may react with his own inferiority feelings because he appears unable to satisfy her. His ability to satisfy is one of his chief masculine ego defenses, and he is highly vulnerable to insecurity in this area.

The second reason for the often poor quality of premarital sex is the general ignorance of the young American male. As implied earlier, it is important that the boy be aware of the girl's psychological state as well as of her physical state. Candlelight, music, sweet nothings whispered in the ear — in a word, romance — are important ingredients to successful sexual experience for the girl. Yet the American male often lacks understanding of these dimensions. If he does understand them, he may be too preoccupied with himself or too embarrassed to do anything about them. In addition he can't admit to others, and *occasionally* even to himself, that he does not know all there is to know about sex. Indeed, the boy who is the biggest braggart about sex often knows the least. Too, most young men reach orgasm very quickly compared with young women. Often the male has ejaculated before the female has become much aroused.

Thus the generally poor environment in which most premarital intercourse must take place and the lack of knowledge and ineptness of the young couple combine to bring many American youth a disappointing introduction to adult sexuality. In light of the special place intimate physical contact can and should play in the life of the family, this is an unfortunate commentary on our society.

The problems just described, although prevalent, do not appear in every case. Some couples can premaritally experience the joys of adult sexuality, but they are probably the exception rather than the rule.

Although sexual intercourse is the end result of the physical intimacy path, it no longer signifies total commitment. Current research does not support the popular idea that "sexual relations and psychological commitment are related." Letitia Anne Peplau and coresearchers (1977) found that sexual intercourse was not significantly related to pair continuance. In the past it usually was. Sexual intercourse was more closely restricted to marriage or at least to a strong commitment to marriage. The shotgun wedding was a common end for the couple caught having premarital sexual relations, especially if a pregnancy resulted. Today sexual relations are not necessarily a precursor to a long-term commitment.

Finding the One and Only: Mate Selection

Chapter 2 pointed out that "love" is the major reason Americans give for marriage. Yet is love really the magic wand that directs our mate selection? Certainly we fall in love — or we think we do at the time. Yet, who we are attracted to and why is a complicated, still to be understood process. Critics who argue against using love as a basis for marriage believe that Americans are seduced by the romantic ideal into ignoring practical considerations that help ensure a successful marriage — for example, social and economic levels, education, age, religion, and so forth. Yet this is not really true. Our social system does take these factors into consideration, and a close inspection of love finds that it does indeed incorporate some of these factors. You don't fall in love with just anybody; on the other hand, there are a great number of "one and onlys."

First of all, there is a field of "desirables," or people to whom you are attracted. Within this field is a smaller group of "availables," those who are free to return your interest — you can meet them, they are not in love with another, they are unmarried, and so forth.

Availability is closely related to how we live. Our communities are organized into neighborhoods according to social class, and in America this generally means by economic level. So the people who live nearby will be socially and economically like us. Thus middle-class whites tend to marry middle-class whites; lower-class whites tend to marry lower-class whites; Catholics tend to marry Catholics. This idea that like marries like, or, more specifically, that we tend to marry within our own group, is called **endogamy**.

There are exceptions to the rule of endogamy, but generally society aims us toward loving — and marrying — someone similar to ourselves. If you don't marry the girl or boy next door, you are likely to marry someone you meet at school. The American system of neighborhood schools and selective college attendance makes education one of the strongest endogamic factors directing mate selection. Or you may find your future mate through your family's social circle, your job, or your church. All of the groups you join tend to some degree to limit their membership to people who are similar in socioeconomic status as well as in their more obvious reasons for being part of the group.

Strange are the ways of love, but even so it seldom happens that a

Endogamy
The inclination or the necessity to marry within a particular group

banker's college-educated daughter falls in love with the uneducated son of a factory worker.

Alan Kerckkoff and Keith Davis (1962) suggest that we select a mate by passing him or her through a series of successive filters (see Figure 3-4). Proximity and "suitability" of background act as the initial filter. Two people have the likelihood of meeting if they live or work close to one another, and they will be interested in further exploration if each seems, at first appearance, suitable to the other. Suitability is determined by one's values, most of which are learned and internalized from one's parents and peers. The second filter is a more thorough exploration of attitudes and values. For example, the two persons question each other about mutual friends, activities, and interests: "Oh, where do you go to school?" "I know some people who go there, do you know Jim Black and Sally Bowles?" "What classes are you taking?" "Really, I'm taking French next semester." "Do you ski? I'm going next week." If the couple's attitudes and interests prove compatible, they will progress toward more subtle personality exploration, finding out whether their needs for affection, independence, security, and so on are also compatible.

This kind of model is useful in understanding that mate selection is an evolving process. However, such an exact fixed set of filters or processes has yet to be proved (Levinger, Senn & Jorgensen, 1970; Kerckhoff, 1977; Rubin & Levinger, 1975).

Theoretically, two principles guide mate selection. Endogamy, as we have seen, is marriage within a certain group, such as a caste, class, or religion. **Exogamy**, on the other hand, is a requirement that people marry outside their group. In our culture requirements to marry outside

Exogamy
The inclination or the necessity to marry outside a particular group

FIGURE 3-4 Mate selection as successive filters.

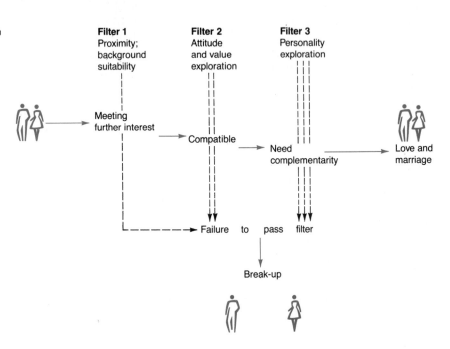

your group are limited to incest and sex; that is, you may not marry a near relative or someone of your own sex. All states forbid marriage between parents and children, siblings (brothers and sisters), grandparents and grandchildren, and children and their uncles and aunts. Most states forbid marriage to first cousins and half-siblings, although some states do not. About half the states forbid marriage between stepparents and stepchildren, and about the same number prohibit marriage between a man and his father's former wife or his son's former wife.

The other rule of exogamy, which until quite recently has been taken for granted, is the requirement that we marry someone of the opposite sex. This helps to ensure reproduction and continuance of the species. In the past few years attempts by homosexuals to obtain more rights have led to a "marriage" ceremony for homosexuals. So far, though, such marriages have no legal value.

Until recently most states had other prohibitions about whom one could marry. These prohibitions were generally termed **miscegenation** laws because they prohibited interracial marriages. Most of these laws were originally aimed at preventing white/Indian marriages, but they also were used to prevent white/black and white/Asian marriages. As recently as the end of World War II, thirty of the forty-eight states had such laws. Gradually, though, some states declared them void; and, finally, in 1967 in a landmark case the U.S. Supreme Court declared all such laws unconstitutional. By chance the defendant's surname was Loving, so the name of the case, *Loving* v. *Virginia*, fits in well with the American romantic ideal.

Miscegenation
Marriage or interbreeding between members of different races

Endogamic and exogamic principles guide our mate selection even though Americans tend to hide such mundane factors under the title of "love."

First Impressions to Engagement

Let us look more specifically at the mate-selection process for you, the individual. First impressions are usually belittled as superficial and unimportant. Yet without them the process cannot begin. A favorable first impression must be made or no further interaction will take place. *Physical attractiveness*, although subjective, tends to create the first appeal (Hatfield & Walster, 1978). This seems true for people of all ages, from children to the elderly. Fair or not, good-looking individuals are given preferential treatment. They are seen as more responsible for good deeds and less responsible for bad ones (Seligman, Paschall & Takata, 1974); their evaluations of others have more potent impact (Sigall & Aronson, 1969); others are more socially responsive to them (Barocas & Karoly, 1972) and more willing to work hard to please them. Physical attractiveness is more important to male evaluations of females than vice versa (Miller & Revinbark, 1970).

It is interesting too that there is a **halo effect** operating in regard to physical attractiveness. The halo effect is the fact that first impressions tend to influence succeeding evaluations. Physically attractive persons are

Halo effect
The tendency for a first impression to influence subsequent judgments

imbued with other positive qualities that might not actually be present. Dion, Berscheid, and Walster (1972) found that both males and females rated pictures of attractive individuals of both sexes as more sexually warm and responding, interesting, poised, sociable, kind, strong, and outgoing than less attractive people. Attractive persons are also seen to be more competent as husbands and wives and to have happier marriages. Thus to be physically attractive is usually an advantage at the first-impression stage of a relationship. This is not always true. Some persons are known to avoid highly attractive persons in order to enhance their own chances of acceptance.

Your impressions of *cognitive compatibility* (how the other thinks, what their interests are, and so forth) are also important in first impressions. In general similarity seems to go with attraction because (1) another's similarity itself is directly reinforcing, (2) another's similar responses support the perceiver's sense of self-esteem and comfort, (3) such responses indicate the other's future compatibility (Huston & Levinger, 1978).

After the first impression has aroused interest, you must consider two factors in choosing a partner. First, you must believe that the potential partner's attributes will be found desirable. Second, there must be a degree of anticipation that the potential partner will react favorably to your invitation of further interaction. Except for traditional females who don't take the initiative in pursuing a relationship because they think it is improper to do so, most people will pursue if the potential partner is in the field of "eligibles" and the two factors mentioned are favorable.

We usually try to further a relationship by various attraction-seeking strategies. In order to draw a potential partner's attraction, we may attempt to buoy the other's esteem by conveying our feelings that we think highly of them. We will probably try to do things for them. We will tend to agree with the other person, and we will attempt to ascribe attractive characteristics to ourselves (Jones & Wortman, 1973).

Attraction tends to lead to *self-disclosure*. Intermediate degrees of disclosure may in turn lead to greater attraction, but this depends on the desirability of the information disclosed. Self-disclosure tends to lead to reciprocity. This phase occurs early in a relationship when a lot of exciting mutual sharing takes place. "Is that the way you feel about it?" "That's great, because I feel the same way." As more is disclosed, excitement increases because the potential for a meaningful relationship seems to be rapidly increasing. However, the speed with which one discloses personal aspects is also important. Disclosure that seems overly quick may arouse suspicions rather than trust (Rubin & Levinger, 1975; 1976).

Stambul and Kelly (1978), using retrospective reports of courtship provided by newlyweds, identified four relationship dimensions that interacted during courtship and finally led to marriage. The four dimensions are: (1) love, (2) conflict and negativity, (3) ambivalence (mixed feelings), and (4) maintenance (problem-solving efforts and attempts to change behavior). Love and maintenance activities were reported to increase as a couple moved from casual dating through serious dating to engagement. Conflict and negativity increased from casual to serious dating and then leveled off, presumably as a consequence of the couple's working out the terms of their relationship. Particularly interesting was the way the dimensions were interrelated at various stages. Early in the cycle, love was associated with efforts to maintain the relationship. Later on, however, love had little to do with maintenance activities. Instead, such activities were associated with conflict. Ambivalence was tied to conflict early in the relationship. Later it had more to do with concerns about love than conflict (Huston & Levinger, 1978).

Although much research has been done on interpersonal attraction, some of which we have been examining, our efforts to predict the evolution of a given individual relationship based on the personal characteristics of the partners have been primitive at best and rather unsuccessful (Huston & Levinger, 1978). In fact, to date it is almost impossible to determine in advance whom one should marry to ensure a successful relationship.

As an example of this complexity, let us look at two marriages, one built on similar needs and one on complementary needs. In a marriage of similar needs, the partners begin with similar interests, energy levels, religion, socioeconomic background, age, and so on. They share many characteristics and hence seem well selected for each other. Ideally their relationship can lead to mutual satisfaction, but this is not always so. If, for example, the partners are competitive, the result can be disastrous. Consider the case of Henry and Hazel:

> Henry and Hazel are alike in most respects, including being computer programmers, but Hazel has advanced more rapidly. Henry, being competitive, feels like a loser and begins to resent his wife. He subtly puts her down and gradually becomes more critical of women in general. The more success Hazel has, the poorer their relationship becomes because Henry cannot accept, let alone find joy in, her success. To him it only points up his weaknesses.

By contrast, a marriage of complementary needs is one in which each partner supplies something that the other lacks. For example, an extrovert may help an introvert become more social; an organized partner may help bring structure to the life of a disorganized partner; a relaxed partner may create an environment that helps ease the stress of a tense partner. Such complementarity can be most beneficial but it cannot be counted on to happen reliably because such differences often begin to polarize the partners rather than drawing them together. For example, consider Carol and Otis:

> Carol is so organized that Otis counts on her to pay the bills, make social arrangements, find the nail clippers, and so on. The more Otis depends on her for these things, the more organized Carol feels she needs to be, and she begins to try to organize Otis. On his part Otis resents this pressure and becomes passively resistant (procrastinates and becomes forgetful and careless). Polarization has occurred.

Unfortunately there are no fully satisfying techniques for selecting marriage partners for lasting satisfaction. Even trial marriages have proved relatively ineffective (Hill, Rubin & Peplau, 1976). By way of summary, we can point out some of the reasons for marrying that reduce marital success chances and, in addition, some helpful selection factors that seem to improve chances for success.

Reasons for Marriage That Tend to Reduce the Chances of Success

1. *Love at first sight*: It is easy to understand falling in love at first sight but hard to justify selecting a marriage partner on this basis alone.
2. *Escape from home*: Rather than dealing with a current relationship, many persons run away, hoping a new person or a new environment will be better. A marriage so conceived is often the first of a series of failures.
3. *Avoiding loneliness*: Loneliness can sometimes drive a person into a hasty marriage. To seek companionship in marriage is a proper goal. However, if overcoming loneliness is one's only motivation for marriage, chances are high that this reason alone will not sustain a long-lasting relationship.
4. *Sexual attraction*: Unfulfilled sexual attraction, or guilt over sexual involvement, is a popular, yet weak, reason for marriage. An unusually fulfilling sexual relationship alone is not reason enough to marry.

Reasons for Marriage That Tend to Increase the Chances of Success

1. *Similar socioeconomic backgrounds*: Social research has clearly demonstrated that a similar socioeconomic status improves the chances of success in marriage.
2. *Similar energy levels*: Similar — or dissimilar — activity levels are fundamental to every other aspect of the relationship. For example, consider a marriage where the energy levels are dissimilar:

> Bill is a quiet person who needs eight to nine hours of sleep to function well the next day. His tempo is slow and deliberate but he finishes everything he starts. His slowness causes him to be habitually late. Joyce, his wife, needs little sleep and appears to be a bundle of energy. She does many things, finishing most of them quickly. She is always ready earlier than Bill if they are going out and seems to be waiting for him and nagging him to hurry. She likes companionship in the evening and dislikes going to bed before midnight. Bill usually wants to go to bed around 10 P.M. and is annoyed if she doesn't accompany him. Over several years, the conflicts engendered by their differing energy levels have grown. They wonder if they should look for new partners better suited to their activity levels.

3. *Openness to growth or desire for stability*: A good relationship can occur between two partners who want stability or between two partners who want growth or change, but differences between partners in these respects are extremely difficult to overcome. For example, consider this marriage where the partners differ:

Mary is comfortable with routine and stability. It makes her feel safe and secure to know exactly what is going to happen today, tomorrow, and next week. On the other hand, her husband, Jack, is spontaneous and dislikes committing himself too far in advance to any plan to action. He says that this allows him freedom and flexibility, which he feels is necessary if a person is to grow and avoid stagnation. Their differing philosophies about growth and stability cause them to continually disagree.

Although finding "the one and only" might seem ideal, our chances of doing this are slim. In fact, within limits any number of persons can become satisfactory and long-lasting partners, for the key to a successful relationship is more in the building and maintenance of the relationship than in the selection of the imaginary perfect mate. The marriage ceremony is really a beginning, not a culmination. The key to successful relationships is not the initial mate-selection process so much as it is the couple's learning to compromise and communicate with one another.

Summary

The onset of puberty signals the beginning of adult sexuality. The age of sexual maturity, however, does not coincide in America with social acceptance of overt sexual behavior, especially sexual intercourse. Marriage is the socially accepted vehicle for sexual intercourse. Because marriage for most Americans does not occur until they are in their late teens or early twenties, there is a period of several years during which there is conflict between the dictates of biology and society. This is called the "sexual stress period."

American dating has been a unique form of courtship and mate selection historically. In a sense it has been America's contribution to the world's various mate-selection systems. American dating has become increasingly less formal, especially in the last twenty years when it can perhaps better be termed "getting together" or "hanging around."

Cohabitation has increased in the past twenty years to such an extent that some theorists now consider it to be a stage in the courtship system. Cohabitation has drawbacks, both legal and psychological, compared with marriage. It would appear that the cohabiting woman is at more of a disadvantage than the cohabiting man. The law is becoming increasingly interested in the cohabitation relationship, but the relationship remains precarious legally.

Although much of our society does not consider premarital intercourse a legitimate outlet of sexual energies, a great deal of premarital intercourse is taking place. There appears to be increasing acceptance of premarital intercourse among American youth despite societal pressures against it. However, because there are social mores against premarital intercourse, those engaging in it often face conflict within themselves. Questions about social, personal, religious, and psychological principles should be answered by anyone contemplating premarital intercourse.

Mate selection and sexuality for the young are handled mainly through the American invention of dating. Although dating varies greatly from person to person and place to place, there is some recognizable pattern to traditional dating, especially outside of large metropolitan areas. American dating is controlled by the youth themselves and involves relative freedom for the young man and woman to be alone together. This intensifies the pressure for the pair to move toward premarital intercourse as a means of handling their sexual drives.

Mate selection is an involved process that is not yet fully understood. However, it is fairly clear that similarities of socioeconomic backgrounds, energy levels, and degrees of restraint help to increase the chances of marital success.

SCENES FROM MARRIAGE

Is Living Together a Bad Idea?

Judith Krantz, novelist and commentator about modern American women, wrote a popular article entitled "Living Together is a Rotten Idea." Her general thesis is that from the woman's standpoint cohabitation is a losing proposition. The cohabiting woman loses her independence, her freedom to make choices, her privacy, all of her mystery, any practical bargaining position in the power structure of love, an opportunity to make a meaningful change in her life by taking a genuine step toward full adult status, the prospect of having a child other than an illegitimate one, and the protection of the law. This is a disturbing list of losses to say the least.

She has given up all of these extraordinarily important elements of her life in return for what is fundamentally little more than a half-assed living arrangement.

Living together is not a true commitment. It is only a commitment that says, "I can leave anytime I wish." As Krantz says, "[It is] not the sink or swim of marriage, but a mere dog paddle at the shallow end of the pool." In essence the lack of commitment makes the relationship at best only "playing house."

Krantz suggests that living together without marriage has become a bourgeois cliché and has developed into the biggest rip-off of women's rights since the invention of the chastity belt. Women are making a series of compromises with themselves that rest on a number of falsehoods that she must devise to rationalize her behavior.

Falsehood number one is, "He is not yet ready to make a total commitment but once we are living together I know its only a matter of time until we marry." Unfortunately, as we pointed out earlier in this chapter, most cohabiting men do not share this assumption. In fact, moving in with a man gives him many reasons not to marry you. Looking at the data on division of housework and the proportion of cohabiting women working to support the relationship monetarily compared to their married sisters, it is clear that the man has a gold mine. He has a built-in housekeeper whom he not only doesn't have to pay, but who herself pays him for doing the work. Marriage means obligations, moral and financial. Why marry when one can have a bedmate-companion-housekeeper for free?

[This is the] only time in recorded history when women who are not literally slaves have made themselves totally available to men without expecting something concrete in return. Who can blame men for taking advantage of such sappy, soft-minded, pseudoidealistic stupidity?

Also there remains deep in many men, the remnants of the "double standard" which said, "It's great to have sex with this woman, but I wouldn't want to marry her." As unfair as it is, many men still assume that if you are willing and eager to have a sexual relationship with him, you will have been or will be that way with other men. The "double standard" says, "You don't marry a promiscuous woman."

Falsehood number two says, "How can you really get to know a person unless you live with them?" This is a very popular belief among cohabitors who equate their relationship with a "test marriage." The idea seems rational and makes good sense in light of the high divorce rate among married couples. Unfortunately cohabiting seems to be just as prone to error as does marriage. To date research on the relation of cohabitation with spouse prior to marriage and the permanence of the marriage seems to show no difference between the cohabitors and the noncohabitors. It is also interesting to note that many who live together feel that their problems with their partner will go away after they marry. Yet as we shall see in Chapter 4, expectations that a person will change in marriage are usually disappointed. The fact that a cohabiting couple is only "playing house" means that it is possible that one's behavior will not be the same in marriage as it is in the cohabiting relationship. That marriage asks of both partners a strong, true, lasting commitment changes the basic relationship greatly from the dating, cohabiting relationship. The two relationships simply aren't usually similar enough to assume that what is true of one will automatically be true of the other.

Falsehood number three says, "We're in love and I trust him completely. Why bring marriage into it? It's just a piece of paper?" But what a piece of paper it is. The legalities of marriage provide protection to both partners. Protection that, no matter how much we are "in love," may be needed if the great love evaporates as America's high divorce rate indicates it often does. Of course, both in cohabitation and marriage one assumes that the legalities will never be needed. How could this loving couple do anything to hurt one another? Yet experience tells us that loving couples more often

than casual couples do hurt one another. The bitterness of many divorced spouses towards one another years after the divorce attest forcefully to this fact. As we saw in the "Living Together and the Law" section of this chapter, cohabiting couples are still open to legal entanglements. However, at this time these entanglements are unpredictable, open to the whimsy of a given state or a given judge. At least in marriage, the rules of breaking up are spelled out, giving each spouse fair consideration and protection.

One story out of many related to this author may suffice to make more meaningful the lack of that piece of paper (marriage certificate) in cohabitation. The couple in question were mature, in love yet reasonable about their relationship. He was divorced and in the settlement had retained ownership of the family home. She lived in a small apartment: when they decided to live together, it seemed only sensible that she move into his home. This she did, and over the next seven years she worked hard to make his house into their home. She had a good job and earned as much as he did, and much of the home improvement was done with her money because she felt it only fair since he made the house payments. However, she did in fact occasionally make the house payment when for some reason he was a little short on cash in a given month.

She wallpapered, painted and gardened over the years, and the home took on much of her personality and became her home as well as his in every way but legally. In the seventh year of their relationship she began to feel increasing distance between them.

Finally she confronted him with her feelings. With some reluctance he told her that he had fallen in love with one of his colleagues whom he now wished to marry. Naturally, since the house belonged to him, she would have to move out to make room for his soon-to-be new bride. It was true that she was free to take the furniture she had bought and all of the things that she had brought with her into the relationship. But how do you take hung wallpaper, wall to wall carpeting, and years past of an attractive garden? Had these things been put into her own home, they would remain even if he didn't. At least with marriage, there would have been some division of property, some possible reimbursement for her years of work. As it was, she had to move out and return to a small apartment, because she had not bothered to save during the seven-year relationship. After all, why should she? She had a home with her beloved partner.

Falsehood number four is, "I'm simply not ready to get married yet, but I don't like being alone and need someone to give my love to." For the young woman who hasn't been away from her family this is particularily dangerous. As we have seen, in the past many young women left their parental homes only to enter marriage. Later in their lives when the marriage failed and they were for the first time cast upon their own, they were helpless and afraid. The young woman who is robbed, by entrance into a cohabitation relationship, of her early years of independence, living alone and learning about her own individuality, is also robbed of experiences that she may never again be able to recapture. To be learning about independence and one's own strengths and weaknesses at age forty after a marriage failure is difficult. The best time to learn about oneself is before one takes on the responsibility of marriage. It is a precious short time and should never be given away lightly. Young adulthood is an exciting time of testing one's wings, reaching for the sky, looking for the limits. To hide from this time in an early marriage is bad enough, but to hide from it in a possibly meaningless cohabitation experience is even worse.

How sad to forfeit the freshest years of life—a time of unbounded freedom and opportunity that will never be repeated—for the lukewarm comforts of premature domesticity.

It is true that some of these things we have been discussing could also apply to men. But it is the man who marries approximately two years later than the woman; it is the man who is most apt to adventure with a friend on a trip to far off places; it is the man who is most likely to enter the military and be forced to test

himself and find out who he is; it is the man who in his work world is most likely to have a career as opposed to only a job. The cards, unfortunately are still stacked in his favor as we shall see in Chapter 6. For him to live with a free companion-housekeeper who also shares her body with him is much less dangerous for him than for her. If she wants to give these things to him for little in return why should he not accept?

In the past, it has been the woman who has controlled sex because it was the woman who had the most to lose. Today it is the woman who must control cohabitation and not enter into it lightly, because it is she who has the most to lose.

Inescapably, a woman who lives with a man without a total commitment on his part risks becoming boring and familiar to him, but without having literally become a part of his family, with all that implies. Her position is more fragile in every way than that of a married woman. She has abandoned her own precious apartness, surrendered her claim to the life of a separate individual—too soon. Much too soon. . . .

What Do You Think?

Do many of your friends cohabitate? What kinds of problems do they have in the cohabitation relationship?

Does the man or the woman usually seem most committed to the relationship?

In cohabitation relationships that have broken up, has the man or the woman initiated the break-up?

Who benefits more from cohabitation, the man or the woman? Why? What are the benefits?

Would you cohabitate? If so, why? If not, why not?

CHAPTER 4

MARRIAGE, INTIMACY, EXPECTATIONS, AND THE FULLY FUNCTIONING PERSON

CONTENTS

4

Marriage is the most intimate of all human interactions. At its heart marriage is an interpersonal relationship between two persons, a man and a woman. Most people try to fulfill their psychological, material, and sexual needs within marriage. To the degree that they are successful, the marriage is successful. We know, however, that success in meeting these needs is difficult to achieve. This is reflected in America's high divorce rate.

You may remember that one of the primary functions of the contemporary American family is to provide emotional gratification to members, help them deal with emotional crises, and grow in the most fulfilling manner possible. In other words marriage and the family *ideally* act as a haven from which individual members can draw support and security when facing the challenges of our rapidly changing, technological society. A fully functioning family helps its members grow, mature, and become self-actualized individuals. A good marriage acts as a buffer against mental health problems — against alienation, loneliness, unhappiness, and emotional depression. In a word marriage can be therapeutic, a curative to the problems of its members.

In this chapter and the next we will explore marriage as an interaction between two individuals. We will examine a philosophy and techniques, and we will look at case histories to help us create marriages that are nurturing and that support self-fulfillment. Although we will be discussing interpersonal relations in the context of marriage, the insights are applicable to any kind of human relationship: boyfriend/girlfriend, employer/employee, parent/child, and so forth.

Engagement and Marriage

Most Americans expect to find fulfillment within marriage. About 95 percent of the population will be married at some time during their life (U.S. Bureau of the Census, 1982). People expect marriage to fulfill all of their psychological, sexual, and material needs. Never before have they asked so much of marriage. Such high expectations contribute to great disappointments. Failure often reflects high hopes, and certainly most Americans enter marriage with high hopes.

Marriage is the culmination of courtship. Traditionally, the final courtship stage has been **engagement**. Until recently this has been a fairly formal stage. But with the increased age for first marriage, the higher number of remarriages, and greater cohabitation among nonmarried couples engagement has become much less formal for some. In a typical engagement the couple makes public announcement of their intention to marry and begins active marriage preparation. Once the engagement is announced, the couple usually begins to make concrete plans for the wedding date, type of wedding, who will be invited, where they will live after marriage, at what level they can afford to live, and so forth.

During the engagement the couple often spend more time with each

Engagement
The final courtship stage before marriage; characterized by public knowledge of the coming marriage

other's families and begin to be treated as kin. Marriage is, after all, the union of two families as well as of two individuals. The families may also arrange to meet. Above all the two persons begin to experience themselves as a social unit. Families and friends as well as the public in general react to them as a pair rather than as separate individuals.

Types of Engagements

There is the short, romantic engagement lasting from two to six months. Time is typically taken up with marriage plans, parties, and intense physical contact. Normally, such a short engagement period fails to lead the couple to more insights into one another's personalities. Indeed, so much time is taken up with marriage preparation that the couple may not have enough time for mutual exploration of their relationship.

The long, separated engagement, such as when one partner is away at college, also presents problems. There are two distinct philosophies of separation: "Absence makes the heart grow fonder" and "Out of sight, out of mind." In reality the latter tends to prevail. Prolonged separation tends to defeat the purposes of the engagement. Also, the question of exclusivity of the relationship is raised. Does one date others during the separation? Dating others may cause feelings of insecurity and jealousy, whereas separation without dating is lonely and may cause hostility and dissatisfaction. In general the separated engagement is usually unsatisfactory to both members of the couple.

Another possibility is the long but inconclusive engagement. Here the couple puts off marriage because of economic considerations, deference to parental demands, or just plain indecisiveness. When a couple is engaged for years but the engagement never culminates in marriage, it is probably a good sign that all is not well between them.

About one in four engaged couples break up temporarily. The causes of breakups appear to be simple loss of interest, recognition of an incompatible relationship, or the desire to reform the prospective mate. The major areas of disagreement tend to be matters of conventionality, families, and friends. However, broken engagements can be considered successful in the sense that the couple had the time during this formal commitment period to look more closely at one another and to realize that marriage would not succeed.

Functions of Engagement

What should an engagement do? How can engagement help the couple achieve a better marriage? Basically, the couple should come to agree on fundamental life arrangements. Where will they live? How will they live? Do they want children? When? Will they both work?

The couple also needs to examine long-range goals in depth. Do they want similar things from life? Are their methods of obtaining these things compatible? Do their likes and dislikes blend? What role will religion play in their lives? How will they relate to one another's family? Friends? Work associates? They may not be able to answer such questions with complete finality, but at least tentative answers should be agreed upon. In fact the most important premarital agreement may be an agreement as to how answers to such questions will be worked out in the future. A couple with a workable, problem-solving approach to life is in a good position to find marital success.

An important part of the engagement is the premarital medical examination, which serves several useful functions. For instance, one of the partners may have a general health problem that will require special care by the other partner. Marrying a diabetic, for example, means that diet will have to be carefully controlled and insulin administered periodically. Or a medical examination may reveal anatomical problems that would interfere with sex and/or conception. The woman's hymen may be totally blocking her vagina, which would make first intercourse difficult. The man may have a low sperm count, which would make conception more difficult. Both persons need to be checked and cured of any possible sexually transmitted disease. The Rh factor in each partner's blood needs to be determined, as this factor is of major importance in future pregnancy. Information on mutually acceptable methods of birth control can be given at this time if the couple has not already chosen such methods. And each partner will have the opportunity to talk over with the physician questions about the coming marriage.

Premarital counseling is good because often there is a blindness that comes with "being in love." It can be helpful to discuss ideas and plans with an objective third person such as a minister, marriage counselor, or mutual friend. A truly successful engagement period leads either to a successful marriage or to a broken engagement. An unsuccessful engagement in all likelihood will lead to marital failure.

Fulfilling Needs in Marriage

Psychological Needs   You may remember from Chapter 1 that one of the basic assumptions on which this book is based is: The family becomes increasingly important to its members as social stability decreases and/or people feel more isolated and alienated.

Mobility, increased anonymity, ever larger and more bureaucratic institutions, and lack of social relatedness all contribute to increasing feelings of loneliness and helplessness. Because of these feelings, our psychological need for intimacy has increased greatly. It is in marriage that most people hope to find intimacy.

> What men and women seek from love today is no longer romantic luxury: it is an essential of emotional survival. More and more they hope to find in intimate love something of personal validity, personal relevance, a confirmation of one's existence. For in today's world, when men and women are made to feel as faceless as numbers on a list, they want intimate love to provide the feelings of worth and identity that preserve meaning and sanity. (Bach & Deutsch, 1970, pp. 14 – 15)

Marriage can supply love and affection, emotional support and loyalty, stability and security, and romantic fulfillment as well as companionship. This is a big order.

Sexual Needs   Marriage is the only legitimate outlet for sexual energies recognized by American society. Indeed, sexual intercourse is a state-mandated part of marriage. If sexual needs are not fulfilled in a marriage, the marriage can be dissolved. Thus American spouses must function as lovers to their mates as well as fulfilling the long list of psychological needs.

Material Needs   "Room and board" is a part of every marriage. Breadwinning and homemaking are essential to survival. Material needs also affect how successfully psychological and sexual needs are met. Marital disruption is considerably higher among families in economic trouble than among families satisfactorily meeting material needs.

Society recognizes that fulfilling these three areas of needs is a valid responsibility of the marriage institution. In fact, so important is the meeting of these needs for individuals that failure to do so is recognized by all states as legitimate reason for divorce.

You and the State: Legal Aspects of Marriage

Every society has some kind of ceremony whereby permanent relationships between the sexes are recognized and given status. The society (or

the state) sets minimum standards for marriage in the interests of order and stability. In Western societies the state is interested in supporting a monogamous marriage, assuring the "legitimacy of issue," protecting property and inheritance rights, and preventing marriages considered unacceptable, such as between close relatives.

In the United States marriage laws are determined by individual states. Although there are differences in requirements, all states recognize marriages contracted in all other states. California law is typical of many state laws relating to marriage:

> Marriage is a personal relation arising out of a civil contract, to which the consent of the parties capable of making that contract is necessary. Consent alone will not constitute marriage; it must be followed by the issuance of a license and solemnized as authorized. (Section 4100, West's Annotated California Codes, 1983, 5)

Marriage in the United States is a contract with obligations set by the state. Like all contracts, the marriage contract must be entered into by mutual consent, the parties must be competent and eligible to enter into the contract, and there is a prescribed form to the contract. All states set minimum age requirements, and most require a medical examination and a waiting period between the examination and license issuance (see Appendix E). However, unlike most contracts, which are between two parties, the marriage contract involves three parties: the man, the woman, and the state. The state prescribes certain duties, privileges, and restrictions. In addition the contract cannot be dissolved by the mutual consent of the man and woman but must be dissolved by state action.

In a few instances a couple may be exempt from the marriage license law. Section 4213 of the California Civil Code allows couples living together to marry without applying for a license, provided they are eighteen or older. A certificate of such marriage must be made by a clergyman, delivered to the parties, and recorded in the records of the clergyman's church. Thirteen states recognize common law marriage if a couple can prove they have lived as husband and wife for seven or more years.*

The state also sets a number of other standards. It limits how closely within family relationships one may marry. It considers a marriage invalid if consent to marry is obtained by fraud or under duress, if there is mental incapacity, if there is physical inability to perform sexually, or if either party is already married.

No particular marriage ceremony is required, but the parties must declare, in the presence of the person solemnizing the marriage, that they take each other as husband and wife, and the marriage must be witnessed, usually by two persons (Section 4206). Although some states are quite specific, there is a general trend away from uniform marriage vows. Traditional vows reflect the permanence expected in marriage by society: ". . . to have and to hold from this day forward, for better or worse, for richer, for poorer, in sickness and in health, to love and to cherish, till death do us part."

About 75 percent of all marriages in the United States take place in a church. The state vests the clergy with the legal right to perform the marriage ceremony. Most faiths in the United States consider marriage a sacrament. God is called on to witness and bless the marriage: "Those whom God hath joined together let no man put asunder."

The marriage ceremony commits the couple to a new status. It sets minimum limits of marital satisfaction. Typical of these directives are those found in Title 8, Husband and Wife, of California's Senate Bill 252:

Husband and wife contract toward each other obligations of mutual respect, fidelity and support.

The husband is the head of the family. He may choose any reasonable place or mode of living, and the wife must conform thereto.

Neither husband or wife has any interest in the property of the other, but neither can be excluded from the other's dwelling (except under certain circumstances recognized by the court).

The respective interests of the husband and wife in community property during the continuance of marriage relations are present, existing and equal interests under the management and control of the husband.

Note that these directives give authority to the man in a number of areas. The feminist movement is working to change such laws so that marriage can truly be an arrangement between equals.

---

*Alabama, Colorado, Georgia, Idaho, Iowa, Kansas, Montana, Ohio, Oklahoma, Pennsylvania, Rhode Island, South Carolina, Texas.

Marriage, then, is much more than "just a piece of paper." It commits the couple to a new set of obligations and responsibilities. In essence the couple in many ways marries the state, and it is the state to whom they must answer if the prescribed responsibilities are not met.

Writing Your Own Marriage Contract

Marriage contract
A written agreement between married partners outlining the responsibilities and obligations of each partner

As we have seen, marriage is a formal contract between the couple and the state and has a set form in each state. Not every couple's needs can best be met by the standard state contract, however; hence an increasing number of couples are writing their own **marriage contracts**. Such a personal contract cannot take the place of the state marriage contract, nor can it reject legally any of the state contract obligations. However, as a supplement to the state contract, it can afford a couple the freedom and privacy to order their personal relationship as they wish. It also can permit them to escape to some degree from the sex-based legacy of legal marriage and to move in the direction of an egalitarian relationship. The couple can formulate an agreement that conforms to contemporary social reality. Personal contracts can also be written by couples who wish to have a relationship but not one of marriage (for example, a cohabiting couple or a couple barred from marriage such as a homosexual couple (Weitzman, 1981).

As Lenore Weitzman suggests, in addition to its legal advantages, a personal contract facilitates open and honest communication and helps prospective partners clarify their expectations. Once the contract agreement has been reached, it serves as a guide for future behavior. Contracts also increase predictability and security by helping couples identify and resolve potential conflicts in advance.

Personal contracts need to be constructed carefully if they are to be legal. For example, when one partner brings to marriage a great deal of wealth that has been accumulated before the marriage, the couple may want to sign a contract that keeps this property separate from the property that may accumulate during the marriage. This is particularly difficult to do in community property states. Such a contract needs to be drawn by an attorney who knows well the state laws governing community property. Any topic may be handled in a personal contract, but such contracts generally cover the following:

- Aims and expectations of the couple
- Duration of the relationship
- Work and career roles
- Income and expense handling and control
- Property owned before the contract and acquired after
- Disposition of prior debts
- Living arrangements
- Responsibility for household tasks
- Surname
- Sexual relations
- Relations with family, friends, and others

- Decisions regarding children (number, rearing, and so forth)
- Religion
- Inheritance and wills
- Resolving disagreements
- Changing and amending the contract
- Dissolution of the relationship

The list of what could be covered is endless. As unromantic as it seems to sit down before marriage with your intended partner and work out some of the details of your future relationship, it is a worthwhile task even if you don't plan to have a written legal contract. As we shall see in this chapter, people's expectations about one another and their relationship are important determinants of behavior. If one partner's expectations differ greatly from the other's and are left unexpressed and unexamined, the chances are great for conflict and disappointment. By going through the steps of working out a personal contract, the couple thereby bring into the open their many attitudes and expectations; appropriate compromises and changes can then be made before major problems arise.

The Transition from Single to Married Life

Married life is indeed different from single life. Suddenly, marriage brings duties and obligations. One is no longer responsible for only oneself but now shares responsibility for two people and perhaps more if children arrive.

Furthermore, one's identity is changed with marriage. No longer are you simply you, you are now Bill's wife or Marge's husband or Randy's father or mother. You become interdependent with the others in your family and lose the independence you had when single. You enter a double-person pattern of life: Planning together, working together, and playing together become more important than what you do as an individual. Decisions now involve the desires of two people and often become a discussion or debate and end in compromise rather than you simply doing what you want (Bowman, 1974).

The transition from dating to establishing a home and family is often a large step for both partners. The couple may have cooked some meals together during courtship, but preparing 1095 meals a year for two on an often tight budget is a far greater challenge. Planning a month's finances is certainly more difficult than raising money for a weekend of skiing. In fact, living within some kind of a family budget is a difficult transition for many newly marrieds. Before marriage they were used to spending their incomes as they wished. Now another person must be consulted, and what they earn must be shared.

Leisure time activities, which are often spontaneous and unplanned when one is single, now must be planned with another person, and often compromises must be worked out. As we shall see with Bill and Marge, conflicts over leisure time pursuits can be difficult to resolve.

New relationships must be developed with both sets of parents after marriage. One's primary relationship is now with one's spouse rather than with one's parents. Also, one must learn to relate with one's in-laws. Before marriage there usually isn't much interaction with the parents of the partner. But after marriage interaction will be more frequent and more important. Failure to build a satisfactory in-law relationship makes married life more difficult inasmuch as the relationship with one's parents is important to each spouse.

The sexual relationship may also involve a transition. Premarital sexuality may have been restrained, covert, and only partially satisfying. Ideally, the marital sexual relationship will become fully expressive and satisfying to both partners. However, this may not occur if one or both have been taught excessive control and repression of sexual impulses. The many sexual technique manuals, the lack of sexual enjoyment, and the increasing interest in sex therapy attest to the problems in this area of the relationship and to the need for greater openness about sex.

There are many other transitions that must be made if a marriage is to be successful. Basically, all the transitions are from the self-centeredness of childhood to the other-centeredness of adulthood. To consider the likes and dislikes of one's partner, to compromise one's desires at times in favor of the other's, to become a team that pulls together rather than in opposing directions, to become a pair that has more going than the sum total of the two individuals making up the pair — these are a few of the things that indicate a successful marriage. If the majority of transitions cannot be made by one or both partners, the chances for a successful marriage are slim.

Bill and Marge — Married Singles

Both Bill and Marge were active singles until they met, fell in love, and married in their midtwenties. Bill's single life pattern had involved a great deal of time for sports, especially trips to the desert to ride his motorcycle with other dirt-bike enthusiasts.

Marge had spent a great deal of time with her office colleagues, going to picnics, bowling on the office team, and window shopping on Saturdays. Sunday was reserved for church. Although she had dated a great deal, her religious background had restricted her sexual activities. She had spent much of her time on dates defending herself. Although she was no prude about her sexuality, she did not feel it necessary to sleep with every date.

As the newness of marriage begins to wear off, both Bill and Marge find themselves somewhat bored and uncomfortable with the other's activities. Marge did go to the desert twice when Bill went motorcycling, but she found it dirty, boring, and lonely because she didn't know the other women and the men were away from camp riding all day.

Bill doesn't like bowling although he tried once or twice. He doesn't like being alone at night either, and so he pressures Marge to give up the bowling team. "After all, why am I married if I have to be alone in the evening?" he complains.

Marge also has difficulty relaxing and enjoying sex with Bill. For so long her impulses, when she was approached sexually, had been to back away and defend herself that she finds it difficult to change. Bill, feeling this tension, takes it as a rejection of himself rather than as a transition stage that Marge has to pass through.

He begins flirting with other women because it makes him feel good when they respond. He even entertains the idea of going out with other women behind Marge's back. "It's Marge's hang-up that our sex life isn't very good," Bill often says.

Gradually, each falls back into old single-life patterns and they spend less and less time together. Although they are still married, they do almost nothing together. Bill spends more time on motorcycle trips, and Marge has joined a second bowling team. Their friends wonder if they ever see one another.

The transition from single to married status does not end the need for change. As time passes, the marriage also will change and require further transitions of both partners. The coming of children, for example, places a whole new set of demands on the married couple.

In general the couple contemplating marriage seldom realize the extent of the changes necessary, both in themselves and in their partner, to make a successful marriage. After all, "love" should take care of all of the transitions from single to married life. "We get along now; of course we'll get along after we marry."

Marriage: A Myriad of Interactions

Each day we interact with numerous people. On the job we talk with colleagues, receive instructions from superiors, and give orders to those who work for us. At stores we talk with salespeople. On our way home we interact with the other drivers or with people on the bus. All of these interactions are relatively simple. For example, when buying something at a store, I simply want to make my purchase. I don't need to know how the salespeople are feeling, how their children are doing in school, how their sex life is, how they feel about their jobs. I need only relate to them as a customer. The interaction begins and ends at a superficial level.

Not so with marriage. The family, perhaps more than any other institution, is an arena of intimate and complex interaction. Not only are there literally hundreds of interactions within a family each day, but they vary in infinite ways. We can think of these interactions as ranging from purely intellectual, with no emotional involvement, to strongly emotional. Note in the following conversations how the interactions move from superficial and distant to ones showing care, commitment, and emotional involvement:

"Good morning. How are you feeling?"

" 'Morning. Fine. How're you?"

"Good morning. How are you feeling? Did you sleep well?"

" 'Morning. I slept fine. Hope you did, too."

"Good morning. I'm really glad to see you looking so well this morning! I'm glad the headache went away."

" 'Morning. It's great not to be in pain. Thanks so much for reminding me to take those aspirin — they really did the trick! Don't know what I'd do without you!"

"Good morning! You know, it's always wonderful to wake up in the morning with you!"

"It makes me feel so good when you say that! I'm so happy with you!"

The first interaction is superficial, a general morning greeting. The next, while still superficial, demonstrates more concern and awareness of the other person. The concern deepens in the next interaction — the first speaker remembers the other's headache of the previous day and is happy that the partner is out of pain. The partner expresses gratitude for the concern and for the aid. And the last interaction demonstrates a deep emotional level of sharing between the partners.

Let's also look at some of the role interactions that go on in a marriage:

What Do You Think?

What kind of marital role expectations do you think you have learned?

Are they similar to the roles your parents fulfilled in their marriage?

What do you think are the two most important roles your spouse should fulfill?

What would you do if your spouse disagreed with you and didn't wish to fulfill one of these two roles you consider important?

man	⟷	woman
lover	⟷	lover
friend	⟷	friend
provider	⟷	provided-for
provider	⟷	provider
spendthrift	⟷	budgeter
father*	⟷	child*
child*	⟷	mother*
child*	⟷	child*
taker	⟷	giver
giver	⟷	taker
teacher	⟷	learner
learner	⟷	teacher
learner	⟷	learner
employer	⟷	worker
worker	⟷	worker
colleague	⟷	colleague
leaning tower	⟷	tower of strength
tower of strength	⟷	leaning tower

*These are not interactions between real children and real parents, but interactions that involve one partner acting like an authority or parent and the other partner reacting as a dependent child. The child/child interaction involves the partners acting like children with each other.

What Factors Influence Marital Success?

Marital satisfaction depends on many factors. In addition each couple may value the factors differently, thus making it difficult to identify general principles. But if we are to understand the dynamics of prolonged, mutually fulfilling marriages, we must identify some of the generally important elements on which they depend.

Several basic factors show up clearly in the literature on marital satisfaction. (Good summaries of this literature can be found in Hicks and Platt, 1970, and Laws, 1971.) These include:

1. *Length of marriage*: Generally, satisfaction is rated higher at the beginning and in the later years of marriages, with a drop in satisfaction experienced in the middle years (see number 2; for a fuller discussion of this factor and the next, see Rollins and Cannon, 1974).

2. *Children*: Children tend to put a strain on marriages, and some of the drop in satisfaction experienced in the middle years of marriages is probably due to the effect of children. Childless couples on the average report greater marital satisfaction.

3. *Adequacy of performance of marital roles*: One study (Chadwick et al., 1976) indicates that "adequacy of role performance of both self and spouse and spouse's conformity to expectations [see also number 5, following] emerged as the strongest predictors of satisfaction." Mary Hicks and Marilyn Platt (1970) found that the husband's performance was crucial because in most cases he was the economic support of the family and his status determined theirs.

4. *Similarity of socioeconomic background*: Having similar religious and social class backgrounds and similar educational levels reduces conflict in a marriage and increases communication. The partners feel they can understand and are understood by each other.

5. *Shared expectations about appropriate marital behavior*: Again, shared expectations reduce conflict and give each partner a sense of security in knowing the other will behave appropriately. The reverse is also true: Marital satisfaction goes down when spouses do not conform to each other's expectations of appropriate behavior.

In that regard Judith L. Laws (1971) found that the wife's conformity to her husband's expectations was more crucial to the marriage's success than the reverse. She also found that wives were more tolerant of disappointment when their husband's behavior did not conform to their expectations than were husbands when their wives did not conform to expectations. James Hawkins and Kathryn Johnson (1969) add that a person who experiences a lack of conformity between his or her expectations and personal behavior will also experience a lowering of marital satisfaction.

Obviously, the list of possibilities is endless! And think of the complications that can arise when children enter the picture. Remember also that cross-interactions can occur, such as between lover and friend or lover and teacher. For example, the friend can interact with the woman, the lover, and so on down the list. Thus when I wake up in the morning and say to my wife "How do you feel?" it means far more than saying the same thing to a passing acquaintance. It could mean, "I am concerned about you" as a friend; "I'd like to have sex with you" as a lover; "Will you be able to work today?" as an employer; and so forth. And to further complicate matters, the spouses may not agree on what the meaning is. She may take his question to mean he'd like to make love before getting up, whereas he really meant to inquire how she was feeling because she had been sick the day before. Complicated, isn't it?

To manage successfully the hundreds of interactions that occur daily in marriage would be a miracle indeed. But to manage them better each day is a worthy and attainable goal. If people can be successful in marriage, the chances are they will also be successful in most other interpersonal relations because other relationships will almost certainly be simpler than the marriage relationship.

Marital Expectations

In a very real sense, humans create their own world. The wonderful complexity of the human brain allows us to plan, organize, and concern ourselves with what we think should be as well as what is; we predict our future and have expectations about ourselves, our world, our marriage, our spouse, and our children. In our earlier discussion of "love," we noted that love often acts like the proverbial "rose-colored glasses" in that we don't see the people we love as they really are, but rather as we wish (expect) them to be.

In essence the world is as we perceive it, and our perceptions are based in part on the input of our senses as well as what we personally do with that input: accept it, reject it, interpret it, change it, color it — essentially, put our own meaning on it. The study of how people experience their world is called **phenomenology**. It is important to realize that most people react to their perceptions of the world rather than to what the world may be in scientific reality. A simple example may clarify this point. Let's say we place a straight metal rod halfway into a pool of clear water. The rod will appear bent or broken because of the refraction of the light waves by the water. Yet because we have measured and examined the rod scientifically, we know it is straight. But how would people react if they knew nothing about light refraction and had never before seen a partially submerged object? To them the rod is bent, and they would act on that perception. On the other hand, most of us have learned that light waves will be refracted by the water and appear bent, so we will assume that the rod is straight even though our eyes tell us it looks bent. In other words, because of our training, we have learned that our perceptions do not always reflect the objective world — we have learned that appearances can be deceptive.

Phenomenology
The study of how people subjectively experience their environment

How does this relate to marriage? In our interactions with other people, we often forget that our perceptions may be deceived by appearances or that our spouse may have different perceptions or even a different "reality." Consider the following situation:

Jim asks his steady out for Friday night. She says she's sorry, but she has to go out of town to visit her grandparents (she is actually going to do this). Jim becomes jealous and angry and accuses her of having a date with someone else. No matter how she reassures him that she is indeed visiting her grandparents, he remains unconvinced. When she returns from her visit, he is even more angry and upset because of her refusal to tell him the truth as he believes it to be.

Jealousy can be a difficult emotion with which to cope. We can see that Jim's behavior is being dictated by his own subjective view of the world, not reality. Yet even though we know and his girl knows that his view is incorrect, the difficulty is just as real as if he were correct. Because he is angry, they may fight and not speak to each other for a week. If Jim finds out from others that she was indeed visiting her grandparents, he will be apologetic and sorry that he acted "that way." Remember, we act on our perceptions, and they are not necessarily the same as objective reality.

The Honeymoon Is Over: Too-High Expectations

One morning, after Jim and Sue have been married for about a year, Sue awakens and "realizes" that Jim is no longer the same man she married. She accuses him of changing for the worse: "You used to think of great things to do in the evenings, and you enjoyed going out all the time. Now you just seem to want to stay home." Jim insists, of course, that he has not changed; he *is* the same person he has always been, and that, indeed, he always said he looked forward to quiet evenings alone with her.

This interaction may be signaling that the "honeymoon" is over for Jim and Sue. This stage is very important in most marriages. It usually means that the unrealistic, overly high expectations about marriage and one's mate created by "love" are being reexamined. In a successful relationship it means that subjective perceptions are becoming more objective, more realistic. It means also that we are at last coming to know our mate as a real human being rather than as a projection of our own expectations.

Unfortunately, some people throw away the real person in favor of their own idealizations. In essence they are in love with their own dreams and ideals and not with the person they married. Originally their mate became the object of their love because the mate met enough of their expectations that they were able to project their total set of expectations onto the mate. But this state of affairs is possible only so long as they are able to overlook and deny the things in the mate that don't fit their idealized image of what a mate should be. Living together day in and day out makes it only a matter of time until each partner is forced to compare ideals with the flesh-and-blood spouse and seldom, if ever, will the two coincide exactly.

"Why can't you be what I
want?"

Romantic ideals lead us to expect so much from our mate and from marriage that disappointment is almost inevitable. How we cope with this disappointment determines, in part, the direction our marriage will take when the honeymoon is over. If we refuse to reexamine our ideals and expectations and instead blame our mate for the discrepancy, then trouble lies ahead. On the other hand, if we realize that the source of disappointment is within, caused by our own unrealistic expectations, we can then look forward to getting to know our mate as a real human being. Further reflection also makes it clear that recognition of our mate as a real human being complete with frailties and problems rather than as some kind of perfect, godlike creature greatly eases the strain on the marriage and on ourselves. No one can live up to perfection. Realizing the humanness of our partner allows us to relax, to be human as well. If my partner can make mistakes and be less than perfect, so can I, thank goodness. Of course, each person can work to become better. But who will ever be perfect?

But, consider what can happen if we are unwilling to give up our expectations of an ideal mate:

Carol, the Perpetual Seeker

Carol's father died when she was eight years old. Her mother never remarried because she felt no other man could live up to her dead husband. Through the years Carol was told how wonderful and perfect her father had been, both as a man and as a husband.

As a teenager Carol fell in love often and quickly, but the romances always ended soon, usually, she said, because the boy would disappoint her in some way. The only romance that lasted

was when she met a boy while on a summer vacation to Califorı
Even though they knew one another for only a month, they cuı-
tinued their romance via mail during the following year. They met
again the next summer. Carol was now nineteen. Three months
after they parted, after school had resumed, and after many letters
declaring their love and loneliness, Carol's friend asked her to
come to California and marry him. Carol assured her mother that
he was the right man: strong, responsible, and loving, just as her
father had been.

They married and everything seemed to go well. However, by
the end of the first year Carol was writing her mother letters telling
how the husband was changing for the worse, how he wasn't
nearly the man Carol had thought him to be. She was questioning
whether he would ever be a good father, and she noted that he
didn't have the drive for success that her dad had at his age.

Two years after marrying, Carol divorced her husband. She had
met an exciting, great man who had given a talk to her women's
sensitivity group. He was all of the things her husband wasn't
and, incidentally, all of the things her father had been. She married
him not long after her divorce was final.

Carol is now thirty years old and married to her third husband,
about whom she complains a great deal.

What Do You Think?

Why does Carol seem to find so little satisfaction with her husbands?

Why did Carol's romance persist so long with her first husband before marriage while all of her earlier relationships dissolved quickly?

What are the qualities of your dream spouse?

How does your relationship with your parents influence your marriage ideals?

How can Carol find satisfaction in marriage?

Love or Marriage?

That disappointment with marriage is almost inevitable makes sense if
we consider that our prevailing cultural view of marriage as expressed
in the mass media is one of overly high romantic expectation. We are
also led to expect that the powerful emotions of romantic love will
remain indefinitely throughout our marriage — "forever."

One of the greatest disappointments newly married couples face is
the fading of romantic love with time. Romantic love depends on an
incomplete sexual and emotional consummation of the relationship.
Physical longing is a tension between desire and fulfillment. In a marriage, where sexual desire is fulfilled, romantic love changes to a more
stable feeling of affection that, although less intense and frenzied than
romantic love, is more durable. However, because we have been flooded
with romantic literature and with movies about love and marriage, we
are often unprepared for this natural change in the emotional quality of
the relationship. For example, let's look at a not untypical couple:

Allison fell in love with Mike when she was sixteen and he was
seventeen. Neither of them had ever been in love before. After
two years they are still deeply in love and Mike persuades Allison
to marry him because he is tired of dealing with their guilt about
premarital sex, worrying about pregnancies, and hiding their intimacy from parents. After two years of marriage, Allison finds
herself not nearly as excited by Mike as she had been earlier. The

couple is struggling to make a living, and she feels that "the bloom is going from the rose." One day, as she listens to a lecture from her art history teacher, she feels a lump in her throat, a thumping in her heart, and a weakness in her knees. This was the way she felt about Mike two years ago, and she suddenly realizes that she doesn't have these feelings for Mike any more. She can't tell Mike, and she is afraid of her feelings for the teacher, so she drops the class and tells Mike it's time for them to have a baby.

It's clear that Allison believes feelings of sexual attraction are "love." Since American folklore says you can't love more than one person (at least at the same time), she must either hide from these feelings of tension and longing, as she does, or believe that she is no longer in love with Mike and perhaps consider a divorce. Narrowly defining love as only "the great turn on" means that all marriages will eventually fail, as that intense feeling fades with time.

Mixed Expectations

Even if expectations about marriage are realistic, spouses may have different expectations about marital roles. This is especially true about roles that each expects the other to play in marriage. Roles that historically have been fulfilled by one sex or the other today are no longer clear-cut. For example, the husband is no longer only the breadwinner and the wife only the homemaker. However, as we have learned, many of our expectations about role behavior have come from our experience with our parents' marriage. And often we are unaware of these expectations. For example, consider the possibilities for conflict in the following marriage:

What Do You Think?

Who do you think should control the money in marriage? Why?

What feelings will Susan have when she asks Randy for money to buy a new dress?

What do you think will happen if she quits her job as he wants?

Who controls the money in your family?

Did your parents have any areas of conflicting expectations? If so, what were they?

Randy and Susan: Who Handles the Money?

In Randy's traditional midwestern family his father played the dominant role. His mother was given an allowance with which to run the house. His father made all of the major money decisions.

In Susan's sophisticated New York family both her mother and her father worked hard at their individual careers. Because they both worked, they decided that each would control his or her own money. While both contributed to a joint checking account used to run the household, individual desires were fulfilled from personal funds. There was seldom any discussion about money decisions because each was free to spend his or her own money.

Randy and Susan marry after Susan has been teaching school for a year and Randy gets a good position with a New York bank. Randy believes that because he has a good job, it is no longer necessary for Susan to work; he can support them both, which he believes is the proper male marriage role. He sees no reason for Susan to have her own bank account. After all, if she wants something, all she has to do is ask him for it.

The increasing diversity of acceptable relationships found in modern America means that children in the future may be raised differently from the way we were. Their expectations of marital roles will also be different from ours. And their marriages may well involve a flexible interchange of roles.

80 Percent I Love You — 20 Percent I Hate You

Many people hold the expectation that their partner will meet all of their needs, indeed that it is the partner's duty to do this if he or she loves you. To the extent that partners fail to live up to this expectation, they are "bad" spouses. However, human beings are complex. It is probably impossible for any two people to completely fulfill one another's needs. If a pair could mutually satisfy even 80 percent of one another's needs, it would be a minor miracle.

The expectation of total need fulfillment within marriage ruins many marital relationships. Even if the minor miracle of your spouse's meeting 80 percent of your needs occurs, destructive interaction often will also occur. As time passes, the spouse with the unmet needs longs to have them satisfied and accuses the partner of failure and indifference: "What's wrong with you that you can't/won't meet my needs?" Conflict will grow because the accused spouse feels unfairly accused, defensive, and inferior. Life will revolve more and more around the negative 20 percent rather than the positive 80 percent. This is especially true if the partners are possessive and block each other from any outside need gratification. Unless such interaction is broken, it is possible for a spouse to suddenly fall out of love and leave the mate for someone else. These sudden departures are catastrophic to all the parties. And the ensuing relationship often fails because of the same dynamics. For example, the newly "in love" spouse has met a person who meets some of the unfulfilled needs and because these needs have become so exaggerated, the person concludes that at last he or she has met the "right" person. "Right" means someone who will meet *all* needs. In the excitement, the person often overlooks the fact that the new love does not fulfill other needs that have long been met by the discarded spouse. Because those needs have always been met, they are taken for granted. But careful inventory of the new love's need meeting potentials might disclose the fact that the new person is incapable of meeting a large portion of the 80 percent that the former spouse met. Hence in a few years the same conflicts will reappear, admittedly over different unmet needs, and the process of disenchantment will reoccur.

Let's take a closer look at this process. We'll call our spouses Carl and Jane. They are very much in love. Their friends are amazed at how compatible and well suited they are to one another. Each expects total fulfillment within the marriage. Jane enjoys staying up late and insists that Carl, who likes to go to bed early to be fresh for work, stay up with her as she hates to be alone. At first Carl obliges, but he gradually returns to his habitual bedtime. But, of course, he can't sleep well because he feels guilty leaving Jane alone, which, she reminds him, demonstrates his lack of love and uncaring attitude. She tries going to bed earlier but also can't sleep well because she isn't sleepy, and so she simply lies there resenting Carl. She begins to tell him how he has failed her, and he responds by listing all the good things he does in the marriage. Jane acknowledges these good things but dismisses them as the wrong things. He doesn't really do the important things that show real love, such as trying to stay up later. Naturally, sex and resentment are incompatible bed partners, and Jane and Carl's sex life slowly disintegrates. They begin to hate the other for not fulfilling their needs, for making them lose their identity in part, and because their sex life has become so unsatisfactory. Then Carl, working overtime one Saturday, spontaneously has intercourse with a co-worker and is soon "in love." Sex is good, reaffirming his manhood, and the woman loves to go to bed early. He divorces Jane and marries his new "right" woman. Unfortunately, they also divorce three years later because Carl can't stand her indifference to housekeeping and cooking. He reminds her periodically during their marriage that Jane had kept a neat house and prepared excellent meals.

Such dynamics are prevalent in "love" marriages. This is true because "love" blinds, reducing the chances of realistic appraisal and alternative seeking. To the person who believes in love as the only basis of marriage, the need to realistically seek alternatives is a signal that love has gone. But:

> The happy, workable, productive marriage does not require love or even the practice of the Golden Rule. To maintain continuously a union based on love is not feasible for most people. Nor is it possible to live in a permanent state of romance. Normal people should not be frustrated or disappointed if they are not in a constant state of love. If they experience the joy of love for ten percent of the time they are married, attempt to treat each other with as much courtesy as they do distinguished strangers, and attempt to make the marriage a workable affair — one where there are some practical advantages and satisfaction for each — the chances are the marriage will endure longer and with more strength than so-called love matches. (Lederer & Jackson, 1968, p. 59)

The Self-Fulfilling Prophecy

There is evidence suggesting that the expectations you hold about another person tend to influence that person in the direction of the expectations (for a more extensive discussion see Rosenthal and Jacobson, 1968). Thus, to hold *slightly* high expectations about another person is not totally unproductive as long as the expectations are close enough to reality that the other person can fulfill them. Remember, though, that to expect something different of a person implies that you don't approve of the person at the present time. Also, expectations that are clearly out of another's reach tell that person that he or she is doomed to failure because the expectations can't be met. Many times this happens to children. They often seem unable to meet their parents' expectations. Sometimes children feel so frustrated by this that they deliberately do the opposite of what their parents desire in an effort to free themselves from impossible expectations. "All right, if you are never satisfied with my schoolwork, no matter how hard I try, I'll stop trying." Such dynamics are often found in marriage. If your mate constantly expects something of you that you can't fulfill, you may begin to feel incompetent, unloved, and unwanted.

On the other hand, positive and realistic expectations about our spouse, or anyone else for that matter, may be fulfilled because the other person will then feel good about himself or herself and will often act on this positive feeling.

It is clear that the closer we can come in our expectations and perceptions to objective reality, the more efficient our behavior will generally be. If we expect impossible or difficult behavior from our mate, we doom both our mate and ourselves to perpetual failure and frustration. If, on the other hand, we accept ourselves and our mate as we are, then we have the makings for an open, communicative, and growing relationship.

The Self-Actualized Person in the Fully Functioning Family

How can we be realistic in our expectations of others and of marriage? Perhaps we can never be totally realistic, but if we can accept ourselves basically for what we are, can feel respect and genuine liking of ourselves, can admit error and failure and start again, can accept criticism, and can be self-supportive rather than self-destructive, then we will be on the right road. Of course, if these were easy steps, we would all be living happily ever after. Although much is known about helping people live more satisfying lives, a great deal remains to be learned. Individuals are complex and vary greatly; no single answer will suffice for everyone. Thus we need many paths by which people can travel to self-actualization. In this chapter and the next we will map some of these directions by examining common marital conflicts and possible solutions to these conflicts. Our first step will be to set up ideal yet realistic goals toward which we may move in our quest for maturity and **mental health**.

Mental health
A mode of being in which a person is free of mental problems and/or disease

Characteristics of Mental Health

The National Association for Mental Health has described mentally healthy people as generally (1) feeling comfortable about themselves, (2) feeling good about other people, and (3) being able to meet the demands of life. We will amplify each of these statements.

Feeling Comfortable about Oneself   Mature people are not bowled over by their own emotions — by fears, anger, love, jealousy, guilt, or worries. They take life's disappointments in their stride. They have a tolerant, easygoing attitude toward themselves as well as others, and they can laugh at themselves. They neither underestimate nor overestimate their abilities. They can accept their own shortcomings. They respect themselves and feel able to deal with most situations that come their way. They get satisfaction from simple everyday pleasures.

Notice that this description recognizes that people's lives have negative aspects — fear, anger, guilt, worries, and disappointments. Mentally healthy people can cope with such negative aspects. They can accept failures without becoming uptight or considering themselves failures because of temporary setbacks. Moreover, they can laugh at themselves, which is something maladjusted people can seldom do.

Feeling Good about Other People   Mature people are able to give love and consider the interests of others. They have personal relationships that are satisfying and lasting. They expect to like and trust others, and they take it for granted that others will like and trust them. They respect the many differences they find in people. They do not push people around, nor do they allow themselves to be pushed around. They can feel part of a group. They feel a sense of responsibility to their neighbors and country.

As you have probably noticed, this description includes a great deal of common sense. Certainly we would expect people who are considerate of other people's interests to have lasting relationships. Furthermore, as we noted before in our discussion of self-fulfilling expectations, if we approach people in an open, friendly, manner, expecting to like them, they will feel warmed by our friendliness and will likely feel friendly toward us. If, on the other hand, we approach people as if we expect them to cheat us, the chances are that they will be suspicious of us and keep their distance.

Another aspect of this description is that it recognizes that people are gregarious, or, as the song says, "People need people." Mature people recognize this need and are also aware of the responsibilities that people have toward one another.

Ability to Meet the Demands of Life   Mature people do something about problems as they arise. They accept responsibilities. They plan ahead and do not fear the future. They welcome new experiences and new ideas and can adjust to changed circumstances. They use their natural capacities. They set realistic goals for themselves. They are able to think for themselves and make their own decisions. They put their best effort into what they do and get satisfaction out of doing it.

Abraham Maslow and Actualization

Self-actualization
The process of developing one's cognitive, emotional, social, and physical potential

Abraham H. Maslow spent a lifetime studying people, especially those he called **self-actualized** people. These were people he believed had reached the highest levels of growth, people who seemed to be realizing their full potentials. They are people at the top of the mental health ladder. Let's take a look at some of the characteristics they share:

1. A more adequate perception of reality and a more comfortable relationship with reality than occur in average people. Self-actualized

people prefer to cope with even unpleasant reality rather than retreat to pleasant fantasies.

2. A high degree of acceptance of themselves, of others, and of the realities of human nature. Self-actualized people are not ashamed of being what they are, and they are not shocked or dismayed to find foibles and shortcomings in themselves or in others.

3. A high degree of spontaneity. Self-actualizing people are able to act freely without undue personal restrictions and unnecessary inhibitions.

4. A focus on problem centeredness. Self-actualizing people seem to focus on problems *outside* themselves. They are not overly self-conscious; they are not problems to themselves. Hence they devote their attention to a task, duty, or mission that seems peculiarly cut out for them.

5. A need for privacy. Self-actualizing people feel comfortable alone with their thoughts and feelings. Aloneness does not frighten them.

6. A high degree of autonomy. Self-actualizing people, as the name implies, for the most part are independent people capable of making their own decisions. They motivate themselves.

7. A continued freshness of appreciation. Self-actualized people show the capacity to appreciate life with the freshness and delight of a child. They can see the unique in many apparently commonplace experiences.

Sidney Jourard (1963) lists such traits as a democratic character structure; a strong ethical sense; an unhostile sense of humor; creativeness; a feeling of belonging to all humanity, including occasional mystical experiences about this sense of connection; and a resistance to **enculturation** (being overly influenced by one's culture).

Enculturation
The process of learning the mores, rules, ways, and manners of a given culture

Let's take a deeper look at this last trait. Self-actualized people, like other individuals, learn from and accept many of their culture's teachings. But they are aware of these cultural beliefs and can be critical of some of them. They are not simply a rubber stamp of the culture. The relationship between mentally healthy people and their culture is one of delicate balance. If there is too much emphasis on culture, then individuality is lost, as it has been in many totalitarian cultures. Yet overemphasis on the individual may lead to anarchy and the ultimate destruction of the culture. Also, extreme nonconformity to one's culture, which may appear to be individuality, is often uncritical control by the culture because the person, to nonconform, must act opposite to the culture — the culture is still controlling the behavior.

Jourard sums up the qualities of the fully healthy person:

Healthy personality is manifested by the individual who has been able to gratify his basic needs through acceptable behavior such that his own personality is no longer a problem to him. He can take himself more or less for granted and devote his energies and thoughts to socially meaningful interests and problems beyond security, or lovability, or status. (Jourard, 1963, p. 7)

Living in the Now

Marriages are constantly troubled because one or both spouses cannot live in the present. Aren't the following remarks familiar? "I'm upset because Christmas now reminds me of how terrible you were last Christmas." "This is a nice dinner but it doesn't compare with the one I want to fix next week."

All phases of time—past, present, and future—are essential for fully functioning people. To retain what has been learned in the past and use it to better cope with the present is an important attribute of maturity. To project into the future and thereby modify the present is another important and perhaps unique characteristic of people. Past and future are used by the healthy person to live a fuller, more creative life in the present.

Just as retention and projection of time can help us behave in a more efficient manner in the present, they can also hamper present behavior. In the preceding comments the present Christmas is being ruined because of the past Christmas. Probably the spouse is now being perfectly pleasant, yet the other is unhappy because he or she is dwelling on the past rather than enjoying the present. People who do not learn from the past are doomed to repeat mistakes, yet people must develop the capacity to learn from the past without becoming entrapped by it.

Much the same can be said of the future. To plan for the future is an important function. Yet people may also hamper their behavior by projecting consequences into the future that keep them from acting in the present. For example, look how a husband's performance fears can create a lonely night for himself and his wife:

> James knows his wife is in a loving mood, but he is tired and fears that if they make love he will fail to satisfy her. When she approaches him, he says he doesn't feel good and goes to the guest room to sleep.

James may have been correct, but, on the other hand, he may not have been. By avoiding the situation, he assured his wife's dissatisfaction.

As we saw, some persons live frustrated lives because their expectations of the future are unrealistic. Remember Carol and her three husbands? Carol projects idealized expectations onto her husbands. Rather than letting them be the persons they are, she expects them to act in a certain manner (like her father). She is so preoccupied with expecting her husband to behave as she thinks he should that she derives no satisfaction from his actual behavior.

People who can let go of past animosities and hurts and who can plan intelligently for the future without belittling the present find a great deal of happiness in the present.

The Goals of Intimacy

It seems clear from the foregoing discussions in this chapter and in Chapters 2 and 3 that to build a satisfying and successful intimate relationship is a difficult and complex task. Many factors will influence the success of such relationships. Certainly if we prepare ourselves to meet the problems so often found in intimate relationships of all kinds, if we know the skills of open communication and problem solving *before* they are needed, before hostilities and inability to communicate make problem solving more difficult, then we stand a better chance of maintaining and fulfilling intimate relationships.

What we are proposing is that marriage be treated as a complex vehicle to personal happiness and that, like any vehicle, preventive maintenance and regular care will minimize faulty operation.

Marriage counselors see many couples whose marriages are so damaged that little if anything can be done to help them. But most American couples begin their marriages "in love." They do not deliberately set out to destroy their love, their partner, or their marriage. Yet it is hard to believe that the couples in the marriage counselor's office or the divorce court ever felt love and affection toward each other. Too often they are bitter, resentful, and spiteful. Their wonderful "love" marriage has become a despised trap, a hated responsibility, an intolerable life situation.

Why? Marriages often become unhappy because we are not taught the arts of "getting along" intimately with others, solving problems and conflicts as they arise, nor are we taught the skills necessary to create a growing and meaningful existence in the face of the pressures and problems of a complex world. According to Paul Popenoe (1974, p. 3): "Far more could be done to handle marital difficulties more intelligently and successfully, and failure to teach how this can be done, both before and after marriage, is a notorious deficiency of contemporary treatment of the subject of marriage."

To get along intimately with another person, to create a fully functioning family, we need to be clear about the basic goals of intimacy. In their most general terms they are identical to some of the functions of the family that we discussed in Chapter 1. In particular they are (1) providing emotional gratification to family members, (2) helping members deal with crises and problems, and (3) helping members grow in the most fulfilling manner possible. The following examples show how a marriage can fulfill these functions.

Emotional Gratification

Pete loves to tinker with things, and he feels important if he can fix something in the house for Gail. Gail loves to knit and Pete loves sweaters, so she feels worthwhile and appreciated when she knits him a sweater. Pete enjoys sex with Gail because of the giving and receiving of affection between them. Gail knows she can sound off when she gets angry, because Pete understands and doesn't put her down. Both partners are having emotional needs met as well as meeting many of the needs of the other.

Dealing with Crises

When Pete has a crisis in the office, he tells Gail about it, and she listens, offers support, asks questions, and, very occasionally, offers advice. When he is through telling her about it, Pete often understands the situation better and feels more ready to either accept or change it.

Growing in a Fulfilling Manner

Gail wants to be less shy, and Pete encourages her to be more assertive with him and to role play assertiveness with others. Gradually, she finds she can overcome her shyness, in large part because Pete encourages and supports her.

Certainly it does not seem to be asking too much of a marriage to supply emotional gratification to the partners, to help them better deal with crises that arise, and to encourage each to grow in a personally fulfilling manner. Yet marriage often fails this assignment or, to put it more accurately, marriage partners often fail to create a marriage in which these positive elements thrive.

The Scenes from Marriage at the end of this chapter, "Warm Fuzzies and Cold Pricklies," will give you some insight into how to go about creating a fulfilling intimate relationship.

Summary

Marriage is the socially accepted relationship through which sexual drives are fulfilled. It is also much more than this — it is the generally accepted mode of life for most Americans. Legally, marriage is a three-way relationship that involves the man, the woman, and the state. The state sets certain eligibility requirements that must be met in order for a couple to marry. The state also prescribes certain obligations that each partner must fulfill in marriage. The marriage ceremony commits a couple to a new status, with certain privileges, obligations, and restrictions. In addition to state-mandated marital obligations, some couples are writing their own marriage contracts, stating goals, obligations, and responsibilities that they wish to be a part of their marriage. Such contracts, if properly written, are considered legal so long as the couple has not disregarded state-mandated duties and obligations.

Marriage is many things, but, more than anything else, it is the constant interaction between the family members and the many roles that each fulfills within the family relationship. How does one interact with another person at the intimate level of marriage? Basically, how we interact will be determined by our attitudes and expectations about marriage and our partner. We assimilate these attitudes and expectations of the larger culture from our parents. When our expectations and attitudes differ from our spouse's, there will usually be conflict in the marriage.

The basic goals of intimacy in a marriage are emotional gratification of each partner, helping each deal with crises, and helping each grow in a fulfilling manner. The ideal goal of family is to provide an environment in which each family member is encouraged and free to become the most actualized person that he or she is capable of becoming. Each family member will have to work toward maintaining his or her own balance and growth while at the same time contributing to the well-being of all others within the family unit. This is a large order and means that all will have to understand themselves and "keep their heads on straight" if they are to help and support the other family members.

Self-actualizing people essentially are people who feel comfortable about themselves and others. They are able to meet most of the demands of life in a realistic fashion. They tend to use their past experiences and ideas about their future in such a way as to enhance the present rather than to escape from it. They are not prisoners of their past but rather are free to use it to improve the present. Intimacy includes the commitment to help each other realize to the fullest possible degree all of the human potential inherent in each individual family member. Granted this is a difficult and at times impossible task, yet it is a worthy goal toward which to strive.

SCENES FROM MARRIAGE

Warm Fuzzies and Cold Pricklies

Once upon a time, a long time ago, there lived two very happy people called Tim and Maggie with two children called John and Lucy. To understand how happy they were, you have to understand how things were in those days. You see, in those happy days everyone was given at birth a small, soft, Fuzzy Bag. Any time people reached into this bag they were able to pull out a Warm Fuzzy. Warm Fuzzies were very much in demand because whenever people were given a Warm Fuzzy, it made them feel warm and fuzzy all over. People who didn't get Warm Fuzzies regularly were in danger of developing a sickness which caused them to shrivel up and die.

In those days it was very easy to get Warm Fuzzies. Any time that somebody felt like it, she might walk up to you and say, "I'd like to have a Warm Fuzzy." You would then reach into your bag and pull out a Fuzzy the size of a little girl's hand. As soon as the Fuzzy saw the light of day, it would smile and blossom into a large, shaggy, Warm Fuzzy. You then would lay it on the person's shoulder or head or lap and it would snuggle up and melt right against her skin and make her feel good all over. People were always asking each other for Warm Fuzzies, and since they were always given freely, getting enough of them was never a problem. There were always plenty to go around and, as a consequence, everyone was happy and felt warm and fuzzy most of the time.

One day a bad witch became angry because everyone was so happy and no one was buying her potions and salves. This witch was very clever and she devised a very wicked plan. One beautiful morning she crept up to Tim while Maggie was playing with their daughter and whispered in his ear, "See here, Tim, look at all the Fuzzies that Maggie is giving to Lucy. You know, if she keeps it up, eventually she is going to run out and then there won't be any left for you."

Tim was astonished. He turned to the witch and said, "Do you mean to tell me that there isn't a Warm Fuzzy in our bag every time we reach into it?"

And the witch said, "No, absolutely not, and once you run out, that's it. You don't have any more." With this she flew away on her broom, laughing and cackling hysterically.

Tim took this to heart and began to notice every time Maggie gave up a Warm Fuzzy to somebody else. Eventually he got very worried and upset because he liked Maggie's Warm Fuzzies very much and did not want to give them up. He certainly did not think it was right for Maggie to be spending all her Warm Fuzzies on the children and on other people. He began to complain every time he saw Maggie giving a Warm Fuzzy to somebody else, and because Maggie liked him very much, she stopped giving Warm Fuzzies to other people as often, and reserved them for him.

The children watched this and soon began to get the idea that it was wrong to give up Warm Fuzzies any time you were asked or felt like it. They, too, became very careful. They would watch their parents closely and whenever they felt that one of their parents was giving too many Fuzzies to others, they also began to object. They began to feel worried whenever they gave away too many Warm Fuzzies. Even though they found a Warm Fuzzy every time they reached into their bag, they reached in less and less and became more and more stingy. Soon people began to notice the lack of Warm Fuzzies, and they began to feel less and less fuzzy. They began to shrivel up and, occasionally, people would die from lack of Warm Fuzzies. More and more people went to the witch to buy her potions and salves even though they didn't seem to work.

Well, the situation was getting very serious indeed. The bad witch who had been watching all of this didn't really want the people to die, so she devised a plan. She gave everyone a bag that was very similar to the Fuzzy Bag except that this one was cold while the Fuzzy Bag was warm. Inside of the witch's bag were Cold Pricklies. These Cold Pricklies did not make people feel warm and fuzzy, they made them feel cold and prickly instead. But, they did prevent people from shriveling up. So from then on, every time somebody said, "I want a Warm Fuzzy," people who were worried about depleting their supply would say, "I can't give you a Warm Fuzzy, but would you like a Cold Prickly?" Sometimes, two people would walk up to each other, thinking they could get a Warm Fuzzy, but then they would change their minds and would wind up giving each other Cold Pricklies. So, the end result was that while very few people were dying, a lot of people were still unhappy and feeling very cold and prickly.

The situation got very complicated because, since the coming of the witch, there were less and less Warm Fuzzies around, so Warm Fuzzies, which used to be thought of as free as air, became extremely valuable. This caused people to do all sorts of things in order to obtain them. Before the witch had appeared, people used to gather in groups of three or four or five, never caring too much who was giving Warm Fuzzies to whom. After the coming of the witch, people began to pair off and to reserve all their Warm Fuzzies for each other exclusively. If ever one of the two persons forgot and gave a Warm Fuzzy to someone else, he or she would immediately feel guilty about it because he or she knew that the partner would probably resent the loss of a Warm Fuzzy. People who could not find a generous partner had to buy their Warm Fuzzies and had to work long hours to earn the money. Another thing which happened was that some people would take Cold Pricklies — which were limitless and freely available — coat them white and fluffy and pass them on as Warm Fuzzies. These counterfeit Warm Fuzzies were really Plastic Fuzzies, and they caused additional difficulties. For instance, two people would get together and freely exchange Plastic Fuzzies, which presumably should make them feel good, but they came away feeling bad instead. Since they thought they had been exchanging Warm Fuzzies, people grew very confused about this, never realizing that their cold prickly feelings were really the result of the Plastic Fuzzies.

So the situation was very, very dismal and it all started because of the witch who made people believe that some day, when least expected, they might reach into their Warm Fuzzy Bag and find no more.

But, not long ago, a young woman with big hips born under the sign of Aquarius came to this unhappy land. She had not heard about the bad witch and was not worried about running out of Warm Fuzzies. She gave them out freely, even when not asked. They called her the Hip Woman and disapproved of her because she was giving the children the idea that they should not worry about running out of Warm Fuzzies. The children liked her very much because they felt good around her and they, too, began to give out Warm Fuzzies whenever they felt like it. The grown-ups became concerned and decided to pass a law to protect the children from depleting their supplies of Warm Fuzzies. The law made it a criminal offense to give out Warm Fuzzies in a reckless manner. The children, however, seemed not to care, and in spite of the law they continued to give each other Warm Fuzzies whenever they felt like it and always when asked. Because there were many, many children, almost as many as grown-ups, it began to look as if maybe they would have their way.

As of now it is hard to say what will happen. Will the grown-up forces of law and order stop the recklessness of the children? Are the grown-ups going to join with the Hip Woman and the children in taking a chance that there will always be as many Warm Fuzzies as needed? Will they remember the days their children are trying to bring back, days when Warm Fuzzies were abundant because people gave them away freely?

Claude M. Steiner

CHAPTER 5

COMMUNICATION IN INTIMATE RELATIONSHIPS

CONTENTS

5

I know you believe you understand what you think I said, but I am not sure you realize that what you heard is not what I meant.

Building and maintaining a marriage that supplies emotional gratification to each partner and helps each to deal with crises and to grow in a fulfilling manner can only be achieved by the active processes of talking, listening, negotiating, and problem solving. We generally call this process *communication*, which is simply conversation with a purpose, a purpose that can be seen as seeking emotional gratification or, more specifically, as avoiding pain and seeking pleasure. Try it yourself. Can you think of any verbal statement that does not have as its ultimate purpose the avoidance of pain or the seeking of pleasure? The definition may seem like semantic manipulation, yet any conversation can be reduced to this fundamental purpose.

In marriage true communication is a mutual understanding, a *knowing* of one another, so that pleasure is maximized and pain minimized for both partners. A possible complication is that the achievement of pleasure for one may cause pain for the other, or that the avoidance of pain for one may add to the pain of another. Thus our definition of successful marital communication must be refined. Successful marital communication is a conversation that leads to pain reduction or pleasure enhancement for one partner, with regard to the impact on the other partner.

Successful communication is the cornerstone of any relationship. Such communication must be open, realistic, tactful, caring, and valued. Maintaining this kind of communication is not always easy unless all family members are committed to the belief that good communication is important to life satisfaction. This sounds simple, yet couples in marital trouble almost always list failure to communicate as one of their major problems.

Good communication is especially important and especially difficult in marriage because of the intensity of emotions in an intimate relationship. High emotional levels tend to interfere with rationality and logic, and thus with clear communication. If you have ever had trouble communicating when you are calm and collected, imagine the potential problems when you are excited and emotionally aroused. Yet, it is only through clear communication that each partner can know the needs of the other. When conflicts arise, the only chance to resolve them is if each partner is able to communicate fairly about the problem, define it clearly, and be open to alternative means of solution. Good communication also helps minimize hostilities. For example, unexpressed dissatisfactions tend to create hostility, but fairly expressed dissatisfaction allows the other partner to understand the problem and to act to reduce the partner's dissatisfactions and thus deflate the hostility.

Conflict management is essential to all intimate relationships. This is true because conflict is bound to occur in any long-lasting relationship. When one considers that two people marry after many years of growing up and learning multiple attitudes, it is surprising that the two can get along at all on an intimate day-to-day basis because what each individual has learned about handling interpersonal relationships will be to a large extent peculiar to that person. For example, one partner may learn that

This chapter was written in collaboration with C. Norman Jacobs, a licensed psychologist in private practice in Santa Barbara, California.

you do not talk about problems until everyone is calm and collected. Sometimes this has meant that a problem is not brought up for several days. The other partner has learned that you always speak your mind immediately. To wait, she or he has been taught, only makes things worse. You can see that these differing beliefs about when to communicate will cause difficulty.

Communication is also affected by the general society. For example, American men are taught to be less communicative, less self-disclosing about their feelings than American women. The traditional American masculine role is one of strength and silence. To be expressive, sensitive, and tender is considered feminine. But obviously the latter three traits are important in good communication even if the traditional masculine role denies them to males. Thus marital communication is certainly affected by general societal values about masculinity and femininity as well as by the individual communicative skills of the partners.

It is important to emphasize this influence of the general society and its institutions. Most people encountering problems in their marriage tend to believe that the problems are personal. That is, they believe that the problems are unique to their partner, their family, themselves, or the immediate circumstances. To place the source of problems within the couple and their marriage reinforces the myth that marriage to the "right" person will solve all problems and result in a happy family life (Feldberg & Kohen, 1976). Certainly many problems are unique to a given family, but it is equally true that many family problems arise because of pressures placed on the family by the general society. For example, stereotypical sex roles may lock a family into rigid patterns of behavior that cause problems for individual family members and therefore stress for the family.

Part of good communication is the ability of a couple to relate to one another in a manner relatively free from cultural or sociological influences, such as sex role stereotypes (Montgomery, 1981). Partners, in other words, should attribute meaning to each other's communications based on personal knowledge of one another, rather than on traditionally accepted interpretations.

> Jane calls her husband Jim "pigheaded," but instead of becoming angry at a traditionally accepted put-down, he laughs and hugs her. Calling him pigheaded is her special way of complimenting him for being properly assertive.

The example also makes it obvious that good communication depends on high levels of agreement between partners on the unique meanings of each other's communications. Jim needed to know his wife's positive meaning in her traditionally negative label, pigheaded, in order to react with a hug rather than with anger. This means that successful communication takes time to develop. It is a learning process between two people. It develops gradually over time. The ultimate goal of successful communication is the achievement of interpersonal understanding.

Such understanding between people in close relationships also implies a certain "richness" in their communication. By this is meant that they have many ways of communicating with one another, even many ways of conveying the same thing (Galvin & Brommel, 1982). Research indicates that marital happiness increases the number of communication styles of the couples, whereas less happily married spouses tend to have fewer communication styles (Honeycutt et al., 1982).

What Causes Communication Failure?

Failure to communicate is not usually an accident. The failure is usually intentional, though not overtly or consciously so. *People choose not to communicate.*

Often when a marriage is disintegrating, the partners say "We just can't communicate" or "We just don't talk to each other any more." They identify a deficiency of communication as the cause, when actually it is not a deficiency but a surplus of negative or aversive communication that causes the disintegration. Of course, a deficiency of talk may eventually replace the unproductive aversive talk, but the deficiency is not the cause of the problem.

Failure to communicate with others usually begins with a breakdown of internal communication. Anger, emotional maladjustment, stress and strain, and faulty perceptions can all lead to blind spots and overly strong defenses. If we become rigid and inflexible, we may be threatened by new experiences and change. Our self-image may become unrealistic, causing us to filter all communications to fit this faulty self-picture. When this happens, it is hard to have good communication.

Not all communication is verbal or positive.

Aversive Communication

Let's return to our basic principle of human behavior: People seek pleasure and avoid pain. And let's refine the principle a bit more: People first avoid pain and then seek pleasure, because in the hierarchy of human needs pain avoidance is basic for survival. This point is crucial in our understanding of communication failure because motivation to communicate will be most urgent when avoiding pain. Unfortunately, the quickest means of changing the spouse who is giving us pain is by threatening him or her. That is, by creating pain with an aversive communication, we get the spouse "off our back." In the long run, communicating via threats is counterproductive because our partner will most likely respond on the same level, creating a "vicious circle" and we both become losers. That is, we respond negatively to our partner's negative response, and the communications continue, each more hostile and aversive, until one of us retreats and stops communicating altogether. This kind of communication is a power struggle in which the winner is the one who generates the most aversion. The loser feels resentful and may engage in typical loser's behavior such as deceit, procrastination, deliberate inadequacy, sarcasm, sullenness, and so forth. Any verbal input by the loser is now likely to be an emotional discharge of the resulting resentment and hostility. Often the loser will begin to meet needs outside the marriage, at which point communication failure will become an intentional goal. The loser stops talking or becomes deliberately misleading because he or she knows that his or her behavior is unacceptable to the winner. Also, the loser stops talking because communication has become so painful.

An example of aversive communication is one that starts out to deal with one conflict but instead brings up a confusing kaleidoscope of other marginally related disagreements, one following on the heels of the other and connected only by the pain each partner causes the other:

"Where did you put my socks?"

"You mean the socks I have to crawl under the bed to find every time I do the laundry?"

"Yes, every time you do the laundry—the second Tuesday of every week."

"With the machine that's always broken, that nobody fixes."

"Because I'm so busy working to pay for tennis lessons and ladies' luncheons."

"And losses at Tuesday night poker bashes."

"I'm sick of this argument."

"Well, you started it."

"How?"

"Well, I can't remember, but you did."

It is important to remember that negative things can be communicated, but there are also positive ways to communicate them (see Table 5-1).

TABLE 5-1 Negative and Positive Responses in Communication

NEGATIVE		POSITIVE[1]	
1. Ordering, directing, commanding	"Stop ordering me around." "You can't buy that." "Don't talk to me like that."	1. Providing self-direction and choice	"You appear very disappointed." "Let's discuss whether that would be a good purchase." "When you talk like that, I feel frightened."
2. Warning, admonishing, threatening	"Listen to me or else." "If you won't, then I'll find someone who will."	2. Seeking causes for differences	"What did I say that turned you off?" "Help me to understand why you don't want to . . ."
3. Exhorting, moralizing, preaching	"You should tell your boss you want that raise."	3. Choosing one of several alternatives	"Which do you think would be best for you, . . . for us, . . . for all involved?"
4. Advising, giving solutions or suggestions	"Why don't you try . . ." "You ought to stay home more."	4. Exploring possibilities	"What could you try?" "Would it help you if . . ."
5. Lecturing, teaching, giving logical arguments	"It makes more sense to do it this way." "The Browns are happy and they don't have a new car."	5. Considering consequences	"Which way seems to get better results for you?" "Let's think about what would result from each decision."
6. Judging, criticizing, blaming	"You are wrong." "It's all your fault." "What a stupid idea!"	6. Sharing responsibility	"Those two statements seem to conflict." "Let's do what we can to solve it." "Let's see if that idea will work."
7. Praising, agreeing, evaluating[2]	"I think you are absolutely correct." "You do so many good things."	7. Expanding openness	"This seems like a difficult decision for you to make." "You sound discouraged. I'll listen."
8. Name calling, ridiculing, shaming, categorizing	"You're no good." "You're just like all the other men/women." "You're a liar."	8. Enhancing self-esteem and uniqueness	"I love you." "I appreciate your understanding." "Your interpretation is different from mine."
9. Interpreting, analyzing, diagnosing	"If you weren't so tired, you could see my point." "You don't care what I think."	9. Increasing sensitivity	"If you prefer, we can discuss this at another time." "Right now, I'm feeling so alone and left out."
10. Reassuring, sympathizing, consoling[2]	"Don't worry about it." "All men/women go through that at some time."	10. Expressing care and concern	"What worries you about that?" "This is an especially difficult time for you."
11. Probing, questioning, interrogating	"Where have you been?" "Now, tell me the real reason you feel that way."	11. Giving freedom and privacy	"I've missed you a lot." "You don't need to explain if you would rather not."
12. Withdrawing, distracting, humoring, diverting	"You're funny when you are mad." "Why don't you tell me something new!"	12. Accepting, giving attention to the other person	"I understand that you are feeling mad because . . ." "That point is something you haven't mentioned before."

Source: From Richard Hunt and Edward Rydman, *Creative Marriage* (Boston: Holbrook, 1976), pp. 50–51.
[1]Most of the positive responses are ways of saying to the partner, "Yes, I'm listening." More explicit listening invitations are "I see," "Tell me about it," "This seems important to you," and "Okay, let's work on it together." As you become aware of negative responses in your interaction with your partner, substitute more positive responses that show your care and concern for him or her.
[2]Praising and reassuring may be negative responses when the other person has a problem because such responses tend to prevent that person from sharing feelings that are more threatening or painful. Don't be too quick to reassure. Later, when the partner has sufficiently explored all of the feelings that are associated with the problem, expressing appreciation and confidence in the partner will be positive.

Can We Really Be Totally Open All the Time?

It is a popular notion now that the more open, the more honest the self-disclosure, the better the communication and thus the better the relationship. Yet research is mixed about this idea. Certainly there is a correlation between openness and satisfaction (Jorgensen & Gaudy, 1980), but it turns out that both too much and too little self-disclosure can reduce satisfaction with a relationship (Cozby, 1973; Galvin & Brommel, 1982).

A. L. Rutledge (1966) has noted that after marriage, restraints tend to be released, so that manners are forgotten, frankness overrides tact, and hostility results. If the hostility and frankness become too overwhelming, the couple tends to limit their self-expression and to withdraw from communication altogether.

B. R. Cutler and W. G. Dyer (1965) have found that nearly half of the "nonadjustive responses" for both husbands and wives come as a result of open sharing of feelings about violated expectations. Contrary to popular belief about the benefits of such sharing, this open communication did not lead to improved relations.

Shirley J. Gilbert, who has studied communication in families, says, "What is being suggested is that there exist pros and cons of openness and that previous research does not suggest the existence of an unequivocal relationship between self-disclosure and satisfaction in human relationships (1976).

The real question is *how* to disclose rather than whether to disclose. What is said (the content), how positive or negative it is, and the levels on which it is said (superficial to deeply meaningful, intellectual to emotional)—all have to be taken into account. For example, M. J. Bienvenu (1970) has found a number of elements that differentiate between good and poor communication for couples. These elements include the handling of anger and of differences, tone of voice, understanding, good listening habits, and self-disclosure. The elements that contribute to poor communication are nagging, conversational discourtesies, and uncommunicativeness.

Certainly both partners must share a willingness to communicate. But equally important is that they learn how to communicate successfully and that they remain aware of each other's weak and sensitive points. For example, people who are insecure, and feel inferior and worthless, tend to be self-deprecating. They also tend to be fearful of open communication and usually react with hostility to what they perceive to be unfair criticisms. On the other hand, people with a high level of self-esteem tend to be comfortable with open communication and are willing to disclose their own feelings and to accept their partner's feelings.

So, how one discloses thoughts and feelings, especially negative ones, strongly influences how the communication will be accepted. Those who believe it is important to keep everything out in the open, to express themselves always to the fullest, must also concern themselves with *how* this is done or they may find such openness backfiring and actually destroying communication rather than enhancing it.

Developing a Flow Chart of Communication

There is a sense of order in successful communication where communications flow smoothly back and forth between sender and receiver. Three general conditions must be met for successful communication to occur:

1. *Commitment*: The partners must be motivated to work on their relationship.
2. *Growth orientation*: The partners must accept the fact that their relationship is dynamic and changing rather than static.
3. *Noncoercive atmosphere*: The partners must feel free to be themselves, to be open, to be honest.

These conditions are difficult to attain; we shall look at each in more detail later. When these three conditions exist, good communication can be attempted. The first step is to "encode" the message and send it to the partner via some communication channel—for example, verbal or written. The partner (receiver) must "decode" that message and, to ensure that it has been correctly received, must feed back what has been decoded to the sender (source). The source either verifies the message or, through correction, negotiation, and problem solving, resends the message and the process is repeated. This circular pattern may have to be repeated several times before successful communication is achieved (see Figure 5-1).

In addition to the three basic conditions, communication requires that five skills be mastered (see Gordon, 1970, for a more thorough discussion of these skills, which we will discuss only briefly):

1. Identifying ownership of the problem.
2. Self-assertion by the owner of the problem.
3. Empathic listening by the other partner.
4. Negotiating.
5. Problem solving.

Commitment

Simply stated, commitment means active involvement in working to build and maintain the relationship as well as commitment to the partner as a person. Couples often seek marriage counselors when so much pain and suffering has occurred that the commitment of one or both marital partners has ceased. There is then little hope of resolution. Often one partner is still committed enough to want counseling, while the other, who has covertly given up hope and commitment, is resistant to counseling and fears being drawn back into a painful trap. Sometimes a noncommitted partner will seek therapy only in the hope that a dependent spouse will become strong enough to survive without the marriage. This situation leads to an added complexity if the dependent partner, sensing abandonment, avoids getting stronger in the hope that the noncommitted partner will stay in the marriage. Overt commitment of both partners is essential to building and maintaining a marriage.

Many uncommitted partners allow the other to plan activities, anticipate problems, make necessary adjustments, and so on. Sometimes this
kind of relationship works. More often than not, the partner with the
greater commitment feels resentment. Paradoxically, the one who cares

FIGURE 5-1 Communications
flow chart. The three conditions necessary to successful
communication are shown at
the top.

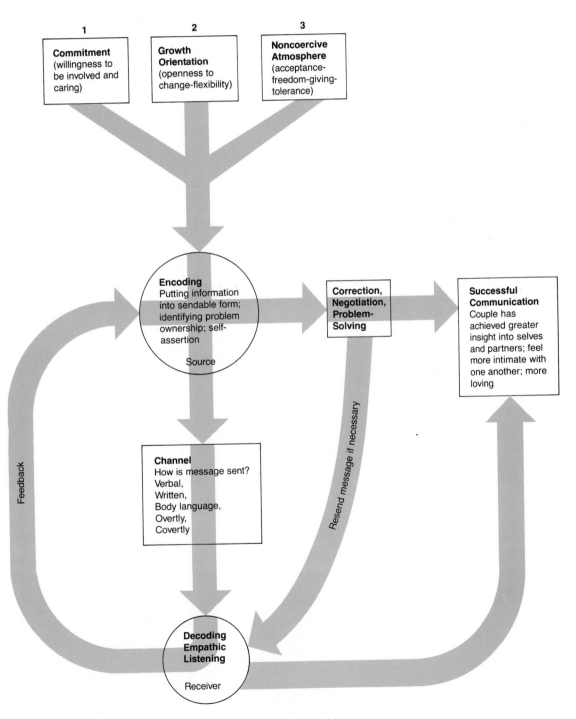

Communications flow chart. The three conditions necessary to successful communication are shown at the top.

the least controls the relationship. This is termed the principle of ''least interest.''

> Alice is more committed to their marriage than is Roger. For their summer vacation she wants to go to San Francisco, whereas he wants to go backpacking. Because he is not as committed to the relationship, it is easy for him to say, ''Go to San Francisco if you want, but I'm going backpacking and you can come along if you like.'' Alice can plead with Roger to consider her desire but, more likely, she will resign herself to going backpacking.

Although commitment is a precondition to effective communication, each partner's commitment to the relationship can be increased through use of the five communication skills, to be discussed later.

Growth Orientation

Individuals change over time. The needs of a forty-year-old person are somewhat different from the needs of a twenty-year-old. Marriage must also change if individual needs are to be continually met within the marriage framework. Yet change is often threatening. It upsets comfortable routine and is therefore often resisted. Such resistance will be futile inasmuch as time does not stand still. So it is far better to accept and plan for change. An individual oriented to growth is someone who incorporates the inevitability of change into his or her lifestyle. This implies not only accepting change but creating intentional and orderly change in a chosen direction.

> Going to a large social gathering was something Helen anticipated with pleasure but that her husband Art dreaded. However, they were both oriented to growth and Art wanted to be more comfortable in social situations. So they decided to work actively on helping Art change his dread to an enjoyment of social interaction. Helen, at Art's suggestion, began to invite one or two couples over to their house, because Art felt more comfortable at home. He soon began to enjoy these small get-togethers, which Helen then gradually expanded. Although Art is still not perfectly at ease away from home in large groups, he is much more comfortable than before and accompanies Helen most of the time.

Had Helen and Art not been growth-oriented, they might have grown apart or become resentful of one another. Helen might have chastised Art for his social inabilities and gone out without him, leaving him home to brood and resent her. On the other hand, Art might have been dictatorial and not allowed Helen to go to large social gatherings, with the likely outcome that she'd have felt entrapped and hostile. Yet, because neither was afraid of change and because each thought that change in Art would be beneficial, they set out deliberately to encourage this process. Notice that both were committed to the change. If only one partner desires change, particularly in the other partner, and the other disagrees, then conflict and diminished communication can result. Successful communication requires noncoercion and a positive regard for each other.

Noncoercive Atmosphere

The goals of marriage will usually be lost if either partner is subjugated in all ways by the other. Free and open communication cannot exist in a one-sided totalitarian relationship. When any two persons share a common goal, the issues of responsibility and authority arise. The situation in marriage is not unlike that in government. A marriage can be laissez-faire, where both partners have freedom of choice and action. It can be democratic, where responsibility is shared and authority is delegated by equitable agreement. A marriage can also be an autocracy, where authority is assigned to a single leader.

Most Americans state they desire to establish a democratic marriage. In reality this pattern is the most difficult to maintain, although it is ultimately the most satisfying.

When power is invested in an authority, a coercive relationship usually results. At least one partner feels a loss of freedom and often both feel this loss because there are ways the subjugated person can manipulate the authority as well as vice versa. Free and open communication usually cannot coexist with coercion.

> Mike and Daphne have been married six months. She pleads with him to give up his weekly poker game because she is afraid to be alone. He feels unfairly restricted and calls her a child. She in turn calls him an immature "jock" who can't give up the boys. One thing leads to another, and he walks out of the room and slams the door. She tearfully runs to the bedroom and locks herself in, leaving him to nurse his guilt. Although he apologizes profusely, she won't come out. So Mike stays home, having had his physical coercion overpowered by her emotional coercion. He is resentful and she is resentful and frightened. The intimacy that they experienced in their courtship is being dissolved by the acid of resentment created by coercive acts committed by both of them.

It is clear that successful communication will not survive long in such an environment. Sharing responsibilities, giving control voluntarily, and feeling relatively free in a relationship greatly facilitate communication.

Instead of the foregoing sequence, Mike and Daphne might have worked out a compromise that would have satisfied both of them. For example, Daphne, knowing how much Mike enjoys his weekly poker session, might have supported him in this desire, in the hope of leading him to respond to her fear of being alone. He could suggest that he reduce the number of times he plays poker. Or perhaps she could plan to visit her parents that evening or do something with a friend. If each saw the other as noncoercive and supportive, compromise solutions would then be far easier to work out.

Communication Skills

When all is going well with a couple, they usually don't think about communication. Yet this is the best time to build communication skills, as disruptive forces are minimal. Later, if and when problems arise, the skills will be there. It is apparently irreconcilable conflicts that destroy relationships. In most cases such conflicts become irreconcilable because the partners have failed to develop communication skills.

Identifying Problem Ownership

Clarifying responsibility or problem ownership is an important first step in communication. This is not always easy. A problem can belong to either partner or it can be jointly shared. The key question is, "Who feels tangibly affected?" That is, to own or share ownership of a problem, we must know and openly admit that we are personally disturbed by it. For example, let's look at the following situation:

> Jane thinks that her husband Ray is losing friends because he drinks heavily and becomes belligerent. But he isn't concerned about his behavior. He thinks people exaggerate his behavior, so he refuses ownership of the problem. Because he doesn't have a problem, no change on his part is necessary.

In addition to accepting ownership of a problem, one must be tangibly affected by it. In the preceding situation if Ray's behavior does not interfere with Jane's friendships, it does not affect her, and she does not own or share ownership of the problem. The fact that she might be concerned for him does not make it her problem. She can, of course, share her observations with him. However, if Jane is tangibly affected by his behavior, she does, at least, share the problem. For example, if their friends stop calling, then her needs are being tangibly interfered with. If she communicates this to Ray and he refuses to admit to it, then, as paradoxical as it may seem, Jane owns the problem. If, however, Ray acknowledges that his behavior is affecting Jane, then the problem is jointly owned.

Assuming ownership of a problem is extremely important, yet we often shun responsibility. Some people think that if they don't pay attention to problems, the problems will disappear. However, the reverse is generally true. In the long run unattended problems usually become worse. Denial effectively cuts off communication and prevents change.

Modern American society has, unfortunately, too often encouraged individuals to "cop out" of problems by supplying many scapegoats on which responsibility can be placed:

"My parents made me this way because they rejected me as a child."

"My father beat my mother when he drank, so I can't relate to men because of my deep hostility at his behavior."

"The establishment controls everything, so why bother to change?"

"American society is racist, I am black, and therefore all my problems are caused by society."

The list could go on and on, but these examples give an idea of what must be avoided if we are to solve personal problems. For instance, it may be true that you have problems because your parents rejected you, but they are still *your* problems. Rejecting parents are not going to suddenly become loving parents in order to solve your problems. Obviously, your parents have problems of their own, but you can't make them solve their problems; you can only work to solve your own. The first step toward solution is assuming responsibility for a problem if it is yours.

We must add an important caution to the discussion of problem ownership. Forcing problem ownership onto your partner can also be "blaming," which is highly destructive. Some people use this aspect of good communication in a negative manner; that is, to *show* the other person that he or she is wrong and that they blame the other person for causing the trouble because "it is *your* problem." We can make the same kind of comment about the next skill we will discuss, self-assertion. One partner can, in essence, attack the other under the guise of being self-assertive, thus perverting a positive communication skill into a disguise for harmful communication.

If the problem is mine, then I will use skill 2, *self-assertion*. If my partner owns the problem, then I will try to use skill 3, *empathic listening*. If we both own the problem, we will alternate these two communication skills.

Self-Assertion   Self-assertion is the process of recognizing and expressing one's feelings, opinions, and attitudes while at the same time being aware of the feelings and needs of others.

Some people are nonassertive. They fail to make their feelings and thoughts known to others. This makes communication almost impossible.

> Mary sees Jim as becoming less affectionate. He doesn't seem to hug her and touch her as much as he used to. Mary always liked the close physical contact and misses it. But it has always been hard for her to talk about her physical desires with anyone, much less a man, and so she says nothing. Her anxiety and discomfort grow. She believes that if Jim really loved her, he would recognize how miserable she feels and give her more physical contact. She becomes increasingly hostile to him until one day he asks, "What's the matter?" She replies, "You ought to know, it's your fault."

Jim is completely in the dark. Mary's nonassertive behavior has precluded successful communication and thus has foreclosed solving the problem.

Some of the personal reasons for nonassertive behavior are fear, feelings of inferiority, lack of confidence, shyness, and embarrassment. Besides personal reasons society and its traditional role expectations may influence nonassertive behavior. For example, in Mary's case she may have incorporated the traditional American feminine role of being passive and nonassertive, of expecting the male to solve her problems. Whatever the reasons, if we can't express our needs, we cannot expect others to magically recognize and fill them for us.

INSET 5-2

"Psyching-Out" the American Male

The traditional sex roles of a strong, silent male and a submissive, emotional female lead to stereotyped behavior and to communication difficulties. Carol Pierce and Janice Sanfaco (1977) have studied and outlined some of this traditional conditioning; they point to the following results:

Women are encouraged from childhood to feel it is better to have a man's approval than a woman's approval.

Women are set in competition with other women for male approval.

Women experience lines of power as going from women to men.

Women are taught to be reactive rather than proactive.

Women learn to live for and through others and to define themselves in terms of others.

Women are expected to be selfless helpers and not to have needs for a lot of space, both territorial and psychological.

On the other hand, men are taught: to be self-sufficient, intact, a closed system; they are not expected to acknowl-edge their dependence needs. . . . Eventually men begin to deny to themselves that they even have such needs. They lose touch with their feelings, become task-oriented, com-partmentalized, mechanical, totally rational and therefore totally dependent on women to fill their needs for nurtur-ing and caring of their own personal relationships and in-teraction with others (women playing the role of facilitator between father and child, adult son and father, man and friends). Men are now ripe for women's "psyching-out."

For women this necessitates the development of mental processes and styles charac-terized by continual fore-thought as to how to "use" another person. Hence, women learn to be schemers. Women often learn to gear their thoughts to what will make a man feel comfortable; the best way to make a man appear pleasing and smart to others; what problems a man needs to talk about; and how to make a man feel fascinat-ing and powerful.

The cost to women in this process is that they learn to deny their own wants and needs and, hence, do not gain a sense of self-esteem, integ-rity as an individual, and au-tonomy. They have little feeling of being powerful enough to shape their environment. Women frequently "psych-out" to get male approval, to com-pete with other women, to manipulate, because these are the modes familiar to them.

Whereas, in those interac-tions characterized by the sharing of straight, factual knowledge, giving orders or advice, and the initiating of sexual encounters, one sees the preponderant type of com-munication behavior of men in a male-dominated world. Many men are now experienc-ing a revolution to learn those behaviors and expressions necessary to grow emotion-ally and to relate in a more personal way.

"Psyching-out" then is a mode of behavior where a person constantly takes on the responsibility of figuring out what is most helpful and pleasing to another person, hoping the result will be that in return he/she will be liked, appreciated, and will receive attention. The problem is that because of role-stereotyping, the same kind of attention is seldom initiated or returned to women, and the giver is fre-quently neither noticed nor appreciated (Pierce & San-faco, 1977, pp. 97–98).

In contrast to nonassertive individuals, aggressive individuals completely bypass tact and recognition of others' needs in expressing their feelings. They demand attention, support, and whatever they want at the moment, often overriding the rights and feelings of others. In fact, they often seem unaware that other people have rights and feelings, and they can hurt other people without being aware of what they are doing. However, not all aggression is destructive. Used in a constructive manner, aggression offers emotional release, lets a partner know how intensely the other partner is feeling, and helps both partners learn how to cope with all kinds of aggressive and emotional behavior.

Self-assertive people, on the other hand, are free to express themselves and are aware of the feelings and needs of others. Self-assertive people's communications are also about themselves rather than critical of other persons. For example, contrast the statement, "This kind of behavior is hard for me to handle and makes me angry even though I don't want to be" with "You make me mad." The second statement is almost useless to successful communication. It judges and places blame on the other person. It will usually only provoke a defensive comment on the part of the person to whom it is said.

It may seem surprising that special help with self-assertion should be required in building a relationship. Many people believe that what is needed is less self-assertion. They see self-seeking assertions and selfishness as the basis of marital difficulty. Remember, though, that our definition of self-assertion includes awareness of the other's feelings and needs. We certainly need to be less destructively aggressive in our relations, but we must not confuse that with being nonassertive.

It is important to be aware that recognition and expression of needs do not necessarily lead to their fulfillment. For example, I may recognize and express my desire to smoke, which is self-assertive. If, however, other people in the room find cigarette smoke unpleasant and tell me so, they are also being assertive. This conflict can be resolved in several ways. I may go outside and smoke, thus satisfying my needs and not interfering with the needs of other people. Or I can recognize that smoking would be more unpleasant to them than pleasant to me and forgo smoking in their presence. In any case I have still been assertive—I have recognized and expressed my need, though I may not have fulfilled my desire. Self-assertion does not mean "getting one's way" all the time.

Note that the definition of self-assertion does include recognizing needs and inner feelings. This is not always easy, as the following example shows:

Alice has to conduct a PTA meeting tomorrow morning, and she is both anxious and resentful about it. She has put off planning the meeting until there is almost no time left. Harry comes home and says, "How about going to the movies tonight?" Alice blows up and says irritatedly, "I still have dinner to cook and dishes to do—as the old saying goes, 'Man works from sunup to sundown, but woman's work is never done.' " Harry responds, "If women have it so tough, why do men get all the ulcers and heart attacks?"

And so the argument rages on without chance of solution because Alice has not recognized the real source of her irritation; namely, her anxiety about the PTA meeting. But, why doesn't she?

Perhaps she doesn't want to admit to herself that she is afraid of conducting the meeting. She avoids thinking about the meeting and thereby avoids the fear that arises when she does. Or maybe she knows she is afraid but doesn't want Harry to see this weakness, so she covers it by starting an irrelevant argument.

Self-assertion requires self-knowledge. That is, successful communication depends in large part on knowing oneself. In any relationship there will be known and unknown dimensions. One way of diagramming and discovering these dimensions is called the Johari window. This is shown in Figure 5-2.

Let's see how to use the Johari window. As you begin a new relationship with another person, one where you both are committed to helping each other grow, you can both draw Johari windows. The easiest window to fill in is that of common knowledge. At the beginning of the relationship, common knowledge will probably only include such things as height, hair color, weight, food preferences. As the relationship continues, you will be able to fill in some of the other's blind spots, perhaps such things as insensitiveness, always wanting one's own way, nervous laughter, bad breath, snoring. Then, as you continue to develop trust in each other, you can begin to fill in your secrets, perhaps feelings of inferiority, fears of homosexuality, being afraid to be alone at night. By now you may be discovering aspects of each other's unknown self; these may be hidden potentials, talents, or weaknesses that are uncovered by the relationship itself, by the interaction between the two of you and your friends. As you get to know each other better, the blind spots and secret areas will become smaller as more information is moved into the common knowledge window.

Of course you don't have to have a new relationship to use the Johari window—it can illuminate behavior and knowledge in ongoing relationships. In fact, the process of exploring new dimensions of the self and the other person is exciting and never ending. Yet, unfortunately, many cou-

FIGURE 5-2   The Johari window.

Things about myself that I . . .

		do know	don't know
Things about myself that the other . . .	does know	**common knowledge**	**my blind spots** (such as an irritating mannerism I'm unaware of)
	does not know	**my secrets** (things I've never shared about myself)	**my unknown self** (things neither you nor I know about myself)

ples share little common knowledge because each has little self-knowledge. People who are afraid to learn about themselves will usually block communication that might lead to self-insight. Aversive reactions, as we saw earlier, are excellent ways to stifle communication. For example, consider the following interaction:

Jim thinks his wife Jane looks unusually good one evening and says, "I really feel proud when men look at you admiringly."
Jane replies angrily, "When you say that, I feel like a showpiece in the marketplace."
"Why don't you get off that feminist trip," he retorts.

Her aversive reply to his statement will probably make him more reluctant to express his feelings the next time. In essence her aversive response punished him for expressing his feelings. But why did she respond aversively? It's hard to know. She may simply have been in a bad mood. Or perhaps she has always felt negative about her appearance and thus needs to deny Jim's statement because it is inconsistent with her self-image. Her appearance might be a blind spot in her Johari window. Regardless of how objectively attractive Jane may be, if her view of herself is negative, that is what she will believe. In this case Jim has failed to listen empathically (see skill 3, following) to understand Jane's feelings. His own response in the interaction shows that he is also avoiding communication.

So we can define the communication skill of self-assertion as learning to assert oneself without making the other person defensive.

Empathic Listening Of all the skills we have been discussing, none is probably more underrated and overlooked than that of being a good listener. We are all very ready to give our opinions and often not really ready to listen to the other's opinion. To be a good listener is an art in itself and much appreciated by most people. To be a good listener may be one of the most therapeutic things we can do for our intimate relationships.

Real listening keeps the focus on the person who is talking. By focusing on the speaker, the listener actively tries to reduce any personal filters that distort the speaker's messages. Usually, though, we as listeners are actively adding to, subtracting from, and in other ways changing the speaker's message. For example, someone says, "I wrapped my car around a tree coming home from a party last night." I might be thinking, "Well, you probably were drinking (inference) and one should not drive when drinking (value judgment)." Although I have no evidence of drinking, I have immediately put my own meaning on the statement. If the speaker recognizes my negative implications, he or she might react with anger or cease talking to me.

Empathic listening, on the other hand, is nonjudgmental and accepting. To the degree that we are secure, we can listen to others without filtering

The ability to listen attentively
is an art to be developed.

their message. To really listen and to understand another means that we
allow our own self to be open to new self-knowledge and change. For the
insecure, however, this can be frightening.

> George is very unsure of Gloria's love for him and fears she may
> one day leave him. At dinner she comments, "I really like tall men
> with beards." George feels his clean-shaven chin and begins to feel
> insecure. He doesn't hear much of the ensuing conversation because
> he is busy trying to decide whether she would like him to grow a
> beard or if she has a crush on another man. He has completely
> filtered out the part about tall men because he is tall and therefore
> not threatened by that.

George has put his own inferences onto Gloria's comment and becomes
increasingly upset as he ponders, not what she actually said, but what he
thinks she meant by what she said.

It is interesting to note that it is easier to listen empathically to a
stranger than to someone close. Married persons often state that some
friend or acquaintance understands them better than their spouse. This
may well be true. Our emotions often get in the way of our hearing. For
example, when George's co-worker says she likes tall men with beards,
George doesn't even think about it, he simply says, "That's nice."

When we listen empathically, what happens to the speaker? The speaker
feels that the listener hears and cares. In essence the speaker feels non-
threatened, noncoerced, and free to speak—one of our preconditions for
successful communication.

Empathic listening has several components. Obviously the listener must feel capable of paying close attention to the speaker. If we are consumed by our own thoughts and problems, we cannot listen to another. But when we know that we cannot listen well, we should point that out (self-assertion) and perhaps arrange to have the discussion at another time. For instance, family members often bring up problems at the end of the day when everyone is tired and hungry or at other inopportune times and then become upset because no one is willing to listen. We all need time, a quiet environment, and a peaceful mind to be good empathic listeners.

We may also need practice to become good listeners. As children we receive plenty of training to enhance our verbal skills, but we seldom receive training for our listening skills. Just as our verbal skills can be improved through training, so too can our listening skills (Garland, 1981).

Part of our attention also needs to be directed to the nonverbal—body language—communications of the speaker. Emotions are reflected throughout the body. Although bodily communication generally is more idiosyncratic than verbal communication, it is often more descriptive of the person's feelings. For example, Mary habitually uses her hands in an erasing motion to wipe away unpleasant thoughts. Ralph pulls at his ear and rubs the back of his neck when being criticized. It takes time to learn what a person's nonverbal communication patterns are, but such patterns are perceived by the empathic listener.

Feedback is another key component of empathic listening. The listener must periodically check perceptions with the speaker. This is best done by rephrasing the speaker's words. This allows the speaker to have reassurance that she or he is being listened to and accurately heard, to have the opportunity to correct the listener's perceptions, and to hear her or his ideas from the listener's perspective. Some examples of feedback are:

Speaker: I'm not getting out of bed today.

Listener: Is there a problem?

Speaker: You're always working.

Listener: I know. Is it interrupting something we need to do?

Speaker: Why don't we get out of this town?

Listener: I don't understand why. I guess you don't like it here.

Speaker: Nobody does any work around here but me.

Listener: It sounds like you feel tired of all the work you have to do.

Note that empathic listening involves an effort on the listener's part to pick up feelings as well as content. If the listener is incorrect, the speaker can correct when the listener feeds back what she or he thinks was said.

Remember, though, that we are discussing enhancing good problem-solving communication. Much communication is for play and fun, to establish contact, or to impart information. To use problem-solving skills in inappropriate situations can *cause* problems. For example, if someone asks you to "Please pass the butter," it would *not* be appropriate to reply, "Oh, you feel like having some butter on your bread." About the best this

Exercises for Sending and Receiving Feeling Messages

People often intermix sending and receiving messages. For example, the speaker may be overconcerned with the effect the message might have on the listener and may thus modify and change the message so that it is not quite what was originally meant. In other words, the sender fails to send a true message because of fear about how it will be received. And, as we have seen, the listener may put a personal interpretation on the message, or may be thinking about how to reply, and thus not concentrate on getting the entire message.

When feelings are involved, as in conflicts between family members, messages are even more likely to get changed.

Practice in sending—self-assertion—and receiving—empathic listening—will help keep the two separate and enhance clear, good communication.

The following exercise should give you and your family and/or friends the opportunity to improve both your ability to assert yourself clearly and your ability to listen effectively. Begin by choosing a speaker and a listener. The speaker should send a brief, personally relevant communication in which she or he recognizes and owns some feeling. The listener then repeats, to the best of his or her ability, the speaker's statement. The others listen attentively and, after the listener has responded, share with the speaker any other feelings they think were involved in the communication but which the speaker did not express. When the message is clearly understood by both speaker and listener, they should change places. All members of the group should have a chance to practice as senders and receivers.

The exercise serves two purposes:

1. The speaker does not receive a critical reaction and therefore does not have to defend the statement. This frees the speaker to deal more honestly with feelings and also to hear the message she or he has communicated.
2. The listener gets practice in effective listening without having to react, interpret, or evaluate. This frees the listener from feeling he or she has to resolve or somehow deal responsibly with the feelings the speaker has expressed, so the listener can concentrate on what is actually being said.

In the practice situation the burden of reaction is lifted from the listener. Thereby he or she may concentrate on receiving the message accurately and clearly. The listener will feel a strong connection with the speaker. On page 165 are examples of poor sending and receiving as well as examples of clear communication where listening and speaking are well separated. (For a thorough discussion of training in communication skills, see Schauble and Hill, 1976.)

remark will do is invoke muttering from the requesting person about ''There you go using that dumb psychology again'' while he reaches for the butter. To know when and how to listen is an invaluable skill, but it too can be misused.

Negotiating   If the problem is jointly owned, then the situation calls for negotiation. In this case the partners alternate between self-assertion and empathic listening. Usually the most distressed partner starts with self-assertion. But because the problem is jointly owned, the listener's feelings

Fighting Fairly in Love and Marriage

Many couples state that their basic problem is that they fight all the time. Yet, rather than a problem, fighting is a normal part of any intimate relationship. The problem is not whether one fights, but how one fights. Fighting is simply a form of communication and all of our principles apply. George Bach is a therapist who gives fight training to help increase intimacy rather than destroy it (see Bach and Wyden, 1968). The following dialogue is an example of pointless fighting. It is followed by the same fight done in a constructive manner. Within the parentheses are Bach and Wyden's analysis of the interactions.

Ralph: I don't like the way the kids handle money.
Betsy: What's the matter with it? They're good kids.
Ralph: Yes, but they haven't learned the value of money.
Betsy: They're just kids. Why not let them have their fun? They'll learn soon enough.
Ralph: No, I think you're spoiling them.
Betsy: How in the world am I doing that?

Ralph: By giving them the idea that money grows on trees.
Betsy: Well, why don't *you* set a better example? You might start by spending less on your pipe collection.
Ralph: What's that got to do with it?
Betsy: Plenty. When the kids see you waste money on nonessentials, they feel they have the same rights.
Ralph: I shop for my pipes. They're very carefully selected.
Betsy: Maybe, but whenever I send you to the market, you always spend more than I would. You're always dragging in stuff we don't really need.
Ralph: OK, OK. I know you're a better shopper at the market, but that's your job, you know, not mine.
Betsy: Well, then, don't blame me for the kids.

After several training sessions, we asked the Snyders to refight the same fight before one of our training groups. Here is how it went the second time around:

Ralph (starting with a specific objective, not a general observation): I want you to stop slipping the kids extra money beyond the allowances I give them.
Betsy (showing Ralph why his idea may be difficult to accomplish): But you're not around. You don't know their needs.
Ralph (spelling out his objective further): I want to know their needs. I want them to come to

me with their money needs.
Betsy (justifying her past practices): Well, you know what goes on. I tell you everything. You know where the money goes.
Ralph (specifying the real issue that this fight is all about): That's fine, but it's not the point. I believe the children should learn more about responsibility—having to justify getting the money from me and spending it wisely.
Betsy (making sure he's serious): You really want to supervise all this piffle?
Ralph (reconfirming the stakes as he sees them): Don't you see the importance of teaching them early responsibility for money matters?
Betsy (specifying the reasons for her opposition): Frankly, no. They are good kids and they're having a good time. I like to give them a little extra now and then. I enjoy it when they have fun. They'll learn responsibility soon enough.
Ralph (sizing up the results of the fight thus far and rechecking his wife for more feedback): I can see we really differ on this issue. Do you understand my position?
Betsy (reconfirming her understanding of Ralph's real objective): Yes, you want us to teach the kids responsibility.
Ralph (seeking a meeting ground, at least in principle): Yes, don't you?
Betsy (agreeing to his principle but dissenting from his method): Yes, but your method would deprive me of some-

INSET 5-4, CONTINUED

thing I enjoy doing, and I don't believe I am overdoing it. You know I'm careful with my money.

Ralph (hardening his stand): Yes, you're a careful shopper and all that—I have no complaints about that—but I must ask you to stop slipping the kids extra money. That's the only way to control careless spending.

Betsy (realizing that she'll probably have to give some ground): I see you really are concerned with this specific issue.

Ralph (elaborating on the reasons for his firm stand): I love the children as much as you do and I don't want to see them develop into careless adults.

Betsy (offering a proposal for a compromise): I don't think they will, but since this seems to mean so much to you, let me suggest something. Why don't you tell me how much you think would be reasonable to

give them "extra" and for what occasions, and I'll stick to it.

Ralph (checking out that Betsy isn't likely to compromise further): You still want to keep giving them extra money?

Betsy (reconfirming her stand): Yes, I do. I enjoy it, as I told you.

Ralph (accepting Betsy's compromise, proposing details on how to make it work, and offering another compromise as a conciliatory gesture): Well, let's sit down and budget how much money they should get from us altogether, for everything every week, how much for extras, and so on. It's not so terribly important to me who gives them the money, as how much and what for.

Betsy (confirming Ralph's acceptance and offering a further implementing proposal showing that she too is now trying to accomplish his objective): OK. Let's

figure it out; then, every weekend, you can sit down with the kids and me and see that we didn't go over the limit.

Ralph (confirming that he understands and approves her latest idea): Yes, I could vary the regular pocket money, depending on how much you've slipped them.

Betsy (offering another suggestion to make sure their new plan will work and maybe show Ralph that she was right about the kids' sense of responsibility after all): Certainly, you can also ask them how much they've spent and what for. Then you would find out all about their needs and learn how responsible they can be.

Ralph (nails down the deal and specifies the date it goes into effect): OK. Let's try it this Saturday (Bach and Wyden, 1968, pp. 65–68).

are also involved, so it is imperative to switch roles relatively often to be sure that each person's communications are understood by the other. Set a time period, say, five to ten minutes, for each partner to speak and then listen. Remember that listening will take extra effort to avoid the temptation of thinking about your side of the problem while the other is speaking, which, of course, interferes with empathic listening.

When roles are exchanged, the partner who was listening should first restate the assertive partner's position (feedback) so that any necessary corrections can be made before going on to his or her own assertions. The very fact of knowing that the speaker's position must be restated to her or his satisfaction before your own position can be presented works wonders to improve listening ability.

This simple procedure of reversing roles and restating the other's position before presenting your own is also amazingly effective in defusing potential emotional outbursts. Much frustration usually builds up because partners do not listen to one another and therefore often feel misunderstood. But with this process even if your partner strongly disagrees with your position, at least you both have the satisfaction of knowing your

INSET 5-5

Additional Suggestions for Constructive Conflict

1. Be specific when you introduce a gripe.
2. Don't just complain, no matter how specifically; ask for a reasonable change that will relieve the gripe.
3. Confine yourself to one issue at a time. Otherwise, without professional guidance, you may skip back and forth, evading the hard ones.
4. Always consider compromise. Remember, your partner's view of reality may be just as real as yours, even though you may differ. There are not many totally objective realities.

5. Do not allow counterdemands to enter the picture until the original demands are clearly understood, and there has been a clear-cut response to them.
6. Never assume that you know what your partner is thinking until you have checked out the assumption in plain language; or assume or predict how he will react, what he will accept or reject. Crystal-ball gazing is not for pairing.
7. Never put labels on a partner. Call him neither a coward, nor a neurotic, nor a child. If you really believed that he was incompetent or suffered from some basic flaw, you probably would not be with him. Do not make sweeping, labeling judgments about his feelings, especially about whether or not they are real or important.
8. Sarcasm is dirty fighting.
9. Forget the past and stay with the here-and-now. What either of you did last year or month or that morning is not

as important as what you are doing and feeling now. And the changes you ask cannot possibly be retroactive. Hurts, grievances, and irritations should be brought up at the very earliest moment, or the partner has the right to suspect that they may have been saved carefully as weapons.
10. Meditate. Take time to consult your real thoughts and feelings before speaking. Your surface reactions may mask something deeper and more important. Don't be afraid to close your eyes and think.
11. Remember that there is never a single winner in an honest intimate fight. Both either win more intimacy, or lose it.

Source: George R. Bach and Ronald M. Deutsch, 1974, *Pairing*. Copyright, David McKay, Inc. Reprinted by permission of the publisher.

position will be heard and understood by the other. This is a large step toward better communication and certainly helps avoid "the dialogue of the deaf" which all too often occurs in marriage.

Problem Solving Now that ownership of the problem has been established, clarification of the problem started, and some of the emotion surrounding the problem discharged, we are ready to solve the problem. Of course, by now the problem will have been greatly diminished, or the partners may even discover, once they have truly expressed themselves and listened to the other, that the problem has disappeared. However, if the couple still think they have a problem, they can now apply the scientific method to solving it. There are seven steps to scientific problem solving:

1. Recognizing and defining the problem.
2. Setting up conditions supportive to problem solving.
3. Brainstorming for possible alternatives (establishing hypotheses).
4. Selecting the best solution.
5. Implementing the solution.
6. Evaluating the solution.
7. Modifying the solution if necessary.

The first two steps have already been accomplished if the couple has used the skills discussed. Step 3, brainstorming, helps to broaden the range of possible solutions. Brainstorming is producing as many ideas as possible in a given time period. That is, if you select a half hour to brainstorm the problem, you both call out any ideas you have as fast as possible—without pausing to evaluate. That is, all ideas are put out regardless of whether they are ridiculous or possible. All too often negative judgments stifle creative thinking, so it is important to suspend any evaluating until both of you have run out of ideas or reached the end of the time period. You can jot down ideas as they occur so you won't forget any—but just jot them down, don't think about them.

Once you have run out of ideas, or time, you can begin to select the best solution. Be sure to read both lists of ideas so that all will be considered. Then use the skills of self-assertion and of empathic listening to evaluate the likely ideas. It is a good idea to decide on an amount of time to spend defending and judging each idea.

Once you agree on the best idea, you must act on, or implement, it. If the problem has been a serious one, it is a good idea to schedule periods when you can both discuss how the solution is working. If the solution has solved the problem, then you will not need to use step 7. If, however, you are still experiencing difficulties, you may have to modify the solution in light of your evaluation sessions. Or you may have to go back to the possible alternatives generated during the brainstorming session and re-select another solution to test.

Communication and Family Conflict

Every intimate relationship will have periods of conflict. Research suggests that conflicts are equally present in happy and unhappy marriages (Vines, 1979). The difference is that in successful marriages the partners have learned how to handle their conflicts and use them to improve their relationship. Murray A. Straus (1979) suggests that if conflict is suppressed, it can result in stagnation and failure to adapt to changed circumstances, and/or it can erode the couple's relationship because of an accumulation of hostility.

Conflict occurs when two or more family members believe that what they desire is incompatible with what other (one or more) family members want (Galvin & Brommel, 1982). Realistic conflicts result from frustration of specific needs, whereas nonrealistic conflicts are characterized by the

"Now let's get the rules straight."

need for tension release of at least one of the partners. By exploring the process of conflict and how it can be used constructively, one can better manage it. Successful management of conflict solves problems and helps a relationship evolve into an ever better one. Recognition of and successful coping with nonrealistic conflict helps reduce tensions and change nonrealistic conflict into realistic conflict, which is usually easier to cope with.

Conflict becomes damaging to a relationship when it is covert or hidden. If one can't confront and work with real conflict, it is nearly impossible to resolve the problem. Generally, hidden conflict relies on one of the following communication strategies: denial, disqualification, displacement, disengagement, and pseudomutuality (Galvin & Brommel, 1982).

Using denial, one partner simply says, "No, I'm not upset. There is no problem," when in fact he or she is upset and there is a problem. Often, however, the person's body language contradicts the words.

Disqualification occurs when a person expresses anger and then discounts it. "I'm sorry I was angry, but I am not feeling well today." Of course, this could be true. It only becomes disqualification when the person intends to cover the emotion and deny that there is a real conflict.

Displacement occurs when emotional reactions are placed elsewhere than on the real conflict source. John is really angry at his wife, but he yells at the children. Thus the source of the conflict is kept hidden.

Disengaged family members simply avoid conflict by avoiding one another. This keeps the conflict from surfacing. Unfortunately, the conflict remains below the surface and creates anger that can't be vented, which adds increased tension to the relationship.

Pseudomutuality represents the other side of the disengagement coin. It characterizes family members who appear to be perfect and to be delighted with each other. In this style of anger a hint of discord is never allowed to spoil the image of perfection. Often only when one member of the "perfect" group develops ulcers, a nervous disorder, or acts in a bizarre manner does the crack in the armor begin to show. Anger in this situation also remains below the surface to the point that the family members lose all ability to deal with it directly. Pretense remains the only possibility (Galvin & Brommel, 1982).

We also need to note the relationship of sexual behavior to these covert strategies. For many couples sex becomes a weapon in guerrilla warfare. Demands for, or avoidance of, sexual activity may be the most effective way of expressing covert hostility.

Overt conflict can also be destructive to a relationship even though the chances of dealing with it are greater than with covert conflict. This chapter doesn't allow space enough to discuss the many destructive overt patterns of conflict. Nevertheless, attacking one's partner, either verbally or physically, is almost always counterproductive.

There is an old saying, "Sticks and stones may break my bones, but words can never hurt me." Unfortunately, verbal abuse often does hurt. Emotional hate terms—"You idiot," "Liar," "I hate you"—and other attacks on a person's self-respect and integrity do real damage if continued over a long period of time. Most people can forgive an occasional verbal attack during an outburst of anger, but if the attacks come often or become the norm for handling conflict, then the partner and the relationship can become damaged.

> Whenever Jane becomes frustrated with her husband, she heaps verbal abuse on him: He has no drive; he is too dumb to get ahead in his job; he is a lousy lover; and so forth. The name calling greatly affects his self-esteem, and he slowly loses self-confidence. He begins to doubt himself, which in turn causes him to act in ways that are self-defeating. What began as name calling and negative labeling has become his reality over time.

Physical violence seldom solves a conflict. Rather, it tends to lead to more violence (Steinmetz & Straus, 1974). Generally, physical violence occurs in families lacking communication skills. One member is increasingly frustrated in his or her relationship and can't communicate with the partner or the children about the conflict. Finally, the frustration becomes so great that one loses control and strikes out physically. And anything that lowers one's inhibitions and/or frustration tolerance—such as alcohol—will also act to increase the possibility of physical violence.

A good review of the communication principles discussed in this chapter is provided by Kathleen Galvin and Bernard Brommel (1982). They characterize successful conflict management as follows:

1. Communication exchange is sequential in which each participant has equal time to express his/her view.
2. Feelings are brought out, not suppressed.
3. People listen to one another with empathy and without constant interruption.
4. The conflict remains focused on the issue and doesn't get sidetracked into other previously unresolved conflict.

INSET 5-6

Topics of Conflict over Time

Percentage of Couples Where One or Both Partners Indicated Any Disagreement in Fourteen Specified Areas

DISAGREEMENT AREAS	PREMARRIAGE (N63) %	Rank	SIX MONTHS (N63) %	Rank	ONE YEAR (N63) %	Rank	FIVE YEARS (N56) %	Rank
1. Husband's job	74	1	75	4	68	6	76	4
2. Wife's job	56	8	63	6	62	10	53	10
3. Household tasks	66	3	87	1	91	1	88	1
4. Handling money	62	6	79	2	76	3	72	6
5. Husband's relatives	49	11	52	10	67	7	72	6
6. Wife's relatives	64	5	56	9	71	4	72	6
7. Husband's friends	61	7	63	6	51	12	52	11
8. Wife's friends	54	10	50	12	46	13	42	12
9. Affection	56	8	65	5	67	7	76	4
10. Children	44	12	48	13	54	11	42	12
11. Religion	25	14	21	14	19	14	28	14
12. Social activities	66	3	51	11	71	4	65	9
13. Time and attention	74	1	76	3	86	2	88	1
14. Sex	41	13	62	8	64	9	78	3

Edward Bader and colleagues (1981) gathered data about topics of conflict over a period of five years. They first interviewed sample couples just before marriage. They then reinterviewed them after six months of marriage, after one year, and again after five years. The table shows the ranking of conflict topics for the couples at each interview time.

Before marriage the man's job and time and attention were the two topics (tied for first) that aroused the most conflict. Six months after marriage, household tasks had become number one, with handling of money second, while time and attention had fallen to third place. At the end of one year of marriage, household tasks were still the number one topic of conflict. Time and attention was second, and handling money was third. At the end of five years, household tasks and time and attention were tied for first, while sex had moved all the way from thirteenth to third. The table makes it clear that the basic job of living together (how we divide the household tasks, how and how much time and attention we give one another, how we handle our money, and so forth) creates the most conflict for couples.

5. Family members respect differences in opinions, values, and wishes of one another.
6. Members believe that solutions are possible and that growth and development will take place.
7. Some semblance of rules has evolved from prior conflicts.
8. Little power or control is exercised by one or more family members over the actions of others.

Summary

Nowhere are communication skills more important than in the marriage relationship. Couples having marital trouble almost always report communication failure as a major problem. Basically, communication failures occur because one or perhaps both partners choose not to communicate or lack the skills of communication.

Although communication problems are often the result of personal problems and inadequacies of the partners, the general society can also facilitate or hinder good communication. Society's support of stereotypical sex roles, especially that of the strong, silent male, restricts good communication.

When most people talk about failure in communication, what they mean is that communication has become too aversive, that it causes too much discomfort. In other words, there is too much negative and hurtful communication rather than no communication. If the aversive communication continues too long, the couple may indeed stop communicating.

Three basic conditions must be met before good communication can be assured. First, there must be a commitment to communicate. Both parties must want to communicate with one another. Second, the partners must be oriented to growth and to improving the relationship. Each must be willing to accept the possibility of change. Third, neither partner must try to coerce the other with communications. Communication should not be so aversive and attacking as to cause a partner to be defensive or to withdraw.

When these basic conditions are met, problem-solving skills can be called into play. Basically, five skills are involved in successful communication. The ownership of the problem must be identified; each partner must be willing to speak up and state his or her position and feelings (self-assertion); each must be a good listener (empathic listening); each must be willing to negotiate; and each must be willing to use problem-solving methods if needed.

Fighting fairly and using problem-solving skills will enhance any relationship and keep it alive and growing. Failure to communicate clearly and fight fairly will usually cause disruption and the ultimate failure of intimate relationships.

SCENES FROM MARRIAGE

Communication Failure and Family Violence

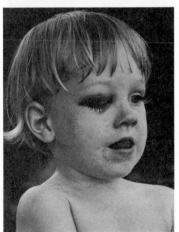

We include a Scene from Marriage on family violence in this chapter because physical violence is most apt to erupt in the family lacking communication skills. Such families often can't talk to one another, don't listen to one another, and simply lack enough communication skills to make themselves understood. Children are often physically violent because they haven't learned how to communicate. In a way adults who cannot communicate remain like children and too often express themselves physically rather than verbally.

In earlier chapters the importance of the family as a source of love, caring, and emotional support has been emphasized. Yet it is also true that the possibility of violence and abuse of family members exists within the poorly functioning family. Family violence is difficult to measure and document because most of it occurs in the privacy of the home, away from public view. In the past few years efforts have been made to increase public awareness of family violence: there have been many newspaper and magazine articles as well as television presentations on the battered wife and the abused child. Such publicity has served to bring family violence more into the open.

Violence between Spouses

The most life-threatening situation that a police officer can enter is a family dispute. Emotions run high and the family members usually see their problems as a private matter and the police officer as an unwanted intruder. Homicide rates are high within families, with about equal numbers of wives killing husbands as husbands killing wives. Physical damage done by one spouse to another usually involves the husband hurting his wife, although the reverse happens too.

In general physical violence flares between spouses who do not have good communication skills. Because of this, frustration and hostility build and finally something triggers an emotional outburst resulting in violent behavior.

Some researchers such as Bach and Wyden (1968) maintain that verbal arguing and fighting are integral to all intimate relationships. They encourage couples to learn how to fight fairly and effectively. Many researchers believe that verbal fighting and aggression will reduce the incidence of physical violence. The idea is that the verbal expression of hostility is cathartic and that "letting it out" will reduce its intensity. In his study of 385 families, however, Murray Straus (1974) found that the greater the amount of verbal aggression, the greater the amount of physical aggression. Physical aggression was less common when people tried to discuss their problems calmly. The use of force for resolving family conflict also acts as a training ground for abuse (Steinmetz, 1977a).

Child Abuse

Mistreatment of children by parents hardly seems compatible with mom, apple pie, and Sunday family outings. Yet there are many parents who physically and emotionally abuse their children. Although statistics are difficult to obtain, it is estimated that at least 1 out of every 500 children dies each year from mistreatment and that another 1 million children are victims of physical abuse or neglect (American Psychological Association, 1976).

In 1973–74, the California Central Registry of Child Abuse reported 17,000 documented cases in this state alone. The problem is so troublesome to California authorities that, as of January 1, 1975, the penal code was amended to increase penalties for child abuse and, perhaps more important, to make it legally mandatory that suspected abuse be reported within thirty-six hours of discovery.

Child Abuse and the Law

The following are paraphrased excerpts from Section I, Section 1161.5, of the California Penal Code, effective January 1, 1975:

Any person who willfully causes or permits a child to suffer, or inflicts thereon unjustifiable physical pain or mental suffering, or willfully permits a child to be placed in a situation dangerous to its person or health, is punishable by imprisonment in the county jail for a period not exceeding one year, or in the state prison for not less than one year nor more than ten years.

Any person who under circumstances other than those likely to produce great bodily harm or death, who willfully causes or permits any child to unjustifiably suffer or permits the child to be injured, or places the child in a dangerous situation is guilty of a misdemeanor.

In any case in which a minor is brought to a physician, dentist [there follows a long list of persons, including teachers, social workers, and so forth], and they determine from observation of the minor that the minor has physical injury or injuries which appear to have been inflicted by other than accidental means by any person, that the minor has been sexually molested, or that any injury prohibited by the terms of Section

273a has been inflicted upon the minor, shall report such fact by telephone and in writing, within thirty-six hours to both the local police authority having jurisdiction and to the juvenile probation department; or, in the alternative, either to the county welfare department, or to the county health department. The report shall state, if known, the name of the minor, the minor's whereabouts, and the character and extent of the injuries or molestation.

Reports and other pertinent information received shall be made available to any licensed physician and surgeon, dentist, resident, intern, podiatrist, chiropractor, or religious practitioner with regard to the patient or client; any director of a county welfare department, school superintendent, supervisor of child welfare and attendance, certified pupil personnel employee, or school principal having a direct interest in the welfare of the minor, and to any probation department, juvenile probation department, or agency offering child protective services.

The most important thing about this law is that it becomes mandatory for those in contact with children to report cases of suspected abuse. This provision helps greatly in uncovering cases that otherwise might be easily hidden.

Three elements must usually be present in a family for child abuse to occur. First, the parent must be a person to whom physical punishment is acceptable. It is often found that the abusive parent was abused as a child. The abusive parent has also often been found to be self-righteous and moralistic and to have unrealistic expectations for the child. The parent often expects things of the child that are impossible for the child's level of development. Second, the child is usually difficult and trying. Third, there is usually a crisis event of some kind. The parent has lost a job or is having marital conflict, or some-

thing else that has reduced the parent's tolerance level is occurring (Helfer & Kempe, 1974; Starr, 1979).

Some cities have created telephone hot lines that a parent may use to receive immediate help if he or she feels unable to cope with the child or children. One program to help abusive parents was started in 1970 in Santa Barbara, California. Claire W. Miles became so concerned about child abuse that she installed an extra phone in her home and advertised in the personal column of the local newspaper asking anyone who knew of an abused child to call the number. Within the next month she received twenty-eight calls, many from parents who abused their children. From this simple beginning the Child Abuse Listening Mediation (CALM) program grew. In the first year CALM was involved in 213 cases. Since that time the program has grown to include educational presentations throughout the country and visits to parents by volunteers, as well as the immediate help offered by telephone.

Help for the Abusive Parent from CALM (Child Abuse Listening Mediation)

A good example of the effectiveness and dedication of CALM volunteers is demonstrated in the following case of a young mother:

The mother has a son three years old. About two years ago, she had a nervous breakdown and was confined for some time in the psychiatric ward of a hospital. Her baby was cared for by grandparents during her confinement. When she was able to take her baby back, she remarked how fat and healthy he was. The improvement in his physical condition seemed to accentuate her feelings of in-

adequacy as a mother, and gave her a feeling of even greater insecurity in her relationship with her son. Her child is hyperactive, and her energy is not often a match for his. She has been trying to toilet train him without much success. When she tries to feed him, he throws food all over and refuses to eat. Then later he cries and is cross because he is hungry. Generally she feels that he does nothing right and everything wrong. She is fearful that he is abnormal in some way.

She would like to take him to a nursery school one or two days a week, so she could just be alone and rest, but she can't afford the private nurseries, which are the only ones who will take a child under three or one in diapers. She said, "I don't know what to do—I can't stand it much longer. Can you help me?"

She was told about the volunteer program, and she agreed to have someone come over the next day. A volunteer was selected who lives near her, and who has seven children of her own, ranging in age from ten to one, including a set of twins three years old.

The volunteer found that the girl has no friends here, since she has recently come from the east. Her relatives are all back there. She is lonely and overanxious and tense from being a twenty-four-hour-a-day mother every day. On the initial visit, she didn't want the volunteer to leave, so the volunteer stayed as long as possible, then took the client and child home with her. For two or three weeks, the volunteer invited her over three mornings a week. She encouraged the girl to use her sewing machine to make kitchen curtains. The client gained assurance that there was nothing abnormal about her child, and through association with the volunteer's twins of the same age, the boy began to eat normally without throwing his food around. The mother observed many traits in the volunteer's children similar to those she had worried about in her son, and in a relatively short time has already expressed a relieved sense of relaxation in her relationship with her son. She is being more realistic in her expectations of him, and is gaining self-confidence in her feelings of being able to care for him more adequately.

Sibling Abuse

Probably the most physical abuse occurs between siblings. Young children have fewer ways to express themselves than do adults. They also have less self-control, and thus their frustrations are often expressed aggressively via physical means. Almost 5 percent of surveyed families reported a sibling's having used a knife or gun at some time. If this statistic is correct, it is estimated that 2.3 million children have been attacked by a sibling or at least threatened with such a weapon (Steinmetz, 1977b, 1978).

Parental Abuse by Children

Although abuse against parents sounds improbable, there are cases where children physically attack and even kill their parents. Such violence tends to occur most often with troubled teenagers. Although physical abuse of parents by their children is limited, verbal and psychological abuse is common. Children place heavy demands on their parents and seldom fail to react at least verbally when they are frustrated. Verbal abuse heaped on parents by teenage children seems to be the norm during that stage of development.

Factors Associated with Family Violence

1. *The cycle of violence*: One of the consistent conclusions of domestic violence research is that individuals who have experienced violent and abusive childhoods are likely to grow into violent adults (Geller, 1980; Geller & Straus, 1979; Straus, 1980; Straus, Geller & Steinmetz, 1980). In other words, violence begets violence.

2. *Socioeconomic status*: There is an inverse relation between parental income and parental violence: Those with incomes below the poverty line have the highest rates of violence (Straus, Geller & Steinmetz, 1980). Parental violence is also related to the father's occupation. The rate of severe violence is higher when the father is a blue-collar worker than when he is a white-collar worker. This conclusion, however, does not mean that domestic violence is confined to lower-class households.

3. *Stress*: A third consistent finding is that family violence rates are directly related to social stress in families. Unemployment, financial problems, pregnancy, being a single-parent family, and alcohol abuse all relate to violence in the family.

4. *Social isolation*: Social isolation increases the risk that severe violence will be directed at children or between spouses. Families who have religious affiliations, a large circle of intimate friends, or who participate in community and social activities report less familial violence.

CHAPTER 6

People Liberation: Changing Masculine and Feminine Roles

CONTENTS

In the musical *Kiss Me Kate*, Kate sings:

I Hate Men

I hate men.
I can't abide 'em even now and then.
Than ever marry one of them, I'd rest a virgin rather,
For husbands are a boring lot and only give you bother.
Of course, I'm awf'lly glad that Mother had to marry Father
But, I hate men.

Of all the types I've ever met within our democracy,
I hate the most, the athlete with his manner bold and brassy,
He may have hair upon his chest but, sister, so has Lassie,
Oh, I hate men!

Their worth upon this earth I dinna ken.
Avoid the trav'ling salesman though a tempting Tom he may be,
From China he will bring you jade and perfume from Araby
But don't forget 'tis he who'll have the fun and thee the baby,
Oh, I hate men.

If thou shouldst wed a bus'nessman, be wary, oh be wary.
He'll tell you he's detained in town on bus'ness necessary,
His bus'ness is the bus'ness which he gives his secretary,
Oh, I hate men!

Her negative feelings about men find their counterpart in *My Fair Lady* when the good Dr. Higgins laments:

I'm an Ordinary Man

I'm an ordinary man,
Who desires nothing more than just the ordinary chance
To live exactly as he likes and do precisely what he wants.

An average man am I,
Of no eccentric whim;
Who wants to live his life free of strife
Doing whatever he thinks is best for him.

Just an ordinary man.

But let a woman in your life
And your serenity is through!
She'll redecorate your home from the cellar to the dome;
Then go on to the enthralling fun of overhauling you.

Oh, let a woman in your life
And you are up against a wall!
Make a plan and you will find she has something else in mind;
And so rather than do either you do something else that neither likes at all.

Later, Dr. Higgins asks:

Why can't a woman be more like a man?

Women are irrational, that's all there is to that!
Their heads are full of cotton, hay and rags!
They're nothing but exasperating, irritating, vacillating, calculating, agitat-
ing, maddening and infuriating hags!

The lyrics in these songs clearly depict some of the stereotypical attitudes held by our society about the characteristics of men and women. Yet
such stereotypes are generally incorrect and, if believed, certainly limit
the interaction between the sexes.

Many theorists are now pointing out the oppressiveness of rigid sex
stereotypes. They note that what we think of as "natural" gender behavior is often learned behavior. They see all people benefiting from a balance
of what we consider "feminine" and "masculine" behaviors. In the future
we may speak of "human" qualities instead of just "masculine" and
"feminine" ones.

Certainly individuals whose choices are not arbitrarily restrained and
who are happy and fulfilled by what they have chosen to do in life can
function better in marriage than people who feel oppressed and dissatisfied. If the partners can share the decisions and responsibilities of marriage in ways that feel right for them, their satisfaction will be greater
than if each is forced into stereotyped behaviors that may not fit. To do
away with role rigidity and stereotyping and to move in the direction of
"people liberation," so that everyone is free to choose a fulfilling lifestyle,
is a proper goal of a free society.

Actually we do not need new roles for the sexes but an acceptance of
the concept of role *equity*. This means that the roles one fulfills are built
on individual strengths and weaknesses in contrast to roles built on preor-
dained stereotypic differences between the sexes. Equity implies the "fair"
distribution of opportunities and constraints (restrictions) without regard
to gender. Equity does not necessarily mean "the same." For example,
perhaps one spouse has more interest in and/or better skills in arithmetic
and bookkeeping and so he or she manages the family finances. If such
an arrangement is freely chosen by the individuals concerned and is believed to be fair, then it is an equitable arrangement. Equity between the
sexes in family life embraces variation, not advocacy of some ideal model
type of family, be it traditional or liberated (free of any set roles). True
equity between the sexes implies true freedom to establish roles within
the relationship that accent the unique personalities of each partner and
that allow each to fulfill his or her own capabilities to the greatest possible
degree. "Constructive liberation" takes into account the fact that people
vary; a relationship that is good for one person may be restrictive for
another. To suggest that a perfectly egalitarian relationship, in which each
partner plays all roles, is the only right and proper one for all couples
offers little more freedom to the partners than did embracing a traditional
relationship as the only proper one. What person can play all roles in a

marital relationship equally well? Rhona and Robert Rapaport (1975) suggest that many who rigidly extol the virtues of a "liberated" relationship are really only suggesting that we move from one prison (traditional roles) to another (liberated roles).

The opening of alternatives makes some people feel threatened and insecure. If roles are tightly prescribed by society and few if any deviate from them, people feel safe and secure. American society encompasses a great deal of diversity, however. People may find that their neighbors have a different lifestyle. Children may point to imperfections in their parents' marital life and question whether people need to get married. Couples may find the mass media criticizing a relationship they may never have seriously questioned. They may read articles praising alternative living arrangements that they were taught were immoral. Confusion, insecurity, anxiety, and resentment often result from such pressures. Unfortunately, these reactions also cause people to cling even more firmly to the status quo. Indeed, the extreme attacks on the "traditional American marriage" mounted by radical feminists, gay liberationists, sexual freedom leagues, and others may have seriously undercut a thoughtful and constructive approach to change within the family structure and certainly contributed to the failure of the Equal Rights Amendment in 1982. The thrust of this chapter is recognition of the value of varying forms of marital roles, with the knowledge that most people will continue partially to choose the traditional roles for some time into the future.

Male = Masculine and Female = Feminine: Not Necessarily So

Simply stated, whether one is male or female is biologically determined. The behaviors—roles—that go along with being male or female, however, are largely learned from one's society. For example, a French male can cry in public over a sad event; an American male, to be considered masculine, will repress tears in public. Both men are male, but a social behavior (role) assigned to their sex differs. We call this assigned behavior in a given society masculine for the male and feminine for the female.

One's sex is determined by the different chromosomal and hormonal influences that lead to the anatomical differences between the sexes. One's **gender** includes not only one's sex but all of the attitudes and behaviors (masculine and feminine) that are expected of one's sex by a given society. Thus sexual identity includes both the physiologically prescribed sex and the socially prescribed gender behaviors.

Gender
Attitudes and behavior associated with each of the two sexes

Norm
Accepted social rules for behavior

Role
Particular type of behavior one is expected to exhibit when occupying a certain place in a group

Norms and Roles

Before we discuss gender development, it is important to understand the meanings of the terms *norm* and *role*. **Norms** are accepted and expected patterns of behavior and beliefs established either formally or informally by a group. Usually the group rewards those who adhere to the norms and places sanctions against those who do not. **Roles** involve people doing

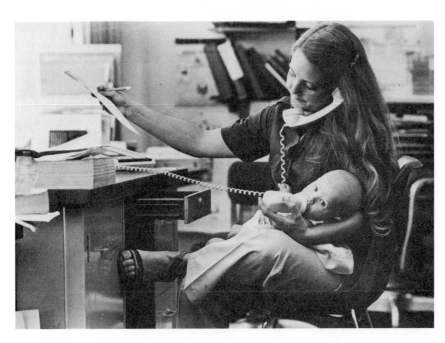

Working mothers often hold
two jobs: office and home.

the activities demanded by the norms. That is, a husband working to
support his family is fulfilling his role as husband and thereby fulfilling
the social norm of husband as supporter of family. Because there are
many norms in a society, there are also many roles that a person plays.
For example, a married woman may fulfill the roles of sexual partner,
chef, mother, homemaker, financial manager, psychologist, and so on. If
she works outside of the marriage, she fulfills roles there too. A married
man may fulfill the roles of breadwinner, sexual partner, father, general
repairman, and so on. The point is that all people play a number of roles
at any given time in their lives. And conflict between roles often occurs
because of the many roles in a complex society. For example, in our society
a woman's mother and wife role may interfere with her career role (see
Chapter 8).

The expectation that people will fulfill their roles, and thus meet social
norms, is strong. Because roles are so taken for granted, most of us
probably are not aware of the pressure to conform. In fact, the expectation
that people behave in prescribed ways probably makes much of life simpler for us. But what happens when people behave in unexpected ways?
To find out how unconscious expected role behavior is, try stepping out
of an expected role and observe the reactions of those around you!

Norms and roles obviously play important parts in marriage, too. That
is, each of us brings to marriage, or to any intimate relationship, a great
number of expectations about what our roles and those of our partner
should be. Many disappointments in marriage stem from frustration of
the role expectations we hold either for ourselves or our spouses (see
Chapter 4). The most obvious example is that of a man who assumes that
the role of wife is restricted to caring for him, the house, and the children.

His wife, however, may believe the role of wife can also include a career and that the role of husband can include household duties and care of children. These conflicting role expectations will undoubtedly cause conflict for this couple.

Norms and roles, when accepted, tend to smooth family functioning. Problems occur when roles and norms are not accepted or when they are unclear. In many societies there are very definite goals for marriage, such as increasing the family's land holdings, adding new workers (children) to the family, or even bringing extra wealth into the family in the form of the wife's dowry. But our society does not set definite goals other than the vague "living happily ever after" we learn about in movies and romantic fiction. And even there "happiness" is not defined.

Furthermore, in societies where roles and norms are stable, people enter marriage with clear ideas of each partner's rights and obligations. In our society, though, almost all norms and roles are being questioned and none more so than those associated with masculinity, femininity, and sexuality. Because the classification of behavior by gender is so central to human society, and to the concept of marriage as we have known it, this chapter will take a closer look at division according to gender and at the expectations, roles, and norms that arise from such division.

How Sex Identity Develops

Three factors determine one's sex identity. First, sex is genetically determined at conception. Second, hormones secreted by glands directed by the genetic configuration produce physical differences. Third, society defines, prescribes, and reinforces the gender aspect of one's sex identity. Problems with any one of these factors can cause faulty sex identity.

Biological Contribution

Every normal person has two sex chromosomes, one inherited from each parent, which determine the biological sex. Women have two X chromosomes (XX), men an X and a Y (XY). Thus if the man's X chromosome combines with the woman's X, the child will be female (XX). If, on the other hand, the man's Y chromosome combines with the woman's X, the child will be male (XY).

At first all embryos have the potential to become either sex (Money & Athanasion, 1973). That is, the already existing tissues of the embryo can become male or female. In order for a male to be produced, the primitive undifferentiated gonad must develop into testes rather than ovaries. The male hormone (a chemical substance) testosterone spurs the development of testes, while another substance (Müllerian-inhibiting substance) simultaneously causes the regression of those embryonic tissues that would become the female reproductive system. In the absence of male hormones, the female organs develop. The hormones have already started working by the time the embryo is six millimeters long, at about two weeks. By the end of the eighth week, the child's sex can be determined by observation of the external genitalia (see Chapter 9, pp. 298–299, for a fuller description of embryonic development).

Note that the male appears to develop only by the addition of the male hormones, which are stimulated by the Y chromosome. Without that stimulation a female develops. This occurrence has led some researchers to conclude that the human embryo is innately feminine (Sherfey, 1972).

By puberty hormonal activity has increased sharply. In girls estrogen (one of the female hormones) affects such female characteristics as breast size, pubic hair, and the filling out of the hips. Estrogen and progesterone (another hormone) also begin the complicated process that leads to changes in the uterine lining and subsequently to the first menstruation, followed about a year later by ovulation (the cycle, mediated by these hormones, that causes an egg to mature each month; see the section in Chapter 9 on female sex organs for a fuller discussion of the menstruation and ovulation processes). It should be noted that some young women begin ovulating at the same time they begin menstruation.

In boys the active hormone is testosterone. At puberty it brings about the secretory activity of the seminal vesicles and the prostate and the regular production of sperm in the testes (see the section in Chapter 9 on male sex organs for a fuller discussion of this process).

Testosterone also affects such male characteristics as larger body size, more powerful muscles, and the ability of blood to carry more oxygen. Castration (removal of the testicles) generally leads to obesity, softer tissues, and a more placid temperament in the male because of the reduction in the quantity of testosterone.

Because every human starts with the potential of becoming either male or female, each as a fully differentiated adult still carries the biological rudiments of the opposite sex. For example, the male has undeveloped nipples on his chest and the female has a penislike clitoris. In a few rare individuals, even though gene determinants have set the sexual direction, the hormones fail to carry out the process. Such persons have characteristics of both sexes, though neither are fully developed, and are called **hermaphrodites**. Hermaphrodites are rare and should not be confused with transsexuals or transvestites. A **transsexual** is a person who believes that he or she is actually of the opposite gender and who may have undergone a sex-change operation as discussed in Inset 6-1. A **transvestite** is a person who enjoys and gains sexual pleasure from dressing as the opposite sex.

The strength of the sex hormones can be seen when pregnant rhesus monkeys are injected with testosterone for twenty-five to fifty days. The genetically female offspring of the injected mothers have malformed external genital structures, which include a scrotum, a small penis, and an obliterated external vaginal orifice. In addition, the behavior of such pseudohermaphroditic females is altered in the direction of normal male behavior (Perez et al., 1971).

The early adaptability of the tissues that grow into mature sexual organs is also quite amazing. Ovaries and vaginas transplanted into castrated male rats within the first twenty-four hours after birth will grow

Hermaphrodite
A person who has both male and female sexual organs, or organs that are indeterminant, such as a clitoris that resembles a penis

Transsexual
A person who has a compulsion or obsession to become a member of the opposite sex through surgical changes

Transvestite
A person who prefers to dress as the opposite sex.

Transsexualism: A Confusion in Sexual Identity

The following excerpt is from Jan Morris's autobiography *Conundrum*:

I was three or perhaps four years old when I realized that I had been born into the wrong body, and should really be a girl. I remember the moment well, and it is the earliest memory of my life.

I was sitting beneath my mother's piano, and her music was falling around me like cataracts, enclosing me as in a cave. . . .

What triggered so bizarre a thought I have long forgotten, but the conviction was unfaltering from the start (Morris, 1974, p. 3).

Morris attended Oxford which led to a glamorous position as correspondent for *The Times* (London). He scored one of the world's historic journalistic coups by climbing 22,000 feet up Mt. Everest with Edmund Hillary and Tenzing Norgay, and flashing first word of their conquest of the peak. The lean, stubble-chinned Morris, whose "manly" stamina made such a feat possible, became a Fleet Street legend. By this time, in spite of his inner contradictions, he married, and he and his wife, daughter of a Ceylonese tea planter, had five children. Eventually he resigned from *The Times* to write books, and in this endeavor, too, he distinguished himself.

However, for all of his outward appearance of normalcy, his inner anguish remained. He consulted physicians, and was advised either to wear gayer clothes or to "soldier on" as a male. His quest for help led him to New York City where he was counseled by Dr. Harry Benjamin, an endocrinologist who has specialized in the study of gender confusion. Dr. Benjamin prescribed female hormone treatments to prepare the way for Morris's sexual changeover. For men, such treatments involve estrogen and progestin to soften the skin and enlarge the breasts. Morris underwent the treatment for eight years and estimates that he swallowed 12,000 pills.

In July, 1972, James Morris took the final, irreversible step. He checked into a Casablanca clinic that specializes in transsexual operations and submit-

and function exactly like normal female organs. This plasticity of the sex tissues quickly vanishes as the hormones cause further differentiation. Transplants of female organs into male rats more than three days old are unsuccessful.

Environmental Contribution

Once a baby is born, society begins to teach the infant its proper gender role and reinforces its sexual identity. In the United States we name our children according to their gender; we give girls pink blankets and boys blue blankets; and at Christmas and birthdays boys receive "masculine" toys and girls "feminine" toys.

In keeping with cultural prescriptions, we show different attitudes toward children of different sexes and we expect and reward their different behaviors. For example, boys are encouraged to engage in rough and tumble activities, whereas girls are discouraged from such activities. (This may explain, in part, why men tend to be more interested in contact sports than women are.) Parents provide guidance to help the child assim-

INSET 6-1, CONTINUED

ted to the surgery. The male-to-female procedure is carried out by amputation of the penis and castration, after which an artificial vagina is created, using scrotal or penile tissue or skin grafts from the hip or thigh. Because the penile tissue is still sensitive, male-to-female transsexuals may experience orgasm, though, of course, pregnancy is impossible.

Today the former James Morris is in virtually every respect a woman, with a new name, the properly androgynous Jan since it is used by both male and females; a new relationship with her former wife (divorced, they regard each other as unofficial "sisters-in-law"); and with her children, who now call their father "Aunt Jan."

James Morris was a very conventional male, who did all of the things that a man was supposed to do. He has turned into a very conventional female, doing the things that a woman is traditionally supposed to do. The new Jan Morris enjoys having men open doors for her, flirt with her, and kiss her. She says, "Women who like to feel cherished by a stronger man have every right to their feelings."

Such cases are extremely rare. It is estimated that about 5,000 individuals in the United States have altered their sex by surgery. For them, biology and the environment had failed to work together to produce a stable sex identity.

When it was active in the sex-change field, Johns Hopkins Medical Center received about 1,500 applications for sex-change operations per year but only performed about six operations per year. Re-searchers there found that the vast majority of persons who think they are transsexual are not and can be helped with psychotherapy. It is interesting to note that Johns Hopkins Medical Center ceased doing sex-change operations in 1979. The follow-up studies of sex-changed persons indicated that the psychological and other gains were minimal and not worth the problems risked with the extensive surgery necessary to accomplish a sex change.

From *Human Sexuality: An Age of Ambiguity*, a title in the Human Behavior series by John Gagon and Bruce Henderson and the editors of Time-Life Books, 1975.

ilate the proper role. Nothing inherent within the child will give rise to the socially sex-appropriate behaviors. Each child must learn—from parents, relatives, teachers, friends—the appropriate behaviors for the culture. (See also p. 432 on accepting the new body image at puberty.)

Because sex roles are learned, it is possible for a society to change masculine and feminine behavior. This is a position taken by feminists. One interesting piece of evidence they point to is those few babies whose ascribed sex differs from their biological sex. Some of these babies have been studied over a twenty-year period, and one researcher (Weitzman, 1975, p. 108) concludes:

In virtually all cases, the sex of assignment (and thus of rearing) proved dominant. Thus, babies assigned as males at birth and brought up as boys by their parents (who were unaware of the child's female genetic and hormonal makeup) thereafter thought of themselves as boys, played with boys' toys, developed boys' sports, preferred boys' clothing, developed male sex fantasies, and in due course fell in love with girls. And the reverse was true for babies who were biologically male but were reared as girls; they followed the typical feminine pattern of development.

In one case one of two identical twins was reassigned as a female following a surgical mishap. At seven months the twin boys were to be circumcised by electrocautery. Because of an electrical malfunction, the penis of one was totally destroyed. Following the recommendations of the doctors, the parents of this little boy elected to have the boy's sex reassigned. At seventeen months the boy came to the Johns Hopkins clinic for the necessary surgical corrections to give him female external genitals. John Money and Anke Ehrhardt reported that since surgery, the parents have made every effort to raise the twins in accord with their assigned sex—one male and one female. According to the reports of the parents, the two children are developing to fit the role expectations of their assigned sex. The mother described her "daughter's" behavior this way (Money & Ehrhardt, 1972, p. 119):

> She likes for me to wipe her face. She doesn't like to be dirty, and yet my son is quite different. I can't wash his face for anything. . . . She seems to be daintier. Maybe it's because I encourage it.

Occasionally, children fail to learn the role that traditionally accompanies their biological sex. This failure can lead to the unusual circumstance of a person being one sex biologically but the opposite sex psychologically, thus resulting in sexual identity confusion.

Biological and Environmental Interaction

There are obvious anatomical and chemical differences between the sexes, but the extent to which they dictate behavioral differences is still not clear. At the present time it appears that the cultural overlay is mainly responsible for behavioral differences.

For example, many women experience premenstrual depression, irritability, and fatigue. These symptoms are caused by the influence of various hormones during certain times of the monthly cycle. Generally such feelings occur during the days before the onset of menstruation. The symptoms, however, can be exaggerated if one's culture has a negative attitude toward menstruation (Bardwick, 1974; Ivey & Bardwick, 1972; Paige, 1973; Angier, 1982). Many cultures, unfortunately, have a "menstrual taboo": Menstruation is seen as something unpleasant and to be avoided. Historically in many cultures the female was isolated during menstruation, and many myths about the dangers of menstrual blood and potential evils existed. If a woman is raised to expect menstruation to be unpleasant and if her society emphasizes the unpleasantness, it is obvious that menstruation will be more difficult for her than need be. She may feel worse than necessary, or she may deny that she feels any different in an effort to minimize the negative cultural stigma. In any case the negative cultural overlay will only serve to make a normal bodily function more mysterious, more troublesome, and less understood than it need be. In our own society we are coming to realize that a more positive attitude toward menstruation leads to a healthier and more positive experience for women. For those women who do suffer from premenstrual syndrome, it is important that they recognize rather than deny its existence so that it can be dealt with both psychologically and medically if necessary.

INSET 6-2

A Theory of Sex Role Development

The old argument over whether environment and learning or genetics and biology determine sex role behavior should not be stated in this either/or form. In truth, of course, it is the interaction of these two great molders of behavior that determines one's actual behavior. The following theory tries to take both into consideration. In the early years (stage 1) biological influence is most clearly seen. Children ten through thirteen (stage 2) demonstrate much more socially influenced behavior. Finally, during adolescence (stage 3), there seems to be a more personal psychological orientation directing sex role behaviors.

Stage 1: Biological Orientation

Level I (6 years): Differences between masculine and feminine are expressed primarily in terms of external bodily differences, such as size, strength, length of hair, etc. Social and psychological differences are recognized but are assumed to be the consequence of these external physical differences. Conformity to sex differences is viewed as necessary in order to maintain gender identity and to allow for the expression of innate gender differences.

Level II (8 years): There is a growing awareness that masculine and feminine traits can exist independently from biological and physical features. Emphasis is placed on the ability of the individual to act according to choice, since he or she is no longer limited by physical or biological constraints. Also the role of training and social conditions is beginning to be recognized. Finally, since children no longer see sex differences as biological necessities, they do not demand the conformity to sex roles characteristic of the younger children.

Stage 2: Societal Orientation

Level III (10 years): Masculine and feminine traits are seen as inherent in the requirements of a system of social roles, and are viewed as fixed and unchangeable. The traits associated with certain adult social roles are assumed to be characteristic of the members of the sex expected to fill those roles. Conformity to masculine and feminine standards is based on the need to satisfy external demands of the social system.

Level IV (12 years): There is a growing awareness that the system of social roles is arbitrary and variable, and may function independently of sex of individual. Stress is put on the individual's freedom to act according to individual self-interest. Conformity is no longer expected.

Stage 3: Psychological Orientation

Level V (14–16 years): Masculine and feminine traits are based on the adoption of an appropriate psychological identity by males and females. These adolescents admit that sex differences are not biologically based and may not be the result of social necessity but these traits are assessed as a central part of men's and women's identities. Deviation is viewed as "sick" or "abnormal," and conformity to external standards is seen as required for maintenance of marriage and the family.

Level VI (18 years): There is an awareness that masculinity and femininity may exist independent from conformity to traditional standards, roles, and behaviors. Sex-stereotyped traits are not assumed to be crucial aspects of personal identity. Principles of equality and freedom are proposed as standards for behavior, and are used to define an ideal model of personal and interpersonal functioning.

Source: Ullian, 1976.

Recent studies of the human brain indicate that there may be gender-related differences in how certain mental processes are controlled and the location of the control area (Goleman, 1978). There are no commonly accepted, observable differences in the physical size, structure, and biochemical components of brains, however, and the degree to which gender-related differences influence behavioral differences is difficult to determine. Table 6-1 looks at some of the stereotypic differences between the sexes and compares them to scientific findings. There seems to be little support for the belief that there are many strong and consistent differences between males and females. Yet when when we examine all of the studies that have been done on the subject of sex differences, there is support for some mild differences. In every case, however, the differences between persons of the same sex on a given characteristic can be greater than the average differences between the sexes.

The reduction of gender role stereotypes—or any behavioral stereotypes—is a worthy goal. Furthermore, to argue endlessly over the relative influence of biology as opposed to environment is a waste of energy. Because we know that culture does influence gender roles to a great extent, it is certainly possible to modify them.

Sweden has moved in the direction of reducing gender role differences. Boys and girls are now required to take identical subjects in school. All jobs are open to both sexes. Laws are applied equally.

Perhaps gender roles in the future will become flexible enough so that individuals will be able to choose roles that maximize their own unique capabilities. Only time will tell.

The Androgynous Person

Androgynous
The quality of having both masculine and feminine characteristics

The concept of the **androgynous** person who exhibits both male (andro) and female (gyno) behavioral characteristics now associated with one or the other sex has become popular among many who are in favor of reducing gender role differences. Abraham Maslow's (1968) self-actualized person (see pp. 136–137 for a fuller discussion of Maslow's ideas) comes close to being such a person, open to both masculine and feminine as well as positive and negative aspects. The self-actualized person has no need to assert dominance or play the coquette. He or she is free to build an individualized role.

To create such adults, society would have to train children for competence in many areas without regard to sex. Following is an idea that has been tried in Sweden.

> In an androgynous society children strive for competence in many areas without regard to sex. They develop motor skills through running and jumping, and hand-eye coordination through needle work, art work, and handling of tools. They learn the skills necessary to take care of themselves, such as cooking, sewing, and household repairs. They play with friends of both sexes, in school as well as out. They engage freely in games of competition as well as games of cooperation with friends of the other sex and friends of the same sex. They learn to respect (or to dislike!) each other on the basis of individual differences, not according to sexual category.

TABLE 6-1   Stereotypic Sex Role Differences Compared with Research Findings[1]

STEREOTYPE	FINDINGS
Perceptual Differences	
Men have: better daylight vision	Mild but in direction of stereotype.
less sensitivity to extreme heat	"
more sensitivity to extreme cold	"
faster reaction times	"
better depth perception	"
better spatial skills	"
Women have: better night vision	"
more sensitivity to touch in all parts of the body	"
better hearing, especially in higher ranges	"
less tolerance of loud sound	"
better manual dexterity and fine coordination	"
Aggression	
Males are more aggressive.	Strong consistent differences in physical aggression.
Females are less aggressive.	
Dependency	
Females are more submissive and dependent.	Weak differences that are more consistent for adults than for children.
Males are more assertive and independent.	
Emotionality	
Females are more emotional and excitable.	Moderate differences on some measures; overall, findings inconclusive.
Males are more controlled and less expressive.	
Verbal Skills	
Females excel in all verbal areas including reading.	Moderate differences, especially for children.
Males are less verbal and have more problems learning to read.	
Math Skills	
Males are better in mathematical skills.	Moderate differences on problem-solving tests, especially after adolescence.
Females are less interested and do less well in mathematics.	

[1]This table has been constructed using four main sources:
1. Maccoby, Eleanor E., Jacklin, Carol N. *The Psychology of Sex Differences*. Palo Alto, Calif.: Stanford University Press, 1974.
2. Goleman, Daniel. "Special Abilities of the Sexes: Do They Begin in the Brain?" *Psychology Today*, Nov., 1978.
3. Frieze, Irene H., et al. *Women and Sex Roles*. New York: W. W. Norton, 1978.
4. McGuiness, Diane, Pribram, Karl. "The Origins of Sensory Bias in the Development of Gender Differences in Perception and Cognition." In Morton Bortner (Ed.) *Cognitive Growth and Development*. Essays in honor of Herbert G. Birch. New York: Brunner-Mazel, 1979.

> Children learn not only self-confidence and a sense of mastery but also attitudes of caring and concern for others. Both sexes are held and touched often as infants and after. They learn to understand and express their own feelings and to recognize the needs and feelings of those around them. Verbal and physical displays of emotion are encouraged as long as they are not harmful to other people. (Lindemann, 1976, pp. 185–86)

Whether this is an ideal that most Americans want to strive for remains to be seen.

Traditional Gender Roles

The depth of most people's belief in gender role stereotypes is often overlooked and is sometimes hard to believe. Most people simply take the various traditional gender role behaviors for granted. See how you react when reading Inset 6-3 which substitutes male terms for female in an imaginary article for a young man about to wed. Reversing the genders often quickly reveals our stereotypes.

To the degree that our behaviors are dictated by stereotypic thinking about gender roles, we close ourselves to potential growth and broader expression. A husband may have a need to express his emotions, yet the masculine stereotype forbids him to cry. A wife may be a natural leader, yet she may suppress leadership behavior because the stereotype says it is not feminine.

Traditional roles historically reflected the woman's childbearing functions and the man's greater physical strength and the necessity to defend his family from attack. A male's status today is still partially determined by his physical prowess, especially during the school years. The traditional role stresses masculine dominance in most areas of life, in the society as well as within the family. The traditional role also allowed men sexual freedom while severely limiting women's sexuality—the **double standard**.

Double standard
Role orientation in which males are allowed more freedom than are females.

The traditional feminine role was essentially the complement of the masculine role. Man was active, so woman was passive and submissive. Wives helped their husbands, took much of their personal identity from their husbands, ran the home and family, and worked outside the home only if necessary. Woman was the source of stability and strength within the home, from which most of the love and affection flowed.

In sociological terms the traditional masculine character traits are those labeled "instrumental." Such traits enable one to accomplish tasks and goals. Being aggressive, self-confident, adventurous, active, and dominant are examples. "Expressive" character traits—being gentle, expressive, loving, and supportive—tend to be used in describing feminine behavior. Notice how the traits often complement one another. For example, the man exhibits aggressiveness, whereas the woman tends to be the opposite, gentle.

It is interesting to note that we find relative agreement between Amer-

INSET 6-3

How to Hold a Wife: A Bridegroom's Guide

Oh, lucky you! You are finally bridegroom to the woman of your dreams!

But don't think for a minute that you can now relax and be assured automatically of marital happiness forever. You will have to *work at it*. While she may have eyes only for you *now*, remember that she is surrounded every day by attractive young men who are all too willing to tempt her away from you. And as the years go by, you will lose some of the handsome muscularity of your youth; you will have to make up in skill and understanding what you will lack in the bloom of youth. It will be up to you to make your physical relationship so exciting, so totally satisfying to her, that she won't be tempted to stray!

Yes, boys, we are talking about SEX. Don't turn away in embarrassment. For if you are to *hold* that wonderful woman, you will have to practice and work hard at making her sex life as marvelous as it can be.

But how?

Here is what you need to know and do to succeed in your marriage, your greatest challenge in life—and the one that will be utterly essential to your wife's future happiness and thus your own.

1. Let's start in with the essentials. You should always be available to your wife whenever she wants you. It is, of course, your husbandly prerogative to say no, but you will be wise to never do so unless you are really ill, for that may tempt her to turn to other men to fulfill her essential needs. She cannot do without sex, so you as a smart husband should always be ready to provide it.

2. That means that you should never let yourself get too tired to perform. The cardinal sin for a husband—and a good way to lose the wife you love—is to fail at your duty to achieve a good erection and to sustain it until your wife is fully satisfied. So never let your work or anything else get in the way of plenty of rest each day, regular but moderate exercise, and plenty of protein in your diet—and stay away from excessive alcohol.

Remember that women's sexual needs vary. Some need it more often than others, and some (lucky you if you are married to a real woman like that!) can achieve multiple orgasms in a single night of love *if* you can do your part!

3. "But how about me?" you may ask. "How about my sexual needs and satisfactions?"

Now man's passion, of course, often does not equal that of woman. But you have a wonderful surprise in store for you, if you concentrate your efforts on your wife's pleasure and don't worry selfishly about your own. For sooner or later you will discover the ecstasy of truly mature male coital orgasm that can be induced only by total surrender to the exquisite sensations of a woman's orgasmic contractions. . . .

4. Remember that your first duty is to your wife: So if you fail to satisfy her (and yourself, too) in the above-described natural way, you should talk to a good psychiatrist who specializes in this kind of problem. She will help you if, for instance, you have not fully accepted the natural masculine role that will bring you the joy of selfless service to others instead of the futile envy of woman's natural leadership role. . . .

5. Now for a subject that may seem trivial: your appearance and dress. Don't overlook it—it is a vital ingredient in marital happiness.

Every woman likes to be proud of how attractive her husband is, so dress to please her. If she likes you to show off your youthful figure, by all means do so! Broad shoulders can be accentuated by turtleneck jerseys (with shoulder pads if needed), as can the well-tapered waist. Small, firm, well-shaped buttocks (very much in fashion this year) can be set off by well-cut . . . pants. . . .

INSET 6-3, CONTINUED		
If you do your job well—for husbandhood is the true career for all manly men, worthy of all your talents—you will	keep your wife happy and hold her for the rest of her days. Remember that marriage for a man should be *life's Great Ad-*	*venture, so relax—relax—relax—and enjoy.* From Jennifer S. MacLeod, *The Village Voice* (February 11, 1971).

ican men and women when they assess the advantages and disadvantages of their gender roles. Essentially, the perceived advantages of one sex are the disadvantages of the other.

> Masculine disadvantages consist overwhelmingly of obligations with a few prohibitions while the disadvantages of the female role arise primarily from prohibitions, with a few obligations. Thus females complain about what they can't do, males about what they must do. Females complain that they cannot be athletic, aggressive, sexually free, or successful in the worlds of work and education; in short, they complain of their passivity. Males complain that they must be aggressive and must succeed; in short, of their activity. The (sanctioned) requirement that males may be active and females passive in a variety of ways is clearly unpleasant to both. (Chafetz, 1974, p. 58)

When persons are polled, however, and asked to describe the ideal man and ideal woman, their descriptions do not follow the stereotypes just described (Tavris, 1978). Both men and women generally agree on similar lists of ideal characteristics for both sexes, leading one to believe that the ideal of the androgynous person is something both sexes would like to seek even though this is difficult to achieve.

Ideal Woman

As Men Describe Her

1. Able to love
2. Warm
3. Stands up for beliefs
4. Gentle
5. Self-confident

As Women Describe Her

1. Able to love
2. Stands up for beliefs
3. Warm
4. Self-confident
5. Gentle

Ideal Man

As Women Describe Him

1. Able to love
2. Stands up for beliefs
3. Warm
4. Self-confident
5. Gentle

As Men Describe Him

1. Able to love
2. Stands up for beliefs
3. Self-confident
4. Fights to protect family
5. Intelligent

If you examine the first five highest-rated traits for the ideal woman and ideal man as seen by each sex, there is a striking similarity. And all of the lists contain some of the positive traits of each sex as seen traditionally.

TABLE 6-2   Positive and Negative Ascribed Character Traits
as Seen by a Cross Section of Americans

POSITIVE	NEGATIVE
WOMEN	
Gentle	Passive
Tactful	Nonassertive
Loving	Cunning
Social	Talkative
Sensitive	Moody
Caring	Subjective
Warm	Dependent
Communicative	Illogical
Sympathetic	Insecure
Socially aware	Submissive
Modest	Shy
MEN	
Strong	Tactless
Aggressive	Rough
Brave	Egotistical
Objective	Unemotional
Logical	Socially unaware
Adventurous	Inconsiderate
Self-confident	Domineering
Decisive	Insensitive
Independent	Loud
Cool under stress	Lacking empathy
Self-reliant	Uncaring

Unfortunately, the attempt to free each gender from the stereotypic role behaviors is, at best, limited. A man who is taught to be competitive and dominant may easily stand up for his beliefs yet have a difficult time being warm and gentle. On the other hand, a woman who is taught to be warm and gentle may have trouble standing up for her beliefs. A man who is only warm and gentle and not aggressive will probably have difficulty being successful in our highly competitive work culture. Successful men in our culture must still be aggressive and make their work their first priority, often leaving the family in second place in their lives. Women who want our culture's stamp of personal achievement often are still the ones who bear children and, by and large, retain the day-to-day responsibility for the children's upbringing. The conflict between the idea of androgyny, the ideal masculine and feminine traits, and the real world of our culture causes each of us to feel confusion, ambiguity, and frustration as we attempt to mold our lives. For example, women are told to expand themselves by seeking careers outside the home yet made to feel guilty if they do not devote themselves to their families. Unfortunately, they are also made to feel guilty by some feminists if they do want to be ''devoted'' to their families.

Gender Roles and the Female Liberation Movement

If people do become freer from past gender role stereotypes, then much credit must be given to the women of America. As Betty Friedan puts it in her recent critique of the feminist movement:

> At the moment, I feel like women are ahead of men, and it's a lonely thing. We still have to deal with men who want to control us in the old way. . . . Is the new man going to come soon enough for us? . . . It's not women versus men any more—the anger's gone. But there can't be that flow between us until men stop playing games, too. Women have made the big leap; men are still stuck. Men have to break out of the mold next. (1981, p. 122)

The women's movement has contributed much toward focusing our attention on gender inequalities and thereby has energized the desire to change these inequalities and thus ourselves. It has brought about profound changes in the relationship between men and women and therefore within the American family.

As women have made changes in their roles, changes in the masculine role have also resulted. Women's liberation, to the extent that it has succeeded, also has meant men's liberation. For example, as more and more women have entered the workforce, more families have become two-paycheck families (Chapter 8). Thus the traditional role of husband as sole

breadwinner for the family has been mitigated. No longer is he solely responsible for fulfilling this function. Shared economic responsibility means more freedom for men. Economic participation by women also means that they have become more independent.

Unfortunately, all of the changes fostered by the women's movement and its allies have not been positive. Failure of the ERA to win ratification, the strength of the prolife attack on permissive abortion, and the antifeminist movement all bear witness to the conflicts that are stirred up when traditional gender roles are challenged.

Women and the Economy

The major restraint to freer role choice is women's inferior economic position in our society. In general a man can earn more than a woman regardless of their individual skills. This economic differential in earning power locks each sex into many traditional roles. For example, a father who would prefer to spend more time at home caring for the family usually cannot afford to do so. In most cases this would mean giving up a portion of his income, income that his wife generally is not able to replace.

Although more and better job opportunities for women are now available, the male/female earnings gap has remained. Table 6-3 shows women's earnings compared with men's earnings in 1981. In 1956 women's earnings averaged 63.3 percent of men's. In 1965 this figure dropped slightly, to 59.9 percent; in 1975 to 58.8 percent; and in 1981 the figure was 59.8 percent. Thus, women's earnings, compared with men's, haven't gained over the past twenty-five years. Note that some "firsts" for women, described in Inset 6-4, tend to be stories of women gaining jobs and positions that historically have been held by men. Opening of more job categories to women is not as important as addressing the inequity of pay between men and women. It is true that a few women may become locomotive engineers, yet most women will continue to seek jobs that women historically have sought. The real stumbling block to freer role choice for both men and women is comparable pay for comparable work. For most of the time since women entered the workforce in large numbers, they have been America's best source of cheap labor. Often they have done work comparable to men's, but, as Table 6-3 clearly demonstrates, they are paid less for it. The differential is so great that the comparable pay question raises serious questions about whether the economy could afford such a step. To follow society's years-long struggle against inflation with an overall increase in women's pay to the level of men's would be an inflationary shock not easily absorbed. The shock is considered by the courts to be so great, in fact, that thus far courts have refused to rule in favor of generally comparable pay for women in all areas of work.

Despite generally lower pay, unemployment seems to hit women just as hard as it hits men. In 1981 the average annual unemployment rate for men age sixteen years and older was 7.4 percent, while for women sixteen years and older it was 7.9 percent. At the high point (December 1982) of unemployment during the recent recession, the unemployment rate na-

---

INSET 6-4

"Firsts" in the ERA Decade

● In 1977 Alice Peurala was elected the first woman president of a major steelworkers' local, the USW's then 5,500-strong Local 65 in Chicago. Peurala, 54, entered union politics after she saw men getting promoted ahead of her ("I was wild; I couldn't believe it"), but was defeated for re-election in 1982 and has returned to her $19,000 factory job.

● In 1972 Sally Priesand, 36, was ordained the first woman rabbi. Since then there have been 60 others. Priesand is now installed at Monmouth Reform Temple in Tinton Falls, N.J.

● In 1977 Dr. Olga Jonasson, 47, was named the first woman head of a major surgical department, at Chicago's Cook County Hospital. "There aren't nearly enough women who strive for the kind of position I have," she says. "And we need a lot more of them."

● Lauded for her eloquence during the 1974 Watergate impeachment hearings, Texas Congresswoman Barbara Jordan appeared at the Democratic National Convention two years later and became the first woman ever to deliver the keynote address. Now 46, she decided not to seek a fourth term in 1978 and teaches at the Lyndon B. Johnson School of Public Affairs in Austin.

● Janet Guthrie, 44, is the first woman to have driven in the Indianapolis 500. Guthrie took part in the '77, '78 and '79 Memorial Day classics and had her best finish in 1978 when she came in ninth place. She is now automotive editor for *Working Woman* and races rarely.

● In 1973 Oakland, Calif., resident Evelyn Hart, 34, was made the first woman locomotive engineer by Southern Pacific. "I got into this because of the money [annual salary: $26,000]," says Hart, who runs a freight train through Northern California. "But that's not why I do it now. It's the challenge."

● In 1973 Ruth Johnson Kline, 30, became the first woman in the U.S. Marine Corps Band (French horn). She quit after eight years because "it was time to do something else," and is now training to become an air traffic controller.

● Sandra Day O'Connor, 52, mother of three, became the first woman justice on the U.S. Supreme Court. Said O'Connor: "Women have a great deal of stamina and strength. It is possible to plan both a family and a career and to enjoy success at both."

● Sally K. Ride, 31, was named the first American woman astronaut chosen for space flight. . . . "I was not an active participant in women's liberation," Ride once said, "but my career at Stanford [where she earned a physics Ph.D.] and my selection as an astronaut would not have happened without the women's movement."

People, July 5, 1982, p. 40.

---

tionally was 11.2 percent for men and 10.3 percent for women (U.S. Department of Labor, March 1983).

Most women tend to be employed in a relatively narrow range of jobs. You can see from Figure 6-1 that 80 percent of employed women tend to fall into only six basic job categories, with 57 percent of them falling into just two categories, clerical and service workers. In some specific job categories as well as in some professions, women have made significant headway in the past ten years. The U.S. Department of Labor (November 1982) reports that in eight major job categories women have become the majority in the last decade. Those categories are insurance adjusters,

TABLE 6-3   Earnings by Occupation, 1981 Weekly Medians

	WOMEN'S PAY	MEN'S PAY
Clerical workers	$220	$328
Computer specialists	355	488
Editors, reporters	324	382
Engineers	371	547
Lawyers	407	574
Nurses	326	344
Physicians	401	495
Sales workers	190	366
Teachers (elementary)	311	379
Waiters	144	200

U.S. Bureau of the Census, May 1982.

examiners and investigators, bill collectors, real estate agents and brokers, photographic process workers, checkers, examiners and inspectors, and production-line assemblers.

Women have made significant progress in professional education. For example only .8 percent of college women left campus with engineering degrees in 1971, whereas 10.4 percent earned such a degree in 1981. A third of the 1981 graduating class of Harvard University's medical school consisted of women. In 1971 only 8.1 percent of law students were women, whereas in 1981 30.2 percent of the graduates were women. In general college attendance more quickly pays greater monetary rewards to women than to men. After graduating from college, young women quickly catch up with and overtake the wage rates of their high school counterparts

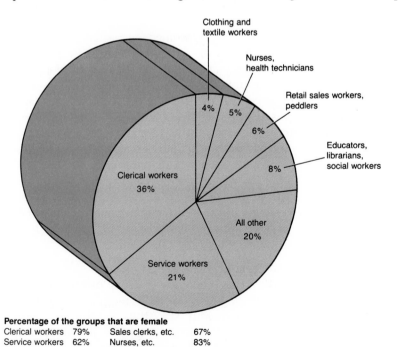

FIGURE 6-1 Occupational profile of the female labor force, 1977. Source: U.S. Department of Labor, 1977.

Percentage of the groups that are female

Clerical workers	79%	Sales clerks, etc.	67%
Service workers	62%	Nurses, etc.	83%
Educators, etc.	64%	Textile workers, etc.	76%

who have opted to go right to work after high school. The college women are outearning the noncollege women within four years of college graduation. College men are taking about ten years before they begin to outearn noncollege men (National Center for Education Statistics, 1982).

The Equal Pay Act of 1963 and the creation of the Equal Opportunity Commission (EOC) under Title VII of the Civil Rights Act of 1964 have greatly helped women to move in the direction of equal pay for equal work, but there is still a long way to go. Barrett (1979, p. 57) concludes:

> The rapid evolution of the law from sanctioning sex discrimination in the guise of protecting the weaker sex, to establishing the principle of equal employment opportunity, and finally to mandating the eradication of discrimination through affirmative action is one of the most significant legislative developments of the post-World War II era. . . .
>
> Equal employment legislation may open new doors for women, but women themselves must be prepared to walk through them.

Although women's earning power and choice of jobs are still more limited than men's, this century has witnessed dramatic changes in women's participation as workers outside the home. In twenty years the number of working women has risen 95 percent. The most startling increases have been among married women, including those with children. During the last two decades the number of two-earner households has increased to 50.4 percent from only 22.4 percent in 1960. The percentage of married women in the labor force has risen from 32 percent to 51 percent during this period. Today, about as many women say they would like to be a wife and mother and hold a full-time outside job (40 percent) as would prefer being a stay-at-home wife and mother (39 percent) ("Gallup Poll," August 8, 1982).

Despite the great increase in working women, or perhaps because of it, many women still see themselves discriminated against in the world of work. A recent Gallup Poll (August 15, 1982) asked the question, "Do you feel that women in this country have equal job opportunities with men, or not?" Fifty-four percent of the women polled answered "no." This percentage has increased since 1975 when only 46 percent answered "no." The increased percentage who felt that they did not have an equal opportunity with men probably reflects heightened awareness of job discrimination rather than an actual increase in discrimination.

What changes can be made in the economic system to make better and fairer use of women in the workforce? Equal pay for equal work is certainly the first necessary change. But this can only become a reality when certain attitudes about working women change. Janet S. Chafetz (1974) lists a number of these attitudes, which she calls myths:

Myth 1: Women are only working for "pin money."
Myth 2: Women aren't worth hiring where any training or investment is necessary because they just get married or pregnant or quit.
Myth 3: Women are weak and frequently sick, thus missing too many days of work. For example, California employers are required to have a couch in every women's restroom in larger firms.

Let's take a closer look at these myths. Although there are some women who work because they enjoy it, rather than out of necessity, many women are the sole breadwinners or major contributors of their families. One-parent families accounted for 21 percent (about one out of five) of the 31.6 million families with children in 1981; 90 percent of these one-parent families were headed by women (U.S. Bureau of the Census, May 1982). In light of present pay levels for women, it is not surprising to learn that approximately half of these women-headed families fall below the poverty line. In addition combating inflation and unemployment has brought many women into the labor market as second earners in their families even when the husband is present.

Myth 2 rests on a factual foundation: Females do quit more often than males. Many things contribute to this, however, such as low pay, over-qualification for available jobs, lack of promotional opportunities, time conflicts between job and marriage responsibilities, and much more. In general people in low-paying jobs have higher quit rates. Because a higher proportion of women have such jobs, their overall quit rate is exaggerated.

Myth 3 is simply untrue. Females average 5.3 sick days per year to males' 5.4 (Suelzle, 1970).

A number of societal rearrangements could help the working mother. First, the quality of care provided for children of working mothers is a matter of public as well as private concern. Traditionally children have been cared for by their own mothers. When the mother works outside the home, other arrangements must be made. Children must be left with nonemployed women, with relatives, or at child-care centers. Although professionally run child-care centers would seem to offer the most advantageous help to working mothers, most women cannot afford even the modest cost of $10 to $15 per day ($200 to $300 per month) that good private centers currently charge. Consequently, in recent years feminists have argued and worked for government funding of day-care centers. They have had limited success on the state level but little on the federal level.

Three objections can be made to government funding of day-care centers. The first objection is that government funding will mean too much government control over childrearing practices. Granted that minimal standards for day-care centers should be established for such things as fire and health precautions, general funding usually provides for much more detailed control. Those who pay the bill usually decide what sort of service will be provided. It is possible that legislation for child-care funding would provide for parental control over governing boards of child-care facilities. The trend, however, in other segments of public education has been in the opposite direction, toward loosening of local community control and greater regulation from the governmental bureaucracy. Government funding for early childhood care is likely to take the direction for children's care out of the hands of parents.

A second objection to governmental funding, especially from a feminist viewpoint, is that it provides a substitute for adequate pay for women workers. In effect the government is giving a subsidy to employers. Because the government is paying for the child care that employees cannot afford, employers can keep wages low and still find workers. Such government funding does benefit the worker but at the same time limits options. If a mother does not like the kind of care provided in the government-funded centers, she has little recourse. She cannot afford to send her children elsewhere, and it is unlikely that she could influence the center's policies to any great extent.

A third objection is that the quality of child care may be poor. Consistency and predictability are crucial to the development of young children. In the past this guidance has been provided by parents. Profamily groups argue that the chances for good care are best with the child's own parents. Parents know the child best; they are ego involved with the child. In daycare centers the quality of care, the philosophy of child care, and the sort of person interacting with the children often is unknown to the parents. If a working mother were paid an adequate wage, she would thereby have a choice of private or public child care and could choose the type of care that best meets her and the child's needs. If women were paid adequate wages, the resulting demand for quality child care would make it profitable to establish child-care centers, and a variety could then be opened, having differing educational policies. Even if parents had little direct influence over the programs offered, they would have some indirect control because they would not have to patronize the centers whose practices were inconsistent with their own values.

For the immediate future government help for early child care would be an improvement over the present situation where children of working mothers often receive only minimal care. In the long run wage scales for women's jobs must be raised to levels comparable to those for men's jobs. That is the best way to help families choose quality child care that will meet their needs.

Second, in addition to better child care, more part-time jobs at good pay could be created. For example, two women could share one job (see Inset 6-5). They could alternate days, or one could work a morning shift and the other an afternoon shift. In Massachusetts, Honeywell, Inc., offers mothers shortened shifts within school hours. These shifts allow mothers time to be with their children and maintain their home and yet contribute economically to the family. In addition, such mothers can participate in the world outside the home and maintain a career without working themselves into exhaustion as so often happens when a woman works all day and then returns to her homemaking job at night.

Third, maternity leaves should be a normal fringe benefit of all jobs. The man who desires to should also be allowed such a leave to participate with his wife in the birth of their child.

Fourth, business should reconsider age limitations in its hiring practices. The woman whose children have left home is often a reliable and conscientious employee. She may need some training if she has been away from the work world for a long time, but given that training she is far freer to devote herself to the job than is her counterpart with children at home, and she is often more stable and experienced in dealing with people than a younger man or woman.

INSET 6-5

Job Sharing

Joan and Pamela, each recently divorced, share quite a bit: a job, a paycheck, a house, and their children.

The two friends persuaded a small company to hire both of them to split one secretarial job. One works while the other cares for the children. This arrangement has numerous advantages. Each woman has a job, which is necessary if she is to make ends meet because neither receives more than a minimum amount of child support. Each saves money that would go to baby-sitters. Each knows the other well so that the children are left with a friend rather than a stranger. The children also remain in their own home rather than being sent away for the day. In addition, each mother has time with her own children. Each has reduced her expenses by sharing the costs of the house.

Each woman works three days one week and two days the following week. This schedule gives the company a full-time secretary while each mother works only half time.

The company has also derived some extra advantages from the job sharing. Occasionally one of the women's children becomes sick. The other woman can cover for her at work. If only one mother were involved, the company would probably have to do without an employee for the day.

Both workers are also fresher and less tired because they are not coping with two full-time jobs every day, mother and employee.

Fifth, employers need to reconsider their position on maintaining child-care facilities at the workplace. An employer supplying child-care facilities provides a number of advantages for working mothers. No extra time must be taken to deliver and pick up the child because the child is at or close to the workplace. Also, because the child is close by, the mother may be able to visit the child on breaks and perhaps have lunch with the child, thus maintaining a higher level of mother/child contact.

With these suggested changes women would have more alternatives and would derive more satisfaction from their work. Business would have better workers, because the person who feels worthwhile and productive in all areas of life does a better job and is less prone to quit. Fair pay and a humane work system that supports rather than hinders home life are worthwhile social goals.

Credit and the Single Woman

Obviously, the lower pay scale for women makes it more difficult for them to obtain credit. For example, for house purchases loan institutions require that the monthly payment be no more than a certain percentage of the borrower's monthly income. The lower the income, the lower the possible loan.

The single, never-married, working woman usually has some credit standing, but the divorced or widowed woman may find herself stranded without credit. Until recently credit standing has been based almost entirely on the husband's income. Even a working wife's income has often been discounted in the belief that she is only a temporary worker.

> Susan and Larry Stevens both worked and earned well above the national average. Both had and used many credit cards. Unfortunately, one day Larry was killed in an automobile accident. Susan decided to move to another city where her parents were living. Although she and Larry had never had any problems obtaining credit, she now finds herself turned down because she has no credit history. Although she had contributed to their joint income during their entire marriage, her past jobs and savings were not considered assets. She is lucky in only one way. If Larry's credit had been bad, she would have had a negative credit history too.

Through the 1975 Equal Credit Opportunity Act, such unfair practices have been curbed to a degree. The act requires that credit rights be spelled out. Credit may not be refused solely on the grounds of sex or marital status. A woman who qualifies for credit does not need a cosigner. Everyone has the right to know on what grounds credit was refused. Everyone has the right to examine the information used in making the credit decision (this must be done within sixty days). A woman's income or savings must be counted as equal to a man's. The credit history of "family accounts" must be considered in extending credit to either spouse, and credit ratings must be established for each partner.

Just how much these regulations will help women remains to be seen, but they are a step in the right direction. Of course, both males and females must be good credit risks if credit is to be obtained. Prompt and consistent payments on loans and accounts is the best way to build a good credit rating.

Women and the Law*

Another restraint on freer sex roles has been the legal structure. Our laws are extremely complicated and have often worked to the detriment of both sexes. In the past laws have considered females to be irresponsible and in need of protection. For example, in California a married woman had to use her husband's home as her legal address, and until a recent change in the law she could not buy or sell stocks or property without her husband's consent and thereby his acceptance of the responsibility for her actions. The current Georgia code (written in 1856) states: "The husband is head of the family and the wife is subject to him; her legal and civil existence is merged in the husband . . . either for her own protection, or for her benefit or for the preservation of public order." This may sound archaic, but recent attempts to change this wording were defeated in the Georgia state legislature.

*Most of the laws governing marriage and sex roles are state laws and hence do not apply throughout the country.

Although many laws remain in effect that are unfair to one or the other sex, the 1970s and '80s have seen much legal change. The changes have been precipitated mainly by women challenging the laws they believed discriminated against them. Changes in laws on living together, divorce, child custody and support, on crimes such as rape and sexual harassment, and on benefits such as social security have resulted.

A change in a law to make the sexes more equal sounds like a worthy goal. Yet some critics see new inequities resulting. For example, divorce laws that ask equal division of property may leave older women who have little work experience much worse off than their former husbands. The divorced woman may rightly have her half of the property but still be unable to support herself. "Rehabilitative alimony" is one legal response to this new problem created by changing laws. The idea is that the ex-husband financially should help the ex-wife retrain herself to become self-supporting.

Many law changes are making work and economic participation fairer to women. One example is the California statute enacted in 1978 making it an unfair employment practice to discriminate on the basis of pregnancy, childbirth, or medically related conditions. This law also requires employers who provide disability insurance programs for their employees to include disability for normal pregnancy as a benefit (AB 1960, Berman, Chapter 1308, Statutes of 1978).

In the criminal courts women have successfully strengthened rape laws. Punishments for rapists have been made stronger. For example, California now prohibits the granting of probation to any person who has been convicted of rape by force or violence (SB 1479, Deukmejian, Chapter 1308, Statutes of 1978). More important, many states have eliminated the humiliating defense tactic of cross-examining the victim about her previous sexual conduct. In 1977 Oregon passed a statute that made it a criminal offense for a husband to rape his wife. This stance is a complete departure from marital law of the past where there was no such thing as "rape" if a couple were married.

Sexual harassment is another legal area that is slowly opening to women (see Inset 6-6). Although the women's movement supports such changes, leaders believe that it will take forever to change the thousands of laws now in effect on a one-by-one basis. They prefer legal change via the Equal Rights Amendment (ERA).

Gender Role Stereotypes

The Traditional Closed Marriage

Marriages that accept traditional gender role assignments have been called "closed marriages" by Nena and George O'Neill. Essentially, they are marriages of possession and reduced freedom. The main tenets of the closed marriage "contract" are:

INSET 6-6

A Steno Who Said "No!"

Adrienne Tomkins says that all she wanted was to get ahead in her career. Tomkins, now 34, was a pool stenographer at the Public Service Electric and Gas Co. in Newark, N.J., when she was offered a tryout position as private secretary to company executive Herbert D. Reppin. Her competency, she was told, would be evaluated in three months.

The day of reckoning, as the green-eyed, auburn-haired Tomkins tells her story, occurred nearly three months later. "Since your evaluation is coming up, why don't we discuss it over lunch?" Reppin asked. Not wanting to hurt her chances for promotion, Tomkins reluctantly agreed.

Reppin took her to a restaurant in a hotel, Tomkins says. he suggested a drink at the bar. "This is my new girl," she quotes him as telling his barmates. After two hours at the bar, Tomkins said she was leaving. Reppin, she says, reminded her that he was her boss. By 3 p.m., Tomkins remembers, he was on his sixth drink and gossiping about office love affairs. "All of a sudden," she says, "I heard him say flat out, 'I want to _____ you. It's the only way we can have a working relationship.' "

Tomkins insists that she tried to leave, but that her boss grabbed her by the wrist and said they were going to a room in the hotel. She talked her way out by saying she had to visit her sick mother. Reppin kissed her, then let her go, Tomkins says. . . .

The day after the ill-fated luncheon date, Tomkins complained to the company's personnel department. The following day, she received a call from a supervisor, who called it "all a big misunderstanding." Furious, Tomkins said she would never return to the job. The supervisor promised to find her a "comparable" position in the company.

The comparable position never materialized. She protested in vain to the staffers of equal-employment-opportunity in the company. "In those days you had to plead sex discrimination," recalls Tomkins. "There was no such thing as 'sexual harassment'." Unbeknownst to her, her personnel folder was filling up with critical appraisals. Eventually, Tomkins was fired.

By now under treatment from a therapist and still caring for her mother, Tomkins went to Federal court. She and her lawyer, Nadine Taub of Rutgers University Law School, charged that Reppin and the company had violated Title VII of the 1964 Civil Rights Act, which forbids sexual discrimination in employment. U.S. District Judge Herbert Stern held that Tomkins could sue the company, but not Reppin. Tomkins appealed and the U.S. Court of Appeals agreed with her, holding that sexual harassment was a form of discrimination and she could sue Reppin.

Before the facts could be de-

Clause 1: Possession or ownership of the mate. (Both the husband and the wife are in bondage to the other: "You belong to me." Belonging *to* someone . . . is very different from the feeling that you belong *with* someone.)

Clause 2: Denial of self. (One sacrifices one's own self and individual identity to the contract.)

Clause 3: Maintenance of the couple-front. (Like Siamese twins, we must always appear as a couple. The marriage in itself becomes your identity card, as though you wouldn't exist without it.)

Clause 4: Rigid role behavior. (Tasks, behavior and attitudes strictly separated

INSET 6-6, CONTINUED
terminated at trial, PSE&G, without admitting fault, offered to settle. The company agreed to pay Tomkins $20,000 plus her legal costs, and to restore her personnel file to its state before her luncheon with Reppin. It agreed to set up a panel to hear sexual-harassment complaints. And it agreed to finance a film—produced by Tomkins and Taub—illustrating Title VII discrimination. . . .

Diane K. Shah with Susan Agrest, *Newsweek*, April 30, 1979.

Man Wins Office Sex Suit

Sexual harassment has become in the past few years a routine basis for lawsuits brought by women against male bosses. But a male employee suing a female supervisor on the same grounds is like the proverbial man biting the proverbial dog. David Huebschen, 33, an employee of the Wisconsin Department of Health and Social Services, is apparently the first male to win such a suit. Last week a federal jury in Madison said that he is due $196,500 in damages, probably the largest amount ever awarded an individual in a sexual harassment case. The sum is to be paid by the state on behalf of Huebschen's former superior, Jacquelyn Rader, 37, and Rader's boss, Bernard Stumbras.

The jury of five women and one man believed Huebschen's contention that Rader demoted him from his job as a disability-insurance supervisor because he refused her sexual advances. Stumbras, an administrator of the state agency, was held liable for not remedying Huebschen's harassment complaints. The verdict will probably be appealed.

Huebschen admitted he did not always feel harassed by Rader's overtures. After an office party in September 1979, the couple met in a motel room but did not actually consummate their tryst, Huebschen says, because he was "too tense." In November, he testified, he told Rader that "the sexual stuff has to stop." Rader soon sent him packing to his old, lower-paying job as a claims adjudicator.

Rader, who like Huebschen is married, denied any affair. Rather, she claimed, it was he who pestered her—unsuccessfully—for dates. Rader said she demoted Huebschen in 1979 because he was an inept supervisor. Yet just three months earlier she had praised his work in a written critique, and a month before that she had recommended him for a pay raise.

The record amount awarded Huebschen was a surprise. "Sexual harassment is a pervasive problem for women, not for men, yet you don't see this kind of award to women," noted Isabelle Pinzler, director of the American Civil Liberties Union's Women's Rights Project. Said Detroit Attorney Allyn Ravitz: "Male or female, every big verdict has got to help."
Time, August 2, 1982.

along predetermined lines, according to outdated concepts of "male" and "female.")

Clause 5:   Absolute fidelity. (Physically and even psychologically binding, through coercion rather than choice.)

Clause 6:   Total exclusivity. (Enforced togetherness will preserve the union.)

You may not agree that this is the kind of psychological contract you agreed to at all. *You* married for love, warmth, companionship. Of course you did. But, subtly, insidiously, often without your even knowing it, the clauses of the closed marriage contract begin to foreclose upon your freedom and your individuality, making you a slave of your marriage (1972, pp. 52–53).

Let's take a closer look at what goes on in a closed marriage.

What Do You Think?

In what ways have stereo-typed sex roles affected this conflict?

Why does Mary seem so dissatisfied?

Why doesn't John allow her to take the class?

What role changes can you suggest that might help alleviate their conflict?

A Closed Marriage

John and Mary Doe both come from lower-middle-class families where the wife's role is oriented toward the home and is secondary to the husband's. Their parents say they are satisfied with marriage and their families. John and Mary met while they were attending community college, and they married about a year and a half later. John is now selling insurance, and Mary is busy at home with their three-year-old son. One evening, the following scene takes place:

"John, can't you stop looking at television for a while?"

"Gee, honey, I'm tired and it's a good mystery. What do you want?"

"Just to talk."

"We can talk later."

"You always say that and when later comes, you want to go to sleep."

"Can't you leave me alone and give me peace? All you do is nag. You want me to make more money, so I have to be out more. Yet you want me to be home. I'm not paying enough attention to you. Well, you can't have it both ways."

At school, Mary had done well and had been an active leader. But now she denies her competitiveness because she fears it is unfeminine. However, she expresses her competitiveness by urging John to earn more, while at the same time belittling his efforts.

Later that same evening, in bed, John tries to be affectionate, but Mary responds by saying, "You wanted to go to sleep, so go to sleep and leave me alone."

"You never seem interested in sex any more."

"Well, you never want to talk to me any more so why should I satisfy your every whim?"

Note how Mary gets back at John by controlling their sexual behavior.

The following conversation is also typical of many:

"John, I'd like to do something besides stay home. There's an interesting art class offered at night that I want to take."

"No, I can't see you being out at night. You should be home with me."

"But it's just one night a week and it doesn't cost much."

"It's not the cost. I just think a wife should be at home with her husband at night."

"Why don't we take it together?"

"No, I haven't got time. You keep me working seven days a week with all your nagging and pushing. I want to do what I want in my little spare time."

"You always do what you want."

"Are you kidding? I'd much rather be at the motorcycle races on Sunday than doing gardening work."

"Well, it seems to me that when you aren't working late, you spend your time at home glued to the TV. That certainly isn't doing what I want. Besides, at least you get to meet adults and be out in the world."

John usually responds to these conversations by withdrawing into work and into watching television. This withdrawal stimulates Mary to try more frantically to gain his attention, which causes John to withdraw further. Thus a vicious circle develops.

Here we have seen a couple trying to conform to gender role stereotypes that don't quite fit. Mary would like to participate in the world; she would like to exercise some of her competitiveness and dominance, yet the traditional role precludes this. Such behavior does not fit her husband's expectations for a wife. By not talking directly about her frustration, Mary does not give John a chance to understand her feelings. Because she does not find her role as fulfilling as she expected and because she and John do not talk about this, she may react in negative ways such as nagging, ridicule, and sexual withdrawal. John may react by withdrawing more, perhaps by coming home later, protesting his "tiredness," and hiding his feelings from Mary, as men have traditionally been taught to do. Once such a cycle is started, breaking it is difficult because of the increasing lack of communication.

In many relationships the partners do conform comfortably to traditional gender role expectations. If both have internalized these roles, there will probably be minimal conflict, but marital growth may also be minimal. Genuine sharing and two-way communication may be minimal too because the traditional masculine role restrains males from sharing their feelings. If partners don't genuinely share their feelings, it becomes difficult for them to make significant changes in their relationship. Without such change stagnation is apt to occur.

If the female has truly internalized the traditional wifely role, she will too often limit herself to a child-centered, home-centered, husband-centered life. She may feel isolated and restricted. She may have to repress other aspects of herself as Mary did to conform to her role as she sees it. Such repression may lead to dissatisfaction and unhappiness. Her husband may find himself married to someone who is virtually dependent on him for the fulfillment of all her needs, for making all decisions, and so on. What begins as an ego trip (the helpless idolizing wife and the strong responsible husband) quickly becomes a heavy burden for many men. Few honest males today would deny that such overwhelming responsibility is difficult and unpleasant, as well as constricting to their own lives (Chafetz, 1974).

The closed marriage locks the husband into a set of roles that may limit his growth as well as the wife's. He may be locked into the role of provider, which tends to give him a different set of commitments than his wife. In our competitive society, where success is measured by individual productivity and achievement, the husband often must manage two marriages: the first to his career and the second to his wife and family. When conflict

Sexual attraction is a strong
motivator.

arises between the two, he may place his job first. This situation may be
difficult for the traditional wife, who is family-centered, to accept. She
may feel cheated and rebuffed by her husband because he appears to
place a lower value on what for her is the most important part of her life.
So long as the economic system is partial to the man, it will be difficult
for him to escape the provider role. In the middle classes the unfortunate
antagonism between male economic success and marital life is difficult to
resolve. One step that can be taken to limit this conflict is for the wife to
participate as much as she can in the husband's life outside the family.
He can encourage this by sharing his career experiences and encouraging
her interest in his work world. This is especially important if the man's
work demands almost total commitment as in medicine or in the ministry.
In such cases, if the wife does not participate, she may risk sharing little
with her husband. Here important factors in marital satisfaction will be
the wife's acceptance of and respect for her husband's commitment, as
well as comfortableness with her own role.

A similar conflict exists for the married career woman. To succeed, she
may have to put even more energy into her career than her husband has
put into his because she must overcome prejudice about career females.
Her husband may become jealous of the attention she gives her career, or
he may resent her encroaching on his domain. Unemployed men who are

dependent on their wife's earnings are likely to suffer feelings of failure and guilt. Some may respond to these feelings with hostility.

Most of our discussion has focused on the middle-class family. The traditional working-class family in many ways has even more rigidly stereotyped marital roles. The wife is expected to be in the home most of the time unless she is working. The man, on the other hand, fulfills much of his social life in his relations with his male friends. Thus sharing activities and joint participation in family matters seem much less important than in middle-class families. However, while shared conjugal roles may have greater potential for mutual satisfaction, they may also lead to conflict, as we have seen. Segregated roles may leave husband and wife with little to say to one another and yet give each a sense of competence and independence. Lillian Rubin (1976) suggests that the lower-economic-class male may be threatened when his wife works because she will contribute a much higher proportion of the family income than would her middle-class counterpart. By maintaining rigid traditional roles in marriage, he is better able to maintain control and a sense of pride and importance. Working wives in these families express satisfaction with their jobs; often their husbands do not. The wife's working broadens her world and opens choices for her. Her husband may feel trapped and oppressed by his work. His choices may be limited by low pay and by the low prestige of his work. Often his own lack of skills entraps him, and he is unable to think about moving ahead economically. He feels as though he is in a dead-end situation and often blames the burdens of his family responsibilities for his unfavorable circumstances.

On the surface the closed traditional marriage may give a couple security and reduce conflict, yet in the long run a marriage based on rigid stereotypical roles will probably create resentments on the part of both partners. The rigidity of the marriage also tends to make the marriage fragile and unable to adjust to new strains and pressures.

An Open Companionship Marriage

An **open marriage** is one in which both members are freer to create their marital roles. By becoming aware of the roles society now expects us to fill and by understanding the role expectations that we have learned, we can begin to choose roles for which we are best suited and that will yield the most satisfactions. Such freedom of choice in itself can cause problems. To make marriage viable, certain tasks must be accomplished. Who will do the necessary tasks that neither partner wants to do? For example, neither partner may want to be tied to a nine-to-five job, yet in most families someone must earn money. The bills must be paid, the children raised, the car fixed, the house cleaned, the in-laws telephoned, and so forth.

In an open marriage the viewpoint is that each mate be committed to the idea of seeking equity in the marriage and to communicating openly any feelings of inequity. This philosophy requires that the couple be willing to experiment and to change if first solutions fail.

Open marriage
A relationship that emphasizes role equality and the freedom for each partner to maximize his or her own potential; may or may not involve extramarital sex

Sally and Jim find, after several years of marriage, that their dissatisfactions with themselves, their marriage, and each other are growing dangerously large. They decide together to take an adult education class called Creative Marriage. The class examines many facets of marriage and family living, first analyzing common marital problem areas and then suggesting creative ways of approaching problems.

Sally and Jim decide that they will rearrange family responsibilities so that each can have more time to do the things he or she wants to do as an individual. They hope that by being freer as individuals, they will also find more joy in doing things together. Because both Sally and Jim work, each felt put upon by the children and the household chores. Sally did most of the chores, but was angry at Jim for doing so little. Even when he did help, he did not do it happily and then Sally felt guilty for not properly fulfilling her role as housewife. Now they make a list of all the things that have to be done each month to keep the family running smoothly. They each pick out the four things they think they are best at. In one case they picked the same thing. Jim thinks he is good at handling money and Sally thinks she is. They decided that, to be equitable, each will handle the money on alternate months. The chores neither wants, they divide between them. They agree to try the new arrangement for two months and then reevaluate.

At the end of the two months, they decided to change how they did the chores neither had wanted to do. Both had felt burdened by the chores even though they did not feel unfairly put upon. They decide that rather than dividing the unwanted chores, each will assume responsibility for all of the chores on alternate weeks. In this way each is completely free of the chores for one week and then totally responsible for them the next week.

To date, this arrangement is working well for Jim and Sally. Each feels freer and less resentful toward the other; at the same time the family is running efficiently.

This kind of exploring can lead to a great deal more satisfaction than limiting oneself to prescribed roles that may or may not fit. However, seeking equity in marriage means that the partners be willing to explore and compromise. Each couple will have to sort responsibilities so as to yield the greatest freedom while maintaining love and intimacy. This is no small task, but the rewards can be large. The Couple's Inventory (see Appendix C) can help you explore your own and your partner's gender role attitudes.

Even with such equity the couple may still be encumbered by the stereotypical gender roles held by the society. For example, Sally and Jim may agree that she is to handle the investments but still find that the banker or stockbroker always asks for him. Be this as it may, each couple can work to realize more freedom within marriage. As one student of changing gender roles suggests:

A society that has gone beyond narrow ideas of femininity and masculinity to the ideal of the self-actualized person offers the widest possible range of choices to its members. It is a society that has reached a level of material comfort that allows it to put resources into human rather than only material development. The real issue is not the liberation of women so much as the liberation of humanity, the establishment of a society where men and women have equal opportunity to fulfill their hopes and dreams unhampered by oppressive and irrelevant sexual stereotypes. (Lindemann, 1976, p. 188)

The idea described here seems at last to be more acceptable to many Americans.

The Movement toward Gender Equality: Some Losses

On the death of the Equal Rights Amendment* in 1982 (and before its resurrection in 1983), *Time* magazine devoted a cover story to the women's liberation movement ("How Long till Equality," 1982). The story began "And yet." Its overriding message was that American women had made large gains in their efforts to achieve equal opportunities with men, "and yet" they hadn't reached equality. "And yet" there had been some losses as well as gains. "And yet" in some areas men may have gained more from the women's movement than have women. The haunting feeling that the women's movement has been successful and yet has failed permeated the story.

More women are working now than ever before, and yet most still hold low-prestige jobs and earn 40 percent less than men. Despite women's economic gains, single-parent families headed by women are more often below the poverty line than other families. There were 301 women state legislators in 1969 and 908 in 1981—"and yet" these 908 legislators represent only 12 percent of the state legislative bodies. In 1982 only 19 of the 435 members of the U.S. House of Representatives were women and only two of the 100 senators. More than one-third of all candidates for M.B.A. degrees are women, and yet only 5 percent of the executives of the top fifty American companies are women. And so the statistics go.

Other writers echo this mixed evaluation of the movement toward gender role equality. Foremost among them is Betty Friedan whose book *The Feminine Mystique* (1963) helped set the women's movement into motion. In 1981, much to the dismay of ardent feminists, Friedan wrote *The Second Stage*, a critique of the movement that pointed out both its failures and

*"Equality of rights under the law shall not be denied or abridged by any state on account of sex. The Congress shall have the power to enforce, by appropriate legislation, the provisions of this article."

The Equal Rights Amendment (ERA) is certainly a simple statement of rights and yet it has provoked ten years of often bitter conflict. On June 30, 1982, the ERA died, three states short of the thirty-eight needed for ratification. Subsequently, it has been reintroduced.

successes but emphasized the need to move in new directions and to abandon some of the dead ends of the first twenty years of women's struggle for equality.

> Though the women's movement has changed all our lives and surpassed our dreams in its magnitude, and our daughters take their own personhood and equality for granted, they—and we [the founders of the movement]—are finding that it is not so easy to *live*, with or without men and children, solely on the basis of the first feminist agenda. I think, in fact, that the women's movement has come about as far as it can in terms of women alone. (pp. 26–27)

Friedan points to the strident militancy of the women's movement that turned off many American housewives who also yearned for greater fulfillment but who loved and cherished their families as well. What did the hue and cry about lesbian rights mean to these women, to their families? How would bra burning make them equal partners with their husbands in the world of work?

"The men still have the power," "ERA has lost so we must fight even harder," "We haven't won yet," suggest some of the feminist leaders. But perhaps winning isn't the point. Perhaps the first stage of the women's movement was too much "we" against "them," women versus men, a power struggle cast only in "win or lose" terms. Polarization was the result rather than cooperation. Gain for me, loss for you, instead of gain for both. Friedan suggests that we have to begin talking about a second stage, a new stage that unlocks us from obsolete power games and the irrelevant sexual battles. Battles that we sometimes may *lose by winning*. Personal liberty and equality cannot be won by one sex at the cost of the other. They can be won for each sex only by both sexes working together in partnership. The women's movement must now become the "women's and men's movement" if a full measure of liberty and equality of sexes is to be realized.

We must make sure that the feminist image does not harden into a confining and defensive radical *feminist mystique* where personal truths are denied and questions unasked because they do not fit the new image of woman.

"I'm suffering from feminist fatigue," writes Lynda Hurst. . . . "After the last dazzle of the [feminist] fireworks, there was deeper darkness. [Women] are perhaps *more enslaved now than [they] have ever been.*" . . .

Don't get me wrong. It's not the women's movement I'm fed up with. . . . It's the "feminist" label—and its paranoid associations—that I've started to resent. I'm developing an urge to run around telling people that I still like raindrops on roses and whiskers on kittens, and that being the local easy-to-bait feminist is getting to be a bore.

I'm tired of having other people (women as well as men) predict my opinion on everything from wedding showers to coed hockey. . . .

I don't want to be stuck today with a feminist label any more than I would have wanted to be known as a "dumb blonde" in the fifties. The libber label limits and shortchanges those who are tagged with it. And the irony is that it emerged from a philosophy that set out to destroy the whole notion of female tagging. (Friedan, 1981, p. 33, italics added)

In discussing the second stage of the movement, Friedan suggests:

The second stage cannot be seen in terms of women alone, our separate personhood or equality with men.

The second stage involves coming to new terms with the family—new terms with love and with work.

The second stage may not even be a women's movement. Men may be at the cutting edge of the second stage.

The second stage has to transcend the battle for equal power in institutions. The second stage will restructure institutions and transform the nature of power itself. (p. 28)

Perhaps the questions of the second stage that must be asked today are more difficult than earlier questions. Perhaps women fear to ask them because the very fact of asking spotlights the failures of the women's movement. Yet the new questions are eminently more important to the successful quest for personal equality and liberty. The very success of the movement is now forcing other questions onto women and indirectly onto men.

- "Has my increased equality really made me freer? Or have men simply let me take on more responsibility while they have reduced their own?"
- "How can I have the career I want, and the kind of marriage I want, and be a good mother?"
- "Can I make it in a man's world, doing it the man's way? What other way is there? But what is it doing to me? Do I want to be like men?"
- "Will the jobs open to me now still be there if I stop to have children?"
- "Does it really work, that business of 'quality, not quantity' of time with my children? How much is enough?"
- "Do men really want an equal woman? Do I really want an equal man?"
- "If I put off having a baby till I'm thirty-eight, and can call my own shots on the job, will I ever have kids?"
- "Am I really freer sexually or have I gained the right to say 'yes' only to have lost the right to say 'no'?"
- "Am I really freer if I have to work to pay my own way?"

● "How can I remain free while at the same time my partner and I make loving, caring, responsible commitments to one another and to our children?"

These and many other questions* must be answered by women seeking broader and more fulfilling roles in American society. Yet, after twenty-five years of thinking *me* first, of *self*-actualization, of *self*-improvement, of *self*-awareness, of Fritz Perls's poster philosophy:

I do my thing, and you do your thing.
I am not in this world to live up to your expectations
And you are not in this world to live up to mine.
You are you, and I am I,
And if by chance, we find each other, it's beautiful.
If not, it can't be helped.

Can Americans, both men and women, make the compromises necessary to build a successful and happy intimate relationship with a person of the opposite sex? Can men and women leave the finding of one another, the building of a family, to chance?

Trying to answer all of these questions would be presumptuous. Yet it is answers to such questions that will determine the future of intimate relationships between the sexes and therefore will direct the kind of families Americans develop in the future. The answers are complex at best. Each change in the feminine role brings about changes in the masculine role. Each change brings some gains and some losses. In some cases losses may outweigh the gains, especially during the transitional period. Certainly to some extent the questions raised by the women's movement have contributed to feelings of discontent and dissatisfaction within women and thereby have caused problems in intimate relationships. The increasing economic freedom of the woman also decreases her dependency on a man. One reaction to this has been for women to leave unsatisfying relationships.

Certainly the gains of equality for women are well discussed; however, the losses engendered by these gains are seldom mentioned. What are some of women's losses? The most important losses seem to revolve around sexuality, childbearing, and childrearing.

Hand in hand with the women's movement came the sexual revolution. Only the latter moved at a faster pace than the former. "The pill" brought reliable contraception to women and allowed couples to separate sexual intercourse from procreation. The gains for women were significant. A woman could reliably plan pregnancies and thereby participate in the work world on different terms. She found new sexual pleasures as the fear of unwanted pregnancy was reduced. She became sexually more equal with men as the double standard broke down. Above all, she gained the freedom to say "yes" to her own sexuality.

Her sexual freedom came so fast that within a few years, young women were embarrassed as much by their virginity as they had been embarrassed in past years by admitting to premarital sexual relations. And the

*Some of these questions are from Friedan, 1981, pp. 34–35.

men loved the change! No more lengthy coaxing, cajoling, necking, and petting. No more necessity to promise love and commitment to get sex. The female who refused sex wasn't "liberated," wasn't "free," wasn't "with it." To say no to sex was to say no to the sexual revolution, to the women's movement, to modern society. To say no was to be old-fashioned. Hence many young women, having won the right to say yes to sex, found that they had lost another right, the right to say no. And the sex they are saying yes to is often sex without love and commitment.

The practical result of the sexual revolution and the women's movement's coming together was to *liberate men, not women*. It was as if men encouraged women's liberation so that they could gain unhindered access to women's bodies. Today's young women complain not about the double standard, or being unfree sexually, or being nonorgasmic. They complain about finding men who care, who will make commitments, who will respect them, who will share responsibility for birth control and pregnancy.

And what of unwanted premarital pregnancy? Men had long been morally obligated to provide for the child they helped to conceive. The shotgun wedding traditionally had served to force the man to provide if he tried to dodge his obligation. Today the term shotgun wedding sounds as if it came from some prehistoric age. Even enlightened parents of the premaritally pregnant girl wouldn't think of such a thing. "They made a mistake. Let's help them get out of it." **Statutory rape** (sexual intercourse with an underage female) is seldom prosecuted and seems as out of date in today's society as does a shotgun wedding. As Deidre English (1981, p. 28) suggests: "If a woman gets pregnant, the man who twenty years ago might have married her may feel today that he is gallant if he splits the cost of an abortion." Legally he is obligated to support the child, yet if he will not acknowledge the child as his, a woman can do little aside from a paternity suit, which is costly, painful, and often unsuccessful.

Statutory rape
Sexual intercourse with an underage female.

Even the expectations for child support are far from the legal norm that support of children must be assumed by both parents. Data from a 1975 poll conducted for the U.S. Commission on the International Women's Year indicated that only 44 percent of divorced mothers were awarded child support, and of those only 47 percent were able to collect it regularly. Another 29 percent of those awarded child support received it only sometimes or rarely. A 1979 U.S. Census Bureau report indicated that of the divorced, separated, remarried and never-married custodial mothers, only about 25 percent actually receive child support (Weitzman, 1981).

Thus for the American man, a combination of the pill, free-choice abortion, the sexual revolution, the women's movement, and unenforced child support laws has freed (liberated?) him from responsibility for his sexual behavior. Of course his failure to assume responsibility may leave him isolated and alienated from what could have been a loving family.

And where have these liberating changes brought the American woman? She has been freed to say yes to her own sexuality. She no longer bargains with her sexuality, offering it in return for commitment. She now assumes full responsibility for her sexual behavior, and she is often solely responsible for birth control and for any pregnancy that may occur.

And the family type that has grown the most rapidly over the past twenty-five years is the single-parent family, of which 90 percent are headed by women. Between 1970 and 1982 all families increased 19 percent, married-couple families increased by 11 percent, and families maintained by a woman with no husband present increased by 71 percent. The two major sources of these single-parent families have been divorce and out-of-wedlock births. During this time period single-parent families maintained by a never-married woman increased 367 percent and those maintained by a divorced woman by 182 percent. Overall, one-parent families now account for 21 percent of all families with children, up from 11 percent in 1970 (U.S. Bureau of the Census, May 1982).

It is true that most single-parent families usually are transitional; that is, most of them become married-couple families in time. However, the greatly increased numbers of such families (even if only temporary) relate directly to the economy, inasmuch as it is the woman-headed, single-parent families that have the most difficult economic struggle. These are the families that disproportionately fall below the poverty line and cost society a disproportionate share of public monies via various welfare programs that help them survive. Their low income is due in part to the differential wage scales that still exist between men and women. Be that as it may, in today's economy a mother alone with her child or children generally has a difficult time economically.

Examined in these terms, the movement toward sexual equality for women appears to have freed the American man, not the American woman. When we look at the American woman today, especially her sexuality and childbearing, a good case can be made that she has never been worse off, never more manipulated by men than she now is. It is little wonder that ERA failed, that some women are looking back to the sanguine days of the housewife happy in her kitchen. But to go back is to give up the real gains. Yet to go blindly forward might mean even greater losses.

It would seem that it is now time to take stock. We need to reevaluate past gender roles so that we can keep those parts that were positive (rather than simply throwing out all traditional roles as bad), and we need to evaluate honestly some of the changes already made so that the beneficial ones may be kept and those that have proved damaging to men and/or women can be rectified.

It is now time for "people liberation." Only when men and women work together to gain equality will it happen. Only when men and women work together in mutual respect and with love and care and commitment to one another will the American family again be strong. This does not mean the American family of old nor some rigidly idealized new family form of the future. It means any family form in which men and women can realize their individual abilities and can come together to rear children who become responsible adults willing to make commitments and assume the responsibilities that make a society great.

Summary

Equity between the sexes, not sameness, is the goal we should be seeking. Yet gaining such a goal is not easy. First, one is born male or female, though this is not always as clear as it may at first seem. Second, one learns from society the roles (masculinity and femininity) that go with one's gender. If a society holds hard and fast stereotypes of gender roles, individuals will find it difficult to achieve equitable roles because variations will be discouraged. For change to occur, individual couples must strive to create equitable roles in their own marriages and at the same time join with others to fight cultural stereotypes. One group working to change stereotypes has been the women's movement. The movement has worked toward the passage of the Equal Rights Amendment (ERA) to end discrimination by sex. Women have also been moving slowly into what have been traditional male fields, and more women than ever, married and unmarried, are now working.

Two important stumbling blocks to people liberation insofar as gender roles are concerned are the economic deprivation of women and laws that discriminate between the sexes. Until women are able to earn the same amount as men for the same work, it will be difficult for couples to change the traditional roles of "man the provider" and "woman the homemaker," if they wish to change them. In addition, many kinds of discrimination are built into our system of laws. For example, women in the past have not been able to establish their own credit if married, though this law has recently been changed. Men are discriminated against by our criminal laws and by the armed forces drafting system.

Open marriage means that a couple is free to establish the most free and satisfying relationship they can. It means that they are free to establish gender roles that best fit them. It also means freedom of choice within the marriage. Some may choose older, traditional roles. In such traditional marriages the roles may be rigid, yet tasks necessary to maintain the marriage are clearly spelled out and each partner knows his or her responsibilities. A specific role assignment may be more comfortable for some inasmuch as it yields efficiency and security. Some may choose to radically alter traditional roles into new but equally rigid roles. Others may opt periodically to change roles and to maintain an always flexible system. The concept of open marriage does not dictate the kind of relationship a couple will have. What it does is to free couples to explore and feel encouraged to make their own choices. One of the basic suppositions on which this book is based, as you'll remember from Chapter 1, is: A free and creative society is one that offers many structural forms by which family functions may be fulfilled. The best marital roles are those that best fit you.

As positive as the movement toward gender equality has been, this movement has also caused people, especially women to suffer some losses. For women these losses center around sexuality, pregnancy, and childrearing. For both sexes there have been losses of commitment, security, and stability within intimate relationships. It is hoped that such losses are transitional. As female liberation moves on to a "second" stage, such losses will disappear as the sexes cooperate and work together to improve and enhance commitment, caring, and loving within the man/woman relationship.

SCENES FROM MARRIAGE

A Popular Look at How the Sexes Differ*

Captain to Laura: *"If it's true we are descended from the ape, it must have been from two different species. There's no likeness between us, is there?"*
The Father, by August Strindberg

So it has begun to seem, and not only in the musings of a misogynist Swedish playwright. Research on the structure of the brain, on the effects of hormones, and in animal behavior, child psychology and anthropology is providing new scientific underpinnings for what August Strindberg and his ilk viscerally guessed: men and women *are* different. They show obvious dissimilarities, of course, in size, anatomy and sexual function. But scientists now believe that they are unlike in more fundamental ways. Men and women seem to *experience* the world differently, not merely because of the ways they were brought up in it, but because they feel it with a different sensitivity of touch, hear it with different aural responses, puzzle out its problems with different cells in their brains.

Hormones seem to be the key to the difference—and an emerging body of evidence suggests that they do far more than trigger the external sexual characteristics of males and females. They actually "masculinize" or "feminize" the brain itself. By looking closely at the neurochemical processes involved, investigators are finding biological explanations for why women might think intuitively, why men seem better at problem-solving, why boys play rougher than girls.

Whether these physiological differences destine men and women for separate roles in society is a different and far more delicate question. The particular way male brains are organized may orient them toward visual-spatial perception, explaining—perhaps—why they are superior at math. Women's brains may make them more verbally disposed, explaining—possibly—why they seem better at languages. Males of most species appear to be hormonally primed for aggression, pointing—it may be—to the long evolutionary record of male dominance over women.

But few of these presumed differences go unchallenged. And whether they imply anything more—about leadership capacities, for example, or that men are biologically suited for the workplace and women for the hearth—is another part of the thicket. The notion that biology is destiny is anathema to feminists and to many male researchers as well. It is their position that sexual stereotyping, reinforced by a male-dominated culture, has more bearing on gender behavior than do hormones.

. . .

The new research has thus revived, in all its old intensity, the wrangle over whether "nature" or "nurture" plays the greater part in behavior. At the same time, it has become a fresh battle ground for feminism, a continuation of the sex war by other means. Spurred by the women's movement, large numbers of female scientists have moved into an area of inquiry once largely populated by men and by male ideas of gender roles. Both male and female investigators have been challenging male-fostered notions of female passivity and submissiveness. But because some are also acknowledging the role of biology, they are catching flak from

*Source: *Newsweek*, "Just How the Sexes Differ," May 18, 1981, pp. 72–83.

hard-core feminists, who fear such findings will be used—as they have been in the past—to deny women equal rights.

. . .

The research comes under indictment on another count: since possibilities for experimentation with humans are limited, it leans heavily on animal studies. Complains Stanford psychologist Eleanor Maccoby, who reviewed the literature on sex differences: "People look at this and say it is all biological. They generalize wildly from a little monkey research." But most researchers are cautious about making the leap from lower primates to Homo sapiens. Human evolution involved a huge increase in brain flexibility that gave rise to human culture. And over the long course of that evolution, humans have become much less the creatures of their hormones than are rats or rhesus monkeys.

Even so, the researchers are providing some fascinating new glimpses into the biology of behavior. Among their odd assortment of laboratory subjects are male canaries whose song repertoire is imprinted, like a player-piano roll, in a cluster of brain cells; virginal female rats that go through the motions of nursing when confronted with rat pups, and young girls who turn "tomboyish" because they were exposed to male hormones before birth.

. . .

To see if hormones play a role in human behavior, John Money of Johns Hopkins University and Anke Ehrhardt of Columbia studied one of nature's own experiments—children exposed to abnormally high levels of androgens (male hormones) before birth because of adrenal-gland mal-

functions. Among other effects discovered, the researchers at Johns Hopkins found that girls born with this disorder exhibited distinctly "tomboyish" behavior, seldom played with dolls and began dating at a later age than other girls.

The much-cited Money-Ehrhardt research has provided a classic context for the nature-nurture debate. Some scientists maintain that the tomboyism was a clear result of the hormone exposure, and they bolster their argument by noting the scores of animal experiments that demonstrate similar effects. But others criticize the study for failing to emphasize that girls with congenital adrenal hyperplasia do not *look* like normal girls at birth; they often require corrective surgery to restore normal female genitals. Thus, the argument goes, they may be treated differently as they grow up, and their behavior could be more the result of an abnormal environment than of abnormal blood chemistry.

The debate rages back and forth. But at least one scientist who has been on both sides, Rutgers psycho-endocrinologist June Reinisch, recently found evidence to buttress the hormonal argument. Over a period of five years Reinisch studied 25 boys and girls born to women who had taken synthetic progestin (a type of androgen) to prevent miscarriages. When the scientist compared them with their unexposed siblings by giving each child a standard aggression test, she found significant differences between the groups. Progestin-exposed males scored twice as high in physical aggression as their normal brothers; twelve of seventeen females scored higher than their unexposed sisters. "This result was

so striking," says Reinisch, "that I sat on the data for a year before publishing."

Reinisch has by no means renounced her belief in the importance of environment. Like many of her colleagues, she suspects that hormones act to "flavor" an individual for one kind of gender behavior or another. But how the individual is brought up is still an important factor. As Robert Goy explains, "It looks as though what the hormone is doing is predisposing the animal to learn a particular social role. It isn't insisting that it learn that role; it's just making it easier. The hormone doesn't prevent behavior from being modified by environmental and social conditions."

As to how the initial "flavor" comes about, researchers now believe that hormones change the very structure of the brain. Some variations in the brains of males and females have been observed in animals. They were found mainly in the hypothalamus and pre-optic regions, which are closely connected to the reproductive functions. In those areas males are generally found to have more and larger "neurons"— nerve cells and their connecting processes. Experiments conducted by Dominique Toran-Allerand of Columbia University using cultures of brain cells from newborn mice have shown that neuronal development can be stimulated by hormones, and this suggests a key to the sexual mystery.

. . .

Many scientists are now convinced that hormones "imprint" sexuality on the brains of a large number of animal species by changing the nerve-cell structure. "Even the way dogs urinate— that's a function that is sex different and is determined by hormones," says Roger Gorski, a UCLA neuro-endocrinologist who has done important experiments with animal brains.

But what about humans? So far, no one has observed structural differences between the brains of males and females in any species more sophisticated than rats. In humans, the best evidence is indirect. For years researchers have known that men's and women's mental functions are organized somewhat differently. Men appear to have more "laterality"—that is, their functions are separately controlled by the left or right hemisphere of the brain, while women's seem diffused through both hemispheres. The first clues to this intriguing disparity came from victims of brain damage. Doctors noticed that male patients were much likelier than females to suffer speech impairment after damage to the left hemisphere and loss of such nonverbal functions as visual-spatial ability when the right hemisphere was damaged. Women showed less functional loss, regardless of the hemisphere involved. Some researchers believe this is because women's brain activity is duplicated in both hemispheres. Women usually mature earlier than men, which means that their hemispheric processes may have less time to draw apart. They retain more nerve-transmission mechanisms in the connective tissue between the two hemispheres (the corpus callosum) and can thus call either or both sides of the brain into play on a given task.

On the whole, women appear to be more dominated by the left, or verbal, hemisphere and men by the right, or visual, side. Researchers McGuinness and Pri-

bram speculate that men generally do better in activities where the two hemispheres don't compete with, and thus hamper, each other, while women may be better able to coordinate the efforts of both hemispheres. This might explain why women seem to think "globally," or intuitively and men concentrate more effectively on specific problem-solving.

A few enterprising researchers have tried to find a direct connection between hormones and human-brain organization. UCLA's Melissa Hines studied 16 pairs of sisters, of whom one in each pair had been prenatally exposed to DES (diethylstilbestrol), a synthetic hormone widely administered to pregnant women during the 1950s to prevent miscarriages. Using audiovisual tests, Hines found what appeared to be striking differences between the exposed and unexposed sisters.

First, Hines played separate nonsense syllables into the women's right and left ears. Normally, the researcher explains, most people—but especially males—report more accurately what they hear with the right ear. In her tests, the hormone-exposed women picked the correct syllable heard with the right ear 20 per cent more often than their unexposed sisters. A test of their right and left visual fields produced comparable results. The implication was that the women's brains had been masculinized. "It is compelling evidence that prenatal hormones influence human behavior due to changes in brain organizations," says Hines. Differences in brain organization may have practical implications for education and medicine. Some researchers believe that teaching methods should take note of right-left brain differences, though past

attempts at such specialized teaching have been ineffective. Other scientists predict clinical benefits. It is useful to know, for example, that females who are brain-damaged at birth will cope with the defects better than males.

. . .

Many researchers contend that a child's awareness of gender is more decisive than biology in shaping sexual differences. "The real problem for determining what influences development in men and women is that they are called boys and girls from the day they are born," says biologist Lewontin. He cites the classic "blue, pink, yellow" experiments. When a group of observers was asked to describe newborn infants dressed in blue diapers, they were characterized as "very active." The same babies dressed in pink diapers evoked descriptions of gentleness. When the babies were wearing yellow, says Lewontin, observers "really got upset. They started to peek inside their diapers to see their sex."

It is clear that sex differences are not set in stone. The relationship between hormones and behavior, in fact, is far more intricate than was suspected until recently. There is growing evidence that it is part of a two-way system of cause-and-effect—what Lewontin calls "a complicated feedback loop between thought and action." Studies show that testosterone levels drop in male rhesus monkeys after they suffer a social setback and surge up when they experience a triumph. Other experiments indicate that emotional stress can change hormonal patterns in pregnant females, which in turn may affect the structure of the fetal brain.

By processes still not understood, biology seems susceptible to social stimuli. Ethel Tobach of New York's American Museum of Natural History cites experiments in which a virgin female rat is presented with a five-day-old rat pup. At first, her response is vague, says Tobach. "But by continuing to present the pup, you can get her to start huddling over it and assuming the nursing posture. How did that come about? There's obviously some biochemical factor that changes. . . . When you have the olfactory, visual, auditory, tactile input of a five-day-old pup all those days, it can change the blood chemistry."

A more enigmatic example, says Tobach, is found in coral-reef fish: "About six species typically form a group of female fish with a male on the outside. If something happens to remove the male, the largest female becomes a functional male, able to produce sperm and impregnate females. It has been done in the lab as well as observed in the natural habitat."

The human parallels are limited. No one expects men or women to undergo spontaneous sex changes, and millennia of biological evolution aren't going to be undone by a century of social change. But it is now widely recognized that, for people as well as animals, biology and culture continually interact. The differences between men and women have been narrowing over evolutionary time, and in recent decades the gap has closed further.

Perhaps the most arresting implication of the research up to now is not that there are undeniable differences between males and females, but that their differences are so small, relative to the possibilities open to them. Human behavior exhibits a plasticity that has enabled men and women to cope with cultural and environmental extremes and has made them—by some measures—the most successful species in history.

David Gelman with John Carey and Eric Gelman in New York, Phyllis Malamud in Boston, Donna Foote in Chicago, Gerald C. Lubenow in San Francisco and Joe Contreras in Los Angeles.

CHAPTER 7

THE FAMILY AS
AN ECONOMIC SYSTEM

CONTENTS

7

Gross national product (GNP)
Total value of a nation's annual output of goods and services

Americans have more money per person than most people on earth. The **gross national product (GNP)** divided by the total population of men, women, and children gives each American more than $10,630 per year (GNP figures based on the year 1981). Table 7-1 indicates how this income compares with other nations'.

Americans also spend more than any other people. Most money is spent by family units to support family members. The family in modern America is the basic economic unit of the society in that it is the major *consumption* unit. In the early years of our country the family was also the major production unit. Ninety percent of the population once worked in agriculture on family-owned farms. Over the years, however, most farm workers became factory workers. Thus today's average family is not directly involved in economic production. Most families support themselves by having one or more of their members work for outside employers. The 1980 census reported a median family (household) income of $16,830, up almost 100 percent from 1969.

As a consuming unit the family exerts great economic influence. A couple anticipating marriage and children is also anticipating separate housing from their parents. This means a refrigerator, stove, furniture, dishes, television, and so on. And how will this new family acquire all of these items? Probably by the use of credit, perhaps not an American invention but certainly an American way of life. How much do Americans owe in installment debt? Approximately $336 billion, or about $1400 per person for outstanding personal credit as of November 1982. About 30 percent of this is accounted for by indebtedness for automobiles ("Auto Loans . . .," 1983).

"Buy now, pay later!" "Why wait? Only $5 per week." These and many more are the economic slogans of modern American society. The extension of credit to the general population has produced a material standard of living the likes of which the world has never seen. We may, on the promise of future payment, acquire and use almost anything that we desire. Not only may we acquire material goods, we may also travel, educate ourselves, and use many services such as medical and dental care, all without

TABLE 7-1 1981 Per Capita Income for the Top Ten and Lowest Ten Countries (Using 1979 Dollar Values)

TOP TEN	DOLLARS PER PERSON	LOWEST TEN	DOLLARS PER PERSON
Kuwait	$17,100	Bhutan	$ 80
Switzerland	13,920	Bangladesh	90
Sweden	11,930	Chad	110
Denmark	11,900	Ethiopia	130
West Germany	11,730	Nepal	130
Belgium	10,920	Mali	140
Norway	10,700	Burma	160
United States	10,630	Afghanistan	170
Netherlands	10,230	Burundi	180
France	9,950	India	190

immediate monetary payment. If the credit system were suddenly ended, the degree to which it supports the economy would become glaringly clear. Traffic congestion would end as the majority of autos would disappear from the roads. Many buildings, both business and residential, would become empty lots or smaller, shabbier versions. Thousands of televisions would disappear from living rooms. A vast amount of furniture would also vanish from our homes. If debtor prisons were reestablished at the same time, practically the entire population would be incarcerated!

Any discussion of marriage must include an analysis of the part that finances will play in the relationship. In the past it was widely believed that money mattered little to the general success of a marriage. Many of the classic studies indicated little if any relationship between amount of money and marital success. Unfortunately these results led many later writers to exclude financial adjustment as a significant influence on the general marital relationship. This was an error. Although the actual amount of money earned by a family may not relate to marital success, each partner's attitude toward money and finance is often crucial.

Money is involved in everything we do, yet few people put much effort into studying personal finance, money management, investment, and budgeting. Most Americans appear more willing to discuss their sex lives than their monetary situation. Asking a person what he or she earns or what something has cost is often considered an affront or at the least an invasion of privacy. But the recent unusual economic climate, a frightening mixture of inflation and recession, has brought economics more strongly into the spotlight than at any time since the Great Depression of the 1930s. It has been a period of extreme economic uncertainty. After several years of high inflation (1973–74 and 1978–81), inflation dropped dramatically in 1982 and 1983. As inflation dropped, the general economic trend was downward, and by September 1982 the rate of unemployment had moved to 10 percent even though more people were employed than ever before. Interest rates, after being at record highs through most of 1980 and 1981, declined significantly in 1982, while the stock market rallied to reach historic highs in late 1982 and early 1983. The 1981 Economic Recovery Tax Act (ERTA) passed by Congress was the largest tax cut ever enacted. But 1982 saw government deficits soaring, and Congress responded by passing the Tax Equity and Fiscal Responsibility Act of 1982 which tightened taxation procedures, partly undoing some of the benefits of ERTA. Throughout all of these economic changes, the future of Social Security retirement benefits was being questioned because increased benefits and rising numbers of claimants were placing severe burdens on the system. Then, in 1983–1984, the economy stabilized and accelerated. Interest rates and unemployment dropped, while inflation remained low.

Such economic uncertainties make it imperative that individuals carefully plan their economic destiny. Those who do not are doomed to lose control of their economic lives. Knowing how to spend, save, borrow, and invest are important ingredients in personal and family happiness.

However, even in good economic times, married couples often quarrel over money. Essentially, quarrels over money revolve around allocation of

INSET 7-1

Comparison of Attitudes toward Money

Answer the following questions* without discussing them with your partner. Then have your partner answer them. If you answer the questions differently, it may indicate points of attitudinal differences and possible conflict. You should each discuss the reasoning behind your answer and how your two positions can be reconciled.

1. Are you comfortable living without a steady income?

*Some of these questions are from Landis, 1970, p. 509.

2. Did your parents have a steady income?

3. Do you consider yourself to come from an economically poor, average, or wealthy background?

4. Do you think that saving is of value in America's inflationary economy?

5. Do you have a savings account? Do you contribute to it regularly?

6. In the past have you postponed buying things until you had saved the money for them, or did you buy immediately, if possible, when you desired something?

7. In the past have you often bought on installment?

8. Do you have credit cards? How many? Do you use them regularly?

9. Do you have money left over at the end of your regular pay period?

10. Do you brag about making a really good buy or finding a real bargain?

11. If it were possible to save $100 a month, what would you do with the money?

12. Possible answers to question 11 are listed below. Rank them in order of importance using 1 for what you would most likely do with the $100 and 10 for what you are least likely to do:

   a. Save it for a rainy day.

   b. Save it so you can buy something for cash rather than on credit.

   c. Invest it.

   d. Use it for recreation.

   e. Use it for payments for a new car.

   f. Use it for travel and adventure.

   g. Use it to buy a home or property.

   h. Use it to improve your present living place.

   i. Divide it in half and let each spouse spend it as he or she chooses.

   j. Use it for an attractive wardrobe, eating out, and entertaining.

resources and control of the allocation. What should we buy? When should we buy? Who should buy? Who should make the spending decisions? Such questions become particularly troublesome if the partners have divergent attitudes about money. For example, consider a person who comes from a background of thrift and practicality and who takes pleasure in making a good buy. Such a person will be excited about buying a used car at wholesale rather than at retail price and will probably brag about the purchase. Any minor problems with the car will not be upsetting because of the value of the "good buy." This person's partner, however, comes from a luxurious environment that places value on achieving precisely what you want and that measures success by an economic standard.

The partner sees a new car, of the appropriate model, as the proper vehicle to buy. A used car, especially a "steal," will be considered a mark of poor taste and economic failure. The married life of such a pair potentially will be filled with conflict over money matters.

Why a "Slavery" System?

Credit buying has allowed the average American a higher standard of living than was ever dreamed possible. It has given Americans the means for a healthier, more fulfilling life about which, in centuries past, one could only dream. Despite these positive results, the system can boomerang and place people in a slavery system that traps them subtly but with psychological cost. This entrapment and loss of freedom usually comes from ignorance of the system and blind acceptance of persuasive and seductive advertising. A clear understanding of economics and the relationship of debt to personal freedom enables people to make the system work for instead of against them.

Credit buying
Purchasing goods by making payments for them over a period of time

"Slavery" appears to be a strange term to use to describe the economic system of one of the freest countries on earth. Yet credit and debt are directly opposed to personal freedom. To contract to pay for a new automobile over a period of thirty-six months, for example, involves gaining the use of the automobile but losing a degree of personal freedom. Regardless of circumstances or what you do with the car, you have promised and legally made yourself responsible to pay a certain amount each month for the next three years. If at the end of one year, you wish to take a lower paying but more satisfying job, or to return to school to improve skills, you would be unable to do so unless you make adequate arrangements to continue payments. If you decide to return the car, this does not cancel the debt. Even if the credit company's policies allow you credit for the money it receives when the car is sold, the chances are that you will still owe because during the first year or two the car depreciates in value faster than the debt is reduced. Although the remaining debt may be small, it still exists, and so does your obligation.

Any debt curtails a certain amount of personal freedom. If you cannot at least partially resist the temptations of credit buying, you can become so obligated as to lose almost all freedom. This modern economic slavery is far more seductive than historical slavery systems based on power. In real slavery a person knows who the enemy is and where to direct hostility engendered by loss of freedom. But in the American economic system it is the individual who has placed himself or herself in the slavery of debt. There is no one but oneself to blame for the predicament. No one is forced to keep buying "goodies" on "easy" installments. Unfortunately, too many small, easy payments can add to heavy sums — often too heavy for the marriage to bear.

Joe and Mary — Slow Drowning in a Sea of Debt

Let's now take a closer look at a hypothetical, newly married young couple and follow them through their first few years of confrontation with the American economic system. This analysis will make clear the slow and often insidious nature of the loss of freedom and eventual economic entrapment suffered by so many families. For many young couples marriage actually means a drastic reduction in their standard of living. Accustomed to living at home, to sharing their parents' standard of living (usually created by twenty years of their parents' earnings), the newlyweds are cast economically on their own. Beginning jobs may be scarce, and pay is low compared with the parents' earnings. If the newlyweds don't understand this and attempt to maintain the parental standard in their new marriage, they are likely to be entrapped in the economic slavery system.

When Did Joe's Entrapment Begin?

Joe's actual entrapment began before his marriage. Joe is shorter than most of the other boys in high school and finds he is not as popular with girls as some of his taller friends. Like most of his friends, he has always been interested in automobiles. He figures that if he had a good car, he would probably be more popular. He also notes that his parents often judge their friends by the cars they drive. Thus he believes that his car should be one of the better ones. He has a job as a stockboy at a local supermarket, and because he lives at home and doesn't have any living expenses, he can use his earnings to pay for the car. It seems so simple. His parents don't object to his buying a car but make it clear that they are in no financial position to help him. So he contracts to pay $200 a month for the next three years. Of course, the $200 is not his only expense now — he has all the expenses of an automobile: tax, license, insurance, gas, upkeep, and, quite likely, modifications (lowering it, turbocharging it, adding mag wheels, a tape deck, or whatever else is popular). (See p. 238 for car costs.)

The automobile is one of the few products in the American inflationary economy that usually loses money.* But the practical reason for the auto, transportation, is rarely considered by young men. For many the car is much more than this. It is an extension of one's ego. (In general the relationship between the strength of ego and the cost of the car is inverse. That is, the weaker the boy's ego, the more important the car.) It is one's means to prestige and status. It gives one a feeling of power because one can make the car do whatever one wants. Many adolescent boys drive hundreds of aimless miles per week. Car theft statistics demonstrate dramatically the importance of the auto to the young American male. FBI national figures show a heavy preponderance of male youth involved in car theft.

*A few cars become classics and, if well maintained, may actually appreciate in value.

Joe soon attracts a wonderful girl with his new symbol. Although she first noticed him because of his new car, Mary finds him to be a nice person, and they are soon going steady. The pressures of the American dating game build up, and they consider themselves deeply in love. Joe is near the end of his senior year in high school and will soon be able to work full time. If he stays at the supermarket and becomes a checker, he will be earning $1000 to $1800 a month. This seems like a fortune compared with the $300 he now receives as part-time help. Both Joe and Mary have also always heard that two can live as cheaply as one — another of the great modern myths.

Setting Up Their New Apartment

Joe and Mary marry and set up housekeeping. At first they are the envy of their friends. They are now independent, out from under parental domination, and can participate in many things that were previously taboo. Soon Joe finds that his salary isn't going as far as he anticipated. Somehow rent, food, and basic necessities are eating huge chunks of his new, large salary. Before his marriage he thought he would have enough to update his car a bit, go on some trips, and model their apartment after those seen in *Playboy*. But now Mary says they need a new washing machine, that this is something all young married couples have to have. When they look at washing machines, the salesperson convinces them that they should buy the deluxe model with five washing speeds and three water temperatures. Of course, it's $70 more than the ordinary machine, but then, according to the salesperson, it's far superior and the payments are the same, just stretched a little longer. Of course, the salesperson doesn't tell them that the motor and all basic parts are the same in both models. But the salesperson does add that there's a special this week on the matching dryer, which they can get for $30 less, with free installation. It's a great opportunity and would only add $2 more per week. Joe is beginning to feel a little nervous about adding these payments to the $200 he is still paying on the car, but Mary does seem quite happy, and he supposes the machines will make life easier for both of them. He still wishes he had his car fixed up though.

Gradually Joe will find that his salary is claimed before he receives it — the couple will reach the point where they no longer have the freedom of decision over their income. One problem is that they are starting off with large purchases, some of which they don't need. A washer and dryer are unnecessary items for a young couple without children.

Credit to Cover Credit

A year after their marriage, their first child is born — with concomitant hospital, doctor, and general care bills. A surprising number of salespersons come knocking at their door to help them get their youngster started off right. First there are disposable diapers, a must for the modern mother.

Yearly Salary Needed by a Family of Four to Maintain Three Different Standards of Living Levels

The typical urban family of four (a thirty-eight-year-old working husband, a non-working wife, a thirteen-year-old son, and an eight-year-old daughter) needed to gross $25,407 in 1981, 9.8 percent more than the year before, to maintain what the government considers a moderate standard of living. The family would have to make $15,323 to maintain a "lower-level" standard of living, and $38,060 to maintain a "higher-level" standard of living.

These annual income levels represent the estimated cost of goods and services and tax obligations that are used to portray three relative stan-

dards of living. The family at each level would have had to earn between $2000 and $8000 more dollars in 1981 than they did in 1980 to maintain their relative level. The income levels are based on cost surveys conducted in metropolitan areas around the country. Seek out the city nearest your home to get an idea of the income needed for your area. Note that there are considerable differences across the country.

From most expensive to least expensive, the following are the rankings of the twenty-five metropolitan areas, with expenses for a four-person family in the fall of 1981:

LOWER		INTERMEDIATE		HIGH	
Anchorage	$22,939	Honolulu	$31,893	Honolulu	$50,317
Honolulu	20,319	Anchorage	31,890	New York	47,230
Seattle	17,124	New York	29,540	Anchorage	45,119
S.F./Oakland	17,080	Boston	29,213	Boston	44,821
Washington	16,702	Washington	27,352	Washington	41,137
Los Angeles	16,618	S.F./Oakland	27,082	S.F./Oakland	40,906
Boston	16,402	Milwaukee	26,875	Milwaukee	39,709
New York	15,705	Philadelphia	26,567	Philadelphia	39,560
San Diego	15,690	Buffalo	26,473	Buffalo	38,990
Philadelphia	15,593	Seattle	25,881	Minneapolis	38,698
Chicago	15,587	Minneapolis	25,799	Los Angeles	38,516
Milwaukee	15,505	Cleveland	25,598	Baltimore	38,090
Baltimore	15,315	Cincinnati	25,475	San Diego	37,722
Cleveland	15,176	Chicago	25,358	Detroit	37,721
Minneapolis	15,118	Detroit	25,208	Cleveland	37,487
Pittsburgh	15,116	Baltimore	25,114	Seattle	37,396
St. Louis	15,112	Los Angeles	25,025	Chicago	37,368
Cincinnati	15,110	Denver	24,820	Kansas City	36,988
Detroit	15,107	San Diego	24,776	Denver	36,979
Denver	15,093	Pittsburgh	24,717	Pittsburgh	36,714
Kansas City	14,925	Kansas City	24,528	Cincinnati	36,599
Houston	14,810	St. Louis	24,498	St. Louis	35,965
Buffalo	14,710	Houston	23,607	Houston	34,728
Atlanta	14,419	Atlanta	23,273	Atlanta	34,623
Dallas	14,392	Dallas	22,678	Dallas	33,769

Source: U.S. Department of Labor, 1981, as reported in the *San Francisco Chronicle*, April 17, 1982.

Then there is a photographer who will take regular pictures of the child so they will have a permanent record of the child's growth. There are toys that will help increase their child's intellectual growth. And, of course, they now need a set of encyclopedias.

One month Joe discovers that his paycheck doesn't quite cover their monthly costs. At first they panic, but then Mary remembers an ad she saw that says all their debts can be wiped out by combining them into one large package loan. In fact, the ad said, "Borrow enough money to get completely out of debt." At the time it didn't seem to make sense, but now it does. With a sigh of relief they go to the finance company and soon have things financially under control again. The discount interest rate is 14 percent, but they don't really care as long as they can meet the payments.

Rather than continue Joe's story, suffice it to say that five years after his marriage, Joe is in bankruptcy court. No, he hadn't gambled on a big investment speculation; he had slowly drowned in a rising sea of debt.

Credit, Borrowing, and Installment Buying

People borrow for two basic reasons: to buy consumer goods and to invest in tangible assets.

Consumer debt is high-priced money because it is used for consumable goods such as cars, furniture, and clothing whose value diminishes with time. **Discount interest** is usually charged for consumer debt. This kind of interest is charged on the total amount of the loan for the entire time period.

Investment debt, or real-property debt, is lower-priced money because it is used for tangible assets such as real estate or businesses whose value is permanent. If for some reason the debt is not paid, the creditor may assume ownership of the asset and sell it to regain the loaned money. **Simple interest** is charged for investment debt. This kind of interest is charged only on the unpaid balance of the loan.

Discount interest
Interest paid on the full amount initially borrowed even though some of the loan is repaid each month

Simple interest
Interest paid only on the unpaid balance of a loan

Examples of Actual Interest Costs

Discount Interest*

If you borrow $1000 for three years at 10 percent interest per year, you must pay $100 per year interest for the use of the money (0.10 × $1000 = $100). Each month you will pay $8.33 interest ($100 ÷ 12 months = $8.33). In addition, you will pay back the principal of $1000 in thirty-six equal monthly installments so that it is all paid off at the end of the three years. The monthly principal payment will be $27.77 ($1000 ÷ 36 = $27.77). Thus your total monthly payment is $36.10, or your interest plus your principal payment ($8.33 + $27.77 = $36.10).

Although you will pay $100 interest each year on your $1000 loan, the fact is that you do not actually have use of the full $1000 for the entire three years. Each month you pay back $27.77 of the loan. As the table shows, at the end of a month (after one payment), you only owe $972.23 ($1000 minus your principal payment of $27.77 = $972.23) of your $1000 loan. Each month what you actually owe (or retain) on the loan is reduced

*Interest rates now vary so rapidly that the rates used in the examples may or may not accurately reflect rates at the time you are reading the text. The general principles hold, however.

TABLE 7-2   Comparative Costs of Consumer Credit

LENDERS	TYPE OF LOAN	ANNUAL PERCENTAGE RATE[1]	REMARKS
Banks	Personal loans (consumer goods) Real-property loans General loans	10–18[2]	60% of all car loans, 30% of other consumer-good loans; real-property loans have lower interest rates because property retains value, which may cover defaulted loans.
Credit cards	Personal loans Cash loans	20[2]	Used as convenience instead of cash; credit is approved for the card rather than individual purchase; no interest charged if bills are paid in full each month; cash in varying amounts, depending on individual's credit rating, may also be borrowed against.
Credit unions	Personal loans Real-property loans	9–15	Voluntary organizations in which members invest their own money and from which they may borrow.
Finance companies	Personal loans Real-property loans	12–40	Direct loans to consumers; also buy installment credit from retailers and collect rest of debt so that retailers can get cash when they need it.
Savings and loan companies	Real-property loans	10–18[2]	Low interest rates because real property has value that may cover defaulted loans.

[1]Interest rates vary because of pressures of inflation and recession.
[2]If the institution charges interest on the *face amount* of the loan over the entire period of the loan, double the listed interest rate to estimate the actual interest rate.

by your principal payment until at the end of the three years (thirty-six payments) your loan is paid off.

		PAYMENTS			
	ORIGINAL LOAN	IINTEREST PAYMENT	PRINCIPAL PAYMENT	TOTAL PER MONTH	BALANCE
First month	$1000	$8.33	$27.77	$36.10	$972.23
Second month		8.33	27.77	36.10	944.56
Third month		8.33	27.77	36.10	916.79

With discount interest the stated interest (10 percent in this case) is paid each year of the loan even though with each payment a portion of the loan has been paid back. The actual interest rate in such a case can be estimated by doubling the stated interest rate (in this case it would be 20 percent). This is done because, on the average, you don't really have the full amount of the loan ($1000) to use. You actually have the full $1000 to use only before you make your first payment. After your first payment, you have only $972.23, as the table shows. After the second payment, you have only $944.56 left, and by the thirty-sixth or last payment you have only $27.77 left. By adding up the amount of loan you actually still have after each payment and dividing by the length of the loan (in this case thirty-six months), you will find that you only have an average of $500 to use. Yet you pay $100 per year interest. This means your actual interest on this loan is 20 percent ($100 interest ÷ $500 average cash available from loan = 20 percent).

Actually, all you have to remember is that on a discount interest loan, you pay interest on the full amount of the loan each year even though you have paid back part of the loan. Such interest is usually figured for the full term of the loan and is added to the face amount of the loan at the time you receive the loan. Thus in our example you would sign for a $1300 debt ($1000 principal + $300 interest = $1300) but only receive $1000. The rule of thumb to figure the actual interest rate on this type of loan is simply to double the stated interest rate. In actuality when figured accurately, the interest rate will exceed slightly the doubled figure.

Credit Card Use

If you maintain a balance on your credit card rather than paying promptly at the end of each month, you are charged interest at 1.65 percent per month, or 19.8 percent per year. In addition there is a one-time transaction charge of 2 percent of each cash advance and 1 percent of each loan advance.

If you are short of money and use your credit card to borrow $100 in cash during your vacation and take three months to pay it back, the loan will cost you $2.00 for the transaction and $1.65 per month interest, or a total of $6.95 for the use of $100 for three months.

Home Loans

If you decide to buy a $100,000 home,* you may receive a loan of $80,000 for thirty years at 13 percent simple interest (interest rates for home loans have varied dramatically in the past few years from lows of 9 percent to highs of 18 percent). Simple interest is charged only on the principal balance. For example, to pay off your $80,000 loan and interest in thirty years, your payments will be $885 per month. Actually, $867 of your first payment will be for interest and $18 will be credited against the principal. Thus for your second payment you will owe interest on a principal of $79,982. Of your second payment $866.50 will be for interest and $18.50 will apply to the principal. Each month you will pay less interest and more against principal. However, at the end of thirty years, while you have paid off the $80,000 loan, you will also have paid about $238,600 in interest! (At present you can deduct interest charges from your taxable income, which somewhat reduces the actual amount of money that interest costs you.)

Table 7-3 shows what monthly payments would be at different rates of interest on a $100,000 house when $20,000 is put down ($80,000 owed) or $50,000 is put down ($50,000 owed).

Because the actual amount of interest charged in credit transactions was often difficult to determine, the Truth in Lending Law was passed in

*Home prices vary greatly from area to area (see p. 255).

TABLE 7-3   Thirty-Year Mortgage on a $100,000 House

	EXAMPLE A	EXAMPLE B
Down payment	$20,000	$50,000
Amount borrowed	80,000	50,000
INTEREST RATE	MONTHLY PAYMENTS	
9%	$ 644	$402
10	702	439
11	762	476
12	823	514
13	885	553
14	948	592
15	1012	632

July 1969. Under the terms of this law, lenders must clearly explain what the credit costs of the transaction will be.

Financial Problems and Marital Strain

Bankruptcy
Being financially insolvent, unable to pay one's bills

The story of Joe and Mary — and of other families like them whose debts increase over the years — is not unusual. One way out of debt problems is to declare **bankruptcy**. The basic law that allows one to do this is Chapter XIII of the National Bankruptcy Act, the Wage Earner Plan. This is not actual bankruptcy, however. First, one goes to court and with the aid of a lawyer draws up a budget and plan for repayment of debts, usually spread over a thirty-six-month period. The plan is filed with the local bankruptcy court; when the plan is accepted, a trustee is appointed who receives the payments and distributes them to the creditors. The trustee is paid 5 percent of the amount distributed. Unfortunately, this plan works for only half of the people who use it.

If the debtor cannot meet the court-supervised payments, the only legal way to cancel the debts is to declare bankruptcy in a U.S. District Court. Declaring bankruptcy means giving up all that a person owns. The court allows one to keep only such essential things as the tools of one's trade, clothing, basic furniture, and, in some cases, one's home (what can be kept varies from state to state). The rest of the assets are sold and the money distributed to the creditors. Even if the assets do not cover the debts, declaring bankruptcy does mean that all debts are legally canceled except for taxes, alimony and child support payments, and any debts that others may have cosigned (which become their debts). Although bankruptcy may rid a person of debts, the person suffers the loss of most property, has a black mark against future credit ratings, has lawyer and court fees to pay, and cannot declare bankruptcy again for six years.

The Bankruptcy Reform Act of 1978 generally makes it easier to plead bankruptcy. Before 1978 state standards varied widely, but now an individual may choose either the state standard exemption or a federal exemption. The federal exemption allows the debtor to keep an interest of up to $7500 in real property used as a residence and up to $1200 in a car. The debtor may also keep an interest up to $200 in each of a number of individual categories such as clothing, jewelry, and so forth. The Act does allow a state to prohibit debtors from choosing the federal exemption, and a number of states have done this.

The immediate effect of the Reform Act was to ease the bankruptcy process and to allow a higher exemption. This led quickly to increased bankruptcy filings. For example, in Illinois bankruptcies increased 80 percent during 1979, the first full year under the Reform Act. Thus at least a portion of the current increase in bankruptcies reflects the liberalization of the bankruptcy laws brought on by the Bankruptcy Reform Act, rather than a reflection of harder economic times ("Turning Back a Tide . . .," 1982). In 1981 there were 456,914 bankruptcies, compared with 240,000 in 1980 and 197,000 in 1979. Most of these personal bankruptcies happened to low- and middle-income families who slowly became overburdened with increasing debts ("Bankruptcy . . .," 1982).

Going through bankruptcy procedures does not seem to help people become more prudent with their purchases. Of those who file for bankruptcy, 80 percent use credit and are in debt trouble again within five years (Miller, 1983, pp. 249–250). Even if a family declares bankruptcy, both spouses may have to work just to keep the family financially afloat. And often the second salary will be more token than real if the family has

small children (see Chapter 8, pp. 268–270). Once the children are in school or are old enough to care for themselves, however, the second salary can be of real help.

But What about Joe and Mary?

Under the court-supervised payment plan, Joe and Mary are slowly paying off their debts, including those incurred by the birth of their second child. Both Joe and Mary resent not being able to buy new things, including a new car now that theirs is so out-of-date, but it seems as if every cent of his salary is earmarked for the old debts. Mary keeps asking him why he doesn't get a better job. At one time he investigated going back to school to qualify for a market manager position. But he would need to spend two years in school, and Mary cannot earn enough to support the family during those two years. Instead, he has taken a second job as a night watchman. He is so tired when he comes home that the least little noise is painful, and he finds himself constantly yelling at the children to be quiet or at Mary to make them be quiet. He also finds he is usually too tired to make love at night. At work he envies the younger, unmarried men who are driving new cars. Why, he wonders, did he get married in the first place? Mary sometimes wonders the same thing.

It is obvious that financial pressures have put a great strain on this marriage. In fact, in view of this pressure and the fact that they married in their teens, it is quite likely that Joe and Mary's marriage will end in divorce.

Are Joe and Mary alone to blame for their predicament? Why didn't they make the system work for them? Why didn't they wait before making major purchases? Why didn't they postpone children for a year in order to get on their feet economically? What are the answers to such questions as these? In the wealthiest nation in the world, how could this couple have been economically strangled? (See the continuation of Joe and Mary's story in Chapter 8.)

The Seductive Society: Credit and Advertising

As so often occurs, the actual behavior found in our society bears little resemblance to the truisms we learn in the family or at school. Buying and spending have quietly taken the place of thrift and saving. Traditional values, though still preached, are often no longer practiced. And in a productive, inflationary economy such as ours, they are no longer even virtues. For example, after an income tax reduction in 1965, President Johnson urged the public to spend the additional money they now had. Even thirty years ago, such a statement would have been heresy. At the time the president made the statement, it went almost unnoticed. Spending is important in a credit, inflationary society. Goods must be kept moving. The failure of the consumer to buy can immediately produce dire consequences for the economy. A slowdown in any one of the basic industries affects the whole economy, not just the one industry.

The auto industry is a good example of this effect. A slowdown in the sale of cars affects literally hundreds of subsidiary industries as well as many other major industries such as steel, rubber, and aluminum. If the consumer fails to buy, production must be cut back, which means laying off workers, thus compounding the problem by loss of these workers' buying power as consumers. In order to keep goods flowing, a new field of endeavor has opened, namely, stimulation and creation of wants and desires in the consumer.

John Kenneth Galbraith, in his classic work *The Affluent Society* (1958), states that the theory of consumer demand in America is based on two broad propositions:

1. The urgency of wants does not diminish appreciably as more of them are satisfied.
2. Wants originate in the personality of the consumer and are capable of indefinite expansion.

These two propositions go a long way toward explaining why actual income bears little resemblance to a family's feeling of economic satisfaction. Many Americans are dissatisfied with the amount of money they make, yet Americans command a better standard of living than has ever before been known. The most dissatisfied group is that of professionals, where income is generally high, but of course so are aspirations. Economic contentment appears to relate more to one's attitudes and values than to actual economic level.

Advertising and need stimulation have become essential parts of the American economic picture. A family or individual has to be made to want new material goods for more than rational, practical reasons. For example, though a well-made automobile can last ten years with care, such longevity for the average car would greatly upset automobile production. The auto industry has met this problem with the yearly model change, or the concept of built-in obsolescence often under the guise of improvement. In all fairness to the auto industry, it should be noted that many yearly model changes are improvements, but, on the other hand, change has often been made for its own sake so that older models appear less desirable.

Today's youth are growing up in a different economic atmosphere than their parents did. The society they know is an affluent society. Even the recent period of relative job scarcity, inflation, and recession has had little effect on spending habits. Restaurants, for example, felt little of the 1982 recession. Buying, spending, credit, and debt are now familiar accompaniments of marital life. The advantages of such a system cannot be denied. Yet youth must also be aware of the dangers of such a system in order to utilize it to their fullest advantage. Joe and Mary became trapped and lost their economic freedom because they never had a chance to stand apart from the system and analyze the negative aspects against which they needed to be on guard.

INSET 7-3

The Cost of Your Car

In its 1981 annual car survey, Hertz Corporation concluded that the cost of owning and operating a compact car averaged 44.6 cents per mile, up 18 percent from 1980. Subcompacts cost the least to operate, 34.3 cents per mile, whereas full-sized vehicles averaged 51.1 cents per mile. The statistics showed that motorists are buying smaller cars equipped with fewer options and are keeping them longer and driving them less in an effort to offset increasing costs. The leasing company found that "sticker shock" was well warranted, with the price of an average compact (automatic transmission, air conditioning, power steering and brakes) increasing $1,167 over 1980 to $7621. The cost of options accounted for 15.2 cents per mile, whereas interest rates accounted for 8.8 cents, insurance and fees 9.1 cents, gasoline 8.8 cents, and maintenance 2.7 cents. Hertz estimated the average driver spends $4437 per year to own and operate a car over four years.

The power of advertising and the ability to immediately satisfy one's needs or desires are a formidable and seductive pair for mature adults to cope with, much less youth. How well can a young couple resist the invitation to use a store's credit again when they have almost paid off their bill? An official-looking check arrives in the mail announcing that they may now obtain $500 more merchandise for nothing down and no increase in the monthly payments that were otherwise about to end. If they understand thoroughly the meaning of what exercising their desires in this manner means, they can make use of some or all of the offer with no danger. On the other hand, another purchase could be the straw that breaks the camel's back if, when added to the rest of their financial debt, it pushes them into economic disaster. The young couple must remember that personal freedom and indebtedness vary inversely. The more debt they take on, the less personal freedom they have.

In *The Affluent Society* (1958, p. 155), Galbraith points out that a "direct link between production and wants is provided by the institutions of modern advertising and salesmanship. These cannot be reconciled with the notion of independently determined desires, for their central function is to create desires — to bring into being wants that previously did not exist." Vance Packard's well-known book *The Hidden Persuaders* (1958) early exposed the extent to which advertising influences the public's attitudes, values, and behavior. He questioned the morality of some advertising techniques that manipulated the consumer into buying regardless of the consequences. In concluding his book, he asked a series of provocative questions that young married couples might well consider:

1. What is the morality of the practice of encouraging housewives to be non-rational and impulsive in buying family food?
2. What is the morality of manipulating small children even before they reach the age where they are legally responsible for their actions?
3. What is the morality of playing upon hidden weaknesses and frailties—such as our anxieties, aggressive feelings, dread of nonconformity, and infantile hangovers—to sell products?
4. What is the morality of developing in the public an attitude of wastefulness toward national resources by encouraging the "psychological obsolescence" of products already in use? (p. 143)

Approximately $14.8 billion was spent on advertising in 1981 (see Table 7-4 for the top 50 advertisers). The majority went toward creating wants and desires, which will in turn add new frustrations to the already monetarily unhappy American family who live at one of the highest material levels in the world.

TABLE 7-4   Fifty Leading National Advertisers, 1981*

RANK	COMPANY	ADVERTISING (millions)	RANK	COMPANY	ADVERTISING (millions)
1	Procter & Gamble	$671.8	26	U.S. Government	189.0
2	Sears, Roebuck & Co.	544.1	27	Unilever U.S.	188.9
3	General Foods Corp.	456.8	28	Anheuser-Busch Co.	187.2
4	Philip Morris Inc.	433.0	29	Heublein Inc.	187.0
5	General Motors Corp.	401.0	30	Dart & Kraft	177.0
6	K Mart Corp.	349.6	31	Esmark Inc.	175.0
7	Nabisco Brands	341.0	32	Gillette Co.	171.9
8	R. J. Reynolds Industries	321.3	33	Beatrice Foods Co.	170.0
9	American Telephone & Telegraph Co.	297.0	34	Consolidated Foods Corp.	166.4
10	Mobil Corp.	293.1	35	General Electric Co.	164.7
			36	H. J. Heinz Co.	160.2
11	Ford Motor Co.	286.7	37	Warner Communications	159.0
12	Warner-Lambert Co.	270.4	38	International Telephone & Telegraph Co.	153.0
13	Colgate-Palmolive Co.	260.0	39	Norton Simon Inc.	149.9
14	PepsiCo Inc.	260.0	40	Richardson-Vicks	149.0
15	McDonald's Corp.	230.2			
16	American Home Products Corp.	209.0	41	Seagram Co. Ltd.	145.0
			42	Loews Corp.	141.4
17	RCA Corp.	208.8	43	Time Inc.	141.1
18	J. C. Penney Co.	208.6	44	American Cyanamid Co.	138.0
19	General Mills Corp.	207.3	45	Chesebrough-Pond's	136.2
20	Bristol-Myers Co.	200.0	46	CBS Inc.	134.0
21	B.A.T. Industries PLC	199.3	47	Pillsbury Co.	131.0
22	Coca-Cola Co.	197.9	48	Schering-Plough Corp.	119.8
23	Johnson & Johnson	195.0	49	Mattel Inc.	110.6
24	Chrysler Corp.	193.0	50	Revlon Inc.	106.6
25	Ralston Purina Co.	193.0			

Source: Advertising Age, September 9, 1982.
*Based on measured media expenditures only; does not include local advertising.

An Alternative: Investment

There is a popular belief that one's chances of earning $1 million are much less than they were for one's grandfather. But the number of millionaires today actually far exceeds the number in grandfather's time. Granted, $1 million may be worth considerably less in buying power today, but it is still a healthy mark of affluence. A gradual inflationary economy is also an economy in which money can be made easily by a person who is intelligent and willing to work. Another important qualification is the ability to stay clear of early economic entrapment, as we have described. For most young people the necessity of gathering the first small amount of capital is crucial — even more so because of the strong tendency of the system to work against them. In the early years they must stay alert to keep the system from entrapping them and thereby canceling their at-

TABLE 7-5   Comparative Standard of Living

COMMODITY	WASHINGTON	MOSCOW	LONDON	PARIS	MUNICH
WEEKLY FOOD BASKET, SELECTED ITEMS:	MINUTES OF WORKTIME UNLESS OTHERWISE SPECIFIED*				
Bread: *1 kg*	16	17	16	18	27
Hamburger meat, beef: *1 kg*	37	123	63	80	70
Sausages: *1 kg*	33	160	51	75	75
Cod: *1 kg*	61	47	72	118	45
Sugar: *1 kg*	9	58	11	9	10
Butter: *1 kg*	55	222	50	47	52
Milk: *1 liter*	6	22	9	8	7
Cheese: *1 kg*	100	185	65	59	65
Eggs: *10*	8	55	16	13	12
Potatoes: *1 kg*	7	7	3	4	4
Cabbage: *1 kg*	9	12	10	9	7
Carrots: *1 kg*	11	19	13	7	10
Apples: *1 kg*	10	92	23	15	15
Tea: *100 g*	10	53	5	17	10
Beer: *1 liter*	11	16	18	7	8
Vodka: *1 liter*	61	452	131	107	74
Cigarettes: *20*	9	15	25	8	16
WEEKLY BASKET, FAMILY OF 4 (HOURS)	18.6	53.5	24.7	22.2	23.3
COSMETICS, DRUGS, ETC.					
Toilet soap: *150 g, small bar*	4	20	5	7	6
Toothpaste: *125 ml*	16	27	13	29	28
Aspirin: *100, cheapest*	5	246	9	21	64
Lipstick: *one*	30	69	60	76	80

Source: National Federation of Independent Business Research and Education Foundation.
*Approximate worktime required for average manufacturing employee to buy selected commodities in retail stores in Washington, D.C., London, Paris, and Munich and at state-fixed prices in Moscow during March 1982. Worktime is based on average take-home pay of male and female manufacturing workers. Income, state, and church taxes (not applicable in France); social security taxes and health insurance premiums (not applicable in USSR); and unemployment insurance (not applicable in USA

tempt to accumulate initial investment capital. If they can win this battle and start on the road to financial success, they will be using the system to their advantage rather than being used by it. When one compares costs of living in America with those in other countries (as in Table 7-5), it is clear that America offers a great deal economically to its citizens.

Thinking about **investments** on even a modest scale is important if a person or a newly married couple are to make the economic system work for instead of against them. Figure 7-1 shows the broad range of investment opportunities from which one can choose. They range from the very conservative bank savings account to the highly speculative gambles for high return on such things as mining and oil exploration. You might ask, "How can the average newly married couple even consider investments? It's all they can do to set up housekeeping in this day of inflation and recession." This is a legitimate question. However, the couple who plan investing into their life, even if only at a later date, have the greatest

Investment
Use of money to earn more money, such as putting it in a business or in stocks

TABLE 7-5, Continued

COMMODITY	WASHINGTON	MOSCOW	LONDON	PARIS	MUNICH
CLOTHING, HOUSEHOLD ITEMS AND SERVICES	MINUTES OF WORKTIME UNLESS OTHERWISE SPECIFIED*				
T-shirt: *cotton, white*	19	185	66	53	50
Panty hose: *one pair*	18	366	18	17	18
Jeans: *Levi's (hours)*	3	46	6	6	7
Men's shoes *(hours)*	8	25	7	7	5
Men's office suit:					
2-piece, rayon, dacron (hours)	25	109	22	13	15
Refrigerator: *cheapest (hours)*	44	155	40	53	42
Television: *color, 56-cm (hours)*	65	701	132	106	143
Electricity: *1/12 annual bill*	253	246	198	265	242
Gas: *1/12 annual bill*	290	39	568	369	125
Water: *1/12 annual bill*	32	123	97	95	37
Telephone rent *(per month)*	119	154	190	119	136
Television and radio license:					
annual, color television (hours)	nil	nil	20	15	13
Shirt laundered: *white, cotton*	10	25	16	18	13
Dry cleaning: *one men's overcoat*	79	92	53	91	54
Haircut: *men, no extras*	63	37	34	108	60
TRANSPORTATION					
Small car: *Ford Escort (months)*	5	53	11	8	6
Gasoline: *regular, 10 liters*	32	185	85	87	61
Taxi fare: *2 mi/3 km*	21	37	52	27	35
Bus fare: *2 mi/3 km*	7	3	11	9	8
MISCELLANEOUS					
Morning paper	3	3	5	7	5
Suburban movies: *best seat*	42	31	53	38	40

and USSR) have been deducted from wages. Family allowances (not applicable in USA) have been added for a family of four. In dollars hourly take-home pay in December 1981 was $5.69 for American workers, $1.35 for Russian workers, $4.13 for British workers, $4.66 for French workers, and $5.00 for West German workers.

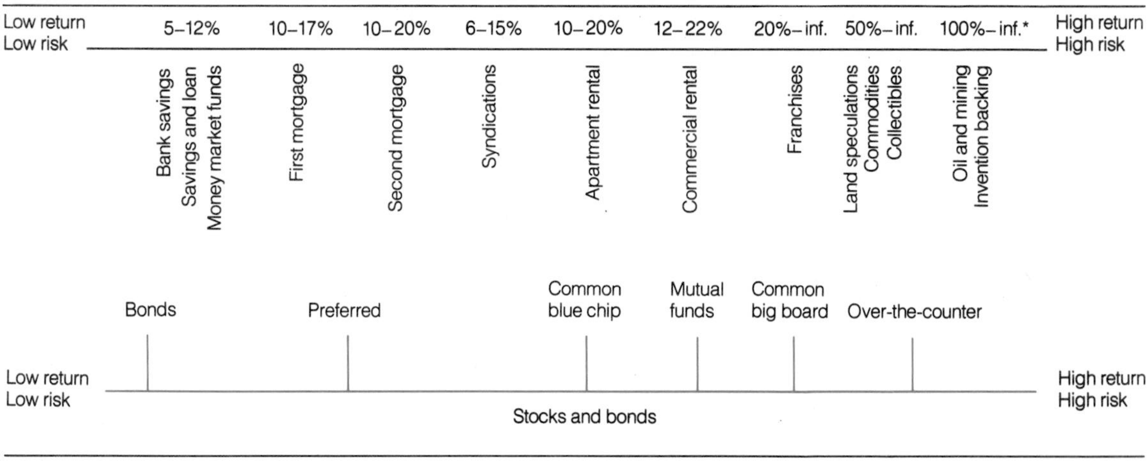

Low return Low risk	5–12%	10–17%	10–20%	6–15%	10–20%	12–22%	20%–inf.	50%–inf.	100%–inf.*	High return High risk
	Bank savings / Savings and loan / Money market funds	First mortgage	Second mortgage	Syndications	Apartment rental	Commercial rental	Franchises	Land speculations / Commodities / Collectibles	Oil and mining / Invention backing	

Low return Low risk	Bonds	Preferred			Common blue chip	Mutual funds	Common big board	Over-the-counter		High return High risk
				Stocks and bonds						

*100%–"inf." means 100% upwards without limit (infinite).

FIGURE 7-1 The investment continuum. Note that the percentage return in successful investments increases as the risk increases. The chances of striking gold are slim, but if you do, the return is great. Percentages also change with economic conditions.

chance of economic prosperity and freedom. A positive attitude toward investment is actually even more important than investment itself. Such an attitude recognizes that "money makes money," that there is value in budgeting and staying free of consumer debt, that controlling one's desires in early years can lead to greater rewards later, and that the American economic system if used properly can free one from economic worries. Even if a couple can put aside only a few dollars a month toward future investments, they stand a good chance of improving their economic position compared with their friends who have no interest or knowledge of investing. (See "Gaining Freedom through Investment, p. 259.)

For example, starting at age 25 to put away $20 per month is the same as putting away $200 per month starting at age forty-five with retirement at age sixty-five. Table 7-6 shows how money grows at 6 percent and at 12 percent compounded daily interest. The figures are predicated on putting aside $100 per month initially until you have $12,000.

Effective Money Management

Effective money management is the first step toward successful investment and the reduction of conflict over money within the family. The most important step in reducing marital conflict over money is to determine ahead of time how most money decisions will be made. There are at least five possible ways in a family to handle monetary decisions: (1) the husband can make all the decisions, (2) the wife can make all the decisions, (3) one spouse can control the income but give the other a household allowance, (4) each spouse can have separate funds and share agreed-on financial obligations, and (5) the spouses can have a joint bank account on which each can draw as necessary (Landis, 1970).

Once a couple reaches an agreement, most day-to-day monetary deci-

TABLE 7-6 $100 per Month Invested at 6% and 12%

YEARS	AMOUNT INVESTED	6%	12%	DIFFERENCE
10	$12,000	$ 16,766	$ 23,586	$ 6,820
20	24,000	46,791	96,838	50,047
30	36,000	100,562	324,351	223,789
40	48,000	196,857	1,030,970	834,113

sions can be handled automatically. The next step in reducing monetary conflict is to agree on a budget (see pp. 246–247). A **budget** is actually a plan of spending to assure attaining what is needed and wanted. For example, a family's income must cover such basic necessities as housing, food, clothing, and transportation and, it is hoped, leave some money for discretionary expenditures such as vacations and recreation. How Americans spend their money is shown in Table 7-7 and Figure 7-2.

The first step is to allot money for necessities. Whatever money is left over can be divided among other wants the family may have. The inflation/recession economy we have been experiencing has made planned spending more important than ever. For example, it is estimated that the spontaneous food shopper spends approximately 10 to 15 percent more for food than the shopper who has a planned food budget and a shopping list of needed items.

Budget
A plan for balancing expenses with estimated income

TABLE 7-7 Summary of Annual Budgets for a Four-Person Family at Three Levels of Living, Urban United States, Autumn 1981

COMPONENT	Lower	Inter-mediate	Higher	Lower	Inter-mediate	Higher
				ITEM AS PERCENTAGE OF TOTAL BUDGET		
Total budget	$15,323	$25,407	$38,060			
Total family consumption	12,069	18,240	25,008			
Food	4,545	5,843	7,366	29%	23%	19%
Housing	2,817	5,546	8,423	18%	21%	22%
Transportation	1,311	2,372	3,075	8	9	8
Clothing	937	1,333	1,947	6	5	5
Personal care	379	508	719	2	2	2
Medical care	1,436	1,443	1,505	9	6	4
Other family consumption[1]	644	1,196	1,972	4	5	5
Other items[2]	621	1,021	1,718	4	6	5
Social Security and disability	1,036	1,703	1,903	7	7	5
Personal income taxes	1,506	4,443	9,340	10	17	25

Note: Because of rounding, sums of individual items may not equal totals.
Source: U.S. Department of Labor, July 1982.
[1]Other family consumption includes average costs for reading materials, recreation, tobacco products, alcoholic beverages, education, and miscellaneous expenditures.
[2]Other items include allowances for gifts and contributions, life insurance, and occupational expenses.

FIGURE 7-2 Annual expenditures for a four-person,
medium-income family.

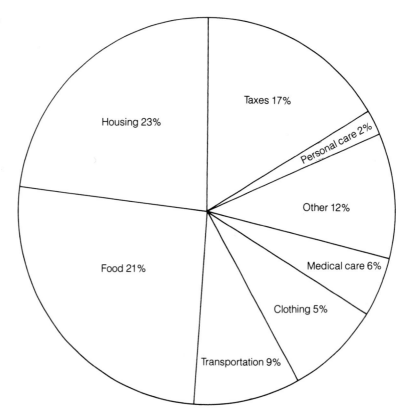

By living within a budget (see Table 7-8 and Inset 7-4), a family can avoid many of the problems that defeated Joe and Mary. In addition, by budgeting even a small amount to savings, they can make investment possible. Saving is really only deferred spending. If immediate spending is deferred, it becomes possible to use the money to earn additional income.

A budget should only be used for a specified time, and then it should be updated to reflect changing family circumstances. For example, the newly married couple may feel well off if both work. They have two incomes and minimal expenses. But danger is ahead if they become accustomed to using up both incomes. For example, if they decide to have

TABLE 7-8   Suggested Budget for Necessities for a Family of Four

ITEM	LOW INCOME PERCENTAGE RANGE	MEDIAN INCOME PERCENTAGE RANGE
Food	25–35	20–30
Housing	25–35	20–30
Transportation	16–20	12–18
Taxes	12–15	20–23
Clothing	10–15	10–15
Health and Insurance	8–12	8–14
Recreation and Savings	4–10	8–12

children, the wife may give up her income, at least for a while. Expenses also increase when children are added to the family. Thus income often drops and expenses rise, which can throw the family into an economic crisis unless they have planned economically for both eventualities.

Another stage that the family must plan for is if and when the children go to college. This usually means a drastic rise in expenditures. The cost of putting a child through college averages between $20,000 to $40,000 if room and board are considered.

After children have become independent, the spouses can usually enjoy a comfortable period of relative affluence. They must, however, plan carefully for their coming retirement. Without such planning the couple may spend their older years in a state of poverty, especially if inflationary pressures exist.

As dull and uninteresting as budget planning may sound, the family that does not put time into planning its finances may face increasing monetary strain, which may even lead to the destruction of the marriage. This is especially true when there is a high rate of inflation.

Inflationary Recession and the Stop-Go Cycle

Not many years ago economists thought that **inflation** and **recession** were opposites and could never occur together. Yet this combination has occurred together at times during the 1970s and 1980s. Effective money management must take into consideration both inflation and recession plus a mix of the two. In an **inflationary recession** economy every possible bad thing is happened at once. Output is falling, unemployment is rising, and inflation continues. Fortunately this state of the economy seldom lasts for long.

This book is not the place for a detailed economic discussion of inflationary recession, although you will need a minimal understanding of it if you are to make the economy work for you rather than against you. Essentially the Democratic party supports an expansionary monetary policy that tends to lead to low unemployment, rapid growth, and high inflation. On the other hand, the Republicans support a conservative economic policy that tends to lower inflation and tolerates a moderately higher level of unemployment. Because inflation, economic growth, and employment all are related, a change in one tends to produce changes in the others. Essentially, the inflation/recession phenomenon occurs when a new political party comes into power and tries to reduce inflation quickly. At the time of the 1980 election double-digit inflation was a major economic problem, and the Republicans were easily voted into office. They quickly put the brakes on inflation but as it slowed, economic growth stagnated and unemployment rose. Theoretically, once inflation is controlled, the economy rejuvenates and starts to grow again, thereby lowering unemployment. The stop-go characteristic of the economy occurs as government control switches between liberal and conservative economic philosophies. Thus the successful money manager must understand inflation as well as recession caused by efforts to slow inflation.

Inflation
A sustained rise in the average of all prices

Recession
A temporary falling off of business activity

Inflationary recession
A falling off of business activity at the same time that prices are rising

INSET 7-4

How to Budget Your Income

Once you decide to do some positive money management, you must figure out a budget and try to stick to it. The budget is a planning tool to help you reduce undirected spending.

Steps in Budget Making

Create a spending plan by following these four basic steps:

1. Analyze past spending by keeping records for a month or two.
2. Determine *fixed expenses*, such as rent, and any other contractual payments that must be made—even if they are infrequent, such as insurance and taxes.

3. Determine *flexible expenses*, such as food and clothing.
4. Balance your fixed plus flexible expenditures with your available income. If a surplus exists, you can apply it toward achieving your goals. If there is a deficit, then you must reexamine your flexible expenditures. You can also reexamine fixed expenses with a view to reducing them in the future.

Note that so-called fixed expenses are only fixed in the short run. In the longer run everything is essentially flexible, or variable. One can adjust one's fixed expenses by changing one's standard of living, if necessary.

The Importance of Keeping Records

Budget making, whether you are a college student, a single person living alone, or the head of a family, will be useless if you don't keep records. The only way to make sure that you are carrying out your budget is by keeping records of what you are actually

spending. The ultimate way to maintain records is to write everything down, but that becomes time consuming and therefore costly. Another way to keep records is to write checks for everything. Records are also important in case of problems with faulty products or services or the Internal Revenue Service.

General Budgeting

Figure 7-3 is a monthly general-budget form that encompasses both estimated and actual cash available and fixed and variable payments.

You will note that the savings category is located under the *Fixed Payments* heading. This is because the money in your savings account may be used to pay such fixed annual expenses as auto, fire, and life insurance, and it is necessary to plan to save in advance for these expenses.

The key to making a budget work for you is to review your figures every month to see how your monthly estimates compare with your spending.

Inflation

Since World War II there have been many, and often revolutionary, social and economic changes. Certainly one of the most noticeable changes, especially in the 1970s and continuing in the 1980s, has been the increasing rate of inflation with which families have had to cope. Each day we are surprised, dismayed, and angry at increased nominal costs of almost everything we buy.* Bread is more than $1 a loaf, yet it seems only yesterday that it was 50¢. The last new car you bought ten years ago cost $4000, tax and license included. Today, the same model is priced closer to $10,000. "Buy now before the price increases," is an often-repeated ad-

*Nominal price is the absolute price in dollars you pay for an item — $1 for a loaf of bread, $10,000 for an automobile.

FIGURE 7-3 A general way to budget.

CASH FORECAST, MONTH OF _____	ESTIMATED	ACTUAL
Cash on hand and in checking account, end of previous period	————————	————————
Savings needed for planned expenses	————————	————————
RECEIPTS		
Net pay	————————	————————
Borrowed	————————	————————
Interest/dividends	————————	————————
Other	————————	————————
Total cash available during period	————————	————————
FIXED PAYMENTS		
Mortgage or rent	————————	————————
Life insurance	————————	————————
Fire insurance	————————	————————
Auto insurance	————————	————————
Medical insurance	————————	————————
Savings	————————	————————
Local taxes	————————	————————
Loan or other debt	————————	————————
Children's allowances	————————	————————
Other	————————	————————
Total fixed payments	————————	————————
FLEXIBLE PAYMENTS		
Water	————————	————————
Electricity	————————	————————
Fuel	————————	————————
Telephone	————————	————————
Medical	————————	————————
Household supplies	————————	————————
Car	————————	————————
Food	————————	————————
Clothing	————————	————————
Nonrecurring large payments	————————	————————
Contributions, recreation, etc.	————————	————————
Other	————————	————————
Total flexible payments	————————	————————
TOTAL ALL PAYMENTS	————————	————————
	————————	————————
RECAPITULATION		
Total cash available	————————	————————
Total payments	————————	————————
Cash balance, end of period	————————	————————

vertisement that feeds our fears about inflation. Those on fixed incomes slowly, month by month, drop farther into poverty. The demands for increased wages, just to stay even with inflation, become more insistent. Public opinion polls find that inflation continually is a major concern. Books on personal finance often begin with a discussion of inflation in the first chapter (Miller, 1979).

Constantly rising prices and recent stagnation of real income (buying power) combine to bring more and more wives into the labor force. A thorough understanding of inflation can help today's family make better use of their resources.

Americans born after 1940 have only known an inflationary economy, one with constantly rising prices. Beginning with World War II, the rate of inflation has averaged 5 to 6 percent a year. The rate dropped at the beginning of the 1960s but then began to rise again until it reached a dramatic double-digit high of 12 percent in 1974. Thereafter it declined until 1978 when it went to 9 percent and 1979 when it reached a new post-World War II high of over 13 percent, the highest rate in 33 years (see Figure 7-4). By 1982, the inflation rate had dropped dramatically to less than 5 percent.

Consumer Price Index (CPI)
A sample of costs of goods and services collected by the Bureau of Labor Statistics, which are then compared with some arbitrarily set base period (now set at 1967)

Prices do not always rise, although younger persons might not believe this. Figure 7-5 shows the **Consumer Price Index (CPI)** since 1860. Declines in the index indicate a recession or depression in the economy. Overall the CPI has risen over 600 percent in the past 100 years. Goods costing $100 in 1967, the new base year, cost $272.40 in December 1981.

It is interesting to examine some of the specific components in the CPI. Take, for example, December 1981: Residential rents have lagged behind other increases (208), while the cost of home ownership has soared ahead of general increases (352.7). Apparel has lagged behind (186.9), while

FIGURE 7-4   Inflation rates. The figures cover each full year. The highest gain was in 1979 when the Consumer Price Index soared to 13.3 percent (U.S. Department of Labor, 1980).

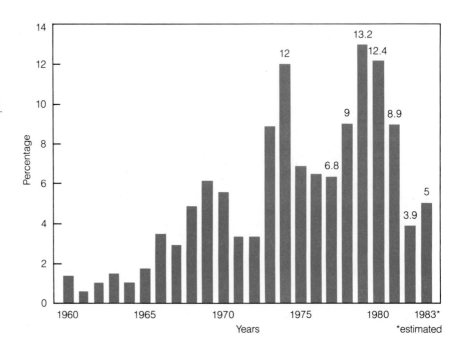

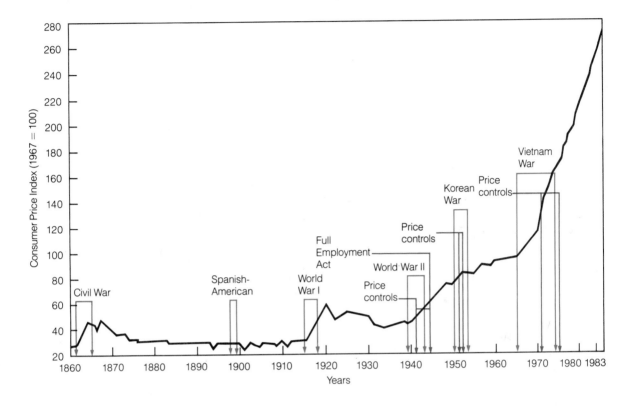

FIGURE 7-5 Consumer Price Index has its ups and downs (mostly ups) (U.S. Department of Labor, 1980).

energy prices have soared (410) (President's Council of Economic Advisors, 1982).* (See Appendix A for a general summary of selected CPI items.)

Inflation rates by themselves only tell half of the story of the American economy. Inflation simply says that the nominal prices have risen. However, income has also risen during this time. If income rises at the same rate as prices, one's buying power remains the same. Thus a more important measure of the economy than just the inflation rate is the *real per capita income*. This is computed by taking the per capita income increase and subtracting the inflation rate. If my income increases 10 percent in a year during which inflation is only 5 percent, my real income (buying power) has increased 5 percent. Most people have actually increased their real income (buying power) since World War II. In the seventies and thus far in the eighties, however, there have been years (such as 1976–1977) when the real per capita income has declined (Table 7-9).

The CPI is the most common indicator used in popular media to measure price fluctuations. Because it is an average, it tends to mask actual price fluctuations for a specific item. Thus it is important that the consumer look at the relative price of a product rather than just at the nominal or absolute price (see Appendix A). Although most goods have greatly increased in nominal price, some relative prices have actually decreased. For example, compared with 1967, the base year, when the CPI was set

*See Inset 7-5 for an explanation of the figures within parentheses.

TABLE 7-9   Gross Weekly Earnings for Private Nonagricultural Workers

	CURRENT DOLLARS	1967 DOLLARS
March 1977	$183.45	$102.95
March 1976[1]	$176.29	$103.40

Source: U.S. Department of Labor, May 1977.
[1]Note that the buying power was actually 45 cents lower in 1977 than it was in 1976.

at 100, the index rose to 276.5 in August 1982, indicating that the CPI-measured average prices had almost tripled in the preceding fifteen years. But television sets rose to only 104 on the index, and so compared with the average CPI gain during these years, their relative price dropped to .37. In other words, television sets did not go up much in absolute cost between 1967 and 1982 and, relative to other goods on the CPI, were much cheaper in 1982 than in 1967. So, although overall prices as measured by the CPI are going up, some goods go up more slowly than others and therefore become relatively better buys.

Some individual goods — such as the popular hand-held digital display calculators — have actually decreased in absolute price during this time. Decrease in price has occurred because of technological breakthroughs that lower production costs in the electronics industry.

Another way to see the relationship between inflation of prices and income is to compare the actual amount of income needed to remain at the same purchasing power level from 1950 to 1981. A family that earned $10,000 in 1950 needed $12,219 in 1960, $16,130 in 1970, and $27,200 in 1981 to retain their initial 1950 purchasing power of $10,000. Table 7-9 shows both the absolute and real weekly earnings for nonagricultural workers in 1976 and 1977.

Although much lip service is paid to the cause of reducing inflation, little was actually done by government until President Reagan took office in 1980. Compared with many other countries, the United States has had a relatively low rate of inflation since World War II. Many countries have experienced 40, 50, and even 100 percent inflation rates per year. The government benefits from mild inflation, as Table 7-10 shows. In recent

TABLE 7-10   A 9.4 Percentage Increase in All Prices and Salaries over a One-Year Period*

	GROSS INCOME	FEDERAL INCOME TAX	EFFECTIVE RATE	AFTER-TAX INCOME IN YEAR 1 DOLLARS
Year 1	$14,000	$1,600	11.4%	$12,400
Year 2	15,316	1,890	12.3	12,164
Year 1	20,000	3,010	15.1	16,990
Year 2	21,880	3,506	16.0	16,646
Year 1	30,000	6,020	20.1	23,980
Year 2	32,820	7,035	21.4	23,361

*Because of graduated income tax rates, even families lucky enough to get raises matching the big increase in living costs wound up losing purchasing power. Here we show how a 9.4 percent inflation outruns a 9.4 percent pay raise.

Brief Explanation of the CPI

The Consumer Price Index (CPI) is a measure of the average change in prices over time in a fixed market basket of goods and services. Effective with the January 1978 index, the Bureau of Labor Statistics began publishing CPI's for two population groups: (1) a new CPI for All Urban Consumers (CPI-U) which covers approximately 80 percent of the total noninstitutional civilian population; and (2) a revised CPI for Urban Wage Earners and Clerical Workers (CPI-W) which represents about half the population covered by the CPI-U. The CPI-U includes, in addition to wage earners and clerical workers, groups which historically have been excluded from CPI coverage, such as professional, managerial, and technical workers, the self-employed, short-term workers, the unemployed, and retirees and others not in the labor force.

The CPI is based on prices of food, clothing, shelter, and fuels, transportation fares, charges for doctors' and dentists' services, drugs, and the other goods and services that people buy for day-to-day living. Prices are collected in 85 urban areas across the country from over 18,000 tenants, 18,000 housing units for property taxes, and about 24,000 establishments — grocery and department stores, hospitals, filling stations, and other types of stores and service establishments. All taxes directly associated with the purchase and use of items are included in the index. Prices of food, fuels, and a few other items are obtained every month in all 85 locations. Prices of most other commodities and services are collected every month in the five largest geographic areas and every other month in other areas. Prices of most goods and services are obtained by personal visits of the Bureau's trained representatives. Mail questionnaires are used to obtain public utility rates, some fuel prices, and certain other items.

In calculating the index, price changes for the various items in each location are averaged together with weights which represent their importance in the spending of the appropriate population group. Local data are then combined to obtain a U.S. city average. Separate indexes are also published for 28 local areas. Area indexes do not measure differences in the level of prices among cities; they only measure the average change in prices for each area since the base period.

The index measures price changes from a designated reference date — 1967 — which equals 100.0. An increase of 22 percent, for example, is shown as 122.0.

years California has been a good example of the increased government income that accrues from inflation. As prices go higher, sales tax revenues increase, and, as Table 7-10 demonstrates, so do income taxes. Despite the big property tax cut embodied in California's Proposition 13 that was passed in 1978, the state surplus of funds remained almost as high (between five and six billion dollars) after the property tax reduction until 1982 when the recession reduced the state's income.

Increased revenue to the government and the politician's fear of recession combine to keep government from doing much about mild inflation, except talking. Increasing energy costs are one of the major causes of recent inflation, along with an inflationary mentality that has been created in the last few years.

Living with Inflation

It appears that some degree of inflation will influence the economy for the foreseeable future, and Americans must take it into consideration if they are to be successful economically. You can combat mild inflation in a number of ways:

1. *Minimize your cash holdings.* Cash obviously loses value at the rate of inflation. If I bury $1000 cash to protect it from theft for a year during which the inflation rate is 10 percent, inflation robs me of $100. At the end of the year I only have $900 in purchasing power.

2. *Select high-yield savings accounts whenever possible.* There are now many savings plans paying interest rates from 5 to 16 percent. In the longer term accounts there are often substantial penalties if you withdraw your funds before the end of the term. Hence one must spread one's savings over a number of different kinds of accounts. For instance, you will want to keep a small balance to cover unexpected expenses in a regular passbook account where you can withdraw at any time without penalty. You will probably only earn between 5 and 6 ½ percent interest on this money. You may want some money in a six-month to one-year term account on which you may earn higher interest, although the higher yields usually require large minimum deposits such as the $10,000 required on T-bill accounts in savings and loan institutions. If you have enough funds, you can place more monies into longer-term, higher-paying savings certificates. (Recent banking deregulation is quickly changing the characteristics of savings accounts.)

3. *Try to have a cost-of-living clause tied to your employment contract.* Many unions have been successful in gaining this for their members. Thus if inflation increases the CPI by 10 percent, cost-of-living clauses take effect and the worker's income is automatically increased to match. This, of course, also acts to maintain the inflation.

4. *Try not to let inflation panic you into buying before you are ready.* We are constantly told to buy now before prices increase. Yet, as we pointed out, some prices may actually decline relative to the CPI even though they go up in absolute terms. Even with large-cost items such as automobiles that have risen in cost as fast as the CPI, you might want to postpone buying. If your present auto has two more years of trouble-free life, then drive it those two additional years and you will probably save more money even though the new car will cost you more in absolute terms two years in the future.

Example: Take a new-car cost of $8000. If you bought the car outright (no payments), you'd lose 10 percent interest per year that the money could be earning in a savings account. Thus in two years you'd lose $1600 of potential interest. If the inflation rate was also 10 percent per year, the car would cost you $1680 more two years from now (10 percent × $8000 = $800 the first year, 10 percent × $8800 = $880 the second year; adding the two yields $1680 as the price increase of the car over two years). Considering that your income stays at least even with inflation, the car will actually cost you relatively less if you buy it two years from now at the higher price, because the money you would have spent on the car earns interest for the two years and your income is higher. Of course, if you don't have the money and must buy the car on credit, these figures will not apply.

5. *Learn about investments.* Money earns money. The wise investor can stay ahead of inflation. For example, real estate has stayed ahead of inflation in many parts of the country. By this, we mean that it has gone up in price faster than the CPI has risen. Unfortunately, inflation brings with it a certain amount of irrationality. Thus we see speculation causing unusual and unpredictable surges in prices. Gold and silver are two good examples of what irrational speculation can do to prices. The small, prudent investor would do well to avoid irrational investments in favor of more predictable ones. (See p. 259.)

6. *An inflationary period tends to favor the borrower.* Money borrowed today is paid back in cheaper dollars in the future.

   Example: I borrow $10,000 at 10 percent interest per year for a five-year period. During that period inflation is 10 percent per year. In essence I am paying nothing for the use of the money. I will have paid $1000 per year or $5000 in simple interest at the end of five years. However, at the end of five years, the $10,000 I pay back is worth *only $5000 in buying power because of the accumulated 50 percent inflation which has halved the value of my dollars.*

7. *Try to buy wisely.* Watch for bargains such as year-end sales and seasonal price reductions (See Appendix B.)

8. *More members of the family can work.* This suggestion is discussed in more detail in Chapter 8. Higher inflation rates are partially responsible for the increasing number of married women seeking employment.

9. *Conserve and save to accumulate investment funds.*

Periods of Reduced Inflation and Mild Recession

The recession of 1981–83 demonstrates what happens when the government makes a strong effort to slow inflation. Unemployment goes up, productivity decreases, and government income falls, while social program (unemployment benefits, and so forth) costs rise. Because such economic problems are much more obvious than the negative effects of creeping inflation, great pressure is brought on government to support at least a mild form of inflation despite the long-term negative effects. You may remember how quickly the hue and cry against inflation that brought President Reagan to office abated when he instituted monetary changes to reduce inflation. In the face of a recession, people quickly forgot about their problems with inflation.

The prudent money manager most likely will live with mild inflation most of the time, thus giving more weight to suggestions about living with inflation than to suggestions about how to deal with a recession. There will be times, however, when the economy slumps. In order to guard against such times, the prudent money manager will want to do the following:

1. Maintain enough liquidity to cover emergencies.
2. Beware of investments wherein a large balloon payment is due in the short-term future. For example, in the late 1970s the inflation rate on well-located real estate was 20 percent or higher per year. Because interest rates were high, many people bought under so-called creative financing plans that included only short-term financing of the mortgages, with the total loan due in three to five years. Buyers assumed that the high rate of inflation would continue and that they could then refinance based on the increased value of the property. When inflation slowed, property values leveled out or fell slightly so that it became impossible to refinance such property, and many persons were unable to meet loan due dates. In some of the most speculative real estate markets, such as southern California, the number of foreclosures increased greatly during the early 1980s.
3. If you are able to foresee a slowing of inflation and resulting economic downturn, try to maintain a larger percent of your assets in cash so that you can take advantage of good buys that may result. In the example just described, there were numerous good buys in real estate as short-term mortgages became due and could not be met by owners who had banked too strongly on inflation to bail them out of their debts.
4. Keep yourself in a financial position that has enough flexibility for you to ride out short-term economic downturns. Judging from the inflation history of the United States during the past 100 years (p. 249), we can probably safely assume that some amount of inflation will remain for the foreseeable future. And as always there will be periodic short-term economic downturns that must be planned for in advance.

A Word about Insurance

Proper use of insurance can protect a family from catastrophic financial setback. Every family must have at least three kinds of insurance: medical, automobile, and, if they own their own home, fire insurance.

Medical coverage is an absolute necessity. Medical costs have become so high that no average family can sustain the expense of a prolonged illness. For a young, healthy couple, coverage can be limited to catastrophic illness with a large deductible, perhaps as high as $500. This is the least expensive type of medical coverage. When children arrive, a policy that covers everyday medical problems and that has a lower deductible should be sought. A family of four may have to pay $100 to $250 per month for medical coverage depending on how comprehensive it is. In addition to insurance plans such as Mutual of Omaha and Blue Cross, there are also prepaid foundation plans such as the Kaiser plan where one may have full medical coverage at a certain facility, hospital, or clinic for a specified yearly fee.

Many employers offer group medical plans as part of their fringe benefits; this helps reduce health coverage costs for their employees. In such cases the family will not need to supply its own medical coverage.

The government is also entering the health field more strongly with Medicare plans of various kinds (Social Security disability and Workmen's Compensation insurance). Many analysts suggest that health services will one day be a branch of government, but for the time being unless you are very poor, you must cover for health emergencies or face potential financial ruin. One example of rising medical costs should suffice to convince you of the importance of medical coverage. A knee cartilage removal cost about $200 in 1950; in 1984 the cost was $3000.

Automobile coverage is also essential. It is so important that many states make it illegal to be uninsured. Property damage and liability are the crucial elements. Covering one's own car for damage is less important unless, of course, it is being purchased through an installment loan, in which case the lender requires coverage for collision damage.

If you own your own home or other real property, you must have fire coverage. This is a mandatory condition of borrowing mortgage money. Because of inflation you should increase such coverage periodically to keep up with rising construction costs. Homeowner's package policies give much more protection than just fire coverage. Usually they include coverage for such things as theft, personal liability, wind and water damage, and personal belongings.

Even if you do not own your own home, it is a good idea to have a personal belongings insurance policy. Such things as stereo equipment, cameras, furniture, and clothing are surprisingly expensive to replace if they are stolen or lost in a fire. Insurance, on the other hand, is relatively inexpensive.

Life insurance is also important, although not an absolute necessity. There are many kinds of life insurance, and newly married couples are often pushed by insurance agents to overinsure or to choose an unnecessarily expensive policy. Remember that the purpose of life insurance is to protect one's estate and provide for the family until the children are independent. The best protection for the least money is term insurance. In term insurance a given amount of insurance is bought for a set period of years, usually five. As one becomes older, the premium becomes higher because the chance of death increases.

Savings life insurance policies are very expensive and should usually be avoided by young couples. For example, a young couple can buy about $16,000 worth of five-year term life insurance for $100 a year, whereas that amount will only pay for $6000 worth of coverage in an insurance plus savings policy. Insurance agents tend to push savings life insurance because both they and their company earn a great deal more on this type of policy. However, the savings aspect of the policy yields only 2 to 3 percent return.* By investing the substantial difference in cost between term and savings life insurance, a couple can have a great deal more

*Starting in 1982 some insurance companies began to offer better savings rates by investing the insured's money in money market funds.

insurance protection and at the same time can accumulate savings at a much faster rate.

Basically, the amount of life insurance a couple needs will depend on the number and ages of their children, their standard of living, and their other investments. What life insurance must do is protect the family if the major monetary contributor should die. It should cover death costs, outstanding debts, and should supply enough money to allow the family to continue functioning. Just how much this will be depends on the individual family. In some families the wife and children may also be insured.

Your Own Home: The End of an American Dream?

Home ownership has been a way of life for most Americans. A higher percentage of Americans (67 percent; U.S. Bureau of the Census, 1983) own their own homes than do persons in any other nation in the world. As you will see in Chapter 13, one's home is a major source of savings for many retired Americans. Depending on the state of the economy, arguments can be made that the costs of home ownership make the investment less attractive than commonly believed. Assuming that the money spent on home ownership is saved and invested wisely, it is probably true that most of the time more money can be made than will accrue through appreciation of a home. A person's home yields many other kinds of personal satisfactions, though, beyond the possibility of economic gain. The American dream of one day owning your own home is therefore more than merely an economic dream.

Unfortunately, for many young couples the dream may not come true. The costs of home ownership have risen so drastically in the past ten years as to place a home out of reach of many Americans. Home prices, mortgage interest rates, property taxes, and utilities costs have all risen at a much faster rate than the overall Consumer Price Index increase. As of December 1982 the overall CPI stood at 292. Home ownership was at 372.9, with interest costs (one subpart of home ownership) at 626.3. Residential rents, it is interesting to note, stood at 230.8. Rents historically have lagged behind general inflation rates by about two years. With the soaring costs of home ownership, rent is one of the consumer's better buys today. Although we hear much grumbling about increasing rents, in relation to the rest of the economy rents simply have not increased as rapidly as most goods and services.

Mortgage interest rates have risen from a low of 6 percent to around 18 percent over the past fifteen years. They are extremely volatile. For example, in the beginning of 1982 they were at record highs, but by the beginning of 1983, they had dropped back to the 12-to-14-percent range. To give you some idea of what these fluctuations mean to prospective home buyers, Table 7-11 shows the amount of income necessary at various interest rates to qualify for a thirty-year, $50,000 mortgage.

TABLE 7-11 Income Needed to Qualify for a Thirty-Year, $50,000 Mortgage*

INTEREST RATE	MONTHLY PAYMENTS	MONTHLY INCOME	ANNUAL INCOME
10%	$439	$1,752	$21,024
12%	514	2,056	24,672
13%	553	2,212	26,544
14%	592	2,368	28,416

*Principal and interest payment.

Although housing prices have risen dramatically over the past fifteen years, the acceleration in prices seems to have leveled off. In many parts of the country, prices actually began to decline in 1982, although not dramatically. A few years earlier — 1978 — the new-house median price had been $61,900 and the used-house median price $53,700. By November 1982 the respective figures had increased to $74,200 and $67,500.

The economy has reacted in a number of ways to try to keep home ownership within reach of the American family. Smaller homes, modular homes, mobile homes, condominiums, and cooperatives have all increased in popularity. Government funding of lower-interest mortgages has also been made available. However, the long-range picture for home ownership by the young American family is not promising.

Summary

The family is the major unit of consumption in the United States. For a family to survive it must have the economic ability to provide food, shelter, and transportation for its members. Ideally, there will also be money to supply pleasurable and recreational activities as well. The family that is economically successful stands a much better chance of cohesiveness than the family that fails economically. For example, the poorest segment of the American society has the highest rate of divorce.

Credit use in the United States has allowed Americans to maintain the world's highest standard of living. Yet this easy availability of credit can also curtail individual and family freedom when it is abused and/or misunderstood. Future payments for present goods or services can lock the person making the agreement into an inflexible life pattern. Money must be earned steadily to meet the payment schedule. For many families the debt burden is so large that almost all funds are allocated automatically to make the many payments due each month. The family has little or no monetary flexibility to meet unforeseen emergencies or to act quickly if a good investment opportunity arises.

On the other hand, a thorough understanding of credit, installment buying, interest costs, and budgeting can work to a family's benefit, allowing them to invest and perhaps to achieve not only economic security but freedom as well. Investments are a means of supplementing income and making money work to produce more money. The family able to save and invest even a small portion of their income is freer of possible economic entrapment and stands a better chance of survival than families who cannot control wants and desires and spend their total income.

Investments can be plotted along a continuum from low risk, low return to high risk, high return. Examples of low-risk, low-return investments are bank savings and savings and loan accounts. Risk and return increase with such investments as first and second mortgages, syndications, apartment houses, commercial property, and franchises. While the rate of return can be very high for such speculations as land, commodities, oil and mining, and invention backing, the risk is too high for young couples with limited funds. The stock market is another investment outlet. Here again there is a continuum from low risk, low return to high risk, high return.

The day-to-day handling of money can be a problem in a family if the partners have different values about money. Conflict can be minimized if the couple decides ahead of time how most monetary decisions will be made. Their choices are: to let the husband make all decisions, to let the wife make all decisions, to let both have separate funds and share agreed-on obligations, or to share a joint account on which each can draw as necessary. Budgeting will also allow them to plan for necessities and to see how their income is spent. Deciding together how to use income left over after meeting necessities is another way to reduce monetary conflict.

Inflation is the number one economic enemy of the newly married couple. Inflation rates have risen in recent years, as have wages. However, at times wages do not rise as rapidly, so that many people find that their real income actually will go down. It is important for families to understand inflation so that they can take steps to guard against it. Proper budgeting and good investments are two steps that a family can take to reduce the unwanted effects of inflation.

Insurance should be considered a necessity. A couple needs medical coverage, automobile coverage, and, if they own a home, fire insurance. Life insurance is also important, though not a necessity. Couples should start with a medical policy that protects them against catastrophic illness and then, as children arrive, change to broader coverage. This pattern should also be followed with life insurance. The couple should buy term insurance, increasing the amount of the coverage as needed to protect family members.

The American dream of home ownership for every family shows strong signs of fading in the face of drastically increased housing prices. Smaller homes, condominiums, and cooperatives will probably be the housing of the future.

SCENES FROM MARRIAGE

Gaining Freedom through Investment

The world of investment has undergone drastic change in the past few years. Investment opportunities for the small investor have greatly expanded. Perhaps the best example is the revolution in banking that occurred with the passing of the Depository Institutions Deregulation Act of 1980. For years checking accounts earned no interest and bank savings accounts earned only minimal interest, 3 to 6 percent per year, which did not even offset inflation.

Savings Accounts

Starting in 1982, however, gradual deregulation allowed banking institutions to offer a greater variety of investment and savings opportunities with much higher interest return to their customers. Because most investors must start by first saving some investment capital, the many new types of accounts allow those savings to start working immediately. Table 7-6 indicated the difference in interest earned over time between a 6 percent return and a 12 percent return. Using the new savings opportunities can thus pay the investor big dividends.

Banks and savings and loan associations are now offering a variety of money market accounts that pay between 7 and 18 percent depending on the market. Investors with a great deal of money, say $100,000 or more, have always been able to invest in a number of money instruments, such as certificates of deposit, that were not limited in interest by law. For the small investor money market funds pool the monies of a number of persons and invest them in high-yield certificates as well as Treasury bills and so forth.

Money market savings accounts are now offered by all savings institutions. Checking accounts also now earn interest on the average balance. A type of checking account, the SuperNow account, pays money market rates so long as the balance is above $2500. If the balance drops below this amount, the institution may pay no interest or a maximum of 5.25 percent, depending on the institution's policies. Because of the partial deregulation of the banking industry, consumers must shop more carefully to maximize their savings and possible checking account returns because there are almost as many plans as institutions.

Once a person has instituted a savings program and has accumulated some capital, one can begin to investigate a broader range of investments. Space allows only a superficial discussion of a few of the many investment opportunities possible. Each person must make her or his own decisions about saving and investing. For example, a young family with small children should lean toward conservative investments that require little personal time because they probably have little free time at this stage in their lives. Each couple must consider their personal interests and their financial goals. For example, the family in which the husband or wife has flexible time (perhaps they own their own business, do free-lance work, teach and have considerable vacation time, and so on) can consider apartment ownership and management. Where time is rigidly structured, the family can investigate the stock market, real estate or business syndicates, mortgage purchase, house trading, and so on.

It is also important to review

TABLE 7-12   Current Value of $10,000 Invested*

5 YEARS AGO		1 YEAR AGO	
Coins	$37,500	Corporate bonds	$14,085
Gold	29,780	Treasury bonds	14,085
Gems	22,467	Money market funds	11,394
Growth funds	21,015	Growth funds	11,022
Platinum	18,663	Passbook savings account	10,572
Money market funds	17,575	NYSE stocks	10,170
Silver	17,400	Single-family existing home	10,149
Single-family existing home	15,148	Old masters painting	10,000
Old masters painting	15,197	Gold	9,250
Treasury bonds	14,896	Silver	8,912
NYSE stocks	14,470	Gems	7,956
Passbook savings account	12,927	Platinum	7,312
Corporate bonds	12,647	Coins	7,140

*Figured as of January 1, 1983.

investment choices often. The economy has shifted so quickly during the past five years that what was an excellent investment one day may have been a poor investment the next. Table 7-12 examines the current value of $10,000 invested in different types of investments. Some interesting facts appear that point out clearly the necessity of continually reviewing investment choices. If you invested in coins five years ago, your $10,000 would be worth $37,500 today. However, if you invested in coins only one year ago, your $10,000 would be worth only $7140 today. In other words, coins were a great investment five years ago but a poor investment during the past year. Notice that stocks were not a particularly good investment five years ago, nor even one year ago (figured as of January 1, 1983). During 1983, however, the stock market soared to record highs.

First Mortgage

Money is loaned with real estate as security for the debt. If the debt is not paid, the land and/or building is taken over by the lender. First mortgages are quite safe so long as no more money is loaned than the property is worth. For example, most savings and loan institutions lend 80 percent or less of the selling or appraised price of a property, thus assuring themselves that their loan will be covered in case the property must be sold to recover the debt. Young couples usually cannot consider buying first mortgages because to do so requires a good deal of money. For example, 80 percent of an $80,000 house is $64,000. Also, the money is usually tied up for a long time, twenty to thirty years in most cases.

Second Mortgage

This kind of investment can be considered by a young couple because the amount of money required can be low. The loan is the same type as a first mortgage but more speculative because it is given after a first mortgage has already been placed against the property. (The first-mortgage holder has first claim on the property in case of default.) A second mortgage is often made when the buyer of a property doesn't have enough cash for the down payment or when money is needed to make up the difference between the price and the first mortgage. Take, for example, a house bought for $65,000, with a $55,000 first mortgage, by a buyer who has only $5000 for the down payment. The buyer is therefore $5000 short of the sales price. A short-term second mortgage of $5000 will make up the difference.

Second mortgages are usually for only a few years, seldom more than seven and more often only for two to three. They can be in any amount, which makes them investment possibilities for young couples. They may be purchased from real estate agencies and money brokers. Ads for both first and second mortgages also may be found in the classified newspaper sections. In general one should not invest more in a second mortgage than the buyer has put down on the property. One should also be sure that the property is worth the price paid, so that in the case of default, sale of the property will realize enough money to cover both the first and second mortgages.

Although the standard interest rate for most second mortgages is 10 percent (in many states it can now be higher), one can often earn more by buying the second at a discount. Let's say that the previous owners of the $65,000 house took the second mortgage of $5000 from the new buyer. However, the previous owners find that they need cash before the mortgage is due. In order to make the second mortgage more attractive, they offer to sell the mortgage at a 10 percent discount. Perhaps $4000 is still due on the mortgage. The discount means that the new investor would get the mortgage of $4000 for $3600, thus effectively increasing the profit margin.

Syndicates

Money for investment is raised by a group of individuals who form a partnership and usually buy real estate or a business. For the young couple, joining such a venture is often possible in the position of a limited partner. There will be a few general partners who actually put the deal together and run the investment on a day-to-day basis. They will also assume the risks beyond each limited partner's investment. All the limited partner does is contribute some minimum amount of money. For example, the limited partner shares might cost $1000 each. The limited partners have no responsibility in the management and no risk other than their initial investment. If the venture is prof-

itable, they share in the profits. Such syndicates are often advertised in the financial pages, but more often one learns about them from other investors and professional money management persons. State laws control the syndicates so that the investor knows how the money will be used and what liabilities will be assumed, as well as what profit will be paid if the venture works well.

Apartment and Commercial Rentals

This kind of investment requires time as well as money because the rentals must be managed and maintained continually. However, apartment management for other owners is a good way for a young couple to get started. They not only make money but learn the fundamentals of property management before actually investing in apartments themselves. Commercial rentals are generally beyond the economic means of young couples, so they won't be discussed here.

If a couple has time and is handy at minor repairs, then buying and living in a duplex or triplex is a good start toward property ownership. The rents help with the payments and maintenance, and in addition the value of a well-located property will follow the upward inflationary trend.

Franchises

This kind of investment involves buying a business such as McDonald's, Radio Shack, Sambo's, or Colonel Sanders' Kentucky Fried Chicken. The advantage is that one starts a business sup-

ported by a large company's reputation, experience, backing, and advertising. The new owner must use the parent company's products and maintain a given standard of service. The price for good franchises is high, but many of the larger companies have loan funds that can help the new owner get started.

Land Speculation and Commodities

These are really speculations rather than investments and should be avoided by the small investor because the risk of loss is high. Both involve gambling on the future desirability of land or the future price of commodities (commodities are farm products such as corn, wheat, cattle, or oats, or raw materials such as copper, silver, gold, or timber).

Let's look at one commodity speculation. Suppose a cattle raiser needs money or decides to avoid the risk of changing prices by entering into a futures' account. The calves are bought at today's prices and then are sold to the futures' account at the going rate for year-old steers. (The cattle raiser still has to feed the calves for the year but has been assured of a moderate profit.) The speculator who buys the account hopes, of course, that the price of beef will be higher when the steers are actually ready for market. Risks are high because such unpredictable things as weather, governmental policies, and the international situation affect commodity prices. For example, remember what happened to the price of beef when wheat reserves were sold to the Soviets and the price of feed for cattle skyrocketed? On the other hand, often so much of a particular commodity is produced that prices drop (this has happened in recent years with milk and pork).

Oil and Mining and Invention Backing

These investments are even more speculative and should not be considered by a young family entering the investment market.

Stocks and Bonds

Another major form of investment is the stock market, or stocks and bonds. We will consider these investments in some detail, starting at the low-risk, low-return end of the continuum and continuing to those investments that involve more risk and also more return.

In general stocks, bonds, and notes of various kinds are bought through stock brokerage firms. These firms are members of various stock exchanges through which they buy and sell. The customer pays a small fee to the brokerage house to buy or sell.

Bonds

Bonds are a form of IOU or promissory note that companies issue when they need funds. Bonds are usually issued in thousand-dollar multiples. The issuing company promises to pay the bondholders a specified amount of interest for a specified amount of time at the end of which the bond will be redeemed for the face amount. Because of this generally low risk, bonds usually offer low interest rates. There are several kinds of bonds: U.S. savings, corporation, and municipal bonds. U.S. savings bonds are the safest investment but are also long term and

low interest. Because of inflation, an investor can actually lose money over the period of the bond. Corporation bonds are relatively safe because the company pledges properties it owns as collateral. Municipal bonds are similar except that a government unit offers the bonds, usually to complete a building or park project. They are relatively safe, but as city finances have become more strained in recent years, there is doubt that some municipal bonds will be repaid at the expiration date. Municipal bonds have the advantage of having their interest exempt from federal income taxes.

Stocks

A stock is a piece of paper (stock certificate) that gives the owner the right to a portion of the assets of the company issuing the stock. Like bonds, stocks are issued when companies need money, usually for expansion. Unlike bondholders, stockholders are part owners of the company they have invested in and can vote at stockholders' meetings. The stocks of large companies are usually listed on stock exchanges, either regional ones around the country or the two largest, the New York Stock Exchange and the American Stock Exchange. These organized exchanges set minimum requirements that must be met by a company to have its stock listed. For example, the New York Stock Exchange specifies that a company must have at least $10 million in tangible assets, at least $2 million in annual earnings, and at least 1 million shares divided among 2000 or more shareholders. Stocks are also sold over the counter in markets that are less organized than the exchanges.

These stocks are usually not traded as often as those listed on the exchanges and are issued by smaller and less well known companies (over-the-counter stocks offer the highest risk and highest return).

1. *Preferred stocks.* These are called preferred because when earnings are distributed or when a company is liquidated or becomes bankrupt, holders of preferred stock are paid first.

2. *Common stocks.* Most stocks are common stocks. They are the last to earn and normally fluctuate more than bonds and preferred stock. Whereas common stocks usually pay dividends, most investors hope to buy the stock at a low price and sell it at a higher price after a rise in the stock market. Blue chip stocks are those of strong companies such as General Motors or IBM. The stronger the company, usually the safer the stock.

Mutual Funds

Mutual funds are companies that buy and sell large blocks of stocks. The investor can buy shares in such companies rather than shares in "real" companies. Each mutual fund stock represents a share of the large and diversified group of shares the fund owns. There are two kinds of mutual funds, closed end and open end. Closed-end funds usually do not issue stock after the initial issue. Many closed-end mutual funds are listed on the New York Stock Exchange, and their shares are readily transferable in the open market and can be bought and sold like other shares. Open-end funds, on the other hand, usually issue more shares as people want them and are not listed on the stock exchange.

The young family should consider diversified investment rather than place all of their capital into one venture. For example, in the stock market the mutual fund is safer than the single stock because it represents a widely diversified holding of stocks. Before considering any investment, though, the family should be sure it has enough insurance for basic security (see A Word about Insurance, pp. 254–255).

Collectibles

Collectibles are tangible goods that usually have in common some degree of (1) rarity, (2) scarcity, (3) demand, (4) popularity, (5) craftsmanship, (6) antiquity, (7) aesthetic qualities of beauty and taste, (8) absolute and/or classical value to society and culture (Van Caspel, 1980). Such things would be rare coins and stamps, art of various kinds, rare books and cars, oriental rugs, antique toys, and so forth.

The naive investor generally should avoid collectibles. It takes a great deal of knowledge to know a valuable coin or to recognize a stamp that has appreciation value. Sometimes a hobby started in one's youth can be turned into a collectible investment.

CHAPTER 8

A REAL REVOLUTION:
THE TWO-JOB FAMILY

CONTENTS

American families have undergone a fundamental change in how they provide for their economic welfare. The new family type is what the Census Bureau describes as a "husband-primary-earner, wife-secondary-earner" family. The long title really denotes that in today's family the woman works outside the home and shares economic support of the family with her husband.

The jobs of the vast majority of working women are not the glamorous professions, the upper management levels of corporate America, nor the government leadership roles depicted by mass media. No, the work world for women is much the same as it is for most men: eight-to-five days, two-week yearly vacations, and often mundane duties. Unlike her husband, though, the working wife must shoulder a second job, that of running her home and family.

As we saw in Chapter 6, women have gained access to a greater variety of jobs as well as to higher-level employment in all areas. There are more women doctors and lawyers. There are more women corporate executives and managers. But these are the exceptions just as they are among men, granted that women are still far less represented than men in these occupations. Although it is a worthy goal to open all types and levels of jobs to women, the reality is that most women will not achieve such occupational ends. The work world for women is still more limited than it is for men, both in pay and in opportunity.

Regardless of the additional problems faced by the working wife, her entrance into the work world and her sharing of the breadwinner role has wrought a revolution in the family and in the overall relationship between the sexes. In years past the working woman generally, and the working wife in particular, was an unusual phenomenon. Before 1900 the labor force included few women. Married women were full-time wives and mothers and were considered negligent in their duty if they worked outside the home. Of the workers in the labor force in 1890, 3.7 million were women. They accounted for 17 percent of all workers and represented 18 percent of the female population over fourteen years of age. Only 4.5 percent of married women were in the labor force (Smith, 1979).

By 1980, 52 percent of the female population over age sixteen were in the labor force (Rank, 1982), compared with 34 percent in 1950. Among married women 51 percent were in the labor force in 1981 (Bureau of Census, 1982), compared with 34.7 percent in 1960 and 44.4 percent in 1975 (Glick & Norton, 1979). The most dramatic and perhaps most significant increase has occurred for women with young children. In 1950 only 12 percent of mothers with one or more children below age six were employed or looking for work. By 1960 this number had risen to 23.3 percent, by 1975 to 36.6 percent, and by 1980 close to half, 45 percent, were in the labor force (Rank, 1982; Glick & Norton, 1979). If we consider the strong past attitudes about the importance of the mother being at home when her children are young, this is an amazing change in behavior and social mores. Number of children at home is no longer strongly related to workforce participation of women (Ferber, 1982).

These statistics clearly show that women are in the workforce as never before. It is equally clear that the role of the woman as homemaker and mother, to the exclusion of employment, is passing. Thus the traditional marriage in which the husband works to support the family while the wife remains home caring for the family has become a minority pattern. Labor department projections indicate that by 1990 this traditional type of family will describe only 25 percent of married women's families (Smith, 1979). Today's American family is a dual-worker family in which both husband and wife work to support the family.

A number of factors have led to the increased numbers of married women working outside the home (Smith, 1979):

1. The constant inflationary pressures of the American economy and the rising expectations about higher standards of living have combined to bring many women into the workforce. The majority of working wives work to help make ends meet. This economic need of the couple is still the major reason most women go to work (Gordon & Kammeyer, 1980). The cost of housing in many areas (see Chapter 7) has risen so greatly that only a two-income family can afford to buy a home. This is just one example of why an inflationary economy works to bring the wife into the labor market.

2. Since World War II real wages have increased dramatically. (Real wages are those that have been adjusted to take inflation into consideration.) Because the woman can now earn much more than in the past (still less than men), the relative cost of staying home with her family all day becomes too large, and more women are drawn into the labor force. One might think that the opposing effect of increased real income for a family — namely, less economic pressure to work and greater financial means to enjoy leisure pursuits — would work to keep women home. However, this effect has not been dominant. One reason might be that desires for increasingly higher standards of living have outpaced the real-income increase. Secondly, in recent years of high inflation, real income has not increased rapidly. Indeed, in some years it has actually declined.

   Thus despite generally increasing real income, women have not remained home to enjoy it but have entered the labor market to participate in the higher wages. Increased income also permits the reduction of unpaid labor in the home by the woman, because labor-saving devices and domestic help can be purchased.

3. There has been a tremendous increase in the kinds of jobs available to women. The importance of physical strength in many industrial jobs has diminished. Service jobs, such as clerical and sales, have expanded greatly. The opportunity for part-time work has also increased. Equal opportunity legislation (Chapter 6, p. 198) has created demands for women in jobs previously unavailable. Because of the greatly increased demand for women workers, their wages have increased, although they remain well below men's wages (Chapter 6, p. 195).

4. Declining birthrates have certainly contributed to women's working more. Women with small children are still the least likely to work

outside of the home, although this is fast changing (Glick, 1979). As the years diminish during which small children are at home, the woman is freer to seek work and fulfillment outside of the home.

5. Increasing education has contributed to women's working outside the home. College attendance by women has gradually increased from only a small percentage fifty years ago to equal or even higher percentages than among men (Glick, 1979). Many colleges now have more women than men enrolled. Better education certainly creates job opportunities. More importantly, the educated person's awareness tends to increase, and as a result, he or she will seek fulfillment as well as the chance to make a broader contribution to society. The role of wife and mother becomes only one of many roles for the educated woman as she becomes more aware of her potential.

6. Attitudes about the role of the woman in the family have changed greatly during this century. In 1930 only 18 percent of surveyed women believed married women should have a full-time job outside of the home (Smith, 1979). Valerie Oppenheimer (1977) reports that in 1964 54 percent of the women surveyed agreed that a working mother could still establish a close relationship with her children. By 1970 that percentage had risen to 73 percent. Today most women also believe that working outside the home is important for personal satisfaction, rather than just for earning additional money. Much of this change in attitude has undoubtedly been brought about by the women's liberation movement.

The Working Wife

Joe and Mary Revisited

In the last chapter (p. 236), you'll remember we left Joe and Mary trying to pay off their debts under a court-supervised bankruptcy payment plan. Mary was busy at home with her second baby. Another, more common scenario for this story is that Mary goes to work to help make ends meet. In this way they are able to avoid the drastic step of bankruptcy, at least for a while and probably indefinitely.

The woman entering the work world is faced with more complicated and, often, more limited choices than her husband. Basically she must choose from three major work patterns:

Pattern A: Working for a few years before marrying or having children, and then settling into the homemaker job for the rest of her life. This was the predominant pattern for white, middle-class women until World War II. Although the numbers of such women are large, their proportion is declining. Today such women are most apt to be: mothers of more than three children, wives of affluent men, and women without high-school education who have meager opportunities in the job market.

Pattern B: Following the same career pattern as men, in that she remains in the paid labor force continuously and full time throughout the years between school and retirement. Women most likely to be in this pattern are women without children, black women, and women in professional and managerial jobs.

Pattern C: Working until she has children, then staying home for a certain amount of time (perhaps five to ten years), and returning to the labor force on a basis that won't conflict with her remaining family responsibilities. This is now the dominant pattern for American women (Howe, 1977).

Most men follow pattern B, and more and more women are entering this pattern also. Both patterns A and C are limited by the job opportunities available. Many employers are hesitant to place young unmarried or newly married women into jobs with long-term advancement potential or higher-level jobs that require extended training. They fear that such women will soon leave the job by choosing one of the other two patterns. Pattern C has special difficulties for the woman returning to work after a long absence. She often finds that her skills are outdated. Too, higher-level jobs may demand too much of her attention, causing conflict with her second job as mother, homemaker, and wife.

Work Availability: A Double-Edged Sword for Married Women

Increasing work availability for women has also meant increasing independence. Not only does this mean increased freedom *within* marriage, but it can also mean increased freedom *from* marriage. There is little doubt that the working woman's ability to support herself has freed her to seek changing roles. As Ralph Smith (1979) says:

> To the extent that employment provides a woman with a reason and the means to postpone marriage, with meaningful roles other than motherhood, and with the ability to support herself after divorce, women's employment has contributed to these changes in marriage formation and dissolution. (1979, pp. 23 – 24)

In the past a woman's inability to support herself trapped her into marriage. She had to have a husband to survive. But with wider economic opportunities, this has become increasingly untrue. She is now able to survive financially; on her own, even when she has children. She does not need to remain trapped in an unhappy, unfulfilling marriage. Thus one edge of the work availability sword is the woman's increased independence from marriage.

Persons with limited resources also have limited freedom and reduced alternatives compared with persons having greater resources. In the past a woman has almost always had fewer economic resources in a marriage and thereby has been more dependent on the marriage (Rank, 1982). Not only has she had fewer alternatives than her husband, but she even had to derive her status from his success. As sociologists Hornung and Mc-Cullough (1981) put it, hers was only "relational property" status — that is, her status was derived from information about the substantive relationship between her and her husband: "Who are you?" "I'm the wife of a doctor." One result of work availability for women, then, is that it frees them to have their own identity. And it frees them from marriage if they so desire.

The other edge of the sword is that through work outside of the home, a woman's family life can be improved and enhanced. Her earnings can increase the family's standard of living. She can help alleviate the family's monetary restraints. For example, when Mary goes to work, she reduces the pressure on Joe. Hopefully this will help him feel happier and more satisfied with his family life. The family can take longer vacations together. They can afford better housing in a nicer neighborhood. They can help their children increase their education. Thus the wife's working can contribute greatly toward the family's well-being and the permanence of the marriage.

In addition to the direct economic advantages of having an additional wage earner in the family, there are numerous other advantages. As mentioned, the husband may be under less economic pressure. The working wife may derive great personal satisfaction from her work just as many men do. By interacting with other adults outside of her family, she may feel more stimulated and fulfilled, especially if she has small children at home. Her self-esteem may increase, with the knowledge that she is more of an equal partner in marriage.

The results of increased independence experienced by the woman who enters the work world are hard to predict. Each individual will react differently. The point is that increased independence for the woman, made possible by her participation in the work world, is now a fact of life. For some women it may effectively end their marriage and harm their family. For others it will greatly enhance their marriage and family. Regardless of the particular case, there is no doubt that women's participation in the world of work has been revolutionary to the individual woman, to women, and to the family and society in general.

What Are the Effects of Female Employment on the Time of Marriage?

As we discussed in the previous section, employment of a married woman can have either positive or negative effects on her marriage. A working woman is more likely to postpone marriage (Moore & Hofferth, 1979; Smith, 1979) because she is able to support herself without marriage. Although this seems to support the idea of employment as an alternative to marriage, overall marriage rates have not declined. About 95 percent

INSET 8-1

Working Women, Health, and Death

Sickness and death may seem like far-fetched consequences of female employment, but when one considers that women have, within the traditional role, made nurturing and home production their principal concern, the loss or diminution of these services might be feared to lead to poorer health among family members. Women, of course, as they opt for the working world, are exposing themselves to job tensions, commuting accidents, and occupational hazards; consequently, their mortality may

rise. Especially given the picture of over-work and strain in households with two full-time earners plus children, it seems possible that less attention can be given to proper diet and rest. Parents cannot afford to take the time to relax or to be ill, so their physical health may deteriorate. Two-job couples may consequently have shorter life spans.

On the other hand, the higher incomes of families with employed wives may provide the wherewithal for an adequate diet and preventive medical care. Husbands who are freed from the omnipresent concern of supporting their families might enjoy lower blood pressure and fewer heart attacks. Husbands may be able to turn down overtime or leave a job that is harmful to their long-term health. These benefits from women's rising labor force participation might lengthen the average life span, particularly among men.

At this time, no studies are known that have addressed

this issue. If it is the case that increases in female employment affect longevity and the incidence of disease, however, the ramifications are enormous. The frequency and length of widowhood would be lessened. Fewer retired people might be unmarried. Pension systems and health care services would be affected. If the strains experienced by two-earner families are reflected even in the incidence of sickness and death, the importance of flexible and part-time employment becomes self-evident. Clearly, this is a topic that merits research attention.

Our speculation at this point is that the long-run effect of women's working will be to equalize the life span, lengthening men's lives but shortening women's. A shorter life span would be less likely, however, to the extent that both sexes reject the aggressive, competitive model of employment (Moore and Hofferth, 1979).

of contemporary American women will marry at some time in their lives (U.S. Bureau of the Census, May 1982). The young woman who works tends to postpone marriage rather than reject it altogether. On the other hand, for older women employment seems to act as a "dowry," particularly for those who have children and are contemplating remarriage (Oppenheimer, 1977; Moore & Hofferth, 1979). Men apparently are more willing to marry a woman with children if she is able to help support the children and herself, thus reducing the economic burden on the new husband.

The age at first marriage has risen slightly in the past few years, a fact that may be due to both the increasing education of women and their greater participation in the work force. Kristin Moore and Sandra Hofferth (1979, p. 29) summarize the effect of women's working on time of marriage as follows:

To the extent that increased employment of women raises occupational aspirations and educational attainment, age at marriage will continue to rise. Employment does not seem to lead many people to develop tastes or life-styles that preclude eventual marriage, however. Nevertheless, there may be a slight increase in the proportion of never married among those who turned 20 during the 1970s to about 7%. Rather than indicating a rejection of marriage, this will probably reflect the inability among some of those who postpone marriage to find a suitable partner when ready for marriage and some increase in the frequency of cohabitation.

How Does Employment of the Wife Affect Divorce and Separation?

As with time of marriage, female employment seems to have differing effects on the possibility of marital disruption. A woman can support herself outside of marriage if necessary. On the other hand, by economically contributing to the marriage, she can improve the quality of her family's life and consequently the stability of her marriage.

Studies on this question yield mixed results. Ivan Nye and Saul Hoffman (1974) reviewed the literature and concluded that families in which the wife is employed are no more likely to separate or divorce than those in which she is not employed. If the wife earns more than the husband, however, or if he is periodically unemployed, the probability of divorce or separation increases (Moore & Hofferth, 1979).

An interesting and controversial side question concerns the effect of welfare aid on marital disruption. Two different research teams have reported that receipt of welfare or income maintenance decreases marital stability (Hoffman & Holmes, 1976; Hannan & Tuma, 1977). In addition, welfare recipiency severely depresses remarriage rates in the first two years after divorce. This negative effect seems to disappear after two years have passed.

The Working Wife's Economic Contribution to the Family

Mary Decides to Go to Work

Joe manages to keep the family afloat financially until their second child is two and one-half years old. Mary and Joe realize, especially with the high inflation rate, that they simply aren't going to make it comfortably on his earnings alone. Mary has heard that a local company is expanding and needs new employees. She applies for a job, receives it, and suddenly finds herself to be a full-time working mother. Although her income is relatively small compared with Joe's, she believes her $900 per month will not only get them out of debt but will allow them a few luxuries they have had to forego. Also, she and Joe hope it will allow them to save a little money toward a house down payment.

Unfortunately, Joe and Mary learn that her $900 does not raise the family income by that amount. Before Mary can go to work, arrangements must be made for child care. They have several choices. Mrs. Smith, an older mother down the street, also needs some extra money and, for $50 per week, is willing to keep both children at her house during Mary's working hours. Joe's mother is also willing to keep them one day a week for free. There is a public day-care center near Mary's work that will care for the children for $45 per week. What the center charges is based on a family's income, so that the weekly costs vary from family to family. Mary decides to leave the children with Mrs. Smith four days a week ($40 per week) and Joe's mother for the remaining day (free). This way the children will be with people they know and will be staying in their own neighborhood as well. If this arrangement doesn't work out, Mary can put them in the day-care center. Thus Mary's monthly child-care costs are $160. This leaves $740 from her paycheck.

Transportation must be considered. There is a bus that goes past her workplace. The route is circuitous and requires her to leave the house one-half hour earlier than she would have to leave if she drove. Taking the bus both ways will cost an additional hour of time per day plus $22 per month ($1 per day). Riding the bus also means that Joe will have to take the children to the sitter's each morning. They decide that buying an older economy car is probably the best solution. With the added car, Mary can help deliver and pick up the children and can be more efficient generally. They borrow $1200 for twenty-four months at 15 percent interest and buy a used car from a friend. The car is in good shape and, other than needing a new set of tires, requires no work. There are additional insurance costs, however. They purchase only liability coverage, thinking that because the car is old, it isn't worth the cost of collision coverage. The total monthly cost for the car is $100. The breakdown is as follows:

Payment	$ 65	Discount interest adds up to $360 for two years. This makes a total debt of $1560. Divide by 24 months to get monthly payment of $65.
Insurance	$ 10	
Gas and maintenance	$ 25	
Total	$100/month	

Subtracting $100 more from Mary's monthly paycheck leaves $640.

Taxes and social security are also deducted from Mary's paycheck. She takes no deductions for the children and finds that another large bite has been taken from her paycheck. In addition, her income added to Joe's puts the family in a higher overall tax bracket. They will receive a refund at the end of the year because of child-care costs and other deductions, but when all is said and done, the taxes and Social Security costs average about $150 per month. Thus, Mary's monthly check shrinks further, to $490.

There are also miscellaneous costs associated with Mary's going to work. She doesn't have as much time for food preparation and household work. She uses more partially prepared foods such as frozen dinners that tend to be more expensive. She also sends more clothing to the laundry. In addition, she has had to buy some new clothes to wear to work. These costs add up to about $100 per month. The bottom line is that her $900-per-month pay adds only about $390 to the family income. This amounts to about 43 percent of her gross pay. In fact, studies indicate that the working mother will spend between 25 and 50 percent of her income in order to work, depending on the age of her children, type of work, and other factors unique to her situation (Vickery, 1979).

Because women tend to hold lower-paying jobs, as we saw in Chapter 6, the actual amount of money they contribute to the family tends to be small. Yet for many families this contribution is increasingly important. In the past, when the working wife was the exception, her work was viewed as a family insurance policy, a buffer against hard times. Today for many families her income has become necessary for survival. What this means is that many families no longer have an economic buffer between themselves and hard times. They become accustomed to living on two incomes; if either is lost, family finances become precarious, if not impossible.

Household Activities

It seems strange to hear a mother of two small children reply to the question "What do you do?" with "Oh, nothing, I'm just a housewife." Obviously, a mother with two small children does a great deal of work for her family inside the home. She certainly doesn't "do nothing." Therefore when she takes a job outside the home, something has to change inside the home. Mothers with children at home average about thirty-six hours per week working in the home (Walker & Woods, 1976). Generally, their time is divided into three major household activities: (1) meal preparation and cleanup, about 30 percent of their time; (2) care of family members, 15 to 25 percent; and (3) clothing and regular house care, 15 percent.

What happens to all of this work when mother takes an outside job? Essentially nothing. It still must be done and mother still does it. She simply cuts down the amount of time she gives to each task and donates much of her leisure time (weekends) to household tasks.

Although seldom discussed, the "just housewife" role usually includes other than homemaking activities. It is the "just housewives" that often do much of the important volunteer work for society. They are the ones who attend the PTA meetings, organize the church rummage sale, help a neighbor, and raise extra money for the children's school by conducting a paper drive. As more and more wives enter the formal work world, our society may experience a loss in the informal work world of the volunteer.

Community service may diminish because the working wife simply won't have time — or if she takes the time, as many do, the energy drain may be too great.

Many people suggest that the husband and children of the working wife will increase the amount of housework they do. Husbands, in fact, are just as likely as wives to agree that they should do more in the households when their wives work (Ferber, 1982), but they do not live up to their professed beliefs or their wives' expectations. Their increase in household work, especially the husband's, is small. Studies yield varying results about increased household work by husbands of working wives. Some show an increase as low as only six minutes a week, while others show as much as a two-hour weekly increase (Moore & Hofferth, 1979).

Although husbands don't appreciably increase their share of household work when their wives go to work, overall they are sharing more household work than they have in the past, whether or not their wives work. This change stems from shifting attitudes about sex roles and the increased emphasis on egalitarian marriage in the United States. Despite this, for many wives one result of going to work is "overload" and strain. They end up doing two jobs, one outside the home and one inside. Their leisure time is greatly reduced. The quality of their household work diminishes. Time becomes their most precious commodity.

It is this "overload" of the working wife, especially the working mother, that families most complain about. In the General Mills report, "American Families at Work" (1981), 63 percent of the working mothers surveyed indicated that they did not have enough time for themselves. It is interesting to note that only 40 percent of the working fathers felt the same way. Both working parents listed lack of time with family and children and long hours on the job as the greatest strains placed on the family when both husband and wife work. Of the working women in the study, 41 percent indicated they would prefer to work part-time.

Mary Seeks Part-Time Work

Mary works for seven months at her new full-time job. This helps get all of their debts paid off. However, she finds that she is increasingly fatigued. She and Joe never seem to have fun together any more. If she does find some free time, all she wants to do is sleep. The house looks unkempt. She hasn't had fun cooking a meal in months. She feels guilty about the little time she is able to spend with the children. She finds herself grumpy and unhappy much of the time. Mary decides, now that they are out of debt, to see if she can find a part-time job. She finally does, and with a sigh of relief, quits her full-time job.

Part-Time Work

As we suggested in Chapter 6 (p. 200), the creation of more and better part-time jobs for mothers with young children would help alleviate the overburden experienced by the full-time working mother. Between 1965 and 1977 the number of workers on voluntary part-time schedules increased nearly three times as rapidly as the number of full-time workers. Most of this increase was among women (see Figure 8-1), so that by 1977 women held nearly 70 percent of the part-time jobs (Barrett, 1979).

Approximately half of all women who work part-time give "taking care of the home" as their reason for preferring part-time work. The part-time schedule reduces the overload on the working mother. Unfortunately, it also reduces her economic contribution to the family. This is due not only to fewer hours worked but also to the lower pay standards for part-time work (see Table 8-1).

On an hourly basis part-time work generally pays 75 percent of full-time work. Part-time work seldom gives fringe benefits, job protection, or advancement opportunities. Those who seek part-time employment are usually assumed to be intermittent workers without long-term commitment to a career. Failure to gain fringe benefits, especially health insurance, combined with low pay in part-time jobs, may keep some people on welfare. Welfare recipients are eligible for free medical care under the Medicaid program, and welfare payments in some cases can be as much as can be earned in a part-time job.

The proportion of women working part-time has increased because of the larger proportion of mothers with young children (like Mary) who

FIGURE 8-1   Growth in part-time employment for men and women. Note: Excludes agricultural workers and part-time workers who want full-time jobs but cannot find them (U.S. Department of Labor 1978).

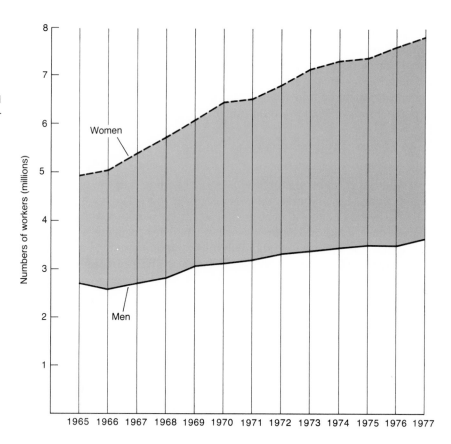

TABLE 8-1   Earnings of Part-Time versus Full-Time Workers by Occupation and Sex, 1977

OCCUPATION*	PERCENTAGE OF THE WORK FORCE ON PART-TIME SCHEDULES	MEDIAN HOURLY EARNINGS		PART-TIME EARNINGS AS A PERCENTAGE OF FULL-TIME EARNINGS
		FULL-TIME	PART-TIME	
WOMEN				
All workers	29	$3.85	$2.87	74
Sales	54	3.05	2.64	86
Clerical	24	3.91	3.06	78
Services (nondomestic)	47	2.95	2.59	88

Source: U.S. Department of Labor, Bureau of Labor Statistics, 1978.
Note: Data for part-time workers include persons who usually work from 1 hour to 34 hours per week. Data for full-time workers include persons who usually work at least 35 hours per week.
*The detailed occupations shown include 70 percent of all female part-time workers.

search for such jobs. Where are part-time jobs to be found? Usually in the occupations where women predominate, the so-called pink-collar occupations. Very few jobs are available for part-time managers. Very few openings exist for accountants, butchers, and machinists to work over the Christmas vacation. At the same time, four out of five waitresses work less than a full year. Department store saleswork is becoming increasingly part-time, and offices are turning more and more to temporary help. Beauty shops always have used part-time people. In the health field (hospitals and so forth), where women make up 75 percent of the workforce (except at the top), shift work and part-time arrangements are commonplace. In teaching, schools are turning increasingly to part-time substitutes in order to save money and live within more restricted budgets. In contrast, in the industries dominated by men, part-time and temporary work is seldom found.

What this means for most mothers is that they will be downwardly mobile in their work rather than upwardly mobile like their husbands. More and better jobs are open to women before they have families, because they can work full-time. After a woman has a family, when she is available for work often determines the job she finds. In the face of demands on her time, the young mother is likely to find that the scheduling of her job is the most important single consideration. Her immediate job choice is dictated in large measure by the time constraints imposed in the short run, and this in turn directs her subsequent career development (Howe, 1977).

However, as more and more mothers enter the workforce and prove to be good workers, part-time jobs may take on more and more of the advantages that come with full-time work. As we saw in Chapter 6, there are some problems for an employer who hires two part-time people to do one full-time job. Social security contributions, for example, will be higher for two workers than for one full-time worker, even if the rates of pay are identical. As the advantages of part-time work are recognized, it is hoped that such inequities for the employer can be removed.

Mary's New Part-Time Job

Mary's new half-time job pays her $350 per month. With her mother-in-law's help, she is able to do away with child-care costs. Transportation costs remain the same, $100 per month, leaving her $250. Taxes and social security are reduced to $70 per month, leaving $180. Miscellaneous costs are also reduced to $50 per month. In the end she contributes $130 extra dollars to the family compared with the $390 she contributed when working full-time. This is just enough to keep them out of debt. There is a great deal less strain on Mary, however, and hence on the family.

Marital Satisfaction When the Wife Works

As with so many areas we have discussed, the question of marital satisfaction is double-edged. The family may gain satisfaction through the wife's economic contribution; the family may lose satisfaction because she is no longer able to supply some of the caring and services she did as a full-time wife and mother. Economic strain may be reduced when she works; psychological and physical strain may be increased.

Moore and Hofferth (1979) find that the research evidence on marital satisfaction when the wife works is mixed. After reviewing many studies, they conclude that wives who work from choice rather than economic necessity, those whose husbands are favorable toward their employment, and those who work part-time are happier with their marriages than full-time housewives.

Although we have spoken mainly of the working wife's economic contribution to the family, Chapter 6 made it clear that her participation in the world of work may also pay her psychological dividends. Work may allow her to use some of her skills that are unused in the homemaker role. She will meet and interact with a wider variety of adults. She will gain more power in relationship to her husband (Rank, 1982). Her feelings of integrity, self-respect, competency, self-determination, and accomplishment may increase if she has desired employment and has successfully solved the problems of working and caring for her family.

The evidence of husbands' satisfactions with marriage when their wife works is also mixed but tends to indicate that they are less satisfied than the wives. As Moore and Hofferth report:

Evidence from other studies suggests that many husbands accept their wives' work grudgingly; that men may have more trouble than women do adapting to nonstereotypical roles; and therefore that men experience greater difficulties resolving the resulting stress. Other researchers note that in going to work a woman is frequently expanding into a new role, one that is higher in status than that of homemaker, while a husband who assumes homemaking functions is adopting a role of lower status — a role that may strain not only his sense of status and identity but his feeling of competence as well. Furthermore, a busy wife may not be able to provide the same level of physical and emotional support that a full-time homemaker can, so a husband may well come to feel he is losing out on all fronts. (1979, p. 121)

On the other hand, a second income can provide the husband additional freedom. He can cut down on moonlighting or overtime work. He might be able to take a temporary reduction in pay to enter a new career or job he finds more satisfying. Increased free time may allow more family enjoyment and leisure time pursuits.

Because of the importance of expectations in human relations (p. 128), what one thinks or expects about something is often as important as what actually happens. Research on marital quality in families where the wife works finds that happiness with the relationship is more related to the congruence between role expectations of one spouse and the role performance of the other spouse than to any particular pattern of roles. It is not simply a matter of whether a woman's working has an impact on marital adjustment but rather the extent to which that behavior violates role expectations, her own as well as her family's (Lewis & Spanier, 1979; Houseknecht & Macke, 1981). If she expected to be a housewife, if her husband expected her to stay home, and if significant others in her environment (parents, in-laws, children, and so forth) have negative attitudes about her working, then the chances are great that marital satisfaction will drop within herself and her family.

Researchers have discovered an interesting social-class difference in marital satisfaction when the wife goes to work: Lower-class families seem to have more adjustment problems than middle-class families. For example, studies report that lower-class sons who have full-time working mothers were less admiring of their fathers (Hoffman, 1974; Gold & Andres, 1978). Lower-class working wives score lower on marital adjustment (Burk & Weir, 1976; Rallings & Nye, 1979). One theory that tries to explain this is that the lower-class woman usually must work in order for the family to survive. Her working is thus a direct statement about her husband's inability to provide for his family and can therefore be seen by him as a threat to his status. In contrast with lower-class women, those in the middle class are more likely to be in the labor force voluntarily rather than out of necessity. One must be careful interpreting social-class differences in marital satisfaction because there are many differing influences on the lower class as compared with the middle class as compared with the upper class. For example, differing educational levels lead to differing attitudes about a mother's entering the work world.

Traditionally, only a small minority of mothers with children under age six have been employed. Two factors have worked to keep the mother of young children out of the labor force. First, the logistics of caring for the children are often insolvable. Second, there has been a long-standing belief that a mother belongs with her children, especially when they are young. Because of earlier studies of the effects of prolonged separation of children from caring parents (orphanage and foster home placements, war orphans, and so forth), many people believe that the mother's absence during the early years will do great harm to the child.

There is a large body of research on both animals and humans that suggests the importance of early maternal nurturing to proper maturing. In each case the research notes that the maternally deprived child has difficulty forming close relationships as an adult. Alice Rossi (1977) notes that it is more important to the survival of humans than to any other mammals to provide prolonged care through intense attachment of mother and infant. She indicates that throughout most of human history infants had extremely close physical contact with their mothers for 70 percent of the day during infancy and for about 30 percent of the day until the middle of the second year. Today most infants have body contact with others less than 25 percent of the day soon after birth, which shortly falls off to 5 percent. J. W. Prescott (1970, 1975, 1976) has demonstrated neurostructural, neuroelectrical, and neurochemical abnormalities of sensory system functioning and development as well as related behavioral deficits associated with sensory deprivation. Others (Schwartz, Money & Robinson, 1981) conclude from such research that it is likely that absence of fondling, stroking, touching, and playing during early years of postnatal brain differentiation may make a person particularly susceptible to attachment and intimacy difficulties later in life. The General Mills study (1981) found that almost twice as many family members believed that the effect of both parents' working outside the home has been negative (52 percent) as believe it has been positive (28 percent).

Yet effective child care by other than the true biological mother does not necessarily lead to severe problems in children. Actual effects of substitute child care are just as difficult to uncover as are the effects of natural parenting. The effects depend on (1) the quality of the substitute care, (2) the characteristics of the child, (3) the mother's reasons for working and the quality and quantity of the time she does spend with the child, and (4) the general social acceptance of substitute child care.

The quality of substitute child care can be excellent. It can provide for the child both physically and psychologically. A loving, caring baby-sitter is often an important and happy influence on a child. Most often (48 percent) working mothers leave their children with other family members. Only about 19 percent leave their children in day-care centers (General Mills, 1981). It would seem that the chances of other family members' giving the child love and attention would be greater than with strangers. Substitute child care cannot be wholly praised or condemned but must be examined as to its specific merits. It can be good or bad for a child, just as the child's biological mother can be.

Individual children will react differently to the partial loss of their mother and the substitution of another manner of care. Their reaction can be positive or negative. A hyperactive, disruptive child may experience much negative feedback in a large day-care center. This same child may thrive with an attentive individual baby-sitter.

If the mother is an unhappy, frustrated homemaker and prefers the work world, her child will probably be better off with a substitute. It is perhaps not the quantity of time a mother spends with her child but rather the quality of time that counts. A working mother may spend less time with her children, but if she makes it high quality time, her relationship with her children may be improved. Note, however, that a generous quantity of time must be spent with children if there is to be quality.

Mary Tries to Improve the Time She Spends with Her Children

When she was a full-time homemaker, Mary found that her two children were always under foot. She never seemed to have a minute's peace. They were calling "Mommy, Mommy, Mommy" so often that she almost never paid attention to it. In fact, sometimes when she heard them, she'd deliberately hide from the children to escape their constant pressure. Now that she works, she finds she enjoys spending time with them. She looks forward to the weekends so she can do projects with them and give them her undivided attention. She spends much less time with them now that she works, but she enjoys that time more than she ever has.

It is interesting to note that daughters of working mothers as compared with daughters of nonworking mothers view women as more competent (Broverman et al., 1972) and view female employment as less threatening to marriage. This seems to indicate that their mothers provided adequate nurturance even though they worked. Obviously, a working mother may shortchange her children. On the other hand, she may also be able to provide for them better.

Jobs, Occupations, and Careers

To this point, we have been discussing women taking jobs in the labor market. However, a short- or long-term job is not the same as a long-term career. Essentially we can place work on an attitudinal continuum according to the degree of commitment (Kahn & Wiener, 1973, p. 153).

Basic attitude toward work as	*Basic additional value fulfilled by work*
1. Interruption	Short-run income
2. Job	Long-term income — some work-oriented values (one works to live)
3. Occupation	Exercise and mastery of gratifying skills — some satisfaction of achievement-oriented values
4. Career	Participating in an important activity or program. Much satisfaction of work-oriented, achievement-oriented, advancement-oriented values
5. Vocation (calling)	Self-identification and self-fulfillment
6. Mission	Near fanatic or single-minded focus on achievement or advancement (one lives to work)

Most women in the labor force occupy one of the first three levels. Although many men also occupy one of these first three levels, there is a far higher percentage of men than women in the latter three categories. This is true because the man traditionally has been the family breadwinner while the woman has been the homemaker. However, as women have increasingly entered the work force, and as attitudes about sex roles have changed, more and more career opportunities are opening to them. The two-career family will become a more visible reality in the future. A career may be denoted by (1) a long-time commitment including a period of formal training, (2) continuity in that one moves to higher and higher levels if successful, (3) mobility in order to follow career demands.

In the families of most career men, the man's career will dictate much of the couple's life. Where they live, how they live, and for how long often will depend on his career demands. These demands are met relatively easily if the wife is a homemaker or works at one of the first three levels. A **dual-career family**, however, can have possible conflict between the partners over career demands as well as other kinds of problems that occur in any family when both partners work. For example, the president of a local community college is married to a woman who is also a high-level school administrator. When he won a new position as president, this meant moving several hundred miles to a new college. After much discussion the couple decided that each should continue his and her own career. They are now a "weekend family." Each spends the week at the job, and they visit each other on the weekends. Because they now have a house in each city, they take turns visiting. This couple does not have children to complicate the situation. Such a lifestyle is not suitable for

Dual-career family
A marriage in which both spouses pursue their own careers

The "Successful Woman as Sex Object" Syndrome

It's not that I'd never seen her before.

Years ago she'd been photographed outside of her apartment building, dressed in a fur coat and bra and panties. Since then she'd been found in similar attire in the theater and hotel lobbies. Usually, of course, you get used to this sort of thing if you live in a city long enough.

But it was a shock to see her in a hospital room. There she was, hair tied back primly, medical chart in her left hand, pen in her right hand, long white jacket over her shoulders, exposing her lacy magenta bra and panties. What was she doing dressed like that in the hospital?

Was it possible? Why, yes! Stop the presses! The Maidenform Woman Had Become a Doctor! According to the caption under this photograph, she was "making the rounds in her elegant Delectables."

At some point when I wasn't looking, everybody's favorite exhibitionist must have ac-

tually gone to medical school. I suppose that I had underestimated her intelligence — —this happens so often with attractive women. I always thought she was a candidate for a cold, not a medical degree. I can only imagine the difficulties she had getting accepted, what with her portfolio and all.

But now any number of magazines are featuring her personal success story. On their pages, the Maidenform Woman is willingly displaying her new bedside manner in living color.

Poised, concerned, even prim, young Dr. Maidenform is photographed looking down compassionately at her bedridden patient. We don't know exactly what the patient thinks of all this. Fortunately for her, his leg is in traction and he can't move.

The other doctors in the ad seem quite unconcerned about her outfit. Dr. Maidenform seems to have made it in a world that is entirely non-sexist. They aren't even glancing in the direction of her non-airbrushed belly button!

Quite frankly, I must admit that the Maidenform Woman cured me of a disease. She cured me of creeping complacency.

Until I saw her, I had become virtually numb to the advertising image of that handy creature, "The New Woman." We are now out of the era of housewife-as-airhead. We've even come a long

way from the era of coming a long way, baby.

We are plunging into the "successful woman as sex object" syndrome. The more real women break out of the mold, the more advertisers force them back in. We are now told that, for all the talk, the New Woman is just the Total Woman in updated gear.

Under the careful dress-for-success suit of an MBA is a woman buying Office Legs for sex appeal. Around the briefcase of a lawyer is a hand shining with high-color nail gloss. Take away the lab coat, the stethoscope and syringe, and the doctor is just another set of "elegant Delectables."

The point in all this isn't especially subtle. As Jean Kilbourne, who has long studied media images of women, said: "It's out of the question that they would ever show a male doctor like that. She is aloof but available. Underneath she is still a sex object."

Kilbourne's favorite entry in this category is a perfume ad that shows the successful woman mixing business with, uh, pleasure. In the first frame we see the busy executive at a business lunch with three men. In the second frame, we see her under the covers with one.

Advertisers have a big investment in this new-old image. I'm not talking about the professional woman market. There are hardly enough women doctors to keep the

(Continued on p. 284)

magenta lace factory in business. But there are now an increasing number of women who see professionals as glamorous and want to identify with them.

The advertisers are betting that these women want, as the Maidenform ad puts it, "just what the doctor ordered." So the doctor is ordered to strip, literally, her professional cover. She is revealed in the flesh, to be — yes, indeed — just another woman insecure about her femininity, just another woman in search of sex appeal, just another woman who needs "silky satin tricot with antique lace scalloping."

Pretty soon, I suppose, she will need it in the Senate, in the Supreme Court, even in the Oval Office. The Maidenform Woman. You never know where she'll turn up (*The Washington Post*, October 12, 1982).

families with small children. Research indicates that families that choose this lifestyle tend to be those free of childrearing responsibilities, older couples, those married longer, those with established careers (Gross, 1980) and those having high educational levels, high-ranking occupations, and high income levels (Kirschner & Wallum, 1983).

An overwhelming proportion of the literature on the dual-career family reports that the impact of dual-career stress is felt most by women. Not only is this true in the woman's family life but in her occupation as well. Occupationally, she takes more risks, sacrifices more, and compromises career ambitions in attempting to make the dual-career pattern work (Skinner, 1980). The stress is reduced for her if she has a supportive husband, one who is willing to leave his job and relocate to advance the wife's career. Strain is also greatly reduced if she is free of childrearing responsibilities (Houseknecht & Macke, 1981).

Marjorie Smith, a trust officer at Chase Manhattan Bank, is up every morning at 6 o'clock. After making breakfast and laying out clothes for her daughter Suzy, 5, she leaves for work. At that point, her husband, Lee, takes over — getting Suzy dressed and walking her to school. At 5 o'clock, after her day at the office, Marjorie picks up their daughter at a day-care center. Once home, the Smiths continue their hectic schedule, doing the laundry, dashing through a supper of soup and sandwiches, and dividing up the other household tasks — grocery shopping by Marjorie, vacuuming by Lee. The only trouble is that the routine rarely works. "The norm is frantic phone calls and schedule changes," says Lee with a laugh. "Valium has to rank with the invention of the wheel."

The Smiths are one of a growing number of couples whose daily life is fraught with the hassle of keeping two careers and a family afloat.

This short description of Marjorie Smith's day may help to give some feeling of the frenetic pace found in many dual-career families, especially those with children still living at home.

If both partners are successful in their careers, it usually means that major career decisions must be made periodically throughout the relationship. Each new decision may serve to upset the balance that has been worked out by the couple. For example, what happens when one spouse is offered an important promotion, but this means moving to another location? Will harm be done to the partner's career? If the new location is not too far away, should one spouse commute? Should they take up two residences? What will this living arrangement do to their relationship? Each time one partner has a major career change, a series of such questions will have to be answered. In most cases, where the couple strives for career equality, the answers will not be easy.

Summary

Many consider the number of women entering the work force to be the major revolution affecting the American family this century. In the past the woman's, and especially the mother's, place was in the home. This is no longer true. Today, in most families the woman is an active participant in the economic support of her family. Her movement into the work world has been speeded recently by the higher rates of inflation that have made it harder for all families to make ends meet.

Although now a permanent and large part of the American labor force, women still earn a disproportionately lower income than their male counterparts. In addition the working mother is often overburdened, carrying out her job as well as being the major worker in the home.

Increasing job availability has also contributed to making women more independent than they have been in the past. This has brought pressure on many husbands, because women now have a realistic alternative to a bad marriage — moving out and supporting their families themselves. A woman's increasing independence can reap rewards for the family. They are financially better off. Her additional earnings may help them invest and start the economy working for them. Pressure is taken off the husband or father to be the only breadwinner. In general a woman's participation in the work world leads to a more egalitarian relationship within the marriage.

Unfortunately, the lower incomes often received by women tend to blunt some of the possible advantages of working. The costs of working, including clothes, transportation, increased taxes, and child care, often make the woman's real economic contribution small and even "not worth it" at times. However, as the woman improves her skills, as she becomes a more indispensable part of the workforce, as she gains political power, as she becomes more career oriented as opposed to job oriented, the pay differential between the male and female worker declines.

SCENES FROM MARRIAGE

Happy Mother's Day: April Fool

If I don't get flowers on Mother's Day, I'll be miserable — and angry. This is my one day of visibility. Although it is tainted with commercial exploitation, I need the recognition and the rewards. But while I may bask briefly in the day's warm glow, I'm not fooled by it for a minute.

Mother's Day is a symbol of our national feeling of guilt for making child care an activity of high rhetoric and low prestige. The cliché that nobody is against motherhood cannot hide the many ways we put mother down.

Mother's job has no status in a society which rewards the single-minded pursuit of money and success. Her role clashes head-on with the real values of an achievement-oriented culture. The qualities needed to nurture, to put the needs of others ahead of your own, are directly opposite to those needed to "make it" in the outside corporate world. A mother's job is to train her children to enter a world whose values differ sharply from those she herself lives by in her relationship with them. No wonder there is confusion on all sides.

Furthermore, mother has no credentials. She is an unpaid amateur, and this gives her low status in a society obsessed with professional, certified expertise. Whatever its past benefits, the professionalization of child care has had the demeaning side effect of reducing mother to a bewildered consumer of expert (and often contradictory) advice. The glory has gone to an ever-increasing army of experts — pediatricians, psychologists and social workers — who have defined her job in terms of their own special doctrines and prejudices. Mother no longer knows best.

Because it is done free and done by women, mother's work should not be devalued. But we all know it is. Can our society ever respect a service freely given? Conditioned by unremunerative mothering at home, women are programed to accept less than adequate compensation for work outside the home as well. The depressing statistic that women earn only 60 cents for every dollar earned by men is by now all too familiar. The slogan "equal pay for equal work" remains, alas, just a slogan.

Raising children is a complex task that stubbornly remains in the private sector of our lives. A mother's imprint on her children and the satisfaction this gives her are personal and private — and they should be. Although nearly everyone feels qualified to judge other people's children, there are no effective yardsticks by which to measure the quality of a mother's work. And there is no way of placing a monetary value on the art of bringing up children or of transferring skills needed to raise children to the "outside" world of work.

The truth is we are stuck in an outdated work pattern. The idea that men worked in the real world while women stayed at home and "only" raised children may have been suited to the days when children were an economic asset instead of an economic burden. In 1981 women work not because of the women's movement or merely for "fulfillment," and certainly not for the patronizing earning of "pin" money. They work because they need the money. You need not be an economist to realize that fewer and fewer people — read women — can afford the luxury of not working. The choice, if any, is between earning a good living and earning a poor one.

It is time we recognized that there is a harsh conflict between the demands of a career and raising a family, no matter how fulfilling and rewarding both may be. It is precisely because they are both rewarding (in different ways) and both demanding of time, energy and resources that the problems are so difficult to tackle.

When my children were younger, I tried a whole range of combinations of working and mothering — full time, part time, working at home and not working at all. All compromises. None fully satisfying. When my profession began to make greater demands on my time, I cut back on my work as did many women who came of age during the 1950s. In all honesty, I cannot say that if I had it to do over again I would make the same choice.

The fact remains that if a mother drops out of her career or job slot for a few years — as I did — her professional development will suffer. Yet, if she continues to work, she will also suffer — from

chronic exhaustion at the very least — and this will make her children and her husband suffer as well. What a choice! Shrinks and other experts glibly counsel mothers to stay home until their children are 3 or 5 or 8 years old and thus "fully developed," and then return to work. They ignore the realities both of the marketplace and of child development.

At a recent professional meeting on time management, a blonde in a gray flannel suit told her eager listeners how she organized her life at home by "scheduling" walks with her daughter as carefully as she planned business meetings. I did not know whether to laugh or cry. The current chic theory that it is possible and desirable to set aside short periods of "quality time" for children is baloney. How can anyone do a demanding job by only working at it an hour or so a day? And after a hard day at the office as well! Chalk up another put-down for mother's work.

Ironically, the women's movement reflects the same dilemma that troubles individual women. The initial concentration on cre-

ating new employment opportunities was a realistic response to priority needs. But progress has had the unintended consequence of making motherhood appear even less appealing to many younger women. There are far more job options for women in their 20s and 30s today. But these women are just as confused about their choices for combining work and childrearing as we were twenty years ago.

There is only cold comfort for all of us in a Wall Street Journal front-page story about a father who stayed home to care for his two small daughters while his wife completed medical school. When he wanted to return to work, an executive recruiter told him: "There isn't a male I know of in an executive position who would accept raising kids as a legitimate excuse for not working for three years."

Happy Mother's Day.

GRACE HECHINGER

CHAPTER 9

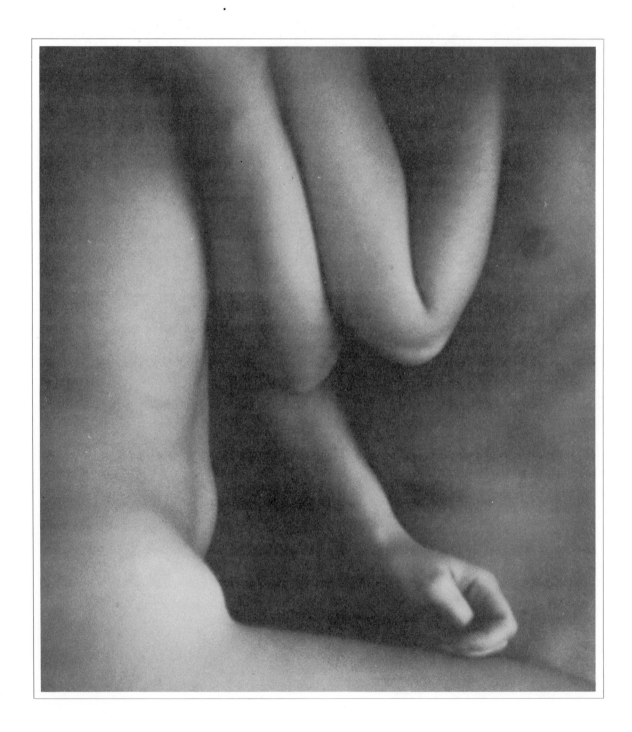

THE BIOLOGICAL FOUNDATION: SEXUALITY

CONTENTS

Friend: What is sex?

Student: Everyone knows what sex is! Sex is for having babies — you know, reproduction.

Friend: I know, but if sex is only for reproduction, why don't humans mate like other animals, once a year or so? Why don't human females go into "heat" to attract males?

Student: Well, human females *are* more sexually receptive at certain times during their monthly cycle, aren't they?

Friend: The evidence on that is mixed, but even if it were true, why are humans interested in sex all the time? Why do they spend so much time talking about, reading about, thinking about, and having sex?

Student: Perhaps sex is for human pleasure.

Friend: But if sex is for fun, why are there so many restrictions on sexual behavior? Why does society try so often to regulate sexual expression? Why does religion try to focus sexual behavior toward some higher purpose?

Student: Well, then, perhaps sex is for love.

Friend: But, what is love exactly? Does sex always mean love? If masturbation is sex, does it mean I love myself if I do it?

Student: Love is emotional closeness that allows you to communicate at an intimate level. Love also makes you feel good about yourself — it enhances your ego. So if sex is love, it does all these things too.

Friend: Certainly sex can be for all of the things you mention. But isn't sex sometimes just for biological release such as when a man has a wet dream during which semen is released? This doesn't sound much like love or ego enhancement, does it?

Student: No, but sex can and should be an expression of love.

Friend: Ah, yes, but what it sometimes is and what it should be are often two different things.

Student: What do you mean?

Friend: Well, is sex an expression of love when it is used to possess another person, such as when a woman is considered to be a man's property? Or when it is used to gain status, such as when a king marries the daughter of another king to increase his holdings and thereby his prestige? Or when it is a part of violence, such as in rape? Or when it is a business, as in prostitution? Or when it is used indirectly, as in advertising where appeals based on sex are made to sell many different products?

Student: Now I'm really confused. Just what is sex?

From this short discussion it is obvious that sex is many things, and, at times, something of a riddle. If sex were only for reproduction, or only an expression of love, or only for fun, there would be little controversy about it and no need to control it. Sex isn't for one purpose, though, but for many. It is this fact that causes people to be so concerned and, at times, confused about the place of sex in their lives.

Human Sexuality in the United States

For better or worse the place of sexuality in American society has changed rapidly in the last twenty-five years. Generally, sexual expression has become freer, more diverse, and more open to public view. The infamous double standard, which promoted sexual expression for men while limiting it for women, has begun to break down in the face of women's liberation. Better understanding of one's own sexuality has become an important goal in many people's lives.

In fact, better understanding and acceptance by women of their sexuality may be one of the revolutionary changes affecting the family and all intimate relationships during the 1980s (Reiss, 1980). Reiss predicts that the incidence of sexual dysfunction will decrease in the 1980s in part because women will gain increasing control over their own sexuality.

Traditionally, the male has set the stage for sexual expression. He has usually initiated and guided sexual encounters. Hence he has been able to engage in sexual activity at the times, in the places, and in the manner he desires. The woman, in turn, reacted to him. Under such circumstances it seems clear that the chances for him to derive pleasure from the sexual contact are far greater than for her. He has sex when he feels interested, ready, and capable. She may or may not feel this same confidence when he initiates sexual interaction. Hence the chances are greater that she will fail to feel satisfied more often than he will. The chances are also greater that she will make excuses to avoid sexual activity because she traditionally has been placed in an automatically defensive, reactive position.

This description sounds as if the man could always have sex when he desired. Of course, this has not been true. When women were strongly restricted in their sexual expression, often it was difficult for a man wanting sexual activity to find a woman who wanted the same. Necking and petting were the norms of sexual conduct for young people through the 1940s and 1950s.

As women have become freer to initiate sexual activity and to express their desires, they have been able to set the stage for sexual expression or at least to share in the decision. Thus women too can pick times for sexual activity when they feel interested, ready, and capable. And if they can pick these times, their chances of sexual satisfaction are increased. There is no need to make excuses to avoid sexual activity if you are the initiator.

As women gain sexual equality, they are able to channel sexuality into their lives in their own way and at their own pace. Sexual equality should serve to reduce sexual dysfunction in both men and women. If each person is free to express himself or herself sexually with a partner and respects that freedom for the partner, then chances of sexual exploitation of one partner by the other are reduced. Without exploitation and manipulation, the chances for sexual fulfillment and enjoyment are greatly increased. Freedom of sexual expression also includes the freedom to say "no."

In a sense greater sexual diversity and freedom create as well as solve problems. Freedom means responsibility. I must assume personal responsibility for my actions if I am free to choose those actions. In the past when the mores, taboos, and traditions tightly surrounded sexual expression, responsibility was removed from the individual. I could always blame the rules for my lack of satisfaction, for my failures, for my unhappiness. But the America of the past few years has rapidly removed the rules from my sexual expression. The decisions are now up to me, and this can be frightening.

Freedom of Choice and Sexual Health

Freedom of sexual choice for the young unmarried individual can be much more threatening than for the married person. The sexual mores in many parts of the American society have changed from supporting postponement of sexual intercourse until marriage to pressuring young people to engage in premarital sex. "Don't be old-fashioned." "Get with it." "Everyone does it." Especially for young women, the harder decision now seems to be to say, "No, I don't wish to have sex." Or, "No, I don't want to have sex at this time." This is quite a change from the old fear of losing one's virginity. A young woman now often feels guilty and inadequate if she doesn't participate in sex. **Virginity** is maligned because it represents past traditions and morality and, of course, it is supported by all the wrong people — parents, grandparents, ministers, and those who aren't liberated.

Virginity
Not having experienced sexual intercourse

Yet, part of a healthy model of sexual behavior is the freedom to choose to participate or not in sexual relations. "It is my body." Respect for me as an individual will allow me this choice. Being coerced into sexual relations, either physically or psychologically, seldom leads to a healthy experience.

Healthy sexual expression is a primary part of human intimacy. As we try to make good decisions about our sexual intimacy, it is helpful to think about what we mean by healthy sex. There is debate over this topic. For some no sexual involvement before marriage is healthy. Others will argue that complete sexual freedom is healthy. In between these two opposing positions, are a variety of less extreme viewpoints. Following are some questions to help you discover foundations to promote "healthy sex."

Does My Sexual Expression Enhance My Self-Esteem?

If my behavior adds to me, increases my self-respect and my positive feelings about myself, and helps me like myself better, then the behavior is most apt to be healthy. Behavior that creates negative self-feelings and causes loss of self-esteem is better avoided. Low self-esteem, as we saw .in Chapter 4, creates many problems, especially in intimate relationships. Thus for any behavior, not just sexual, each of us can ask: Does my behavior increase my self-esteem?

INSET 9-1

Cleansing the Mother Tongue

Wanda: I got in late, Ralph. What happened today on *Search for Yesterday*?

Ralph: The usual, my sweet. Craig is still sowing his wild oats. Fenwick is wife swapping with Brent. Cybelle attended her first orgy, where she fornicated with Brad, the recently rehabilitated pervert.

Wanda: (Sigh) You really must do something about your language.

Ralph: What's the matter? Is it too dirty?

Wanda: Too old. We don't use those kinds of words any more. To begin with, wife swapping is sexist. It implies that women are property. It was changed years ago to mate swapping, then to swinging. Now someone suggests we call it ''expanding the circle of love.'' That may be a bit much . . .

Ralph: Not at all, dearest. Circle expansion is fine with me. Where else did I go wrong?

Wanda: Fornication. To anyone born after 1900 and not employed by the Ayatullah Khomeini, it is known as premarital or nonmarital sex, and adultery is extramarital sex, comarital sex or just extra sex. Orgy is now simply group sex. Since you spent a year reading *The Joy of Sex* and *More Joy*, you may remember that Alex Comfort suggests we call orgies ''sharing.''

Ralph: I love that word, Wanda. It brings out the total selflessness of an evening spent slaving over the needs of other people.

Wanda: Not everyone shares your sexual values.

Ralph: Certainly not promiscuous people, dearest. Give me more of your sexual euphemisms. What do we call perverts these days?

Wanda: The last pervert died in 1957, Ralph. Nowadays we have sexual minorities and sexual variations, some of them involving sexual aids and sexual toys, and all of them indulged in by folks with alternate sexual preferences. Perversion is a nasty, judgmental word that is likely to hurt the feelings of variants everywhere.

Ralph: There's no stopping progress, Wanda. Since there are no more perverts, I assume parents no longer have to worry about child molesters, but do you think they could keep a nonjudgmental eye out for pedophilic variants?

Wanda: Don't be smart, Ralph. And I want you to stop using the word promiscuous. That's a male word for women who do what men have always done.

Ralph: What's the modern term?

Wanda: Sexual variety or casual sex. Helen Gurley Brown suggests that a woman who sleeps with two or more men in one week can simply be called ''multifriended.''

Ralph: You can never have too many friends, Wanda. O.K. I'm beginning to get the hang of this. An affair is now a relationship. In the '50s we lusted after loose girls and pushovers, but in the '80s men search for their sexual identities with liberated women. Homosexuals are gay, and tots who play doctor are engaged in sexual rehearsal play. My dirty books are pornography, but yours are erotica. A woman who has never had an orgasm is not frigid or even nonorgasmic, but preorgasmic. Bluebeard, Catherine the Great and Erroll Flynn were multifriended, but I am married and single-friended with a woefully constricted circle of love. How am I doing so far?

Wanda: It's you, Ralph. Totally offensive.

Ralph: Let's plod on, my love. What's modernspeak for masturbation? Self-enhancement?

Wanda: Self-help, self-pleasuring, automanipulation, the first step in the process of sexualization, self-remedy for orgasmic dysfunction.

INSET 9-1, CONTINUED

Ralph: And you don't even have to dress for it! What about foreplay?

Wanda: Out. It implies that what you males do is the main event. Foreplay is now genital pleasuring, sexual expressiveness or a high stage of sensate-focus exercises.

Ralph: I suppose all this is done with a significant other in a primary meaningful relationship.

Wanda: Not necessarily, stodgy one. It can be in a satellite relationship, or with a partner you have just met and may not encounter again.

Ralph: You mean a one-night stand.

Wanda: A shabby, reactionary term. Call it a brief encounter. Helen Gurley Brown suggests we label it an instant liaison or a one-night friendship.

Ralph: Not good enough, my pet. Helen is trying hard. But a successful euphemism should be poured into Latinate verbiage for true obfuscation. How about a uninocturnal relationship? Or if it's a noonie, call it a self-limiting quotidian encounter.

Wanda: Ralph, I'm experiencing oral desire-phase dysfunction.

Ralph: What's that?

Wanda: I don't want to talk about it any more.

Ralph: But we must, beloved. We must cleanse the mother tongue of preliberation pettifoggery. I assume that mistress, kept woman, bimbo and paramour are somehow offensive, but what about the term prostitute?

Wanda: There's no good word yet. Those in the business don't seem to like it very much, so we tried working girl, which changed quickly to working woman, but that's the name of a magazine that appeals to female executives.

Ralph: Hmmm. I guess ladies of the evening won't do. How about strolling sexual facilitators? Or freelance orgasmetricians?

Wanda: You are a difficult man, Ralph.

Ralph: And one ever eager to learn, light of my life. Now let me recast today's soapy occurrences on *Search for Yesterday*. Our friend Craig is expressing his sexual needs in a heartfelt but brief interpersonal exchange with a woman whose name he didn't catch. Fenwick and Brent are having extra sex in multilateral interfamilial relationships with each other's spouses. Cybelle attended a sharing, where, amid an enormous pile of bodies, she encountered one belonging to Brad, the well-known variant, thus augmenting her sexual growth. Say good night, Wanda.

Wanda: Ralph, I promise you'll pay for this (Leo, 1982, p. 78).

Is My Sexual Expression Voluntary (Freely Chosen)?

Answering this question is not always easy. Obviously, rape is not voluntary sexual expression and not health enhancing. Other situations, however, are not always so clear-cut. Is my behavior voluntary when I have sex out of fear of losing my boyfriend if I don't? Perhaps it is, yet the element of fear raises a doubt. Does the fear make me think I must do it? Does the fear rob me of voluntary choice? Does the fear cause me to overlook the broader question: If I will lose him only because I will not have sex at this time, is he really someone with whom I want to have an intimate relationship? If my decision is really mine, independent of peer and social pressure, then the chances increase that my chosen behavior will be healthy.

Is My Sexual Expression Enjoyable and Gratifying?

This may sound like a strange question to ask. Isn't all sex fun and enjoyable? It generally will be if it is healthy, but we often find that it is not. Many people report disappointment with their early sexual encounters. A few people report that they seldom derive much joy from sex. For most, however, positive answers to the first two questions will help answer this question positively. In general enjoyable and gratifying sexual expression tends to occur most often within intimate all-encompassing relationships. This not to deny that at times sex for sex is gratifying. However, close intimate relationships that involve one in many ways — intellectually, emotionally, socially, and physically — tend to promote healthy sexual relations.

Will My Sexual Expression Lead to an Unwanted Pregnancy?

Sexual activity leading to wanted children is healthy. Sexual relations using birth control methods and thereby avoiding unwanted children can also be healthy. Some persons, for religious reasons, will disagree with the latter statement. For them healthy sex might mean abstinence if children are not desired at a given time. For most people, though, sex leading to unwanted pregnancy is not sexually healthy. We will discuss the problems of unwanted children in Chapters 10 and 11. Taking steps to prevent unwanted pregnancy is an important element in healthy sexual expression.

Will My Sexual Expression Pass a Sexually Transmitted Disease to My Partner?

It is obvious in the medical sense that healthy sex does not transmit sexually transmitted disease (STD). Thus knowledge of STD and taking precautions against it must be a part of healthy sexual expression.

In a sense healthy sex is knowledgeable sex. Knowing oneself so that self-esteem may be enhanced, knowing how to make voluntary choices and being independent enough to make them, knowing what is enjoyable and gratifying, knowing how to prevent unwanted pregnancies, and knowing how to guard against and what to do about sexual diseases — these are the foundation blocks to healthy sexual expression. In a nutshell: "Knowledge breeds responsible behavior, ignorance just breeds" (Canfield, 1979).

Human Sexuality Compared with Other Species'

No society has ever been found where sexual behavior was unregulated. True, regulations vary greatly — one spouse, multiple spouses, free selection of sexual partners, rigidly controlled selection, and so forth. Ac-

What Do You Think?

What do you think is the major purpose of human sexuality? Why?

Do we need any controls on human sexuality? Why or why not?

What controls would you have if you believe they are needed?

If there were no controls, how would the institution of marriage be affected?

tually, the specific regulations include almost any arrangements imaginable if one takes a cross-cultural view of sexuality. Within a given culture, however, the regulations, whatever they may be, are usually strictly enforced through taboos, mores, laws, and/or religious edicts. To transgress may bring swift and sometimes severe punishment, as in the case of stoning to death an adulterous woman, as is done in some Middle Eastern cultures.

Why do humans surround sex with regulations? Certainly among lower animals sex is controlled, but the controls are usually identical throughout the species, dictated by built-in biological mechanisms. Humans have regulated sex precisely because their biology has granted them sexual freedom of choice. Sexual behavior can occur at any time in humans. Among animals sexual behavior occurs only periodically, depending on the estrous cycle of the female in all mammals below primates. For mammals sexual behavior is for reproduction. Thus, sexual responsiveness is tied directly to the period of maximum fertility in the female. The female gives clues, such as odor change and genital swelling, to which the male responds.

In lower animals sexual behavior is controlled by lower brain centers and spinal reflexes activated by hormonal changes. In general the larger the brain cortex, the higher the species and the more control the animal has over its own responses. So we come to humans with their large cortex and what do we find? Earth's sexiest animal (Gotwald & Golden, 1981). An animal with few built-in restraints and hence many variations in sexual behavior. Without built-in guidelines, human sexuality is dependent on learning, and because different societies and groups teach different things about sexuality, many variations in sexual attitudes and behavior exist. Sexual compatibility, in part, depends on finding another person who shares your attitudes about sex.

Because sex for human beings is less tied to reproduction, sexual expression can serve other purposes as well. For example, Desmond Morris notes:

> The vast bulk of copulation in our species is obviously concerned, not with producing offspring, but with cementing the pair-bond by producing mutual rewards for sexual partners. The repeated attainment of sexual consummation for a mated pair is clearly, then, not some kind of sophisticated, decadent outgrowth of modern civilization, but a deep-rooted, biologically based, and evolutionarily sound tendency in our species. (1971, pp. 65 – 66)

Human sexuality differs significantly from that of other animals in several other important ways besides the greater freedom from instinctive direction. It appears that human females are the only females capable of intense orgasmic response. The sexual behavior of the human male, however, still resembles the sexual behavior of male primates; it depends largely on outside perceptual stimuli and is under partial control of the female in that she usually triggers it (Barclay, 1971). Of course, with the human this trigger can be indirect, such as when a person fantasizes.

Another important difference is that human females are not necessarily more sexually responsive during ovulation as are most other animals.

Sex Knowledge Inventory

Sex is a subject that most people think they know a lot about. Let's see if we do. Mark the following statements true or false. Answers may be found on p. 298.

1. Women generally reach the peak of their sex drive later than men.

2. It is possible to ejaculate without having a total erection.

3. Sperm from one testicle produce males and from the other, females.

4. A person is likely to contract STD when using a toilet seat recently used by an infected person.

5. If a person has gonorrhea once and is cured, he or she is now immune and will never get it again.

6. Certain foods increase the sex drive.

7. Premature ejaculation is an unusual problem for young men.

8. The penis inserted into the vagina (sexual intercourse) is the only normal method of sex.

9. It is potentially harmful for a woman to take part in sports during menstruation.

10. A woman who has had her uterus removed can still have an orgasm.

11. During sexual intercourse a woman may suffer from vaginal spasms that can trap the male's penis and prevent him from withdrawing it.

12. The cause of impotence is almost always psychological.

13. For a certain time period after orgasm, the woman cannot respond to further sexual stimulation.

14. For a certain time period after orgasm, the man cannot respond to further sexual stimulation.

15. Taking birth control pills will delay a woman's menopause.

16. The size of the penis is fixed by hereditary factors and little can be done by way of exercise, drugs, and so on to increase its size.

17. If a woman doesn't have a hymen, this is proof that she is not a virgin.

18. As soon as a female starts to menstruate, she can become pregnant.

19. About 80 percent of women infected with gonorrhea show no symptoms.

20. The penis of the male and the clitoris of the female are analogous organs.

There seems to be no particular time during the menstrual cycle when *all* women experience heightened sexual desire (McCary & McCary, 1982). A few women seem to become more sexually aroused at midcycle when they are most fertile (Adams, Gold & Burt, 1978). However, of twenty-eight studies on this subject, thirteen revealed that women's sexual desire peaks just after the menstrual flow begins. It is possible that this relates to her reduced fear of pregnancy. Nine studies showed the peak to be just before the menstrual flow, and six located the peak midway in the menstrual cycle (Cavanagh, 1969). According to A. M. Barclay, "This difference, coupled with the development of the orgasm in females, might tentatively be interpreted to mean that humans are the only species to derive pleasure out of sexual behavior without becoming involved in its reproductive aspects" (1971, p. 61).

The major difference between humans and animals remains that much of human sexuality depends on what the individual thinks rather than on biology. Compared with other species', human sexuality is:

1. Pervasive, involving humans psychologically as well as physiologically.
2. Under conscious control rather than instinctual biological control.
3. Affected by learning and social factors and thus is more variable within the species.
4. Largely directed by an individual's beliefs and attitudes.
5. Less directly attached to reproduction.
6. Able to serve other purposes such as pair bonding and communication.
7. More of a source of pleasure.

Marriage is society's sanctioned arrangement for sexual relations. Sex is one of the foundations of most human intimate relationships. Sex is the basis of the family — procreation — and the survival of the species. Sex is communication and closeness. It can be pleasuring in its most exciting and satisfying form. Certainly it is proper to study marriage by viewing humans as the sexual creatures they are. And though thoughts and attitudes toward sex are the most important part of human sexuality, we must start with the biological foundations if we are to fully understand sexuality and the male/female bond.

Human Sexual Anatomy

When describing human anatomy, we think in terms of two descriptions, male and female. Yet the development of male and female anatomical structures rests on a common tissue foundation. As described in Chapter 6, hormonal action triggered by chromosomal makeup differentiates the tissues into male and female organs. Figures 9-1 and 9-2 show this differentiation, as well as the homologues (similar in origin and structure but not necessarily in function) of external and internal male and female genitals. The contrast between the sexes begins around the fifth or sixth week after conception.

It is interesting that human sex organs have always been of great interest to people, more so than other organs. Many past societies have glorified the genitals in their arts. But the advent of Christianity brought a more negative attitude toward sexuality in general, limiting it to reproduction and denying its more pleasurable aspects. The interest in sexuality went underground, so to speak, and graphic display of sexual activities became known as pornography.

Genitals
The external reproductive organs

Although the **genitals** have been studied medically in modern American society, only recently have they been studied as organs of sexuality. As one gynecologist puts it:

> Gynecology is a subspecialty concerned with the diagnosis and treatment of diseases of the female genital tract. . . . Gynecology requires four years of residency. It is a thorough and intensive program that has consistently produced

Undifferentiated

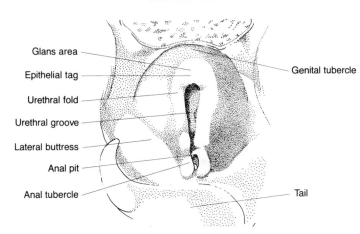

FIGURE 9-1 External male and female genitals: development from undifferentiated to differentiated stage.

Glans area

Epithelial tag

Urethral fold

Urethral groove

Lateral buttress

Anal pit

Anal tubercle

Genital tubercle

Tail

Male　　　　　**Embryo**　　　　　**Female**

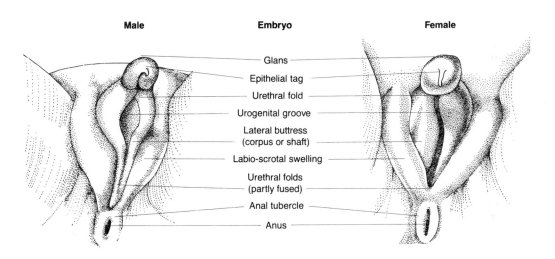

Glans

Epithelial tag

Urethral fold

Urogenital groove

Lateral buttress
(corpus or shaft)

Labio-scrotal swelling

Urethral folds
(partly fused)

Anal tubercle

Anus

Fully Developed

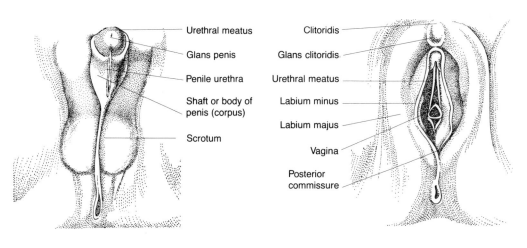

Urethral meatus

Glans penis

Penile urethra

Shaft or body of
penis (corpus)

Scrotum

Clitoridis

Glans clitoridis

Urethral meatus

Labium minus

Labium majus

Vagina

Posterior
commissure

UNDIFFERENTIATED

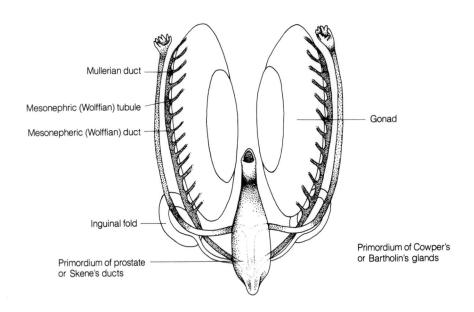

Mullerian duct

Mesonephric (Wolffian) tubule

Mesonepheric (Wolffian) duct

Gonad

Inguinal fold

Primordium of prostate
or Skene's ducts

Primordium of Cowper's
or Bartholin's glands

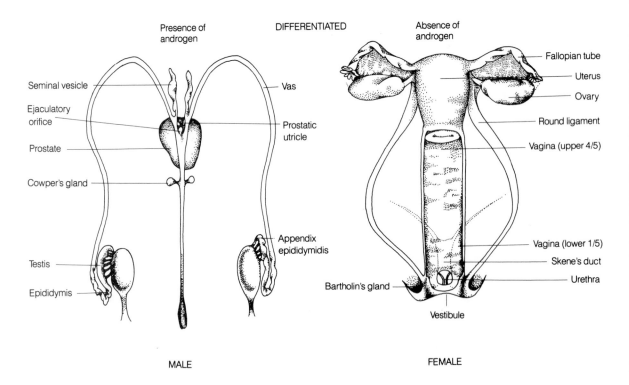

Presence of
androgen

DIFFERENTIATED

Absence of
androgen

Seminal vesicle

Ejaculatory
orifice

Prostate

Cowper's gland

Testis

Epididymis

Vas

Prostatic
utricle

Appendix
epididymidis

Fallopian tube

Uterus

Ovary

Round ligament

Vagina (upper 4/5)

Vagina (lower 1/5)

Skene's duct

Urethra

Bartholin's gland

Vestibule

MALE

FEMALE

FIGURE 9-2   Internal male and female genitals: development from undifferentiated to
differentiated stage.

highly skilled and extremely well qualified practitioners. . . . Yet under these ideal circumstances, in a discipline focused entirely on the genital tract, in my four years of training there was absolutely no time devoted to the consideration of sexuality. It was never even mentioned. Our consideration of the vagina involved its tensile strength, its supports, its distensibility, its bacterial flora. . . . The vagina as a source of pleasure was simply never mentioned. (Neubardt, 1971, p. 2)

Fortunately, medical schools have begun to correct this oversight and to study human sexuality. For example, at a recent regional meeting of the Society for the Scientific Study of Sex the following papers were presented: "Feminine Sexual Hygiene," "Penile Sensitivity, Aging and Degree of Sexual Activity," "Clitoral Adhesions: Myth or Reality," and "The Vaginal Clasp."

Male Sex Organs

Although most people's interest focuses on the external organs of both sexes because of their obvious sexual connotations, the internal ones are regarded as the primary organs of procreation (see Figures 9-3, 9-4, and 9-5).

The testes in the male produce *spermatozoa* (or sperm for short). If the coiled tubules within the testes that produce and store the sperm were straightened out, they would be several hundred feet long. Other special cells within the testes produce the important hormone **testosterone**. It is this hormone that directs the developing tissue toward maleness and, at adolescence, causes the maturing of the sexual organs and the appearance of secondary sexual characteristics such as deepening voice and facial and body hair. Figures 9-5 and 9-6 show the course taken by the sperm in ejaculation. Sperm are matured and stored in the *epididymis*. With ejaculation they travel up the *vas deferens* where it joins the duct of the *seminal vesicle* in the lower abdomen. The two seminal vesicles produce a secretion, **semen**, which increases the volume of the ejaculatory fluid, which empties into the ejaculatory ducts. These ducts then empty into the *urethra*, which is the canal extending through the penis. (The urethra is the canal through which urine also is discharged, but urine and semen can never pass through at the same time. Sexual arousal and ejaculation inhibit the ability to urinate.) The *prostate gland* surrounds the first part of the urethra as it leaves the bladder. This gland secretes a thin fluid that helps alkalize the seminal fluid. In addition the muscle part of the prostate helps propel the ejaculatory fluid out of the penis. The last contribution to the seminal fluid comes from the *Cowper's glands*, two pea-sized structures flanking the urethra. During sexual arousal they secrete an alkaline fluid that further neutralizes the acidic environment of the urethra and provides penile lubrication to facilitate intercourse.

The process of **ejaculation** begins with contractions of the ducts leading from the *seminiferous tubules* in the testes and simply continues on through the system. The actual amount of ejaculate varies according to the male's physical condition, age, and the time elapsed between ejaculations. Usu-

Testosterone
An important component of the male sex hormone androgen; responsible for inducing and maintaining the male secondary sexual characteristics

Semen
The secretion of the male reproductive organs that is ejaculated from the penis during orgasm and contains the sperm cells

Ejaculation
The expulsion of semen by the male during orgasm

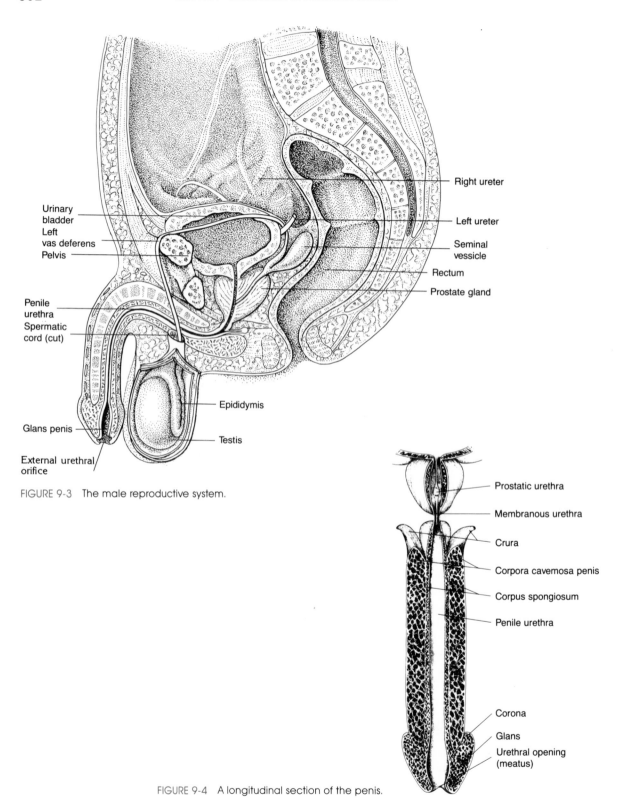

FIGURE 9-3   The male reproductive system.

FIGURE 9-4   A longitudinal section of the penis.

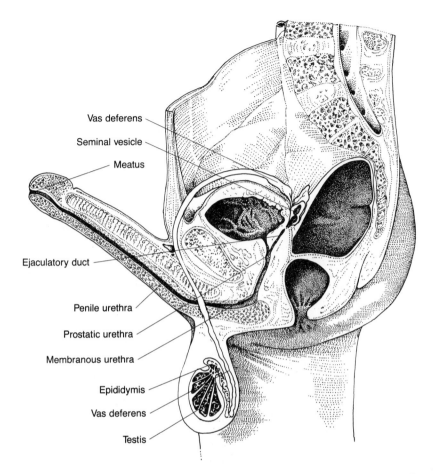

FIGURE 9-5 The passage of sperm.

Vas deferens

Seminal vesicle

Meatus

Ejaculatory duct

Penile urethra

Prostatic urethra

Membranous urethra

Epididymis

Vas deferens

Testis

ally about a teaspoon of fluid is ejaculated; it contains about 300 million sperm. To be considered of normal fertility, the ejaculate must contain a minumum of 60 to 100 million sperm per cubic centimeter of semen.

The strength of the ejaculatory response also varies: The semen may simply ooze out of the urethra or may be discharged as far as several feet beyond the penis. The ejaculatory amount is reestablished in the healthy male within twenty-four hours.

Ejaculation is accompanied by a highly pleasurable sensation known as *orgasm*. (This will be discussed more fully later.) Figure 9-6 diagrams the route taken by the sperm for fertilization to take place. The testes are particularly sensitive to temperature and must remain slightly cooler than the body to produce viable sperm. Hence when the temperature is hot, the sac containing them will hang down farther. When the temperature is cold, the testicles will be pulled up close to the body. Occasionally, the testicles don't descend into the scrotum properly and sterility results. Surgery and hormone treatment usually can correct this (McCary & McCary, 1982). Sometimes only one testicle descends, but one is usually enough to ensure fertility.

In order to have intercourse, it is necessary for the male to have an erection. He does not have voluntary control of this and cannot always be

FIGURE 9-6   The route of a sperm during ejaculation from its origin to its fertilization of an egg.

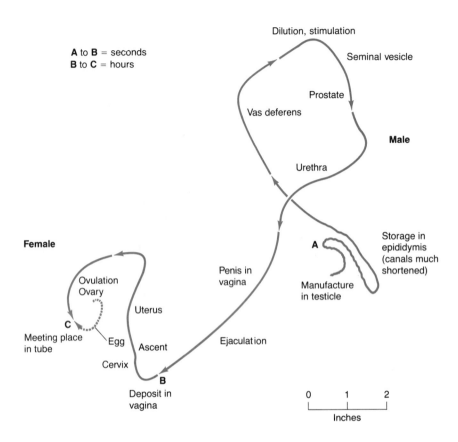

Impotence
Usually temporary inability of a man to experience erection; may be caused by either physical or psychological factors

sure that he will be capable of intercourse. This fact sometimes leads to sexual insecurity in males. Failure to achieve and hold an erection long enough for sexual intercourse is called **impotence**. Both erection and ejaculation can occur without physical stimulation, such as with a nocturnal emission that usually is accompanied by an erotic dream.

Figure 9-4 shows the three cylindrical bodies of spongy erectile tissue that run the length of the penis. Sexual arousal causes the dilation of blood vessels within the penis, and small valvelike structures (polsters) emit blood into the vascular spaces of the erectile tissue. Because the rate of blood inflow is greater than the rate of outflow, the volume of blood in the penis increases. As the erectile tissue becomes engorged with blood, the penis stiffens into an erection. The average penis is three to four inches long in a flaccid state and six to seven inches long when erect. Size variations are less in the erect state than they are in the flaccid state and are not related to virility.

Modern technology has succeeded in duplicating the erection's mechanism. Brantley Scott, a urologist at St. Luke's Episcopal Hospital in Houston, Texas, has successfully implanted a mechanical device to aid men who cannot become erect. The device consists of two silicone rubber cylinders implanted into the penis, a bulb in the scrotum, and a liquid-containing reservoir in the pelvic region. Repeated pumping of the bulb

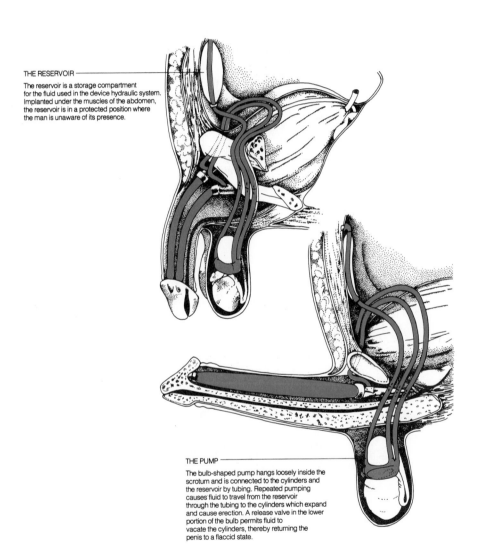

THE RESERVOIR

The reservoir is a storage compartment
for the fluid used in the device hydraulic system.
Implanted under the muscles of the abdomen,
the reservoir is in a protected position where
the man is unaware of its presence.

THE PUMP

The bulb-shaped pump hangs loosely inside the
scrotum and is connected to the cylinders and
the reservoir by tubing. Repeated pumping
causes fluid to travel from the reservoir
through the tubing to the cylinders which expand
and cause erection. A release valve in the lower
portion of the bulb permits fluid to
vacate the cylinders, thereby returning the
penis to a flaccid state.

FIGURE 9-7 The inflatable penile prosthesis. The operation of the inflatable penile
prosthesis mimics the natural action of the erection process. A miniature hydraulic system
transfers fluid to implanted cylinders, which causes the cylinders to fill and expand,
creating an erection. When an erection is no longer desired, the man activates a
deflation mechanism to return the penis to a normal flaccid state.

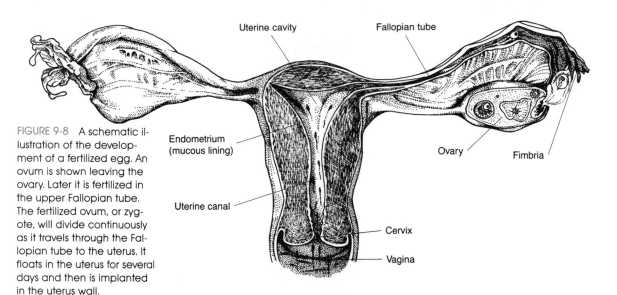

FIGURE 9-8   A schematic illustration of the development of a fertilized egg. An ovum is shown leaving the ovary. Later it is fertilized in the upper Fallopian tube. The fertilized ovum, or zygote, will divide continuously as it travels through the Fallopian tube to the uterus. It floats in the uterus for several days and then is implanted in the uterus wall.

Ovum
The female reproductive cell (egg) that when fertilized develops into a new member of the same species

Ovaries
The female sex glands in which the ova (eggs) are formed

causes the liquid to flow into the cylinders, creating an erection. The penis remains erect until a release valve is squeezed to evacuate the fluid back to the reservoir (see Figure 9-7).

Female Sex Organs

As we did with the male sperm, let us trace the course of development and ultimate fertilization of the female egg (**ovum**). Eggs are released from the female gonads or **ovaries**. Each ovary contains an estimated 50,000 to 200,000 tiny sacs or *follicles*, but only 250 to 400 will become active during a woman's lifetime and produce eggs (see Figure 9-8). Each

FIGURE 9-9   Sperm swim toward a mature ovum and swarm around it until one of them penetrates the outer edge of the egg.

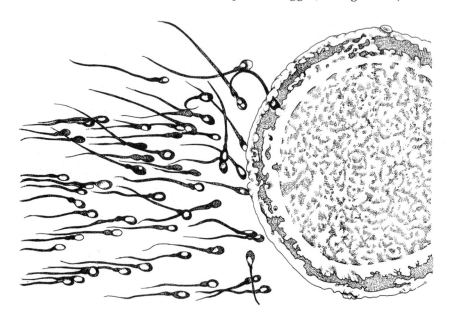

woman is born with a lifetime supply of eggs and does not actually produce them as the male produces sperm. After puberty normally once every twenty-eight days one egg will ripen and burst from a follicle and will enter the **Fallopian tube**, where fertilization may occur.

Each month, normally, a ripe egg is produced and released, to travel through the Fallopian tubes to the uterus where, if fertilized, it will implant in the blood-rich uterine lining that has built up during the month to receive it. This cycle is known as the menstrual cycle, and release of the ripe egg from the follicle is called **ovulation**. If the egg is not fertilized, it will be shed, along with the thickened uterine lining, as menstrual flow. The easiest way to describe this process is to label the first day of menstrual flow as day 1 because it is easy to observe. On an average the cycle lasts twenty-eight days, with menstruation lasting five days. Individuals may vary considerably from these averages.

Follicle-stimulating hormones (FSH) are released from the anterior lobe of the pituitary gland, which is a pealike gland suspended from the base of the brain. The follicle-stimulating hormone activates the ovarian follicles, and two to thirty-two eggs begin to ripen. The follicles mature at different rates of speed. By the tenth day the most mature follicles look like rounded, fluid-filled sacs. The maturing follicles begin to produce **estrogen**, which prepares the uterus for implantation of the fertilized egg. At this time one of the follicles speeds its growth. The others, developed to various extents, regress and die. Occasionally a woman may produce more than one ripe egg per cycle and thus be prone to multiple births. Recently, many women who took certain chemicals designed to increase their fertility have had multiple births, indicating that the chemicals stimulate numerous follicles to continue ripening (see Inset 9-3).

By about day 13, the egg is ready to be released. This is accomplished by the *luteinizing hormone (LH)*, also produced by the pituitary gland. The luteinizing hormone causes the follicle to rupture, which is ovulation.

The egg survives for about twenty-four hours. Sperm, on the other hand, can normally survive from one to three days after being deposited in the vagina. If ovulation occurs between the twelfth and sixteenth days of the cycle, intercourse any time between the ninth and the eighteenth days might cause pregnancy (see Figure 9-12).

As the egg has been developing, estrogen has also worked to enrich and thicken the uterine lining, or *endometrium* (see Figure 9-13). Blood engorges the tissue to provide a nourishing environment for the fertilized egg. If fertilization does occur, the fertilized egg will be implanted in the thickened uterine wall, and the menstrual cycle will be suspended for the duration of the pregnancy (see Chapter 11). Usually, however, fertilization does not take place, and the menstrual cycle is completed. Without fertilization the estrogen level falls and the thickened uterine lining, as well as the remnants of the unfertilized egg, are shed, as **menstruation**, through the cervix and vagina. About two ounces of blood are lost in an average menstrual period. There may be some cramps in the pelvic region as well as general discomfort at this time. Many women also report some fatigue, irritability, depression, and psychic distress just before menstruation. This

Fallopian tubes
The two tubes in the female reproductive system that link the ovaries to the uterus; passageway for eggs

Ovulation
The regular monthly process in the fertile woman whereby an ovarian follicle ruptures and releases a mature ovum (egg)

Estrogen
Often called the "female hormone"; directs the differentiation of embryonic tissue into female genitals and of prenatal brain tissue that governs female physiological functions; responsible for the development of female secondary sexual characteristics

Menstruation
The discharge of blood from the uterus through the vagina, normally occurs every twenty-eight days in women from puberty to menopause

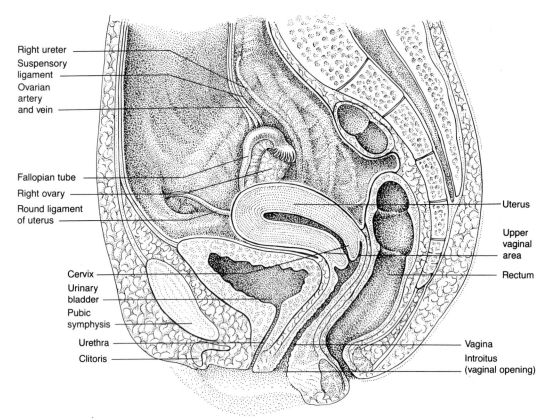

Right ureter

Suspensory ligament

Ovarian artery and vein

Fallopian tube

Right ovary

Round ligament of uterus

Cervix

Urinary bladder

Pubic symphysis

Urethra

Clitoris

Uterus

Upper vaginal area

Rectum

Vagina

Introitus (vaginal opening)

FIGURE 9-10   The female reproductive system.

FIGURE 9-11   External female genitals.

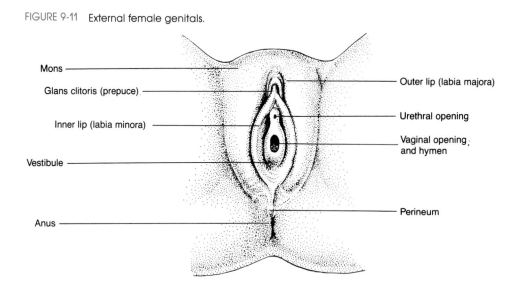

Mons

Glans clitoris (prepuce)

Inner lip (labia minora)

Vestibule

Anus

Outer lip (labia majora)

Urethral opening

Vaginal opening and hymen

Perineum

INSET 9-3

Fertility Drugs: A Mixed Blessing

"They just kept coming. We weren't expecting anything like this."

Mark Levy, 27, of Fairfield, Ohio, had good reason to be surprised and excited. . . . His wife Pamela, 28 and previously childless, had just given birth to quintuplets — a phenomenon that until recently happened only once in every 41 million births. But quintuple deliveries and other multiple births have become more commonplace lately; Pamela, like thousands of other women, had been taking a fertility drug called Pergonal. Doctors estimate that women who become pregnant after treatment with Pergonal are many times more likely, and women who take another fertility drug called Clomid slightly more likely, than other women to have more than one baby.

The Levy quints are doing well, and their parents seem to be adjusting to the startling increase in the size of their family. But many of the multiple births that result from the use of fertility drugs turn out to be mixed blessings at best. The infants are usually born prematurely, and because of overcrowding within the womb are likely to suffer even more problems than most "preemies." The prospect of multiple births also puts a strain on pregnant women. They are usually dismayed when they first hear the news. In fact, many families feel that they are simply unprepared — physically, financially, and emotionally — to cope with more than one new baby at a time. Most women nonetheless profess to be delighted after they find themselves the mothers of twins, triplets, or even quints.

Multiple births are not the only problems that go with fertility drugs. Though many, perhaps even the majority of women who take fertility drugs experience no ill effects, a number develop potentially serious illnesses. Researchers found that women who took Clomid occasionally developed ovarian cysts, which, without skillful treatment, can rupture and cause internal hemorrhaging and death. The incidence of cysts is higher with Pergonal.

Casual Use Most fertility experts insist that the drugs are indeed safe — if they are used with care and discretion. Unfortunately, says Manhattan gynecologist Edward Stim, who rarely prescribes the drugs, they are sometimes given on a casual, "Why not give it a try?" basis. Clomid, a synthetic hormone-like drug, seems to work by stimulating the pituitary gland to release hormones that help to ripen the ovum. Pergonal, a hormonal extract from the urine of postmenopausal women, primes the ovaries so that another hormone — human chorionic gonadotropin or HCG — can ensure the release of the ovum. Neither treatment should be used unless doctors have first determined that a woman's inability to have a baby is caused by a failure to ovulate, which accounts for only 5 to 10 percent of all cases of infertility.* The experts urge that patients be monitored carefully to prevent the development of cysts.

Some doctors feel that women faced with giving birth to litters should consider having abortions. "If there are more than three fetuses, it's a disaster," says one fertility expert. But Dr. Robert Kistner of Harvard Medical School, a pioneer in Clomid treatment, feels that multiple pregnancies can and should be prevented before they start. Kistner treats women who do not respond to Clomid alone by priming them first with small doses of Clomid and Pergonal then checking their

*More common causes: male sterility and infections that scar the lining of the uterus and Fallopian tubes.

INSET 9-3, CONTINUED		
estrogen (female hormone) levels to estimate how many eggs they are about to release.	gests the ripening of more than two eggs, he withholds the drug; the small doses of Clomid and Pergonal alone are insufficient to produce ovulation. Kistner's system appears to be effective. Of 80 patients	treated with Clomid and Pergonal in sequence, most of those with simple ovulation problems became pregnant and had babies. Only one woman had more than one baby, and she had only twins.
If his test indicates that the patient will yield only one or two, he administers HCG to trigger release. If the test sug-		

premenstrual tension is probably the result of the shifts in hormonal levels.

Toxic shock syndrome (TSS) is a new problem that recently has come to public attention via well-publicized lawsuits against some tampon-manufacturing firms. The cause of TSS is unknown, but a bacterium, *Staphylococcus aureus*, is suspected. The continuous use of tampons during menstruation may favor the growth of this bacterium ("Toxic Shock . . . ," 1980). In actuality the problem is rare. It is characterized by sudden onset, with symptoms such as vomiting, diarrhea, fever, skin rash, and a drop in blood pressure. Despite the glare of publicity surrounding the tampon's relationship to toxic shock syndrome, there is little scientific evidence at this time as to just what the relationship is.

The remaining organs of the female reproductive system, the *vagina*, *clitoris*, and other external genitals (Figure 9-11) are important to sexual behavior. The vagina is about three and a half inches long when it is relaxed and can stretch considerably during intercourse and childbirth (see Chapter 11). The clitoris is important to female sexuality, being highly erogenous. It is located just under the upper part of the labia minora (Figure 9-11).

Menopause

Menopause
The cessation of ovulation, menstruation, and fertility in the woman; usually occurs between ages forty-six and fifty-one

The cessation of the menstrual cycle in women is termed **menopause** or the climacteric. Menopause occurs between the ages of forty-six and fifty-one. Menstruation does not stop suddenly but usually phases out over a period of time not exceeding two years. So long as a woman has any menstrual periods, no matter how irregular, the possibility of ovulation and therefore conception remains.

Because of the changing hormonal balances during menopause, a woman may experience some unpleasant symptoms such as "hot flashes," excessive fatigue, dizziness, muscular aches and pains, and emotional upset. Some women also worry that menopausal changes will bring decreased or changed sexual interest and desire. In actuality menopause does not seem to decrease sexual desire. In fact, many women report increased sexual desire because they no longer worry about pregnancy.

Estrogen therapy may be prescribed to help reduce negative symptoms. Because of this use, estrogen gained a reputation for slowing down the general aging process. Although it was widely prescribed during the 1960s, several studies appear to link it to the development of uterine cancer (Smith et al., 1975; Ziel & Fickle, 1975). At this time it is suggested that estrogen therapy be limited to the control of serious negative menopausal reactions and not be prescribed over extended time periods inasmuch as it does not appear to have any real value in retarding the aging process. Also, recent research indicates that far fewer women suffer serious negative symptoms from menopause than we have believed (Bruck, 1979), thus reducing even further the need for estrogen therapy.

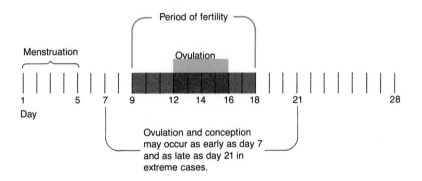

FIGURE 9-12 Timing of the menstrual cycle.

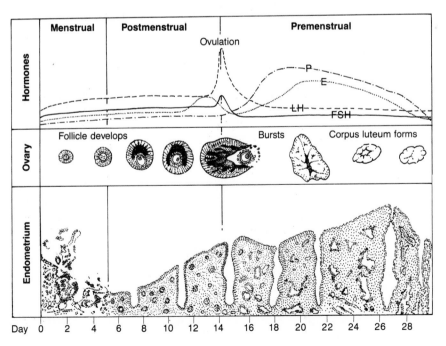

FIGURE 9-13 Lining buildup. galley 265

The Physiology of the Sexual Response

Only recently have we begun to understand the physiology of the human sexual response. In a series of controversial studies, William H. Masters and Virginia E. Johnson (1966) pioneered research using human subjects engaged in sexual activities. Before these studies most of our knowledge was derived from animal research. Among other techniques Masters and Johnson photographed the inside of the vagina during sexual arousal and orgasm. As controversial as this research was, it opened a new field of study, gave us a new understanding of the human sexual response, and paved the way for providing programs to help those having sexual difficulties. Recently Masters and Johnson's work has been criticized for methodological errors and slipshod reporting. (See Zilbergeld and Evans, 1980, for an overview of this criticism.) Yet it was their pioneering efforts that finally brought scientific research to bear on human sexuality.

Masters and Johnson divide the sexual response of both men and women into four phases: *excitement*, *plateau*, *orgasm*, and *resolution*. A partial description of these phases follows. The responses in all the stages for both females and males are usually independent of the type of stimulation that produces them. In other words the basic physiological reactions are the same regardless of whether they are produced through manual manipulation, penile insertion, or in some other manner.

The Female Sexual Response

Sexual response begins with the excitement phase, which may last anywhere from a few minutes to several hours. The breasts swell with blood. The skin may also be flushed; the nipples may become erect; and there may be general muscle contractions in the thighs, back, abdomen, and throughout the body. The **clitoris** becomes engorged with blood (tumescent); vagina walls then begin to sweat a lubricating fluid that facilitates the entrance of the penis. The inner portion of the vagina balloons, increasing in size, and the uterus may have irregular contractions. The labia minora (inner vaginal lips) increase in size. Blood pressure, heart rate, and breathing rates all increase.

The next phase, the plateau phase, lasts from only a few seconds to about three minutes. Tumescence and the sex flush reach their peak. Muscle tension is high and the woman experiences a complete physical and emotional absorption with the impending climax. The clitoris withdraws beneath its hood and can only be stimulated indirectly. (The idea that direct stimulation of the clitoris is necessary for female orgasm is untrue. Indirect stimulation is effective, and, in fact, the heightened clitoral sensitivity during this phase may make direct stimulation uncomfortable.) Muscle rigidity reaches a peak as shown by the facial grimace, rigid neck, arched back, and tense thighs and buttocks. The labia minora change color dramatically. (In women who have not borne a child, the color will become pink to bright red. In women who have had children, the color will become pink to a deep wine.) Blood accumulates in the

Clitoris
A small organ situated at the upper end of the female genitals that becomes erect with sexual arousal; homologous with the penis

arteries and veins around the vagina, uterus, and other pelvic organs. This pelvic congestion is relieved by the orgasmic phase.

The third phase, **orgasm**, is the most intense. During orgasm, most of the built-up neuromuscular tension is discharged in three to ten seconds. Orgasm is so all absorbing that most sensory awareness of the external environment is lost. The whole body responds though the sensation of orgasm is centered in the pelvis.

Orgasm
The climax of excitement in sexual activity

> Of all the widespread muscle responses, the muscle contractions . . . that surround the lower third of the vagina cause the most unique phenomenon. These muscles contract against the engorged veins that surround that part of the vagina and force the blood out of them. This creates the orgasm. These contractions, in turn, cause the lower third of the vagina and the nearby upper labia minora to contract a number of times. (Kogan, 1973, p. 86)

Although it is generally recognized that women do not ejaculate as men do, researchers (Addiego et al., 1980) report isolated cases in which women have experienced an ejaculatory-type phenomenon. The researchers claim to have evidence that "some women ejaculate a fluid which contains the product of the 'female prostate,' . . . which is homologous to the male prostate" (p. 100). Their evidence suggests that such responses occur most frequently from stimulation of the so-called Gräfenberg spot (G spot), an area located on the front wall of the vagina halfway between the top of the pubic bone and the cervix. It lies along the urethra, just below the neck of the bladder. The G spot ranges in size from that of a dime to a quarter. This research remains suspect, though, because even the existence of the Gräfenberg spot is questionable at this time. Researchers Perry and Whipple (1982) report finding the G spot in 400 of their sample women. Masters and Johnson (1982), however, were unable to replicate this finding. Because areas of the body can be eroticized psychologically, Masters and Johnson suggest that perhaps some women have located a psychological pleasure spot within a certain area of the vagina and that there is no physiological basis for the increased sensation. It is also interesting to note that those few women, seen over the years in the Masters and Johnson laboratory, who show considerable fluid discharge with orgasm secrete fluid that has essentially the chemical makeup of urine, although some claim the fluid is similar to prostatic fluid (Mahoney, 1982). The fluid bears no chemical similarity to male semen.

In the last phase, resolution, the body returns to its normal prestimulated condition, usually within ten or fifteen minutes. If orgasm does not take place, the resolution phase may last as long as twelve hours or more. Women have the capacity of repeating the four-phase cycle immediately after resolution and can experience multiple orgasms if stimulation is continued.

The Male Sexual Response

The four stages of the sexual response cycle cause the same changes in the male as they do in the female, with a few additions. For example, during excitement the penis (as well as breasts and nipples) becomes engorged with blood until it erects. Also, the sperm begin their journey from the epididymis to the penis.

The next and major difference occurs during the orgasmic phase. Orgasm for the male is reached by the ejaculation of the semen and sperm through the penis.

Once the male ejaculates, penile detumescence (loss of erection) usually follows quickly in the resolution phase, though complete detumescence takes longer. Unlike the female, who can reach repeated orgasms, the male usually experiences a refractory (recovery) period during which he cannot become sexually aroused. This period may last only a few minutes or it may last up to several hours, depending on such factors as age, health, and desire. Recent research has found that not all men have an immediate complete refractory stage. Some men are able to keep an erection or partial erection after they ejaculate and continue to enjoy sex for a while (Nass, Libby & Fisher, forthcoming). Because in our society the male has usually been taught that it takes time to become sexually aroused again after ejaculation, the refractory period may be partially due to psychological as well as physiological factors.

The male who is sexually aroused for a length of time without ejaculating may experience aching in his testicles and a general tension. These sensations can last for an hour or two. Such tension may be relieved by masturbation if a sexual partner is unavailable.

Variations in Sexual Response

Although Masters and Johnson's early work suggested that all persons follow this four-phase pattern, later research indicates that there may be more individual variation than first thought (Hartman & Fithian, 1972, 1979; Nass, Libby & Fisher, forthcoming). This later research suggests four variations on the basic pattern of sexual response described by Masters & Johnson. Some people appear to orgasm as they're approaching the peak of heartbeat and breathing, some as they hit the peak, some on their way down, and a few have orgasms that are so gradual the researchers can't tell when they start although it is obvious when they end.

Masters and Johnson believed that the woman's orgasm was identified by vaginal contractions and that without these the woman's sexual response was not an orgasm. They concluded that women experience only one kind of orgasm, although earlier researchers had described two kinds of female orgasms, clitoral and vaginal. At first it appeared that the Masters and Johnson research had settled the question of one type or two types, but the question has been reopened. Shere Hite (1976), for example, found that during intercourse many women experience a peak of tension followed by total relaxation, without any sensation of involuntary contractions in the vaginal area. Some researchers think that such women are having mild vaginal contractions but aren't aware of them because muscles all over their bodies are contracted (Kerr, 1977). Many of the women in Hite's survey also believe that there is a subjective difference between intercourse orgasms and those brought on by masturbation or oral sex where there is little or no penetration. These women describe the intercourse orgasms as more "diffuse" and whole-body involving, whereas the nonintercourse orgasms are more intense and localized. Some women found the former more satisfying, and some found the latter more satisfying.

Other researchers (Singer & Singer, 1972) suggest that there may be three kinds of female orgasms. The first is a vulval or clitoral orgasm, as Masters and Johnson described. The second is a uterine or upper orgasm during which breathing changes lead to involuntary breath holding (because of a strong contraction in the muscle at the back of the throat) and then to explosive exhalation. This orgasm is not accompanied by vaginal contractions. The researchers suggest that the third type is a blending of these two.

Although much research has been done on the female orgasm, we still do not have a definitive answer about its nature. What is clear is that females have a greater diversity of sensation and reaction to a sexual stimulation than males do. Therefore when a woman reads a popular description of what she "should" be feeling and how she "should" be reacting to sexual stimulation, she must be aware that the description may or may not fit her. If the description does not fit her, she need not necessarily label her sexual responses as inadequate.

Some Myths Unmasked

Masters and Johnson's research put to rest a number of myths about human sexuality. First, it established beyond question that women can have multiple orgasms. It also established that, within normal ranges, the size of the penis and vagina have little to do with the experience of orgasm. For example, the back two-thirds of the vagina is practically without nerve endings and plays little part in orgasm. Most of the stimulation occurs in the front third of the vagina, the labia minora, and the clitoris. A larger penile circumference may increase a woman's sexual sensation by placing pressure on the vaginal ring muscles thus causing pleasurable tugging of the labia minora. Further, a longer penis may heighten sensations by thrusting against the cervix (Keller, 1976; McCary & McCary, 1982). On the other hand, too large a penis may be uncomfortable for the woman, detracting from her sensual enjoyment.

Masters and Johnson also revealed that it is not essential to stimulate the clitoris directly for orgasm to occur, though such stimulation produces the quickest orgasm for most women. And they found that the myth that the female responds more slowly is not necessarily true. When she regulates the rhythm and intensity of her own sexual stimuli, the time required for her to reach orgasm is about the same as for the male. The female's much-discussed slowness in arousal is probably due to cultural repression rather than to some physiological difference.

Partners often believe that to achieve complete sexual satisfaction they should try to experience orgasm simultaneously. As pleasant as this may be, there is no reason why partners must always reach orgasm at the same point in time. In fact, doing so may hinder spontaneity and may deprive each of being fully aware of the other's pleasure. They may find it equally satisfying for one to orgasm at a different time in the love-making sequence than the other.

In addition to these specific findings, Masters and Johnson's work changed our ideas about other general aspects of sexuality. For example, masturbation is now considered by many sexologists to be an important and necessary part of sexual expression rather than a taboo behavior. Some women who have never experienced orgasm can learn how by first learning the techniques of masturbation. Once they have learned how to orgasm, they can transfer the learning to sex with their partners. The rationale behind this is that so many emotions surround sex (for example, shame and guilt about the failure to achieve orgasm, disappointment and perhaps insecurity on the part of the partner) that it becomes almost impossible for some women to enjoy sex or to change their behavior. The direct stimulation of masturbation encourages orgasm. Too, being alone may ease the emotional tension associated with sex.

In general Americans' attitudes toward sexual expression have become more open as they have learned more about their sexuality. Rather than ignoring and/or hiding sexuality, it is important to understand it so that you may use it to enhance your life and bring greater joy and intimacy to your intimate relationships.

Differences between Male and Female Sexuality

There are a number of basic differences between male and female sexuality that are well documented, yet controversial. These differences stem from both biological and cultural sources (see Chapter 6 for a discussion of the biological and cultural background of male/female differences).

Figure 9-14 diagrams some general differences in sexual drive between men and women across their adult life span. There is considerable debate over the source of these differences. Some researchers, such as sociobiologist Edward O. Wilson (1978), suggest that these dissimilarities stem from inborn differences in biological makeup between males and females. Most sociologists and psychologists believe that the differences stem from the socialization processes that teach men and women their sex roles and the place of sexual behavior in their lives. The truth probably lies somewhere in between these two views, with both nature (biology) and nurture (culture) combining in some manner to create the differences between the sexes.

Because puberty begins on the average about two years earlier in females than in males, young girls develop an interest in sexuality earlier than boys do (area A of Figure 9-14). This interest is usually displayed as "boy craziness." During this period most boys remain essentially uninterested in girls. When puberty does arrive in young men, their sexual interests and desires soar above those of like-aged girls. From age fifteen through age twenty-five, males are at the height of their sexual drive.

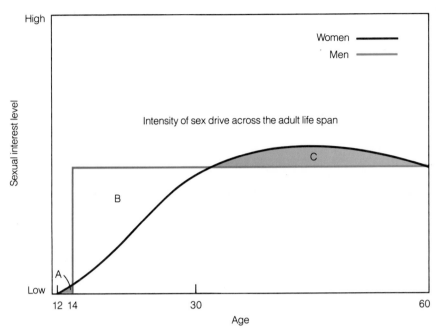

FIGURE 9-14 Intensity of sex drive across the adult life span.

Most similarily-aged females perceive their male counterparts as "preoccupied with sex" during this period (area B on Figure 9-14), whereas the male's major thought is "I don't get enough sex." (See Scenes from Marriage on page 328.) During this time periodic **masturbation** is common among young men.

Various studies indicate an 86 to 96 percent incidence of masturbation among men, while the same studies indicate only a 47 to 69 percent rate among women (Nass, Libby & Fisher, 1981). These studies are misleading to some degree because they look at the incidence of masturbation over one's entire lifetime. Most men have masturbated in their early youth, whereas relatively few women have. Women's masturbation rates climb slowly over the age span to reach the levels reported, whereas the men's rates are reached early in their lives. The male during his teens and twenties (area B in Figure 9-14) simply is a much more sexual creature than the female. The female's sexual drive gradually increases, reaching its peak when the woman is between thirty and forty years of age. Because of some females' multiorgasmic capability, they may become even more sexual than males in later years (area C in Figure 9-14).

To some extent Figure 9-14 indicates that males and females are somewhat incompatible across their sexual lives. If we consider only sexual drive, older men and younger women and older women and younger men make the most compatible partners sexually. Margaret Mead, in fact, suggested that a sexually compatible culture would be one in which older men married very young women, who on the death of their first husbands would be left economically secure. These women in turn could marry young sexually compatible men whom they could help to a good

Masturbation
Stimulation of the genital organs, usually to orgasm, by means other than intercourse

economic start. Although such an idea intellectually may solve the problem of differing sex-drive strength between men and women at different ages, it is hardly apt to find wide acceptance in our culture. Thus men and women will have to work out compromises in their sex lives as their sex drives vary over time and clash periodically.

Certainly, in the young teens males are far more genitally oriented than females, who are more socially oriented. When young males are sexually stimulated, there is an increased flow of seminal fluid. This buildup causes a preoccupation with the genital area and the need to ejaculate.

Males generally are aroused more easily and directly by visual stimuli or mental imagery caused by pictures of nude women and pornography than are women (Barclay, 1971). Women are also aroused but at times don't recognize their arousal (Heiman, 1975). Their reactions to various sexually provocative materials are more complex, with much depending on the type of material. In addition they are more apt to react negatively to sexually explicit material than are men (Nass, Libby & Fisher, forthcoming).

Sexual fantasies play an important part in both men's and women's sex lives. Such fantasies can be important to sexual arousal. Gathering information on people's sexual fantasies is difficult because they are regarded as private and intimate. Too, one's fantasies will be influenced by personal experiences as well as by societal mores regarding sex. Although the details of people's fantasies vary greatly, certain general themes have been found in both sexes. Masters and Johnson (1982) report the top five fantasy contents for heterosexual men and women as follows:

Heterosexual Male	*Heterosexual Female*
1. Replacement of established partner	1. Replacement of established partner
2. Forced sexual encounter	2. Forced sexual encounter
3. Observation of sexual activity	3. Observation of sexual activity
4. Cross-sex encounters	4. Idyllic encounters with unknown men
5. Group sex experiences	5. Cross-sex encounters

Probably the most outstanding thing about these lists is their similarity. Their general similarity masks more specific gender differences, however. For example, women tend to surround sexual fantasies with more romantic images than do men (Wilson & Lang, 1981; Friday, 1974). Masters and Johnson point out that fantasy content will change with time, personal experience, and one's culture. They also note that analysis of fantasy content for diagnostic purposes is usually nonproductive. For example, it is sometimes said that a person who fantasizes about same-sex experiences may be a "latent homosexual." Yet both heterosexual men and women report such fantasies, and both homosexual men and women report fantasizing about heterosexual relations. We do not label homosexuals who fantasize about heterosexual relations as "latent heterosexuals."

Researchers have found that about one in four married women had not experienced orgasm at age twenty-five, and it appears that about one in

The Hite Report on Male Sexuality*

Hite's new report suggests that men and women share far more sexual fears and romantic fantasies than has been commonly supposed. Like the women depicted in her first book, many of the 7,239 men who participated in the second study said they felt trapped by sexual stereotypes, craved emotional intimacy — and found themselves unable to talk openly about their sexual angers, anxieties and desires. Exclaims one man: "What a hell of a way to live. Our sexual definitions and ideals are a mess, and they bring pain and sorrow to us all."

Source: Waters et al., 1981, p. 104.
*Caution: This study is based on a volunteer sample (see p. 27).

Her most provocative findings challenge the traditional belief that heterosexual men are most satisfied by intercourse. "The myth is that intercourse is the greatest thrill that men can have," Hite says. "Surprisingly, most men said they could have a stronger orgasm physically during masturbation." Even so, almost all heterosexual respondents (who comprised 87 percent of Hite's sample) said they enjoyed intercourse more than masturbation or oral sex. Their reasons were more psychological and emotional than physical. Only 3 percent of those sampled mentioned orgasm when asked, "Why do you like intercourse?" The most common responses cited physical closeness, sensations of masculinity, acceptance and love. From that, Hite concluded that intercourse may be the only activity during which many men feel free to express emotion. "It is the closest you can be to a person," said one respondent, "and for a moment or an hour it overcomes the loneliness and separation of life."

Despite the pleasure they found in intercourse, many men in the Hite report expressed ambivalence about the "macho" obligations it involves. Nearly a third of heterosexual respondents said they sometimes had intercourse simply because it seemed to be expected of them; many complained about the escalating pressures to initiate sex, to get and maintain frequent erections, to control the timing of ejaculations and to satisfy their partners' orgasmic needs. "If anything goes wrong, I'm blamed for it," said one man. Over and over again, the men in Hite's sample expressed resentment at being typecast as the ever-ready, do-it-all maestros of sexual relations — although some of the same men admitted being intimidated by sexually aggressive females. Asked about their feelings, many men seemed to be filled with rage. "Yes, I usually take the initial sexual advance . . . and every other advance . . . and I'm damned tired of it," said one. "*I* make the first phone call, *I* make the first date . . . *I* touch her and *I* [make love to] her. . . . It's no wonder we grow up to think of women as objects, because that's exactly what many women act like."

ten women never experience orgasm (Kinsey, 1953). By contrast, the average male by his wedding day has already had 1523 orgasms (Kinsey, 1948). As Lloyd Saxton (1977) summarizes: "It is not surprising, then, that the average male often feels betrayed and dejected by the indifferent sexuality or antisexuality of his wife." To the degree that this difference is cultural — and probably most of it is — women may become more overtly interested in sex as the double standard declines and as they learn more about their own sexuality.

INSET 9-5

The Redbook Report on Sexual Relationships*

In a survey of more than 26,000 women and men the following findings stood out:

Achieving orgasm is not the determining factor of a satisfying sex life for either men or women.

Source: "The Redbook Report . . .," 1980, p. 73.
*Caution: This study is based on a volunteer sample (see p. 27).

Failure to reach orgasm is considered "no big thing" by almost 7 of every 10 women in good or excellent sexual relationships.

At least 95 percent of the men with the best sex lives have orgasms nearly every time they have sex. But so do 95 percent of the men with the worst sexual relationships.

Good communication with one's partner is the factor most strongly related to having a good sexual relationship.

Superior sexual communication skills are reported by 85 percent of the men and 82 percent of the women who have the best sex lives.

When men and women talk about sex, they talk about the quantity more than the quality.

Frequency is also the topic most argued about. Oral sex is the next most argued about.

Women who can assert themselves in an argument are happier with their sex lives than women who rate low in assertiveness.

Among women who report unsatisfying sexual relationships, nearly 1 in 4 is too embarrassed to talk about sex with her partner.

Men are more open in discussing sex than women are.

Surprisingly, men are also more likely to say that they communicate well about their feelings.

What Do You Think?

What differences between male and female sexuality have you found troublesome?

There has always been a double standard of sexual conduct for the sexes in America. How does this affect sexual differences between the sexes?

Must sex and love always go together? Why or why not?

Another important difference is that the degree of sexual response variation is far wider in women than in men. Some women never achieve orgasm and some only when they are thirty to forty years of age. At the other extreme some women have frequent multiple orgasms. Neither of these extremes is true for males (Masters & Johnson, 1966). There is also an interesting difference in the reported subjective feelings of pleasure with repeated orgasm. Women who experience multiple orgasms usually find their second and third orgasmic episodes the most pleasurable. But most men report greater pleasure from the first ejaculation rather than from a repeated orgasmic experience (Masters & Johnson, 1966). This might be explained in part by the relatively greater volume of seminal fluid in the first ejaculation, especially following a period of continence.

Another difference is that females tend to have a cyclic increase in sexual desire related to the menstrual cycle. Most women report increased sexual desire just before menstruation and a few report increased sexual desire right afterward. Evidence also indicates increased female sexual arousal close to ovulation (Adams, Gold & Burt, 1978). There is little counterpart of this cyclical heightened desire in the male. It is also interesting to note that sterilized women report an increase in sexual enjoyment because they are free of fear of pregnancy. Such differences should be understood so that they do not cause misunderstanding or conflict.

Sex and Drugs

People have long sought the ideal **aphrodisiac**, a substance that would arouse sexual desire. Thus far the search has failed, although folklore is extensive about the use of such things as powdered rhinoceros horn and "Spanish fly," or cantharis. Alcohol is the most widely used sexual stimulant in America, but in reality it is a depressant and inhibits the sexual response in males if ingested in large amounts (Wilson & Lawson, 1978; Wilson & Abrams, 1978). Long-term alcohol consumption increases the production of a liver enzyme that destroys testosterone, thereby reducing sexual desire (Rubin et al., 1976). Sexual-response times for erection and ejaculation are also increasingly reduced as alcohol ingestion increases (Kolodny, 1982). In women the effects of alcohol are somewhat more mixed than in men. Researchers (Malatesta, 1982) found that women have a more difficult time achieving orgasm and experience less orgasmic intensity. Despite this, women believed (self-reports) that they experienced increased sexual arousal and increased pleasure. Alcohol's reputation as an aphrodisiac apparently stems from its psychological effects: It loosens controls and inhibitions, thereby indirectly stimulating sexual behavior.

Marijuana has mixed effects on sexuality. There is no evidence of heightened physical reactions, but there is some sense distortion that probably heightens sexual sensitivity with a compatible partner (Kogan, 1973). As a true aphrodisiac, however, it is a failure, as it appears to have neither a positive nor a negative effect on sexual desire (Mendelson, 1976). There is some evidence that those who use marijuana heavily for prolonged periods have a higher incidence of impotence than nonusers, probably because testosterone levels drop (Maugh, 1975; Jones & Jones, 1977; Kolodny et al., 1974). Feelings of increased sexuality probably stem from reduced inhibitions and the relaxing of tensions as in the case of alcohol.

Robert Kolodny (1982) reported research in which five groups using different levels of marijuana were studied for sexual dysfunction. The following table catalogs the results.

Aphrodisiac
A chemical or other substance used to induce erotic arousal or to relieve impotence or infertility

Male Sexual Dysfunction and Chronic Marijuana Use

	N	SECONDARY IMPOTENCE	PREMATURE EJACULATION
Control group (no use)	225	8.4%	14.2%
Group A (less than once a week)	272	8.5%	13.2%
Group B (1 to 2 times a week)	342	7.3%	14.0%
Group C (3, 4, and 5 times a week)	117	13.7%	12.8%
Group D (daily use)	94	19.2%	16.0%

Infrequent marijuana use showed no effects on either secondary impotence or premature ejaculation. Chronic marijuana use, however, was clearly related to secondary impotence but apparently unrelated to premature ejaculation. Those using marijuana every day showed almost two and a half times more secondary impotence than those using it less than three times a week.

LSD, by distorting time, may seem to prolong the sexual experience. However, a bad "trip" (frightening hallucinations, and so forth) can have disastrous effects on one's sexuality (Jones & Jones, 1977).

Amphetamines (speed) act as stimulants, in that the male can maintain a prolonged erection, but their long-term use destroys general health as well as sex drive and ultimately leads to impotence. Cocaine has similar effects. For the female, because these drugs have a drying effect on vaginal secretions, prolonged intercourse may be uncomfortable unless extra lubrication is supplied. Some cocaine users believe that placing the substance directly on the end of the penis and on the clitoris heightens sensitivity. The opposite is true. Cocaine is an anesthetic to the touch sense and so acts to deaden the area to which it is applied. It is interesting to note also that because of the high expense of cocaine, offering it to a person of the opposite sex is almost always secondarily an invitation to have sexual interaction as well.

The Roman philosopher Seneca knew the best aphrodisiac: "I show you a philtre [potion], without medicaments, without herbs, without witch's incantations. It is this: If you want to be loved, love" (quoted in Wedeck, 1962, p. 302). Masters and Johnson echo this when they say that intimacy — being close to another in all ways — is the best stimulant to eroticism.

Anaphrodisiac
A drug or medicine that reduces sexual desire

Anaphrodisiacs are drugs that decrease sexual desire and activity. Perhaps the best known is saltpeter (potassium nitrate). Saltpeter acts as a diuretic and, because of frequent urination, may act to deter sexual activity. However, it has no known direct physiological effect on sexual behavior.

There are four groups of drugs that impair sexual functioning. *Sedatives* such as barbiturates and narcotics can suppress sexual interest and response. *Antiandrogens* are drugs that counter the effect of androgen on the brain and thus diminish sexual responsivness. *Anticholenergic* and *antiadrenergic* drugs work to diminish sexual response by blocking the blood vessels and nerves connected to the genitals. These drugs are used to treat diseases of the eye, high blood pressure, and circulatory problems. Two drugs commonly used to treat hypertension, reserpine and methyldopa, cause loss of sexual interest and erectile incompetence (Gotwald & Golden, 1981). *Psychotropic drugs* such as tranquilizers and muscle relaxants may cause ejaculatory and erectile difficulties.

As the discussion shows, there are a number of drugs with known anaphrodisiac qualities. On the other hand, drugs with aphrodisiac qualities are less understood and many times are surrounded by unsubstantiated "old wives' " tales.

Sex and the Aging Process

For some inexplicable reason the myth has grown up that for older persons sex is a thing of the past, an indulgence for the young. Yet we find that the natural function of sex remains as we age, just as the other natural functions do, albeit in changing forms. We don't expect at age seventy to run as fast or to have the physical strength we had at age twenty. Yet we accept these changes, and we don't give up jogging or lifting. Likewise, changes in our sexual functioning don't mean that we shouldn't still use it.

Masters and Johnson (1981) indicate that there are three criteria for continuing sexual activity regardless of age. First, a person must have good general health. Second, one needs an interesting and interested sexual partner. Third, past fifty years of age, the sexual organs must be used. "Use it or lose it," is their advice to aging people, especially males.

One is never too old for love.

As a man moves past his midfifties, he may notice four changes in his basic sexual physiology. First, it may take him longer to achieve a full erection even with overt sexual stimulation, and he may experience fewer spontaneous erections. What has been a pattern when he was younger of rapid erective response to real or imagined sexual opportunity becomes slowed and more dependent on his partner's direct physical approach. Second, he may notice a reduction in expulsive pressure and, third, a reduction in the volume of seminal fluid during ejaculation. As a fourth change he may notice an occasional reduction or loss of ejaculatory demand. Aging men continue to have a high level of interest in the sensual pleasure specific to sex, but subjectively their felt need to ejaculate may be reduced. Perhaps one out of three or four times that aging men have intercourse they may not experience the need to ejaculate. It's not that they can't if they force the issue; they just don't feel the need to ejaculate.

Knowledge of such changes is important to both the man and to his partner. If a man does not anticipate and understand these changes associated with aging, he may develop fears about his sexual performance and such fears may rob him of his sexual desires. If his partner does not understand these changes, she may question her own sexuality when confronted by the changes. For example, his slower erective response may be interpreted as loss of interest in her. If he doesn't ejaculate regularly, she may be concerned that he doesn't need her.

The aging process also brings a number of changes in the woman's sexual facility. The lubricating fluid produced by the older woman is diminished in volume and is produced at a slower rate. The vaginal walls lose some of their elasticity, which can lead to the creation of small fissures in the lining of the vagina with sudden penile penetration or long-continued coital thrusting. Just as with the aging male, more time should be allocated for precoital stimulation. If neither partner evidences a sense of urgency in sexual interaction, erections and lubrication usually develop satisfactorily. Even with the physiological changes mentioned, it is important to remember that the psychologically appreciated levels of sensual pleasure derived from sex continue unabated (Masters & Johnson, 1981).

Older men and women are losing their sexual involvement far earlier than necessary because there has been little effort to educate them to the physiologic facts of aging sexual function. Older people are and should continue to be sexually responsive human beings.

Sexually Transmitted Disease (STD)

Sexually transmitted disease (STD)
Any contagious disease communicated mainly by sexual interaction

Unfortunately, no discussion of human sexuality is complete without mention of the most social of human diseases, an oft-found bedmate, **sexually transmitted disease (STD)** (Table 9-1). The incidence of such disease in the United States has been drastically reduced by the use of antibiotics such as penicillin. Recently, however, there has been an epidemic of some kinds of STD. In fact, next to the common cold, gonorrhea is the most common infectious disease in the United States. In 1978

TABLE 9-1   Sexually Transmitted Disease (STD)

DISEASE	CAUSE	INCUBATION PERIOD[1]	CHARACTERISTICS	TREATMENT[2]
Primary syphilis	Bacteria	7 – 90 days (usually 3 weeks)	Small, painless sore or chancre, usually on genitals but also on other parts of the body	Penicillin and broad spectrum antibiotics
Secondary syphilis	Untreated primary		Skin rashes or completely latent, enlarged lymph glands	Same
Tertiary syphilis	Untreated primary		Possible invasion of central nervous system, causing various paralyses; heart trouble; insanity	Same
Gonorrhea	Bacteria	3 – 5 days	Discharge, burning, pain, swelling of genitals and glands; possible loss of erectile ability in males who delay treatment, with chance of permanent sterility; 80% of infected females asymptomatic	Same
Chancroid	Bacteria	2 – 6 days	Shallow, painful ulcers, swollen lymph glands in groin	Sulfa drugs, broad spectrum antibiotics
Lymphogranuloma venereum	Virus	5 – 30 days	First, small blisters, then swollen lymph glands; may affect kidneys	Broad spectrum antibiotics
Genital herpes	Virus	Unknown	Blisters in genital area; very persistent	Pain-relieving ointments

Note: As soon as you suspect any sexually transmitted disease, or notice any symptoms, consult your doctor, local health clinic, or local or state health department. Both syphilis and gonorrhea, in particular, can be easily treated if detected early; if not, both can become recurrent, with dire results.

[1]If sexually transmitted disease is diagnosed, all sexual partners during the infected person's incubation period and up to discovery of the disease should be examined medically.

[2]Local health clinics or local and state health departments will have more detailed information on current treatment and follow-up.

approximately 3 million people were treated for gonorrhea in the United States (American Social Health Association, 1978). In contrast, only about 100,000 new cases of syphilis were treated that same year. Over 75 percent of reported STD occurs in young adults age 15 to 30. In 1980 it was estimated that one out of two high school students will have contracted gonorrhea by the time they graduate (U.S. Department of Health, Education, and Welfare, 1975). Since these statistics are based on reported cases, in all likelihood they underestimate the actual level of STD.

Of the various kinds of STD, genital herpes is the one people are discussing the most. Genital herpes appears to be infecting Americans at an epidemic rate, yet the disease was practically unknown to the public just a few years ago. Of the five types of human herpes, types I and II are those at the center of the current epidemic. Type I is most familiar as the cause of cold sores; Type II causes genital lesions. The two types are similar, with Type I also able to cause genital problems.

The first symptom of genital herpes is usually an itching or tingling sensation. Blisters appear within two to fifteen days after infection. The moist blisters ooze a fluid that is extremely infectious. After one to three weeks they gradually dry up and disappear. The infected area is extremely sensitive and sore to the touch. For this reason genital herpes precludes sexual activity when it is in an active state. Also, the friction of sexual activity can reactivate the herpes sores unless they are completely healed.

Because the herpes virus remains in the body once it has been contracted, it can be activated at any time. The exact causes of reactivation are not known. It is clear that stress, sunshine, and nutritional and environmental changes are related (McKean, 1981). Indeed herpes is so related to a person's moods and emotions that learning to remain calm and under emotional control is one of the most effective preventives against its reactivation.

At this time there is no cure for genital herpes, only treatment for its symptoms. Acyclovir (trade name Zovirax), a creamy salve, alleviates symptoms and speeds healing. Unfortunately, it is less effective on subsequent episodes and does nothing to reduce the frequency of outbreak. There is some evidence that taken in oral form it reduces both the severity and frequency of outbreak.

Because no cure exists, many herpes sufferers have sought help from one another. A national group that encourages this self-help is the Herpes Resource Center in Palo Alto, California. It has about 30,000 members in forty-five chapters known as "help groups." The chapters function as group therapy sessions, letting newcomers talk about their problems and assuring those with herpes that they are not alone.

Although herpes is not as physically threatening as syphilis, its incurability is so discomforting and it is becoming so widespread that it is beginning to put a damper on indiscriminate sexual contacts. A recent *Time* magazine article concluded:

> For now, herpes cannot be defeated, only cozened into an uneasy, lifelong truce. It is a melancholy fact that it has rekindled old fears. But perhaps not so unhappily, it may be a prime mover in helping to bring to a close an era of mindless promiscuity. The monogamous now have one more reason to remain so. For all the distress it has brought, the troublesome little bug may inadvertently be ushering in a period in which sex is linked more firmly to commitment and trust. ("The New Scarlet Letter," 1982, p. 66)

Another sexually related disease that is making headlines is acquired immune deficiency syndrome (AIDS). Although AIDS affects very few people, the fact that it often leads to death makes it frightening. The survival rate is about 20 percent at this time. AIDS first was observed in the male homosexual population (72 percent of all cases) and in intravenous drug users (17 percent). First fully described in 1980, the disease destroys the immune system, leaving victims prey to all manner of viruses and bacteria. As of March 1983 about 913 people in the United States had the disease and 228 others had already died ("Battling, . . .," 1983).

At least three factors play a role in the resurgence of STD. First, because the pill has become the major method of birth control, the condom, with its built-in protective barrier against STD infection, is no longer so widely used. Second, the antibiotics themselves have lulled people into apathy. "Who cares about VD, it's easy to cure," appears to be a common attitude. (Although this is partly true, cure depends on prompt treatment; furthermore, new forms of antibiotic-resistant strains of the infecting organisms are appearing.) Third, the increased sexual activity among the young, especially the increased number of sexual partners, has contributed to the widespread outbreak of STD.

If you, your spouse, or a sexual partner suspect an STD, have a medical examination as soon as possible. In most cases the disease does not "go away," even though some of its symptoms may change or even disappear. Begun early, treatment is effective; delayed, the disease may recur or become more dangerous. Also, anyone seeking treatment will be treated with confidentiality. If a sexually transmitted disease is diagnosed, all persons who have had recent sexual contact with·the carrier should be notified and should also be examined. With increased public awareness of STD, it is hoped that the incidence can be cut back to earlier low levels.

Summary

Sexuality pervades the life of humans. This is mainly because human sex is to a great extent free from instinctual control. Although sexuality is a biological necessity, much of the way in which sex is manifested is learned. For this reason there is far greater variation in sexual behavior among humans than among other animals. All human societies try to control sexual expression, but the controls vary from one society to another. Because of the variability of sexual expression and the often conflicting teachings about sexuality, there is confusion both within societies and within individuals about sexuality. In all societies, human sexuality serves purposes other than procreation — such as communication, strengthening the male/female bond, increasing intimacy, pleasuring, having fun, and generally reducing tension.

Our understanding of sexual physiology has increased greatly as science and medicine have learned more about the functioning of the body. It is clear that males and females are physiologically similar, having developed their sexual organs from common structures. There are timing differences in function, however. Another major difference is the cyclical preparation for pregnancy that the female goes through each month.

Basically, both males and females share the same physical responses during sexual activity. These are called the excitement, plateau, orgasmic, and resolution stages. It is during the orgasmic stage that the major difference between the sexes takes place: the ejaculation of the male. Also, the male usually goes through a refractory period after the resolution stage before he can have another erection.

Unfortunately, sexually transmitted disease too often accompanies sexual activity. The two major STD are syphilis and gonorrhea, both of which are increasing. This increase is attributed to use of the pill rather than the condom, people's believing that modern drugs have eliminated the diseases, and, most of all, to youth's increased sexual activity and variety of sexual partners. Genital herpes has increased to epidemic proportions and may serve to slow the sexual revolution by encouraging more careful choices of sexual partners.

SCENES FROM MARRIAGE

What Are Your Biggest Problems or Complaints about Sex?

Human sexuality has come out of the shadows into the spotlight, or so it seems. Textbooks and college courses on the subject abound. "How to" manuals become best sellers. Workshops are given for nonorgasmic women or to help men who have problems with premature ejaculation.

Surely we all know everything there is to know about sexuality! Yet each year I find that students in my marriage and family courses are filled with questions and complaints about their sexuality. Perhaps in some convoluted way the very fact that today everyone is supposed to know all about human sexuality makes it more difficult to become knowledgeable. To ask a question is to display ignorance and, of course, no one is ignorant about sex anymore.

As one of many exercises, my students answer anonymously the following question: "What are your biggest complaints or problems in the area of sex?"* It is interesting to note that females write much more on the subject and describe many more problems than do the males. The fact that females are more expressive in answering this question might indicate that they are more troubled by their sexuality. On the other hand, perhaps they are simply more open about it than the males. Or maybe they just write more and better. You be the judge as you read a random selection of student responses to the question.

Females

● After dating a guy steadily for awhile, I start to feel this pres-

*My colleague Henry Bagish has used this question exercise for years, and it is from him that I got the idea.

sure to go farther than just necking and petting. Is it just me? Do guys really expect to go all the way with a girl they are going steady with for a long time? I have broken off a lot of relationships because I felt that I must go to bed with a guy. I am amazed at how many guys expect you to just do it, like it wasn't a big deal.

● It seems when you're with a guy he wants one thing, and then they don't want to see you anymore.

● My problems in the area of sex are the moral questions: Is it right to have sex before marriage? I will, probably, but not until I am in a lasting relationship, and some love is there. I find myself sexually attracted to males before I know them emotionally. This is difficult because I'm not sure if there is any emotion in it too.

● Communication (understanding).

● Because my boyfriend is away at college, I feel that I'm not able to develop a good sexual relationship with him. We see each other about once a month, and since we both live at home, it's difficult.

● Another problem I have with sex is that I become frustrated if things don't go well, which in turn makes me think about it too much and hinders the enjoyment. I also feel that my boyfriend needs sex more than I do. I'm not saying I don't enjoy it, but I do have a certain tolerance for doing without that may not equal his.

● Too many people have sex without having any personal feelings toward the person.

● Basically the problem of the still-existing double standard. Men are allowed to enjoy casual sex in our culture without acquiring a negative label, whereas a woman enjoying sex for the sake of sex can risk her "good reputation" unless she is very discreet in her choice of casual partners. I have had, fortunately, very many nice partners (with the ability to keep their mouths shut) and am friends with all of them.

● One thing I feel is that young girls are being pressured at too early an age nowadays to engage in sexual activities that they really do not feel ready for. I think it is because through the media our culture places a lot of importance on sex and sexuality, and they are influenced to follow these standards.

● My biggest complaint about sex is that, to me, it's such a definite step toward total commitment to a person. When I do have intercourse, I want it to be with the person I marry. I want this part of me to belong to only one person. Sometimes this bothers me, because it's such a hard thing for some people (men) to accept.

● My biggest complaint about sex is having to deal with the rubber and creams. *I will not use the pill.*

● I don't orgasm during intercourse. This is more of a concern to my partner than to me. I've had many orgasms through various foreplay-type activities. If the angle is wrong during sexual intercourse it can be pretty painful.

● Not enough responsibility taken by men in the area of contraception. Not enough communication between partners. There should be more sex education for younger men and women, especially in the area of venereal disease and contraception. Young women and men should be taught about their sexuality with a positive and healthy aspect, and that they should recognize their sexual drives and not abuse them.

● Problems: I honestly don't feel my partner and I have any *major* problems. We openly communicate with each other what we like, dislike, feel, or would like to try. The only area that seems a problem occasionally is when one partner feels sexually stimulated and the other doesn't — but we are working on it. Communication seems to be the key that unlocks all the problems. Thank God he gave both of us the feelings to empathize with one another!

● My biggest problem is trying not to get pregnant. The birth control methods that are the most effective are the ones that have the worst side effects. I realize that for some people there are no unfavorable side effects, but there are also those who *do* have unfavorable side effects. I don't know if I'm willing to take those chances or not (for example the pill or the IUD).

● My complaint is that the female is the one that has to go through all the hassles of birth control, pregnancy, and abortion. The male doesn't have to worry about these things and doesn't know what it's like. I wish scientists could come up with a pill for *men* instead of women.

● Many people just want to jump right into bed and "do it." The preliminaries are totally skipped. All it seems my partners want is a piece of action. Is all the romance dead?

● I give love to the full extent and often feel I don't get as much in return. I need more affection and shows of love to make me know I'm good. The physical aspect of my sex life is great; my lover is the best I've ever had. It's the emotional aspect that is sometimes lacking. I need romance.

● My attitude was pretty sour on sex before. I feel this is because I started at a very young age (14) and I only did it because I wanted to know what the big fuss was all about. The only thing I felt after losing my virginity was mild pain — bleeding — no sensation of pleasure at all. I thought, "If that's all it is, who needs it?" I didn't have sex again for two years. All the other attempts until this relationship were just as sour for me. The love feelings make all the difference!

Males

● The hang-ups people have about sex. If both partners want to share sex, then what's wrong?

● Never get enough.

● Many of the times that I have had opportunities to have sex, anxiety seems to set in and I back out. Too much pressure on being "good."

● My biggest complaint is pressure from friends and acquaintances. Hey, we're doing it, why aren't you? I'm not out for a quickie. I don't want my first time to be a one-nighter.

● Not enough! Actually my need for *intimacy* and *love* is greater than having actual intercourse. Self-respect and integrity is too great to indulge in numerous, casual affairs just to have *sex* (without some emotional worth and support acknowledged by the other person). Don't want to be like most other guys (as they seem). I have a *great* need to "become a friend," and then I have a *love* relationship with a girl special to me. In this case I *would* engage in sex (lovemaking).

● There was one girl that I went with for about six months. At first we were kind of nervous (although it wasn't our *first* time). But after a while we had so much fun. There was no thinking, worrying, analyzing, etc. It was just the way it should be. Free. Love. We broke up. I really miss her and what we had going. I find myself really wanting that kind of relationship again, *now*. Frustrating in a way. But it'll come again.

• I really hate it when the girls expect us males to start and do everything. They want equality and all but want us to start all the seduction games.

• No complaints or problems except not having the usual socially accepted ideals about sex outside of marriage. At times I get teased by people who don't understand my religiously based ideas.

• Basically, I do not feel as though I have that natural tendency or trait to attract the opposite sex. I consider myself fairly good looking (not that I'm a Robert Redford or anything), but the vibrations just don't seem to flow between myself and the opposite sex. It could be that, often I am reluctant to open a conversation or advance into an existing one. Whatever it is I am *not* satisfied with my sex life or my love life.

• It's a problem sometimes finding a place to have sex.

• (1) Can't get enough, (2) can't last all night, (3) VD, (4) possibly getting my partner pregnant.

• I have learned that in order to have a good sexual relationship you need to have communication which I am currently working on with my girlfriend. That seems to be one of our problems, lack of communication. Second problem: My girlfriend does not have an orgasm most of the time when we are having sex. It is very hard for her to tell me what pleases her.

• Trying to keep from having an orgasm for a prolonged period of time for the satisfaction of my lover, and not accomplishing it.

• I hate the idea that some girls have that sex is the only thing a man wants out of a relationship.

• Finding someone that I feel is worth it, emotionally and physically.

• A big one used to be in the area of commitment after the fact. I didn't want commitment, but girls seemed to need it.

• Expectations of orgasm for the woman and trying to live up to this expectation.

• It probably seems weird for a male not to have sex at this age, but not really. I have a high regard toward sex. I don't want to have it because it's what everyone else is doing. It's got to be with someone I really love. As of yet I haven't felt that love. Some people may think me weird, but it's the way I feel.

• My sex life is completely open after several years of dealing with problems and fears. My only complaint is I don't receive enough sex.

• Sometimes too superficial, too short, too exploited, often too much importance placed on the sexual conquest.

• Not enough variety.

• That the man is expected to make the "first move." This is obviously indicative of my lack of ability to tell when a woman is interested in having a sexual relationship with me. This is generally the rule (there are exceptions), not only in sexual relations but in dating patterns as well.

• I don't think I have any, at least I am told that too. But many fe-

males are incompatible, they find it not as serious, they have traditional problems or fears that are imprinted in them. This creates problems, restructure of their minds — at times it is really time consuming. For some it's worth it to wait the time, but some just can't change. Unfortunately.

• It has become a need rather than a thrill.

• There's not enough of it.

• I find it difficult to just lay back and receive sexual pleasure. I often feel like I must always be participating, or giving instead of just receiving and enjoying. Otherwise I have no problems or complaints that I am aware of.

• I have a big appetite and don't always feel that I get enough.

• As far as contraception goes, I think, since girls/women have more *reasonable* alternatives to take, that they should be the ones taking action against getting pregnant, instead of the traditional pressure put on men when one does get pregnant.

• Sometimes it's made up to be such a big *deal*. It seems like there is so much pressure: "To be a virgin, or not to be. Do you go to bed with more than one person? Did you do OK? Did she have fun, should I worry about it? Yes, no, maybe? Confusion!"

What Do You Think?

What seems to be the women's greatest complaint?

What seems to be the men's biggest complaint?

Is there a difference in complaints between the sexes?

If there is, why do you think it exists?

How do these complaints square with your own complaints?	Do you think that the complaints have changed from the complaints your parents had when they were your age?	In what way might your parents' complaints be different from young people's complaints today?

CHAPTER 10

FAMILY PLANNING

CONTENTS

10

The place and function of children within the family and within the culture varies from culture to culture and over time. In countries with high infant mortality, women have to bear many children to ensure that at least a few will reach adulthood. Pregnancy for women living in such a country may be nearly a perpetual state. In other cultures a male heir may be the major aim of reproduction. Years ago when the United States was still an agricultural nation, it was important to have many children to help work the land; children were major economic contributors to the family. In today's urban America, however, the costs of rearing children far outweigh their economic contributions to the family. Thus from a strictly economic viewpoint, children have changed from being assets to being liabilities. The Department of Agriculture estimates that in rearing a child to age eighteen an average family spends $60,000 to $100,000.

Modern contraceptive techniques give couples free choice about the number and timing of children. These same techniques also have population control ramifications. Countries such as India that chronically suffer from overpopulation can initiate programs to reduce birthrates and thereby gain some control over burgeoning populations. Also, as we have already discussed, efficient birth control has brought a revolution in our standards of sexual conduct.

Family Planning in America Today

The ideal family is one that allows all children to grow up in the most healthful manner possible. Aside from environmental considerations, this definition implies that: (1) children are wanted by both partners, (2) the partners are healthy enough physically and psychologically to supply love and security to children, (3) family economics are such that children can be properly nourished and kept physically healthy, and (4) the family can supply the children with sufficient educational opportunity to learn the skills necessary to survive and enjoy success within the culture.

A Child Should Be Wanted

The most important prerequisite to an ideal family is that children should be wanted by their parents. Unwanted children are often social problems. Unwanted children are more often abused children. Unwanted children are more likely than others to grow up in psychologically unhealthy homes, are more likely than others to become delinquents, and, when they become parents, are more likely to be poor parents themselves and breed another generation of unwanted children. "This is a vicious circle if ever there was one. . . . It is ruinous to the social system" (Hardin, 1964).

When motherhood is no longer culturally compulsory, there will certainly be less of it. Women are now beginning to think and do more about development of self, of their individual resources. Far from being selfish, such development is probably our only hope. That means more alternatives for women. And more alternatives mean more selective, better, happier, motherhood — and childhood and husbandhood (or manhood) and peoplehood. It is not a question of whether or not children are sweet and marvelous to have and rear; the question is, even if that's so, whether or not one wants to pay the price for it. It doesn't make sense any more to pretend women need babies, when what they really need is themselves. (Rollin, 1970, p. 27)

Whatever the reason, parents who do not want a child should not have one.

It is difficult to say just what the effects of being unwanted are on a child, but they are often negative. At one extreme are the many battered children, having been beaten by fathers and mothers who could not cope with them. While not showing such devastating results, a Czechoslovakian study (Matĕjcĕk, Dytrych & Schüller, 1979) of 110 boys and 110 girls born in 1961 to 1963 to women denied legal abortion on initial request and again on subsequent appeal showed negative characteristics in the children when compared with a matched group of children whose mothers had not requested an abortion. In general, those children born of mothers denied an abortion: (1) had a higher incidence of illness and hospitalization, (2) had slightly poorer school marks, (3) showed somewhat poorer social integration into their peer group, (4) had come to the attention of school counseling centers more often, (5) had a less stable family life, and (6) showed generally poorer adaptation, more frustration, and increased irritability (especially the boys).

A review of the data from the continuing longitudinal study of the Czechoslovakian children makes clear that a woman's original rejecting attitude toward her pregnancy does not inevitably lead to behavioral difficulties in the child. The belief that every child unwanted during pregnancy remains unwanted is not necessarily true. It is equally untrue that the birth of an originally unwanted child causes a complete change in maternal attitude. Not every woman who becomes a mother will love her child. In sum the study confirms the risk of unfavorable developmental consequences for the unwanted child and thus the desirability of preventing unwanted pregnancies (David & Baldwin, 1979).

Are We Ready for Children?

The first question a couple should answer when thinking about raising a family is, "Do we really want children?" The answer rests on resolving questions such as the following: "How much time do we want for just each other and establishing a home? How much more education do we want or need for the jobs and income we want? Are we ready to give a baby the attention and love it needs? Can we afford to provide it with the food, clothing, and education we want for it? Can a child successfully fit into the style of life we feel is best for ourselves?

Most family planning experts advise young couples to wait awhile before having their first child. Waiting gives them time to make the important early adjustments to each other, to enjoy one another's individual

Are you ready for children?

attention, and to build some economic stability before adding the responsibility of a child.

The decision to have children is one of the most important marital decisions, and yet it is often made haphazardly. Having children generally means assuming long-term responsibilities, usually for eighteen to twenty years or more. When children are young, great amounts of time and energy and money must be devoted to their well-being. Adolescence usually brings a period of unrest, strain, and conflict. If higher education is desired, financial strains on the family will be greatly increased. There is almost no time when children do not make heavy demands on their parents, sometimes even long after they have become adults.

Having children also brings many rewards. There is joy in watching a child grow and become competent and assume a responsible role in society. There is joy in learning to know another person intimately. There is just plain fun in doing things together as a family. (For further discussion see Chapter 12, p. 411.)

Remaining Childless

Reliable contraception allows those couples who desire so to remain childless. Although the mass media has in the recent past played up reports of large numbers of American women choosing to remain childless, government population reports tend to show otherwise. What is clear is that women are having fewer children. In addition, they are postponing both marriage and childbirth. For example, the median age at first marriage remained between 20.2 and 20.4 years for women who first married between 1950 and 1969. However, delayed marriages have increased the median age to 22.5 years for women marrying in 1982 (U.S. Bureau of the Census, 1983). Women born in 1880 had the highest proportion who remained childless since records have been maintained, 22 percent. In this century the highest has been 15 percent childlessness among women born during the 1920 – 24 period (U.S. Bureau of the Census, 1980). The best current estimates of childlessness and parenthood in the United States among currently married women ages fifteen to forty-four are: 2 percent are voluntarily childless, 2 percent are involuntarily childless, 15 percent are temporarily childless (they indicate they will have children in the future), and 81 percent are parents (Bachrach & Mosher, 1982).

Remaining childless after marriage is more acceptable in the 1980s than it has been in the recent past. During the 1950s and early 1960s, to marry and postpone having children (or worse yet, deciding not to have any children) brought a great deal of societal criticism. Parents of the newly married couple dropped hints about how nice it would be to become grandparents. Friends who already had children wondered if perhaps something was wrong with one of the partner's reproductive capabilities. Others saw the couple as selfish and preoccupied with themselves. Fortunately, such pressures on the newly married couple have lessened. It is interesting to note that men today are significantly more likely to regard childlessness as disadvantageous than are women (Blake, 1979). Just why this is so is unclear.

Childlessness offers numerous advantages to the couple. The major advantage is increased freedom. The couple does not have the responsibilities of children. They are monetarily less encumbered. Their time and money are their own to devote to their careers, each other, hobbies, travels, and adult life in general. Often the childless couple is a two-career family where both partners are free to invest their energies in their work and meet during leisure times for mutual enjoyment. Although the differences are not great, research does lend support to the idea that childlessness is related to enhanced marital adjustment and satisfaction (Houseknecht, 1979).

Birth Control

Modern techniques of **birth control**, though far from perfect, have made better family planning possible. The idea of birth control has long been a part of human life. The oldest written records mentioning birth control date back to the reign of Amenemhet III in Egypt around 1850 B.C. Women were advised to put a pastelike substance in the vagina to block male sperm from reaching the egg. Pliny's *Natural History*, written in the first century A.D., lists many methods of birth control: potions to be taken orally, magical objects, suppositories and tampons of primitive sorts, and physical action such as jumping to expel the semen. Most of the time such early birth control methods were unsuccessful.

Two ancient birth control methods did evolve into the first effective contraceptive techniques. First, the ancient attempts to block the cervix so

Birth control
Deliberate limitation of the number of children born

that sperm could not penetrate to the egg evolved into the vaginal diaphragm and cervical cap when vulcanized rubber was invented. The most sophisticated historical prototype of the modern cervical cap was the use of a half lemon, squeezed of its contents and inserted over the cervix; the residual citric acid, which is mildly spermicidal (causing the death of sperm), provided additional protection (Peel and Potts, 1970). Second, early attempts to cover the penis evolved into the modern condom. Starting in the sixteenth century, the penis was covered to protect it from venereal infection. In the 1840s manufacturers began to make condoms of inexpensive rubber and later of latex.

Despite the long history of birth control, modern birth control and family planning have had a difficult and eventful emergence. Englishman Francis Place, the father of fifteen children, was the founder of the birth control movement. In the 1820s he posted handbills advising contraception to counteract the effects of the growing industrialization and urbanization that he believed were creating poverty. His handbills recommended that women place a piece of sponge tied with a string into the vagina before intercourse and remove it afterward by pulling the string. (Note that one of the newest birth control devices is a sponge treated with a spermicide.)

In the United States people such as Margaret Sanger waged a long hard battle that lasted well into this century. The Puritan morality in the United States opposed birth control. Although contraceptives were advised for the highest ethical reasons as a means of avoiding poverty, misery, and marital discord, their promoters were accused of immorality and often were brought to trial and fined. In 1873 Congress passed the Comstock Law prohibiting the distribution of contraceptive information through the mail. Numerous states also passed repressive laws. For example, the right of physicians to prescribe contraceptives was a legal issue in Connecticut until 1965 when the state law banning prescription of contraceptive devices was overthrown by the U.S. Supreme Court in *Griswold and Duxton v. State of Connecticut.*

Infanticide
The deliberate killing of infants as a population control measure or for some other purpose

Of course, family planning is possible without the aid of mechanical contraceptive devices. **Infanticide** has been practiced historically in many cultures, though it is no longer acceptable by modern ethical standards. Postponing marriage acts as an effective birth deterrent, providing illegitimacy is controlled. In China today marriage is discouraged until the woman is twenty-four and the man is twenty-seven. Rigid peer group control has reduced illegitimacy to a low level. Discouraging early marriage and controlling illegitimacy have reduced the Chinese fertility rate considerably (see Sidel, 1974).

Withdrawal and abstinence also reduce fertility rates. France, for example, has long had a relatively stable population of near 50 million. Inasmuch as contraception is frowned on by the Catholic church, population stability has been achieved mainly by withdrawal (coitus interruptus), even though it is only fifty percent effective. Other methods of sexual outlet, such as masturbation, oral sex, and homosexuality, serve a contraceptive purpose as well as a sexual purpose.

Although various chemical and mechanical means of birth control are

Chinese Infanticide Rate Up

The killing of unwanted female babies is occurring with such frequency in China that the sex ratio is being upset, an official Chinese report says.

The China Youth News said recent letters received from across the nation report abandonment of female babies on the streets and drownings of the unwanted children.

It said statistics from communes already indicate an imbalance in the sex ratio in the last two years because of infanticide.

"Is there anything on earth more heinous than this?" asked the newspaper report. . . .

China's tough birth control policy allows only one child per couple in urban areas and a maximum of two in the countryside. Couples who exceed limitations risk economic penalties and forced abortions.

For young couples clinging to "feudalistic thinking" that favors men over women, the pressure is to have a son, even if it means killing a female baby born first, the newspaper said.

The traditional Chinese belief was that a son could provide more labor as he grew up, take better care of his parents when they retired and carry on the family name.

A daughter was viewed as a financial burden who eventually would change her name once married and care for her in-laws first.

The China Youth News did not give the number of communes surveyed, but said three of every five of their babies were boys. If the trend continues, the report said, the male-female balance will be damaged artificially.

"The law governing human development and propagation requires the rough balance between men and women in society," the newspaper said.

"In two decades, if this phenomenon goes unchecked, there will appear a serious social problem in which a large group of men will be unable to find spouses."

The newspaper stressed the current marriage law demands both sons and daughters care for their parents and said in many cases the daughters provide better comfort and support.

China's census in July showed there were 106 men in the country to every 100 women ("Chinese Infanticide Rate Up," 1982).

widely used in the United States (about 68 percent of married couples), agreement on such methods is by no means universal. The Roman Catholic and Mormon churches each have official doctrines banning "artificial" methods of birth control (although Catholic women use the pill at about the same rate as other women) (U.S. Department of Health and Human Services, 1982). Some minority group members also discourage birth control in an effort to increase their proportion of the population. Still others may have some personal aversion to using birth control methods. However, the vast majority of Americans do practice birth control at times, using many of the specific methods we will describe in the next section.

Contraceptive Methods

Although family planning in itself is generally healthful, methods of implementing it may have mixed results insofar as health is concerned. Table 10-1 examines the various contraceptive devices, describes them, and in-

TABLE 10-1   Contraceptives

POPULAR NAME	DESCRIPTION	EFFECTIVENESS (PREGNANCIES PER 100 WOMEN USING METHOD FOR 1 YEAR)
The pill (oral contraceptive; consultation with physician required)	Contains synthetic hormones (estrogens and progestin) to inhibit ovulation. The body reacts as if pregnancy has occurred and so does not release an egg. No egg — no conception. The pills are usually taken for 20 or 21 consecutive days; menstruation begins shortly thereafter.	Combined pills, 2*
IUD (intrauterine device; consultation with physician required)	Metal or plastic object that comes in various shapes and is placed within the uterus and left there. Exactly how it works is not known. Hypotheses are that endocrine changes occur, that the fertilized egg cannot implant in the uterine wall because of irritation, that spontaneous abortion is caused.	3 – 6
Diaphragm and jelly (consultation with physician required)	Flexible hemispherical rubber dome inserted into the vagina to block entrance to the cervix, thus providing a barrier to sperm. Usually used with spermicidal cream or jelly.	10 – 16
Chemical methods	Numerous products to be inserted into the vagina to block sperm from the uterus and/or to act as a spermicide. Vaginal foams are creams packed under pressure (like foam shaving cream) and inserted with an applicator. Vaginal suppositories are small cone-shaped objects that melt in the vagina; vaginal tablets also melt in the vagina.	13 – 17 (More effective when used in conjunction with another method, such as the diaphragm.)
Condom	Thin, strong sheath or cover, usually of latex, worn over the penis to prevent sperm from entering the vagina.	7 – 14
Withdrawal (coitus interruptus)	Man withdraws penis from vagina before ejaculation of semen.	16 – 18
Rhythm	Abstinence from intercourse during fertile period each month.	10 – 29

Note: Individuals vary in their reaction to contraceptive devices. Advantages and disadvantages listed are general ones.

*If taken regularly pregnancy will not occur. If one or more pills are missed, there is a chance of pregnancy. Combination pills contain both estrogen and progesterone.

Source: U.S. Department of Health and Human Services, May 1980.

ADVANTAGES	DISADVANTAGES	COST
Simple to take, removed from sexual act, highly reliable, reversible. Useful side effects: relief of premenstrual tension, reduction in menstrual flow, regularization of menstruation, relief of acne.	Weight gain (5 – 50% of users), breast enlargement and sensitivity; some users have increased headaches, nausea, and spotting. Increased possibility of vein thrombosis (blood clotting) and slight increase in blood pressure. Must be taken regularly. A causal relationship to cancer can neither be established nor refuted.	$9 – $13 per month
Once inserted, user need do nothing more about birth control. High reliability, reversible, relatively inexpensive. Must be checked periodically to see if still in place.	Insertion procedure requires specialist and may be uncomfortable and painful. Uterine cramping, increased menstrual bleeding. Between 4 – 30 percent are expelled in first year after insertion. Occasional perforation of the uterine wall. Occasional pregnancy that is complicated by the presence of the IUD. Associated with pelvic inflammatory disease.	$50 – $100 for insertion
Can be left in place up to 24 hours. Reliable, harmless, reversible. Can be inserted up to 2 hours before intercourse.	Disliked by many women because it requires self-manipulation of genitals to insert and is messy because of the cream. If improperly fitted, it will fail. Must be refitted periodically, especially after pregnancy. Psychological aversion may make its use inconsistent.	$40 – $75 for fitting
Foams appear to be most effective, followed by creams, jellies, suppositories, tablets. Harmless, simple, reversible, easily available.	Minor irritations and temporary burning sensation. Messy. Must be used just before intercourse and reapplied for each act of intercourse.	$7 – $9 for month's supply
Simple to obtain and use; free of objectionable side effects. Quality control has improved with government regulation. Protection against various sexually transmitted diseases.	Must be applied just before intercourse. Can slip off, especially after ejaculation when penis returns to flaccid state. Occasional rupture. Interferes with sensation and spontaneity.	50¢ each and up
Simple, costless, requires no other devices.	Requires great control by the male. Possible semen leakage before ejaculation. Possible psychological reaction against necessary control and ejaculation outside the vagina. May severely limit sexual gratification of both partners.	
Approved by the Roman Catholic church. Costless, requires no other devices.	Woman's menstrual period must be regular. Demands accurate date keeping and strong self-control. Difficult to determine fertile period exactly.	

dicates their effectiveness as well as possible side effects. Effectiveness is stated as the number of sexually active women out of 100 who become pregnant in the course of one year when using each method. Without some method of birth control, between 80 and 90 out of 100 sexually active women would get pregnant in the course of one year.

Planning a family requires deciding how many children are desired and how far apart they should be. Questions about birth control must also be answered: "Who will be responsible for using a birth control method? What method will be used? How will the method chosen affect our sex lives? What will be the cost of the method?" These questions need to be discussed and a mutually acceptable birth control method decided on by each couple.

Contraceptive
Any agent used to prevent conception

The general requirements for an *ideal* **contraceptive** — which does not exist yet though research continues — are that it should be harmless, reliable, free of objectionable side effects, inexpensive, simple, reversible in effect, removed from the sexual act, and should give protection against venereal disease (Guttmacher, 1969). Although the following contraceptives do not fulfill all of these requirements, they do meet many of them.

Condom
A sheath, usually made of thin rubber, designed to cover the penis during intercourse; used for contraceptive purposes and to control sexually transmitted disease

The Condom   The **condom** is a sheath of very thin latex or animal gut that fits over the penis and stops sperm from entering the vagina when ejaculation occurs. The condom should be placed on the penis as soon as the penis is erect, to ensure that none of the preejaculatory fluid (which contains sperm) gets into the vagina. Either the man or the woman can put the rolled-up condom over the head of the penis and unroll it to the base of the penis, leaving a small space at the tip to collect the semen. Both partners must be careful not to puncture the condom with their fingernails or rings. After ejaculation either partner should hold the condom tightly around the base of the penis as the man withdraws so that no semen will spill from the now loose condom, enabling sperm to find their way to the uterus.

The condom has always been a popular method of contraception in the United States and though briefly eclipsed by the pill and the IUD, it is now coming back into widespread use because of the possible dangerous side effects of other birth control methods. Condoms are openly displayed and sold in forty-six states and thus are easily acquired. They have an additional advantage in that they afford protection against sexually transmitted disease. Their disadvantages are that they diminish sensation and interfere with spontaneity.

As noted in Table 10-1, the risk of pregnancy with condom use is quite low. At least some of the pregnancies occur because of careless removal of the condom. Some may occur because of a puncture in the condom. Both risks can be reduced if, in addition to the male's using a condom, the female uses a vaginal spermicide.

Diaphragm
A contraceptive device consisting of a hemispherical thin rubber that is placed within the vagina covering the cervix

The Diaphragm   The diaphragm is a dome-shaped cup of thin latex stretched over a collapsible metal ring. It is available on prescription from a doctor. Because of differences in the size of the vaginal opening, the diaphragm has to be carefully fitted to ensure that it adequately covers the mouth of the cervix and is comfortable. The fitting should be checked

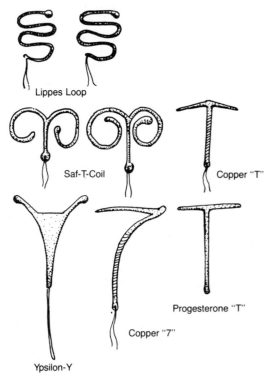

Lippes Loop

Saf-T-Coil

Copper "T"

Progesterone "T"

Copper "7"

Ypsilon-Y

(a) Some commonly used IUD's

Cream or jelly

Spring (coil-spring type)

Dome of soft rubber

(b) A diaphragm; spermicidal cream is squeezed into cup and around the rim before insertion.

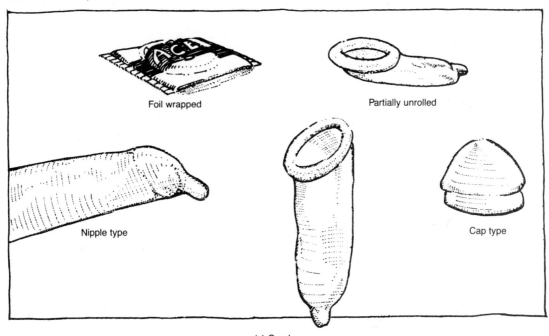

Foil wrapped

Partially unrolled

Nipple type

Cap type

(c) Condoms

Types of contraception.

FIGURE 10-1 Types of contraception.

every two years, as well as after childbirth, abortion, or a weight loss of more than ten pounds.

Once she has been fitted properly, the woman can insert the diaphragm, either dome up or down, whichever feels more comfortable. Before insertion, she should spread a spermicidal jelly or cream over the surface of the dome that will lie against the cervix. Then she squeezes the diaphragm flat with one hand, holds the labia apart with the other, and pushes the diaphragm up along the back of the vagina as far as it will go. Then she tucks the front rim behind the pubic bone. It helps if she squats, lies down, or stands with one foot raised while inserting the diaphragm. After it is inserted, she should feel the cervix through the dome to make sure that it is completely covered.

The diaphragm can be inserted just before intercourse or it can be inserted several hours ahead of time. If it is inserted more than two hours before intercourse, additional spermicide should be inserted into the vagina, or the diaphragm should be taken out and spermicide reapplied to it. Spermicide should be used again before any additional acts of intercourse. The diaphragm must be left in place for six hours after the last intercourse to give the spermicide enough time to kill all sperm.

The diaphragm is removed by hooking the front rim from behind the pubic bone with a finger and pulling it out. It should be washed with mild soap and water, rinsed, and gently patted dry. It should also be examined in front of a bright light for holes or cracks. It is usually dusted with cornstarch before being put away.

As noted in Table 10-1, the diaphragm is highly effective when used with a spermicide. In addition, it has no physical side effects. However, like the condom, it dampens spontaneity. It also loses effectiveness when fresh spermicide is not used for additional intercourse, and many persons do not like to break the "mood" of sexuality by taking time to use additional spermicide. It is disliked by some women who do not like to touch their genitals.

The main causes of pregnancy with diaphragm use are inaccurate fitting and incorrect insertion. Sometimes, too, the vaginal walls expand during sexual stimulation and dislodge the diaphragm.

A variation on the type of diaphragm just described is the Vorhauer sponge (trade name, "Today"). It is a soft, round polyurethane sponge permeated with spermicide. Although the use of sponges for contraception is centuries old, dating back more than 3000 years to the Egyptians, modern materials and spermicides make the sponge more effective and reliable. It has numerous advantages over the standard diaphragm. It does not have to be fitted by a doctor because it automatically conforms to the woman's shape and size. It remains effective for twenty-four hours regardless of how often the woman has intercourse. It is not messy or awkward. A small polyester loop attached to the sponge makes removal easy. Its cost is about $1.

The Intrauterine Device (IUD)   The intrauterine device is a stainless steel or plastic loop, ring, or spiral that is inserted into the uterus by a doctor.

A sterile device is used to insert the IUD into the cervical canal and a plunger is used to push it into the uterus. The protruding threads are trimmed so that only an inch or an inch and a half remain in the upper vagina. Usually they can't be felt during intercourse. The best time for insertion (and removal) is during menstruation because the cervical canal is most open then and there is no possibility of an unsuspected pregnancy.

Just how or why the IUD works is still unknown. As Table 10-1 notes, theories range from its producing biochemical changes, interfering with the implantation of eggs, interfering with the movement of eggs or sperm, to its causing spontaneous abortions. As also noted in the table, the IUD is quite effective, second to the pill in overall effectiveness. Its other advantages are that, once inserted, it can be used indefinitely and requires nothing further; it doesn't interrupt sexual activity; it is fully reversible; and it has a low long-term cost.

However, it has quite a few disadvantages. The most common is abnormal menstrual bleeding. Bleeding starts sooner, lasts longer, and becomes heavier after IUD insertion. Bleeding and spotting between periods are also fairly common. Women who have never been pregnant often experience pain, mostly uterine cramps and backache. The uterine cramps usually disappear in a few days, though they may be severe enough to require removal of the IUD.

Intrauterine devices are spontaneously expelled in about 10 percent of women who try them, and if the woman does not notice the expulsion, an unwanted pregnancy may result. Most expulsions occur during menstruation, so it is a good idea to check sanitary pads or tampons for the device. The threads can also be checked periodically to make sure the device is still in place.

A more serious complication that may occur is pelvic inflammatory disease. About 2 to 3 percent of women using the device may develop the disease, usually in the first two weeks after insertion. Most of these inflammations are mild and can be treated with antibiotics. In rare cases the IUD may puncture the wall of the uterus and migrate into the abdominal cavity, requiring surgery. Pelvic infection, usually caused by bacteria, also seems to be more common among IUD users ("IUD Debate," 1980; Piatrow, Rinehart & Schmidt, 1979).

Most of the risk of pregnancy occurs during the first few months of IUD use; therefore an additional method of contraception should be used for that period. The failure rate tends to decline rapidly after the first year of use. Pregnancy may occur with the device in place, but the rate of spontaneous abortion for such pregnancies is 40 percent (compared with 15 percent for all pregnancies). There is little additional risk of birth defects for babies born of such pregnancies. The device usually remains in place during the pregnancy and is expelled during the delivery. One particular brand, the Dalkon Shield, has been taken off the market because there was an unusually high pregnancy rate among its users, and when pregnancy did occur, its users developed uterine infections at a much higher rate than nonusers ("Doubts about IUDs," 1974).

The Pill   The pill, or oral contraceptive, is a combination of the hormones estrogen and progesterone, and must be prescribed by a doctor. The daily ingestion of these hormones bluffs the body into thinking it is pregnant so it stops further ovulation. Because no mature eggs are released, pregnancy cannot take place. In addition, the hormones act to thicken the mucus covering the cervix, thus inhibiting sperm entry.

Until recently, two kinds of pills were available, the combination pill and the sequential pill. However, the Federal Drug Administration requested withdrawal of the sequential pill because it appears to pose an increased risk of cancer of the uterine lining compared with combination pills ("Pills . . .," 1976). The combination pill is a monthly supply of twenty or twenty-one tablets. The woman takes pill 1 on day 5 of her menstrual cycle, counting the first day of the cycle as day 1. She takes another pill each day until all the pills have been taken. Menstruation usually begins two to four days after the past pill.

The pill should be taken at about the same time each day. If a pill is forgotten, it should be taken as soon as possible, and the next pill should be taken at the scheduled time. If two pills have been forgotten, an additional form of contraception should be used for the rest of the cycle.

If menstruation does not occur when expected, a new series of pills should be started a week after the end of the last series. If a period doesn't begin after this series, a doctor should be consulted.

During the first month of the first pill cycle, an additional method of contraception should be used to ensure complete protection.

As Table 10-1 notes, the pill, taken properly, is the most effective method of contraception today. It is relatively simple to use, does not affect spontaneity, is inexpensive, and is reversible. However, irregular use does not afford protection. The pill is also the most widely used method. As many as 8 million American women used the pill in 1975. In 1977 this had dropped to 6 million, mainly because of increased surgical sterilization ("Fewer American Women . . .," 1979; Mosher, 1982) and fear of a possible link between the pill and cancer.

The pill's side effects range from relatively minor disturbances to serious ones. Among the former are symptoms of early pregnancy (morning sickness, weight gain, and swollen breasts, for example), which may occur during the first few months of pill use. The symptoms usually disappear by the fourth month. Other problems include depression, nervousness, alteration in sex drive, dizziness, headaches, bleeding between periods, and vaginal discharge. Yeast fungus infections are also more common in women taking the pill. The more serious side effects include blood clot problems and the possibility of a link between pill use and uterine cancer. Although the incidence of fatal blood clots is low (about thirteen deaths among 1 million pill users in one year), women with any history of unusual blood clotting or who have had strokes, heart disease or defects or any form of cancer should not use the pill (for a more complete discussion of oral contraceptives, see Hatcher et al., 1980; McCary & McCary, 1982).

The arguments over the relationship of pill use and cancer continue and may only be resolved at some time in the future when large numbers of women have been using the pill over many years. If there is a relationship, it appears to be minimal at this time; the chance of death from cancer caused by pill use is far less than the chance of death in childbirth.

Another form of the pill, the minipill, is taken throughout the month, even during menstruation, thus eliminating the necessity of counting pills and stopping and restarting a series. The minipill helps do away with many of the negative side effects we have been discussing. Many of these side effects are related to the estrogen component of the regular pill. Minipills contain only progestin. They do not stop ovulation or interfere with menstruation. Instead, they make the reproductive system resistant to sperm or ovum transport. Should fertilization take place, they also impede implantation. Their effectiveness is slightly less than the regular pill (Hatcher et al., 1980; McCary & McCary, 1982).

Rhythm   The rhythm method of contraception is based on the fact that usually only one egg per month is produced. Because the egg only lives for twenty-four to forty-eight hours if it is not fertilized, and because the longest period that sperm released into the uterus are capable of living is forty-eight to seventy-two hours, conception theoretically can occur only during four days of any cycle. Predicting this four-day period is what is so difficult. If each woman had an absolutely regular monthly cycle, then rhythm would be much more reliable than it is. Unfortunately, all women do not have regular cycles. In fact, about 15 percent have such irregular periods that the rhythm method cannot be used at all.

To use the rhythm method, a woman keeps track of her menstrual periods for a full year. Counting the day menstruation begins as day 1, she notes the length of the shortest time before menstruation starts again and also the longest time. If her cycle is always the same length, she subtracts 18 from the number of days in the cycle, which gives the first unsafe day. Subtracting 11 gives the last unsafe day. For example, a woman with a regular twenty-eight-day cycle would find that the first unsafe day is the tenth day of her cycle and the last is the seventeenth day. Thus she should not engage in intercourse from the tenth to the eighteenth days. Figure 10-2 shows the twenty-eight-day cycle.

If a woman's cycle is slightly irregular, she can still determine unsafe days by using the formula. In this case she subtracts 18 from her shortest cycle to determine the first unsafe day, and 11 from her longest cycle to find the last unsafe day. Table 10-2 gives the unsafe days for periods of varying duration.

A breath and saliva test may soon allow women to more accurately predict their optimum fertile days. Scientists recently reported that they have found a correlation between levels of mouth odor and saliva chemicals and fluctuations in basic body temperature during the menstrual cycle. By using simple tests on saliva samples, a woman will be able to recognize when she is ovulating and thus know exactly when to avoid intercourse if she does not want to become pregnant (Kosteli & Preti, 1982).

Vaginal Spermicides (Chemical Methods)   Spermicides (sperm-killing agents) come as foams, creams, jellies, foaming tablets, and supposito-

FIGURE 10-2   **The 28-day cycle.**

1 Menstruation begins	2	3	4	5	6	7
8	9	10	11	12	13	14
		Intercourse on these days leaves live sperm to fertilize egg.		Ripe egg may also be released on these days.		
15	16	17	18	19	20	21
Ripe egg may be released on any of these days.		Egg may still be present.				
22	23	24	25	26	27	28
1 Menstruation begins again.						

ries. Foams are the most effective because they form the most dense and evenly distributed barrier to the cervical opening. Tablets and suppositories, which melt in the vagina, are the least effective.

Foams are packed under pressure (like shaving cream) and have an applicator attached to the nozzle. Creams and jellies come in tubes with an applicator. A short time before intercourse, the woman (or the man)

TABLE 10-2   How to Figure the Safe and Unsafe Days

LENGTH OF SHORTEST PERIOD	FIRST UNSAFE DAY AFTER START OF ANY PERIOD	LENGTH OF LONGEST PERIOD	LAST UNSAFE DAY AFTER START OF ANY PERIOD
21 days	3rd day	21 days	10th day
22 days	4th day	22 days	11th day
23 days	5th day	23 days	12th day
24 days	6th day	24 days	13th day
25 days	7th day	25 days	14th day
26 days	8th day	26 days	15th day
27 days	9th day	27 days	16th day
28 days	10th day	28 days	17th day
29 days	11th day	29 days	18th day
30 days	12th day	30 days	19th day
31 days	13th day	31 days	20th day
32 days	14th day	32 days	21st day
33 days	15th day	33 days	22nd day
34 days	16th day	34 days	23rd day
35 days	17th day	35 days	24th day
36 days	18th day	36 days	25th day
37 days	19th day	37 days	26th day
38 days	20th day	38 days	27th day

places the applicator into the vagina (like a sanitary tampon) and pushes the plunger. The effectiveness of vaginal spermicides only lasts for about half an hour, so another application is necessary before each act of intercourse.

Vaginal spermicides are generally harmless, relatively easy to use, readily available in most drugstores, and do not require a prescription. However, as Table 10-1 shows, they are not very effective, though their effectiveness can be increased by using them with a diaphragm. Other disadvantages are that they are messy, may interrupt the sexual mood, must be reapplied for each act of intercourse, and sometimes cause a burning sensation or irritation. If the latter persists, a doctor should be consulted.

Withdrawal (Coitus Interruptus)   Withdrawal is simply what the name implies, in that just before ejaculation the male withdraws his penis from the vagina. Withdrawal is probably the oldest known form of contraception. It is free, requires no preparation, and is always available. However, as Table 10-1 points out, it has a high failure rate. Other disadvantages include the necessity of tremendous control by the male, plus the fear that withdrawal may not be in time, which can destroy sexual pleasure for both partners. The woman also may be denied satisfaction if the male must withdraw before she reaches orgasm. Also, there may be some semen leakage before withdrawal, which can cause pregnancy.

Douche   A douche is a stream of water applied to a body part to cleanse or treat it. As a contraceptive method water is washed through the vagina by the use of a douche syringe. Used as contraception, douching is probably useless and may in fact serve to wash sperm into the uterus, thus increasing the chances of pregnancy. A number of commercial douches are available, but their use should be limited. Using a substance other than water can cause a bacterial imbalance in the vagina, leading to yeast and other infections.

Sterilization

Sterilization is the most effective and permanent means of birth control. Despite the fact that in many cases it is irreversible, more and more Americans are choosing sterilization as a means of contraception. The Association for Voluntary Sterilization estimates that 10 to 12 million people in the United States have been voluntarily sterilized and about 1 million more are being sterilized each year. The Association further estimates that about 90 million people in the world are now sterilized. In 1965 18 percent of American couples intending no more births were protected by sterilization. In 1976 43 percent of such couples were so protected (Mosher, 1982).

Sterilization
Any procedure (usually surgical) by which an individual is made incapable of reproduction

Vasectomy   **Vasectomy** is the surgical sterilization of the male. It is done in a doctor's office under local anesthetic and takes about thirty minutes. Small incisions are made in the scrotum, and the vasa deferentia, which

Vasectomy
A sterilization procedure for males involving the surgical cutting of the vas deferens

FIGURE 10-3   Male reproductive system, showing effects of vasectomy. Note that in actual sterilization, surgery is performed on both sides of body.

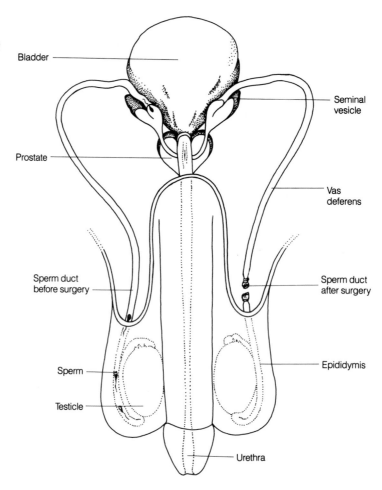

Bladder

Seminal vesicle

Prostate

Vas deferens

Sperm duct before surgery

Sperm duct after surgery

Epididymis

Sperm

Testicle

Urethra

carry the sperm from the testes, are cut and tied. The male may feel a dull ache in the surgical area and in the lower abdomen. Aspirin and an ice bag help relieve these feelings. Usually the man can return to work in two days.

He can have sex again as soon as he doesn't feel any discomfort, usually in about a week. An additional method of contraception must be used for several weeks after the operation because live sperm are still in parts of the reproductive system.

Although the male will continue to produce sperm after the operation, the sperm will now be absorbed into his body. His seminal fluid will be reduced only slightly. Hormone output will be normal, and he will not experience any physical changes in his sex drive. Some males do experience negative psychological side effects. For example, some equate the vasectomy with castration and feel less sexual (Kogan, 1973). Such feelings may interfere with sexual ability. Postvasectomy psychological problems occur in perhaps 3 to 15 percent of men (Lear, 1969; Wolfers, 1970). On the other hand, many men report they feel freer and more satisfied with sex after a vasectomy (Kogan, 1973).

In about 1 percent of vasectomies, a severed vas deferens rejoins itself so that sperm can again travel through the duct and be ejaculated (Insel & Roth, 1976). Because of this possibility, a yearly visit to a doctor so that semen can be examined is a good safety precaution.

A promising new nonsurgical alternative to vasectomy is a process called *vas sclerosing*. In this procedure the wall of the vas deferens is injected with small quantities of material that produces scarring, thus blocking the passageway. The technique greatly reduces the risks inherent in any surgical process, as well as overcoming the psychological objections that some men have to cutting in the genital area (McCary & McCary, 1982).

One of the major drawbacks of vasectomy or other sterilization is that in many cases it is irreversible. Thus the husband and wife should be sure to discuss the matter thoroughly before deciding on this method of contraception.

If reversal is desired, the tubes can be reconnected in about 40 percent of vasectomies (Guttmacher, 1973b). Doctors at the University of California Medical Center in San Francisco have recently reported much higher success with reversal operations using improved techniques. In selected cases up to 50 percent of men undergoing microsurgical vasovasotomy (reconnecting the vasa, or tubes) subsequently ejaculate sperm and three-quarters are able to impregnate their wives (Brody, 1979; Willscher, 1980).

Tubal Ligation   **Tubal ligation** is the surgical sterilization of the female. Until recently it has been a much more difficult operation than vasectomy because the Fallopian tubes lie more deeply within the body than the

Tubal ligation
A sterilization procedure for females in which the Fallopian tubes are cut or tied

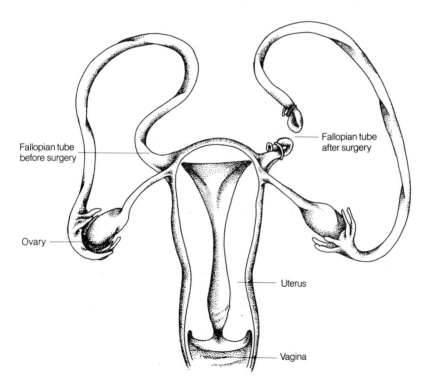

FIGURE 10-4 Female reproductive system, showing effects of tubal ligation. Note that in actual sterilization, surgery is performed on both sides of body.

Fallopian tube before surgery

Fallopian tube after surgery

Ovary

Uterus

Vagina

vasa deferentia. The operation, done in a hospital rather than a doctor's office, requires a general anesthetic and a hospital stay of about three to four days. One or two small incisions are made in the abdominal wall, the Fallopian tubes are located and each is severed, a small section of each is removed, and then the two ends of each tube are tied. Incisions can also be made through the vaginal wall, which will not leave a scar and requires shorter hospitalization (however, recent pregnancy or obesity make this approach more difficult or impossible). Both procedures take about thirty minutes.

Besides being more difficult than vasectomies, tubal ligation is also riskier. About 7 percent of the women experience problems after the operation, mainly from infections (Insel & Roth, 1976). Some women also experience abdominal discomfort and menstrual irregularity. Most women, however, have no aftereffects and continue to have a regular menstrual cycle.

Laparoscopy
A sterilization procedure for females involving the use of a telescope instrument (laparoscope) to locate the Fallopian tubes, which are then cauterized

A more recent procedure is called **laparoscopy**. Again, it is a hospital procedure that requires a general anesthetic. However, the operation takes only fifteen minutes and does not require overnight hospitalization. A tiny incision is made in the abdomen and a small light-containing tube (laparoscope) is inserted so the surgeon can see the Fallopian tubes. The surgeon then inserts another small tube carrying high-intensity radio waves that burn out sections of the Fallopian tubes. The incision is so small that only a stitch or two is needed; hence the procedure is often referred to as Band-Aid surgery. Most women leave the hospital two to four hours after surgery.

Both forms of tubal ligation have a failure rate of about 3 in every 1000 cases (Insel & Roth, 1976). Attempts to reverse the sterilization have been about 70 percent successful (Hatcher et al., 1980).

Women who have been sterilized tend to report an increase in sexual enjoyment because they are now free of the fear of pregnancy. A few women report reduced sexual enjoyment because of the loss of fertility that they may equate with femininity (Easley, 1972).

Hysterectomy
Surgical removal of a female's uterus; results in sterilization

Although a **hysterectomy**, which is the surgical removal of the uterus, does end fertility, it is an extreme procedure and should be used only when a woman has uterine cancer or other problems of the uterus and not just for birth control reasons.

Tomorrow's Contraceptives

As probably became obvious in the discussion of the different contraceptive methods, the ideal method is still to be discovered. Researchers hope to find a safe, simple, and reversible contraceptive. They also want to find one that does not need to be taken every day and that doesn't require a doctor's prescription. The following lists will give you a better idea of some of the recent research in contraception.

Possible Future Female Methods

1. *One-time plant*: An elongated plastic capsule filled with synthetic progestin would be inserted into an arm or leg where it would remain in the fatty layer just under the skin. The progestin would be released at a regulated rate, fooling the woman's body into thinking she is already pregnant so that no new eggs will be released. If she wishes to become pregnant, the capsule could be easy to remove. However, there are presently serious disadvantages to the use of progestin. These include uterine bleeding and delays of a year or longer in the return of ovulatory cycles (Insel & Roth, 1976).

2. *Continuous low-dosage progestin*: Again, the constant presence of progestin would fool the body into thinking it is already pregnant, and no new eggs will be released. Possible sources of the progestin would be: implanted capsule as just described, removable vaginal insert, pill, long-term injection, IUD, or perhaps through skin contact with a progestin-impregnated ring or cosmetic. However, the same problems as previously noted are still likely to occur.

3. *Immunization against eggs or sperm*: Theoretically a woman could be sensitized against her own egg cells (or against sperm) so that she would produce antibodies that would inactivate the eggs or sperm as if they were a foreign disease. So far, though, human testing has not been undertaken because researchers do not know how long the immunity would last or how to control it, and they are worried that the allergic reaction could upset other disease-fighting systems (Insel & Roth, 1976).

4. *Once-a-month pill*: A combination estrogen/progestin pill that has to be taken only once a month would eliminate the accidents that now occur among pill takers who forget to take a pill or two during the monthly cycle.

5. *Postcoital estrogen pill (morning-after pill)*: A form of morning-after pill is already in use. It contains large doses of artificial estrogen and is taken for five days after unprotected intercourse. However, the large doses have caused nausea, vomiting, and other undesirable changes in metabolism. Also, there is some evidence that the synthetic estrogen used in the pill may cause cancer. Continued research may discover a less dangerous form of estrogen.

6. *Long-term injection*: Long-term (every ninety days) injections of progestin have been found to be almost completely effective in preventing pregnancy. However, progestin has the disadvantages already described. Researchers are trying to discover a safe combination of estrogen and progestin that will also be effective, perhaps for periods of as long as six months.

7. *Once-a-month injection*: A lower dosage of estrogen and progestin might be safe and only have to be injected every month. It might be possible to package the hypodermic needles already loaded, much as insulin is now packaged for diabetics.

8. *Reversible tubal occlusion*: Instead of cutting and tying the Fallopian tubes, attempts have been made to plug them by injecting liquid

silicone. In animal experiments, however, such plugs have been easily dislodged (Insel & Roth, 1976). Other substances may not dislodge so easily, however. Because the plug could be removed, the woman could later decide to become pregnant.

9. *Improved ovulation-detecting devices*: If ovulation can be pinpointed accurately, then rhythm can become a reliable method of birth control. A small, battery-run device called an Ovulometer has come on the market. The device registers changes in body temperature and voltage that occur during ovulation. By touching her body with electrodes, a woman can tell if ovulation has taken place ("Device May Pinpoint . . .," 1976).

10. *Contraceptive nasal spray*: Hormones contained in the spray go directly to the area of the brain that regulates ovulation and act to stop ovulation. So far, five inhalations a month have kept rhesus monkeys from becoming pregnant.

11. *Breath/saliva test*: Both analysis of a woman's breath and her saliva can reveal time of ovulation (Kostelic & Preti, 1982).

12. *Tissue-adhesive injection*: A tissue-adhesive substance — somewhat like a quick-acting glue — could be injected into the Fallopian tubes to block them.

Possible Future Male Methods

1. *One-time implant*: This would be an as-yet-undiscovered chemical that would prevent sperm from being produced. The chemical would be placed into a plastic capsule that would be implanted in an arm or leg and would slowly release the chemical into the body. If the male decided to have children, the capsule could be easily removed. Although some chemicals have been found to suppress sperm production in animal experiments, side effects in humans have been severe.

2. *Immunization against sperm*: The male would be sensitized to his own sperm so that he would produce antibodies that would attack them as if they were a foreign disease. As noted for female immunization, however, human testing has not been undertaken because researchers do not know how long immunity would last, how to control it, or what effect it would have on other immune reactions.

3. *Once-a-month or daily pill*: Some combinations of hormones or chemicals will prevent maturation of sperm when taken orally. So far a safe combination has not yet been discovered.

4. *Long-term injection*: A sperm suppressor would be injected every three to six months. Again, no safe suppressor has been discovered to date.

5. *Reversible vasectomy*: Instead of cutting and tying the vasa deferentia, they would be plugged with some substance. Experimenters have tried blocking the flow of sperm with removable clips and plugs, but so far these have damaged the vasa (tubes) and have interfered with full restoration of fertility. In some cases the sperm have made a new path around the plug, so that birth control was not achieved. Another technique has involved implanting small mechanical valves. In the closed position the valves prevent sperm from reaching the penis. If fertility

is desired, another operation is performed to change the valves to the open position. A possible problem with all vasectomy reversals is that some vasectomized men develop antibodies to their sperm, which may persist after the reversal and counteract fertilization (Insel & Roth, 1976).

Abortion

In the United States the 1960s witnessed mounting interest in **abortion** as a method of birth control. Although each state had restrictive legislation against abortion, many illegal abortions nevertheless were performed, which sometimes killed and often harmed the expectant mother because of nonsterile or otherwise inadequate procedures.

Other countries successfully use abortion to control population, and to help women avoid unwanted pregnancies. Japan, for example, was plagued by overpopulation for years, until in 1948 it enacted the Eugenic Protection Act that, in essence, allowed any woman to obtain a legal abortion. Consequently, abortion became a major method of birth control. It has been estimated that for every birth prevented by contraceptive devices in Japan, two births are prevented by abortion (Hart, 1967). In the first eight years after the act was passed, the birth rate fell from 34.3 to 17 per 1000, and it has remained at this lower level (Hart, 1967). In addition to the liberalized abortion policy, Japan has also mounted a massive educational campaign to make the populace aware of the need to reduce family size.

After a number of states liberalized their abortion laws, the U.S. Supreme Court on January 22, 1973, in *Roe* v. *Wade* and *Doe* v. *Bolton*, made abortion on request a possibility for the entire country. Essentially, the Court ruled that the fetus is not a person as defined by the Constitution and therefore does not possess constitutional rights. "We do not resolve the difficult question of when life begins. When those trained in the respective disciplines of medicine, philosophy, and theology are unable to arrive at any consensus, the judiciary . . . is not in a position to speculate as to the answer."

More specifically, the Court said that in the first trimester (twelve weeks) of pregnancy no state may interfere in any way with a woman's decision to have an abortion as long as it is performed by a physician. In the second trimester (thirteen to twenty-five weeks) a state may lay down medical guidelines to protect the woman's health. Most states that do permit abortion permit it by choice only through the twentieth week. After that there must be clear medical evidence that the mother's health is endangered or that the baby will be irreparably defective. Only in the last trimester may states ban abortion, and even then an abortion may be performed if continued pregnancy endangers the life or health of the mother.

The proponents of abortion on request believed they had won a final victory, yet this conclusion has proved premature. Abortion has become

Abortion
Induced or spontaneous termination of a pregnancy before the fetus is capable of surviving on its own

one of the most emotional issues in politics and morality that the nation now faces. On one side are the crusaders "for life," otherwise known as "right-to-lifers," who argue on religious and moral grounds that abortion is murder and thus should be outlawed. On the other hand are the crusaders "for choice" who contend that abortion is a right that any woman has to the control of her own body and thereby of her life.

One reason why the conflict continues is that the American public is fairly evenly divided on the question. A 1977 national poll by Yankelovich indicated that 48 percent approved abortion while 44 percent did not ("The New Morality," 1977). ABC-Harris polls indicate that 60 percent of Americans approve of the Supreme Court decision legalizing abortion. However, the National Opinion Research Center shows that the circumstances of the pregnancy greatly influence one's attitude about abortion. More than 80 percent of those sampled favor abortions in cases of rape and incest or when the pregnancy threatens the mother's life. But only 40 percent favor abortions for less compelling reasons ("The Battle over

Abortion," 1981). A Gallup Poll in June 1983 found 50 percent of Americans favoring the 1973 Court ruling while 43 percent were opposed ("Public Remains Closely Divided . . .," 1983).

The rapidly increasing number of abortions after the 1973 Court decision also fueled the conflict. Although it is difficult to guess the number of illegal abortions performed before 1973, the number of legal abortions has at least doubled to around 1.5 million last year. One-third of all pregnancies in the nation were ended by abortion in 1980. Presently America's abortion rate of 30.2 per 1000 women age 15 to 44 ranks fourth in the world. Only Russia, 180 per 1000 (1970); Rumania, 88 per 1000 (1979); and Cuba, 52.1 per 1000 (1978) rank higher ("The Battle over Abortion," 1981).

The prolife movement's ultimate goal is to add a "Human Life Amendment" to the Constitution that would reverse the Supreme Court's decision. Most recently Senator Jessie Helms and Representative Henry Hyde introduced a congressional bill amendment (Human Life Statute) to do what the Supreme Court said it could not do; namely, define "life." The bill simply says, "For the purpose of enforcing the obligation of the States under the 14th amendment not to deprive persons of life without due process of law, human life shall be deemed to exist from conception" ("The Battle over Abortion," 1981, p. 22). The effect of the bill would be to allow states to pass laws defining abortion as murder. The bill was defeated by filibuster in August of 1982 but will certainly resurface in subsequent congressional sessions.

Congress has passed bills cutting off most federal funds for abortions, and such restrictions have been upheld by the Supreme Court. Federally financed abortions have dropped from a high of 300,000 to essentially zero. Battles are also going on in many states to limit abortions within the context of the 1973 decision and to cut off state funds for abortion purposes. Such steps seem to support the idea that there is a growing trend toward a more conservative view of abortion (Ebaugh & Haney, 1980).

Another part of the debate concerns the right of the father to participate in the abortion decision. Current laws exclude him from the decision, allowing that it is the mother-to-be's body and therefore under her control. A husband in Maryland, though, recently went to court to block his wife from having an abortion that she sought against his wishes. After several lower court decisions and the ensuing abortion, the Maryland Court of Appeals has agreed to hear the case (*The Washington Post*, October 11, 1982). The case is expected to be an important debate over the role that a father can and should play in the abortion decision. In an interesting twist the lawyers may argue that Maryland's child abuse law can be applied to a fetus being aborted.

Where the continuing debate will go is anybody's guess, but one thing is sure: The question of abortion will remain a controversial one for some time.

The debate over induced abortion tends to cloud the physical act of abortion itself. First of all, spontaneous abortion occurs in 10 percent or more of all diagnosed first pregnancies by the end of the tenth week. If

Abortion on Demand Is Everyone's Right

The proabortionists believe a woman's body belongs to her, so she should have the right to determine whether to pursue pregnancy to completion. They believe that laws governing abortion are an unconstitutional invasion of privacy.

They also argue that overpopulation is a major threat to civilization and humanity. Thus to fail to use every acceptable method to reduce population growth is immoral and shortsighted and will ultimately lead to world disaster.

They further argue that it is more immoral to have unwanted children than it is to seek abortion. The unwanted child suffers and becomes the source of many of society's problems. Problems are cre-ated both for and by un-wanted children.

Garret Hardin, professor of biology at the University of California at Santa Barbara and an outspoken proponent of free abortion, has pointed out that:

Critics of abortion generally see it as an exclusively negative thing, a means of nonfulfillment only. What they fail to realize is that abortion, like other means of birth control, can lead to fulfillment in the life of a woman. A woman who aborts this year because she is in poor health, neurotic, economically harassed, unmarried, on the verge of divorce, or immature may well decide to have some other child five years from now — a wanted child. If her need for abortion is frustrated, she may never know the joy of a wanted child. (Hardin, 1964)

The American Friends Service Committee makes the following statement:

We believe that every child should be wanted by and born into a family that is able to feed, clothe, educate, and, above all, love him; that the family is the basic unit of our society and that the married life of the parents should encompass sexual activity whether or not for purposes of procreation; that an appropriate contra-ception, which spaces children and eliminates the fear of unwanted pregnancies, strengthens family ties and establishes a sense of responsible parenthood; that in view of the problem of overpopulation, every couple has a responsibility to society as well as to their own family not to overburden the world with more lives than it can sustain.

We believe that responsible parenthood demands consideration not only of the number of children individual parents want but also of the effect of that number on society as a whole. (American Friends Service Committee, 1970)

Abortion is not as dangerous to the mother as is childbirth. The maternal death rate in New York is 29 per 100,000 births, whereas the death rate from legal abortions is only 3.5 per 100,000 abortions. Deaths from pregnancy and birth in England are about 20 per 100,000 deliveries. In Japan the death rate is about 8 per 100,000 from abortions.

Women have always sought abortions and always will. By making abortion illegal, society fosters a black market in abortions and increases the woman's chances of injury and death.

undiagnosed first pregnancies are taken into account, the figure is probably closer to 25 percent. Interestingly, a high percentage of spontaneously aborted embryos are abnormal. There is also evidence that emotional shock plays a role in spontaneous abortions as well as abnormalities of the reproductive process. There is also some evidence that excessive manipulation of the cervix during induced abortion is related to later spontaneous abortions.

INSET 10-3

Abortion Is Murder

Antiabortion groups believe that abortion is murder and that inasmuch as murder is not condoned in our society, we should not condone abortion.

An important factor is just when the fetus can be termed "life." Quickening, the first awareness of fetal movement by the mother, has been used in the past to decide when abortion should no longer be undertaken. If one accepts this, then before quickening occurs, abortion would be acceptable because the fetus is not yet considered alive. However, the embryo is actually alive from the minute that conception occurs. Most medical authorities indicate that abortions are relatively safe physically up until the twelfth week of pregnancy; the Supreme Court's decision also used the twelfth week as a point of demarcation. But by the twelfth week the embryo is clearly recognizable as a living human being. It is three inches long, weighs one ounce, has nails beginning to appear on toes and fingers, has a beating heart, has eyes, and its gender can be determined (see Chapter 11).

Social utility is not a viable criterion in matters that involve life and death and essential liberties. Although a huge proportion of unhappy lives and a whole network of social ills can be traced to the unwanted child, no one can predict with certainty how a child will turn out. No one can say that an unwanted child won't later be wanted and loved. How many people, even unhappy ones or ones in trouble from time to time, seriously wish they had never been born? The social utility argument reduces human life to the value of a machine — how well does it work (Lessard, 1972)?

Antiabortion groups believe that easy availability of abortions will lead to promiscuity. The Christian heritage in the United States not only bans abortion but has a great deal to say about sexual mores. By making abortion freely available, promiscuous behavior is encouraged because the consequences of the act are removed. The possibility of pregnancy means that one needs to contemplate sexual intercourse in a responsible manner inasmuch as it is possible that the act will involve a child for whom responsibility must be taken. Free abortion leads to irresponsible sexual activity because one need not be responsible for a child even if pregnancy does occur.

Abortion can lead to severe psychological trauma. The feelings of guilt, the frustrated desire to have had the child, and the feelings of responsibility for the death of the child — all these and many more psychological reactions can and do occur and are as much a threat to the mother's health as the continued pregnancy.

Evidence is also beginning to demonstrate physical problems associated with abortion. In Athens, Greece, during 1966 to 1968, 29 percent of 8312 previously pregnant women admitted for delivery acknowledged one or more previous induced abortions. In the group admitting previous abortion, the average number of abortions per woman was two. Of this group the percentage of stillbirths (born dead) and premature births was double that of the control group (the remaining 71 percent). Another study from Greece indicates that about one-third of all women subjected to induced abortion were permanently infertile (Pantelakis et al., 1973). Thus far, however, such findings have not been reported in the United States. Approximately 1.5 million abortions were performed in the United States in 1980, and very few negative aftereffects have been reported to date. But this is an area in which more research should be undertaken.

Dilatation and curettage (D and C)
An abortion-inducing procedure that involves dilating the cervix and scraping out the contents of the uterus with a metal instrument (curette)

Vacuum aspiration
An abortion-inducing procedure in which the contents of the uterus are removed by suction

Saline abortion
An abortion-inducing procedure in which a salt solution is injected into the amniotic sac to kill the fetus, which is then expelled via uterine contractions

What Do You Think?

It is one thing to debate intellectually the right of abortion. How do you personally feel at the gut level? If female could you have an abortion easily? If male could you counsel your partner to have an abortion?

Do you know anyone who has had an abortion? How does that person feel about it?

Will making abortion on request common affect our society, especially the family? How?

Should a wife have the right of abortion without consulting her husband?

Abortion is a fairly simple procedure, though it can be more unpleasant than abortion advocates claim. The major method of legal abortion used to be **dilatation and curettage (D and C)**. In this method the cervix is dilated by the insertion of increasingly larger metal dilators until its opening is about as big around as a fountain pen. At this point a curette (a surgical instrument) is used to scrape out the contents of the uterus. An ovum forceps (a long, grasping surgical instrument) may also be used. The woman is instructed not to have sexual intercourse for several weeks, and she may take from ten days to two weeks to fully recover from the procedure.

Vacuum aspiration is now the preferred method of abortion because it takes less time, involves less loss of blood, and has a shorter recovery period than a D and C. In this method the cervix is dilated by a speculum (an expanding instrument), and a vacuum-suction tube is inserted into the uterus. A curette and electric pump are attached to the tubing, and suction is applied to the uterine cavity. The uterus is emptied in about twenty to thirty seconds. The doctor will sometimes also scrape the uterine lining with a metal curette. The procedure takes five to ten minutes. The woman may return home after a rest of a few hours in a recovery area. She is usually instructed not to have sexual intercourse and not to use tampons for a week or two after the abortion (see Figure 10-5).

After the fourteenth week, a different method, called the **saline abortion**, must be used because the fetus is now too large to be removed by suction, and a D and C performed now may cause complications. By this time the safest abortion is to stimulate the uterus to push the fetus out; in other words, to cause a miscarriage. When a fetus dies, the uterus naturally begins to contract and expel the dead fetus. In order to kill the fetus, a local anesthetic is given the mother and a long needle is inserted through her abdominal wall into the uterine cavity. The amniotic sac (see Chapter 11) is punctured and some of its fluid is removed. An equal amount of 20-percent salt solution is then injected into the sac. The injection must be done slowly and carefully to avoid introducing the salt solution into the woman's circulatory system. She must be awake so that she can report any pain or other symptoms. Once the fetus is dead, the uterus begins to contract in about six to forty-eight hours. Eventually the amniotic sac breaks and the fetus is expelled. In up to 50 percent of the cases, the placenta does not come out automatically and a gentle pull on the umbilical cord is necessary to remove it. In about 10 percent of cases, a D and C must be performed to remove any remaining pieces of the placenta. The saline procedure should be carried out in a hospital, and the woman should remain there until the abortion process is complete. The recovery period is longer than for other forms of abortion, and complications are more frequent. Therefore, although it should be a considered decision, the decision to have an abortion should be reached as quickly as possible.

A new chemical abortion procedure that may make the preceding methods obsolete is being used in Sweden. A synthetic prostaglandin is the chemical used in a suppository that is placed into the vagina. The chem-

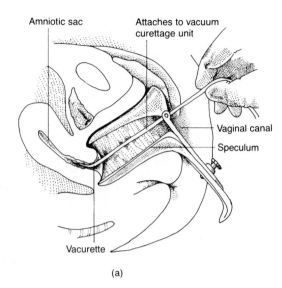

Amniotic sac

Attaches to vacuum
curettage unit

Vaginal canal

Speculum

Vacurette

(a)

FIGURE 10-5 Vacuum aspi-
ration, an abortion method,
takes only five to ten minutes; it can be performed up
to the twelfth week of pregnancy. (a) The vacuum aspiration process. (b) An
operating unit for vacuum
aspiration.

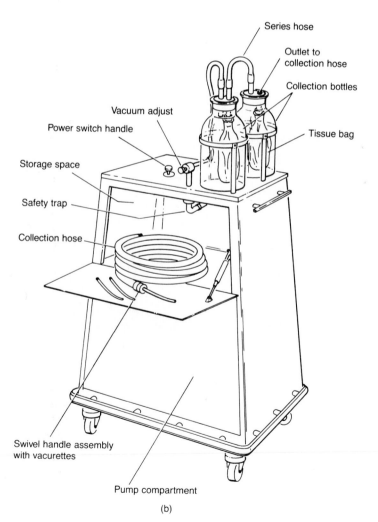

Series hose

Outlet to
collection hose

Collection bottles

Tissue bag

Vacuum adjust

Power switch handle

Storage space

Safety trap

Collection hose

Swivel handle assembly
with vacurettes

Pump compartment

(b)

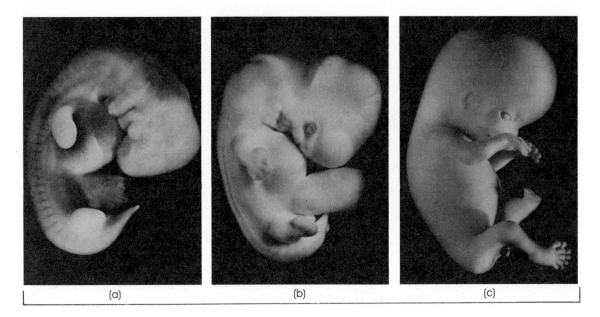

(a)	(b)	(c)

FIGURE 10-6 Examples of fetal development, at: (a) 4.7 weeks; (b) about 6 weeks; (c) about 9.5 weeks.

ical causes muscle contractions within one to five hours after a "missed period." The uterine contractions lead to abortion.

The decision to have an abortion may not be easy and should not be made lightly. Whenever possible, it is wise for the woman considering an abortion to discuss the decision with the prospective father, parents, physicians, counselors, and/or knowledgeable and concerned friends.

Professional abortion counseling can be obtained at local Planned Parenthood chapters and in most states with the Clergy Consultation Service on Abortion. Both agencies are listed in local telephone directories. Abortion is not recommended as a means of birth control and should be used only as a last resort. A woman who is well informed about sex and contraceptive devices usually will not be faced with having to make an abortion decision.

Infertility

Although many people think only of contraception when hearing the phrase "family planning," problems of infertility are also important aspects of family planning. The U.S. Public Health Service estimates that 25 percent of married couples cannot have any children or as many as they want because they are infertile or subfertile (Mosher, 1980). Infertile for a male means that he is not producing viable sperm and for a female that she is either not producing viable eggs or has some other condition that makes it impossible to successfully maintain a pregnancy. Alan Guttmacher (1969) estimates that about one-third of all married couples do conceive the first month they try and that about 60 percent conceive within the first three months.

Essentially, there are three phases in the treatment of infertility: education, detection, and therapy. Young couples should persist in trying to conceive for at least one year. If they are not successful, they should seek help from a physician. Often if the couple learns more about how conception occurs and the possible reasons for failure to conceive, they will feel less tense and anxious and thus increase the chances of conception.

Prerequisites of Fertility

There are at least nine biological prerequisites for achieving conception (Guttmacher, 1969). Four pertain to the male:

1. Healthy live sperm must be produced in sufficient numbers. Ordinarily a single normal testicle is all that is required, though usually both assume an equal role in producing sperm. To function properly, a testicle must be in the scrotal sac. In the male embryo each testicle is formed in the abdomen and descends into the scrotum during the seventh month of intrauterine life. Infrequently, one or both testicles fail to descend. If they have not descended by five or six years of age, the boy is usually treated with a hormone to stimulate testicular growth. This makes the testicle heavier, which in some instances brings about descent. If hormone treatment fails, surgery is performed, usually when the boy is about eight.
2. Seminal fluid (the whitish, sticky material ejaculated at orgasm) must be secreted in the proper amount and composition to transport the sperm.
3. An unobstructed seminal "thruway" must exist from the testicle to the end of the penis.
4. The ability to achieve and sustain an erection and to ejaculate within the vagina must be present.

The other five biological requirements for reproduction pertain to the female:

1. At least one ovary must function normally enough to produce a mature egg.
2. A normal-sized uterus must be properly prepared by chemicals (hormones) fed into the bloodstream by the ovary to become the "home" of the developing fetus.
3. An unobstructed genital tract, from the vagina up through the Fallopian tubes to the ovary, must exist to enable the egg to pass down and the sperm to pass up.
4. A uterine environment must adequately nourish and protect the unborn child until it is able to live in the outside world.
5. Miscarriage must be avoided, and the infant must be delivered safely.

It is not uncommon for couples seeking fertility help to conceive before treatment begins and for adoptive parents to conceive shortly after they decide on adoption. Clearly, emotional and psychological factors are tremendously important to the process of conception. Psychological factors account for approximately one-quarter of subfertility cases (Guttmacher, 1969).

Causes of Infertility

Infertility
Inability to produce children

Males account for about 33 percent of **infertility** problems (Kogan, 1973). For example, impotence, the inability to gain or maintain an erection, precludes sexual intercourse and thus conception. Often impotence is psychological in nature, though it can be caused by alcohol, general fatigue, or a debilitating disease. Low sperm count is another possible reason for infertility. An ejaculation that contains fewer than 100 to 150 million sperm limits the possibility of conception. Infectious diseases such as mumps can damage sperm production. Sterility can also occur if the testes have not descended into the scrotum, because the higher temperature of the body reduces production of healthy sperm. Also, undescended testes are often abnormal in some way, which is why they didn't descend and which also affects production of healthy sperm. A prolonged and untreated sexually transmitted disease can cause permanent sterility.

If a couple consults a physician — as they should about their apparent infertility — it is easier to test the man first because fertility tests for the male are quite simple compared with those for the female. Basically, the tests involve collecting a sample of ejaculate and analyzing it for the number and activity level of sperm as well as for abnormal sperm.

Unfortunately, some men tie fertility and manhood closely together. They consider an examination for possible fertility problems an attack on their manhood and may be unwilling to cooperate. Both partners, however, must share in the search for a solution to infertility.

In a woman both vaginal infections and ovarian abnormalities can cause infertility. A woman must ovulate if she is to conceive. Almost all mature women menstruate, but in about 15 percent of a normal woman's cycles an egg is not released (Young, 1961). In a few women, even though they menstruate, ovulation seldom occurs, making them almost infertile.

A woman may have a problem conceiving if the tract from the vagina through the uterus and Fallopian tubes to the ovary is blocked. If the egg and sperm cannot meet, conception cannot occur. It is possible to determine if the Fallopian tubes are open by filling them with an opaque fluid and X-raying them.

Another possible problem can arise from the chemical environment of the woman's reproductive organs. Too acid an environment quickly kills sperm. Also, the chemical environment may make implantation of the fertilized egg into the uterine wall difficult or impossible. In the latter case the woman may conceive and then spontaneously abort (miscarry) the embryo.

Methods of Treatment

Artificial insemination
Induction of semen into the
vagina or uterus by artificial
means

When the cause of infertility rests with the husband **artificial insemination** is sometimes used to induce conception. This consists of taking sperm from the husband, if possible, or from an anonymous donor, if not, and injecting the sperm into the wife's vagina during her fertile period. Even if the husband's sperm count is low, his ejaculate can be collected and the concentration of sperm increased to bring it within the normal range necessary for fertilization. It is interesting to note that, for reasons unknown, artificial insemination results in a marked preponderance of males being conceived. Sperm banks have been established where sperm is frozen and stored for later use; it seems to remain viable for long periods. Sperm that has been frozen for up to three years has been used for successful human fertilization. Japanese researchers recently reported successfully inseminating a cow with frozen bull sperm eighteen years old ("18-Year-Old-Sperm . . .," 1982).

There are numerous controversies surrounding artificial insemination, especially when the sperm comes from someone other than the husband. Questions of legitimacy and parental responsibility have arisen. Biologically, though, it is a perfectly acceptable manner of overcoming a man's infertility.

When the cause of infertility is the woman's failure to ovulate, *fertility drugs* have been used to stimulate the ovary to ovulate. However, the drugs often overstimulate ovulation and cause multiple births. Overstimulation may be reduced by the discovery of the chemical structure and the subsequent synthesis of the luteinizing-hormone-releasing factor of the hypothalamus, which controls the release of the egg from the ovary (see Kogan, 1973, p. 216).

When it is impossible to correct a woman's infertility, another woman may be hired to bear a child for the couple. Such a woman is termed a **surrogate mother**. She is usually paid between $15,000 and $20,000 compensation. Normally she is fertilized via artificial insemination using the husband's sperm. Once the baby is born, it is legally adopted by the infertile couple. There are a number of organizations throughout the United States that bring infertile couples together with potential surrogate mothers. The organizations act to screen and match the parties as well as to handle the complex legal problems of adoption and payment. Because it is illegal in every state to buy or sell a child, payment must be made to compensate the surrogate mother, not for the child, but for such things as taking the risk of pregnancy and childbirth and for the loss of work because of pregnancy. The contract in each situation is unique and may specify such things as no drinking or smoking during pregnancy. Generally all contracts stipulate the following:

On the Part of the Surrogate

1. The surrogate agrees to terminate maternal rights and allow adoption by the couple.
2. The surrogate must not seek the identity of the adoptive parents unless this is mutually agreeable.
3. Should the surrogate breach the contract and decide to keep the child, she must reimburse the adoptive couple for all payment, expenses, and legal fees.
4. The surrogate agrees to abort the fetus if an abnormality is discovered during pregnancy.

Surrogate mother
A woman who becomes pregnant and gives birth to a child for another woman who is incapable of giving birth

On the Part of the Adoptive Couple

1. The couple are required to take out an insurance policy on the surrogate mother and on the biological father (husband), with the child named as beneficiary.
2. The couple agrees to compensate the surrogate at a reduced rate if she should miscarry.
3. The couple agree not to seek the surrogate's identity unless this is mutually agreeable.
4. The couple agrees to accept all babies should multiple births occur.
5. The couple agrees to accept the child should it not be born normal.
6. The couple must show proof of marriage and wife's infertility.

The potential legal problems are complex. Even though a contract is signed, what actually happens when a surrogate mother decides to keep the child, as has recently occurred in California ("Surrogate Mother . . .," 1981)? Or what happens if the parents-to-be decide they don't want the child, as happened when a surrogate mother gave birth to a mentally defective child? To solve such questions, surrogate mother bills are being introduced in a number of state legislatures. To date, however, none has become law (MacDonald, 1982).

The use of a surrogate mother is a method of last resort. However, the procedure informally is as old as history. In days past it was not unusual for a woman to have a child and give it to another couple, infertile or not. This often happened with an illegitimate birth that was hidden from public view. For example, a daughter has an illegitimate child that is then passed off as her parent's child — her new brother or sister.

Sex therapy is being used to help couples with nonphysical problems that affect their sex life and their ability to conceive. Obviously, intercourse is necessary for conception to occur. But if a couple is having problems with premature ejaculation, impotence, or lack of sexual enjoyment, they may avoid having intercourse..

Sex therapists usually use techniques devised by Masters and Johnson and others to guide the couple to a more satisfactory sexual relationship. (See Masters and Johnson, 1970, and Leiblum and Pervin, 1980, for a fuller discussion of these techniques.) In general the couple is seen together. To reduce their performance expectations and fear of sexual failure, they are prohibited from having intercourse for a period of time. The therapists give them a series of exercises, which they perform at home and then discuss with the therapists. The discussions also deal with sexuality in general and with the couple's specific problems. In the exercises they learn to explore each other in sensual, rather than specifically sexual, ways. They learn not only to give and receive pleasure but what gives the partner pleasure. As they become more knowledgeable and relaxed about sexuality, they are led, through further structured exercises, to increased comfortableness with intercourse.

Sex therapy has suffered from a sudden popularity that is leading to ethical problems. For example, some therapists are having intercourse with their clients in the name of therapy. Others are using sexual surrogates (substitute partners) to help their clients overcome sexual problems

Sex therapy
Therapy of any kind designed to help persons overcome sexual problems.

A Sperm Bank for Nobel Prize Winners

Robert K. Graham, 74, a wealthy California businessman, calls it a "moderately expensive hobby." Fairly interesting too. Graham collects sperm from Nobel-prizewinning scientists — five so far — and offers it to young women who have high IQs. According to the Los Angeles *Times*, which broke the story last week, Graham has shipped frozen sperm to several unidentified women, and three of them — all on the East Coast — are pregnant. Says he: "This is just the beginning."

Graham several years ago began writing to Nobel laureates, asking for sperm donations. Five said yes, and Graham made collections in the San Francisco and San Diego areas for his subterranean sperm bank — the Hermann J. Muller Repository for Germinal Choice — built on his ten-acre estate in Escondido, Calif.

A member of Mensa, a group of 33,000 people who have IQ scores in the top 2%,

Graham first revealed his project last summer in an interview published in the Mensa *Bulletin*. He was seeking to place his Nobel sperm with bright women who were healthy, under 35 and preferably married to a sterile man. Two dozen women applied, and those who were chosen received physical descriptions of the anonymous Nobel donors — plus Graham's own assessments. "A very famous scientist," he wrote on the description of one of the five available mail-order fathers (to whom he assigned numbers 10 through 14), "a mover and a shaker, almost a superman." Replied one of the women: "I'm very excited about this. . . . I'm tentatively going to select No. 13 because he's the youngest of the donors and has the highest IQ." As a condition for receiving Nobel sperm, the applicants agreed to send Graham regular reports on the pregnancy and, after birth, on the child's health and IQ.

So far only one of the sperm donors has revealed himself to the press: Laureate William Shockley (Physics, 1956), whose genetics opinions are regularly attacked as racist. Says he: "I don't regard myself as a perfect human being or the ideal candidate, but I am endorsing Graham's concept of increasing the people at the top of the population." Steve Broder, who directs a Southern California sperm bank called Cryobank and is a former adviser to Graham,

says he saw "three or maybe four" Nobelists donating to the depository. "I see nothing extraordinary in all this," he adds. "It's quite normal for potential mothers to come in and ask for sperm with a high IQ."

Many Nobel winners are taking a dim view of Graham's project. Stanford's Burton Richter (Physics, 1976) reports that his students are beginning to ask whether he supplements his salary with stud fees. "It's somewhat weird," he says. "What they are trying to do is create an intellectual superman, and selecting winning Nobel Prize scientists is not the way to do it." Charles H. Townes (Physics, 1964) of the University of California at Berkeley dismissed the project as "snobbish," and the Salk Institute's Dr. Renato Dulbecco (Medicine, 1975) disqualified himself. Said he: "I was vasectomized long ago."

Graham's project may not even make good sense on its own terms. Nobel sperm may be bright, but the donors are usually far along in years. Shockley, for example, is 70, and recent studies suggest that the chance of having a mongoloid child increases not only with the mother's age, but with the father's too, especially if he is 55 or older ("Superkids? . . .," 1980). The first children conceived using Graham's sperm bank were born in 1982. Thus it is still too early to know if especially bright children have resulted.

(see Kaplan, 1974, 1979). Although such practices might be justified on theoretical grounds, ethical and moral questions are involved. Masters and Johnson have commented that they think only half a dozen of the many sex therapy clinics are legitimate, using well-trained staff and proven procedures (Masters et al., 1980). To help rectify abuses, they organized a series of multidisciplinary meetings to identify and discuss the primary ethical issues pertinent to sex therapy and research. From the proceedings, published in 1977 as *Ethical Issues in Sex Therapy and Research*, came a set of "Ethics Guidelines for Sex Therapists, Sex Counselors, and Sex Researchers" (Masters et al., 1980). Recently several state legislatures have considered licensure regulations for sex counselors. In California sex counselors are required to have master's degrees and supervised training.

Despite these ethical and moral problems, sex therapy is a breakthrough in the treatment not only of infertility problems resulting from impotence and frigidity, but all sexual problems.

In the past, for example, an impotent male had little chance to overcome his problem because he failed every time he attempted intercourse. Getting and maintaining an erection is a complex interaction between a man's chemistry and his psychological state of being. No matter how physically healthy a man is, if he is psychologically "in the wrong place," he will not become erect. Failure causes worry and fear that he will fail again. Such worry and fear work against achieving an erection. A vicious circle is thus created wherein the more he tries to become erect, the less chance he has of being successful. As success declines, the man often loses his sexual desires. Sex therapy can break this pattern of fear, failure, and more fear by setting up situations in which the man can be successful, thus lessening his fears and increasing his future chances of success and thereby rekindling his sexual desires ("In Search of Sexual Desire," 1983).

Much the same is true for the nonorgasmic woman. In her case failure to achieve orgasm does not hinder her ability to become pregnant, but it may lead to lack of interest in and/or fear of sex and thus lower her frequency of intercourse, which will reduce her chances of becoming pregnant.

For the woman who cannot become pregnant, it is now possible for a human egg to be fertilized outside her body and then implanted within her uterus. Louise Brown, born in July 1978 in England, was the first such "test-tube baby." The first baby born in the United States as a result of this technique — in vitro fertilization — was born in December 1981. Since that time over 100 children have been born in both England and the United States (including a sister to Louise Brown) using implantation of the already fertilized egg. This technique is discussed in detail in the Scenes from Marriage at the end of this chapter.

Summary

Family planning is an important part of marriage. The decision to have children should be just that, a decision, made rationally by the couple. Yet many pregnancies are unplanned, the resultant children unwanted, and the consequences to the marriage often devastating. The couple should ask themselves if they can help all their children grow into adulthood in the most healthful possible manner. They should not only want the children they have, they themselves should be healthy and economically equipped to feed, clothe, and educate their children.

Birth control has a long but somewhat unsuccessful history. Technological advances have led to more reliable contraceptive methods, though the perfect contraceptive has yet to be invented. The pill, IUD, condom, and diaphragm are all popular and effective methods of birth control. Less effective methods, ranging from the most to the least effective, are vaginal spermicides, rhythm, withdrawal, and douches.

Abortion laws have been revised, making abortion on demand a reality. The revisions have generated a great amount of controversy, and it is quite possible that more restrictive laws may again be introduced. Be that as it may, abortion is a presently available method of birth control, though it is one that requires much thought before undertaking.

Sterilization as a form of birth control has also become increasingly popular during the 1970s. Although usually irreversible, advances in technique are opening up the possibility of reversible sterilization procedures.

Family planning also helps couples to have children when fertility problems exist. Increased understanding of reproduction has helped solve some of the problems that cause infertility. Probably 15 to 20 percent of American couples have some infertility problem. Beginning with the 1970s, in addition to correction of physical problems such as low sperm count, failure to ovulate, blocked Fallopian tubes, and so on, efforts have been made to help couples who have sexual problems that stem from their upbringing or from some psychological problem. The couple who cannot successfully have sexual relations will not be able to have children, unless by artificial insemination. Sex therapy, although controversial, is proving helpful to such couples.

In general the couple who plan their family realistically and who control reproduction increase their chances of having a happy sex life and a fulfilling marriage. To leave reproduction to chance too often leads to problems and unhappiness.

The First Test-Tube Baby*

She was born at 11:47 P.M. with a lusty yell, and it was a cry heard round the brave new world. Louise Brown, blond, blue-eyed and just under 6 pounds, was the first child in history to be conceived outside her mother's body. Her birth last week in a dowdy British mill town was in its way a first coming — variously hailed as a medical miracle, an ethical mistake and the beginning of a new age of genetic manipulation. But perhaps more important, as Dr. Patrick Steptoe proudly reported, "The anxieties are over. We've got a nice, healthy, normal baby."

Steptoe and his medical collaborator, physiologist Robert Edwards, had achieved their breakthrough with just a minor variation on the technique they had been developing for twelve years, and the crucial element was apparently timing: the fertilized egg, reimplanted in Louise's mother's womb slightly ahead of earlier schedules, survived for almost the normal nine months to a Caesarean birth. But that was enough to promise fresh hope for millions of childless women, hundreds of whom immediately besieged Steptoe with requests to help them conceive children.

There were widespread misgivings over the next possible steps: surrogate mothers who might rent out their wombs, or tailor-made babies whose genes might be altered in the test tube. "I fear that we may be slipping away from doctoring the patient to doctoring the race," said Father William Smith of New York's Catholic archdiocese.

Few doubted, however, that Louise's birth represented a ma-

*Source: "All about That Baby." *Newsweek*, August 7, 1978, pp. 66 – 72.

jor advance in medical research, with the promise of additional breakthroughs in embryo research, the understanding of birth defects and their prevention, treatment of infertility and — paradoxically—the development of new contraceptives.

From Rabbits to People

Steptoe and Edwards had few precedents to guide them in their development of the test-tube-baby technique. The first report of an in-vitro fertilization came in 1936 from Dr. Gregory Pincus of Harvard University; he united a rabbit egg and sperm. Eight years later Dr. John Rock, also of Harvard and, like Pincus, a major figure in the development of the contraceptive pill, claimed to have fertilized a human egg outside the body and watched it divide into three cells. In 1961, Dr. Daniele Petrucci of the University of Bologna shocked the world with his claim — backed up by movie films — that he had fertilized twenty separate human eggs in vitro. There were even rumors that Petrucci had reimplanted some of them. But so bizarre did the idea of test-tube babies appear to most scientists and laymen that the research was either ignored or greeted with outraged disbelief.

The scientific community was hardly more receptive when Steptoe and Edwards started their historic collaboration, and in the early years the pair proceeded cautiously. Edwards took the lead in perfecting means of fertilizing human eggs and improving the chemical solutions necessary to keep them alive and healthy outside the body. Steptoe, in the meantime, worked on the mechanical technique of removing ova from would-be mothers and returning the dividing, fertilized eggs to the womb. His major contribution — and perhaps the most important event in the chain that led to last week's birth — was to pioneer use of the laparoscope. A foot-long tube equipped with its own eyepiece and internal lighting, it can be inserted through a small slit in a woman's abdomen and used to select a ripening egg that a suction needle can then remove from her ovaries.

Success came slowly. In 1970, the pair reported in the journal *Nature* that fertilized human ova had grown to the eight- and sixteen-cell stage, and a few years later they started serious efforts to reimplant such test-tube ova, which are no larger than the period at the end of this sentence.

Conceived in a Cottage

In 1975, Steptoe and Edwards produced their first definite pregnancy, but the embryo reimplanted itself in the patient's diseased Fallopian tube rather than in the uterus, and it miscarried after ten weeks. The researchers nonetheless remained confident they were on the right track, and continued to make small alterations in the procedure.

Lesley Brown was an excellent subject. "She was in an age group that was highly suitable," explained Steptoe in a news conference last week, "not too old and highly fertile." Shortly after her visits started two years ago, Steptoe removed Mrs. Brown's diseased Fallopian tubes. That operation destroyed any faint chance that she might be able to conceive normally, but it gave the obstetrician an unobstructed internal view of his patient's ovaries when he took the first step in creating Louise. At that point, Mrs. Brown was given hormone treatment to stimulate egg production before she made the crucial visit to Oldham, for the actual conception of her child. It took place in Dr. Kershaw's Cottage Hospital, a little-used brick building originally donated to the town by an Edwardian eccentric.

Operating in the institution's tiny, white-tiled surgical theater, Steptoe extracted an egg from his patient. Edwards placed the egg in a small jar, where it was mixed with John Brown's sperm and sustained by special fluids. Once fertilized, the egg was transferred to another nutrient solution. The researchers monitored the egg as it divided into two, four and, finally — after more than 50 hours — eight cells.

Now came the crucial point of difference. In previous experiments, Steptoe and Edwards had tried to simulate the natural development of the egg, which is normally fertilized within the Fallopian tube and has multiplied into 64 or more cells by the time it reaches the womb. But new research with rhesus monkeys — though it involved only implantation of conventionally fertilized eggs — suggested that an embryo as small as two cells might survive in the uterus. So the researchers decided to reimplant Lesley Brown's ovum at the eight-cell stage, reducing the complexities of sustaining its development outside her body. She had already received a second batch of hormones to prepare her womb chemically to receive the embryo.

The Brown fetus survived and thrived. Lesley Brown checked into the Oldham Hospital's maternity ward, where she assumed the name Rita Ferguson, to allow doctors to monitor her around the clock. Other mothers told reporters that she was quiet and subdued, spending her time knitting, watching television and doing crossword puzzles. She chewed gum, developed a craving for mints, and couldn't resist disobeying Steptoe's orders by taking an occasional puff from a cigarette — and blowing the smoke out a window to conceal it.

Premature but Beautiful

Steptoe had expected the birth to occur sometime this week, but when Lesley developed a mild case of high blood pressure, threatening complications in the delivery, he decided to deliver the baby immediately by Caesarean section. In a ten-minute conventional operation, he left the mother with a horizontal "bikini cut" and brought forth Louise, several days premature and weighing just 5 pounds 12 ounces. The baby's looks benefited from the operation: because they don't have to struggle through the birth canal, babies delivered by Caesarean section tend to look prettier than children who undergo normal births. "She has a marvelous complexion, not red and wrinkly at all," boasted her father to the Daily Mail. Edwards, a godfather of sorts, added a unique view: "The last time I saw the baby it was just eight cells in a test tube. It was beautiful then, and it's still beautiful now."

CHAPTER 11

PREGNANCY AND BIRTH

11

In their sun-paled plaid maternity bathing suits,
the pregnant young women . . . going along the water's edge,
heads higher than the line of the sea . . . bellies swollen stately.

Faces and limbs freckled in every hollow,
burnished in the ball of the shoulder, the tip of the nose. . . .
The light in their eyes stealing sparkle
from the far hard edge of the sea.

John Updike, When Everyone Was Pregnant

Despite all the talk about effective birth control methods, zero population growth, and sex as a means of communication rather than reproduction, most Americans do have children, and most of the children are desired, cared for, loved, and a source of happiness (along with some heartache) to their parents. Indeed the birth rate has risen from a low of 14.5 babies per 1000 population in 1975 to approximately 17 per 1000 in 1982. As we saw in the last chapter, relatively few American women remain childless throughout their lives. In this century the highest proportion of women having no children was 15 percent among women born between 1920 and 1924. These women reached the peak of their childbearing years during the Great Depression and World War II when many factors combined to increase the possibility of childlessness (U.S. Bureau of the Census, December 1980).

Conception

For a mother listening to her six-foot son discuss the finer points of football, for a father escorting his lovely twenty-two-year-old daughter down the aisle, it may be difficult to remember the beginnings: the love-making; the missed menstrual period that led mother to think, "Maybe I'm pregnant"; the thrill of feeling a tiny, yet-unseen foot kick; the scary feelings when labor started; the movielike rush to the hospital; holding the red, wrinkled seven-pound newborn son or daughter and counting all of the fingers and toes to make sure they are all there; the long discussion over the name; the wet spot on dad's suit after the hugging the baby goodbye before going to work; the first tooth, the first sickness, the first bicycle, the first day of school, the first date, high school graduation, marriage — then the new cycle when suddenly a little one hugs them and says "Hi grandad, hi grandma."

All of us, with our billions and billions of cells and complex organs, have grown from the union of two microscopic cells — the ovum, or egg cell, (about 0.004 inch in diameter) and the sperm (about 0.00125 inch in diameter) — and we weighed only 0.005 of a milligram or one-twenty-millionth of an ounce at conception!

The possibility of **conception** begins with ovulation, the release of one mature egg (containing twenty-three chromosomes, fat droplets, protein substances, and nutrient fluid, all surrounded by a tough gelatinous sub-

Conception
Fertilization of the egg by the sperm to start a new human life

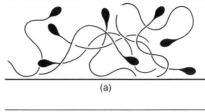

(a)

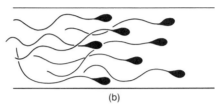

(b)

FIGURE 11-1 Sperm wander aimlessly when no egg is present (a), but all move toward the egg when it is present (b).

stance or membrane) to find its way to the Fallopian tube and begin a three-day journey to the uterus. Fertilization must occur within twenty-four hours of ovulation or the egg will die and be expelled.

A sperm cell, the other necessary ingredient for conception, like the egg contains twenty-three chromosomes within its nucleus (the head), but it also contains a tail that gives it mobility. There are about 200 to 400 million sperm in an average ejaculation. They are so minute that enough of them to repopulate the earth could be stored in a space the size of an aspirin tablet.

When sperm are deposited in the vagina after an ejaculation, they are affected by the presence of an egg. If an egg isn't present, sperm will swim erratically in all directions. But if an egg is present, they will swim directly toward it (see Figure 11-1). By using their tails, they can swim at a rate of three to four centimeters an hour (Katchadourian and Lunde, 1972). Their great numbers are necessary because the job of reaching the egg is so arduous that only a few thousand will reach the Fallopian tube that contains the egg. Many will die in the acidic environment of the vagina. Many will also go up the wrong tube or get lost along the way. Those that do reach the egg will have to overcome another obstacle — the tough outer membrane of the egg. Each sperm that reaches the egg will release a bit of enzyme to help dissolve the egg's membrane. Finally, one sperm will manage to enter the egg and will fertilize it. Once this occurs, the egg will become impervious to all remaining sperm and they will die.

Sperm remain viable within the female reproductive tract for about forty-eight hours; the egg remains viable for about twenty-four hours.* Thus conception can only occur during approximately three days of each twenty-eight-day cycle. For example, if intercourse occurs more than forty-eight hours before ovulation, the sperm will die, and if it occurs more than twenty-four hours after ovulation, the egg will have died. The rhythm method of birth control is based on this fact (see Chapter 10).

Within thirty-six hours after fertilization, the egg divides in half, and then divides again. The dividing continues as the egg moves down the

*The average length of life of the sperm and egg are approximate. It may be that their lives will be shorter or longer depending in part on the chemistry of the reproductive system of the woman at the time.

Uterus
The hollow, pear-shaped organ in females within which the fetus develops; the womb

Fallopian tube, with the cells getting smaller with each division (see Figure 11-2). By the time the floating mass of cells reaches the **uterus** (in about three to four days), it will contain about thirty-six cells. This cluster, called a *blastocyst*, then becomes hollow at the center. The outermost shell of cells, called the *trophoblast*, multiplies faster, attaches the blastocyst to the uterine walls, and eventually becomes the placenta, umbilical cord, and amniotic sac. The inner cells separate into three layers. The innermost layer (the *endoderm*) will become the inner body parts; the middle layer (the *mesoderm*) will become muscle, bone, blood, kidneys, and sex glands; and the outer layer (the *ectoderm*) will eventually become skin, hair, and nervous tissue (see The Course of Prenatal Development, pp. 382–385).

On the sixth or seventh day after fertilization, the blastocyst will be implanted in the uterine wall and the cells will begin to draw nourishment from the uterine lining.

Boy or Girl?

Sex determination takes place at conception. The female egg always carries an X chromosome. The sperm, however, may be either of two types, one carrying an X chromosome and the other a Y chromosome. If the egg has been fertilized by an X sperm, then the child will be female (XX). If,

FIGURE 11-2 Cell division after conception.

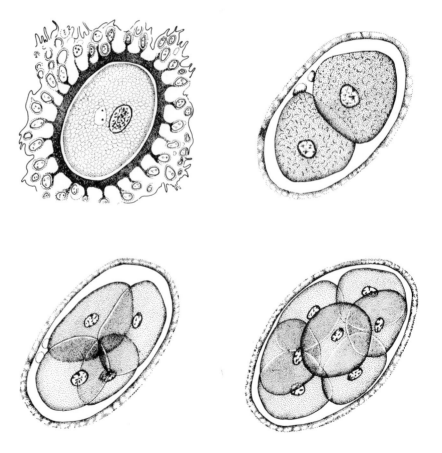

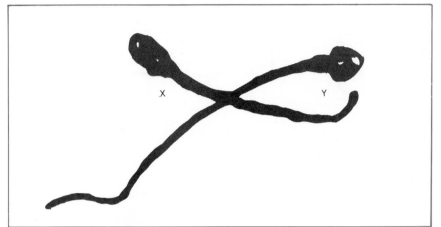

FIGURE 11-3 Microscopic view showing the difference between X-bearing sperm (with larger, oval-shaped head) and Y-bearing sperm (with smaller head, longer tail).

on the other hand, the egg has been fertilized by a Y sperm, then the child will be male (XY) (see Chapter 6 for a complete discussion). It is believed that Y sperm (androsperm) have a small spearlike body with a long tail and that X sperm (gynosperm) have a larger oval-shaped head and a shorter tail. These differences have not yet been proved conclusively (McCary & McCary, 1982).

Many more males are conceived than females. In fact, approximately 140 males are conceived for every 100 females. However, only 106 males are born for every 100 females. We have no conclusive evidence why this is so. Some suggest that the Y sperm move more quickly than the X sperm, thus more reach the egg earlier. Actually, the male is the weaker sex insofar as survival is concerned. In all age groups up to age eighty, males perish at a greater rate than females (see Table 11-1).

Multiple Births

The human female normally conceives only one child at a time, so multiple births have always been unusual. Twins occur about once in every 90 births, triplets once in 9000 births, and quadruplets once in 500,000 births (Katchadourian and Lunde, 1972). Mortality rates are significantly higher for multiple births. The infants are often born somewhat prematurely and are usually smaller than normal in size. The Dionne quintuplets, five girls, weighed a total of thirteen pounds, six ounces at birth (generally, a baby weighs about seven and a half pounds).

Most twins are *fraternal*, which means they developed from two separate eggs that were fertilized simultaneously. Such twins are no more similar in physical characteristics than are any other siblings (brothers or sisters). About a third of twins are *identical*, which means they developed from the subdivision of a single fertilized egg, and usually shared a common placenta. Unlike fraternal twins, their genetic makeup is identical, so they have very similar physical characteristics and are always the same sex.

TABLE 11-1 Male Deaths per 100 Female Deaths, U.S., 1970

AGE	MALE DEATHS
Under 1	139.6
1 – 4	122.1
5 – 14	174.0
15 – 24	277.5
25 – 34	204.8
35 – 44	161.5
45 – 54	171.6
55 – 59	193.1
60 – 64	189.4
65 – 69	159.2
70 – 74	133.8
75 – 79	108.6
80 – 84	89.5
85 and over	64.5
Total, all ages	128.2

Source: U.S. National Center for Health Statistics, 1970.

Note: These data do not cover deaths of U.S. civilians or members of the armed forces that occurred outside the U.S.

Recently, the so-called fertility drugs have contributed to the multiple birth phenomenon (see Inset 9-2, p. 309). In such cases women who fail to ovulate properly have been given a gonadotropin to stimulate proper ovulation. In numerous instances the use of these hormones has caused multiple births. In one case an Australian woman gave birth to nine infants, none of whom survived. With increased understanding of the reproductive functions, the risk of multiple births may be reduced.

Pregnancy

How does a woman know if she is pregnant? Because the union of the egg and the sperm does not produce any overt feelings or sensations, the question "Am I pregnant?" isn't easy to answer in the early stages of pregnancy. Although pregnancy is the most common reason for menstruation to stop suddenly in a healthy female, it is certainly not the only reason. For example a woman may miss a period because of stress, illness, or emotional upset. In addition about 20 percent of pregnant women have a slight flow or spotting, usually during implantation of the fertilized egg into the uterine wall (Katchadourian and Lunde, 1972; Schulz, 1979). In about two to three weeks after the missed period, some symptoms of pregnancy generally occur. The most common is feeling nauseous

INSET 11-1

How to Help Direct Sex Determination

Landrum B. Shettles (1972) aroused much interest and considerable debate with his article *"Predetermining Children's Sex."* After numerous correlational studies, he offers the following suggestions to help determine the sex of one's offspring.

A male offspring is more apt to be conceived if:

1. An alkaline douche is used immediately before intercourse. (Add two tablespoons of baking soda to one quart of water.)
2. Intercourse takes place as soon after ovulation as possible.
3. Penile penetration is as deep as possible.
4. The woman achieves orgasm.

A female is more apt to be conceived if these recommendations are reversed.

Shettles' reasoning is as follows: To favor the birth of a boy, it is logical to create an environment in which the smaller, more numerous Y sperms can outdistance the larger X sperms. The age (viability) of the sperm and egg are also important factors in determining whether conception occurs. The availability of a fresh sperm and fresh egg favors a male birth. A fresh egg and an older sperm favors a female birth; this combination is more likely if sexual intercourse occurs two or three days before ovulation. Deep penile penetration during emission results in the deposition of the sperm near the favorable alkaline secretions within the cervix. This, combined with the alkaline orgasmal secretions and an alkaline douche, makes it possible for the Y sperm to outdistance the X sperm in the journey to the awaiting egg. By using such concepts, couples reportedly can select the genetic sex of their children with an 80 to 85 percent chance of success. However, some scientists have dismissed Shettles' suggestions as invalid (Whelan, 1974).

in the morning (morning sickness), though vomiting usually doesn't occur. The nausea usually disappears by the twelfth week of pregnancy. Breasts and nipples usually begin to undergo changes in shape and coloration. The breasts will become fuller, the areolae (the pigmented areas around the nipples) will begin to darken, and veins will become more prominent. Sometimes the breasts will tingle, throb, or hurt because of the swelling. There may be an increased need to urinate, partly because the growing uterus is pressing against the bladder and partly because of the hormonal changes that are taking place. Somewhere around the twelfth week of pregnancy, the uterus will be higher in the abdomen and will no longer press against the bladder, so urination will return to normal. The hormonal changes may also cause feelings of fatigue and sleepiness. Some women find that they need to sleep more often and for longer periods and are always tired during the first few months of pregnancy. Sometimes there are increased vaginal secretions. However, some women do not experience any of these symptoms, some experience only a few; few experience them severely.

Pregnancy may also have some cosmetic effects. Skin blemishes will often abate, and the complexion will look healthy and glowing. In the

FIGURE 11-4 Negative and positive pregnancy test reactions. In a negative test agglutination (clumping) will be visible within two minutes. In a positive test no agglutination will occur at two minutes.

NEGATIVE

POSITIVE

latter stages of pregnancy stretch marks may appear on the abdomen, although most of them will disappear after birth.

Pregnancy Tests

Usually a physician can tell if a woman is pregnant by a simple pelvic examination. It is possible to feel the uterine enlargement and softening of the cervix by manual examination after six to eight weeks of pregnancy. However, because most women want to know as soon as possible if they are pregnant, chemical tests are used to discover pregnancy earlier.

Usually a test of agglutination, the clumping together of human chorionic gonadotropin (HCG), is used. This process takes only a few minutes and can be used beginning one to fourteen days after menstruation should have started. The test involves taking a morning urine specimen, placing a drop of it on a slide, then adding the proper chemicals. In a negative reaction agglutination will be visible in two minutes. If the woman is pregnant, no agglutination will occur at two minutes (see Figure 11-4).

Several tests examine the woman's blood serum, also seeking changed levels of HCG. One is called radioimmunoassay (RIA). This test takes about seventy-two hours of incubation to get a reading. A newer test is the Biocept-G technique that has reduced the necessary incubation period to thirty minutes and gives accurate results within a few days after a missed menstrual period. In this case a blood sample is mixed with radioactive iodine with which the HCG will react if present.

The tests are considered 95 to 98 percent accurate but can give inaccurate results if they are performed too early (before enough hormone shows up in the urine) or if there are errors in handling or storing or labeling the urine (Boston Women's Health Book Collective, 1976; Nass, Libby & Fisher, 1981). Sometimes it may take several tests to determine if a woman is pregnant because she may produce very low levels of hormone and there may not be enough in her urine to give a positive result even though she is pregnant. It is rare for a pregnancy test to give a positive result when the woman is not pregnant.

False pregnancy (pseudocyesis) is also possible, in which the early physical signs may be present though the woman is not really pregnant. Pregnancy tests, which are inexpensive, will clarify the situation and usually end the symptoms (unless there is a physical problem causing the symptoms).

Because the menstrual cycle is easily affected by one's emotions, uneasiness about engaging in sexual activity may disrupt a woman's monthly cycle enough to delay her period or even cause her to skip a period altogether. Unfortunately, emotional reaction and physical reaction interact to increase her problems in this case. For example, if a woman has sex and worries that she might be pregnant, the worry may actually postpone her period, causing her further worry, which further upsets her menstrual timing, which causes further worry, and so on. A pregnancy test is a way to resolve the worry.

Since 1976 a number of home pregnancy-test kits have come on the market, selling for around $10 ("Home Tests . . .," 1979). They work on the same system as the HCG tests we have already discussed and may be used from seven to ten days after a menstrual period is missed. Although the accuracy of these tests is high if they are used correctly, misuse can lead to false conclusions. Doctors fear that diagnostic errors with such home tests may lead to serious health hazards. For example, the early stages of uterine cancer may produce a false positive reading and thereby delay treatment of the cancer. A false negative would lead a woman to conclude that she is not pregnant and she may well continue to take drugs or to smoke, thereby threatening the well-being of her unborn child. A doctor's visit costs money, but it is well worth the precaution if you think you are pregnant. There are also clinics, such as those run by Planned Parenthood, that give pregnancy tests for a minimal charge or for nothing.

The following comments capture some of the feelings that a woman may have as the early signs of pregnancy begin to appear.

Your period is late.

Well, there's nothing unusual in that, you tell yourself. You just need a good night's sleep, or maybe you're catching a cold.

After a few days, you say, "It's late because I'm anxious." You try to think about something else. You try so hard you can hardly bring yourself to wake up in the morning — as long as you stay asleep, you don't have to think about anything at all. "I'm exhausted," you say, "that's why it's late."

After a week has gone by, it begins to look as if your period is not just late, it is altogether absent.

Even that is not so unusual. You have heard of many women who have skipped periods completely during times of stress or illness. You begin to search your memory for other things you have heard — about hot baths that bring on delayed menstruation, about running up five flights of stairs, jumping off porches, taking laxatives. But mixed in with the hearsay and old wives' tales, you cannot force out of your mind one hard fact:

You had intercourse last month, so the odds are more than even that you are pregnant.

This is somehow unthinkable if you have not planned to be pregnant, and especially if you have never been pregnant before. It is *your* body, known, familiar; you realize in an abstract way that it is equipped for pregnancy, but the idea that it should suddenly begin to function in this strange and unfamiliar way without your willing or intending it seems utterly unreasonable. How can it happen to you? (Guttmacher, 1973a, pp. 1 – 2)

The DES Controversy

DES (diethylstilbestrol) is a synthetic estrogen. During the 1940s doctors in Boston prescribed DES for pregnant women who had histories of miscarriage, bleeding, or diabetes, on the belief that low estrogen levels accounted for the problems. In 1948 they reviewed 632 pregnancies treated with DES in fifteen states and found that the treatment had reduced the pregnancy problems.

Based in part on these generally positive findings, other physicians began to prescribe DES to pregnant women. In 1966 a form of vaginal cancer, clear cell adenocarcinoma, began to appear in young women between the ages of fourteen and twenty-two. Such cancer had been extremely rare in young women heretofore. After much investigation David Poskanzer and Howard Ulfelder revealed a significant link between the cancer and exposure to DES before birth. In 1971 a registry was established to gather more information on this rare condition. By 1978 a total of 350 cases had been reported. In about two-thirds of these cases, the mothers of the women exhibiting the cancer had been given DES during pregnancy.

The research seems to show a clear link between exposure to DES before birth and increased risk of vaginal or cervical cancer. However, the risk is not high, being estimated at no more than 1.4 per thousand exposed daughters up to age twenty-four, and the risk may be even lower. The point of the DES story is: When one is pregnant, the safest course is to avoid ingestion of all drugs as much as possible. Unlike thalidomide, the effect of DES on a few fetuses was very limited and only appeared years later.

Adapted from Annabel Hecht. "DES: The Drug with Unexpected Legacies." *FDA Consumer*, May 1979, pp. 14 – 17.

The Course of Prenatal Development

Prenatal
Existing or occurring before birth

Embryo
The developing organism from the second to the eighth week of pregnancy, characterized by differentiation of organs and tissues into their human form

Fetus
The developing organism from the eighth week after conception until birth

Congenital defect
A condition existing at birth or before, as distinguished from a genetic defect

The average duration of pregnancy is 266 days, or 38 weeks, from the time of conception. For the first two months the developing baby is called an **embryo**; after that it is called a **fetus**. The change in name denotes that all of the parts are now present. The sequence of its development is shown in Table 11-2.

Environmental Causes of Congenital Problems

Although the developing fetus is in a well-protected environment, negative influences from outside may still affect it. Sometimes these outside elements cause birth defects, which are called **congenital defects**. (These should not be confused with **genetic defects**, which are inherited through the genes.) Alan Guttmacher estimates that some 15 million persons in the United States suffer from some sort of congenital defect (Guttmacher, 1973b). The U.S. National Center for Health Statistics (1979) also estimates that about 1300 children aged one through four die each year because of congenital problems.

The developing fetus gets its nourishment from the mother's blood through the **umbilical cord** and **placenta**. There is no direct intermingling of the blood, though some substances the mother takes in can be transmitted to the fetus. When you consider the extremely small size of the fetus during its early months, you can see how a small amount of a substance can do a lot of harm. We'll take a look at some of the more common causes of congenital problems next. Remember that this is an area where much has still to be learned. Therefore if you are pregnant it is wise to avoid taking any drugs, especially during the first three months, and also to eliminate the use of alcohol and cigarettes throughout the pregnancy.

Drugs   If the mother is addicted to a narcotic, especially heroin (and also methadone), the child will be born addicted and will suffer withdrawal symptoms if it is not given heroin and then gradually withdrawn from it.

Furthermore, most common prescription drugs affect the fetus. According to The Boston Women's Health Book Collective (1976, p. 256), "Some antihistamines may produce malformations. General anesthetics at high concentrations may produce malformations. Cortisone reaches the fetus and placenta and may cause alterations. Antithyroid may cause goiter in infants. And tetracycline may cause deformities in babies' bones and stain their teeth." *The New York Times* (December 12, 1974) adds:

> Among the drugs known to damage the human fetus are the antibiotics streptomycin, tetracycline, and sulfonamides taken near the end of pregnancy; excessive amounts of vitamins A, D, B_6, and K; certain barbiturates, opiates, and other central nervous system depressants when taken near the time of delivery; and the synthetic hormone progestin, which can masculinize the female fetus.
>
> In addition, animal studies have implicated such common drugs as aspirin, antinausea compounds, phenobarbital, and the tranquilizer chlorpromazine as possible causes of fetal abnormalities.

The article also mentions that two commonly prescribed tranquilizers, Librium and Equanil/Miltown, may cause defects when taken early in pregnancy (for a more complete discussion of the effects of drugs on the fetus, see Bowes et al., 1970).

The saddest and most widely publicized instance of drug-related birth defects came from the widespread use of thalidomide. Thalidomide was a very effective sleeping pill and tranquilizer, believed to be safer than most other sedatives. It was widely used in Europe during the 1960s and was sampled by many women in the United States before cases of seriously deformed babies began to receive attention. Many of these children had only small, flipperlike appendages attached to their shoulders rather than arms and hands. Others had stunted arms and legs. Needless to say, the drug was taken off the market, and legislation requiring more stringent testing of drugs in this country was passed.

Infectious Diseases   Certain infectious diseases contracted by the mother, especially during the first three months of pregnancy, may harm the developing fetus. The best known of these is German measles (rubella), which can cause blindness, deafness, or heart defects in the child. Some

Genetic defect
An abnormality in the development of the fetus that is inherited through the genes, as distinguished from a congenital defect

Umbilical cord
A flexible cordlike structure connecting the fetus to the placenta and through which the fetus is fed and waste products are discharged

Placenta
The organ that connects the fetus to the uterus by means of the umbilical cord

TABLE 11-2 Prenatal Development

TIME ELAPSED	EMBRYONIC OR FETAL CHARACTERISTICS	ILLUSTRATIONS
28 days 4 weeks 1 month	¼ – ½ inch long head is one-third of embryo brain has lobes, and rudimentary nervous system appears as hollow tube heart begins to beat blood vessels form and blood flows through them simple kidneys, liver, and digestive tract appear rudiments of eyes, ears, and nose appear small tail	
56 days 8 weeks 2 months	2 inches long $\frac{1}{30}$ of an ounce in weight human face with eyes, ears, nose, lips, tongue arms have pawlike hands almost all internal organs begin to develop brain coordinates functioning of other organs heart beats steadily and blood circulates complete cartilage skeleton, beginning to be replaced by bone tail beginning to be absorbed now called a fetus sex organs begin to differentiate	
84 days 12 weeks 3 months	3 inches long 1 ounce in weight begins to be active number of nerve-muscle connections almost triples sucking reflex begins to appear can swallow and may even breathe eyelids fused shut (will stay shut until the 6th month), but eyes are sensitive to light internal organs begin to function	
112 days 16 weeks 4 months	6 – 7 inches long 4 ounces in weight body now growing faster than head skin on hands and feet forms individual patterns eyebrows and head hair begin to show fine, downylike hair (lanugo) covers body movements may now be felt	

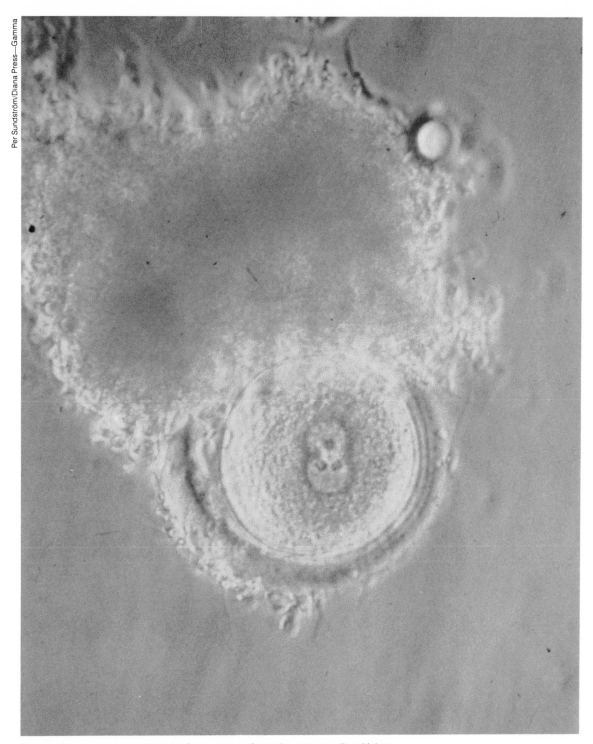

The round egg can be seen emerging from a group of cumulus-corona cells, which at ovulation completely surround the egg. On the egg's surface are thousands of spermatazoa, which look like small needles. The egg has been fertilized, and the two round structures in the center contain the chromosomes from the mother and father.

Spermatozoa in early stages of penetration on the moonlike landscape of the egg's shell.

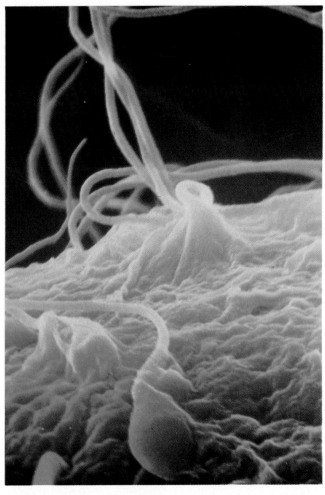

The womb (uterine wall) is prepared for implantation of the embryo. The surface is folded and consists of many kinds of blood-enriched cells.

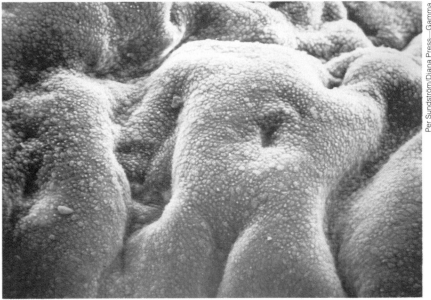

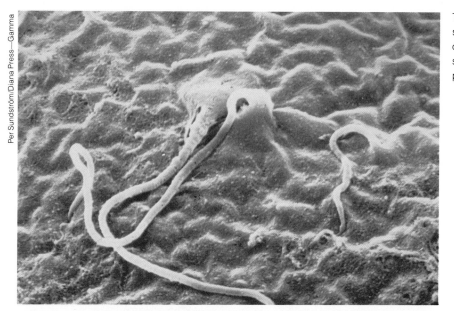

Three spermatozoa in different stages of penetration. Only part of the tail is seen of the leading spermatozoa (to the right of the photograph).

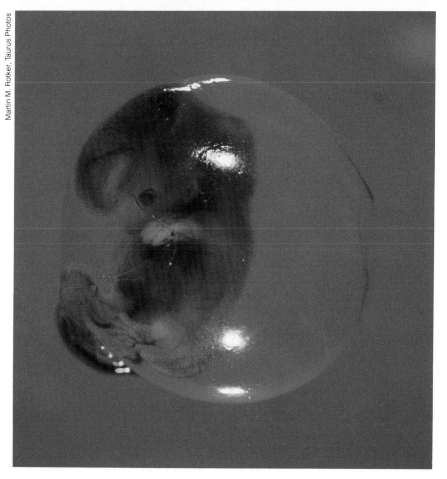

Human embryo in amniotic sac, approximately 8 weeks old.

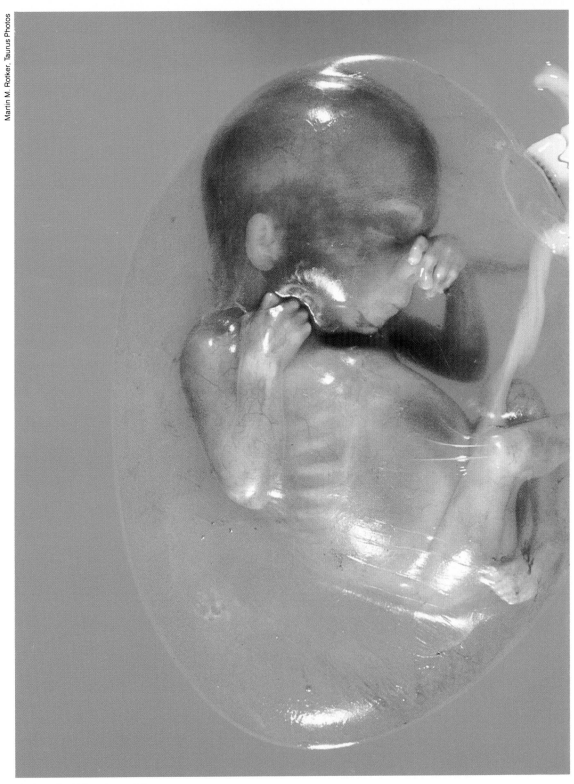

A 16-week-old fetus in amniotic sac.

TIME ELAPSED	EMBRYONIC OR FETAL CHARACTERISTICS	ILLUSTRATIONS
140 days 20 weeks 5 months	10 – 12 inches long 8 – 16 ounces in weight skeleton hardens nails form on fingers and toes skin covered with cheesy wax heartbeat now loud enough to be heard with stethoscope muscles are stronger definite strong kicking and turning can be startled by noises	
168 days 24 weeks 6 months	12 – 14 inches long 1½ pounds in weight can open and close eyelids grows eyelashes much more active, exercising muscles may suck thumb may be able to breathe if born prematurely	
196 days 28 weeks 7 months	15 inches long 2½ pounds in weight begins to develop fatty tissue internal organs (especially respiratory and digestive) still developing has fair chance of survival if born now	
224 days 32 weeks 8 months	16½ inches long 4 pounds in weight fatty layer complete	
266 days 38 weeks 9 months	Birth 19 – 20 inches long 6 – 8 pounds in weight (average) 95 percent of full-term babies born alive in the United States will survive	

women who contract German measles elect to have an abortion rather than risk having a deformed child.

Sexually transmitted diseases also affect the fetus. Herpes (see p. 325), for example, can cause a spontaneous abortion, inflammation of the brain, or other brain damage. Syphilis and gonorrhea can be contracted by the newborn baby. If the mother has syphilis, the baby will have the symptoms of the second and last syphilitic stages (see pp. 324–325). Gonorrhea can affect the newborn's eyesight; as a precaution, silver nitrate or another prophylactic agent is applied to the eyes of all newborns. This safeguard has almost totally eradicated the problem.

Radiation   Radiation, of course, penetrates the mother's body, so it will also reach and affect the fetus. The worst abnormalities occur if the mother is X-rayed during the first three months of pregnancy, when the embryo's major organs are developing. Even one pelvic X ray can cause gross fetal defects during this period. Thus, if pregnancy is suspected, the woman should avoid all X rays, even dental X rays. According to B. A. Kogan:

> Radiation reaching the testes or ovaries, and thereby the reproductive cells, can cause changes in the structure of DNA (genes). Mutation rates are increased by radiation. Since over 99 percent of mutations are harmful and since they do accumulate in man, the threat to future generations is apparent. Depending on the amount, moreover, radiation may cause chromosomal breaks and translocations. So another danger of radiation is related to chromosomal aberrations. Thus radiation may be one of the causes of a wide variety of genetic disorders, ranging from the mental retardation of phenylketonuria to the mental retardation of Mongolism. (1973, p. 167)

Rh factor
An element found in the blood of most people that can adversely affect fetal development if the parents differ on the element (Rh negative versus Rh positive)

Rh Blood Disease   The **Rh factor** (named for the rhesus monkey, in whose blood it was first isolated) is a chemical that lies on the surface of the red blood cells in most people. People with the chemical are considered Rh positive; those without are Rh negative. Only about 15 percent of white and 7 percent of black Americans are Rh negative. If a child inherits Rh-positive blood from the father but the mother is Rh-negative, the fetus's Rh-positive factor is perceived as a foreign substance by the mother's body. Like a disease, it causes the mother's body to produce antibodies in her blood. If these enter the fetus through a capillary rupture in the placental membrane, they destroy red blood cells, which can lead to anemia, jaundice, and eventual death unless corrective steps are taken. Only small amounts, if any, of the child's antibody-stimulating Rh factor reach the mother through the placenta during pregnancy, so the first child is usually safe. However, during delivery, the afterbirth (placenta and remaining umbilical cord) loosens and bleeds, releasing the Rh-positive substance into the mother, which then causes her system to produce antibodies. Once these are produced, she is much more easily stimulated to produce them during future pregnancies involving Rh-positive children. Each succeeding child will be more affected than the previous one. With complete replacement of the child's blood at birth, many can be saved. An even better treatment is now available that essentially can eradicate Rh problems. An Rh immunoglobulin that blocks the mother's immunity system can be injected into the mother, thereby preventing production of the antibodies that attack the red blood cells of the fetus. Before this treatment became available, about 10,000 infants died and another 20,000 had major birth defects because of Rh complications (Apgar & Beck, 1973).

Smoking   Heavy smoking adversely affects pregnancy. It increases the risk of spontaneous abortion, of premature birth, and of low birth weight in babies brought to term. Premature birth and low birth weight increase the chances of infant sickness and death. Babies of smoking mothers also remain smaller for some time than babies of nonsmoking mothers. Pregnant women are advised to cut down on their smoking or stop altogether ("Smoking and the Fetus," 1978; "Pregnant Women and Smoking," 1980).

Alcohol   Fetal alcohol syndrome (FAS), first identified in 1973, affects a large proportion of babies born to chronically alcoholic mothers. FAS includes retarded growth, subnormal intelligence, and lagging motor development. Affected infants also show alcohol withdrawal symptoms such as tremors, irritability, and spontaneous seizures. Even when the children are of normal intelligence, they often have a disproportionate amount of academic failure (Shaywitz, Cohen & Shaywitz, 1980).

What about moderate drinking during pregnancy? Even moderate occasional social drinking has been shown to have possible harmful effects. In a study of over 30,000 women, researchers found that those who drank as few as one to three drinks per day had a higher risk of miscarriage during the second trimester than women who did not drink (Harlap & Shiono, 1980). Another study found that only 8.1 percent of nondrinking mothers miscarried, whereas 17 percent of women who drank twice a week or more miscarried (Kline et al., 1980).

Controlling Birth Defects

Once a woman learns that she is pregnant, she should arrange for regular visits to a physician. Regular prenatal care will help avoid birth defects and dispel any fears she may have.

Diet   The expectant mother should eat a well-balanced diet with plenty of fluids. Inasmuch as the mother's diet has a direct effect on the fetus, she should consult her doctor if there is any doubt about the adequacy of the diet. Protein and vitamin deficiencies can cause physical weakness, stunted growth, rickets, scurvy, and even mental retardation in the fetus (Montagu, 1962). Poor diets can also cause spontaneous abortions and miscarriages or lead to stillborn children.

An inadequate diet leaves the mother more prone to illness and complications during pregnancy, both of which may cause premature birth and/or low birth weight. As we have seen, premature and low-birth-weight babies are more prone to illness and possible death than normal-term babies.

Good nutrition helps prevent stillbirth, brain damage, and retardation in the child as well as infections and anemia in the mother. It lessens complications during pregnancy, helping mothers feel better and have strong, lively babies.

Amniocentesis   A test has been developed for detecting genetically caused birth defects, such as Down's syndrome (formerly called mongolism), amino acid disorders, hemophilia, and muscular dystrophy, to name some of the more common disorders. The procedure, called **amniocentesis**, involves taking a sample of the amniotic fluid and studying sloughed-off fetal cells found in it. Amniocentesis should be done between the fourteenth and sixteenth weeks of pregnancy. The test can be performed in a doctor's office, though the laboratory work will take another fourteen to eighteen days to complete. In addition the fetus's sex can be recognized by this test.

It is well to have the test if you have already had a child with a hereditary biochemical disease, if you are a carrier of hemophilia or muscular dystrophy, if you have already had a child with a genetic abnormality, and if you are over forty because the risk of having a child with a genetic abnormality increases with age. If the test indicates the presence of a birth defect, the woman, her husband, and the doctor can discuss their options, including possible abortion.

Ultrasound in Obstetrics   **Ultrasound** sonography, because it is safe and noninvasive, has become a major means of obtaining data about the placenta, fetus, and fetal organs during pregnancy. It can replace the X ray as a method of viewing the developing child in the uterus, thus avoiding radiation exposure for both mother and child (Hobbins, 1979). It is also simple compared with X ray because the picture is immediately available.

Ultrasound works on the principle that different tissues give off different-speed echoes to high-frequency sound waves directed at them. Thus by moving a transducer (sound emitter) across the mother's abdomen, one can create an echogram outline of the various organs/fetus. Using a "real time" transducer that gives off several simultaneous signals from slightly differing sources, one can obtain a picture showing movement of the different organs, such as the heart. The echogram allows the physician to learn about the position, size, and state of development of the fetus at any time after about the first ten weeks of pregnancy. For example, the procedure can tell a physician if the fetus will be born in the normal head-first position or in some problem position.

Fetoscopy   **Fetoscopy**, a delicate procedure usually performed some fifteen to twenty weeks into pregnancy, allows direct examination of the fetus. To date it is still considered experimental. First, an ultrasound scan locates the fetus, the umbilical cord, and the placenta. The physician then makes a small incision in the abdomen and inserts a pencil-lead-thin tube into the amniotic sac. The tube contains an endoscope with fiber-optic bundles that transmit light. This light-containing tube enables the physician to see tiny areas of the fetus. By inserting biopsy forceps into the tube, the physician can take a 1mm skin sample from the fetus. A blood sample can also be drawn by inserting a needle through the tube and

Amniocentesis
A prenatal diagnostic procedure in which a long hollow needle is inserted through the mother's abdomen into the amniotic sac to obtain a sample of amniotic fluid, which is analyzed for signs of defect or disease

Ultrasound
Sound waves directed at the fetus that yield a visual picture of the fetus; used to detect potential problems in fetal development

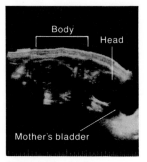
Sonograph of fetus.

Fetoscopy
Examining the fetus through a small viewing tube inserted into the mother's uterus

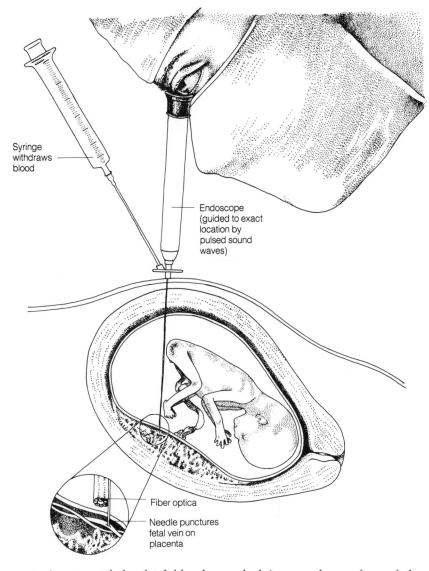

FIGURE 11-5 The fetoscopy procedure.

Syringe
withdraws
blood

Endoscope
(guided to exact
location by
pulsed sound
waves)

Fiber optica

Needle punctures
fetal vein on
placenta

puncturing one of the fetal blood vessels lying on the surface of the placenta. The technique induces miscarriage in about 5 percent of the cases, while the rate for amniocentesis is less than 1 percent ("Testing Fetuses," 1980).

Intercourse during Pregnancy

Although some people regard intercourse during pregnancy with suspicion, research indicates that it is usually not harmful (Masters & Johnson, 1966; Rosen, 1980). Indeed, the couple should not lose the close contact as well as physical enjoyment afforded through intercourse. There is evidence that for some women erotic feelings increase during the second trimester of pregnancy. By the third trimester, however, most women lose sexual interest to a degree.

Couples should exercise some care to avoid excessive pressure on the woman's abdomen, deep penile penetration, and infection. Because the uterine contractions of orgasm are similar to labor contractions, intercourse during the last three weeks of pregnancy should be avoided. Also, spotting or bleeding or pain contraindicates intercourse. In the later stages of pregnancy, the rear entry position with the wife lying on her side is usually the most comfortable (McCary & McCary, 1982).

If a woman has miscarried or has been warned that she is apt to miscarry, she should avoid intercourse during the first three months of pregnancy, especially around the time her period would be due. In most normal pregnancies intercourse poses no real threat. Indeed, some doctors suggest that the contractions of orgasm are helpful to pregnancy because they strengthen the uterine muscles. Intercourse also provides exercise for the muscles of the pelvic floor. And focusing on the feelings of complete relaxation after orgasm can help one learn to relax during labor contractions.

Many women report that sex is important to them during pregnancy. They believe that continued sexual contact maintains close emotional ties with their husbands. To them their husbands' interest shows acceptance of the pregnancy and of their changing body shape. In other words, sexual contact means tenderness, caring, sharing, and love. Many women also feel freer in their sexual behavior because they obviously no longer need fear pregnancy.

To hold one another, to caress, to be intimate is important as birth draws near. It will help allay anxieties and let both partners know that they are not alone but have loving support.

Birth

By the time nine months have passed, the mother-to-be is usually anxious to have her child. She has probably gained twenty to twenty-five pounds. This extra weight is distributed approximately as follows:

Amniotic fluid	2 pounds
Baby	7 – 8 pounds
Breast enlargement	2 pounds
Placenta	1 pound
Retained fluids and fat	6+ pounds
Uterine enlargement	2 pounds

There are two objections to gaining too much weight: Excessive weight can strain the circulatory system and heart, and many women find it difficult to lose the extra weight after the baby is born. On the other hand, dieting during pregnancy to remain within an arbitrary weight-gain limit is also risky because, as we pointed out earlier, good nutrition is important during pregnancy.

Although 266 days is the average length of time a child is carried, the normal range varies from 240 days to 300 days. It is therefore difficult for

FIGURE 11-6 The position of the fetus before birth.

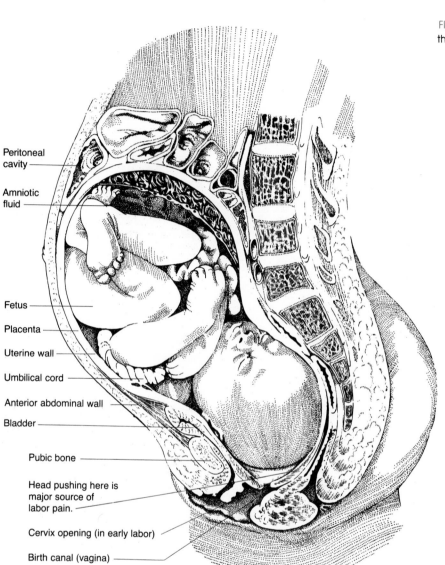

Peritoneal cavity

Amniotic fluid

Fetus

Placenta

Uterine wall

Umbilical cord

Anterior abdominal wall

Bladder

Pubic bone

Head pushing here is major source of labor pain.

Cervix opening (in early labor)

Birth canal (vagina)

the physician to be exact when estimating the time of delivery. In fact, there is only about a 50 percent chance that a child will be born within a week of the date the doctor determines. In general the expected birth date will probably come and go without any sign of imminent birth. Although this can be wearisome for the expectant mother, it is perfectly normal.

Labor

Three to four weeks before birth, the fetus "drops" slightly lower in the uterus (called *lightening*) and is normally in a head-first position (see Figures 11-6 and 11-7). The cervix (the opening to the uterus) begins to soften and dilate (open). There may be occasional contractions of the

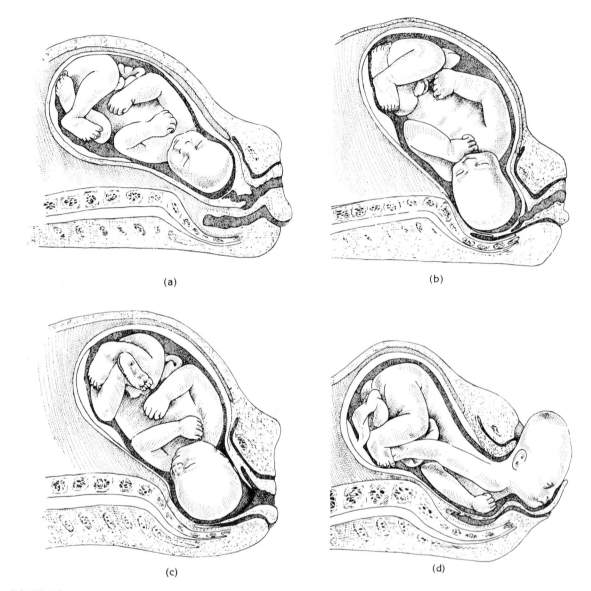

(a)

(b)

(c)

(d)

FIGURE 11-7   Events in the birth process: (a) before labor begins; (b) early stages of labor, dilation of cervix begins; (c) cervix completely dilated; baby's head starts to turn; (d) late stage of labor; baby's head begins to emerge.

Labor
Changes in a woman's body as it prepares to deliver a child, consisting mainly of muscle contractions and dilation of the cervix

Amniotic fluid
The fluid that surrounds and insulates the fetus in the mother's womb

uterus, which the first-time pregnant woman may mistake for labor (false labor). These early contractions are irregular and are usually not painful.

Essentially, there are three stages to **labor**. The first two are illustrated in Figure 11-7. The *first stage* is the longest, lasting eight to twenty hours on the average for the first child and three to eight hours for subsequent children (Kogan, 1973). During this time the cervix must dilate enough for the baby to pass through. (The contracted and closed cervix has held the baby in the uterus until now.) The sac of **amniotic fluid**, a salt solution that suspends, cushions, and maintains the embryo at an even temperature, will break some time during the labor process, except in about 10 percent of women who experience breaking shortly before labor begins. The uterine contractions become more frequent and longer lasting until the baby finally descends into the birth canal (vagina). During this first stage there is little the mother can do except rest, try to relax, and remain as comfortable as possible.

At first the contractions may be thirty minutes apart, but gradually they will come more often until they will be occurring every few minutes. The expectant mother should go to the hospital as soon as she ascertains that she is having regular labor pains (see Inset 11-3).

Transition is the term used to describe the baby coming through the cervix and the commencement of the second stage of labor. In the *second stage* the uterine contractions push the child down through the vagina into the outside world with about a hundred pounds of force. During this stage the mother can actively help the process by pushing or bearing down, thereby adding another fifteen pounds or so to the pressure created by the uterine contractions. This stage may be as short as fifteen to twenty minutes or can last an hour or two.

The *third stage* is delivering the afterbirth or detached placenta, which occurs five to twenty minutes after the birth of the child. During this time the uterus contracts and begins to return to its normal size, and there is minor bleeding.

Although there is a certain amount of pain connected with a normal birth, knowledge of the birth process and the source of labor pain and a relaxed and confident mental attitude will reduce such pain to a minimum. It is wise for both expectant parents to take childbirth preparation classes. Local Red Cross units, county health facilities, and adult education programs usually offer such courses. As mentioned earlier, prenatal care from a doctor should be sought as soon as one becomes pregnant. Although most births are normal, a small number will be abnormal, such as when the child presents buttocks first (breech presentation) rather than head first (see Figure 11-8). In many cases the doctor can recognize the potential problem and be prepared ahead of time.

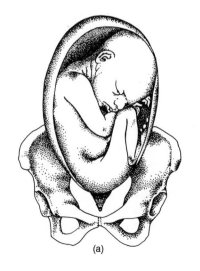
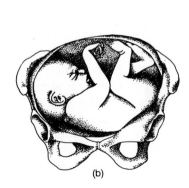

FIGURE 11-8 Atypical fetal positions at birth: (a) breech presentation, with fetus in buttocks-first position; (b) transverse position, with fetus's head at one side of the uterus and its buttocks at the other.

(a)   (b)

INSET 11-3

Guide to First-Stage Labor Progress

Signs of Labor

1. Bloody show/mucous plug
2. Gush of water
3. Contractions

Real labor will include #3 and may or may not include #1 and #2. You may have "false labor" for days or weeks before the onset of real labor. Your due date is not always the best guide as to when labor will start.

Ways to Check for Real Labor

1. Change of activity does not change contractions.
2. Contractions increase in length.
3. Contractions become closer together.
4. Contractions increase in intensity.

Call the Doctor When

1. Contractions are 10 minutes apart or less, lasting 45–60 seconds or more for 1 hour.
2. Bag of water breaks.
3. Anything more than a bloody show appears from vagina.
4. Anything unusual happens.

Early Labor

1. The cervix is thinning and opening or dilating slightly.
2. Labor is generally easy at this point and spirits high.
3. Continue your activities and pay attention — it's fun.

It's the Real Thing

1. Contractions are regular now and the cervix is opening.
2. Spirits are high but the realization that labor is work is starting to dawn.
3. Relax and use slow easy abdominal breathing. Going to bed is not necessary unless desired.

Late Labor

1. This is really hard work. Contractions are intense and close.
2. It takes real concentration on relaxation and abdominal breathing.
3. Birth is getting near.

Transition

1. Confusion is perhaps the best definition. Changing gears going from first-stage contractions to second-stage contractions.
2. Contractions may get closer together or farther apart.
3. Ride with each contraction; it may be your last in first stage.
4. The urge to push signals second stage.

Fetal Monitoring

Fetal monitoring
Using various instruments to measure the vital signs of the fetus during the birth process

Within the past few years **fetal monitoring** during birth has become more widely used. During labor electronic sensors are placed on the mother's abdomen, and in the second stage of birth an electrode is attached to the baby's scalp. These electrodes record the baby's heartbeat as well as the uterine contractions. Ultrasound techniques also display a picture of the baby and offer another measure of heart beat. These monitoring techniques allow the physician to closely monitor the baby's condition. Fetal distress can be recognized quickly.

Considerable criticism has been aimed at this kind of technical monitoring, mainly because it is associated with increased caesarean-section births. However, many claim that such monitoring has reduced infant mortality rates. It seems obvious that monitoring of both mother and baby during birth can be important to successful birth. Whether monitoring leads to unnecessary caesarean births, as some critics claim, is a separate question that should be investigated rather than put forward as an argument to cease monitoring.

Caesarean Section

From as early as 1882, under certain circumstances such as when a baby is too large to pass through the mother's pelvis, or when labor is very long and hard, the baby has been removed via a **caesarean section**. In this operation an incision is made through the abdominal and uterine walls and the baby is removed. The recovery period is longer than for a normal birth. Although many people believe to the contrary, it is possible for a woman to have several babies in this manner or to have one by caesarean section and the next normally.

Caesarean section
The delivery of a baby by means of a surgical incision through the mother's abdominal and uterine walls

Recently the percentage of C-section births has increased, rising to around 15 percent of all births (National Institute of Health, 1981) and even higher in specific hospitals. This has led to controversy, because the C-section is more traumatic to the mother's body than is natural birth. Interestingly, it is far less traumatic to the child because there is no prolonged pressure on the child as there is in the normal birth process.

The hospitals contend that better monitoring of the child just before birth and throughout the process leads to early recognition of possible problems and that many of these can be headed off by a C-section. They admit that monitoring has led to a higher proportion of C-sections, but it has also served to reduce infant mortality.

The popular but erroneous legend that Julius Caesar was delivered surgically gives the operation its name. Probably the term *caesarean* originated from an ancient Roman law, which was later incorporated into a legal code called the Lex Caesarea. This statute, aimed at trying to save the child's life, made it mandatory that an operation be performed on a woman who might otherwise die in the advanced stages of pregnancy (McCary & McCary, 1982).

Birth Pain

The uterine contractions, which are simple muscle contractions, usually don't cause pain, though prolonged or overly strong contractions can cause cramping. The majority of pain arises from the pressure of the baby's head (the largest and hardest part of the baby at the time of birth) against the cervix, the opening into the birth canal. In the early stages of labor, the contractions of the uterus push the child's head against the still-contracted cervix and this point becomes the major source of pain. By trying to relax at the onset of a contraction, by breathing more shallowly so as to raise the diaphragm from the uterus, and by lying on her side with knees somewhat drawn up, a woman can reduce labor pain to a minimum.

Once the child's head passes through the cervix, there is little or no pain as it passes on through the vagina. Hormonal action has softened

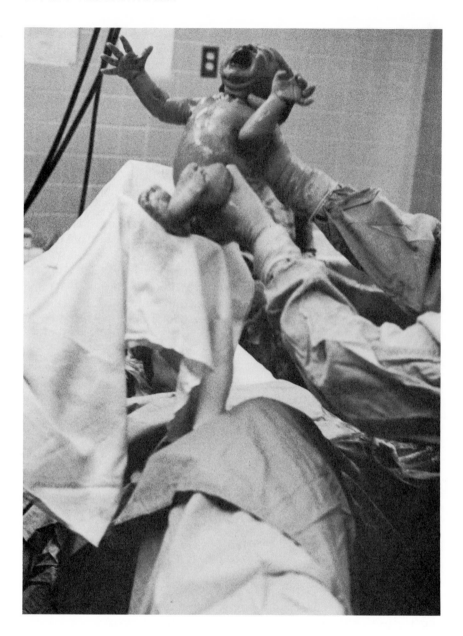

the vagina to such an extent by this point that it can stretch up to seven times its normal size. An additional difficulty may occur at birth as the child passes out of the mother into the outside world. There is often a slight tearing of the perineum, or skin between the vaginal and anal openings, because the skin may have to stretch beyond its limits to allow the infant to exit. In most cases the doctor will make a small incision called an *episiotomy* so that the skin does not tear. The incision is sewn after the delivery. Sometimes massage can be used to stretch the skin enough so tearing will not occur, especially if the newborn is small.

Natural Childbirth

In recent years many women, especially young women having their first child, have sought an alternative to the automatic use of anesthesia and the rather mechanical way many American hospitals have handled childbirth. Many years ago (1932) Grantly Dick-Read coined the phrase **natural childbirth** and suggested in his book *Childbirth without Fear* that understanding of birth procedures by the mother could break the pattern of fear, tension, and pain too often associated with childbirth (Dick-Read, 1972). Natural childbirth thus means knowledgeable childbirth, not simply childbirth without anesthesia or at home.

Natural childbirth
Birth wherein the parents have learned about the birthing process and participate via exercises such as breathing techniques so as to minimize pain

General anesthesia for childbirth has become much less popular, even in hospitals, because it slows labor and depresses the child's activity, making the birth more difficult even though less painful. The caudal or spinal block is now administered in about 10 to 20 percent of births. The spinal block produces a temporary loss of feeling below the waist. It is normally given in stage two of labor, when the baby has passed into the birth canal or vagina. Advocates of natural childbirth question the value of this procedure because most of the mother's pain is over once the child is in the birth canal.

More common today is paracervical anesthesia, which involves injection of novocaine or a similar pain-killing substance into the area around the cervix. This quickly deadens the area, blocking out the pain. It is similar to being injected in the gums around a tooth that is to be filled. The anesthetic action is localized and has little if any effect on the baby, and the mother is completely conscious and able to participate in the birth.

Hypnosis is also being used more frequently during labor and delivery to help relax the mother and reduce her sensations of pain. It is particularly useful for women who cannot tolerate the drugs used in anesthesia. It cannot be used with everyone and requires a doctor knowledgeable with its use. Those who use it report relaxed and relatively uncomplicated deliveries.

Today, more and more physicians are letting the woman decide whether she wants an anesthetic and if so, what type. It is important that the expectant mother is informed of the benefits and disadvantages of the available forms of anesthesia so that she can make her choice intelligently.

A couple interested in natural childbirth will find that numerous sources of training and information are available.* As mentioned earlier, Red Cross facilities, county medical units, and evening adult schools often provide childbirth preparation classes. The classes provide information on the birth process, what to expect, and how to facilitate the natural processes. The woman is also taught physical exercises that will help prepare her body for the coming birth. She learns techniques of breathing to help the

---

*There are a number of sources of free information on natural childbirth. You can write to the: American Society for Psychoprophylaxis in Obstetrics, 36 West 96th Street, New York, NY 10025; the Association of Mothers for Educated Childbirth (concerned with home delivery), Box 9030, Far Rockaway, NY 11691; and the International Childbirth Education Association/Education Committee, Box 22, Hillside, NJ 07205.

natural processes along and to reduce the amount of pain she would otherwise experience.

We have already noted that one of the basic principles underlying natural childbirth is that knowledge reduces fear and reduced fear means less tension and pain. The other basic principle of natural childbirth is to make the mother and father active participants in the birth of their child rather than passive spectators. For instance, controlled breathing (with the father helping to pace the breathing) supplies the right amount of oxygen to the working muscles, giving them the energy they need to function efficiently. Voluntarily relaxing the other muscles helps to focus all energy on the laboring muscles. Another aspect of breathing exercises is to focus attention on responding to the contractions, which keeps attention from focusing on the pain. The Boston Women's Health Book Collective notes that selective attention doesn't

> give our minds time or room to register that we might be feeling pain. As a result, some women say they never really felt any pain during labor; others say that feelings of pain kept surfacing but that they were almost always able to control those feelings with increased concentration on the breathing techniques. One woman wrote that there was a kind of beauty in her acceptance of the pain she felt: "I don't think pain is necessarily bad. I had a short, hard labor, and it was clear to me that the incredible euphoria that I experienced afterward was in part a function of the fact that it was very painful. It really was almost positive pain, really worth it in retrospect." (1976, p. 275)

Inasmuch as the couple has decided to have the child together, it is also important that they learn together about the processes involved and that the husband is not kept a spectator during labor and delivery. The couple will want to know if the hospital they plan to use will allow the father into the labor and delivery rooms so that he can be there to give psychological support and comfort to the mother. During the early stages of labor, he will be able to remind her of what to do as the contractions increase. He can keep track of the time intervals between contractions, monitor her breathing, remind her to relax, massage her (if she finds that a help), and keep her informed of her progress. In other words, he can help by *sharing* the experience with her. Several birthing methods (including Bradley and Lamaze) urge the husband to learn about the birth process and actively participate. This also facilitates father/child bonding.

Once the baby has passed through the cervix into the birth canal (vagina) and the doctor is present, things will happen so fast and the woman will be so involved with the imminent birth that the husband's presence and help will be less important.

Rooming-In

Rooming-in
The practice of placing the newborn in the mother's room after delivery so that the mother (and father) can care for it

More and more hospitals are allowing rooming-in, which means that the mother is allowed to keep her baby with her, rather than having the child remain in a nursery. Rooming-in is especially helpful to the breastfeeding mother. Both mother and newborn benefit from the physical closeness, and the child will cry less because it will get attention and be fed when hungry. Many hospitals are planning for rooming-in by connecting the nursery to the mother's room, allowing her free access to her infant. In these hospitals the baby is placed in a drawerlike crib that the mother may pull into her room whenever she wants. If she is tired, she simply places the child into the drawer and pushes the infant back into the nursery where it is cared for.

Alternative Birth Centers

Some hospitals have created **alternative birth centers**, homelike settings for childbirth. Relatives and friends are allowed to visit during much of the childbirth process. Barring complications, childbirth takes place in the same room that the mother is in during her entire stay at the center. Couples interested in such birth centers usually must apply in advance. The mother-to-be must be examined to be as certain as possible that she will have a normal delivery. In addition, the birth center usually requires that the couple attend childbirth classes. Birth centers serve as a compromise between normal hospital birth and home birth. It is part of the continuing trend by hospitals to make childbirth less mechanical and more an experience in which the couple participates as fully as possible. There are also approximately 150 out-of-hospital birth centers now operating (Echegaray, 1982).

Alternative birth center
A special birth center that creates a homelike atmosphere for birth

Home Births

Some women elect **home birth** rather than having their children in a hospital. At home the woman is in familiar surroundings, can choose her own attendants, and can follow whatever procedures soothe and encourage her (have music playing, for example). At home birth is also a family affair.

Home birth
Giving birth at one's home rather than in a hospital

The immediate question that comes to mind is, how safe is home birth? In Europe where home birth is common, statistics indicate that home birth is just as safe as hospital birth (Boston Women's Health Book Collective, 1976). American doctors do not agree and cite many instances of tragedy with home birth that could have been avoided in a hospital. The amount of risk can be reduced by careful prenatal screening of the mother and by providing backup emergency care. If the prenatal screening indicates conditions that might involve a complicated delivery, then the woman should have her baby in a hospital that has the facilities to deal with possible problems.

The emergency backup for a home delivery should include a person who is medically qualified (either a doctor, paraprofessional, nurse, or midwife) to deal with any unforeseen problems. In the future it may be possible to set up some kind of mobile birth unit staffed by trained personnel. The unit, perhaps housed in a converted motor home, could either be parked outside the home or brought to the house by calling an emergency number. In case of emergency, the mother could be quickly shifted to the unit, which would contain any necessary equipment. Remember,

Midwife
A person, usually a woman, trained to assist in childbirth or, in some countries, to perform delivery

though, that birth is a normal process; 85 to 95 percent of births do not involve any difficulties (Boston Women's Health Book Collective, 1976).

The **midwife**, although a medically qualified person, is not accepted by many. Midwives are used in home delivery in many modern countries such as Sweden and the Netherlands and were used in our country until the turn of the century, yet the organized medical profession as well as many others believe that delivery in the hospital by doctors is much safer. In addition, they believe that it would be difficult to enforce standards of competence if home delivery by midwives became widespread. England, on the other hand, has set high standards and has trained midwives since 1902. At the present time about 80,000 women are registered as midwives in England, of which about 21,000 are actively practicing. In 1970 about 75 percent of all births were midwife-assisted ("British Birth Survey 1970," 1975). In England the obstetrician is the leader of the birth team and the midwife does the practical work. In the United States certified nurse-midwives (CNM) are registered nurses who practice legally in the hospital setting. Some states limit them from performing home births.*

As interest in home births increases and as hospital costs soar (it now costs over $2500 to have a baby with standard hospitalization and delivery), the idea of midwifery is returning in the United States. For example, at the Booth Maternity Center in Philadelphia, the number of midwive-assisted births has risen steadily from 254 in 1971 to 1212 in 1976 (Dillon et al., 1978). Some states now have licensed training programs for midwives.

Breastfeeding

Attached to the natural childbirth philosophy is a strong emphasis on breastfeeding. There are many reasons for this emphasis, such as the fact that breastfeeding is more natural. The major reason that psychologists advocate breastfeeding, however, is that it brings the mother and child into close, warm physical contact. Inasmuch as feeding is the infant's first social contact, many experts such as Erik Erikson (1963) and Ashley Montagu (1972) believe that this loving contact is necessary to the development of security and basic trust in the infant. Another advantage of breastfeeding derives from the secretion of *colostrum*. This substance is present in the breast immediately after birth and is secreted until the milk flows, usually three to four days after birth. It has a high protein content, but, most important, it is high in antibodies and helps make the child immune to many infectious diseases during infancy. Breastfeeding also causes hormones to be released that speed the uterus's return to normal. One should also count the warm, loving feelings that arise in the nursing mother as another advantage to breastfeeding.

The new mother needs to prepare for breastfeeding as well as understand the natural process if she is to be successful. Her breasts will be

*For information on your state's midwife regulations plus a list of CNMs in your area, contact: The American College of Nurse-Midwives, 1522 K Street Northwest, Suite 1120, Washington, DC 20005.

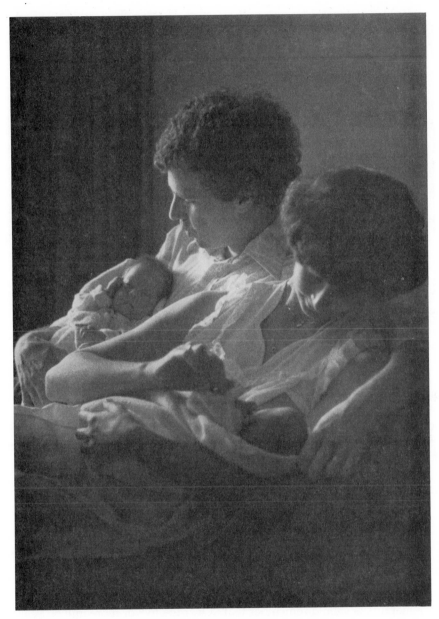

Nursing should be a time of warmth and affection.

engorged, congested, and painful for the first few days after birth. How-ever, mothers who have rooming-in and who begin to breastfeed the baby from birth onward (the sucking reflex of a baby born to an unanesthetized mother is very strong), on the baby's demand, usually do not experience engorgement. The act of breastfeeding itself soon relieves the congestion.

Before birth it is helpful if the mother massages her nipples to prepare them for the child's sucking. Otherwise, the nipples sometimes become chafed and sore. If this happens, exposing the nipples to the air will help.

Some Speculations about Breastfeeding and Sex

Only recently is breastfeeding beginning to come into vogue after forty years of unpopularity. One might ask why breastfeeding fell into disrepute. Although some new mothers claim that they can't breastfeed, investigation reveals few women who, for physiological reasons, cannot breastfeed. Rather it appears to be a problem of attitude or lack of knowledge.

One reason for a poor attitude may be the close association that has developed between a woman's breasts and her sexuality. Breast size and shape have, since World War II, become increasingly important to attractiveness and sexuality. But one need only remember the popularity of the flat-chested look of the 1920s flapper era to realize that large breasts have not always implied sexuality. In fact, in most primitive societies the breast is left exposed because its primary function is for feeding rather than sexual arousal.

Because of the association between breasts and sexuality, some women may be afraid that breastfeeding will ruin their figure and decrease their sex appeal. In reality this need not happen. If the new mother exercises and watches her diet, she should be able to return her figure to normal within a reasonable time.

The woman who thinks of breasts only in sexual terms may also feel guilty about the pleasurable sensations she feels when her child nurses. She may confuse the maternal feelings elicited by the nursing with sexual feelings and feel guilt because of the deeply ingrained taboos surrounding incest.

Why do you think American women abandoned breastfeeding for so many years?

Milk normally begins to flow between the third and fourth day. The baby is biologically prepared to maintain itself during these days, because it normally has a little surplus fat that sustains it until milk flow begins. Thus the mother does not need to worry that she will not be able to satisfy the infant's hunger during the first few days.* In the words of Ashley Montagu, she should remember that "Over the five or more million years of human evolution, and as a consequence of seventy-five million years of mammalian evolution, breastfeeding has constituted the most successful means of administering to the needs of the dependent, precariously born human neonate" (1972, p. 80).

Many new parents may decide to bottle feed. With bottle feeding it is important to make sure the baby receives the holding and close bodily contact that breastfeeding supplies. The father can participate as well, in providing holding and physical contact for the baby.

*For those wishing more information on breastfeeding, contact La Leche League International, 9616 Minneapolis Avenue, Franklin Park, IL 60131.

At times the father is a forgotten person immediately after birth. Not only does the mother occasionally suffer mild depression after birth, but the father may also suffer feelings of neglect, jealousy, and simply "being left out" after childbirth. The more of a partnership, the more sharing a couple can have in the whole process of conception, pregnancy, and child-birth, the more satisfaction both the father and mother will receive.

Postpartum Emotional Changes

The first few weeks and months of motherhood are known as the *postpartum period*. About 60 percent of all women who bear children report a mild degree of emotional depression following the birth, and another 10 percent report severe depression (Clark, 1983).

> Some of us are high, some are mellow, some of us are lethargic and depressed, or we are irritable and cry easily. Mood swings are common. We are confused and a little scared, because our moods do not resemble the way we are accustomed to feel, let alone the way we are expected to feel. If this is our first baby

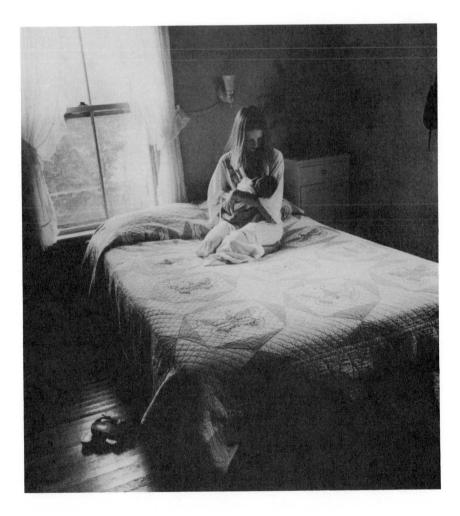

we may feel lonely and isolated from adult society. The special attention and consideration many of us receive as expectant mothers shift to the baby and we too are expected to put the baby's needs before our own. (Boston Women's Health Book Collective, 1973, p. 207)

Most women experience this mild postpartum depression between the second and fourth days after delivery. This may be due in part to the changing chemical balance within the women's body as it readjusts to the nonpregnant state. This readjustment takes about six weeks. Some suggest that it results because of the separation of the woman and her newborn immediately after birth (if there is no rooming-in) (Klaus et al., 1972). For most this depression passes quickly. The general emotional reactions to parenthood, especially with the first child, continue for a much longer period.

Summary

Pregnancy and childbirth are an integral part of most marriages. Despite the drop in the birthrate and the increasing number of couples expressing the desire to remain childless, childbearing and rearing will be a part of the majority of people's lives. Knowledge of pregnancy and the birth process is important to the act of birth itself. Those who are knowledgeable stand a better chance of having a simple, uncomplicated childbirth.

Both the egg and sperm cells are among the smallest in the body, yet they contain all of the genetic material necessary to create the adult human being. Both contribute the same number of chromosomes, twenty-three, but the sperm is also responsible for the sex of the child. There are two kinds of sperm, an X sperm, which creates a female, and a Y sperm, which creates a male. Many more males are conceived than females, but by the end of the first year of life, there are almost equal numbers of males and females. This is because the death rate for males at all stages of life after conception is higher than the rate for females.

Pregnancy takes several weeks before it becomes recognizable, though some pregnancy tests can determine pregnancy by the end of the third week. A missed menstrual period is usually the first sign. Other signs might be breast tenderness and coloration change, slight morning sickness, and the necessity of more frequent urination.

The average pregnancy is 266 days, or 38 weeks. During this time the mother should eat a good diet and be under the care of a physician. She should avoid medicines and being X-rayed, as well as stressful life events, if possible. The developing fetus can be affected by the environment. For example, if the mother is addicted to narcotics, or has an infectious disease such as German measles or a sexually transmitted disease, or is a heavy smoker, the child may be damaged. Any resulting defects in the child are called congenital defects. Genetic defects are caused by the chromosomes and genes. By removing a small amount of amniotic fluid — a process termed amniocentesis—doctors can analyze it for certain genetic defects such as Down's syndrome and thus discover defects, if any, before birth.

The birth process is generally divided into three stages. The first is the labor stage, during which the cervix relaxes and opens and the uterus contracts periodically in an effort to push the infant into the birth canal (vagina). In the second stage these contractions, with help from the mother, push the child through the birth canal into the outside world. The third stage comes shortly after the baby has been delivered when the placenta or afterbirth is expelled.

In recent years more and more emphasis has been placed on the mother and the father's participating as much as they can in the birth of the child. Natural childbirth means knowledgeable childbirth, with the use of drugs reduced to a minimum. Breastfeeding is being encouraged, as is rooming-in, or keeping the baby with the mother immediately after birth rather than removing it to the hospital nursery.

Philosophically, those encouraging natural childbirth believe that for a couple to share together the miracle of creating life can be an emotional high point. They suggest that care and planning be made a part of pregnancy so that the birth process will function smoothly and the parents will be able to derive the most pleasure and satisfaction from the entire process of bringing a child into the world.

Birth without Violence: The Leboyer Method

What makes being born so frightful is the intensity, the boundless scope and variety of the experience, its suffocating richness.

People say — and believe — that a newborn baby feels nothing. He feels everything.

Everything — utterly, without choice or filter or discrimination.

Birth is a tidal wave of sensation, surpassing anything we can imagine. A sensory experience so vast we can barely conceive of it.

The baby's senses are at work. Totally. They are sharp and open — new.

What are our senses compared to theirs?

And the sensations of birth are rendered still more intense by contrast with what life was before.

Admittedly, these sensations are not yet organized into integrated, coherent perceptions. Which makes them all the stronger, all the more violent, unbearable — literally maddening. (Leboyer, 1975, pp. 15–16)

Many theorists have hypothesized that the trauma of birth leaves an indelible mark on human personality. One of Freud's early followers, Otto Rank, suggested that the birth trauma is the major source of later problems that center around insecurity, because it is this trauma that marks humans with a basic anxiety about life. . . .

The child emerges out of the quiet, warm, dark, secure environment of the womb into a bright, loud, cooler world, and its source of oxygen and nutrition, the umbilical cord, is immediately severed. The child is hung upside down, slapped, cleaned, and made to function immediately on its own. Little wonder that the child screams, clenches its fist, and has an agonized look on its face. The sensation of the air rushing into its lungs for the first time must be a searing experience. Add to this all of the other new experiences, and life must seem a cacophony of terrifying intensity.

Frederick Leboyer simply tells us to listen to the child. Let the child guide us through the first few minutes after birth. Leboyer's four basic steps are simple. First, once delivery is imminent, reduce the light and be quiet. The infant's vision and hearing will then not be immediately assaulted. Second, as soon as the infant is out, place it comfortably on the mother's warm abdomen, which will serve as a nest for the child. Let the child retain the prebirth curved position of the spine until ready of its own accord to straighten and stretch. Third, do not cut the umbilical cord until the child's own systems are functioning smoothly, six to ten minutes after birth. This way the child is doubly supplied with oxygen and there will be no period of possible deficit and related alarm reaction and ensuing terror. During this time the mother and doctor gently massage the child, simulating the environmental contact the child has so long enjoyed within the mother. Fourth, once the cord stops pulsating, it is cut and the baby is bathed in water similar in temperature to the familiar environment from which it recently emerged. During this time also the baby is held and massaged gently. The hands make love to the child, not briskly rubbing nor timidly caressing, but deeply and slowly massaging just as the child felt within the womb. The child makes contact with the world at a pace that is comfortable for it. And how long might this be? Perhaps ten to twenty minutes is all. Is this too much to ask for a child at this most eventful time in its life?

And what of the Leboyer-born children's later personalities? It might be too early to tell, but they seem noticeably different, especially in their unusually avid interest in the world around them. Does fear and terror at birth cause many of the problems felt by adult humans? Will reducing the impact of birth on the child help that child become an adult with fewer problems? Only time will tell. But shouldn't we try to reduce birth trauma and see what happens?

On the other hand, there are many doctors who feel that the Leboyer method either does nothing or, in fact, may cause harm, although exactly what the harmful effects might be is unclear. A recent study conducted at McMaster University Medical Centre in Hamilton, Ontario, compared 28 infants delivered by the Leboyer method with 26 who had routine deliveries. The study reported no differences between the infants ("No Difference Seen . . .," 1980).

CHAPTER 12

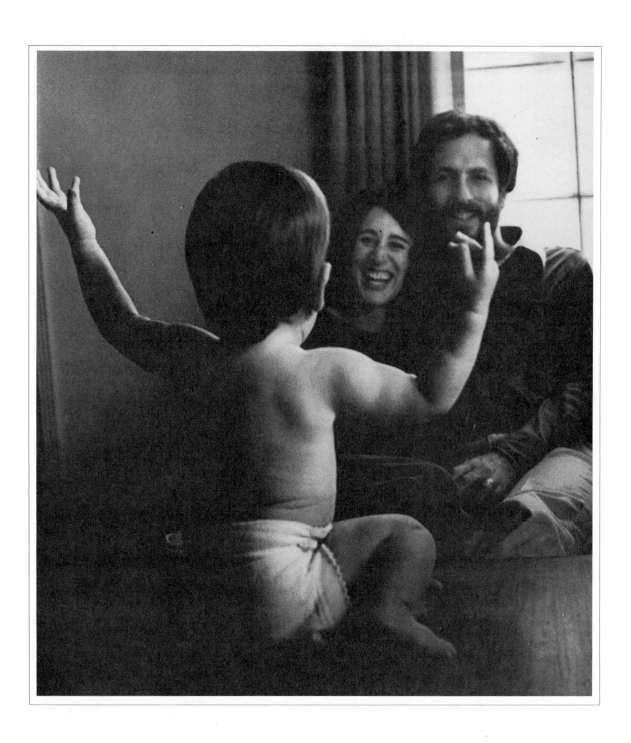

THE CHALLENGE OF PARENTHOOD

CONTENTS

12

Marriage and parenthood have often seemed synonymous in the past. Having children was the major goal of marriage. Many popular sayings supported this goal:

- Marriage means children.
- Having children is the essence of woman's self-realization.
- Reproduction is woman's biological destiny.
- It is the duty of all families to produce children to replenish the society.
- Children prove the manliness of the father.
- Children prove the competence and womanliness of the mother.
- Be fruitful and multiply.
- Having children is humanity's way to immortality; children extend one-self into the future.
- Children are an economic asset, needed hands for necessary labor.

The beliefs of the past often remain to encumber the present long after the original reasons for the belief have disappeared. So it is with repro-duction and parenthood. For thousands of years humans had to repro-duce — had to be parents — if the species was to survive. And they had little choice in the matter because the pleasure of sexual relations usually meant pregnancy.

Historically marriage has implied having and rearing children. Indeed the primary function of the family was to provide a continuing replace-ment of individuals so that the human species and the particular society continue to exist.

Yet the dogma of the past has quietly become the liability of the present, for uncontrolled reproduction today means the ultimate demise of the species, not its survival. In the past high infant mortality, uncontrolled disease, and war meant that society had to press all families to reproduce at a high level in order to maintain the population. Women were pregnant during most of their fertile years. Even today in many underdeveloped countries, infant mortality runs as high as 200 per 1000 live births, and because of malnutrition and disease many women see fewer than half of their children reach maturity.

In developed countries the infant mortality rate has been cut to less than 25 per 1000 live births. Some countries, such as those in Scandinavia, have an infant mortality rate as low as 13 to 15 per 1000 live births. The infant mortality rate in the United States in 1977 was 14 per 1000 live births, the lowest ever recorded (World Almanac and Book of Facts, 1983).

Children by Choice

Reduced infant mortality through greater control of disease and pestilence has removed the necessity for most families to have large numbers of children. Because a much larger percentage of children now reach adult-hood, a family may safely limit the number of children they produce to the number they actually desire. Hence the historical pressure on the family to reproduce continuously will have to be modified. The problems of overpopulation pose one of the greatest threats to the survival of the human species. Let's take a look at how population has increased. It took the human population until 1830 to reach one billion. But by 1930 — just 100 years later — another billion had been added. The fourth billion arrived in 1975, and by the end of the century it is predicted that we will be adding a billion persons to the world population every five years.

Knowledge of overpopulation dangers, improved and readily available birth control methods, and legal abortions have combined to give newly married American couples greater freedom from unwanted pregnancy. Although the social expectation to have children remains, couples are less likely to be thought of as selfish hedonists or as infertile if they remain childless. America's birthrate today is near its lowest point, approximately two children per marriage, or 16 births per 1000 population in 1981. Many underdeveloped countries, on the other hand, have birthrates of 40 to 50 per 1000 population. If America's birthrate continues at the zero population growth level, the population will reach a high in the year 2015 and start downward around 2020, depending on the amount of immigration.

The number of children overwhelmingly preferred by Americans today is two (Glick, 1979; David & Baldwin, 1979), whereas in 1945 only 23 percent of the public stated one or two as the ideal number of children. Larger numbers of young educated women are stating a "no children" preference today than at any time in the past. However, stating such a preference and living by it are two different things. According to Ira Reiss (1980), childlessness among married couples is actually not increasing much, although there is some increase among college-educated partners (see p. 336).

Why Are Children Wanted?

The reasons, conscious or unconscious, a couple decides to have children strongly affect the way the child is treated and reared. Because species survival, political reasons, and economic factors are no longer relevant to having children in modern society, people's personal reasons for wanting children need to be investigated. Many of the personal reasons have a selfish element. It is this selfish element that, when frustrated by the child, so often leads to feelings of disappointment and failure on the part of parents. Bernard Berelson (1972) lists six basic personal reasons for having children; each has a large selfish component.

1. *Personal power*: Children give parents *personal power*. First, there is the power over children, which during the early years of childhood is an absolute power. Second, having children sometimes gives one parent power over the other. The woman may use the children to bind the man to her, or the man may do the same. Children can also represent increased political and/or economic power as in societies where mar-

riage alliances are arranged to control power. In America the Kennedy or Rockefeller families come to mind when we think of children as potential power.

2. *Personal competence*: Children also offer proof of *personal competence* in an essential human role. "Look what I can do; see how virile I am; see how fertile I am."

3. *Personal status*: Tied closely to personal competence is the *personal status* conferred by parenthood. "I have contributed to the society; I can produce and achieve."

4. *Personal extension*: Children are also a form of *personal extension*, immortality, life after death. "After all, my children are a part of me, both physically and psychologically."

5. *Personal experience*: The simple *personal experience* of having children is rewarding. A parent can feel: "the deep curiosity as to how the child will turn out; the renewal of self in the second chance; the reliving of one's own childhood; the redemptive opportunity; the challenge to shape another human being; the sheer creativity and self-realization involved."

6. *Personal pleasure*: The experience of having children can produce *personal pleasure*, the love involved in having wanted children, caring for them, and enjoying them.

Of course, there are many other personal reasons for having children. For example: "Children will make me an adult." "I'll have something of my own." "People will pay attention to me." "I'll have someone to help and to love." "A child will save my marriage," and so on. As we shall see in the next section, the idea that children will save a marriage is erroneous. The increased complications of parenthood usually will hasten the end of a troubled marriage.

To know and understand our reasons for having children is a small step in the right direction. And to understand that the resultant child is an individual in his or her own right and that this new individual has no responsibility to fulfill our needs and reasons for producing him or her is a *big* step in the direction of enlightened childrearing.

What Effects Do Children Have on a Marriage?

This question is a complicated one involving many factors. Certainly, the readiness of the parents for pregnancy and ensuing parenting is crucial. We have already discussed the importance of planning parenthood so that the child is wanted. Yet even parents who want a child will experience ambivalence toward actually having one. Are we *really* ready? How much freedom will I lose? Can we afford a child? Will I be a successful parent? Such questions will arise continually for any expectant parent.

Unplanned pregnancies make such questions infinitely more difficult.

Couples often feel trapped into parenthood by an unexpected pregnancy. They are not ready for nor have they consented to parenthood. Thus they are often angry and resentful, especially the prospective father because he has the least control over the pregnancy. An unwed father, for example, has virtually no legal rights in deciding what shall be done about an unwanted pregnancy. Yet he is legally responsible for the newborn child.

In studying readiness for fatherhood, researchers have identified four major factors that men think are most important in making the decision to become a parent (May, 1982). The most basic factor is whether a man has ever wanted to become a father. If he has always thought that he would one day have children, then the transition to actual fatherhood is easier. The second factor is that he regard the overall stability of the couple's relationship as important. Researchers have found that the husband's positive perception of marital adjustment was strongly associated with high pregnancy acceptance on his part (Porter & Demeuth, 1979). Relative financial security is the third major factor. If a man perceived

Never a minute to oneself with children.

that, as a couple, they were doing about as well as could be expected and if their situation was similar to his expectation of acceptable financial position, then he felt much more ready for parenthood. The couple's objective financial picture proved less important than these more subjective evaluations. The last factor identified was a sense that he had completed the childless part of his life. If the man had set certain life goals for himself, ones that would best be met before starting a family, then completion of most of these enhanced a feeling of readiness for fatherhood.

Men may have more trouble working out parenthood readiness questions than women. This is because they rarely seek out support or help in dealing with such questions (Tognoli, 1980). They are more prone than women to keep their concerns to themselves. They are reluctant to discuss them with their pregnant spouses for fear of upsetting the spouse and "making matters worse" (May, 1979; Roehner, 1976).

Although women seem to better handle readiness for parenthood, they too must confront meaningful life choices. In years past there was not much choice for the woman, as the parenting/homemaking role was often the only role open to her. In those days, however, the homemaking role was a much larger and more varied role than it is today. Women were productive members of farm and craft teams along with their husbands. Children either shared in the work of the household or were left to amuse themselves. These mothers were usually not lonely or isolated because the world came into their homes in the form of farmhands, relatives, customers, and so on. Such women had no reason to complain of the boredom and solitude of spending ten-hour days alone with their children (Rossi, 1964). In addition to being mothers, they contributed to their family and their society in other important and productive ways.

Today the homemaking role has been drastically reduced in scope. The general affluence — especially of the American 'middle-class family — the small nuclear family structure, the trend toward women's liberation, and the removal of economic production from the home into the factory all combine to decrease satisfactions deriving from a narrow and exaggerated maternal/homemaking role. The modern woman has many other choices available to her, which make readiness for parenthood an increasingly difficult choice for her to make. (See Chapters 6 and 8 for further discussion.)

Today, the idea that a mother must remain continually in the home with her children is losing credence as more and more mothers join the workforce. The supposedly negative effects that absent mothers, baby-sitters, and child-care centers have on children have not been found. The majority of studies find no significant differences in the emotional adjustment of the children of working mothers versus nonworking mothers when good child care is available (Nye & Hoffman, 1974; Peterson, 1961; Smith, 1979).

Regardless of the state of parenthood preparation and readiness, many recent studies suggest that the presence of children in the family on the average lowers the marital happiness or satisfaction of the parents (Glenn & McLanahan, 1981; Campbell, 1981; Miller & Sollie, 1980; Glenn & Weaver, 1978; Waldron & Routh, 1981). Many couples report that their happiest time in marriage was before the arrival of the first child and after the departure of the last (Bell, 1975). The trends reported by these studies are not new. For example, study of the research done during the 1960s on family stability and happiness also indicates that children more often detract from, rather than contribute to, marital happiness (Hicks & Platt, 1970). Of course, most of this research involves group data and averages. The effect that children will have on your own marital relationship will depend on your understanding and tolerance of the natural demands and strains that the presence of children creates.

Despite the negativeness of some research findings, most parents express overall satisfaction with children and the parenting role (Chilman, 1980a). In one large national survey of parents with children under age thirteen, 73 percent of the fathers and mothers expressed satisfaction with the fun and enjoyment they derived from family life. Ninety percent of the parents said they would have children again (Yankelovich et al., 1977).

At first glance it may seem that parents' expression of satisfaction with their children contradicts the general evidence of reduced marital satisfaction when children enter the family. The answer to this apparent contradiction is that both negative and positive expressions are genuine. Parenthood, in many ways, is a paradox (Hoffman & Manis, 1978). On the one hand are problems of contending with a demanding child. On the other hand are the joys of knowing you are important to someone. The paradoxical character of parenthood is not simply a function of the fact that both of these experiences are part of parenthood, but that the "lows" and "highs" are so extreme and so intense that you want to cry at one moment and laugh at the next.

Colleen (Monday afternoon) — I never realized that an infant could be so demanding. I never get a moment's peace when she's awake, not even to go to the bathroom. I can't even say "wait a minute" because she is too young to understand (10 months). I feel like my whole life has been taken over by a tyrant. All she does is demand — me! me! me! I've lost my identity, my individuality to a word — "mother."

Colleen (Tuesday morning) — I'm glad I have her. It's neat to know she is a part of me and of Bob. She is a real little person who is perfect and loves me and needs me. She makes me feel successful at something, helping another. It makes me feel good to know that I was able to produce a child and be a parent. (LaRossa & LaRossa, 1981, p. 177)

The fact is that children add enormously to the complexity of family relationships. For example, a couple must contend with communication in only two directions. Add one child and this becomes six-way communication; add two children, and there is now twelve-way communication (see Figure 12-1).

Prospective parents can become better-prepared parents by reading and taking classes about parenthood. Yet even with a thorough preparation, bringing the first new baby home is an exciting, happy, and frightening experience for new parents. No matter how much learning about children they have done, they can never be sure that what they are doing is correct. If the baby cries, they worry. If it doesn't cry, they still worry.

What Do You Think?

In what ways have you caused trouble between your parents?

How could they have avoided any of these problems?

Overall, do you think that having children improved your parents' marriage? How?

Harmed your parents' marriage? How?

Assuming that you have children, what do you think are some of the ways that they might positively influence your relation with your spouse? Negatively influence your relationship?

FIGURE 12-1   Adding children complicates communication.

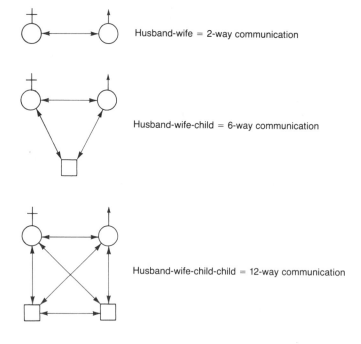

Husband-wife = 2-way communication

Husband-wife-child = 6-way communication

Husband-wife-child-child = 12-way communication

They will have to adjust to the feeding routine. The mother cannot venture far from the baby, especially if she is breastfeeding. The father has to adjust to being in second place in the wife's time and attention. An infant is demanding of both of these if nothing else.

Prospective parents sometimes forget that children will be with them for perhaps twenty or more years, and that their effect on the marriage will be profound. A spouse who becomes unpleasant or a marital relationship that sours can be left behind via divorce. But you cannot divorce a child who is unpleasant and frustrating. Parents are morally and legally responsible to provide care and shelter until the children are of age.

Traditionalization of the Marital Relationship

Examining a couple's relationship after a child enters the family points clearly to the overriding change that occurs. In almost all cases — except the two-career family that can afford to place child care almost fully in the hands of others — the parents' relationship moves in the traditional direction. The mother assumes most of the parenting and household roles (even if she works), while the father turns toward the work world. This occurs even when the couple believe in and work for an egalitarian home-making relationship (Entwisle & Doering, 1980; LaRossa & LaRossa, 1981).

There are several theories that try to account for this traditionalization phenomenon. Alice Rossi (1977, p. 17, p. 24) argues for a physiological theory in which hormonal changes in women during pregnancy, birth, and nursing establish "a clear link between sexuality and maternalism." New mothers receive "erotogenic pleasure" from nursing their infants, which means, according to Rossi, that "there may be biologically based potential for heightened maternal investment in the child, at least through the first months of life, that exceeds the potential for investment by men in fatherhood." Implicitly answering the traditionalization question, Rossi goes on to say that "significant residues of greater maternal than paternal attachment may then persist into later stages of the parent-child relationship."

Personality theories of socialization can be used to account for traditionalization. Early sex role socialization can also be used as an explanation. Such socialization, usually modeled from one's parents, is deeply ingrained. Because our society gives little or no formal education for parenthood, we tend to act out these parenting models when we have our own children. As young people we may be egalitarian in philosophy, among our peers and early in marriage before parenting becomes part of our relationship. But when children arrive, we fall into behavior patterns to which we were early socialized and which, in most cases, tend to be traditional.

A sociological explanation of traditionalization can also explain much simply by examining the social constraints placed on parenting by the general society in relation to the nature of the human infant. As we discussed in Chapter 1 (p. 13), the human infant is born in the most dependent state of any animal. A human baby is so dependent that without continuous care from an adult, it will not survive. The infant's demands are also nonnegotiable — it cannot be told to "wait until tomorrow." Thus in the early life of the child there must be continual adult supervision, a demand that interacts with the social realities. As we saw in Chapter 6 (p. 195), economic reality for most couples is that the man can earn more money. The coming of a child increases the economic burden on the family. If the husband can earn more than the wife, who will go out to work and who will stay home to care for the child? The answer is obvious.

If mother breastfeeds and the society frowns on breastfeeding in public, social pressure here too keeps her at home with her infant. If workplaces do not have infant-care facilities, as most do not, how can mother go to work? And if she goes, much of what she earns is taken by the costs of outside child care (p. 273).

Continuous adult care of the infant also means that one partner's "winning" (being free to pursue his or her own interests outside of parenting) means that the other must "lose" (forgo his or her interests for the sake of the baby). It is this constant time demand of the young child that causes much of the conflict between parents. As Ralph and Maureen LaRossa state: "It is this basic pattern — child dependency resulting in continuous need for care, which means scarcity of time, which leads to conflicts of interest and often conflict behavior — that cuts across the experiences of all couples in our sample" (1981, p. 47).

It is the loss of free time that bothers new parents the most.

Colleen—I do still have some time to myself, for example, when she is taking her nap. But it isn't really totally free time for me to use any way I wish. I'm still "on call." Bob tries to give to me free time by staying home with her and letting me go out. But if he has been at work all day, he also needs some free time so it is hard for him too. (from the author's files)

The Father's Role in Parenting

Colleen touches on a basic conflict between most new fathers and mothers. How much do they share the parenting duties? The movement toward traditionalization in new parents' relations means that the ideal of sharing (if it was an ideal before birth) is slowly lost. If the new mother stops work and remains home to parent, the father assumes few of the childrearing duties once the "baby honeymoon" passes (Cordell et al., 1980). Mothers claim that the period of help given by the father when the new baby arrives home ends quickly (usually within a few months).

Even when the mother goes back to work after the birth, studies have found that the wife's employment has a negligible impact on the husband's housework and childcare responsibilities (Berk & Berk, 1979; Pleck & Rustad, 1980; Robinson, 1977). Most fathers, even those who share childrearing obligations, fail to appreciate the everyday life of a mother with small children. They help — but as an appreciated helper who never really assumes full responsibility. In a sense mothers feel more trapped than fathers because they have no one to hand their job to, whereas fathers do — mother. Robinson (1977) found that housewives spend seven times as much time as employed men in child-care activities, and employed mothers twice as much. Even this is misleading because 50 percent of men's care activities involve play with the child.

Many fathers indicate that their work in supporting the family is the most important part of their parenting role and so feel that they need to do little else with the children, especially if their wives are not working.

> Jean and Jim have two children, a boy age ten and a girl age eight. Jim believes that because he is at work all day, it is Jean's duty to keep the children "out of his hair" when he gets home so that he can relax and recuperate. Jean resents this, believing that she, too, has worked all day. She has also had full responsibility for the children since school was out. She has asked Jim to watch the children occasionally on Saturday or Sunday so that she may have a day off, but he thinks weekends should be a family time.

Even if such attitudes represent the new father's viewpoint, he is still faced with a number of tasks (Barnhill et al., 1979).

1. *Decision-making*: The father must make the decision to accept the reality of having a child.
2. *Mourning*: While the new father gains the role of father, he also undergoes a substantial loss. He loses personal and economic freedom, some of his wife's attention, and much of their relationship's flexibility.
3. *Empathic responding*: The husband who participates in the pregnancy and birth will feel more closely involved with his wife and hence with

the new child. This developmental task may be missed by the nonin-volved father. Such fathers often feel unknowing about and later some-what alienated from their children.

4. *Integrating*: The child must be integrated into the spatial, temporal, and social life space of the family. The question "How much time does the husband spend with his wife, and how much time does he spend with the mother of his child?" is answered by the way in which the father integrates these "fathering" and "husbanding" responsibilities.

5. *Establishing new family boundaries*: The new father must now also alter his role as an individual in his extended family. He has moved between generations, becoming primarily a parent rather than a son. In addi-tion, he becomes connected in a whole new series of family relation-ships transforming his siblings into aunts and uncles, his parents into grandparents, etc.

6. *Synergizing*: The father's last task is developing a sense of trust in the adequacy of the child, the marriage, the family, and himself. This includes integration of the previous five tasks into a coherent life style, along with the acceptance of his own imperfections and those of his family. Synergizing refers to a state of enhancement that occurs if the father is able to achieve this new husband-father level and function successfully in it.

Even though the American father has not shared equally in the parent-ing role, recent social changes indicate that he may be participating more in the future. The historical characterization of the harsh, austere, disci-plinarian father is being replaced by a more humanistic, affectionate, caring kind of father. Liberation of the woman's role also works to liberate the father's traditional role, freeing him to be more loving than he has been in the past. Father participation in childbirth, long closed to him, is now more and more encouraged (Chapter 11). As more women move into careers, more men will have to share a larger portion of the parenting role. A few men are experimenting with fulfilling the home and parent role that used to be limited to their wives while their wives move out into the work world. Although these examples are limited, they are still indic-ative of a trend to bring more parenting into the father's role. Most experts agree that this would be rewarding to all concerned.

Fathering is drastically reduced when families break up. In most cases children go with their mother, and their father's contact with them is greatly reduced. Many ex-husbands are just as happy to escape their parental duties. However, many others desire to maintain their father role. But, even for those who do, the logistics of being with the children enough to remain effective defeat many absent fathers. Contact with the children usually means contact with the ex-wife, which may be painful. The fath-er's living situation is often unconducive to having the children stay with him. New commitments limit his time. In most cases even when the father desires to retain his role with the children, studies indicate that his contact with the children declines rapidly.

For a few fathers the breakup of the marriage means coming to know their children better. When they have the children, they are prepared in advance and so devote time to them, whereas they might not have when the family was intact. More fathers (although very few percentagewise) are obtaining custody of their children, and for them parenting becomes a central responsibility. (For further reading on the father's role in child development, see Parke, 1981; LeMasters & DeFrain, 1983).

Parental Effectiveness

And a woman who held a babe against her bosom said, Speak to us of Children.
And he said:
Your children are not your children.
They are the sons and daughters of Life's longing for itself.
They come through you but not from you,
And though they are with you yet they belong not to you.
You may give them your love but not your thoughts,
For they have their own thoughts.
You may house their bodies but not their souls,
For their souls dwell in the house of tomorrow, which you cannot visit, not
*   even in your dreams.*
You may strive to be like them, but seek not to make them like you.
For life goes not backward nor tarries with yesterday.
You are the bows from which your children as living arrows are sent forth.
The archer sees the mark upon the path of the infinite, and He bends you with
*   His might that His arrows may go swift and far.*
Let your bending in the archer's hand be for gladness;
For even as He loves the arrow that flies, so He loves also the bow that is stable.

Khalil Gibran, *The Prophet*

What Do You Think?

Do you want children at some time in the future? Why or why not?

If you want to have children, how many do you want? Why?

In what ways do you think your parents were successful in their parenting? In what ways were they unsuccessful?

How would you change the ways in which your parents raised you? Why?

Most people take on the job of parenthood assuming they will be successful: "Of course, we can be good parents." Yet raising children is an extremely demanding job. Certainly it is time-consuming, lasting for twenty years or more. What qualifications do expectant parents consider themselves to have? They all have parents, and all have been children. But, as we know from our own experience as children, all parents fail in their job to some degree. Some failure, especially in the eyes of one's children, seems to be an integral part of parenting.

There is no question but that your parents failed you as parents. All parents fail their children, and yours are no exception. No parent is ever adequate for the job of being a parent, and there is no way not to fail at it. No parent ever has enough love, or wisdom, or maturity, or whatever. No parent ever totally succeeds. (Close, 1968)

Because of this phenomenon, great amounts of advice flow forth from almost everywhere — grandparents, doctors, clergy, popular magazines, child experts — all describing how best to rear children. Benjamin Spock, known to millions of parents for his advice about childrearing (*Baby and Child Care* has sold more volumes than any other book except the Bible), has observed:

> A great many of our efforts as professionals to help parents have instead complicated the life of parents — especially conscientious and highly sensitive parents. It has made them somewhat timid with their children — hesitant to be firm. They are a little scared of their children because they feel as parents they are being judged by their neighbors, relatives, and the world on how well they succeed. They are scared of doing the wrong thing. (Spock, 1980)

And of course a great deal of advice comes from the children themselves who are as yet unblessed with their own children. What fifteen-year-old doesn't know exactly how bad his or her parents are and how to be the perfect parent?

The problem with all this advice is that there is no agreement about the best method to successfully bring up children. In a sense children come to live with their parents; their parents do not go to live with them. Parents need not think they must relinquish their lives completely in favor of the child's development. Parental growth and development go hand in hand with child growth and development.

Good parents love their children but are also honest enough to know that there will be days when they are angry with them, unfair with them, and in other ways terrible with them. Secure children will survive such episodes.

There is no single correct way to rear children. If children are wanted, respected, and appreciated, they will be secure. If they are secure, they usually will also be flexible and resilient. What is important is for the parents to be honest and true to themselves. Small children are very empathetic; that is, they have the ability to feel as another is feeling. They respond to their parents' feelings as well as to their actions. Parents who are naturally authoritarian will fail in coping with their children if they attempt to act permissively because they have read that permissiveness is a beneficial way of interacting with children. The children will feel the tension in their parents and will respond to that rather than to the parents' overt actions. Thus parents who attempt to be something other than what they are, no matter how theoretically beneficial the results are supposed to be, will generally fail. Parental sincerity is one of the necessary ingredients of successful childrearing. By and large, the pervasive emotional tone used by the parents in raising children affects subsequent development more than either the particular techniques of child rearing (e.g., permissiveness, restrictiveness, punishment, reward) or the cohesiveness of the marital unit (whether it is stable or broken by divorce or death).

Overconcern and overprotection can also cause problems for children. Children need increasing degrees of freedom if they are to grow into independent adults. This means that they must have freedom to fail as well as to succeed. They need to experience the consequences of their actions, unless, of course, the consequences are dangerous to their well-being. Consequences teach children how to judge behavior. Parents who always shield children from failure are doing them a disfavor. The children

Reprinted by permission of Jules Feiffer. Dist. Field Newspaper Syndicate.

will not be able to modify their behavior to make it more successful because they will be ignorant of the results. Overprotection can sometimes even be dangerous. For example, children taken to beach resorts need to know about and have water skills as soon as possible. Knowledge and skill are the best protection against accidents. Parents who take their children to the beach and then scream hysterically at them the moment they start toward the water are doing only one thing, teaching them to fear the water. Any lifeguard knows that fear of the water may lead to panic if there is trouble, and that panic is the swimmer's worst enemy. It is true that parents need to be aware of small children's activities on the beach. But concern should be shown by helping them learn about the ocean and by showing them how to have fun in the water and gain confidence in their abilities rather than making them fearful. The best protection for children at a beach is early swimming lessons and then watching them to make sure they are not too far out.

It is also important to remember that the family and the child are not isolated from the broader society. Parents are the first to be blamed for their children's faults. Yet the influences on the child from sources outside the family become increasingly powerful as the child grows older. School, peers, friends, and the mass media all exert influence on both parents and children. For example, it is difficult for parents to express their opposition to marijuana use when their teenager's friends are using it and the media present numerous experts giving opinions that it is not as detrimental to health as either alcohol or tobacco. But if their child is caught using it, most often it is the parents who are first blamed, not peers or media.

Parents have the most difficult task in the world — to rear happy, healthy children in an incredibly complex environment. The vast majority of parents love their children and do the best job they can. Our society puts the tremendous responsibility of childrearing almost totally on the parent, even though parents in reality are only one influence, albeit a major one, among many influences on the development of children. Our economic system, schools, religious organizations, mass media, and many other institutions and pressure groups impinge on the child's world. Often these influences are positive and help the parent in the task of rearing and socializing children. Unfortunately, these influences sometimes can be negative, countering the direction parents wish their children to take (LeMasters & DeFrain, 1983).

Parenting then is not something done only by parents. How parenting is accomplished and the results of the parenting are influenced both by the family and the larger society surrounding the family. Parents must pay attention to the society as well as to their children. To expect children to become adults reflecting only the values and behaviors of their immediate family is unrealistic. The effective parent must also be the concerned citizen and must actively work to better the society at large.

Stimulation and Development

Stimulation is necessary for the development of basic behavioral capacities. Early deprivation of stimulation generally produces slower learning later in life. Early stimulation, on the other hand, enhances development and later learning. For example, various research evidence suggests that "given the present state of our knowledge, the best physical environment in which to rear a child is one that gives him experience with a variety of physical objects which he can manipulate and control freely with minimal restriction. Experiences will give him an opportunity to develop basic motor skills which he can later apply to more specific learning situations" (Scott, 1968, p. 114).

The emphasis on early childhood education and intervention, beginning with the Head Start program in the early 1960s, reflects recognition of the importance of early environmental stimulation for children. Although there is controversy over the effects of Head Start experiences and the contribution to lasting change in the child made by such experiences, there is little doubt that the preschool years are important to the cognitive development of the child (Weinberg, 1979).

Some stress in childhood — which is a kind of stimulation — may also be related to achievement. In a study of over 400 famous twentieth-century men and women (Goertzel & Goertzel, 1962), two conclusions seemed to indicate that a child need not be protected from all stress and strain; that, indeed, some manageable stress stimulates achievement:

1. Three-fourths of the children were troubled — by poverty; by a broken home; by rejecting, overpossessive, estranged, or dominating parents; by financial ups and downs; by physical handicaps; or by parental dissatisfaction over the children's school failures or vocational choices.
2. Handicaps such as blindness, deafness; being crippled, sickly, homely, undersized or overweight; or having a speech defect occurred in the

childhoods of over one-fourth of the sample. In many of these individuals the need to compensate for such handicaps is seen by them as a determining factor in their drive for achievement.

This study included individuals from all fields and countries, such as Konrad Adenauer, Louis Armstrong, Lionel Barrymore, Hugo Black, Alexander Graham Bell, Pearl Buck, and Gertrude Stein.

This doesn't mean that parents should deliberately introduce stress into their children's lives. Rather, it means that parents may relax and be less concerned if their children are placed in a stressful situation. Children who are secure in the love and warmth of their parents will be able to survive and, in fact, grow in the face of stress. For example, moving away from a neighborhood, from places of familiarity and friends, can be upsetting. Yet studies of the effect of long-distance moves on children show little negative effect. The children seem to make friends easily, the school change is not difficult, and any disturbance in their behavior dissipates quickly (Barrett & Noble, 1973).

Childrearing, Discipline, and Control

TABLE 12-1   Percentage of Parents Using Various Disciplinary Methods

METHOD	PERCENTAGE
Yelling at or scolding children	52
Spanking children	50
Making children stay in their rooms	38
Not allowing children to play	32
Not letting children watch television	25
Making children go to bed	23
Threatening children	15
Giving children extra chores	12
Taking away an allowance	9

Source: Adapted from General Mills, 1977.

For many parents control of their children is accomplished in a haphazard manner. If parents liked their own parents, they tend to copy their childrearing methods. If parents disliked their own parents' methods, they tend to do the opposite. In either case parents' own experiences as children influence how they themselves parent. The General Mills American Family Report indicates that most parents overwhelmingly use negative techniques to control their children. Table 12-1 shows the percentage of parents reporting use of various disciplinary methods.

Unfortunately, negative control methods tend to have negative side effects because they serve as model behaviors. A child who is screamed at tends to become a child who screams to get his or her way. A child who is treated negatively tends to become a negative child. A child who is punished violently tends to learn that violence is how to change another's behavior. Hostility, low self-esteem, feeling of inferiority and insecurity are frequent reactions of children who are reared by basically negative methods.

Rather than having only a few control techniques, automatically used, parents must work toward having a variety of well-understood childrearing methods. Each child and each situation will be somewhat unique. Therefore, parents should try to react in accordance with each situation. First one tries to understand the child and the problem, then one tries to clearly identify what changes are necessary, and finally one attempts to accomplish the changes in the best possible manner. Thus childrearing becomes a rational, thoughtful, directive process, as opposed to an irrational, reactive process.

In general controlling children can be accomplished by using many different methods that vary in intensity from mild to strong. Many parents use a strong method such as punishment when, in fact, a mild method

Parental guidance is an important part of child-rearing.

such as distraction might have worked equally well. By first trying milder methods, many of the negative side effects of punishment can be eliminated or at least reduced. Table 12-2 outlines a continuum of mild to strong methods. One must consider the age of the child when using this table. A two-year-old will not understand item 3c, an appeal to his sense of fair play, because this ethical concept has not yet been grasped.

Directing a child's behavior ahead of time is preferable to and much easier than being unprepared and surprised by a child's behavior and then trying to react properly. For example, if you give a child a difficult task, stay close (1b, proximity control) so that you can offer help if it is needed (2a).

Firm routines (2c) reduce conflict and the number of overt decisions necessary. For example, an orderly routine at bedtime accomplishes tooth brushing, elimination, getting into pajamas, story reading, and lights off. In a sense the child is on automatic pilot, and little conflict arises once the routine is established. Such routines are only helpful in certain areas of life and probably work best with the preschool and early school child. Distraction (2b) is helpful with small children; they usually have short

What Do You Think?

What were the major methods of control used by your parents when you were a child?

How did you react to these methods as a child?

What do you think of them as an adult? Did they work? Why or why not?

Which methods would you use with your children? Why?

What will you do if you and your spouse disagree on control methods?

TABLE 12-2   Mild to Strong Child Control Methods

1. Supporting the child's self-control
   a. Signal interference (catch the child's eye, frown, say something)
   b. Proximity control (get physically close to the child)
   c. Planful ignoring (children often do "bad" things to get attention and if they don't get it, they will cease the behavior because they are not getting what they want)
   d. Painless removal (remove the child from the problem source)

2. Situational assistance
   a. Give help
   b. Distraction or restructuring a situation
   c. Support of firm routines
   d. Restraint
   e. Getting set in advance

3. Reality and ethical appraisals
   a. Showing consequences to behaviors
   b. Marginal use of interpretation
   c. Appealing to sense of reason and fair play (not useful until child is intellectually able to understand such concepts)

4. Reward and contracting
   a. Rewards (payoffs) should be immediate
   b. Initial contracts should call for and reward small pieces of behavior (a reward for picking up toys, rather than a reward for keeping room clean for a week)
   c. Reward performance after it occurs
   d. Contract must be fair to all parties
   e. Terms of contract must be clear and understood
   f. Contract must be honest
   g. Contract should be positive
   h. Contract must be used consistently
   i. Contract must have a method of change to cope with failures

5. Punishment: See Inset 12-1

interest spans, and their attention is easily shifted from one focus to another. Saying "no" to a child immediately creates a confrontation. ("Don't touch the expensive art book.") However, presenting an alternative and saying "do this" does not necessarily create such a confrontation. ("Why don't you look at this coloring book?" — while handing it to the child.)

The Growing Child in the Family

The essence of children is growing, changing, maturing, and becoming, rather than sameness. Parents must themselves constantly change in their relationship to the growing child. Just about the time they have adapted and learned to cope with a totally dependent child, they will need to change and learn to deal with a suddenly mobile, yet still irresponsible two-year-old. Then the school years follow, when the increasing influence of peers signals declining parental influence. Puberty and adolescence serve as the launching stage for the once small, dependent child to go

Using Discipline and Punishment Effectively

Whether one agrees or not with the use of punishment as a means of teaching children, studies of parental control indicate that it is still the major method used by most parents. Unfortunately, punishment does not always work and, in addition, it has negative side effects such as anger and hostility.

If punishment is used, the parent needs to understand a few simple principles that help maximize its usefulness and minimize the negative side effects. If mild punishment is to be effective, there needs to be alternative behavior open to the child. For example, if a child is punished for turning on the television rather than dressing for school, the punishment will work better if the child knows when he or she can watch TV. In this case the child knows that there is another way to do what he or she wants that will not result in punishment. In addition punishment works best if the child is not highly motivated.

For example, a child eats just before dinner. If the child missed lunch, chances are she or he is very hungry (highly motivated), and punishment will probably not be very effective in keeping the child from eating. If there are alternatives and if the child is not highly motivated, then following the guidelines based on psychological learning theory set forth here will help achieve desired goals while keeping punishment to a minimum.

1. Consider the individual child and the potential negative side effects. *Example*: Randy reacts strongly to punishment, and the reaction lasts for a considerable length of time. He is better controlled by reward or distraction. If punishment is used, it is mild. Michelle is not at all sensitive to punishment. She can be punished, her behavior will change, and there are no lasting side effects.

2. Punish as soon after the act as possible. *Example*: Children are bright, but it is hard for them to associate an act with punishment that comes many hours after the act. The mother who at 10 A.M. tells the child to "Just wait until your father comes home, you will get it," does little more than turn father into an ogre. By the time the father arrives home, little change of behavior will be derived from punishment.

3. If possible let the punishment flow from the act. *Example*: A child is constantly warned when he reaches toward a hot stove, but behavior change will take time. The child who touches the hot stove is immediately punished by his own action, understands what the word *hot* means, and has learned in one trial. Obviously, one cannot always set up a situation where punishment flows from the act, but when possible it is more efficient.

4. Make the punishment educational and be sure that children understand what their alternatives are. *Example*: Many young children really do not understand exactly what they have done and what new behavior is desired. Mary was punished when her mother found her at the cookie jar before dinner. Later Mary found some cookies on the counter and was again punished. Mary did not understand that she was being punished for eating cookies the first time. She thought her mother did not want her around the cookie jar for fear she might break it. Also, she did not understand that she could have cookies after dinner.

5. Keep the punishment as mild as possible and keep it devoid of emotion. *Example*: Jimmy's mother became so exasperated that she lost her temper and spanked him. By losing her own temper, she increased the emotional atmosphere, causing Jimmy to become even more upset. She also modeled overt anger.

6. Try to punish the act, not the child. *Example*: "You are a bad boy. We don't love you when you are bad." This is a threatening and upsetting statement to a child and really is unnecessary. Generally, it is the particular act that is bad rather than the child. When the child changes the behavior, there is no longer a need for punishment, hence the child's relationships should immediately return to normal. By directing punishment at only the act, the child will not continue to be punished by thinking he or she as an individual is bad and unworthy of love ("I don't like your behavior so please change it. I like you, however."

into the world on his or her own to establish a new family and repeat the cycle. As the child grows and changes, the family also changes. In infancy, for example, the mother usually remains close to the child. During elementary school she often becomes a chauffeur, taking the child to a friend's home, music lessons, after-school sports, and so on. Change and growth in the child means parental and family change.

One way of viewing these changes is to see them as a series of social and developmental situations involving problematic encounters with the environment. These situations involve normal "problems" children must "solve" if they are to function fully. This section will focus on *psychosocial* stages rather than biological developmental stages, though the two are interrelated.

Erik Erikson (1963) identifies eight psychosocial developmental stages, each with important tasks, that describe the human life cycle from infancy through old age.* In each of these stages children must establish new orientations to themselves and their environment, especially their social environment. Each stage requires a new level of social interaction and can shape the personality in either negative or positive ways. For example, if children cope successfully with the problems and resultant stress that come into focus in a given stage, they gain additional strengths to become fully functioning. On the other hand, if children cannot cope with the problems of a particular stage, they will, in effect, invest continuing energy into this stage, becoming to some extent *fixated*, or arrested in development. For example, an adult who handles frustration by always throwing a temper tantrum has failed to move out of the early childhood stage when temper tantrums were the only manner of handling frustration. Such an individual is not coping successfully with the stress and problems of adult life.

Notice in Figure 12-2 that each stage can be carried down the chart into adulthood. For example, trust versus mistrust influences all succeeding stages. A person who successfully gains basic trust is then better prepared to cope with the ensuing developmental stages. The reverse is also

---

*Erikson's stages are theoretical, of course, and though there is controversy over the exact nature of developmental stages, the idea of stages is useful in helping parents understand the changing nature of the growing child and themselves.

Stages								
1 Infancy Oral-sensory 1st year	**Trust versus Mistrust** (mothering, feeding)							
2 Toddler Muscular-anal 2 to 3 years		**Autonomy versus Shame, Doubt** (toilet training, self-control)						
3 Early Childhood Locomotor- genital 4 to 5 years			**Initiative versus Guilt** (increased freedom and sexual identity)					
4 School age Latency 6 to 11 years				**Industry versus Inferiority** (working together, school)				
5 Puberty and Adolescence 12 to 18 years					**Identity versus Role-Diffusion** (adult role)			
6 Young adulthood						**Intimacy versus Isolation** (love and marriage)		
7 Adulthood, middle age							**Generativity versus Self-Absorption** (broadening concerns beyond self)	
8 Maturity, old age								**Integrity versus Despair**

FIGURE 12-2   Erikson's eight developmental stages.

true. A mistrusting individual will have more trouble coping with ensuing stages than a trusting person will.

Let's now take a closer look at the first six stages.

Infancy: The Oral-Sensory Stage: Trust versus Mistrust (First Year)

Human beings undergo a longer period of dependence than any other species. In the first years children are completely dependent on parents or other adults for survival and are unable to contribute to the family because their responses to the environment are quite limited. Thus their development of trust depends on the quality of care they receive from their parents or the adults who care for them. The prolonged period of dependence makes the child more amenable to socialization (learning the ways of the society). Sometimes, however, a child will be too strongly or wrongly socialized in the early stages and thereby will suffer from needless inhibitions as an adult. Such inhibitions are easily recognized by modern-day youth as "hang-ups."

The first year, when the infant must have total care to survive, is a difficult adjustment for many new parents because they have enjoyed relatively great personal freedom as well as time to devote to one another. Overnight a newcomer usurps that freedom and has first call on their time. Not only does the infant demand personal time and attention, but many other considerations arise. To go to a movie now means the additional time and cost involved in finding and paying a baby-sitter. To take a Sunday drive means taking along special food, diapers, car seat, and so forth. But for the couple who really want children, the challenge and fun of watching a new human grow and learn can offset many of the problems entailed in the new parental roles.

During this first year the husband must make the adjustment to sharing the wife's love and attention. This can be difficult for a husband who is accustomed to being the center of "his" wife's life. Now suddenly the baby takes priority. As we mentioned earlier, it is not uncommon for a new father to feel some resentment and jealousy over this change in his position. Although most couples are financially strained at this time in their marriage, it is important that they arrange times to be by themselves and that they remember to pay attention to their own relationship. In the past this was easier to do because often relatives were close by who could watch the infant. Today getting time together usually means paying someone to take care of the child. Such money is well spent if it gives the couple an opportunity to improve their own relationship. Their relationship is the primary one, and if it is good the chances are greater that the parents/children relationship will be good also.

Children learn trust through living in a trusting environment. This means that their needs are satisfied on a regular basis and that interactions with the environment are positive, stable, and satisfying. Parents whose relationship is good are better able to supply this kind of environment.

The term *oral-sensory* derives from the fact that eating and the infant's mouth and senses are its major means of knowing the world at this stage.

Toddler: The Muscular-Anal Stage: Autonomy versus Shame and Doubt (Two to Three Years of Age)

As children develop motor and mental capacities, opportunities to explore and manipulate the environment increase. From successful exploration and manipulation emerges a sense of autonomy and self-control. If the child is unsuccessful or made to feel unsuccessful by too-high parental expectations, then feelings of shame and doubt may arise. This is a time of great learning. Children learn to walk, to talk, to feed and dress themselves, to say "no," and so forth. If parents thought the infant demanding, they learn what "demanding" really can be with their two- and three-year-olds. It seems there is not a minute's peace. The relationship between the parents can suffer during this time because of the constant demands and ensuing fatigue and frustrations engendered by the child's insatiable demands. On the other hand, it is exciting to see the child's skills rapidly developing. First steps, first words, and curiosity all make this period one of quick change for child and parent alike.

During this stage parents should try to create a stimulating environment for the child. As we mentioned earlier, stimulation appears to enhance learning skills. Alphabet books, creative toys that are strong enough to withstand the rough treatment given by most two- and three-year-olds, picture books, and an endless answering of questions all help stimulate the child. Toilet training, which also occurs during this period, needs to be approached in a positive way with humor if it is to be easily accomplished. Once the child is toilet trained, it will be of great relief to parents since the messy job of diaper changing and cleaning is over.

The name of this stage denotes the increasing activity of the child and the toilet-training tasks.

Early Childhood: The Locomotor-Genital Stage: Initiative versus Guilt (Four to Five Years of Age)

Children become increasingly capable of self-initiated activities, which is a source of pride for parents. It is exciting to see children's capabilities increase. With each passing month they seem more mature, to have more personality, and to become more fun to interact with. As their capabilities and interests expand, so must the parents'. Where children's energy comes from is a constant source of amazement and bewilderment to often-tired parents. However, school is just around the corner and with it comes a breath of free time.

Children who do not increase their capabilities, perhaps because of accident or illness, may feel guilty and inadequate about their chances of success in school.

Locomotor indicates that the child is now very active in the environment; *genital* refers to sex-organ interest and exploration.

School Age: The Latency Stage: Industry versus Inferiority (Six to Eleven Years of Age)

At last the children are in school and for a few hours a day the house is peaceful. Now the children's peers begin to play a more active part in the family's life. Relationships broaden considerably as parents also become PTA members, den mothers, or little-league coaches. This is often a period of relative family tranquility insofar as the child is concerned.

The children's increasing independence also affects the parents. They find that what other parents allow their children to do becomes an important influence on their own children. "Mom, everyone else can do this, why can't I?" becomes a major means for children to try to get their own way.

The children have new ideas, a new vocabulary, and broader desires, all of which can conflict with parental values. Reports about the children's behavior may also come from other parents, teachers, and authorities. How the children are doing at school becomes a source of concern.

Also, children become increasingly expensive as they grow. They eat more, their clothes cost more, and money is needed for school and leisure activities.

Yet for most families the elementary school years go smoothly. Children become more interesting, more individual, and increasingly independent. More important for the parents is their own increased freedom because the children are now away from home for part of the day.

During this time it is especially important for parents to work together in childrearing. By this time children are aware and insightful and can work their parents against one another to achieve their ends unless the parents coordinate. Children can cause conflict between their parents, particularly if the parents differ widely in their philosophy of childrearing.

Latency refers to the general sexual quietness of this stage, although there is more sexual activity than Freud or Erikson thought.

The Puberty-Adolescence Stage: Identity versus Role Diffusion (Twelve to Eighteen Years of Age)

Puberty
Biological changes a child goes through to become an adult capable of reproduction

Adolescence
The general social as well as biological changes a child experiences in becoming an adult

The tranquility of the elementary school years is often shattered by the arrival of puberty. The internal physiological revolution causes children to requestion many earlier adjustments. **Puberty** signifies the biological changes every child, regardless of culture, must pass through to mature sexually. **Adolescence** is a broader term that encompasses puberty as well as the social and cultural conditions that must be met to become an adult. The adolescent period in Western societies tends to be exaggerated and prolonged, with a great deal of ambiguity and marked inconsistencies of role. Adolescents are often confused about proper behavior and what is expected of them. They are not yet adults but at the same time not allowed to remain children. For example, an eighteen-year-old boy may enter the armed services and participate in battle, yet in many states he may not legally drink beer. The fact that prolonged adolescence is a cultural artifact does not lessen the problems of the period.

The problems of puberty and adolescence fall into four main categories:

1. Accepting a new body image and appropriate sexual expression.
2. Establishing independence and a sense of personal identity.
3. Forming good peer group relations.
4. Developing goals and a philosophy of life.

It is during this stage that peer influence becomes stronger than parental influence. What friends say is more important than what parents say. The major problem facing parents now is how to give up their control, how to have enough faith in the child to "let go."

Parents, entering the midyears of their lives, are also facing problems of requestioning and reordering their lives (see Chapter 13). They must begin to think about coping with the "empty-nest" period of their lives as their adolescent children grow into young adulthood and leave home to establish their own families.

The Young Adulthood Stage: Intimacy versus Isolation

Although some children leave the family in their late teens, many remain longer, especially if they choose to go on to higher education. Seeking a vocation and a mate are the major goals of this period. In the past, success in these two tasks ended children's dependence on the family. Today, however, parents often continue to support their children for several more years of schooling and may sometimes support a beginning family if a child marries during school. This can be a financially strained period for the family. In addition, studies indicate that the presence in the home of unmarried sons and daughters over eighteen can be a strain on their parents' relationship. Both husbands and wives often report that this period when older children are living at home is a dissatisfying time in their marriage.

TRY TO SEE IT MY WAY. I AM NEARLY TWENTY AND IF I WAS EVER GOING TO MAKE THE BREAK NOW WAS THE TIME TO DO IT IMAGINE HALF MY GIRL FRIENDS WERE ALREADY SEPARATED FROM THEIR HUSBANDS AND HERE I WAS STILL LIVING AT HOME!

SO I TOLD MY PARENTS I WAS MOVING OUT

THEN I SLEPT ON TOP OF THE BED SO I WOULDN'T WRINKLE ANY SHEETS. SNEAKED SOME BREAKFAST IN THE MORNING AND GOT OUT BEFORE ANYONE WAS UP.

I'VE BEEN LIVING THAT WAY FOR TWO MONTHS NOW.

YOU CAN'T IMAGINE THE YELLING AND SCREAMING MY FATHER SAID "YOU'RE BREAKING YOUR MOTHER'S HEART!" MY MOTHER SAID "WHAT WAS MY CRIME? WHAT WAS MY TERRIBLE CRIME?"

AND BEFORE I KNEW IT WE WERE IN THE MIDDLE OF A BIG ARGUMENT AND I TOLD THEM THEY BOTH NEEDED ANALYSIS AND THEY TOLD ME I HAD A FILTHY MOUTH AND SUDDENLY I WAS OUT ON THE STREET WITH MY RAINCOAT, MY SUITCASE AND MY TENNIS RACKET BUT I HAD NO PLACE TO MOVE!

SO I LOOKED AROUND DOWNTOWN AND EVERYTHING WAS TOO EXPENSIVE AND EVENING CAME AND ALL MY GIRL FRIENDS HAD RECONCILED WITH THEIR HUSBANDS SO THERE WAS ABSOLUTELY NO PLACE I COULD SPEND THE NIGHT

WELL, FRANKLY WHAT ON EARTH COULD I DO? I WAITED TILL IT WAS WAY PAST MY PARENTS BEDTIME - THEN I SNEAKED BACK INTO THE HOUSE AND SET THE ALARM IN MY BEDROOM FOR SIX THE NEXT MORNING.

EVERY NIGHT AFTER MIDNIGHT I SNEAK INTO MY BEDROOM, SLEEP ON TOP OF THE BED TILL SIX THE NEXT MORNING, HAVE BREAKFAST AND SNEAK OUT

AND EVERY DAY I CALL UP MY PARENTS FROM THE DOWNSTAIRS DRUGSTORE AND THEY YELL AND CRY AT ME TO COME BACK. BUT, OF COURSE, I ALWAYS TELL THEM NO.

I'LL NEVER GIVE UP MY INDEPENDENCE.

John is twenty, living at home with his parents, William and Jan. John works and contributes a little toward the food budget. However, his parents find that his living at home strains their relationship. John has a new car and insists that because it is new, it should have a place in the garage. His father often transports clients in his car, and though it is older he feels that it must be parked inside so it remains clean. Jan often intercedes in her son's behalf, "Oh, William, it's his first car, let him use the garage." This angers William, and he sometimes feels as though it's two against one. He also has wanted a den for years and would like to convert John's bedroom into one. When he encourages John to look for his own place, Jan feels that he is "just throwing him out." "We should be happy that he wants to be with us." However, Jan does find it difficult when John has his friends over. They take the living room and television, leaving her and William with little to do but retreat to their bedroom.

Ideally, by the time their children are grown, parents like and love them and take pride in a job well done. Now, after twenty or more years the marital relationship again concerns just two people, husband and wife. Sometimes parents discover that their relationship has been forfeited because of the urgency of parenthood. In this case they face a period of discovery and rediscovery, of building a new relationship between the husband and wife, or of emptiness. Parents must work to maintain their relationship all through the period of childrearing. If they fail to do this, their relationship may become simply "for the children." In this case when the children leave, there may be no relationship between the husband and wife (see Chapter 13).

Broader Parenting

Perhaps the dissatisfaction and decreased marital happiness felt by some parents result from the American nuclear family where one father and one mother are expected to give a child total parenting: all the care, love, and attention that is necessary for healthy growth. But most societies, including America historically, do not expect one father and one mother to supply 100 percent of a child's needs. Grandmothers and grandfathers, aunts and uncles (blood relatives or not), older siblings, and many others also supply parenting to children.

In many American suburban families, children and their parents (especially children and their mothers) are basically alone together. The parents cannot get away from the small child for a needed rest and participation in adult activities, nor can the child get away from the parents. The nuclear family often is too isolated from friends and relatives who occasionally might serve as substitute parents. For example, consider Susan and her mother:

> Susan and her mother have always disagreed but recently, with puberty, the conflict has intensified to such a point that the entire family is in constant turmoil. Susan and her mother simply cannot communicate at this time. Susan feels that her mother doesn't understand her, and her mother feels that Susan is too defensive to talk to and won't listen. Susan says her mother is old-fashioned and behind the times. Her mother feels that Susan lacks respect for her elders and is insensitive to others in general.
>
> Susan relies on her girlfriends for advice. Yet she needs a female adult with whom she can communicate her fear and anxieties about becoming an adult and from whom she can learn. In the past Susan could have turned to a grandmother or an aunt who lived in the family or nearby.

What if parents find they can't be good parents for a particular child? The child will be trapped in the setting for years. Again, in the past this child could possibly have lived with relatives who, by temperament, might be better suited to act as his or her parents. Children were sometimes traded between families for short periods, spent summers on a farm, were helped to grow by numerous adults and older children. This extended family meant that no one person or couple was responsible for total parenting. Some critics of the nuclear family suggest that the nuclear family pattern of parents and children always alone together contributes to creating problems in children rather than preventing them. Inasmuch as the reality of the nuclear family is the only reality small children may know, they cannot correct misperceptions. Because they have no other basis by which to compare how adults act, it is difficult for them to recognize problems and to reorient themselves.

Broader parenting might be supplied by trading care of children with other families, volunteer community nursery schools, business-supplied day-care centers for workers, and expanding the nuclear family to again include relatives. Volunteering to work in a community nursery is also a way for prospective parents to gain experience with children.

Parents without Pregnancy: Adoption

We usually think of adoption as the resort of a couple who cannot conceive children. However, there are many other reasons for adoption. A couple may not be able to care for their children, for example, so friends or relatives may adopt the children in order to give them a home. Or a couple may feel strongly about the problems of overpopulation and decide to adopt rather than add to the population. Or a husband or wife may wish to adopt their spouse's other children by a prior marriage in order to become their legal parent as well as their stepparent.

The choice to adopt a child is just that, a reasoned decision, a choice made by a couple after a great deal of deliberation and thought. As such the decision-making process leading to adoption makes an ideal model that all couples desiring children can follow. Adoption takes time, and certain requirements such as family stability, finances, and housing must be met by the prospective parents.

Adoptive parents have some advantages as well as disadvantages compared with natural parents. For example, adoptive parents may choose

Some families adopt cross-racially.

their child. To some degree they may pick genetic, physical and mental characteristics of the child. They may bypass some of the earlier years of childhood if they desire. On the other hand, they do not experience pregnancy and birth, which help to focus the couple on impending parenthood. Of course, some may consider this another advantage of adoption.

A unique parenting problem faced by adoptive parents is that of deciding whether to share the knowledge of adoption with the child and if so, when? Experts believe the best course is to inform the child from the beginning, but this is sometimes difficult for parents to do. They may fear that such information will affect the child's love for them. They may want to tell them but simply keep avoiding it until it seems too late. Most adoption agencies, such as The Children's Home Society, supply counseling to prospective adoptive parents on how to handle telling the child. The problems created for both parents and children if the children find out about their adoptive status from others are usually greater and often do harm to the parent/child relationship. The basic trust of the children in their parents may be weakened or perhaps even destroyed if the parents aren't the ones to tell them.

At some time in their lives many adoptive children feel the need to know something about their natural parents. In most legal adoptions, however, records identifying the true parents are unavailable. Some adults who were adopted as children are pressuring states to make information about their real parents available. A few states are moving toward opening adoption records to adopted persons when they reach legal age.

For many years legal adoption was a drawn-out process wherein prospective parents went through a strenuous screening process to establish their parental suitability. Recently such screening has been minimized and the long wait for an adoptive child reduced. Also, in a few cases, especially with older children, single persons are being allowed to adopt.

Adoption works to give parentless children a home and family as well as to give childless couples children. Unfortunately, not all parentless children are easily adoptable. Many minority children are never adopted. Children with defects and health problems seldom are sought by prospective adoptive parents. For the most part such children are reared in various kinds of institutions or by a series of short-term foster home placements.

The Single-Parent Family

The single-parent family is the fastest growing family form in the United States. In 1982 about 13.7 million children (25 percent of all children) lived with only one parent, 66 percent more than in 1970 (12 percent of all children). Of these children living with one parent, 90 percent lived with their mothers and 10 percent with their fathers. This proportion has remained constant over the past several decades.

The racial distribution of single-parent households is disproportionate. In white households having children, 19 percent were headed by one parent, as were 31 percent of Spanish-origin households, whereas 53 percent, just over half, of black households had only one parent present.

Single-parent families derive from a number of sources. The largest percentage of one-parent families result from divorce. In 1981, of the children who lived only with their mothers, 41 percent had a mother who was divorced, 25 percent had a mother who was separated, and 19 percent had a mother who had never married. One-parent families also result from the death of a parent (U.S. Bureau of the Census, May 1983).

The increase in single-parent families is due mainly to the rapid increase in divorce rates over the past decade. The number of children with divorced mothers has doubled since 1970. Although the actual number of children is far smaller, the number with a never-married mother has tripled. This dramatic change is not really a great increase in illegitimacy but rather a dramatic increase in the number of unwed mothers who opt to keep their child (94 percent of adolescent unwed mothers). The so-called teenage pregnancy epidemic of the 1970s turns out to be more of a teenage baby-keeping epidemic (Scharf, 1979). And because these mothers had been a major source of babies for adoption agencies, such agencies are now having a difficult time finding enough children to keep up with the demand.

As we have noted, the rising divorce rate has been the major contributing factor to the increase in single-parent families. Beginning in 1975, however, the divorce rate began to level out (Chapter 14), and so we can expect the rate of increase of single-parent families to also show a decline. Remember also that single-parent families tend to be transitional because marriage rates for single parents are high (Reiss, 1980).

Although family form (single-parent, nuclear, three-generation, foster, and so forth) affects children, the old idea that *only* the traditional two-parent, father/mother family does a good job in rearing children is passing (Marotz-Baden et al., 1979). However, there is little doubt that single parenting has more inherent problems than does two-parent childrearing. In many ways the problems of the single-parent family are exaggerated duplicates of the working mother's problems.

The majority of single-parent families are women and their children. Thus for them all of the problems encountered by the working mother are present (see Chapter 8). Low pay, child-care problems, overburden caused by working and continuing to shoulder household and childrearing duties face the single mother. The single father may face these same problems, except that his pay is usually better. A problem that most fathers face is that the home and child-care burdens are new and, at first, often frightening.

Single-parent families headed by women with small earning power suffer numerous logistic problems. Caring for small children during working hours without exorbitant cost is a major concern. Finding adequate housing in a satisfactory neighborhood is often impossible. Even in small cities female-headed families are concentrated in less desirable blocks of the city (Roncek, Bell & Chaldin, 1980). Larger amounts of welfare aid go

Basic Parenting, the Working Mother, and the Single-Parent Family

Education, particularly character formation, is the essential family task, for the obvious reason that children are first formed by families. If the family does not lay the needed psychic foundation, then it falls to the schools to try to do it. To date, however, the schools have not been an adequate substitute for the family in the forming of basic character in the young.

For the educational mission of the family, character formation, it *is* essential to have active and involved parenthood, accorded sufficient time and commitment, at least for the children's formative years, especially from birth until age six but preferably until the end of adolescence. What children require above all are parents who care and who educate, who have a commitment to parenting and the energy to back up their commitment, and who have a relationship to emulate. Hence parents who are overworked, habitually drunk or drugged, or consumed by their own personal problems are unable to provide effective basic parenting.

Basic parenting *does* tend to conflict with both parents' working full time outside the home, therefore basic parenting for the single parent often is nearly impossible. In any other industry if you remove a million employees without reducing the job requirements very much, nobody would deny that the industry is woefully shorthanded. If we take a million women out of a million households—as we have to work outside of home—and replace them with precious little in child-care services, few baby-sitters, and little more grandparenting, then the parenting "industry" is woefully shorthanded (and television sets and the streets are overworked). This is not an argument for women to stay home and do parenting, but for *someone* to do more of it (Etzioni, 1983). It is estimated that there were more than 6.5 million "latchkey kids" in 1983. These are children who must fend for themselves because they have no parenting adults at home much of the time (Long, 1983).

As part of the ideology that tries to legitimate absent parenting, it has been argued that "quality" counts; that if you cannot spend much time with your child, you can make up for this by making the minutes you do provide "count." Pop psychologists who promote this notion do not cite any data to show that one can make minutes into quality time on order. Indeed, it is more plausible that quality time occurs when one has longer stretches of "quantity" time. Most important, there is no evidence that quality time can make up for long stretches of no time, of parental absence (Etzioni, 1983).

In general the increasing incidence of both parents' working and greater numbers of single-parent families mean that the chances for successful parenting are reduced and that lack of character development in America's children may soon become the nation's number one problem if it isn't already.

to these families than to any others, which is indicative of the financial difficulties they face.

Social isolation is one of the problems faced by any single parent. Juggling work, home maintenance, and child-care duties usually leaves one little time for either social interaction or self-improvement activities. Emotional isolation is a second major problem. Having no other adult in the home with whom to interact often leads to feelings of loneliness and a sense of powerlessness. If one is a separated or divorced unmarried parent, emotional isolation may be increased by the social stigma that is sometimes attached to these statuses. The early-widowed parent, on the other hand, will experience sympathy and support from society.

Many single parents attempt to alleviate the isolation as well as reduce living expenses by making greater use of shared living arrangements. One study indicates that 23 percent of the single-parent sample had a second adult (usually a relative) living in the household, whereas only 9 percent of the two-parent families shared their household with another adult (Smith, 1980).

The Adolescent Parent

Single adolescent parents face all of these problems while they themselves are still working toward self-identity, maturity, and attaining worthwhile vocational skills.*

A study using 1000 thirty-year-olds selected from the 1960 Project Talent participants found that 10 percent of the men and 31 percent of the women had a child during adolesence. Higher incidences of adolescent parenting occurred among blacks and low socioeconomic and low ability groups. Adolescent parenting appeared to negatively affect a number of aspects of the individual's life.

The most immediate consequence of adolescent parenting was termination of school attendance. This directly affected employability so that the adolescent parents were still employed in lower paying jobs at age thirty compared with nonadolescent parents in the sample.

Having children at a young age also appears to be related to marital dissolution. In a recent study 21 percent of the adolescent parents were or had been separated or divorced compared with 11 percent of the entire sample (Russ-Eft, Sprenger & Beever, 1979).

Many studies have been done on the consequences of early childbearing. The results of these studies have been summarized by Chilman (1980b) under two headings: consequences for teenage parents and consequences for the children of adolescent parents.

Consequences for Teenage Parents   Teenage childbearing is a major factor in dropping out of high school. Adolescent mothers tend to do poorly in school and have low interest in school before pregnancy occurs. Despite efforts by high schools to encourage pregnant students to continue their education, pregnancy often triggers school drop out. However, half or more of these dropouts do return to school in later life, often in early middle age.

Larger family size is also likely if the first birth occurs before the mother is age seventeen, particularly if she is black and married. The majority of unmarried adolescent parents marry within a few years of the first child's birth, but such early marriages are more prone to later disruption than are later marriages.

---

*About 60 percent of all unwed mothers are teenagers (Honig, 1978).

It is interesting to note that women who have been adolescent mothers are especially apt to be welfare dependent compared with the general population. On the other hand, the availability of welfare assistance helps such mothers to return to school.

Consequences for Children of Adolescent Parents   Cognitive development seems to be lower for the children of adolescent mothers, with sons more adversely affected than daughters. This tends to show up in reduced school performance. Such lowered development seems to be reduced if there is another adult in the home. A higher percentage of these children (9 percent) tend to be slower in overall development when compared with other children (4 percent). There is also a slight tendency for these children to repeat the parental pattern of early childbearing and/or marriage, as well as to have large families.

Perhaps the greatest objection to adolescent parenthood is the fact that the parents assume responsibilities and obligations before they themselves are complete individuals. Their chances for self-growth through extended education, travel, and broadened experiences are reduced because of their parenting responsibilities. One purpose of the usual prolonged adolescence in America has been to allow young persons some freedom from adult responsibilities so that they can concentrate on their own personal development. "To go as far as you can," "to make the most of yourself" are American ideals sought for the young. Very early parenthood almost always works against such ideals.

Summary

Parenthood remains one of the major functions of marriage. Despite decreasing emphasis on it and more tolerance of childlessness for married couples, the majority of married couples will become parents.

Planning for parenthood, improving parenting skills, working as a parent team, and understanding the course of development a child passes through in becoming an adult are all important to successful parenting. In addition, understanding how children will affect the parental relationship is crucial. No one method has yet been discovered whereby parents can assure the successful upbringing of their children. The fact is that parenthood is a difficult and everchanging job that demands intelligence, flexibility, emotional warmth, and stability as well as a goodly portion of courage.

Children will affect their parents in many ways. Bringing the first baby home immediately changes the lifestyle of the parents. Suddenly they have a dependent and demanding person to take care of who, at first, contributes little to the family. Not only is room taken up in the family's living place, but additional funds are needed to care for the new family member. Dad and Mom will both come second to the infant's demands. Although one can divorce a troublesome spouse, there is little that parents can do to escape a troublesome child. Legally and morally, children are the parents' responsibility until they reach legal adulthood. Even then, parents in many cases will still shoulder responsibility for their children, for example when they go to graduate school.

Erik Erikson identifies eight psychosocial developmental stages that describe the human life cycle from infancy through old age. The first six are important to parents. They are the oral-sensory stage (first year), the muscular-anal stage (two to three years), the locomotor-genital stage (four to five years), the latency stage (six to eleven years), the puberty-adolescence stage (twelve to eighteen years), and the young adulthood stage (eighteen to thirty, approximately). Each stage has certain tasks that the child must accomplish to become a successful adult. By knowing at what stage a child is and the kinds of tasks that characterize the stage, parents can better understand the child and plan activities that are optimally helpful.

Broader parenting would help parents to do a better job. Having alternative sources of parenting available would serve a number of helpful purposes. First, parents would have time-out periods from their children. This would allow them to concentrate for a short period on themselves and their relationship and would give them a respite from the burdens and responsibilities of the children. Second, the children would have a broader set of influences and greater stimulation. They would also learn to cope with new and different kinds of people. In general their experience base would be broader.

Adoption is another avenue to parenthood. It has the advantages of contributing to population control as well as allowing parents greater choice in selection of the children they want. It does, however, have the difficulty of having to tell the children that they are adopted.

The single-parent family, although usually transitory, is more common today than ever before. Such a family faces many problems, but with support is capable of doing a good childrearing job. Adolescent parents also face special problems, the main one being that the parents themselves are still in the process of becoming fully functioning adults and parenthood tends to make this job harder.

Parenthood is an important part of most marriages. Good planning will help make parenthood a positive factor in marriages.

SCENES FROM MARRIAGE

Television as a Surrogate Parent

In most American homes three parents mind the children: the father, the mother, and television. Indeed with the increasing incidence of single-parent (especially mother only) families, television has perhaps replaced father for a good many children. Certainly it can be said of the generations born in the 1960s or later that they are a product of the television age.

By age sixteen most children in the United States have spent more time watching television than going to school (Liebert & Poulas, 1975; Singer, 1983). The average child watches two to six hours of television every day (Liebert, Neale & Davidson, 1973; Singer, 1983).

What effects does all of this TV viewing have on children? Everyone is interested in the answers to this question, even the federal government. For example, in 1968 after the assassination of Robert Kennedy, President Johnson formed a commission to inquire into the relationship between violence and mass media (mainly television). The commission's report, titled *Task Force on Mass Media and Violence*, concluded that the short-range effect on those who see violent acts portrayed on television is that they learn to perform such acts and may imitate them in a similar situation. Over the long term exposure to media violence socializes audiences into the norms, attitudes, and values of violence.

Over the years there has been a great deal of research on this violence question as well as on television's overall effect on viewers. As yet the answers remain somewhat unclear and equivocal. For instance, recent research (Singer, Singer & Sherrod, 1979; Singer & Singer, 1981) on three-

and four-year-olds attending nursery school correlated their behavior during free play — their imaginativeness, emotionality, aggression, cooperation, interaction, and mood — with their parents' reports of television watching by the child. A strong relationship was found between frequent physical aggression and frequent viewing of all but educational children's programs. Viewing of educational programs, on the other hand, was found to be related to prosocial behavior and to using mature language in school. This research example reflects the mixed findings about television viewing that emerge from current research. The one clear fact that emerges is that television is indeed an important influence on children and is, *perhaps*, as influential as are parents themselves (Rubinstein, 1983).

It is also clear that television is affecting the whole American society, not just the children. For example, in a recent Florida murder case a fifteen-year-old was convicted of killing his elderly neighbor despite the plea of "involuntary subliminal television intoxication." On a worldwide level it is obvious too that many terrorist acts are perpetrated to bring media attention to the people or the "cause" espoused by the terrorist group (Schorr, 1981).

If the conclusions of the various government studies about the relationship between violence and observed violence on television are correct, then those raised on television will have problems with violence control. It is estimated that by the time of high school graduation, the average American young person will have seen 18,000 televised murders (Brody,

TABLE 12-3

	NETWORK	ACTS OF VIOLENCE PER HOUR
Prime-Time Shows		
Walking Tall	NBC	25
Vegas	ABC	18
Lobo	NBC	18
Greatest American Hero	ABC	18
Incredible Hulk	CBS	14
Magnum P.I.	CBS	14
Hart to Hart	ABC	14
Dukes of Hazzard	CBS	14
B.J. and the Bear	NBC	14
Fantasy Island	ABC	11
Saturday Morning Cartoons		
Thundarr the Barbarian	ABC	64
Daffy Duck	NBC	52
Bugs Bunny/Road Runner	CBS	51
Superfriends	ABC	38
Richie Rich/Scooby Doo	ABC	30
Plastiman	ABC	28
Heathcliff and Dingbat	ABC	28
Fonz	ABC	28
Tom and Jerry	CBS	27
Popeye	CBS	26

1975). The National Coalition on Television Violence compiled the data shown in Table 12-3, which was drawn from televised violence between February and May of 1981:

Because television has a strong impact on viewers, especially youthful viewers (even though we don't always know exactly the results on the viewers), it is important for parents to consider its place in their home. What roles should television play? How can it be used to promote prosocial rather than antisocial behavior?

How can it improve children's cognitive development rather than retard it (Carew, 1980)?

A few concerned parents who object to the strong and often negative influence of television on their children opt to have no television. Yet as the children grow and begin to visit friends, this strategy can backfire because the children end up watching at friends' houses, thus limiting parents' control over television input in their childrens' lives. Inasmuch as 95 percent of American homes contain television, the best course of action for parents is to set up supervised viewing for their children. First, parents will need to consider the place of television in their own lives. For instance, if a mother has the TV turned on all day for company while she is alone at home, she will need to decide whether she wants to continue this.

Once the parents determine their own preferences about television's place in their lives, then they will need to set appropriate ground rules for their children. These rules should include:

1. How much time per day, per week the children may devote to television
2. The actual time of the day or evening that television may be watched
3. The kinds of programs that may be watched
4. The amount of adult attention and discussion to be given during and after television viewing (as such parental interaction with the child mitigates the negative effects of viewing)
5. How much to use television as a reward in order to influence other kinds of behavior besides television viewing

The parent who is unwilling or unable to set some controls on his/her children's use of television abrogates parental responsibility, thus leaving television as the main parent influencing the children.

CHAPTER 13

FAMILY LIFE STAGES:
MIDLIFE CRISIS TO SURVIVING SPOUSE

CONTENTS

13

The flush of love and the excitement of exploring a new relationship effectively keep most newly married couples from thinking about later stages of their relationship. After all who can think about children leaving home when no children have yet arrived? What possible relevance can retirement have for a twenty-three-year-old man receiving his first job promotion? And what newly married woman can be thinking about the very real likelihood that she will spend the last ten to fifteen years of her life as a widow, alone and without this man she now loves so much?

Yet, these are important questions with which almost all married couples must come to grips at some time in their lives. Perhaps one way that you can make such questions relevant is to consider them in the context of your parent's and grandparent's lives. We cannot expect to live our lives identically to our relatives' because we are different individuals and the times in which we live change. Yet their lives may serve as a preview for some of the changes that will come into our own lives.

If we have children, then the day will come when our children leave home. This is a change that we will have to face just as did our parents and their parents before them. The couple who thinks about and prepares for these inevitable family life changes before they occur stands a better chance of adapting to them in a creative and growth-oriented manner.

Any family relationship can change, just as individuals within the relationship can and do change. Change does not mean the end of the relationship. Indeed, lack of change over time is usually unhealthy and may ultimately lead to the demise of the relationship.

Marriage changes, just as people change. Change can be for the better or the worse. If a marriage changes too much for the worse, then it may end. On the other hand, individuals and families can grow in positive directions to become stronger, more intimate, more communicative, more need-fulfilling, more supportive, and more loving. Because change cannot be avoided, the real question to answer becomes, "Will I cope with the changes in my life and family in a positive, growth-oriented way?" To answer this question, we must first consider the changes that can be expected.

An Overview of Family Life Stages

Dividing family life into stages will help us gain better understanding of the changes that people go through as they move from birth to death. A developmental stage approach has long been taken in studying children, as we saw in Chapter 12. The prenatal stage, infancy, preschool, school, prepuberty, puberty, adolescence, and young adulthood are all well-known developmental stages in the life of the maturing human.

What about stages in the life of a maturing marriage? If we examine the general kinds of problems faced at various marital stages, we find that for the average American couple there are six important periods in a long-term marriage: (1) newly married, (2) early parenthood, (3) later parenthood, (4) empty nest (middle age), (5) retirement, and (6) widowed singleness.

The problems of the *newly married* stage revolve around adjusting to each other, establishing a home, setting directions to the relationship, learning to confront the world as a pair rather than as individuals, and learning to work together to achieve mutually agreed-on goals. These problems have already been discussed in various parts of preceding chapters.

The arrival of children places a couple in the parental role. This change will compound the problems of a newly married couple, especially if children arrive shortly after marriage, before the couple has had much time to work out the problems of the first stage.

Early parenthood covers pregnancy, birth, infants, toddlers, preschoolers, and elementary school children. When puberty arrives and the children move into junior and senior high school, college, and the young adult world, the problems parents face change drastically. So drastic are the changes that it becomes worthwhile to examine this period in marriage separately — hence the third stage, *later parenthood*. As we saw in Chapter 12, adolescence is actually a combination of puberty — the biological maturing of the child — and the social expectations placed on the child to behave in an adult manner. America, like many western cultures, does not sharply define entrance into adulthood. In fact, the adolescent period in America is nebulous, conflicting and confused because it extends well beyond the achievement of biological maturity. Because of this, many parents find later parenthood to be a trying time. Children become increasingly independent and demanding of freedom, yet parents legally and ethically are still responsible for their children's actions. Finances, too, can be strained, especially if the children go on to higher education. This is also a time for parents of adjusting to their children's adult sexuality and mate selection process, which culminates in the acceptance of a new family as the children marry and reproduce.

Finally, the last child leaves home and the *empty nest* or *middle-age* stage begins. For many couples the parental role continues in that they may still give monetary and psychological support to the newly married children. In the grandparent role as well, parents often continue many parental behaviors because children are still part of the couple's lives at times. For others, especially mothers who were child-centered, the empty-nest stage can be one of loneliness and loss if the children move far away or reject continued parenting. New interests and goals must be developed to replace the lost parenting functions. The husband may need to assist his wife to reorient her life away from the children and this in turn will usually influence his own. Fathers or career-oriented mothers survive this stage more easily than traditional mothers, because many of their goals and fulfillments lie outside the family in the work world. Thus their feelings of loss when the children leave are usually less severe.

The empty-nest stage may be a period during which the husband and wife draw closer. During the earlier marital years many wives devoted their energies to the children, their husbands devoted themselves to their work. Husband and wife may well have grown emotionally apart. Now, when the children are gone may be the time for a couple to renew their life together, to reinvest in one another, to lay the foundation to the next marital stage, *retirement*.

Increasing life expectancy, automation, and America's emphasis on youth have combined to almost double the length of retirement in the average worker's life during this century. The retiring worker faces the problem of adjusting to leisure after years of basing much of his or her self-worth on working and income production. In addition our work ethic says that stature is gained by a work orientation, not leisure. Retirement equals obsolescence in the view of American society. For the productive worker retirement presents the choice: adjust or be miserable.

In a sense retirement for the man is similar to the empty-nest stage for the traditional child-centered wife. It is now he who must cope with lack of purpose and feelings of uselessness. For those who cannot find substitute goals, retirement can be an unhappy period. Indeed, for some it is literally a short-lived period in that death often arrives shortly after retirement for those who cannot seem to adjust. On the other hand, especially for those that have been financially successful, retirement may mean rebirth rather than death. It may signal a new beginning, expanding interests, and rediscovery of the marital partner. Poor health and poverty are the two greatest enemies of the retired. Indeed economic necessity forces some 30 percent of men to continue working after age sixty-five.

Inevitably one of the marital partners dies, and so the final marital stage is usually a return to *widowed singleness*. In 1982 there were about 10.7 million widows in the United States, approximately 5.5 times the 1.9 million widowers (U.S. Bureau of the Census, May 1983). These statistics point clearly to the fact that widowhood is a far greater possibility than is becoming a widower. Although the percentage of widowed persons in the general population has dropped this century, just as with retirement, the number of years that widowed singleness may be expected to last has risen dramatically. For example, half of those women widowed at age sixty-five can expect fifteen more years of life. Thus, especially for women, this final marital stage can be lengthy.

Being widowed is predominantly an older person's problem. For younger widowed persons remarriage is the solution of choice. With advancing age, however, remarriage becomes increasingly remote. In 1975 only 1 percent of brides and 2 percent of grooms were sixty-five years old and over (Glick, 1979). For the widowed person who does remarry, being widowed may not be the last stage of marriage. Remarriage will reinstate an earlier marital stage.

Because we have already discussed in earlier chapters the first three family life stages — newly married and early and later parenthood — we will devote the remainder of this chapter to the last three stages, the empty nest, retirement, and widow/widowerhood.

The Empty Nest: Middlescence

For most couples middle age — the **empty-nest stage** — starts when the children become independent and ends when retirement draws near. Although these figures are arbitrary, most people are in this stage between the ages of forty and sixty.

The Census Bureau uses the age of forty-five to denote the onset of middle age. Better than using an arbitrary age range, however, is to delimit this stage by the kinds of changes and problems that occur. For example, a very young mother might face empty-nest changes by the time she is thirty-five years old.

Historically, middle age is a relatively new stage in marriage. For persons born in 1900, life expectancy was about forty-seven years. Today, life expectancy for women is 77.7 years and about 70 for men. The much shorter life spans before 1900 made it such that most wives buried their husbands before the last child left home. As Paul Glick points out:

> In 1890 women bore their last child at thirty-two, buried their husband at age fifty-three and attended their last child's wedding at age fifty-five. (1955, p. 4)

> In 1975 women bore their last child at age thirty, attended their last child's wedding at fifty-two, and buried their husband at age sixty-five. (1977, p. 6)

Thus for most marriages before 1900, there was no period of return to simply being a couple again. Yet today such a period is not only likely, but the chances are great that it will last for fifteen to twenty years.

The changes faced during middle age can be somewhat different for men and women. If the woman has not had a career, her adjustment centers on no longer being needed by her children, whereas the man's problems usually revolve around his vocation and feelings of achievement and success.

For both partners, however, middle age reactivates many of the questions that each thought had been answered much earlier in their lives. Indeed many of the questions that arise resemble those struggled with when the partners were adolescents: "Who am I?" "Where am I going?" "How will I get there?" "What is life all about?" "How do I handle my changing sexuality?" Hence the term **middlescence** has been coined to describe this stage.

Writers who compare middle age with adolescence and who discover an identity crisis in both periods disagree over what this crisis means (Kerckhoff, 1976). Some see middle age characterized by trying to avoid the recurring bizarre, irrational, sexually confused questions that first occurred at adolescence (McMorrow, 1974). Others suggest that although middle age may be frustrating and upsetting, such problems can also be growth producing:

> There are significant parallels between adolescence and middle age. The task of the adolescent is to integrate into life not only his sexuality but the powerful resurgence of idealism. . . . Now in middle life there is a sudden breaking through of this suppressed and neglected . . . element in life. . . . We come

Empty-nest stage
Period in a marriage that begins when the last child leaves home and continues until either spouse retires or dies

Middlescence
The second adolescence experienced in middle age, usually involving reevaluation of one's life

A December-May
relationship.

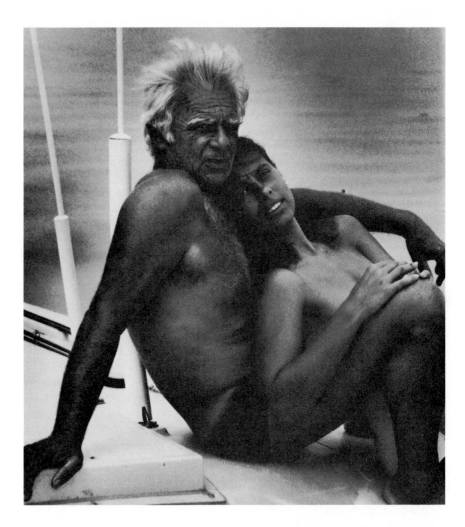

then to the central question. *What is the second half of life for?* Man has always asked himself "What are we here for?" "What is the purpose of life?" "What is our prime duty?" But in practice, ordinary people find that the cares of bringing up a family obliterate these philosophical questions. We are too busy earning our livings and running our homes and caring for our children. We have no doubt that this is our duty and purpose in life. It is when the children go that the ancient (existential) questions become acutely personal for the second half of life. (Brayshaw, 1962, p. 360)

Those suggesting that the crisis of middle age is useful say: "Middlescence is the opportunity for going on with the identity crisis of the first adolescence. It is our second chance to find out what it really means to 'do your own thing,' to sing your own song, to be deeply true to yourself. It is a time for finding one's own truths at last, and thereby to become free to discover one's real identity" (LeShan, 1973). In describing the pain and danger that middle-aged people will experience in reexamining their identities, Eda LeShan compares the process with a lobster's periodic shedding of its shell: It makes the lobster vulnerable, but allows it to grow.

For some, then, it is no wonder that they choose to use their marriage as an escape from facing the existential challenges of middle age. They do not ask the important questions because it is safer to assume that marriage is answer enough. "Who am I?" "I am Mr. or Mrs. Jones." "What is my life all about?" "I am a wife or husband." "I do my duty to the family and help keep it running smoothly." "Where am I going?" "We hope to take a trip to Cape Cod next summer." "My marriage is the answer to all existential questions." "My marriage is my existence."

But to the couples who take the risk, the crisis of middle age can offer a chance to grow, and its problems can become a vehicle for growth. Marriage enrichment for the middle-aged couple is not to be focused on the improvement of marriage so much as on the improvement of the humans in it. According to LeShan (1973):

> One of the most valuable attributes of marriage is that one's partner can truly be one's best friend, and friendship was never more important. If one defines a friend as someone who loves you in spite of knowing your faults and weaknesses, and has even better dreams for your fulfillment than you have for yourself, it can surely be the foundation for what each of us needs most in middle age — permission to continue to quest for one's own identity.

It is not so much what actually happens to us in middle age as it is our attitude about it that really counts. We all experience some kind of crisis in this as in other stages, but how do we use the crisis? If we use it for further growth and expansion of our lives, then our marriage, our relationships, and we ourselves may all benefit and make the second half of our lives even more fulfilling than the first half.

The Authenticity Crisis of Midlife

Speaking of the **midlife crisis** Gail Sheehy writes:

> Deep down a change begins to register in those gut-level perceptions of safety and danger, time and no time, aliveness and stagnation. I start with a vague feeling. . . .
>
> I have reached some sort of meridian in my life. I had better take a survey, reexamine where I have been, and reevaluate how I am going to spend my resources from here on. Why am I doing all this? What do I really believe in?
>
> Underneath this vague feeling is the fact, as yet unacknowledged, that there is a down side to life, a back of the mountain, and that I have only so much time before the dark to find my own truth. As such thoughts grow, the continuity of the life cycle is disrupted. Somewhere between thirty-five and forty-five if we let ourselves, most of us will have a full-out authenticity crisis. (1977, p. 350)

Midlife crisis
The questioning of one's worth and values, usually beginning sometime in one's forties or early fifties

There is infinite variety in the way individuals face the questions that arise when they realize that life is finite. Some people simply look the other way and avoid the questions. Others try to change their external world by relocating, finding a new spouse or a new job. Others seek internal changes such as a new set of values or a new philosophy of life.

Obviously a person's life circumstances influence the questions and their answers. A child-centered mother out of the occupational world for twenty years may feel panic as she realizes that she will soon be unneeded by her children. Another mother who has always worked in addition to raising her children may be happy that her children will no longer need her, thus freeing some time to pursue long-neglected interests. Because of these individual differences, our discussion of the midlife changes must remain general. Some individuals will experience the things we discuss, others may not, and yet others may experience things that are not discussed. Despite these limitations it is worthwhile to examine the middle years of life, because we will all pass through them.

For the traditional wife and mother, the midlife crisis will revolve around the growing independence of her children and finally their move from home. She has to face her partial failure as a parent. She faces feelings of loss and uselessness because she is no longer needed. Her feelings are somewhat akin to the man's feelings when he retires. She often faces reentry to the work world where she may not have used her skills for twenty years. She faces a renewal of her earlier "pair" relationship. She faces the biological boundary of the end of her childbearing years. "No more children even if I wanted them." This and the accent on youth in America will cause her to reevaluate her sexuality, asking: "Am I still attractive to men?" "Is there more to sex than I have experienced?" She, as well as her husband, will become aware of death in a personal way as one of their parents and then the other dies. This event causes many people to direct their thoughts for the first time to the inescapableness of death, to realize that their lives will end too. In addition to these changes, American women must now face the questions of changing identity and roles aroused by the women's movement.

Thus we see that the midlife changes faced by women are broad and profound. And both the woman and her husband face the turmoil within each other created by this stage. If her husband is unhappy and dissatisfied with his work, this adds to her own crisis. If she decides to actively embrace the women's liberation movement, this may add to the stress and strain felt by her husband.

The typical husband's midlife crisis revolves around his work world rather than around his family. This is particularly true for the highly successful man. In a competitive economic society such as ours, a person must devote a great deal of energy to his or her work to achieve success. The male is often forced to handle two marriages, the first to his work and the second (in importance also) to his family.

Thus his midlife crisis centers on letting go of the impossible dream of youth. He begins to recognize that not all of his dreams will be achieved. For those few men who have fulfilled their dreams, the midlife question becomes, "What do I do now?" Most men, however, must cope with disillusionment. The feeling that the dream was counterfeit, the vague feeling of having been cheated, "the dream isn't really what I thought it would be," and the growing awareness that perhaps "I won't ever achieve my dreams" are the questions that cause turmoil.

America's emphasis on youth will also cause the man problems. "If I haven't achieved it by now, I won't get any more chances." Younger

Changing Careers at Midlife

Five years ago Jane and Bill Smith and their two older children left their home in Santa Barbara where they were a mathematician and a teacher, respectively. Now they're back as a physician and lawyer-to-be. Bill, an internist with a local medical group, used to be a systems analyst with a large research and development firm. Jane is scheduled to take her bar exam early this year after having taught elementary school for years.

"I read about a program at the University of Miami where they retrain people with Ph.D.s in the biological sciences to become M.D.s," said Bill. "There was at the time a plethora of Ph.D.s and a lack of M.D.s. Then they let a few people in with degrees in the physical sciences"—he has a doctorate in math—"and discovered that they did just as well."

He spent two years in the accelerated medical school program, which he calls the time of "learning the language," then three years in a Veteran's Administration hospital for his internship and residency, "where I really learned to be a doctor."

Bill said he'd never been exposed much to the hospital environment until he began singing in a barbershop quartet, which was often invited to entertain in rest homes and hospitals. He said he'd had the field of medicine "in the back of my mind" for a long time before he applied. He thought that medicine would be a more self-sufficient career than computers.

"I enjoy the work itself. I never took math home. Nobody cares about the answers except people in the field. However, I never get tired of medicine. When I get home, I get out the medical journals and the texts."

"I knew there'd be 700 applicants and only 28 selected so I didn't get my hopes up. They called for an interview, and three weeks later called again to say that I was 29th, the 'first alternate.' I figured that they told this to many people, so we bought a ping-pong table and settled back into our old routine."

Classes began in Miami on July 1. On July 5, after an afternoon of tennis, the couple arrived home to a telephone call from Miami asking, "Can you come tomorrow?" A student had dropped out making room for the first alternate.

Making a quick decision, he packed up and left the next day, leaving Jane to sell the house and furniture plus complete a summer job that she had undertaken.

Bill said the only courses he had in undergraduate school that applied to medical school were a year in chemistry and a course in physiology. But based on his medical school test scores, the lack of preliminary courses wasn't too difficult a problem. "Math training involves more rational thought and medicine is simply more memorization at first."

During his residency his wife took the opportunity to go to law school. When they returned to Santa Barbara she did some volunteer work in the consumer fraud division of the district attorney's office. "Now I'm spending all my time studying for the bar," she said.

As a teacher Jane said she "was always interested in the political side of teaching. I'm interested in educational law—children's rights, parents' and teachers' rights. I don't think anyone is working in that area here." She said that she was considering this career change even before Bill made his change.

For both spouses to make such dramatic midlife changes is certainly unusual. Yet this true story points out that families can make major and dramatic changes and survive and be rejuvenated.

competitive men can become a threat to job security. The subtle comments about retirement may take on a personal significance.

Unfortunately, this dream disillusionment usually carries over into the man's family. He doubts himself, he doubts his family. He may even blame them for his failure to achieve the dreams of his youth. "If it hadn't been for the family burdens, I'd have made it."

Along with general self-doubts come doubts about sexuality. Unlike his wife's, though, these doubts usually revolve less around physical attractiveness. They occur at a time when his wife's sexuality is at its highest peak and revolve around performance. This, combined with women's liberation influencing his wife to be more aware and assertive of her own sexuality, can make his self-doubts extremely strong. Self-doubt can be the male's greatest enemy to satisfactory sexual relations.

In some cases a rather interesting partial exchange of roles takes place at this time of life. The woman becomes more interested in the world outside her family. She becomes more responsive to her own aggressiveness and competitive feelings. She returns to the work world, to school, to an interest in public affairs and causes. Her husband becomes more receptive to his long-repressed affiliative and loving promptings. He renews his interest in the family and in social issues outside of his work. He becomes more caring in the way that mother has been caring within the family. Unfortunately, the children are no longer receptive to his new-found parental caring since they are busy seeking their own independence (Zube, 1982).

Overall, then, for both a man and a woman, midlife usually means rethinking and reevaluating one's life. It is a time of restructuring. The resulting turmoil may destroy the marriage and family or it may result in a revitalized marriage. By recognizing and squarely confronting the issues of midlife, the chances increase that the results will be positive and growth producing rather than negative and destructive.

Retirement

Retirement usually signals the beginning of disengagement. In many nonindustrialized societies this is a gradual process. The hardest physical labor is performed by young men and women at the peak of their physical condition. As they age and their own offspring grow to maturity, they assume more administrative and supervisory duties while their children take on the harder physical labor. Ideally, the following generation is ready to take over by the time the parental generation begins to slow down. To some extent this gradual tapering off of duties and the smooth transition of tasks from one generation to the next was done on the farm in rural America.

By contrast, in the American urban setting retirement is usually abrupt, based on reaching a certain arbitrary age or having worked for some specified number of years. In a sense age categories of employability are

created (Winch, 1971). For example, child labor laws hold the child out of the labor force, whereas mandatory retirement plans force older workers out of the labor market at an arbitrary age. In 1979, changes in retirement laws raised the earliest time that mandatory retirement can become effective from 65 years to 70 years.

The abruptness of retirement can cause severe adjustment problems for the newly unneeded worker. The woman in the traditional mothering role faces her retirement at the earlier empty-nest stage. For her, though, retirement comes gradually as one by one her children gain independence. The working spouse, on the other hand, is suddenly placed in a totally new role. After forty to fifty years of going to work, they receive a gold watch and pats on the back and are told to go fishing and enjoy their new leisure time (and feelings of uselessness). They are thrust into a new lifestyle that for most retirees is characterized by less income, declining health, and increasing loneliness. They miss their colleagues and the status that was derived from their job. The common question asked by a new acquaintance, "What do you do?" is now answered by, "Nothing, I'm retired." Because so much of the career person's self-image is defined by work identity, retirement often means some kind of identity crisis (Darnley, 1975).

A few seem able to find happiness in the "doing nothing" role. "It's great not to have to get up every morning and go to work." Yet most cannot "do nothing" easily and happily after years of working. Many retirees continue to do odd jobs or continue as part-time employees if their occupation permits. For example, a retired school teacher may occasionally substitute teach. Some retirees change activities entirely and start a new vocation or avocation. They may decide to open their own business or actively pursue some long-suppressed interest such as writing or painting. Perhaps they busy themselves with volunteer work. There are numerous examples of people being retired and then returning to the work world. Konrad Adenauer assumed the leadership of postwar Germany at the age of seventy-three and actively guided Germany to a powerful world position for fourteen years until the age of eighty-seven.

Generally, those who had broad interests or are able to develop new interests quickly make the best adjustment to retirement. Older persons who age optimally are those who stay active and manage to resist the shrinkage of their social world. They maintain the activities of middle age as long as possible and then find substitutes for the activities they are forced to relinquish: substitutes for work when forced to retire, substitutes for friends and loved ones lost to death (Havighurst, Neugarten & Tobin, 1968).

Elizabeth Hill and Lorraine Dorfman (1982) investigated the reactions of housewives to the early years of their husband's retirement. Table 13-1 lists some of the positive and negative aspects mentioned by these wives. In addition, the researchers asked what suggestions these wives had for other women whose husbands were soon to retire. The most frequent suggestions were:

- Wives should try to keep their husbands busy in retirement
- Wives should try to continue their own preretirement activities

TABLE 13-1   Reaction of Housewives to the Retirement of Their Husbands

POSITIVE ASPECTS OF RETIREMENT	PERCENTAGE OF WIVES MENTIONING	NEGATIVE ASPECTS OF RETIREMENT	PERCENTAGE OF WIVES MENTIONING
Time available to do what you want	81	Financial problems	36
Increased companionship	67	Husbands' not having enough to do	31
Time flexibility	33	Too much togetherness	22
Increased participation of husbands in household tasks	28		
Decrease in own household responsibilities	22		
Husbands happier	22		

Source: Hill and Dorfman, 1982.

TABLE 13-2   Summary of Annual Budgets for a Retired Couple at Three Levels of Living, Urban United States, Autumn 1981*

COMPONENT	LOWER BUDGET	INTERMEDIATE BUDGET	HIGHER BUDGET
Total budget*	$7,220	$10,226	$15,078
Total family consumption	6,914	9,611	13,960
Food	2,183	2,898	3,642
Housing	2,377	3,393	5,307
Transportation	553	1,073	1,960
Clothing	244	409	629
Personal care	198	290	424
Medical care	1,085	1,091	1,098
Other family consumption	275	457	901
Other items	311	615	1,118

*The total budget is defined as the sum of "total family consumption" and "other items"; income taxes are not included in total budgets.

NOTE: Because of rounding, sums of individual items may not equal totals.

Source: Monthly Labor Review, 1982.

- Couple should do more together
- Wife should plan to maintain some privacy

Although most of the literature on retirement concerns men, questions of retirement are becoming ever more important for women as well. As we saw in Chapter 8, more and more women are entering the work force. Although past research (Lowenthal, Thurnher & Chiriboga, 1975) has indicated that retirement does not hold the significance for women it does for men, it still is an important transition period in a working woman's life. One reason postulated for retirement's being less significant for working women is that many women experience several roles (wife, mother, homemaker) throughout their life cycle that they perceive to be as important as the role of worker. However, this aspect may well change as more and more women seek lifelong careers. Just as men must prepare for retirement, so must the working woman prepare for this transition (Johnson & Price-Bonham, 1980).

Money and health seem to be the two most important factors influencing the success of not only retirement but the general adjustment to old age. It takes a great deal of money to live free of economic worries (see Table 13-2). Generally, the retiree's income is more than halved on retirement. Over all, one of every three elderly persons is in a state of severe economic deprivation (Butler, 1973). Finding free time for leisure activities is one of the full-time employees' loudest complaints. It is ironic that when they finally retire and get enough free time, many have little money available to pursue desires other than those of subsistence. Financial status directly creates the quality of life for the retired couple. Can they travel, indulge their hobbies, and eat well as the television ads depict? They can only if they are financially well off.

How Do Couples Judge Their Marriages at Each of the Family Life Cycle Stages?

The following eight-stage family life cycle was developed by Spanier et al. (1975, p. 270).

I Beginning families
Couples married less than 5 years with no children

II Childbearing families
Oldest child, birth to 2 years, 11 months

III Families with preschool children

Oldest child, 3 years to 5 years, 11 months

IV Families with schoolage children
Oldest child, 6 years to 12 years, 11 months

V Families with teenagers
Oldest child, 13 years to 20 years, 11 months

VI Families as launching centers
First child gone to last child's leaving home

VII Families in the middle years
Empty nest to retirement

VIII Aging families
Retirement to death of first spouse

Childless families
Families with no children after five years of marriage

Evidence (see Figure 13-1) suggests a general drop in marital satisfaction for both partners, beginning shortly after marriage, bottoming out in the 4th stage (families with schoolage children) and rising thereafter but never regaining the level of satisfaction first found in marriage. Note how the satisfaction levels rise considerably during the last two stages.

There is considerable controversy over this research (Spanier et al., 1975), but it seems clear that feelings of marital satisfaction will change in relation to the various marital developmental stages as well as the general life stages through which each individual passes.

The retiree not only must have planned well economically for retirement but must also have planned for a potentially long-term period with increased life expectancy. Inflation is the retired person's greatest enemy. Those retired on an essentially fixed income fall further and further behind with each passing day of inflation. A retiree may be financially well off on retirement but may have dropped into poverty ten years later because of continued inflation and the shrinking value of the dollar.

Health is the other major influence on people's adjustment to retirement and old age. About 40 percent of those over sixty-five have long-term chronic conditions such as high blood pressure that interfere to some degree with their daily activities (U.S. Office of Human Development, 1976). Although government programs such as Medicare help the elderly cope financially with health problems, such benefits need to be supplemented monetarily. Thus money may compound health problems to further reduce the quality of life for the retired. With the high costs of medical care, there are few people who can be completely safe from financial disaster brought on by prolonged or severe health problems.

Assuming that monetary and health problems are not overwhelming,

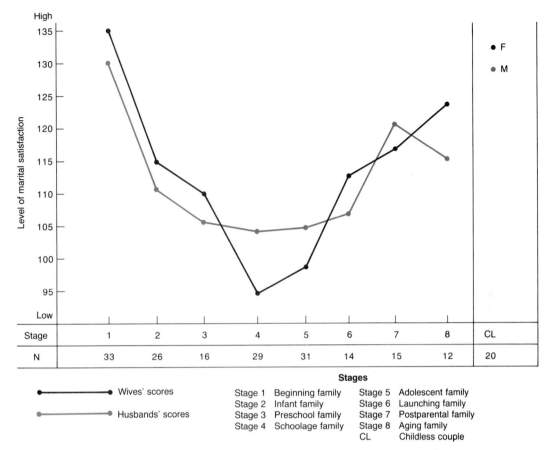

FIGURE 13-1   Spouses' mean scores on the Locke-Wallace Marital Adjustment Scale by stage in the family life cycle (Spanier et al., 1975).

many couples report that the retired period of their lives is one of enjoyment and marital happiness. They are able, often for the first time, to be together without jobs and children placing demands on them. They can travel and pursue hobbies and long-neglected interests. They can attend to one another with a concentration not available since they first dated. In some ways a successful retirement is like courting. After years of facing the demands of work and family, after growing apart in some ways, retirement provides the time needed to renew the relationship, make discoveries about each other, and revive the long-past courtship that first brought the couple together (see Inset 13-3).

Loss of a Spouse: A Return to Singleness

One can be faced with the death of a spouse at any stage of marriage. A spouse can die of disease or accident at any time. However, problems of the young widower or widow are much different from the problems spouses

INSET 13-3

Her New Life Begins on a Jarring Note

The morning after the wedding she found herself standing in her nightgown in the doorway of her daughter's room experiencing the void. I almost feel as if she's died, the woman thought wryly. Stop it. She's on her honeymoon, surely some of the happiest days of her life.

But later, as she packed away some childhood artifacts to be put in the attic for the grandchildren, the hollowness returned. Her daughter was not planning any babies right away. It would be a long time before she might need a grandmother's help.

The woman heard the question echoing in her head again: Of what use am I, really? What's my function now? She became angry at herself for permitting the question, in this form, and the anger diffused toward her husband.

Riding home in the car after the wedding, they'd had the worst fight of their marriage. "You're actually glad they're all gone," she had cried out.

"Of course. It's over—we've done our job," he had said.

"What's over?" she had flared. "You sound as if you're planning to cut our children right out of your life." She had known at the time that she was overstating; obviously he loved the kids.

But finally he had said those bitter words: "You became a different woman with the first baby. All those years you were a mother first and a wife second. Sometimes I felt I was at the bottom of your list, right after the dog."

Outrageous and cruel. Not true. Not true at all. He'd had too much champagne, and now suddenly he was like a wounded little boy: "You never had time for me. Your mind was always somewhere else. If a child sneezed you were out of my arms in a flash, like a mother bear defending her cubs in mortal danger."

Sex, that was it. "Yes, that is it," he had said. "But also when we were talking, or not talking. Or trying to do something together as adults, just the two of us. Evenings out, we'd talk about the kids. I couldn't get you off it. And we never took a vacation on our own."

"I thought you loved our family vacations," she had cried.

"I did. I do," he had groaned. "What's the use? A man can't ever fight Motherhood — all that virtue."

What do you want from me, she had finally asked in a small, tight voice.

"I want us to be lovers again, the way we were before the kids came. There's only the two of us now. We've got the rest of our lives to live together, alone. And it's got to get better than it has been—or else."

Suddenly now, just thinking about that brutal threat, she became weak and had to sit down. Yes, it happened all the time: Men and their midlife crises. Looking for young bodies, young women to flatter their egos.

And yes, in all those frenzied months of the wedding preparations, he had become distant. Maybe he already had a mistress. She tried to think when they had last made love. Was it possible that something terrible was about to happen to her?

No, surely not. Surely he knew how much she loved and respected him. He looked so sad that morning when he left for work, so tired. He wasn't a young man anymore. But he's right, she thought, I can be a better wife to him. If it isn't too late.

At the bottom of her despair that morning in the kitchen she unscrewed her jar of instant coffee, and found inside his scrawled note: "Dear Wife, grow old with me. The best is yet to be, the last of life, for which the first was made. — Robert Browning & Your Husband."

She read it again and again. Then, when she had exhausted her tears, she reached eagerly for the phone to begin her new life.

Source: Sanderson, 1982.

face when they lose their partner at the end of their lives and find themselves alone after the many years of marital partnership. For the young person who loses a spouse, remarriage is most often the solution. For those over sixty-five, as we saw earlier, remarriage is rare, occurring with only about 2 percent of men and 1 percent of women.

Regardless of age, loss of a spouse involves all of the processes that occur whenever one loses a loved one. Grief, feelings of guilt, despair, anger, remorse, depression, turning away from and yet to others at the same time are all normal reactions. Given time, most of us can overcome our emotional distress at losing a spouse and can go on with our lives. For a few long-married couples death of one precipitates the death of the remaining partner. This often occurs when a woman has taken most of her self-identity from her husband (Inset 13-5).

Widowedness as the Last Stage of Marriage

As we saw in the overview of family life stages, the last stage of marriage is overwhelmingly one of widowhood. There are approximately five times more widows over the age of sixty-five than there are widowers (Glick, 1979).

Widowers, in contrast to widows, generally exhibit more severe problems of disorganization. They have higher rates of suicide, physical illness, mental illness, alcoholism, and accidents ("The Plight . . .," 1974). A recent study also shows that their overall mortality rate was 26 percent higher than that for matching (age, schooling, smokers, nonsmokers, and so forth) married men. For widows the mortality rate was only 3.8 percent higher than for matching married women. It is interesting to note that there was no evidence that either men or women were significantly more likely to die in the early months of bereavement. Rather, death resulted later and seemed related to the stressful life situation of the widowed person rather than to an immediate reaction to the death of a spouse. Another interesting fact uncovered was that remarriage by widowers dramatically lowered their mortality rates. In men under fifty-five who remarried, and about half of them did, the death rate was 70 percent lower than for those who did not remarry. In men age 55 to 64, the death rate was 50 percent lower. Such data tend to support our assumption that marriage can promote health. One finding of this same study that applies to both widowers and widows was the dramatic rise in mortality rates, three to four times, if a widowed person moved into a retirement or nursing home because of illness or inability to live with other family members ("Not So Merry Widowers," 1981). Despite these negative findings about the problems of widowers, the social problems caused by aging center on the far larger numbers of widows in the American society.

As of March 1982 about 12 percent, or 10,796,000, of women age fifteen and over were widows. Of these widows 7.5 million were over sixty-five. Only 2.2 percent, or 1,861,000, of men were widowers, and 1,300,000 of these were over sixty-five (U.S. Bureau of the Census, May 1983). Only about half of the population age sixty-five and older still live with a spouse. The problems of widowhood are for the most part the problems generally faced in old age but faced alone without the spouse.

Death of a Wife: A Young Father Alone

Jim was only twenty-eight when Jane was killed in an auto accident while returning from her job. He was left with his son, Mike, who was four years old.

"At first, everyone rushed over and wanted to keep Mike for me. Some of our friends almost couldn't accept 'no' for an answer. Yet I felt that Mike needed to be with me and certainly I needed him.

"It is also amazing to remember who came over the first few days. People that we had hardly known brought food. At first when they asked what they could do, I replied, 'Nothing.' Yet they were so obviously disappointed that I finally tried to think of something for them to do. This seemed to make them feel better, although I'm not sure it helped me. In a way I needed things to do, things to distract me from my grief at least for a short time.

"Although I certainly mourned at first, I found that I was often too angry to mourn. I wanted revenge on the other driver, and I was particularly mad at the city for allowing such a dangerous intersection to exist without stop signs. At times I was even angry at my wife for driving so poorly, but this always made me feel guilty. Actually I think I was angry at the whole world. Why did events conspire to take her away from me?

"I had a lot of remorse for things I had put off doing with and for Jane. We really should have spent the money and gone home to see her parents last Christmas. Why hadn't I told her I loved her more often? In many ways at first I felt I had failed her.

"However as time passed I realized that perhaps she had failed me just a little also. At first I could only think of the good things. To think of bad things between us when she wasn't there to defend herself just seemed terrible. Gradually though I have been able to see her, our relationship, as it really was, with both good and bad. I want to preserve her memory for myself and our son, but I want it to be a realistic memory, not a case of heroine worship. I do fantasize about her, especially when I'm alone, and it really helps me to relive some of the memories, but I know that they can't substitute for the present. I must keep living and carrying forward for myself and our son.

"Although I'm not dating yet, I will in the future. She'd not want me to remain alone the rest of my life. Right now, though, I prefer to be alone with our son, with my thoughts and memories. I need time to understand what has happened, time to be sad. I need time for grief, time to adjust to my new single-parent role, time to ease the pain. I'll be ready for a new relationship only after I have laid the old one gently and lovingly to rest. When the time comes, I will look forward to marrying again."

In rural America many retired parents received monetary and housing support from their grown children. A century ago one tended to grow old on the farm within the family setting. Grandparents gradually turned the farm over to their children, remaining on the farm, giving advice, fulfilling the grandparent role, and being active family members until they died. As America urbanized, however, children tended to move away from their parents and to establish independent households within the cities. Often both partners worked at jobs that took them out of the home. Living space diminished so that no room was available for other than the immediate nuclear family. As the children who had moved to the cities grew older, there was no farm to which they could return, and thus urbanization slowly moved the care of the elderly out of the children's reach.

Today many Americans own their homes, which often gives them refuge and a major asset in their later years. More than two-thirds of the elderly remain in their home until death (Streib, 1972). Another 25 percent over sixty-five live with a child. Despite the large amount of generally negative publicity about institutional care for the elderly, only about 2 percent of those in their late sixties live in institutions such as nursing homes (Glick, 1979). The remaining elderly live in a variety of circumstances: with relatives other than children, with roommates, and in rented quarters. Perhaps half a million are well enough off monetarily to buy or lease living quarters in exclusive retirement communities such as Arizona's Sun City or California's Leisure World.

With the increasing longevity of Americans, the phenomenon of the four-generation family has arisen. It is estimated that half of all persons over sixty-five with living children are members of four-generation families. This does not mean that they live with their families but rather that they are great grandparents. The great-grandmother role is relatively new in society. Great grandchildren can be a source of joy and fulfillment just as can grandchildren. On the other hand, the generational gap is so large that great grandchildren can also be a source of bewilderment as their lifestyles become increasingly different from those of the oldest generation (Shanas, 1980).

The fact that children no longer automatically care for their aging parents means that governmental agencies have had to be created to help the elderly. Government-regulated retirement programs and social security have been established to help economically. Medicare and nutrition programs such as Meals on Wheels have been established to help in the area of health. The National Council on Aging publishes a directory of special housing for the elderly. Licensing and supervision of institutional facilities for the aged is being tightened. The elderly themselves are organizing as a power bloc (the Grey Panthers, for example) to work toward improvement of care and broadening opportunities for people in their later years. In 1979, mandatory retirement rules were successfully challenged in court, leading to increasing the age at which retirement can be required, from sixty-five to seventy years. Now, those who wish to work longer, and are able to do so, may. Thus some of the problems the elderly face, especially economic worries, are postponed. Programs such as the Retired Senior Volunteer program, which pays out-of-pocket expenses to those involved in community activities and projects, and the Senior Corps of Retired Executives, which pays them to counsel small businesses, are springing up to keep the elderly active and useful. All of these things bode well for

TABLE 13-3 Time necessary for elderly widows to adjust and begin developing a new life after the death of a spouse

TIME NEEDED	PERCENTAGE
2–11 months	25
One year	20
1–2 years	23
Over 2 years	16
Other	16

us as we move into the later years of our lives. The majority of elderly report that they are satisfied with their family relations (Seelbach & Hansen, 1980). Yet the question remains, "If possible, isn't the bosom of the family, the center of intimate relationships, the place to age gracefully and to die with dignity and care surrounding us?"

We pointed out earlier that most people finally do make an adjustment to the death of a loved one. In her study of elderly Chicago widows, Helena Lopata (1979) reports the figures for adjustment periods shown in Table 13-3. A few widows reported that they would never be able to establish a new life, but only time will tell if their feeling is correct. Lopata makes several interesting points about her sample of widows that probably hold true for many widows. Many of them had never been alone in a home, having gone from the home of their parents directly into one established with marriage. In addition, many of the widows had no occupational skills, never having worked other than perhaps in a few odd jobs before marriage. Their traditional socialization was to be passive about the world outside of their home environment. They had always depended on a family support system. Thus their socialization and consequent life experiences did not adequately prepare them to start a life alone when their spouse passed away.

These factors should diminish as more and more women enter the workforce and establish a more independent lifestyle. The women's movement's emphasis on individual identity for all women, even when married, should also work to negate the factors Lopata found. The upsurge of interest in death and bereavement has also helped the widow cope with her new role. More understanding and empathy has been extended to her. For example, programs using widows to counsel other widows have been helpful in reducing the adjustment period (Silverman, 1970).* The Widows Consultation Center in New Jersey carries on an experimental program of group discussion that has been successful (Hiltz, 1975).

Remarriage is perhaps the best solution for the widow or widower. Yet, as we saw earlier, few over sixty-five actually remarry. For widows the lack of available older men is the major obstacle. Some researchers (Lasswell, 1973; Duberman, 1977) suggest that polygyny might be an appropriate solution. If the few available older men were allowed more than one wife, remarriage opportunities would be more abundant for older widows. Another way to alleviate the problem would be for women to marry men eight to ten years younger than themselves (Glick, 1979). This would necessitate a change in the long-standing American tradition of women marrying men one to two years older than themselves.

Many elderly, out of necessity, do live with other older people of both sexes. Living together without marriage is probably more common among the elderly than it is among the young, although current census data do not differentiate by age such "live together" households.

*See Scenes from Marriage at the end of the chapter for more details.

Doctor's Wife

My grandmother died only a few months after my grandfather did even though she was in good health and had seldom been sick in her life. My grandfather was a strong independent man who worshiped my grandmother and took especially good care of her. He never allowed her to work or to want for anything and remained much in love with her, often publicly displaying his affection, until he died.

He was an old-fashioned family doctor who made house calls and thought of his patients as his family. My grandmother's entire identity revolved around being "doctor's wife" (that is how she often referred to herself). Her life was his life, and in hindsight I realize she never developed any of her own interests. In fact, she seemed to have no interests outside of his interests. As "doctor's wife" she took care of him, the family, and the house. When the children became independent, she became even more attentive to him and didn't develop any other interests to replace the missing children.

With the arrival of grandchildren, she became the happy mother all over again, caring for the grandchildren as often as she could. When grandfather died, we all tried to visit her often and invited her to visit our families. She told us to give her a little time to adjust and that for the present she preferred to stay home. About three months later I found her lying in grandfather's bed having passed away from an apparent heart attack. In retrospect I think that she had died in spirit when grandfather passed away. The death certificate indicates "heart attack" as the cause of death.

When I think about it, I had no grandmother. My grandmother was "doctor's wife." When he died, her identity died and soon thereafter her body. I prefer to substitute "broken heart" for "heart attack" on the death certificate.

The Grandparenting Role

For many retired, widowed, and elderly persons, fulfilling the role of grandparent can bring back many of the joys and satisfactions of family life. Grandchildren can mean companionship, renewal of intimate contact, the joy of physical contact, and the fulfillment of again being needed and useful.

As with the retirement and widowed stages of marriage, so grandparenting has been greatly extended by increased life expectancy. Most children have a relationship with one or more grandparents throughout their youth. It is quite possible today for a person's period of grandparenting to be longer than the period in which their own children were at home. Of course, younger grandparents, still married, employed, and living in their own homes do not have the same needs to grandparent that the older, retired, and perhaps widowed grandparents do.

For older grandparents the role might be described as "pleasure without responsibility." They can enjoy the grandchildren without the obligation and responsibilities they had to shoulder for their own children. For some the grandparent role gives a second chance to be an even better parent, especially for males. "I can be, and I can do for my grandchildren things I could never do for my own kids. I was too busy to enjoy my own, but my grandchildren are different" (Neugarten & Weinstein, 1973, p. 507). Association with grandchildren can yield a great deal of physical contact for the widow or widower. This is one of the things most often reported missed after one's spouse dies.

In the past the stereotype of the elderly person has excluded the close physical contact of sexual activity. Yet we know today that this is erroneous. Physical contact is an important source of intimacy and emotional gratification, regardless of age (Lasswell, 1973, p. 523).

> The new knowledge that we have about both male and female changes in sexual functioning is going to cause a new kind of sexual revolution — that of the "over fifties"! We now know that menopause has no effect on sexual drive unless the woman thinks it will have such an effect, and then she is only responding to her own negative expectations. And with men, the decrease in testosterone production plays a very small role in decreasing sexual interest, if any.

Although sexual intercourse may be unavailable to the average older widow, much physical warmth can be had with grandchildren. Hugging, kissing, and affection gained from grandchildren can go a long way toward replacing the physical satisfaction earlier had in marriage.

Many grandparents also report feelings of biological and psychological renewal from interacting with their grandchildren: "I feel young again." "I see a future." As fulfilling as the grandparental role might be, many grandparents miss out on it because of the great distance from them that their children live. Retired grandparents who can afford to often move closer to their children in order to increase their family association. Divorce, too, can remove grandchildren from reach of grandparents. Courts are just now beginning to recognize grandparental visitation rights. Of course, with the high remarriage rates, some older persons become foster grandparents. Although grandparenting is no panacea to the problems of aging, it can yield a great deal of comfort and satisfaction.

Summary

Families, like the people within them, span a long period of time. And just as individuals change over time, so too do families. In this chapter we have tried to trace what some of the common changes might be. Because most of the book is concerned with the early family stages, we have examined only the middle and later stages in this chapter.

When the last child leaves home, the empty-nest stage begins. This is usually a time of reassessment for both husband and wife — reassessment of how their lives will change now that the children are gone. What will they do with the time that used to be devoted to mothering and fathering? How have they lived their lives to date; how do they want to live them in the future? What new directions should they undertake? What will be their relationship with their adult children? Between themselves? How will they fulfill the grandparent role? What role will sexuality play in their middle years?

Retirement enters one's thoughts during the middle years. When it finally comes, the family will have adjustments to make. Time demands will change abruptly; monetary circumstances may shift downward; and feelings of uselessness may have to be coped with by one or both of the spouses leaving the world of work that has for so long been a part of their identity.

At the last, death must be faced as one spouse, usually the husband, dies. For many there is a return to singleness in the later years. The period of being widowed, in fact, may be increasingly longer as life expectancy continues to rise.

Despite the death of one spouse, the family often remains active. Grandparenting can bring small children back into one's life and yield new satisfactions to those aging within the family. For some, however, old age may mean being without family for the first time.

SCENES FROM MARRIAGE

Living as a Widow: Only the Name's the Same

"The funeral was over and suddenly I was all alone," said the grieving widow whose whole life had been wrapped up in being wife and mother. Her children were all grown up and gone. Now her husband. "No one to shop for, no one to talk to. The loneliness was so awful I thought I would go out of my mind." . . .

In the case of Mrs. J., she sat at home, depressed, listening to church music that she and her husband once enjoyed together. One moment, she was determined to find a new home, the next morose and immobilized. Move or stay? She couldn't make up her mind.

Other widows can be encountered after adjustment and reentry into the world around them. Such as Judge Lucille Buell who was sworn in . . . as a Family Court judge in Westchester County and who promptly cited her "broad experience in living" — "I was a wife, now I'm a widow. I am a mother [of two college students], a teacher, and a lawyer." . . .

Of all the widowed in America, 85 percent are women. They are neither single nor married, divorced nor separated. They are free — but for what?

Mostly, they are Americans looking for roles. Their search goes on without guidelines, with limited sympathy, and with little attention to their problems. As one expert has noted, widows are social pioneers looking for their place in American society.

As the life span increases, American women are becoming widows later in life and also spending more years as widows.

"The problem in American society — to the extent that a wom-an's identity is based on being a wife — is that the widow has no place to go," says Dr. Helena Zananiecki Lopata, a foremost expert on widowhood. "She can't be a widow, really, and she can't go back to being single. If she can't be a wife, can't be a widow, can't be single, her identity has to come from something else."

That search for identity, built on the ashes of a husband's death, strikes women unprepared, even when a long illness is involved. Widowhood is something that is not discussed, that is faced suddenly in the full force of grief, surrounded by well-meaning sons and daughters, relatives and friends. They are well-meaning but impatient. Concerned, but filled with misunderstanding and easy, often bad advice.

Widows have been largely left out of the vast American industry of professionalized advice-giving. Toddlers and teenagers get special attention, the just-married and the newly-divorced are recognized as special categories, and so are addicts, alcoholics, the unemployed, and the disabled. But not widows. They are expected to wipe their tears and get going. But how and where?

The fewer resources a woman had as a wife the less she is able to cope as a widow. The less money she has, the greater the effort it will take. The more empty the circle of her relatives and friends, the greater her isolation. The less education and the fewer the skills she has, the fewer her options are. The less flexible she has been as a wife, the more difficult her adjustment as a widow will be. . . .

On the practical side, widows confront the legal, financial, and everyday problems commonly handled by husbands in a male-dominated society. They are called upon to perform actions and make decisions they have never faced before.

Finally, in finding their new place in society, they need a new sort of marriage — of attitude and frame of mind with information, know-how, and opportunity. . . .

In general, widows help widows better than anyone else does. This has been evident in the various programs that do exist, particularly the Widow-to-Widow Program developed under the auspices of the Laboratory of Community Psychiatry at Harvard University. Its director, Dr. Phyllis Rolfe Silverman, describes the many advantages a widow possesses as a caregiver: "As a teacher, as a role model, as a bridge person, she helps make order out of the chaos of grief and provides the widow direction in the role transition." . . .

From sympathy and empathy, from a chance to talk to someone who shared the same experience, the widows then could move on to practical questions like legal assistance, social activities, or job-hunting. The idea was so successful that it is being picked up in more places than Dr. Silverman can keep track of. . . .

The death of her spouse often places the widow in a "crisis situation." At the Center in New York, the only professional service of its kind devoted exclusively to widows, the aim is clearly set forth: "Three out of every four wives in the United States eventually face widowhood. Despite this stark fact, no organized effort to help them meet their problems and build new lives for

themselves existed until the Widows Consultation Center was established in 1970 as a nonprofit, nonsectarian agency."

The Center, whose constant backlog involves a month-long wait, receives a stream of inquiries from all over the country about a many-sided approach that is required in all programs for the widowed. Crisis intervention, in the form of counseling sessions and therapy, helps through the periods of depression that come immediately and often much later. Assistance in solving practical problems is provided by legal and financial experts. (In one example, a widow with $300,000 in the bank felt that she couldn't even afford a taxi.) The Center offers social opportunities along with various group activities. In a variant on the Widow-to-Widow Program, clients who have worked out their own difficulties get involved in helping others. One volunteer-client comes to the center every week and phones widows who are alone and suffering from isolation. . . .

The widows expressed this feeling in various ways: "I don't think anyone who hasn't experienced it can understand the void that is left after losing a companion of so many years — all the happy little things that come up and you think, 'Oh, I must share that' — and there isn't anyone there to share it with." . . .

As expected, Dr. Lopata's research showed that the "more deeply the couple were involved" the more difficult the adjustment. But she adds a counsel that might not occur to a well-meaning relative or friend: the widow "must be allowed to grieve." Specialists use the term, "grief work," and

it is the first step on the widow's way back.

Instead of encouraging the widow to forget her loss (impossible, anyhow), relatives and friends must allow her to work through her grief. She faces an emotional trial involving sorrow, guilt, loneliness, and fear. The experts recommend that a widow be encouraged to cry if she wishes, to talk of her late husband, and to describe how bad she feels.

Based on her own first-hand work, Dr. Silverman warns that it is a mistake to judge a widow's state of mind from the fact that her behavior may seem composed at the time of the funeral. For initially the widow is numb, and in handling duties connected with the funeral she is still acting as her husband's wife. "It is safe to say the real anguish and distress have not yet begun," Dr. Silverman says.

As the widow becomes aware of the finality of the loss, the fact that her husband is gone hits home. It can take her up to two years to accept this fact, and the process of grieving is necessary to her adjustment. If the process is avoided, Dr. Silverman says, it can create its own problems. But when faced it is a "prologue to the future."

Besides "grief work," Dr. Lopata cites four needs that all widows have: namely, companionship, solution of immediate problems, building of competence and self-confidence, and help in reengagement in the world around them. It is in meeting these needs that relatives, friends, and agencies can aid widows in helping themselves.

Widows appreciate someone

"just being there" as they learn to live alone. One widow spoke of "loneliness — nobody to talk to." Another spoke of coming home to an empty house: "It's a very lonely life — you have friends, you feel happy when you're with them, but you have to come home to an empty house." This need for companionship is complicated by the *ups* and *downs* of a widow's state of mind. Those close to her should have a special understanding and patience; they should stand by her, not avoid her. . . .

Generally speaking, a widow should avoid making any important decisions during the first year of widowhood because the chance of making mistakes is great. Her outlook will change after she works through her grief and adjusts to being on her own.

Dr. Lopata is emphatic about a widow's doing her own decision-making: "No one should make decisions for her, unless absolutely necessary to avoid a serious disaster." Instead of advice that increases dependency, independence should be encouraged. . . .

Finally, widows need assistance in getting reconnected with society. "Keep busy" is one frequent piece of advice that makes sense. In the beginning, activity is escape from loneliness, then it takes on meaning for its own sake. It plugs the widow into the life around her. . . .

The goal is to stop being *widows* and to start being individuals — women who have lost a husband and learned to begin again on their own. . . .

"I looked around and I saw people worse off than me; they had no money or no family. One woman I know really died after her husband went. The way I was going that could happen to me; I wasn't sure that I wanted that to happen. Then I began to take stock. I was doing things I had never done before, going to meetings [of a widow group], driving people there. People were counting on me. I was needed. I was the one who was always so helpless and here I was helping someone else. I never thought I could change like that. . . .

And I knew then that I had to go on living."

EDWARD WAKIN

CHAPTER 14

THE DISSOLUTION OF MARRIAGE

CONTENTS

14

"In sickness and in health, till death do us part." This traditional part of the marriage ceremony might well be changed to the following in modern America: "In happiness and in good health, till divorce do us part."

A hundred years ago in this country, thirty out of every 1000 marriages were ended each year by the death of one of the spouses. Only three marriages in 1000 were ended by divorce. Today those figures are nearly reversed. Divorce, separation, and desertion finish many marriages today rather than death.

Introduction: Let No Man Put Asunder

It seems obvious that the "love match" marriage based on romance and self-gratification — in other words, on the fulfillment of all one's needs — must suffer from a high rate of failure. Americans ask a great deal of marriage, and the higher the stakes the higher the chances of failure.

The rate of divorce in this country has been rising throughout the century. In 1900 there was about one divorce for every twelve marriages. By 1922 there was one divorce for every eight marriages, and in the late 1940s there was approximately one divorce for every three and a half marriages. This peak probably occurred as a result of dislocations arising from World War II. From 1950 to 1970 the ratio of divorce to marriage leveled off at approximately one divorce for every four marriages. But beginning in 1968 the divorce rate again started to rise until by 1976 it reached an all-time high and then leveled out in 1977 (Glick & Norton, 1977). The number of divorced women heading families increased between 1970 and 1981, going from 7.45 million to 11.41 million (U.S. Bureau of the Census, June 1982).

However, divorce statistics do not yield a complete picture of the incidence of broken marriage. Legal separation claims another 3 percent of all marriages. Desertion, another manner of breaking a marriage, is especially prevalent among the poor, although obtaining statistics on desertion is difficult because such facts may not appear in any records. Usually it is the husband who leaves, although more wives are now deserting than in the past (Todres, 1978).

In any case it appears that dissolution of American marriages is relatively commonplace and becoming more so in the 1970s and '80s. Some family experts have begun to call American marriages "throwaway marriages." A better name is **serial marriages**; that is, Americans tend to marry, divorce, and marry again. Today, 41 percent of all American married couples have divorce in the background of one or both (Glick, 1980). A high divorce rate apparently does not mean that Americans are disenchanted with marriage, however, because the divorced remarry in great numbers and relatively quickly (see Chapter 15).

It is important to remember that statistics on divorce and separation must be interpreted cautiously. For example, the crude divorce rate, the ratio of divorces to each 1000 persons within the population, is greatly influenced by birthrate. A decrease in birthrate will produce a higher

Serial marriage
Marrying, divorcing, and marrying again; a series of legal marriages

TABLE 14-1 Number of Divorces and Divorce Rates

YEAR	NUMBER OF DIVORCES	PERCENT CHANGE FROM PREVIOUS YEAR	RATE PER 1000 TOTAL POPULATION	RATE PER 1000 MARRIED WOMEN 15 YEARS AND OVER
1983	1,175,000	− .01	5.0	
1982	1,180,000	− .03	5.1	
1981	1,219,000	+ .03	5.3	
1980	1,182,000	.00	5.2	
1979	1,181,000	+ .04	5.3	22.8
1978	1,130,000	+ .03	5.1	21.9
1977	1,090,000	+ .006	5.0	21.3
1976	1,083,000	+ 4.5	5.0	27.7
1975	1,036,000	+ 6.0	4.9	20.3
1974	977,000	+ 6.8	4.6	19.3
1973	915,000	+ 8.3	4.4	13.2
1972	845,000	+ 9.3	4.1	17.0
1971	773,000	+ 9.2	3.7	15.8
1965	479,000	+ 6.4	2.5	10.6
1960	393,000	− .5	2.2	9.2
1955	377,000	− .5	2.3	9.3
1950	385,144	− 3.0	2.6	10.3
1946	610,000	+ 25.8	4.3	17.9
1941	293,000	+ 11.0	2.2	9.4

Source: U.S. National Center for Health Statistics, *Vital and Health Statistics*, ser. 21, no. 29, "Divorces and Divorce Rates: United States," table 1; and *Monthly Vital Statistics Report*, vol. 27, no. 5, suppl., "Advance Report: Final Divorce Statistics, 1976," table 1, and vol. 27, "Provisional Statistics: Births, Marriages, Divorces, and Deaths for 1978," page 1; and unpublished base for rate per 1000 married women 15 years and over. Some of the data from 1978 to 1982 supplied by Arthur J. Norton, personal communication, June 20, 1983.

percentage of divorce, presuming the total number of divorces remains stable. Because the birthrate has been at an all-time low in America, some of the increase in crude divorce rate is accounted for by this fact. Also, as John Crosby (1980, p. 57) points out, "Divorce statistics tell us very little about the institution of marriage except that some people choose to dissolve their marriage and others have this choice made for them by their spouses." To conclude that the institution of marriage and the family is in a state of decay and breakdown based on divorce statistics is not valid.

Divorce: The Legalities

Historically, the American attitude toward divorce has been negative, stemming mainly from the majority Christian heritage. The stigma has a long history. Nearly two thousand years ago, only "sinful pagans" divorced freely; "virtuous, spiritual Christians" did not. After some centuries, in fact, divorce was formally forbidden by the Church and made legally impossible (there was no civil marriage or civil divorce until recent centuries). To this day civil divorces of Catholics, even in non-Catholic countries, are not recognized by the Catholic church, and those Catholics who obtain such a divorce and remarry are considered to be in a state of sin and therefore ineligible for communion, although they are no longer excommunicated.

Italy allowed divorce for the first time in December 1970. Italy's new divorce law is hardly liberal, yet it took years of effort to gain any kind of divorce law. Couples seeking divorce must be legally separated for at least five years (when separation is mutual) and for six or more years when one partner is opposed. Other grounds cited in the new law are: foreign divorce or remarriage by one spouse, long prison sentences, incest, attempted murder of family members, criminal insanity, and nonconsummation of the marriage sexually. Adultery is not included as a ground for divorce.

For many, attitudes have changed to make divorce a legitimate option and to create an acceptance of divorce as a right and proper way to end an unsuccessful marriage.

The Conservative versus Liberal Battle over Divorce

Divorce laws vary from extreme restriction, such as in Argentina and Spain where no divorce is allowed, to extreme permissiveness, such as in Japan where divorce is granted simply on mutual consent. Even within the United States there is great variety because divorce, as well as marriage, is regulated by individual states. For example, until 1949 divorce was not allowed in South Carolina. From 1787 until 1966, adultery was the only grounds for divorce in New York, a situation that led to the creation of businesses that planned and documented "adulterous" situations for couples seeking divorce but uninvolved in real adultery. Since 1969 California has allowed divorce essentially by mutual consent, having dropped the old idea of adversary proceedings in which one member of the marriage had to be proved guilty of behavior that would give the other partner some state-defined ground for divorce.

The reason for such variety in divorce laws is the old philosophic battle between those who believe that stringent divorce laws will curtail marriage failure and those who believe that marriages fail regardless of the strictness of divorce legislation. The latter also believe that unrealistic laws do more harm than good.

Until the advent of Christianity, governments in the Western world did not regulate marriage or divorce. In republican Rome, for example, it was customary to marry simply by living together with the stated intention of becoming husband and wife. No ceremony was required. The Roman state recognized a marriage as dissolved when the parties separated.

The Christians, partially in reaction to the hedonistic Roman society, advocated strict control of sexuality and hence strict regulation of marriage and divorce. In the Christian ethic marriage became indissoluble except by death. Sexual intercourse was permitted only within marriage and was therefore limited to only one partner. Marriage was not only an assumption of responsibility for spouse and offspring but a sacrament by which the marriage partners acknowledged their belief in and responsibilities to God and their faith in Christ. The Protestant Reformation reestablished the idea of divorce when Martin Luther claimed that marriage was not a sacrament but a "worldly thing." He considered it justifiable for a husband to leave his wife if she committed adultery. This viewpoint brought back the idea of permissible divorce, but along with it came the idea that one spouse had to be proved a transgressor, thus introducing the adversary approach to divorce that has remained in the Western world to this day. Because religion and government were closely related, laws concerning marriage and divorce came into effect.

Thus the state laid down certain grounds for divorce, rules that if broken by one spouse allowed the other to divorce. And because one spouse had to be proved a wrongdoer, punishments were often established. For example, in the American colonies it was common to deny the guilty spouse the right of remarriage if a divorce was granted. Today payment by one spouse to the other (alimony) is sometimes used to punish the guilty spouse rather than simply to help a spouse become reestablished. The adversary/punishment approach to divorce remained the only approach in America until the latter half of the twentieth century.

Slowly the idea that a marriage might be terminated simply because it had broken down, without placing blame on one party or the other, began to find its way into the law of action (how laws are actually applied) and recently into the law of the books (how the laws are written).

The Legal Sham of Divorce

All states set grounds on which a divorce can be granted. Some of these grounds have been adultery, mental and/or physical cruelty, desertion, alcoholism, impotency, nonsupport, insanity, felony conviction or imprisonment, drug addiction, and pregnancy at marriage. To obtain a divorce, one of the partners had to prove the other guilty of having transgressed in at least one of the areas accepted by the particular state in which they lived. In addition, all states banned *collusion* (the two agreeing and working together to obtain their divorce) or moving to another state if the only purpose was to take advantage of more lenient divorce laws. Thus if the letter of the law was followed, divorce would have to be an action taken by one spouse against the other who would have to be proved guilty of conduct the state of residence found unacceptable and therefore grounds for divorce.

Depending on the particular state, we find such absurdities as drunkenness being twenty-two times more common as grounds for divorce in Florida than in Maryland. This is because of the difference in the state divorce laws and not because Florida residents necessarily drink more. The most extreme example was New York where, until 1966, when the law was changed to allow other grounds for divorce, adultery was the only acceptable reason. In New York the partner proved guilty of adultery was not allowed to remarry for three years and then only if the court removed the restriction because of the "guilty" partner's good conduct. There was no room in the laws on the books for a couple to agree to a rational divorce where the goal would be to minimize the problems faced by each.

Yet the law in practice was often quite different. Only some 10 to 15 percent of divorces are *contested* (in other words, in most divorces both partners agree to the divorce). And as long as both partners agree to the divorce and do not fight it in court, divorces have been granted fairly freely and without much substantiation of charges, regardless of the laws on the books. The American divorce system, in essence, has been restrictive in writing and permissive in practice. The courts usually do not inquire into questions of collusion, residence, or grounds. They accept the word of the party in court and do not pursue such questions unless asked to do so by the parties and their lawyers. In a sense America's varying divorce laws are a true democratic compromise. The conservatives have strict laws on the books, and the liberals have permissive courts.

All states attach residency requirements to divorce. Each state now recognizes divorce in every other state if the other state's residency requirements have been met. And this "if" is not checked in the usual uncontested divorce. Theoretically states do not recognize foreign divorces unless one party actually lives or has lived in the foreign country. But the formal law again differs from the informal action, and the state will do nothing about a foreign divorce even if neither party lives abroad unless a complaint is received. However, if a complaint is received and the divorce is contested, states may invalidate a divorce where residency requirements have not been met. In cases of remarriage spouses have sometimes been prosecuted for bigamy when the divorce to the former spouse has been invalidated. (See Appendix F for state divorce requirements.)

Because the states vary so in their divorce laws, efforts have been made to develop uniform laws for marriage and divorce that all states could adopt. Representative panels of experts have drafted a basic law and have submitted it to the states for acceptance by their legislatures. This process has been attempted several times in the United States, beginning in 1892 when the National Conference of Commissioners on Uniform State Laws deliberated the divorce law. A more recent attempt was made in 1970. To date none of these efforts to unify state laws has met with much success (see Monahan, 1973, p. 353).

The Move toward No-Fault Divorce

For many years the Interprofessional Commission on Marriage and Divorce Laws has advocated elimination of the "proof of guilt" (adversary) procedure and substitution of "what are the best interests of the family."

California led the way in doing this when it passed a "dissolution of marriage" law (Senate Bill 252) in 1969 that became the model for other states to follow. The law removed fault — the question of who was to blame. Grounds were reduced to (1) irreconcilable differences that have caused irremedial breakdown of the marriage or (2) incurable insanity. Section 4507 of the bill defined irreconcilable differences as those grounds that are determined by the court to be substantial reasons for not continuing the marriage and that make it appear that the marriage should be dissolved.

The California law also simplified property allocation by dividing property equally under most circumstances. Child support remained the responsibility of both husband and wife. By 1983 all states had enacted some type of **no-fault** or modified-fault **divorce** proceedings.

Although from a legal view California's two grounds are quite vague and open to varied interpretation, in practice this has meant that the California courts simply ask the petitioner if his or her marriage has broken down because of irreconcilable differences. The court does not inquire into the nature of the differences, though the court can order a delay or continuance of not more than thirty days if in its opinion there is a reasonable possibility of reconciliation. The California law has a unique section that bars evidence of misconduct on the part of either spouse:

> In any pleadings or proceedings for legal separation or dissolution of marriage under this part, . . . evidence of specific acts of misconduct shall be improper and inadmissible, except where child custody is in issue and such evidence is relevant. (*West's Annotated California Codes*, Section 4509, 1983, p. 280)

To date the last point has been ignored by the courts.

Because misconduct of one partner or the other is no longer considered, property settlements, support, and alimony awards are no longer used as punishment. California is one of seven states in which all property acquired during marriage is considered community property belonging equally to each spouse.* As long as the parties to the divorce agree and have divided their community property approximately evenly, the courts do not involve themselves in property settlements. The courts do set up support requirements for minor children, deeming such minors the responsibility of both parents until they are of age. In practice this generally means that the children live with the mother and the father pays.

Although fault is no longer determined, the judge still has the right to award alimony, though now not as punishment for wrong-doing.

> In any judgment decreeing the dissolution of a marriage or a legal separation of the parties, the court may order a party to pay for the support of the other party any amount, and for such a period of time, as the court may deem just and reasonable having regard for the circumstances of the respective parties, including duration of marriage, and the ability of the supported spouse to engage in gainful employment without interfering with the interests of the children. (*West's Annotated California Codes*, Section 4801, 1983, p. 629)

In most cases the wife will receive alimony until she is able to get onto her feet financially. Often the wife has devoted herself exclusively to the family for years and has lost what marketable skills she may once have had. In addition, if she is older, finding a job is even more difficult. The judges are tending to award limited-term alimony on the basis of need. For example, in one case the court awarded a wife funds for a college education on the grounds that she had provided such an education for her husband by working to put him through school when they first married and now it would be fair for him to do the same for her. A number of California counties are using the following rough guidelines in awarding alimony. If the marriage has lasted less than twelve years, support will not exceed half the duration of the marriage. In marriages of twenty

No-fault divorce
Divorce proceedings that do not place blame for the divorce on one spouse or the other

---

*The other states are Alaska, Idaho, Louisiana, Nevada, Texas, and Washington.

years or more, awards of support may be given until remarriage. Generally, under no-fault proceedings the amount and duration of alimony have been drastically reduced (Williams, 1977).

The simplified California law has encouraged a new trend in divorce, namely, "do-it-yourself" divorce. Retaining an attorney in order to obtain a divorce in the past has been mandatory, if for no other reason than to help interpret complicated divorce laws.

Although many attorneys work hard as marriage counselors and do all they can to minimize the problems of divorce, others seem to intensify problems rather than minimize them:

> And because these divorce proceedings are handled by two lawyers, each of whom is being paid to demonstrate his/her own abilities, what is fair is often completely overlooked in favor of what can be gotten away with. Too many lawyers representing husbands feel they can justify their fees only by working out arrangements by which the husband pays too little. Too many wives' lawyers feel satisfied only when they can point out how little the husband has left. (Sheresky & Mannes, 1972, p. x)

Such sentiments are often expressed by recently divorced people. Of course, it might be that the lawyer has simply become the scapegoat. On the other hand, the legal profession may need clearer guidelines for handling divorce as well as some training in counseling and interpersonal relations. Regardless of whether attorneys are involved or not, the couple that can work out differences before approaching a lawyer and the court are in a much better position to obtain a fair and equitable divorce.

It is important that attorneys who handle divorce cases (1) realize that there are psychological as well as legal factors to the termination of marital contracts and (2) attend to these factors as they process their cases. Failure to recognize the psychological aspects in this area of law can lead to a multiplicity of problems and further complicate an already difficult situation. This is not to suggest that lawyers become marriage counselors, but to point out the nonlegal issues that directly affect a divorce action (Sabalis & Ayers, 1977).

Many Californians are going directly to the courts, following simplified procedures from guidebooks written by sympathetic lawyers or knowledgeable citizens, and obtaining their own divorces for the cost of filing ($90 to $150). However, a do-it-yourself approach to divorce is not recommended unless the partners are relatively friendly, in agreement on all matters, including child support, and do not have large assets.

On January 1, 1979, a new law called "summary dissolution" took effect in California. This permits couples who meet several qualifications to get divorced without making court appearances. To qualify the marriage must not be more than five years in duration and the couple must have no children, less than $2000 in debts, no interest in real property, and not more than $10,000 worth of community property excluding automobiles. Also, neither party may have separate property assets exceeding $10,000 (*West's Annotated California Codes*, 1983).

Legal steps in obtaining a divorce vary slightly from state to state. Using California as a representative state, you must take the following steps to obtain a divorce.

INSET 14-1

Humanizing Divorce Procedures*

TERM	CRIMINAL MEANING	DIVORCE MEANING
Custody	Holding of a criminal in jail	Giving of a child to a parent by the courts
Custodian	Prison guard	Parent having legal custody of the child after a divorce
Visitation	Friends and relatives visiting the person jailed	The noncustody parent visiting his/her child
Defendant	Person against whom legal action is taken	Person being sued for divorce
Plaintiff	Person or state taking legal action against defendant	Person suing for divorce
Suit	Legal action to secure justice	Legal action to secure divorce

Because the courts have for so long considered divorce an adversary procedure, it has been difficult for those in the legal profession to think in no-fault terms. Most of the legal terminology of divorce is derived from criminal law, thus the language used by attorneys and the courts is derived from that same background.

A lawyer is also traditionally trained to take the side of his/her client and to do the best possible for them. Thus it is difficult for many lawyers to let go of that training (in fact, unethical to do so) and concern themselves with the entire family unit. Perhaps not every lawyer should handle

*These thoughts were shared in a talk given at the California Council on Family Relations Annual Conference held in Santa Barbara, California, September 26–28, 1980. The talk, entitled, "Drawing Individual and Family Strengths from the Divorce Process," was given by Meyer Elkin, California conciliation court pioneer.

divorces. Family law specialization is already a reality in many states. Such a specialization should lead the lawyer to think in terms of protecting all members of the family. The family law attorney must think beyond the divorce, especially if children are involved, inasmuch as "parents are forever." All divorce really does is to rearrange family relationships, not end them.

The family law attorney should encourage self-determination on the part of the divorcing couple. They each have strengths and weaknesses and are often better judges of how to change their relationship than are attorneys and courts. The traditional attorney is trained to do everything for his client rather than encourage the client to take control of the process as much as possible. The family law attorney must learn to become a facilitator to the couple, complementing

their strengths and weaknesses.

Emotions are not permissible facts in a court of law. Yet emotions *are* facts in most divorce proceedings. They must be considered because the close intimacy of marriage usually cannot be dissolved without them.

In recent years the law has recognized the need for family support during the crises of divorce. No-fault divorce, conciliation courts, joint child custody, and family law specialization for attorneys are all steps in the direction of humanizing divorce. The changes in the law are not enough; we must also work to bring the ideas of no fault and family well-being into the consciousness of those working in the legal system. For example, the table shows how the legal terms used in divorce come from criminal law, which is adversary law.

1. The first papers must be filed with the county clerk. They include a statistical form and confidential questionnaire (some counties) giving information that the court will find helpful; a petition stating the basic information about your marriage and telling the court what you want done; and a summons or message from the court to the respondent, telling him or her that a petition has been filed.

2. A copy of the summons and of the petition and, in some counties, of the questionnaire must be served on the spouse.

3. The second papers must be filed after a minimum thirty-day wait from the date of service on the spouse. At this time you file the proof of service, a request for entry of default, and a financial declaration. The request for default indicates that your spouse will not fight the divorce so that you can move toward an uncontested hearing.

4. A date for a hearing is now set.

5. At the hearing the judge will ask you to state your name, that the facts on the petition are true, your residency, and the grounds on which the divorce is being sought. He may then talk with you about children, property, and bills, using the information you have supplied him. At this time you will receive the interlocutory judgment which clears the way for the marriage to be dissolved after the waiting period.

6. The request for final judgment cannot be filed until at least six months after the papers have been served and two months after entry of the interlocutory judgment. When the final papers are filed, the marriage is officially dissolved and you are divorced.

Strict versus Liberal Divorce Laws

Those favoring strict divorce laws claim that such laws act to strengthen marriage by forcing couples to work out their problems and assume responsibility for making their marriage work. Such persons consider divorce a sign of individual failure in marriage. In reality divorce per se is not the problem; the problem is marital breakdown. And laws may preclude divorce, but they cannot prevent marriage breakdown. Laws may deny the freedom to remarry by denying divorce, but they cannot prevent a man and a woman from living together.

Those favoring more liberal divorce laws accuse strict laws of creating undue animosity and hardship, of leading to perjury and the falsification of evidence, and of simply being unenforceable (see, for example, Rheinstein, 1972; Weitzman, 1981).

However, simple studies comparing divorce rates and the restrictiveness of divorce laws find there is a relationship. The more permissive the state's divorce laws, the higher the divorce rate and vice versa (see, for example, Stetson & Wright, 1975; Rheinstein, 1972). But the divorce rate is not necessarily an accurate reflection of marital breakdown. For example, the incidence of separation and desertion tends to be higher in states with restrictive divorce laws.

Strict divorce laws are one of society's attempts to legislate successful marriage. A better approach might be to make marriages harder to enter. The waiting period between the issuance of a marriage license and the actual marriage could be longer. Premarital counseling could be required. Trial marriages could be sanctioned. More couples seem to be forsaking formal marriage and simply living together, at least for a while, in what appears to be a trial union. This trend might lead to lower divorce rates, although research to date does not support this supposition.

The real issue is whether the law can make marriage successful. It seems doubtful. This does not mean there should be no state involvement in marriage. Certainly assigning responsibility for children, assuring some order in property inheritance, and guarding against fraud and misrepresentation are legitimate state concerns. But beyond those concerns, states' efforts to legislate successful marriage have not worked. Laws that support good human relations might be more helpful. For example, if a couple finds insurmountable obstacles to success in their marriage, then the laws should support their efforts to dissolve the marriage in the most amicable and beneficial manner.

Some Cautions about No-Fault Divorce

There is little question that the implementation of no-fault divorce procedures has eased the trauma of divorce by focusing on the demise of the marriage rather than on the guilt of one of the spouses. The fear that easier divorce laws would lead to skyrocketing divorce rates has not proved to be absolutely true (Dixon & Weitzman, 1980). Divorce rates have increased since the first no-fault law in 1970, but many factors have contributed. California, which pioneered the legal changes, ranked eighteenth in 1976 among the fifty states in number of divorces per 1000 population. From 1969 to 1977 the California divorce rate increased 54 percent, while the national rate increased 56 percent (Maher, 1979).

The enthusiasm for no-fault and do-it-yourself divorces, however, must be tempered. Divorce for most people is traumatic and involves many negative consequences, even under the best of circumstances.

Although on first appearance a divorce settlement that splits assets and responsibilities equally between the couple seems fair and equitable, it favors the man in the majority of cases. This is because the woman's earning power is usually less than the man's. Due mainly to the growing divorce rates, female-headed families with children have increased greatly in the past fifteen years until in 1982 they represented about 11.3 percent of all families (U.S. Bureau of the Census, May 1983). As a group these families have the hardest time financially. Approximately 50 percent live below the official poverty line (U.S. Bureau of the Census, June 1981). About 40 percent spend some time on welfare. Perhaps economic settlements should not be evenly divided at the time of divorce but should take into consideration the lower earning power of the woman, especially if she assumes custody of the children, as occurs in most cases.

Property settlements agreed to by the divorcing couple have been found to be incomplete and, at times, grossly unfair to one of the pair (Weitzman, 1981). An amicable agreement reached by a divorcing couple based on present circumstances may be totally inappropriate at some time in the future (Leslie, 1979). Studies of property settlements in California

INSET 14-2

Divorce and Dad

Pay But Don't Interfere I left home because it seemed easier for Elaine and the kids. After all, I was but one person, they were three. The children could remain in their schools with their friends and have the security of living in the home they had grown up in. I figured I'd come to visit often. I hoped that our separation and divorce would have minimal impact on the children and felt that the family remaining in our home was the way to achieve this.

It certainly hasn't worked out as I first imagined. Visiting the children often is no simple matter. Elaine has a new husband, the children have their friends and activities. And I seem to be busier than ever.

At first I'd just drop by to see the children when time permitted, but this usually upset everyone concerned. Elaine felt I was hanging around too much and even accused me of spying on her. Actually there might have been a little truth in this accusa-tion, especially when she started dating. The children usually didn't have time for me because they had plans of their own. I felt rejected by them.

Next, Elaine and I tried to work out a permanent visita-tion schedule. I was to take the children one evening a week and one weekend a month. Then she accused me of rejecting the children be-cause I wouldn't commit more time to them. But my work schedule only had a few times when I was sure I would be free and thus able to take the children.

At first, the set visiting times worked out well. I'd have something great planned for the children. Soon, however, Elaine told me that I was spoiling them. She said that they were always upset and out of their routine when I brought them home. Would I mind not doing this and that with them. Gradually the list of prohibitions lengthened. She had the house, the children, and my money to support the kids, yet I seemed to have fewer and fewer rights and privileges with them.

Be sure child support pay-ments arrive promptly but please leave the children alone became more and more Elaine's message.

Since she remarried, my only parental role seems to be financial. I really have no say on what the children do. I feel like I'm being taken every time I write a child support check.

The Missing Dad When Bill and I divorced, I wanted him to see our two children as often as possible and told the judge that he could have unlimited visitation rights. Bill seemed happy and said he looked for-ward to seeing the children often, both at my place and taking them to his new home. A year has now gone by and Bill almost never visits the children. Each time I ask him about it, he has another ex-cuse. At first he told me that he was too busy getting moved into his place. Then he was working a lot of overtime and was just too pooped to visit. Later, he said his new girl-friend was not comfortable with his visiting here. When I suggested that he take the children to his place, he told me that they did not allow children, something he hadn't realized when he moved in, he said.

I think that the children really need their dad. It is im-portant to them and they miss him. They ask where he is and why he doesn't come more often. I'm embarrassed when they ask since I don't know what to tell them. I really think he just doesn't care.

Even though the court or-dered him to pay $200 a month for child support, he is very irregular about the payment and often I have to remind him that it is due. This makes it very uncomfortable, too. Between asking him to visit the children more often and reminding him to send the

INSET 14-2, CONTINUED

child support payment, all I seem to do is nag him. In fact, he accuses me of being a worse nag than when we were married, but what can I do?

Divorced Dad Wins $25,000 from Ex-Wife In a verdict described as precedent-setting, a divorced father has been awarded $25,000 because of the serious emotional problems he claims were caused by his ex-wife's refusal to permit visits with their daughters.

A Fairfax County Circuit Court jury of three men and four women made the award to Harold H. Memmer, a civilian Army worker at Fort Belvoir in northern Virginia. Legal experts believe the verdict is the first of its kind.

Memmer claimed that his ex-wife, who has since remarried and lives in Evansville, Ind., had encouraged the girls, aged 13 and 20, not to talk to him.

Source: "Divorced Dad . . .," 1980.

have suggested that divorcing mothers are faring more poorly under the no-fault system than they did under the former system (Seal, 1979; Dixon & Weitzman, 1980, 1982). However, in a study similar to Karen Seal's California study, Charles Welch and Sharon Price-Bonham (1983) found that there were few changes in how mothers fared in Georgia and Washington after no-fault systems were instituted, although this study was limited to one county in each state.

It is interesting to note that in the past women have been the major partner to institute divorce proceedings. However, several studies indicate that after no-fault divorce legislation becomes law, men become the major partner filing for divorce (Gunter, 1977; Gunter & Johnson, 1978). Although the studies do not suggest the reasons for this reversal, it might be that equal property division does in fact favor the male as we have suggested (Weitzman, 1981).

Such cautions are not meant to negate the advantages and the basic civility that no-fault divorce laws have brought to the procedure. They are simply meant to warn the reader that divorce under any circumstances is difficult and if not a legal trial certainly an emotional one.

Divorce But Not the End of the Relationship

Many people who contemplate divorce see it as ending their miseries, ending forever a relationship that has become intolerable. Yet this is not always true and certainly is almost never true if children are involved. Divorced persons often remain bound to one another by children, love, hate, friendship, business matters, dependence, moral obligations, the need to dominate or rescue, or habit (Price-Bonham et al., 1983). It is increasingly recognized that divorce does not necessarily dissolve a family unit and, in the case of children, may result in a **binuclear** family.

Every state has provisions for modifying judgments made by the court at the time of divorce. Requests for change of custody, of support, or of alimony can be made by either spouse at any time. If you believe marital problems end with divorce, you should attend "father's day" in court. Many larger cities set aside specific days when motions are heard relative to an errant father's neglect in paying child support or to a vengeful

What Do You Think?

How hard do you think it is for a father to have a relationship with his children after divorce?

How do you think the father in the first story should handle the situation?

What should the former wife do to get Bill to visit more often and make payments on time?

In your experience which of the two cases seems to occur more often? Why?

Binuclear family
A family that includes children from two nuclear families; occurs when one or both of the divorced parents remarry

mother's refusal to permit her former husband to visit their children. Sometimes these hearings are emotionally packed scenes, replete with name calling, charges, and countercharges.

In August 1975 a federal law (Public Law 93–647) went into effect that permits wives access to federal data — IRS records, social security, and so on — to locate deserting former spouses who have failed to pay alimony and/or child support. The law also allows the IRS collection service to freeze bank accounts administratively (without going to court) after all other actions have been taken and the errant parent still refuses to pay. Nonpayment of child support is a felony punishable by a $1000 fine and/or one year in state prison. Since the enactment of this law, many errant fathers have been forced into making their support and alimony payments.

On the positive side many former spouses become good friends after the pain of divorce fades. Some divorced couples remain business partners. Even after remarriage of one or both, there may be friendly interaction between the couples and the new spouse or spouses. Children usually tie a couple together long after divorce. Divorce thus may not be an end to a relationship at all but may only mean that the relationship has changed. Those who look to divorce as a final solution to their marital problems will probably be in for a surprise, especially if children are involved and the marriage is of relatively long duration.

Ann Goetting's (1979) study of 180 divorced and remarried men and women emphasized the lack of prescribed roles for former spouses. Respondents indicated a high degree of consensus about the following: (1) former spouses should inform one another of emergency situations involving the children, (2) former spouses should not discuss current marital problems, (3) it is appropriate for a spouse to periodically request and be given extra time with his/her children. In contrast there was low consensus regarding: (1) extra financial support, (2) willingness to socialize, (3) perpetuation of rapport, (4) reciprocal influence in childrearing behavior, and (5) the former husband caring for the children (Price-Bonham et al., 1983).

Some professionals discourage relationships with former spouses. They contend that these continuing attachments drain energies that could be more productively spent in forming new relationships. They argue that the best policy for childless couples is to sever all ties.

In general it must be remembered that one's former spouse still has all the characteristics that attracted one to him or her in the first place. Therefore it seems unrealistic to expect that one will totally and forever more dislike a spouse one is divorcing. Some suggest that the best divorce adjustment is probably gained through an "amicable divorce" (Blood & Blood, 1979). This offers a minimum of conflict and develops through a process of gradual deescalation from a marital to a friendship relationship.

Toward a Model of Marital Dissolution

Numerous sociologists have proposed theories to explain why marriages are sometimes dissolved. Although we cannot cover the great volume of

Social Factors Related to Marital Dissolution

Persons living in the west, south, central, mountain, and Pacific regions of the United States have divorce rates that are significantly higher than for other regions (Glenn & Shelton, 1983).

Divorce rates rise during as well as after wars.

Divorce rates rise in times of prosperity and decline in periods of economic depression.

Divorce rates vary by region, generally increasing from east to west.

Divorced persons are overrepresented in urban areas and underrepresented in rural areas.

Independent of the effects of socioeconomic status, blacks tend to be more prone to divorce than are whites.

Generally, the higher the educational level, the lower the divorce rate.

Marriages entered into before age twenty are far likelier to end in divorce. For example, women who marry between fourteen and seventeen are three times as likely to divorce as women who marry at ages twenty to twenty-four (Spanier & Glick, 1981).

Persons whose family of origin has been broken by divorce or separation are themselves more likely to divorce.

marriage stability and instability data from which the theorists draw, it is insightful to examine at least one theory of marital dissolution. John Edwards and Janice Saunders (1981) propose a model of the marital dissolution decision that incorporates much of the previous research on divorce.

First, they point out that each marriage exists within a social context, a context that influences the decision to terminate a marriage. Inset 14-3 lists some of these general social factors that influence marital dissolution. Such social factors become part of the predisposing background characteristics each person brings to marriage. In general the largest and most consistent body of research dealing with marital dissolution indicates that the greater the discrepancy between individual background characteristics of the partners, the greater the chance of divorce. It is interesting to note that our socialization as men or women greatly influences our expectations about marriage. The expectations are sometimes so different between the sexes that some researchers have suggested, "There are two marriages in every marital union, his and hers" (Bernard, 1972, p. 15).

These predisposing background characteristics of each marital partner represent stage A in the model diagram (Figure 14-1). Stage B is represented by the degree of adjustment achieved by the partners during their courtship. Essentially it means that the better the mate selection process, the greater the chances of a successful marriage. Stage C represents the state of the marital relationship. Marital congruity means that the couple is in agreement on most aspects of their relationship. To have high congruity in a marriage does not necessarily mean the relationship is conflict

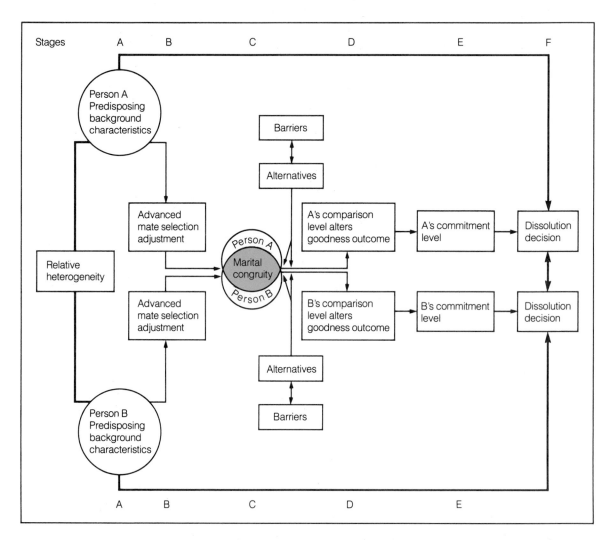

FIGURE 14-1 A social-psychological model of the dissolution decision (adapted from Edwards & Saunders, 1983).

free. If both spouses agree that conflict is an acceptable part of their relationship, then conflict will not cause them great marital problems. Essentially the idea of congruence relates to our earlier discussion of a couple's expectations (Chapter 4). If expectations are realistic and similar between spouses, then there is high congruence, and the likelihood of divorce diminishes.

Stage D represents the spouses' evaluation of their relationship, the perceived barriers to divorce, and the perceived goodness of their alternatives to the present relationship. If a relationship is judged highly satisfactory, if there are many barriers to divorce, and if there are few attractive alternatives, then the chance of divorce is slight (Levinger, 1965, 1979; Udry, 1981).

On the other hand, when these factors are reversed, the chance of divorce increases. Richard Udry's (1981) research indicates that marital alternatives in today's society may be a better predictor of divorce than marital satisfaction. This conclusion would seem to support the idea (Farber, 1964) that our marriage system is one in which we are all permanently available as a spouse. In other words, even if we are married, we remain partially open to a new relationship. Udry (1981) suggests that in arriving at an assessment of personal alternatives, individuals are in some way taking inventory of their resources and are considering what kind of life the alternatives would provide them if they were cut off from their present spouses. But they are also making an assessment of the value of their spouses — that is, those qualities, skills, or contributions the spouses bring to the marriage. Could they get someone better? It might be supposed that individuals consider among their own assets their education, income-producing capacity, sexual attractiveness, age, and number of children they already have. But they must also consider their spouse's assets and wonder if they could command more or less than their present partner in today's marriage market. This line of reasoning leads to the hypothesis that the greater a person's resources, the greater his or her perception of marital alternatives, while the lower the spouse's resources, the greater the individual's marital alternatives.

For divorce to occur, the advantages of the perceived alternatives would have to outweigh the strengths of the barriers to divorce. Barriers include such things as moral prescriptions, family pressure, feelings of obligation, concern for one's children, religious directives, divorce laws, and general level of community acceptance of divorce. During the past twenty years we have witnessed a lessening of the barriers to divorce and an increase in the demand for personal satisfaction and fulfillment. It is little wonder, if this divorce model be correct, that the perceived alternatives have become a strong influence toward divorce. "Maybe I can do better with a new spouse" becomes an increasingly attractive possibility.

Stage E represents one's commitment to the marriage. It indicates the extent to which one's personal needs and self-interests are bound up in and met by a particular relationship and no other. Commitment is the determination to continue a relationship, an attitude that may or may not be shared equally by the pair (Reiss, 1980). In the face of America's high divorce rate, it is little wonder that more and more Americans are talking about lack of commitment as one of the great ills of our society (Etzioni, 1983).

Stage F represents one's decision to remain or not in a given marriage. A model of divorce such as this is useful in helping us realize that many factors influence marital stability. Looking for a single cause of marital disruption, as many of the state laws have done in the past, is too simplistic.

Emotional Divorce and the Emotions of Divorce

Paul Bohannan (1970) has described what he terms the "six stations" of divorce. First is the *emotional divorce*, which centers upon the problem of the deteriorating marriage. It begins before the second station, the *legal divorce*, and may go on long after the legal divorce. It brings forth the kind of thinking and questioning described in Inset 14-4 and may go on for

A divorce is seldom pleasant

several years. It is only when one finally lets go of the former spouse emotionally that one really becomes free. Yet the third and fourth stations, the *economic* and *coparental divorce*, may mean restraints on freedom for years. The fifth station is the *community divorce*, the reactions of friends and the community to the divorce. The last station is the *psychic divorce*, where the major task is regaining individual autonomy.

Divorce is not a spontaneous, spur-of-the-moment act as marriage can be. In most cases dissolution occurs slowly, and divorce is the culmination of a prolonged period of gradual alienation. In many cases some two years elapse between a couple's first serious thought of divorce and the decree. Willard Waller (1967) delineates the following aspects in the alienation process:

1. Early in the process there is a disturbance in the sex life and affectional response. Rapport is lost, with an attempt to compensate for its lack in some cases. Emotional divorce begins here.
2. The possibility of divorce is first mentioned. This tends to clarify the relationship somewhat, with the initiator taking the lead and the partner remaining passive through the divorce cycle.

3. The appearance of solidarity is broken before the public. The fiction of solidarity is important as a face-saver. Once it is broken, the marriage cannot be the same again.
4. The decision to divorce is made, usually after long discussion, although at times it is made without forethought.
5. A severe crisis of separation follows. Severing a meaningful relationship is a traumatic experience at best, even though it is felt to be the only alternative.
6. Final severance comes with the actual divorce. This may come after a long period of delay and separation. While it is usually thought of as closing the case, the actual legal procedure is necessary before the next stage of the final adaptation can begin.
7. A period of mental conflict and reconstruction closes the case. The former partners enter new social worlds and full estrangement takes place.

So, long before legal divorce, a couple may find themselves beginning the process of emotional divorce. Often the beginnings of the process are not noticeable. What usually happens involves such things as a subtle withdrawing of one partner from the other, erecting barriers that slowly shield each from hurt by the other, gradually shifting concern from "us" to "me," meeting more and more psychological needs outside of the marriage, and finally, the erosion of the couple's sexual life together. The actual facts or events that lead up to divorce are as varied as the individuals who marry, but one thing that always happens is that each begins to concentrate on the other's weaknesses, shortcomings, and failures rather than on their strengths. The "20 percent I hate you" becomes the point of attention, rather than the "80 percent I love you" (see Chapter 4, pages 133–134). The inability to accept the partner the way he or she is or the inability to accept unwanted change in the partner is at the root of most emotional divorces.

Although many breakups occur during the first few years of marriage, with the peak occurring about three years after marriage, nearly 40 percent of all broken marriages have lasted ten or more years. The median duration of a marriage at the time of divorce in the United States is approximately seven years (Glick & Norton, 1977). A couple usually decide on a legal divorce only after years of worsening relations.

Once legal divorce is initiated, many emotions will be experienced — essentially the emotions of loss, the grief felt at the death of a loved one. For a lucky few — perhaps those divorcing quickly after marriage — grief and mourning will not occur. Indeed, for a very few happiness and joy over regaining freedom may be the major emotions experienced (see Table 14-2). But for most there will be a period of denial — it really isn't happening — followed by grief, mourning, and a mixture of the following:

- *Self-pity*: Why did this happen to me?
- *Vengeance*: I'm going to get even!
- *Despair*: I feel like going to sleep and never waking up again.
- *Wounded pride*: I'm not as great as I thought I was.
- *Anguish*: I don't know how I can hurt so much.
- *Guilt*: I'm really to blame for everything.
- *Loneliness*: Why don't our friends ever call me?
- *Fear*: No one else will want to marry me.

TABLE 14-2   Characterization of the Divorce Experience and Perceptions of "Best" and "Worst" Periods

	COMBINED SAMPLE	FEMALE	MALE
Characterization of Divorce Experience			
Traumatic, a nightmare	23%	27%	16%
Stressful, but bearable	40%	40%	40%
Unsettling, but easier than expected	20%	19%	24%
Relatively painless	17%	13%	20%
Most Difficult Period			
Before decision to divorce	55%	58%	50%
After decision, but before final decree	22%	20%	25%
Just after the divorce	21%	19%	23%
Now	3%	3%	3%

Adapted from: Albrecht, 1980.

- *Distrust*: He (or she) is probably conniving with attorneys to take all the property.
- *Withdrawal*: I don't feel like seeing anyone.
- *Relief*: Well, at least it's over, a decision has finally been made.

Unfortunately, unlike the grief and mourning at the death of a loved one, our society offers no ritual, no prescribed behaviors for the survivor of divorce. The community does not feel it necessary to help as it does in bereavement. Indeed the fact that the spouse still lives often denies the divorced person the opportunity to come to a final acceptance of the breakup because there is always a chance, no matter how small, of recovering the spouse. For some rejected spouses this little chance is exaggerated and becomes the sustaining theme of their life for a long time after the legal divorce. Children and monetary involvement are often reasons for continued association. Even in cases where marital breakup is hostile and bitter, the loneliness following the breakup may spur a mate to wish the spouse were home, even if only to fight with and ease the loneliness.

Many divorced people may feel a resurgence of hurt, hostility, and rejection on learning of the former spouse's new relationships. To hear that one's former mate is remarrying is often upsetting and may arouse past hostilities and regrets.

It is probably important that anger be a part of divorce, for it is anger that will finally break the emotional bonds that remain between the former spouses. Not until these bonds are finally broken will each be free. Fortunately, for most divorcing couples a turning point comes when their energies can finally turn from destruction to construction once again.

Creative Divorce and Rebirth

Divorce is the death of a relationship, but it can also be the rebirth of an individual. Just as death is difficult, so is rebirth. Once the mourning and

INSET 14-4

Divorce: A Personal Tragedy

How can I be missing her after all of the fighting and yelling we've been doing the past year or two? It's so nice to be in my own place and have peace and quiet. Damn, it sure is lonely. It's great to be a bachelor again, but after fifteen years of married life, who wants to chase women and play all those games? Wonder why the kids don't call? Keeping house is sure a drag. I wonder what she's doing. Do you suppose she is nicer to her dates than she was to me?

What really went wrong? Two nice kids, a good job, nice home, and I certainly loved her when we married. But she has been so unaffectionate and cold over the years. She never seemed to have time for me. Or was it that I never had time for her? When we dated, she was so flexible. She'd do anything with me, but after our first child she seemed to become so conservative. She wouldn't do anything daring. I had so little leisure time what with working so hard to give the family a good life. Why couldn't she do what I wanted when I was free? It's really all her fault. Of course, I could have included her more in my work world. Maybe if I had shared more of my business problems with her, she'd have been more understanding. It's true I am awfully short-tempered when the pressure is on. Certainly I didn't listen to her much any more. It seemed as if she only bitched and complained. I get enough of that at the office. You don't suppose there was another person? Maybe it was all my fault. A failure at marriage, that's me. Never thought it could happen to me. When did it start? Who first thought of divorce? Maybe the idea came because all our friends seemed to be divorcing.

On and on the thoughts of this newly divorced man go. Anger, guilt, frustration, conflict, insecurity, and emotional upheaval are the bedmates of divorce. "Our culture says that marriage is forever and yet I failed to make a go of it. Why?" The whys keep churning up thoughts, and endless questioning follows marital breakdown. There are so many questions, doubts, and fears.

grief begin to subside, the newly divorced individual faces important choices about life directions. What does one do newly alone? Seek the immediate security of a new marriage? Prepare to live alone the rest of one's life? Make all new friends or keep old friends? Maintain ties to the past relationship? Escape into the work world? Seek counseling? Experiment with sexual involvements?

More and more professionals as well as divorced persons themselves are saying, "Use the pain and suffering of divorce to learn about yourself. Seek the rebirth of a new, more insightful, more capable person out of the wreckage of failure."

Divorce Counseling and Mediation

Divorce mediation is a process utilizing one or two professional mediators (a lawyer and/or a mental health worker) who meet with both husband and wife to help them resolve conflicts, reach decisions, and negotiate agreements regarding the dissolution of their marriage (Ruman & Lamm, 1983). Such counseling is gaining popularity, especially since no-fault divorce proceedings have replaced adversary methods. Usually the first phase is predivorce counseling, which centers upon the imminent decision whether to divorce or not. At this point there is still a possibility of saving the marriage. The counselor acts as an objective third party (mediator) to help the person contemplating divorce come to a good decision. The spouses do not abdicate the decision making but are helped to decide for themselves (Coogler, Weber & McKenry, 1979; Haynes, 1981). Divorce counseling per se begins when the decision is made and lawyers and/or legal proceedings enter the picture. Such counseling can help the individuals cope with the many conflicting feelings that arise as well as better understand the legalities and alternatives available.

The third phase of divorce counseling occurs after the divorce is final and is aimed at helping the person get life started again (see Fisher, 1973). In a few states some divorce counseling is available through the courts, and occasionally courts require such counseling. Conciliation courts usually attempt to ameliorate the negative effects of marital failure. Their goal at first is trying to save the marriage, but failing that to help ensure an equitable divorce, "to protect the rights of children and to promote the public welfare by preserving, promoting, and protecting family life and the institution of matrimony, and to provide means for the reconciliation of spouses and the amicable settlement of domestic and family controversies" (*West's Annotated California Codes*, 1983, p. 72).

Those seeking counseling should not expect to find support for *their* side nor advice that if followed will resolve their problems. They should also not expect to see and feel immediate improvement in themselves and their relationship with the former spouse. Rather, they will find clarification and help in assessing strengths and weaknesses so they can move toward better understanding and clearer communication. The better the couple's communication and understanding, the less traumatic the divorce will be, for both themselves and their children if there are any.

Children and Divorce

Generally, it has been thought that divorce always has negative effects on the children involved. Because of this belief many couples have remained together only for the sake of the children, and others postponed divorce until the children were grown. Yet the effects of divorce on children are not at all clear. There is no doubt that the immediate effects are unsettling. Long-term effects are probably mixed. Some children may suffer long-term damage. Others may be much better off after a divorce than they were when the conflicting parents were together. An unhappy marriage is an unhappy home for children, and if divorce promotes parental happiness, then children should also benefit. Although this folk wisdom sounds reasonable, long-term study of divorced families only partially supports it.

Judith Wallerstein and Joan Kelley (1980) did a long-term study of sixty families that had gone through divorce. They interviewed them close to the time of divorce, eighteen months later, and again after five years.

Our overall conclusion is that divorce produces not a single pattern in people's lives, but at least three patterns, with many variations. Among both adults and children five years afterward, we found about a quarter to be resilient (those for whom the divorce was successful), half muddling through, coping when and as they could, and a final quarter to be bruised: failing to recover from the divorce or looking back to the predivorce family with intense longing. Some in each group had been that way before and continued unchanged; for the rest, we found roughly equal numbers for whom the divorce seemed connected to improvement and to decline. (p. 67)

What factors appear associated with the 25 percent who adapted well to the divorce? Not surprisingly, children with strong, well-integrated personalities who were well adjusted before the divorce were making the best adjustments. Children did significantly better when both parents continued to be a part of their lives on a regular basis. This was true only when the parents themselves were able to work out a satisfactory and nondestructive postdivorce relationship. Aside from these two factors, it was difficult to predict which children would do well and which would not.

One thing is clear: Divorced parents who fight via their children will probably cause their children harm. One parent may try to turn the children against the former spouse. Visitation rights may become attempts by the visiting parent to lure the child away from the custodial parent. The "Disneyland Dad" syndrome in which the visiting parent indulges the child may cause conflict with the custodial parent who thinks that the "ex" is spoiling the children. Parents need to speak openly about the divorce but without speaking negatively about the former mate. Unless divorced parents can work out some mutually acceptable relationship that holds conflict to a minimum, adjustment will remain difficult for the children. In extreme cases recurring court battles may be fought over the children. Or perhaps **child snatching** may occur, which is frightening and confusing as well as possibly dangerous to the child.

Child snatching
The taking of children from the custodial spouse by the noncustodial spouse after a divorce

Although not much studied, the role of former grandparents can also be important to children. Divorce not only removes the children from one parent but also from at least one set of grandparents. Grandparents who are one step removed from the conflicts of a divorce may be able to offer their grandchildren relative security and affection during the trying times. As of 1983 forty-three states recognized grandparent visitation rights (Press, 1983).

Studies (see Wallerstein & Kelley, 1980, for discussion) comparing adults from divorced (divorce occurring when the person was a child) and intact families find that the adults from divorced families more often characterized their childhood as unhappy. They are more likely to suffer from feelings of worthlessness, guilt, and despair. Yet such findings might occur because of the kind of relationship their parents had before divorce rather than because of the divorce itself.

What is clear at this time is that we cannot fully understand the effects of divorce on children. There will be immediate effects, usually negative, that will vary from child to child. For some children there will be lasting effects that will influence them as adults (Magrab, 1978). It is also clear that the divorced family is usually less adaptive economically, socially, and psychologically to the raising of children than the two-parent family. The one-parent family lacks the support and buffering effect of another adult (Wallerstein & Kelley, 1980).

Fortunately most divorced people remarry, thereby reconstituting the two-parent family. Of course in this case children must establish a new successful relationship with the stepparent, which is a problem unto itself.

Despite the general acceptance of divorce in our society, it remains for most parents an unpleasant and traumatic experience and for most children a trying and difficult problem with which to cope.

Types of Child Custody

Courts have four choices when awarding custody of children in a divorce proceeding. First and most common is *sole custody*. In this case the children are assigned to one parent who has sole responsibility for physically raising the children. Seventy percent of all custody is sole custody, and 90 percent of sole custody is mother custody.

Joint custody is where the children divide their time between both parents and both parents share in all of the various decisions about their children. At present there is an increasing trend for courts to award joint custody. The perceived advantages are: Both parents continue parenting roles; the arrangement avoids sudden termination of a child's relationship with one parent; and it lessens many of the burdens of constant child-care experienced by most single parents. Joint custody, however, forces the parents to maintain a relationship and if they cannot do this successfully, there are negative impacts on the children (Abarbanel, 1979; Benedek & Benedek, 1979).

Split custody is when the children are divided between the parents. In most cases the father takes the boys and the mother the girls. This method has the major drawback of separating the children from one another.

The fourth choice is when the court awards *custody to someone other than a parent* or parents. This is seldom done unless both parents are highly incompetent or offer such a poor environment for the children that the court decides parental custody would be harmful to the child. In most such cases grandparents or other near relatives gain custody of the children.

Creative Divorce

The phrase "creative divorce" was popularized by Mel Krantzler (1973) in his book of that name and has come to stand for a movement that declares:

> Divorce is not an end, it is a new beginning.
> Divorce does not mean the decay and destruction of marriage and the family in America, rather it means renewed effort to improve marriage and the family.
> Divorce is the beginning of a new enriching and enlivening voyage of self-discovery that makes me a happier and stronger person than I was before.
> Through divorce, a painful and emotional crisis, I learned that what I went through was what all divorced people go through — first a recognition that a relationship has died, then a period of mourning, and finally a slow, painful emotional readjustment to the facts of single life. I experienced the pitfalls along the way — the wallowing in self-pity, the refusal to let go of the old relationship, the repetition of old ways in relating to new people, the confusion of past emotions with present reality — and I emerged the better for it. (p. 30)

Such attitudes are a far cry from the feelings most persons initially experience at the breakup of their marriage. Yet it makes a great deal of sense to use divorce as a learning situation rather than seeing it only as a failure from which nothing good can be derived.

Many groups have sprung up to help the newly divorced move in a positive direction. "We Care" is an organization of volunteers who do just what their name implies — care and help those in mourning, whether it be over the death of a loved one or the death of a relationship. Parents Without Partners (PWP) is a nationwide organization, whose primary goal is that of educating single parents in childrearing. Its overall purpose is to help alleviate some of the isolation that makes it difficult for single parents to provide for themselves and their children a reasonable equivalent of normal family life. Many adult education facilities, churches, and other service-oriented organizations offer workshops and group experiences for the newly divorced.

A word of warning, however, is in order. Recently a myth of romantic divorce has grown up. Perhaps it has appeared as a defense against guilt on the part of the growing numbers of divorced persons in the American society. In essence it stresses only those things perceived as positive about divorce. It tries to make divorce an exciting romantic adventure in the ongoing stream of life. However, this myth of happy-ever-after-the-divorce that stresses only the joys of greater freedom and the delights of self-discovery hardly prepares the divorcing couple for the traumas and stresses they will find in reaching these goals (Hetherington et al., 1977).

Problems of the Newly Divorced

The major dangers facing the newly divorced are prolonged retreat from social contact, jumping quickly into a new marriage, leading a life based on hope that the spouse will return, or leading a life based on hostility and getting back at the former mate. Certainly the first step after any loss may be one of momentary retreat, a turn inward, a time of contemplation, of avoidance of all situations reminding one of the hurt and disappointment, guilt and shame of failure. Unfortunately though, some divorced people make such a reaction their lifestyle. In essence such people die psychologically and end their lives in every way but physically.

What Do You Think?

What do you think is the single most important thing that a newly divorced person can do to start on the road to recovery? Why?

What are some things the newly divorced person should avoid doing if he or she wants to speed recovery?

If you were advising a newly divorced person, what would you tell him or her? Why?

A larger group of divorced persons seek a new relationship as quickly as possible. Discounting those who had a satisfying relationship with someone else before their divorce and are now fulfilling it as soon as possible, there are many who can't stand the thought of failure and/or being alone and thus rush into the first available relationship. These people usually have not had time to reassess themselves or their motives. The idea of facing themselves and the challenges of becoming an independent person are simply too frightening. These are often people who have never really been alone. They married early, and in a sense they may never have grown up psychologically. Even though their first marriage may have been unsatisfying, marriage is still preferable to assuming responsibility for oneself. By rushing into a new marriage, they will likely make the same mistakes over again.

We have already looked at some of the problems of attempting to hold onto a past relationship. Living by false hope serves only to lock the person's life into a kind of prolonged alternation of hope and disappoint-

INSET 14-6

Getting On with Your Life

Just how long it takes to make the decision to get on with your life will vary, but inevitably this step must come. Each person must do it in his or her own way, at his or her own speed, and stumble over the obstacles as best he or she can. It's tough, but you must keep moving forward.

The following are tools that can be used effectively. Remember, determination is the key.

1. Be good to yourself; protect the inner child. Turn on your childlike personality; do things to make your inner self feel good.

2. Stay away from guilt trips — he said this, she said that, my fault, his fault, and so on — stay out of that deadly trap. The relationship is over, the marriage didn't jell, remember the good times, and let go.

3. Avoid bitterness and hostility at all costs. They will only hurt *you*.

4. Take a realistic appraisal of yourself: Focus on your good points; stay out of self-recrimination; keep reminding yourself that you are lovable, worthwhile, unique, special — there has never been nor shall there ever be one exactly like you.

5. Stay in the now. Plan time and activities for your internal child. The childlike portion of you is dependent on approval from yourself and others, so give it permission to cry, to express the hurt, and then to laugh and be free.

6. Reach out to others, don't close yourself off — turn on, be excited, get into other people and find something good about them.

7. Make a list of short-range and long-range goals, and do something to activate them.

8. Recognize fear as a useful tool. Fear gives you caution, and with caution there is discrimination, and with discrimination there are useful decisions.

9. Trust your intuitional hunches, be spontaneous; have faith and trust in yourself. Try not to rule out the possibility that all that has happened has a purpose, that in every negative there is a positive to be learned.

Divorce is not a failure, failure only happens when you give up. It's a new lifetime, a new beginning, a new ball game — get with it, dig in, and enjoy it.

ment. However, a life based on continuing anger and harassment of a former spouse may be the most destructive reaction of all, because the former spouse is harmed as well as the mate seeking revenge. The horror stories connected with this reaction to divorce are enough to keep people from ever marrying. The stories usually involve one of the spouses' taking the divorced spouse back to court time and again in an effort to (consciously or unconsciously) punish him or her. Fortunately, few divorced persons react for long in this fashion.

Community divorce, Bohannan's fifth station of divorce, describes problems and changes in one's lifestyle and in one's community of friends that occur on divorce. When one marries, single friends are gradually replaced by married couple friends. When one divorces, there is usually another change of friends. Unfortunately changes of friendship after divorce tend to be more complicated both for the person newly divorced and for the couple's friends. Some friends may side with one or the other person when a couple divorces. Remaining friends with a newly divorced person is difficult for at least two reasons. The divorcing couple cause their married friends to reexamine their own marriages. Often a divorcing couple will inadvertently cause trouble in the marriages of their friends. There is conflict over which partner to remain friends with. Also, the newly single person may be viewed as a threat or at least as a "fifth wheel" by still-married friends. Generally the newly divorced person will find that old friendships tend to fade and to be replaced by new friendships, often ones in which the new friends share some of the same kinds of problems as the newly divorced.

Most divorced persons start to date within the first year after their separation. The new dating partners also bring with them a new circle of friends. Thus for most divorced persons there will be a gradual change in their larger community of friends and contacts.

Reasons for America's High Divorce Rate

The reasons for America's high divorce rate are many and varied. There are the personal reasons that a divorcing couple gives, such as communication breakdown, sexual failure, or overuse of alcohol. More important, though, are the overriding influences that affect all marriages. The general social problems that have their roots deeply in American society and philosophy affect all relationships.

First, as we have mentioned, Americans ask a great deal of modern marriage — perhaps too much. High expectations often lead to disappointment and failure. Ask nothing, receive nothing, and nothing is disappointing. Ask a great deal, receive a little, and unhappiness often follows. Divorce in this context may not mean the failure of the institution of marriage. Rather, it may mean an attempt to improve one's marriage, to improve the institution.

Tied closely to Americans' high expectations of marriage is the relative freedom allowed individuals in making marital choices. The first basic assumption of this book, that a free and creative society will offer many structural forms of the family by which family functions may be fulfilled, acts as a second cause for America's high divorce rate. Many choices breed a certain amount of dissatisfaction. Is the grass greener on the other side of the fence? Might some alternative be better than what I have? Being surrounded by married friends who see marriage as you do and who are committed to it adds strength and durability to one's own marriage. But being surrounded by those who don't support your concept of marriage, who suggest and/or live alternate forms, who deride and chide the kind of marriage you have is disruptive of your own marital patterns. Although such disruptions might lead to a better present marriage, they are just as apt to lead to marital complications.

Changing sex roles are also a part of American interest in the general concept of change and its benefits. All those who question traditional sex roles place pressure on the institution of marriage. For example, a woman who decides that the role of mother is not for her, who seeks a career and leaves the caring of her children to her husband, is bound to face some disapproval from her family and friends. Certainly the same holds true for the husband who decides at forty to quit his job as an accountant, cease supporting his family, and begin writing adventure stories. Although the end result of sex role changes may be "people liberation," transitory results will continue to be marital disruption for some. Because the changing roles of women and men are listed as a major cause of divorce does not mean that such change will not, in the long run, be good for the family. Certainly many of those advocating change believe the family will benefit.

Another reason for the high divorce rate is America's heterogeneity. There are so many kinds of people, so many beliefs, attitudes, and value systems that family and marriage mean many and differing things to various Americans. Even though people tend to marry people with similar backgrounds, there will still be differences in belief and attitude. For example, consider the situation of a female college graduate interested in pursuing both a family life and a career; she marries an engineer from a traditional family background who believes the wife's place is in the home. Conflict seems inevitable.

Stemming also from America's heterogeneity is the higher incidence of mixed marriages. People of differing marital and family values and philosophies are more apt to marry in America simply because they are here and freedom of marital choice is encouraged. When such persons marry, building a successful and enduring marriage is more difficult because of their many differences.

A list of the general reasons for marital failure would be remiss if it failed to include social upheaval, economic problems, and the general state of health of the society. Certainly the stresses and strains brought on by the Vietnam War took their toll of marriage. Spouses were separated, children disagreed with their parents about the war, and there were periods of riot and social disorganization, all of which strained the family institution.

Continuing economic worries triggered by the unusual inflation/recession economy of the past few years have brought failure to many American marriages. Living in a minority group, living in poverty (Mott & Moore, 1979), and being in a society during turmoil are all factors accounting for marital instability.

Marital failure is highest among the poor, becoming progressively lower as economic status rises. Some data show divorce rates five times higher for low-status husbands compared with high-status husbands, though the gap lessened during the 1960s and 1970s (Burchinal & Chancellor, 1962; Glick, 1975).

Acceptance of divorce by Americans is an important factor in the rising divorce rates. The stigma of divorce has largely vanished over the past thirty years. In fact, a forty-year-old divorcée is probably less stigmatized than a forty-year-old woman who has never been married. General social acceptance is also noticeable in the trend toward more lenient divorce laws.

Last — and certainly emphasized throughout this book — are the personal inadequacies, failures, and problems that contribute to each individual divorce. Regardless of the magnitude of social problems and pressures that disrupt marriage, the ultimate decision to end a relationship is made by one or both spouses.

Reducing Divorce Rates

Paul Glick (1975), after a thorough review of American marriage and divorce statistics, lists a number of steps that might reduce divorce. He suggests first that more effective marriage and family training be given at home and in the schools. Certainly such courses in the schools are increasingly popular, and it is hoped that such an interest by young persons will lead to sounder partner choices and improved marriages.

Glick also advocates more scientific methods of mate selection than the current haphazard system based largely on emotion. Periodic marital checkups through visits to trained marriage counselors should be encouraged. As pointed out earlier, by the time most couples in difficulty seek help, their marriage is beyond help. Facing problems before they are insoluble, building problem-solving techniques into marriage, heading off divorce with help, if necessary, are needed elements in American marriage. Changing marriage laws to encourage couples to take their entry into marriage more seriously would also help reduce the necessity of divorce.

California took a step in the direction of stricter marriage laws in Assembly Bill 402 (*West's Annotated California Codes*, 1983), which became effective in 1970. This law, the first of its kind, empowers the courts to require premarital counseling of any couple applying for a marriage license if either party is under eighteen years of age and if the court deems such counseling necessary. In Los Angeles County the courts acted to make such counseling mandatory (Elkin, 1977).

Child-care centers would help give couples with young children more time for one another and more time to work positively on their marriage. Many couples simply do not have time for their marriage in the early childrearing/work-oriented years. Later, when they have time because the children are finally capable of independence and economic stability has been achieved, there is often not enough left of the marriage to be salvaged, much less improved.

Certainly we need to give at least as much time to the good aspects of marriage as we do to the negative aspects. Giving publicity to ways in which marriage can be improved, to successfully married couples, and concentrating on relationship improvement will be of more value than exaggerating the problems inherent in marriage.

Summary

A means of dissolving marriage has existed in almost every society. Divorce is America's mode of ending unsatisfactory marriages. The divorce rate has increased drastically during this century, probably reflecting Americans' changing expectations for marriage and tolerance of change. But even during these years the divorce laws in the books and the divorce laws in practice have been quite different from each other. In general fairly strict laws are on the books, while the law in practice is permissive and getting more so.

Generally, divorce is arrived at after a long period of gradually deteriorating relations. Indeed long before legal divorce and perhaps long after it as well, a couple will go through the suffering of an emotional divorce. Divorce is complicated by the presence of children and/or considerable property.

In the past few years all states have instituted some form of no-fault divorce. In these proceedings neither party has to be proved guilty of breaking some rule leading to grounds (a legal reason) for divorce. The only thing that must be proved is that the marriage has suffered an irremediable breakdown. By doing away with faultfinding, divorce procedures have been considerably simplified.

Divorce does not necessarily mean the end of a relationship, especially if children are involved. Visitation and financial obligations usually mean that the man and woman will have considerable interaction even after divorce. Such association may be difficult. Divorce counseling before as well as after divorce can help couples make satisfactory adjustments to the change in their lives.

Although divorce is traumatic for most persons, more people are beginning to look to the positive things that can be gained. Getting on with one's life, having a new start, and the learning of new insights into oneself are all possible advantages of divorce, as painful as it may be.

SCENES FROM MARRIAGE

Single Again

My first reaction when I realized my marriage was really over, after more than twenty years, was fear, rage, and despair. Even though we'd never really gotten along well together, he was all I knew. I was engaged at fifteen and couldn't wait to get out of high school to get married. I was a mother at eighteen and spent the next twenty years doing what I'd always wanted to do — care for a home, a husband, and children.

Then along came a young woman who wasn't tied to a house and children. She made him feel unique and young. I had no car, very little money, almost no experience at getting along in the outside world. I decided it was best to leave the big, comfortable home I'd been so proud of. I couldn't see a way to make the payments on it, and everyone in town knew I had been put aside for a younger model. My ego was shattered, my children's world torn apart. I moved back to my old home town. It was a small place, and my mother and sisters were there. I could find a job I could walk to until I could do better. My family had no money, but I needed their moral support badly.

My seventeen-year-old daughter dropped out of high school and moved into an apartment with an older girlfriend. My nineteen-year-old son had an apartment with a friend, and wanted to stay where he was. Neither of them wanted to take sides. My fifteen-year-old tried it with me for a few weeks, but was unhappy without the friends he'd known all his life. I let him move back with his father.

Now I was really heartsick. I felt so terribly old and worn out. I had two little boys who had not run out on me — one was seven and one twelve. I had to move to a tiny four-room house in bad repair, and for a few weeks all I could do was to feel sorry for myself, for the boys . . . and pray. I looked for work, but I was so limited in what I could do. No car, no training, no experience, no longer young. . . . I put up a good front for my boys and for the rest of my family. I had one sister who'd been divorced shortly before me, and she was a great morale-booster.

There was a period when I tried to figure out what I'd done wrong. Finally, I decided that whatever mistakes I'd made, I had been loyal to him and had really tried in every way I knew to make him happy. . . . I went to the library and checked out every book I could dealing with overcoming self-doubt and failure. Did you know that every really successful person has only found success after apparent failure? . . .

I made friends in the same boat that I was. There were plenty of them in my small home town. Too many men and women had been left behind because someone more interesting had come along. I came to know some of them well, and reached the conclusion that the one who is left is not necessarily the failure. The most common complaint seemed to be that they had been poor bed partners. But I think that's because it's one skill that no one else can comment on. Other people can observe how you dress, whether you're a good cook and keep a clean house, but if someone else does know how you are in that department, they're not likely to admit it. . . .

After a few months that seemed much longer, I found a job within walking distance and a larger, better house. My boys made some new friends and things began looking up. I decided that we could make a great life for ourselves. I knew I had to learn to make decisions for myself, and if the older children had been with us I would have leaned on them too much. They were doing well where they were and they came to see me often.

So I sat down and talked things over with myself. "You're young, not yet forty, intelligent, attractive. You always knew that someday the kids would no longer need you. Now you can do what you planned on doing when they were older." As I recovered from the blow to my ego, I was actually glad to be rid of a husband who had never seemed satisfied with me. . . .

With five children to take care of, it wasn't anything new to have to face problems and to make decisions. But in the past, if things went wrong, I had had someone else to share the blame. I don't now. I laughed when I first realized that I, and only I, was responsible for my own mistakes. I faced the fact that to be happy I had to avoid blaming my ex-husband or anyone else for my unhappiness.

I studied and thought about what I really wanted out of life. This took some doing, because all my life I'd tried to be what I thought someone else wanted me to be. It's not easy to look at yourself objectively. I'm still learning how. I've found that even though some ugly things come to the surface of my mind, letting them surface is the only way to deal with them. It's a tremendous feeling to get rid of negative feelings that you've been burying for years. Each time I got rid of one, I'd feel lighter, freer. My ex-husband had had such different ideas from mine that I couldn't accept them, or even understand how he could believe as he did. I wanted to spend our free time with a quiet group at home most of the time. He liked partying. Our ideas about raising the kids were different and so many other things that I wonder how we lived together for twenty years — and why we did. Even the children are all better satisfied now that we're apart.

Yesterday is dead and gone. I can't do anything to change it, but I can do something about today and tomorrow. It wasn't easy, but the hardest thing was deciding that I could do it. It's hard to face a completely different life style that you didn't choose, and then try to make it the greatest thing that ever happened. It can be done. . . .

I've learned a lot of things about myself that I like knowing. I'm good at math. Isn't that great? I've learned how to look for a job. I've learned how to say no to a date I don't want, and how to encourage a date I do. All those years while I was cooking, cleaning, sewing, doing PTA and Cub Scout work my mind wasn't dead — just resting. It took only a short time for it to wake up and get moving. I'm not looking for a replacement for my ex-husband. I'm not the same person I was even two years ago. I'm more self-confident, more comfortable around people, a bit slimmer, and I walk taller now. I like men, in fact, I love them. But if and when I do remarry, it'll be a whole new ball game. He won't have to live with the ghost of an unhappy marriage. . . .

Feel sorry for myself? Not any more. A couple of months ago, I did something I wouldn't have dreamed of doing two years ago. . . . I was in a dead-end job with no chance for advancement. There was little social life in the small town and few eligible men. I went to Brazoria County, looked around, asked some questions and went back home to turn in my resignation. I put my furniture up for sale and we moved. I work at a newspaper now — a job I've always dreamed of. The pay is better, the hours are better, there's a great PWP (Parents Without Partners) group and lots of other opportunities to meet people and lead an even fuller life.

TINCY LACON

CHAPTER 15

REMARRIAGE:
A GROWING WAY OF AMERICAN LIFE

CONTENTS

15

"It seems to me that John and Helen were just divorced, and here's an invitation to Helen's wedding."

"Not only that, but I met John and his new girlfriend at lunch yesterday and from the way they were acting, I'll bet we'll soon get an invitation to their wedding."

"It's hard to understand. They were so eager to escape their marriage and now it seems they can hardly wait to get back into another marriage."

Divorced people as a group are not against marriage. For every age group remarriage rates are higher than first-marriage rates, remarriage rates for men are higher than for women, and remarriage rates for the divorced are higher than for those widowed.

Statistically there are few single divorced people in America's population. Five out of six divorced men remarry and three out of four divorced women remarry ("Divorced Men . . .," 1981). Not only do divorced persons remarry in large numbers but they tend to remarry quickly. Approximately 50 percent of divorced people remarry within three years (Glick & Norton, 1977), and two-thirds are remarried within five years (U.S. Bureau of the Census, 1977). Today, about one in every three marriages (32 percent) is a remarriage for at least one of the new mates (Norton, 1982).

From these statistics it is safe to conclude that remarriage is an important aspect of marriage in the United States. Considering the rise in divorce rates, the lengthening life span, and the younger ages at which Americans divorce (about 30 percent of divorcing husbands and 60 percent of the wives are in their twenties at the time of divorce), it would appear that the incidence of remarriage will remain high in the future. What Americans experience is not monogamy, but serial monogamy — that is, several spouses over a lifetime but only one at a time. **Reconstituted**, or blended, **family** is another useful term to describe this trend in marriage.

Reconstituted family
Husband and wife, at least one of whom has been married before, and one or more children from previous marriage

Historically, remarriage is not new or novel. But the early death of one spouse has been the reason for remarriage in the past. Today it is divorce. Although the widowed do continue to remarry, they stay single longer than the divorced and their remarriage rates are lower.

Returning to the Single Life

Many people married for some time, burdened with the responsibilities of a growing family and missing the flush of romance that brought them together with their mate, feel pangs of envy when their friends divorce and reenter the single world. Remembering their dating and courting days, they relive nostalgic memories of the excitement of the "new date" and the boundless energies that one expended as a young person pursuing and being pursued. Except for a few persons, such dreams on the part of the married are just that, dreams.

Both for men and women, and especially for those married for some years, the return to the single world can be frightening. "Can I be successful as a single person?" is a question that cannot at first be answered. Most people have experienced a severe blow to their self-esteem with the divorce, and they are reluctant to face the potential rejections involved with meeting new people. For some the idea may be so threatening that they don't return to the single life but remain hidden in the safety of their own aloneness until remaining alone the rest of their life appears to be even more threatening, and they eventually venture out into the single world.

Just when divorced persons are ready to return to the single life varies greatly. For most it takes about one year after divorce to get themselves emotionally back together again (Weiss, 1975). Those who had an ongoing extramarital relationship are in a different position and often remarry as soon as legally possible.

Learning to date and relate to the opposite sex as a single person is especially difficult for anyone who has been married for a long time because his or her self-image has for so long been that of a married person, part of a couple. Once the divorced (or widowed) persons reenter the social world, though, they are often surprised at the number who share their newly single status. Except for the very young divorced, most reenter a world of single but formerly married people rather than one of the never married. This helps to ease the transition inasmuch as those they meet have also experienced marital collapse. There is a certain empathy, which helps newly divorced people feel more acceptable. They often feel better by realizing they aren't alone. In fact, the discovery that they can meet and interact with people of the opposite sex in their new single role can be exciting and heartening. "Maybe I'm not such a failure after all" is a common response.

Initial sexual experimentation is often a reaction of the newly divorced person, especially the person who has been rejected by the spouse and who did not want a divorce. To be desired sexually is a boost to shattered self-esteem. To be close to another person physically, to be held, touched, and sexually pleasured makes the rejected person feel loved and cared for as well as verifying his or her sexual desirability. For these reasons newly divorced persons are perhaps easily available for sexual encounters. Therefore the newly divorced person must guard against sexual exploitation and not make the error of equating sex with love.

The newly divorced do have the problem of meeting new people. Sometimes friends, relatives, and business associates supply new acquaintances. Organizations such as Parents Without Partners and We Care become meeting places. Often the lofty educational and helping goals of these groups are secondary to their social functions. The lofty goals may make it easier for people to join activities without appearing to be "people hunting."

Many singles clubs make introductions to others their major purpose. Such clubs sometimes can frighten and intimidate those just recuperating from marital failure, who are uncomfortable with attending singles fetes that have a "meat market" atmosphere.

Although long used in Europe, the personal newspaper advertisement

is relatively new in the United States. Discounting the ads for sexual partners in underground newspapers, there is a growing use of legitimate classified advertising to seek desirable companions and would-be mates, especially by divorced persons. Inserting an ad such as the following in a moderately large metropolitan newspaper will bring forty to fifty replies to females and a dozen to males.

ATTRACTIVE refined widow seeks real gentleman, 60s. Home loving, likes music, trips, books, gardening; financially secure; who wants to enjoy lasting companionship.

EXPERIENCED sailboat skipper, fifties, single, yacht club member, wants to meet compatible outdoor gal who would like to go sailing with me.

MAN seeking intelligent, independent, intuitive female companion (21–35) for social events. Send photo.

MALE 39, desires pleasant, attractive easy-going female. Enjoys good home life, occasional outdoor activities, flying, fishing, ghost towning. Photo & phone.

RETIRED lady loves nature, fine music. Sincere, kind, honest, sense of humor; wants same as bus travel companion or share your trans. No smoking.

Those using such ads should take precautions to make sure that the person one decides to meet is sincere. Using a post office box or telephone number rather than one's home address and arranging for the first meeting to be in a public place are sensible safeguards.

Technology has found a place in the formerly marrieds' new single life in the form of computer dating. For a fee information is fed into a large bank of personal information on many single clients and a match is made from stated interests, hobbies, habits, education, age, and so on. The pair then meet. Some agencies estimate that about 25 percent of their clients eventually marry someone they met through the computer's selection. Other agencies make a videotape interview with each client. Questions are asked about background, interests, feelings about sexual relations, and the qualities sought in prospective dates. The client then has the opportunity to look at videotapes of people who share interests and/or meet the qualifications. Videotapes have the advantage in giving an overall impression of the person before any meeting.

There are many other ways to meet new people. The major factor in meeting new people is the active participation of the newly divorced in the singles' world. Unless one is out in society, meeting new people is difficult. Probably the newly divorced in the small town setting stands the poorest chance of meeting someone new.

Regardless of how meeting people is done, the high remarriage rates indicate that meeting new prospective mates is accomplished by most people who divorce. And the new mate tends to be in the same situation; that is, divorced people marry divorced people. Dates often come from the person's present group of acquaintances.

Remarriage—Will I Make the Same Mistake Again?

High remarriage rates among divorced people indicate, as noted earlier, that the divorced are still interested in marriage and the role of "being married." The fact is that most activities in the American culture, for better or worse, revolve around the married pair, the couple. High remarriage rates seem to suggest that it is important to have someone with whom to share, to be intimate, to feel closeness, and to experience a part of something larger than oneself.

To love and be loved are important to most Americans. As unhappy as a marriage may have been, for most there was a time when love and closeness were experienced. Indeed, loss of this intimacy may have been a major part of the decision to leave the marriage. Certainly, finding intimacy is a factor in most remarriages just as it was in the first marriage.

The route to marriage for young unmarried Americans is fairly clear (see Chapters 2 and 3). You date, you fall in love, you become engaged, you marry. In second marriages, though, the simplicity of ignorance has been replaced by the knowledge and, for some, the anxiety of past experience. Some formerly married people may rush quickly into a new marriage, but for many the road to remarriage is cautious and uneasy. The divorced may have many negative emotions attached to marriage because of their past marital problems. Often they have prior commitments, children, and perhaps economic responsibilities, which must be maintained along with the new marriage.

The partners in a remarriage must deal with all of the problems any newly married pair faces. In addition, they must deal with attitudes and sensitivities within themselves that were fostered by their first marriage. They may enter remarriage with many prejudices for and against the marital relationship. They need to divest themselves of these if they are to face the new partner freely and build a new relationship that is appropriate to both. In a remarriage the mate is new and must be responded to as the individual she or he is, not in light of what the past spouse was. An additional task in every remarriage, then, is the effort partners must make to free themselves from inappropriate attitudes and behaviors stemming from the first marriage. In essence second marriages are built on top of first marriages (Furstenberg, 1979, p. 16).

Bob and Carol, Ted and Alice: Are You Still Married to Your Ex-mate?

Bob had been married for twelve years to Alice, had two children by the marriage, and was established economically when his marriage ended in divorce. Two years later he married Carol, eight years his junior, who had one child by her previous husband, Ted.

Bob and Carol both approached their marriage carefully, giving much thought to their relationship. Both agree that their new marriage is a big improvement over their past marriages. They find that their biggest problem is making sure they react to one another as individuals rather than on the basis of their past relationships. This is not always easy.

Bob's past wife, Alice, is emotionally volatile, which both attracted and repulsed him. He liked Alice's displays of happiness and enthusiasm but hated her temper fits and general unhappiness.

Carol is placid and even-tempered. In fact, these personality characteristics, in part, were what drew him to her. However, when they do things together, he keeps asking her if she is having fun, is she enjoying herself? He asks her so often that Carol is bugged by what she considers to be his harassment of her. One day she blew up at him over this. He reacted strongly to her negative emotional display. Once everything was calm again, they both discovered that the problem grew out of his past marriage. Bob simply expected Carol to show her enjoyment in the same way Alice had. He was not relating to Carol as an individual but was reacting in light of his past experiences with Alice. When Carol blew up at him, his reaction was much larger than necessary. Her emotional blast activated all of his past dislike of Alice's temper fits.

Inasmuch as most divorced persons marry other divorced persons, the story about Bob and Alice clearly shows that another couple is involved in such remarriages, namely the former spouses. This phantom couple often dictates to the newly remarried pair, if not directly through the courts and divorce settlements, then indirectly via years of previous interaction. For example, both Bob and Carol are reacting to one another but in addition they are reacting in light of their interactions with their past spouses.

A remarriage between divorced persons is more difficult than a first marriage for a number of reasons besides the influence, often negative, of past spouses. First, each mate may have problems of self-esteem with which to cope. Second, the divorced are less apt to tolerate a poor second marriage. They have been through divorce and know that they have survived. Life after divorce is not an unknown any longer and is therefore less threatening than before. Divorced persons may end a problematic remarriage more quickly than they ended their first marriage.

Third, the past relationship is never really over. Even if the Bob, Carol, and Alice kind of dynamics are successfully overcome, the past marriage can still directly affect the new marriage. For example, payments to a former spouse may be resented by the new spouse, especially if the current marriage seems shortchanged monetarily.

Fourth, if children are involved in the remarriage, there will be a great many more complications, as we shall see in the next section. Last, the society around the remarrying person tends to expect another failure. "He (she) couldn't make it the first time, so he'll (she'll) probably fail this time, too." "After all, most divorced persons don't learn, they usually remarry the same kind of person as their earlier spouse." "Once a failure always a failure." These are just some of the folk "wisdoms" about the divorced. This lack of support can create a climate of distrust in the minds of the remarried couple themselves. Community support is almost always present for a first marriage. Indeed the whole society usually applauds the young couple who announce their plans to marry. "This is the right thing to do," everyone seems to tell them.

Despite such problems many remarriages do last. Only a small percentage of Americans divorce more than once. What are the statistics on success and failure of second marriages? Unfortunately, the statistics do not present a clear picture. Some studies comparing the divorce rates of first marriages with those of second marriages do report that a remarriage is more likely to break up than a first marriage (McCarthy, 1978; Becker, Landes & Michael, 1976; Cherlin, 1977, 1978; Bumpass & Sweet, 1977; Glick & Norton, 1977). However, these studies do not take into account the small group of divorce-prone people who marry and divorce often. Other studies find that remarriages are no more likely to end in divorce or separation than are first marriages (see, for example, Riley & Spreitzer, 1974).

Perhaps more important than divorce-rate comparisons are the subjective evaluations made by those remarrying. A comparison of the reported marital happiness of divorced and never-divorced white respondents to three national surveys revealed little difference between the two groups. The comparison concluded that remarriages of divorced persons that do not end quickly in divorce are probably, as a whole, almost as successful as intact first marriages (Glenn & Weaver, 1977). Stan Albrecht (1979) also found that remarriages were happy marriages. However, none of the variables that had often been noted in the past as good predictors of marital satisfaction among first married couples (presence of children, age at marriage, social class, and similarity of religion) seemed to be strongly related to remarriage satisfaction. Remarriages seem to be judged by different criteria than first marriages, perhaps because they are based on different factors. (Perhaps the romantic illusion is gone for those remarrying.) Glenn & Weaver (1977) conclude that divorce and remarriage seem to have been effective mechanisms for replacing poor marriages with good ones and for keeping the level of marital happiness fairly high.

Even though statistics are mixed on the success of remarriages, it is clear that a great many are successful despite the extra problems facing those remarrying. As divorce becomes more prevalent and acceptable, the problems facing those wishing to remarry may diminish. Perhaps social support for remarriage will be greater in the future as more and more people marry more than once during their lifetimes.

His, Hers, and Ours

For many years children in the home precluded the parents' divorcing. Everyone "knew" the dire consequences to children if divorce occurred. Many couples stayed together for years after their marriage had failed in order to spare the children the trauma of divorce. In fact, the divorce of parents as soon as the last child leaves home often comes as a surprise to children who have always thought of their parents as happily married.

But staying together for the children's sake is no longer as prevalent as it once was. Some people are reasoning that strained and conflict-ridden families are as harmful to children as are divorcing families. "Those persons in discordant marriages who divorce and remarry are often taking positive steps to improve their home situation, and hence may provide a more healthy environment for children than was possible for the original intact family" (Wilson et al., 1975). Regardless of one's philosophy on the question of divorce involving children, the number of such divorces is going up dramatically. Since 1922 the number of divorces involving children has increased six times. Just since 1950 the number has doubled. About 1 million children were involved in divorce proceedings in 1976 (Glick, 1979b). It is estimated that about 7 million children live with a **stepparent**. The proportion of children living with their mother only has more than doubled since 1960, from 8 percent to 20 percent in 1982 (U.S. Bureau of the Census, May 1983). Only about 67 percent of all children under eighteen live with both natural parents who have been married only once (Glick & Norton, 1977).

Many people believe that the divorced person who has custody of the children stands much less chance of remarriage. In actuality, if age is held constant, having children does not seem to significantly influence one's chances of remarriage (see Bell, 1975, p. 571). In fact, remarriages may well involve at least three different sets of children. Both spouses may bring their own children into the new marriage, and in addition they may decide to have children together. Hence his, hers, and ours is often a correct description of the children in a reconstituted family.

Stepparent
The husband or wife of one's parent by a later marriage

Literature is replete with many examples of the poor treatment accorded stepchildren. The ogre stepparent is a popular stereotype in fairy tales and other children's stories. Yet there is little evidence to support this stereotype in reality. The research on stepchildren is somewhat mixed. Certainly the transition to a new parent is not always easy. The very young child or the grown-up child seems to adapt the easiest. Generally children remain with their biological mother and the stepparent is a new father. Because ties are usually closest to the mother, this is probably an advantage for most children. A frequent impression is that more children are now being placed in the custody of the father. In absolute numbers this is true (1,203,000 children living with the father only in 1981 compared with 748,000 in 1970). But the same rate of increase has occurred for children living with a divorced mother. Consequently, a fairly constant 10 percent of all children living with a divorced parent live with the father (U.S. Bureau of the Census, June 1982).

Several studies report that divorce and remarriage seem to have few detrimental effects on children (for example, Burchinal, 1964; Wilson et al., 1975). One study (Cox, 1960) comparing college students on the dean's honor role and on probation, controlling for intelligence, found a higher proportion of those on the honor role to be from divorced families.

However, counselors and therapists report that stepchildren and stepparents do have a great deal of trouble in their relationships. Perhaps the reason that the data on stepchildren are mixed is because each situation is unique and one cannot generalize about the effects of divorce or a stepparent on children. It may well be that if a child is well adjusted and of healthy personality, breakup of the family will be coped with successfully and will lead to a more mature, independent child. If the child is unstable, then divorce may cause even greater maladjustment.

To learn what effect divorce and remarriage have on a child, we would need to know the answers to the following questions: What were the preconditions to the divorce (much fighting; calm, quick decision; long, slow decision; emotional; rational, and so on)? How well adjusted was the child? What age was the child? With which parent did the child go? Did the child want to go with that parent? What kind of person is the stepparent? How long was the child given to adjust to the stepparent? How many siblings went with the child into the remarriage? Were other children present from the stepparent? What sort of family atmosphere was created? Did the natural parent support or disrupt the child's adjustment? With so many questions to answer, it is not so surprising that the research findings are mixed. The only valid conclusion is that some children suffer more than others from divorce and remarriage.

For divorcing parents who want and need to know how to reduce the negative consequences of divorce and remarriage on their children, probably the single best thing they can do is to maintain a reasonable relationship with the divorced mate. Fighting over children or using them against a former spouse will lead to negative consequences for the child.

Stepparents face additional problems beyond those of natural parents. To begin with they must follow a preceding parent. If the child and the natural parent had a positive relationship, the child is apt to feel resentful and hostile to the stepparent. The child may also feel disloyal to the departed parent if a good relationship is established with the stepparent. Often a child feels rejected and unloved by the parent who leaves the household. In this case the child may cling more tightly to the remaining parent as a source of security and continuity. Thus the remaining parent's subsequent marriage can be threatening to the child. "This stepparent is going to take my last parent away from me." The stepparent may be met with anger and hostility. When the child's relationship with the departed parent was not good, hostility remaining from this prior relationship can be displaced onto the stepparent.

Because of the constant comparison made by children between biological parents and stepparents, many stepparents make the mistake of trying too hard, especially at first. Usually it is better for the stepparent to move slowly, because it takes time for the child to adjust to the new situation and to reevaluate the past parental relationship (see Inset 15-1). It is also important to the child to figure out just what the remaining parent's feelings are toward the new mate. Making this adjustment is even more difficult when the stepparent tries to replace the natural parent, especially if the child is still seeing his or her real parent. Probably the best course for the stepparent is to take on a supplemental role, meeting the needs of the child not met by the previous parent. In this way the stepparent eases direct competition with the natural parent.

When a remarried family has children of its own, additional problems may arise with stepchildren. The stepchild may feel even more displaced and alienated. The remaining parent may seem to have been taken away first by the new stepparent and now by *their* new child. At least some evidence refutes this idea. Of remarried families who had children together, 78 percent rated their relationships with stepchildren as excellent, whereas only 53 percent of those who did not have children together rated their stepchildren relationships as excellent (Duberman, 1973). Perhaps having brothers or sisters takes the focus off the stepchild, allowing a more natural adjustment for both parent and child.

The role of parent is often difficult. The role of stepparent can even be more difficult, yet an empathic, caring stepparent can give a great deal to a child. The stepparent can be an additional source of love and support. The stepparent can supply friendship and, by making the family a two-parent family again, solve some of the childrearing problems of the single parent. When a stepparent enters a child's life when the child is young, it is possible and often happens that the child comes to look on the stepparent as his or her real parent, alleviating the child's feelings of loss.

Although we have spoken only of stepparents, it is important to realize that the blended family will bring another set of kin into the relationships. By and large, new kin do not replace old kin but add to those from the first marriage. For example, there will now be stepgrandparents. There will probably be the new spouse of the noncustodial parent. A blended family's immediate family tree can be unimaginably complex. As an extreme imagine the many relationships of the following blended family:

The Ten Commandments of Stepparenting

The natural family presents hazards enough to peaceful coexistence. Add one or two stepparents, and perhaps a set of ready-made brothers and sisters, and a return to the law of the jungle is virtually ensured. Some guidelines for survival include the following advice for stepparents:

1. *Provide neutral territory.* Just as the Romans had gods that lived in the house and protected it, stepchildren have a strong sense of ownership. The questions: "Whose house is it? Whose spirit presides here?" are central issues. Even the very young child recognizes that the prior occupation of a territory confers a certain power. When two sets of children are brought together one regards itself as the "main family" and the other as a subfamily, . . . and the determining factor is whose house gets to be the family home. One school of thought suggests that when a couple remarries they should move to a new house, even if it means

selling the family heirlooms. If it is impossible to finance a move to neutral territory, it is important to provide a special, inviolate place which belongs to each child individually.
2. *Don't try to fit a preconceived role.* When dealing with children the best course is to be straight right from the start. Each parent is an individual with all his or her faults, peculiarities and emotions, and the children are just going to have to get used to this parent. Certainly a stepparent should make every effort to be kind, intelligent and a good sport, but that does not mean being saccharine sweet. Children have excellent radar for detecting phoniness, and are quick to lose respect for any adult who will let them walk all over him or her.
3. *Set limits and enforce them.* One of the most difficult areas for a natural parent and stepparent living together is to decide on disciplinary measures. The natural parent has a tendency to feel that the stepparent is being unreasonable in demands that the children behave in a certain way. If the parents fight between themselves about discipline, the children will quickly force a wedge between them. It is important that the parents themselves work out the rules in advance and support one another when the rules need to be enforced. . . .
4. *Allow an outlet for feelings by the children for natural parents.* It is often difficult for the

stepparent to accept that his or her stepchildren will maintain a natural affection for their natural parent who is no longer living in the household. The stepparent may take this as a personal rejection. Children need to be allowed to express feelings about the natural parent who is absent. This needs to be supported in a neutral way so that the children do not feel disloyal.
5. *Expect ambivalence.* Stepparents are often alarmed when children appear on successive days or successive hours to show both emotions of strong love and strong hate toward them. Ambivalence is normal in all human relationships, but nowhere is it more accentuated than in the feelings of the stepchild towards the stepparent.
6. *Avoid mealtime misery.* For many stepfamilies meals are an excruciating experience. This, after all, is the time when the dreams of blissful family life confront reality. Most individuals cling to a belief in the power of food to make people happy. . . . Since it is the stepmother who is most often charged with serving the emotionally laden daily bread, she often leaves the table feeling thoroughly rejected. If the status quo becomes totally unbearable, it is forgivable to decide that peace is more important and turn a blind eye, at least temporarily, to nutrition. Some suggested strategies include: daily vitamins, rid the house of all "junk"

INSET 15-1, CONTINUED

foods, let the children fix their own meals, eat out a lot, and/or let father do some of the cooking so he can share in the rejection. Stepfathers tend to be less concerned about food refusal but more concerned about table manners.

7. *Don't expect instant love.* One of the problems facing a new stepparent is the expectation of feeling love for the child and for that love to be returned. It takes time for emotional bonds to be forged, and sometimes this never occurs. All stepparents must acknowledge that eventuality.

Alternately, nonacceptance by the children is often a major problem. Some children make it very clear that "*You* are not *my* mother or father!" This can be very painful or anger provoking, especially if it is the stepparent who is doing the cooking and laundry, and giving allowances. Most children under three have little problem adapting with relative ease. Children over five have more difficulty. . . .

8. *Don't take all the responsibility. The child has some too.* Ultimately, how well the stepparent gets along with the stepchild depends in part upon the kind of child he or she is. Children, like adults, come in all types and sizes. Some are simply more lovable than others. If the new stepmother has envisioned herself as the mother of a cuddly little tot and finds herself with a sullen, vindictive twelve-year-old who regards her with considerable suspicion, she is likely to experience considerable disappointment. Like it or not, the stepparent has to take what he or she gets. But that doesn't mean taking all the guilt for a less than perfect relationship.

9. *Be patient.* The words to remember here are "things take time." The first few months and often years have many difficult periods. The support and encouragement of other parents who have had other similar experiences can be an invaluable aid.

10. *Maintain the primacy of the marital relationship.* It has been our experience that most stepparenting relationships have resulted from divorce by one or both members of the couple. There is a certain amount of guilt left over about the breakup of the previous relationship which may spill over into the present relationship and create difficulties when there are arguments. The couple needs to remember that their relationship is primary in the family. The children need to be shown that the parents get along together, can settle disputes, and most of all will not be divided by the children. While parenting may be a central element in the couple's relationship, both partners need to commit time and energy to the development of a strong couple relationship; this bond includes, but is greater than, their parental responsibilities.

Source: Turnbull & Turnbull, 1983.

Ex-husband (with two children in custody of their natural mother) marries new wife with two children in her custody. They have two children. Ex-wife also remarries man with two children, one in his custody and one in the custody of his ex-wife who has also remarried and had a child with her second husband who also has custody of one child from his previous marriage. The ex-husband's parents are also divorced and both have remarried. Thus when he remarries, his children have two complete sets of grandparents on his side, plus one set on the mother's side, plus perhaps two sets on the stepfather's side.

The example could go to any level of complexity; indeed trying to sort out all of the relationships in some blended families becomes an impossible task. When one considers the complexities of the blended family, it is surprising that as many remarriages are as successful as seem to be.

Mary Ann Lamanna and Agnes Riedmann (1981) also point out the inadequacy of family law in dealing with the blended family. For example, there are no provisions for balancing husbands' financial obligations to spouses and children from current and previous marriages. What are the support rights of stepchildren in stepfamilies or in stepfamilies that end in divorce (Kargman, 1983)? And although all states have laws governing sexual relations between blood relatives, many states do not cover sexual relations between members of reconstituted families.

Those Who Choose to Remain Single

As we have found, Americans divorce in great numbers, and they also remarry in great numbers. Yet, some 20 percent of those divorcing choose not to remarry — for many reasons. For instance, persons who were married a long time may wish to remarry but find their choice of prospective mates limited by the discrepancy between their age and the younger age of prospective partners. This is especially true for the older divorced or widowed woman, in part because of men's shorter life expectancy. In the later years, after sixty, there are far fewer men than women generally.

A few who choose not to remarry may be unable to give up the lost spouse psychologically. This is especially true of the widowed who sometimes feel disloyal to the deceased spouse. Often the children of the widowed spouse discourage marriage as being disloyal to their deceased parent or because they are fearful a new stepparent may take what is rightfully theirs.

But probably most who choose to remain single simply do not want to assume the responsibilities of marriage again. They may have adjusted well to single life and may enjoy the freedom to do as they please; they find meeting new people stimulating, and so on. Or they may not have adjusted to single life but feel that their life is still better than it was when they were married. They may feel so bitter about their previous marriage that they generalize this bitterness to all marriages and perhaps generally to the opposite sex. There are those who are afraid to take the risk again. A few may wish to remarry but set such high demands for the second mate, trying to ensure success, that no one can ever meet their high expectations.

Regardless of the reasons why a person remains single after divorce, he or she may have some difficulties because American society remains marriage oriented. Loneliness, loss of previous friends, job discrimination, loan discrimination, and general disapproval of the divorced single person still remain to some degree. It is partially because of these pressures that most divorced people seek remarriage.

Summary

High remarriage rates indicate that the high divorce rates do not necessarily mean that Americans are disenchanted with marriage as an institution. Rather, high divorce rates may mean that Americans have high expectations for marriage as well as the freedom to end marriage when their expectations are not fulfilled.

The majority of divorced persons remarry, most of them within a few years of divorce. A few remarry as soon as possible, but the rest are usually cast into single life for at least a short period of time. The adjustment to single life is often difficult, especially for those who have been married a long time. Learning to date and interrelate with the opposite sex as a single person after many years of marriage is especially difficult because the newly single person's self-image has for so long been that of a married person, part of a couple. The newly single person may also be insecure and may suffer from feelings of failure and guilt. These feelings make it hard to relate to new persons.

Remarriage is sought by most divorced persons. Yet this is often a difficult choice because the idea of marriage evokes negative attitudes based on a negative experience with marriage. People marrying for a second time carry with them attitudes and expectations from their first marital experience. In many cases they also continue to have to cope with their first family. Visiting children, child support, and alimony payments may add to the adjustment problems in the second marriage.

Children from prior marriages often add to the responsibilities of second marriage. Becoming a stepparent to the new spouse's children is not easy. A second family may have children from several sources. Each spouse may have children from his or her previous marriage and in time they may have children together. Children from previous marriages often mean continued interaction between the formerly married couple when the former mate visits with or takes the children periodically. Many remarriages, especially when children from the previous marriage are present, actually become relationships among four adults. The remarried pair naturally have their own relationship, but in addition each will have some level of relationship with the divorced spouse.

About 20 percent of those divorcing never remarry. For these single life becomes permanent. However, as divorce rates rise, the likelihood of remarriage rises because there are more potential partners. At present about one in four American marriages involves at least one person who was formerly married. Remarriage, then, has definitely become a way of life for a significant number of Americans.

Divorce and Remarriage: A Child's Perspective*

Children face a number of changed life experiences following divorce. First and foremost, there is a *change in parent/child relations*. Usually *father will be absent* from the home (90 percent of the cases). Thus his role will be *fulfilled by the mother*, the mother's boyfriend, or a stepparent in the case of remarriage. The real father may drop out of his relationship with the child, maintain a partial intermittent relationship, or in a minority of cases actually improve his relationship with his children. The latter occurs when a divorced father tries to stay involved and, at times, has the children completely to himself. At such times he must give the children his full attention because mother is not there to attend to them as she was during the marriage. Research suggests that frequent availability of the father is associated with positive adjustment, especially for boys.

Another change for the child is often a *downward shift economically*, accompanied by practical problems of living. In most cases divorced mothers are less well off economically than when they were married. There is often a move to more modest housing. The move may involve the loss of friends, neighborhood, and familiar school.

Mother usually must work. If she had not done so before, the child may experience a double loss (both parents) because now mother is also gone much of the time. Her working, yet being solely responsible for mothering and home duties, contributes to an overload on her and to a *more chaotic lifestyle*

*This material has been adapted in part from: E. Mavis Hetherington. "Divorce: A Child's Perspective." *American Psychologist*, October 1979, 851–65.

(erratic meals, and so forth) for the family. This, of course, contributes to the child's feelings of loss of attention and affection. Being tired, feeling harassed, and generally overextended strains the mother's relationship with her children. Also, the presence of a second parent can serve as a protective buffer between the other parent and the child. When there is only one parent and the parent/child relationship has problems, there is nowhere else to turn.

Children are usually asked to *grow up faster* in one-parent families. They must be more self-sufficient and assume more responsibilities. This can be positive if the child copes successfully or it can lead to feelings of being overwhelmed, of incompetence, and of resentment on the child's part.

Children must cope with *new adults* vying for the parents' attention and affection if the parents date others or remarry. Oftentimes parents beginning to date again find it difficult to deal openly with the subject of their dating and may simply avoid discussing it, assuming the attitude that "this is one thing the children will just have to understand and accept." Therefore in many instances the subject is never really dealt with. The occurrence of parental dating brings a new influence into the child's world. Before, the children were the main focus of the custodial parent's affection, time, and energy. Even with the noncustodial parent's dating, visitation time is now often shared with another adult. The person being dated is often viewed as an intruder usurping time and affection.

A child's acceptance of the reality of his or her parents' divorce may be impeded by the conscious or unconscious hope for a reconciliation between the parents. Dating is thereby troublesome because it implies that reconciliation will not happen. The feelings of being abandoned by the absent parent are often carried a step further by parental dating, which arouses fears that the remaining parent will abandon them also.

A child may, on the other hand, feel genuine affection for the dating partner but wonder whether if by liking the new person, he or she is being loyal to the missing parent. This dilemma can cause a child a great deal of conflict and guilt.

Measuring the effect of divorce on a child's well-being is difficult. Parents tend to minimize the effect so as to avoid their own feelings of guilt. And children themselves aren't able to understand, much less describe, the effects they feel. There is no question that a traumatic life change affects children, but the exact effects will be unique to a given child. The circumstances of the parental breakup, the age and temperament of the child, the other support systems in the child's life such as grandparents, the sex of the child, and the practical problems that are created by the breakup will all influence the child's reaction to the parents' separation and divorce. Generally, the better the relationship that the parents can maintain, the easier it is for the children.

CHAPTER 16

ACTIVELY SEEKING MARITAL GROWTH AND FULFILLMENT

CONTENTS

16

The family is still the "place where, when you go there, they have to take you in."

Robert Frost, *The Death of the Hired Man*

We began our journey of marriage and family study saying, "What an exciting — and essential — field of study: intimate relationships." What better way to end this journey than by examining ideal families. What could my intimate family life be like if I could make it the best possible? Even if I succeed in solving the major problems that will surely arise in my marriage, can I build a marital relationship that is better than just satisfactory? Can my mate and I create an intimate relationship that is secure and comfortable, yet growing and exciting at the same time? Will my family be able to rear children that care about themselves and the community of which they are a part? Children who will grow into adults who are able themselves to be intimate, caring, and loving?

One of the basic assumptions on which this book is based is that the fully functioning family can act as a buffer against mental and physical illness. What can we do to make our family relationships more fully functioning? Although everything we have discussed thus far bears on this question, this concluding chapter will specifically attend to the goal of seeking marital growth and fulfillment. The first step is to summarize the qualities found in strong and healthy families.

Qualities of Strong Families*

Researchers have begun to study strong, healthy, successful families. Those doing the research point out that volumes have been written about what is wrong with the family but little has been written about what is right in the successful family. "We don't learn how to do anything by looking only at how it *shouldn't* be done. We learn most effectively by examining how to do something correctly and by studying a positive model" (Stinnett, 1979, p. 24). Such research suggests six qualities shared by all strong and successful families.

1. *Appreciation*: This first quality is one of the most important. It emerged from the research in many ways and seemed to permeate the family. The family members give each other many positive psychological reinforcements and make each other feel good about themselves. Each of us likes to be with people who make us feel good about ourselves, yet many families fall into interactional patterns where they make each other feel bad. One general difficulty we have about expressing appreciation is that we fear that others will take it as empty flattery, that we are not sincere. In strong families members are able to find good qualities in one another and to express appreciation for them.
2. *Spending time together*: A second quality found among strong families is that they do a lot of things together. It is not a "false" togetherness; it is not a "smothering" type of togetherness. They genuinely enjoy

*Some of this material has been adapted from "In Search of Strong Families," by Nick Stinnett. In N. Stinnett, B. Chesser, and J. DeFrain (Eds.), *Building Family Strengths*. Lincoln: University of Nebraska Press, 1979, pp. 23–30.

being together. Another important point is that these families structure their lifestyles so that they can spend time together. They make it happen. And this togetherness exists in all areas of their lives — eating meals, recreation, work. Much of the time together is spent in active interaction rather than in passive activities such as watching television.

3. *Good communication patterns*: The third quality was not a surprise. The strong families have good communication patterns. They spend time talking with each other. This is closely related to the fact that they spend a lot of time together. It's hard for people to communicate if they do not spend time with each other. Family therapist Virginia Satir has stated that often families are so fragmented, so busy, and spend so little time together that they communicate with each other through rumor.

Another important aspect of communication is that these families listen well. By being good listeners, they are saying to one another, "You respect me enough to listen to what I have to say. I'm interested enough to listen too."

Another factor related to communication is that these families do fight. They get angry at each other, but they get conflict out in the open and are able to discuss the problem. They share their feelings about alternative ways of dealing with the problem and of selecting a solution that is best for everybody.

4. *Commitment*: A fourth characteristic of these strong families is a high degree of commitment. They are deeply committed to promoting each others' happiness and welfare. They are also very committed to the family group, as reflected by the fact that they invest much of their time and energies in the family. "The individual family member is integrated into a web of mutual affection and respect. By belonging and being committed to something greater than oneself, there is less chance that individualism will sour into alienation or egocentrism" (Gardner, 1981, p. 94).

Some of the most informative research on commitment has been done in communes. One of the main differences found between successful and unsuccessful groups was commitment. Those communes that are the most successful, that last the longest, that are the most satisfying in terms of the relationships are those in which there is a great deal of commitment — to each other and to the group. Commitment in the communes is reflected in the amount of time the members spent together. The same is true with strong families.

All of us are busy and sometimes feel that we are being pulled in a thousand different directions at the same time. The strong families experience the same problem. One interesting approach these families used when life got too hectic — to the extent that they were not spending as much together as they wanted — they would sit down and make a list of the different activities in which they were involved. They would go over that list critically and inevitably would find some things that they really did not want to be doing, or that did not give much happiness, or that were not very important to them. So they would scratch those activities and involvements off the list. This would free time for their families, would relieve some of the pressure. As a result they were happier with their lives in general and more satisfied with their family relationships.

This idea sounds simple, but how many of us do it? We too often get involved and not always because we want to be. We act as if we cannot change the situation, but we do have a choice. An important point about strong families is that they take the initiative to structure their lifestyle in a way that enhances the quality of their family relationships and their satisfaction. They are on the "offensive." They do not just react; they make things happen. There is a great deal that families can do to make life more enjoyable. These strong families exercise that ability.

5. *High degree of religious orientation*: The fifth quality that these families express is a high degree of religious orientation. This finding agrees with research from the past forty years, which shows a positive relationship between religion, marriage happiness, and successful family relationships. Of course, we know that there are persons who are not religious who have happy marriages and good family relationships. Nevertheless these strong families went to church together often and participated in religious activities together. Most of them, although not all of them, were members of organized churches. Perhaps the underlying factor is not an overt religious orientation, but rather a strongly held and shared value system. Family members believe in something and those beliefs are shared by all family members.

6. *Ability to deal with crises in a positive manner*: The final quality that these families have is the ability to deal with crises and problems in a positive way. Not that they enjoy crises, but they are able to handle them constructively. They manage, even in the darkest of situations, to look at the situation and to see some positive element, no matter how small, and to focus on it. For example, in a particular crisis it may be that they rely to a greater extent on each other and a developed trust they have in each other. They are able to unite in dealing with the crisis instead of being fragmented by it. They deal with the problem and are supportive of each other.

It does not seem unreasonable that family members exhibit such characteristics as we have listed. We usually start our family with mutual appreciation, wanting to spend time together, feeling committed, and trying to communicate well. Yet many families seem to lose these characteristics as time passes. How can a family keep these characteristics? How can they get them back if they start to lose them? The first step is awareness. A second step is to consciously work to maintain and improve them.

"... And They Lived Happily Ever After"

The American scenario of marriage has always included "and they lived happily ever after." This meant that once you found the right person, fell

truly in love, and married, all your problems would be over. Of course this is a fairy tale. We all know that married couples will certainly face problems.

Yet the persistence of this fairy tale, even at only the unconscious level, hampers many Americans' efforts to realize the fullest possible potentials in their marriages. To find out if this fairy tale influences you, examine your reaction to the following statement: "All married couples should periodically seek to improve their marriage through direct participation in therapy, counseling, or marriage enrichment programs."

What do you think? Following are some typical reactions:

- "It might be a good idea if the couple is unhappy or having problems."
- "I know couples who need some help, but Jane and I are already getting along pretty well. It wouldn't help us."
- "We already know what our problems are. All we need to do is. . . ."
- "I'd be embarrassed to seek outside help for my marriage. It would mean I was a personal failure."
- "We're so busy now, what with work, the children, and social engagements, we wouldn't have time for any of those things."

- "John is a good husband [Mary is a good wife]. I really couldn't ask him [her] to participate in anything like that. He [she] would feel I wasn't happy with him [her] or our marriage."
- "I could be happier, but overall our marriage is fine."

It is true that not all married couples need to seek counseling. But it is also true that marriage needs to be more than just maintained to be successful.

Although an analogy between marriage and the automobile is superficial and a gross oversimplification, it may clarify this point. An unmaintained car quickly malfunctions and wears out; a well-maintained car gives less trouble and lasts longer. However, over and beyond maintenance a car may be modified to run better (faster, smoother, more economically, and so on) and improved (buying better tires, or changing the carburetion, exhaust, compression, gearing, and so on). Most Americans spend most of their adult lives married. Yet they expend little time and energy improving their marriage. At best they often just maintain it. If the marriage becomes too bad, they leave it to seek a new marriage that will be better. The new marriage (car) may be better for a while, but without maintenance and improvement, it too will soon malfunction.

Some Americans expend a fair amount of energy seeking a new mode of marriage. Perhaps communes are the answer. Maybe just living together and avoiding legal marriage is the answer. Yet disenchantment quickly grows with the "improved" alternatives to marriage. The new commune member who had communications problems with the spouse finds that communicating intimately with seven other people is even more difficult. The cohabiting couple who thought that limited commitment was the way to avoid the humdrum in their life together soon find that a prolonged lack of commitment leads to increasing insecurity and discomfort. Perhaps the energies spent seeking some ideal alternative to marriage might be better spent working on marriage itself.

After all most of us married the people we did because we loved them, wanted to be with them, wanted to do things for them. We married out of our own decision in most cases. We started out supposedly with the best of all things going for us, "love." Where did it go? Why wasn't it able to conquer all of our problems? Might it be that the fairy tale "and they lived happily ever after" kept us from deliberately setting about to build a better marriage? Did we think that love would automatically take care of everything?

In reality a number of factors combine to keep most Americans from taking a more active part in improving their marriages. The fairy tale we have been discussing has been called the "myth of naturalism" (see Vincent, 1973). This is the feeling that marriage is "natural," that it will take care of itself if we select the right partner. That is, many people believe that outside forces may support or hinder their marriage but that married couples need do little for marriages to function well, especially when the outside forces are good (full employment, little societal stress, and so on).

Another factor is the general "privatism" that pervades American culture. "It's nobody else's business" is a common attitude we seem to share about our problems in general and our marriages in particular. Marriage is a private affair. Our intimate and personal lives are not to be shared publicly — that's bad taste. To seek outside activities to improve marriage means sharing personal information about marriage, which is an invasion of privacy.

A third factor is the cynicism that treats marriage as a joke and thus heads off attempts to improve it (Mace & Mace, 1974). "You should have known better than to get married. Don't complain to me about your problems." This attitude contradicts the romantic concept of marriage but acts just as strongly to keep people from deliberately seeking to improve their marriages. "Why would anyone want to improve this dumb institution?" Even though American society is marriage oriented, there is still a great deal of ridicule of "being married." Facing up to and countering the antifamily themes found in American society is an important step toward revitalizing marriage and the family (Etzioni, 1983).

Despite these factors there is a growing trend toward actively seeking marriage improvement. For example, more than 60,000 couples have participated in the Roman Catholic Marriage Encounter program since it started in 1967. Although created for Catholics, it is open to all couples who wish to participate. Such programs are indicative that the idea of marriage improvement is finding a place.

In order to improve a marriage, it is necessary to believe that relationships can be improved. In other words, the myth of naturalism must be overcome. A marriage will not just naturally take care of itself. In addition the privatism and cynicism that surround marriage must be reduced if effective steps are to be taken to enrich a marriage.

To improve their marriage, a couple must work on three things: (1) themselves as individuals, (2) their relationship, and (3) the economic environment within which the marriage exists. We have already looked at these elements. For example, in Chapter 4 we discussed the self-actualized person in the fully functioning family; in Chapter 7 we examined marriage as an economic institution and found that the economics of one's marriage will drastically affect the marital relationship; in Chapter 5 we looked at ways to improve communication within a relationship.

This final chapter will stress the idea that every person does have the ability to improve his or her marriage. Marriages tend to get into trouble because many people believe that they can't do much about their marriage and because many of us simply don't take the time to nourish our marriage and make it healthier.

Although this chapter deals specifically with activities designed to improve one's marital relationship, it is important that a couple work to improve the other two influences on marriage; namely, themselves as individuals and their economic situation. Neglect of any one of these influences or emphasis on only one can still lead to marital failure. In fact, a couple can be extremely successful in one of the three areas and still fail miserably at marriage, as the two following cases demonstrate.

> Bill and Susan both worked to buy the many things they wanted: a house, fine furnishings, nice clothing, a fancy car, and so on. Bill even held two jobs for a while. Certainly no one could fault their industriousness and hard work. In time their marital affluence became the envy of all who knew them. Then, after seven years of marriage, they divorced. Their friends were surprised. "They had everything, why should they divorce?" Unfortunately they didn't have much of a relationship other than to say hello and goodby as each went off to work. In addition each worked so hard that neither had time for self-improvement. No self-improvement usually means eventual boredom and this often portends failure.

Bill and Susan were successful with their marital economic environment but did not pay enough attention to improving themselves as individuals or to improving their relationship.

> Jack and Mary believed that the key to successful marriage was self-improvement. Both took extension classes in areas of their own interest. They attended sensitivity training groups and personal expansion workshops. Unfortunately they could seldom attend these functions together because of conflicting work schedules. Soon they were so busy improving themselves that they had little time for one another. The house was a shambles, the yard was weeds, and their relationship disappeared under a maze of "do your own thing" self-improvements.
>
> After seven years they divorced. Their friends were surprised. "After all, they're so dynamic and interesting, why should they divorce?" Unfortunately they became so self-oriented that their relationship disappeared and their living environment became unimportant.

Jack and Mary worked so hard to improve themselves individually that they had no time for each other or for their home.

Both of these scenarios happen every day. And the second is becoming more prevalent with the growing interest in the human potential movement. The very concepts used in this book — self-actualization, self-fulfillment, and human growth orientation — can all be taken to such an individual extreme that marriage is disrupted.

> A possible fallacy of the human potential movement is making self-fulfillment the central goal, while seemingly ignoring the fact that the human being is essentially a relationship-oriented and interactional creature. If an educational or therapeutic goal is to unlock human potential, there must be a corresponding focus on marriage and family relationships. (Cromwell & Thomas, 1976, p. 15)

More and more family researchers as well as general observers of American society see excessive hedonism as America's greatest enemy. Stressing individuality at the expense of mutuality overlooks the importance of successful human relationships, which many see as a basic human need, even for successful individual functioning. Amitai Etzioni (1983) suggests that mutuality, the basic need for interpersonal bonds, is not something each person creates on his/her own, which each then brings to the relationship. Rather it is constructed by individuals working with one another, mutually. It is this mutual working together that is the essence of the healthy family.

To make marriage as rewarding and fulfilling as possible, a couple must be committed first to the idea that "effective family relationships do not just happen, they are the result of deliberate efforts by members of the family unit" (Cromwell & Thomas, 1976). Then they must be prepared to work on all three facets of marriage: to improve themselves as individuals, to improve their interactional relationship, and to improve their economic environment.

Such a commitment helps a couple anticipate problems before they arise rather than simply reacting to them. When there is commitment to active management and creative guidance of a marriage, the marriage can become richly fulfilling and growth enhancing, both for the family as a social unit and for the individuals within the family.

A Short Overview of Marriage Improvement Programs

Many helping techniques are now available to families. Some aim at solving existing problems, others aim at general family improvement. We will briefly examine some of these techniques, in the hope of accomplishing two goals. First, it may help families seek out experiences that may benefit them. Second, it may alert families to some of the possible dangers involved in unselective, nondiscriminative participation in some of the popular techniques.

Help for family problems in the past has usually come from relatives, friends, ministers, and family doctors. The idea of enriching family life and of improving already adequate marriages simply did not occur to most married people. Marriage traditionally was an institution for child-rearing, economic support, and proper fulfillment of marital duties defined in terms of masculine and feminine roles. If there were problems in these areas, help might be sought. If not the marriage was fine.

Marriage in modern America, however, more and more has been given responsibility for individual happiness and emotional fulfillment. The criteria used to judge a marriage have gradually shifted from how well each member fulfills roles and performs proper marital functions to the personal contentment, fulfillment, and happiness each individual in the marriage feels.

Working to improve one's
marriage

Marital complaints now concern sex-role dissatisfaction, unequal growth
and personal fulfillment opportunities, feelings of personal unhappiness,
and feelings that the marriage is shortchanging the individual partners.
That is, more and more marriage problems revolve around personal dissatisfactions than around traditional marital functioning. The "me" in
marriage seems to have become more important than the "us" or the
marriage itself. Perhaps there is too much "me" in modern American
marriages.

Emphasis on emotional fulfillment as the most important aspect of
marriage makes an enduring marital union much more difficult to attain.
According to one authority, "Emotional fulfillment has always occurred
in the family; probably more so in the past than is usual today. But it was
never before seen as the primary function of the family. It was a lucky
'by-product' (Putney, 1972). For example, when Australia was first colo-
nized by male convicts, there was a brisk trade in mail-order wives because there were no available women in the country. Most of these marriages
seem to have been successful for the simple reason

that the prospective husband and wife expected things of each other that the
other could provide. The man needed assistance and companionship of a woman

in the arduous task of making a farm, and he wanted sons to help him. He expected certain skills in his wife, but all girls raised in rural England were likely to have them. Her expectations were similarly pragmatic. She expected him to know farming, to work hard, and to protect her. Neither thought of the other as a happiness machine. If they found happiness together more often than American couples do, it may have been they were not looking so hard for it. They fulfilled each other because they shared a life; they did not share a life in the hope of being fulfilled. (Putney, 1972)

The search for emotional fulfillment has led to many new methods to gain this end. Sensitivity training, encounter groups, family enrichment weekends, sex therapy, sexuality workshops, communication improvement groups, massage and bodily awareness training, psychodrama, women's and men's liberation groups, and many other experiential activities have sprung up in recent years to help Americans enrich their lives.

Although this chapter's overview cannot hope to do justice to the many marriage improvement techniques that are emerging, let's take a brief look at some typical ones before we examine marriage enrichment in more detail.

1. *Courses on marriage and the family*: These are offered by most colleges. They aim to help people better understand the institution of marriage. Many schools offer even more specialized courses, often in the evening, on marital communication, economics of marriage, childrearing, and so on.
2. *Encounter groups*: These consist of group interactions, usually with strangers, where the masks and games used by the marital partners to manipulate one another and to conceal real feelings that may be unpleasant to one or both are stripped away. The group actively confronts the person, forcing him or her to examine some problems and the faulty methods that might have been used to solve or deny problems. There is a great deal of emotion released by such groups. Couples contemplating attending an encounter group should carefully consider the guidelines suggested on page 539.
3. *Family enrichment weekends*: These involve the entire family in a retreat setting where they work together to improve their family life. The family may concentrate on learning new activities that can be shared. They may listen to lectures, see films, and share other learning experiences. They may interact with other families, learning through the experiences of others. They may participate in exercises designed to improve family communication or general family functioning.
4. *Women's and men's consciousness raising groups*: These groups center their discussions and exercises on helping people escape from stereotypical sex roles and liberate the parts of their personalities that have been submerged in the sex role. For example, women may work to become more assertive, believing that the typical feminine role has been too passive. Men, on the other hand, may work to be more expressive of feeling, because the typical masculine role has repressed emotional

display and worked against the man's being communicative of his feelings.

5. *Married couples' communication workshops*: These workshops may be on-going groups or weekend workshops in which communication is the center of attention. Role playing, learning how to fight fairly, under-standing communication processes, and actively practicing in front of the group all help the couple toward better communication. An impor-tant aspect of this is the critique made by the group after a couple communicates about something that causes a problem for them.

6. *Massage and bodily awareness training*: This training is often a part of sexuality workshops. It is aimed at developing the couple's awareness of their own bodies as well as teaching each the techniques involved in physically pleasuring the other through massage. The art of physical relaxation is part of bodily awareness training.

7. *Psychodrama*: This is a form of psychotherapy developed by J. L. Mor-eno. It is used to dramatize problems by acting them out with other group members as the players. In the case of marriage enrichment, it is used to help individuals in the family better understand the roles of other family members. This understanding is accomplished mainly through timely changes of role by the individuals participating in the drama under the direction of the group leader. Shifting roles also helps each player understand how the other person in the drama feels and sees the situation.

8. *Sensitivity training*: This training consists of exercises in touching, con-centrating and heightening awareness, and empathy for the feelings of one's mate, which increase each mate's sensitivity for the other as well as increasing self-awareness.

9. *Sex therapy and sexuality workshops*: These focus on a couple's sexual relationship. Sex therapy is used to overcome sexual problems. Sex-uality workshops are designed more to help couples improve this as-pect of their relationship than to cure severe problems. Such a workshop assumes that there are no major sexual problems. The goal is to heighten sexual awareness so that the couple's sexual relations may be enriched. Films, discussion, mutual exploration, sensitivity, and massage and bodily awareness techniques are all used to reduce inhibitions and expand the couple's sexual awareness.

There are many other techniques, but these give an idea of what is available.

Suggested Guidelines for Choosing Marriage Improvement Programs

Unfortunately with popularity comes misuse. The large demand for such programs has brought untrained and, occasionally, unscrupulous people into the fields of marriage counseling and marriage enrichment. For ex-ample, it is relatively simple as well as monetarily rewarding to run a weekend encounter group of some kind. All you need is a place where the people can meet. Some participants have also found that not all such experiences are beneficial, nor do they always accomplish what is claimed. In a minority of cases, unexpected repercussions such as divorce, job change, and even hospitalization for mental disturbance have occurred after some supposedly beneficial group experience. Consider what happened to the following couple because one partner could not tolerate the intensity of the group experience.

> John and Mary have been married for eleven years and have two children. He has always been shy and uncomfortable among people, but despite this he has worked out a stable, satisfying relationship with Mary. She is more socially oriented than John. She began to attend a series of group encounter sessions out of curiosity. As her interest increased, she decided that John would benefit from a group experience. She asked him to attend a weekend marathon. Unfortunately, the group turned its attention too strongly on John's shyness, causing him acute discomfort that finally resulted in his fleeing from the group. He remained away from his home and work for ten days. On returning he demanded a divorce because he felt that he was an inadequate husband. Fortunately psychotherapeutic help was available and John was able to work out the problems raised by the group encounter.

Couples seeking marital enrichment or help for marital problems are advised to check out carefully the people offering such services. They should also discuss the kind of experiences they want and make sure that the agreed-on experiences are indeed what is offered. For example, if a couple decides that they would like to improve their sexual relations and can do so by seeking some general sensitivity training (learning to feel more comfortable with their bodies, to be more aware, to give and accept bodily pleasure), they might be rudely shocked if the group leader has a nude encounter group with the goal of examining closely each person's emotional hang-ups about sex.

Couples who have a reasonably satisfactory marriage can use the following guidelines in choosing a marriage enrichment activity:

1. Choose the activity together and participate together if possible.
2. If only one mate can participate, do so with the consent of the other and bring the other into the activity as much as possible by sharing your experiences.
3. In general avoid the one-shot weekend group as it is often too intense and no follow-up is available if needed.
4. Never jump into a group experience on impulse. Give it a lot of thought, understanding that such experiences may be painful in the course of leading to growth.
5. Do not participate in groups where the people are friends and associates if the group's goal is total openness and emotional expression. What occurs in a group session should be privileged information.

6. Don't remain with a group that seems to have an ax to grind, that insists that everybody be a certain type of person or that all *must* participate in every activity.
7. Participate in groups that have a formal connection with a local professional on whom you can check. The local professional is also a source of follow-up if necessary.
8. A group of six to sixteen members is optimum size. Too small a group may result in scapegoating, whereas too large a group cannot operate effectively. (Some of these guidelines come from Shostrom, 1969.)

Such cautions are not meant to dissuade couples from trying to improve their marriages. They are simply meant to help couples select experiences that are beneficial and supportive rather than threatening and disruptive. Legitimate marriage counselors throughout the United States are working to upgrade their profession and tighten the rules guiding counseling practices. Many states now have licensing provisions for marriage and family counseling.

The foremost organization in the nation for accrediting and certifying marriage counselors is The American Association of Marriage and Family Therapists, 225 Yale Avenue, Claremont, California 91711. At no charge it will supply you with a list of three or more accredited marriage counselors in your area. Psychologists are also active in marital counseling and enrichment training. Membership in the American Psychological Association (APA) indicates that the member has met minimum training requirements and has agreed to abide by a strict set of ethics in client relationships. The American Association of Sex Educators and Counselors has established certification standards for sex therapists. You can receive a copy of these standards and a list of certified sex therapists by writing to Sex Therapy Certification Committee, American Association of Sex Educators and Counselors, Suite 304, 5010 Wisconsin Avenue N.W., Washington, D.C. 20016. In addition more than 350 marriage and family-oriented nonprofit social service organizations throughout the nation are affiliated with the Family Service Association of America, 44 East 23rd Street, New York, New York 10010, and the National Association of Social Workers, Suite 600, 1425 H Street N.W., Washington, D.C. 20005. Many churches also offer family counseling and enrichment programs. In fact, some churches have been pioneers in the marriage enrichment movement. Whenever seeking help, regardless of recommendations, always check the person's credentials.

An Ounce of Prevention is Worth a Pound of Cure: Marriage Enrichment

Only recently have those working in the field of marriage and family counseling turned their attention away from marital problems and focused on marriage enrichment. "What we are now seeking to do, late in the day when the scene is already strewn with marital wrecks, is to equip married couples with the insight and training that will keep their marriages in such good order that the danger of going on the rocks will be as far as possible avoided" (Mace & Mace, 1974, p. 133).

Past marital services have been remedial in nature. When a couple had a marital problem, they could seek help from numerous sources. Marriage enrichment places the emphasis on the preventive concept of facilitating positive growth. In other words, the goal is to help couples with "good" marriages further improve their relationship.

> Marriage enrichment programs are for couples who have what they perceive to be a fairly well functioning marriage and who wish to make their marriage even more mutually satisfying.
>
> Such programs are generally concerned with enhancing the couple's communication, emotional life, or sexual relationship, fostering marriage strengths and developing marriage potential while maintaining a consistent and primary focus on the relationship of the couple. (Otto, 1975, p. 137)

Some people in the field make a distinction between marriage enrichment and family life enrichment programs. The latter involve not only the primary couple but the entire family in the program. They are designed for the family without severe problems.

If couples are to direct and improve their marriage, they must increase their awareness. You can't improve anything unless you recognize what is taking place. It is helpful to organize awareness into four subcategories (see Hill, 1961): topical, self, partner, and relationship. Marriage enrichment programs usually spend a great deal of time helping couples or families to become more aware in each of these categories.

For example, sensitivity training exercises help you focus on your internal sensory, thinking, and emotional processes. A realistic picture of yourself, openness to your feelings, minimal defensiveness, and eliminating some emotional hang-ups are goals sought by enrichment programs in the category of self-awareness.

Partner awareness involves knowing accurately what your partner is experiencing in terms of his or her own self-awareness (see Miller et al., 1975). For example, how does this behavior affect my partner? Is my partner happy, sad, or indifferent? How can I best communicate with my partner? What does my partner think or feel about this? Answering such questions accurately is the goal of partner awareness training.

Relationship awareness shifts the focus from the behavior of one individual to the interactional patterns of the couple or the entire family. For example, who starts an argument, who continues it, and who ends the interaction? Does each individual contribute self-disclosures, feeling inputs, negative and positive communications? Does the couple play unproductive games? If so, who initiates the game? What are the rules by which the family interacts?

> Every interrelationship has boundaries, constraints that either encourage or discourage certain types of awareness and various types of behavior. These

A Family Life Enrichment Weekend

Mr. and Mrs. Smith have been married for fifteen years. They have two children, Colin, thirteen, and Beth, ten. Their church recently started a series of family retreat weekends at a nearby mountain camp. After some discussion, the family agreed that it would be fun and rewarding to go on one of the weekends.

Early Saturday morning they arrive at the camp and move into one of the cabins. Inasmuch as nothing is scheduled until lunch, the family explores the camp and surroundings. There is a small lake with boating and fishing, a tennis court, volleyball court, and plenty of hiking trails.

At noon the twenty families gather in the cafeteria/meeting hall for lunch. Everyone is given a name tag and the leaders are introduced. After lunch each family introduces themselves. Much to the children's delight, there are many other children present. The leaders assign each family to one of five family subgroups. After lunch the family groups meet and the four families become better acquainted. The group leader then introduces the first work session entitled ''Becoming More Aware.'' There are exercises in identification of feelings and attention is given to feelings the participants would like to have more of and those they would like to experience less.

After a break the group leader discusses methods the families might use to reduce unwanted feelings and increase desired feelings. Each family then practices some of these methods while the others observe. After a family finishes, there is a general critique of their experience.

The families are free after the work session until dinner. After dinner short movies on various developmental problems are shown to the children. At the same time the parents attend a sexuality workshop. The parents are shown massage techniques designed to relax and give physical pleasure. They are asked to practice the techniques in their individual cabins. They are assured of privacy because the children will be occupied for at least another hour. The children meanwhile are asked to form small groups and discuss how the children shown in the films can be helped to meet the developmental problems portrayed.

Next morning, the first work session is devoted to the theme ''Being Free.'' This involves learning openness to experiencing each other. The children of the four families talk to one another about things they like and don't like while the parents sit and listen. Then the roles are reversed. Afterward, each family exchanges children. They are then given a hypothetical problem to work out. Each newly constituted family has a half hour to work on the problem while the other families observe.

At noon each family group eats together and then uses the hour recreational period to do something together, such as hiking, boating, fishing, or whatever they agreed on.

The afternoon work session again separates the parents and children. In each case the assignment is the same. The children are asked to form family groups where some children play the parents' roles. They are given problems to work out as a family unit. The parents also form family groups with some parents taking children's roles.

In the final dinner meeting all of the families come together. Both the families and the leaders try to summarize the experiences of the weekend and their significance. Then the leaders outline several homework assignments, one of which each family has to choose and promise to work on at home.

rules are usually outside our direct awareness and operate to create and maintain meaning and order.

We like to conceptualize rules in terms of who can do what, where, when, and how, for what length of time. This can be applied to any issue in a relationship. (Miller et al., 1975, p. 147)

For example, is personal criticism allowed in a family? Who is allowed to criticize, when, and to what degree? What is a family's mode of handling conflicts? Some talk directly about issues and try actively to solve them. Other families pretend that conflicts don't exist and ignore them, hoping they will go away. Others deal with the issue in some stereotypical manner that usually fails to solve the conflict but allows the ventilation of hostility.

Topical awareness is less important than the three we have just discussed. Topical awareness encompasses references to events, objects, ideas, places, and people, topics that constitute most of everyday conversation. By increasing topical awareness, the couple can focus on their interests, where they differ, where they coincide. They can find areas in which they can work and play together. They can recognize and tolerate those areas of their spouse's interests that they don't share.

Another purpose of marriage enrichment programs is to help couples and families develop a game plan for handling disputes and conflicts. What are the rules, how are they clarified, and what procedure can change them? "If you haven't a set of rules before the game starts, the game is likely to degenerate into a series of arguments and squabbles, and so it is with relationships" (Miller et al., 1975, p. 147). Thus most marriage enrichment programs spend a great deal of time on the development of communication skills. For example, identifying problem ownership, self-assertion, empathic listening, negotiation, and problem solving are all emphasized. Generally, the kinds of skills discussed in Chapter 5 are taught and practiced in enrichment programs.

Esteem building is another area of concern in enrichment programs. Better communication can equip a person to be more destructive as well as constructive. We sometimes forget this when lauding the improvement of communication skills. By emphasizing esteem building, by making the intent or spirit with which something is said positive, by valuing both the self and the partner, communication becomes constructive and growth enhancing. Esteem building is particularly difficult for a partner who feels devalued and inferior, thus enrichment programs stress the importance of building a relationship that acts to negate such feelings, that supports valued, positive, high-esteem feelings in family members.

The fact that a family is interested in and open to the idea of marriage enrichment is an extremely important strength. Certainly the kinds of goals sought in the marriage enrichment movement are worthwhile. These goals, however, are not as important as the general attitude toward marriage taken by a family. The family that takes an active role in guiding, improving, and working on better family relations is the family that stands the greatest chance of leading a long, happy, and meaningful life.

What Do You Think?

What do you see as the major benefits such an experience could provide a family?

Would you be willing to participate with your family in such an experience? Why or why not?

Do you have any friends who have participated in any kind of marriage enrichment experience? How did they respond to it?

Marriage with Purpose: Effective Management

Popular lore has it that the love marriage simply happens (the myth of naturalism that we discussed earlier). If we are in love, then the other factors necessary to a successful relationship and marriage will fall into place automatically, magically. There is no reason to worry about problems ahead of time. Of course there will be differences but they can be worked out successfully by any couple truly "in love."

It is almost a sacrilege to suggest that people entering love relationships should make a conscious effort to guide and build their relationship. In fact, many will argue that it is the attempted guidance and control of a relationship that ruins it. Their advice is to "relax and let it happen." This attitude implies a great tolerance on the part of each individual, because what happens may not be something the other wants. How tolerant are we? Does love mean that we must never judge our mate? Are we to accept any behavior from our mate in an effort to just "let it happen"?

Most people are tolerant only up to some given point, after which certain behavior becomes unacceptable. Most of us are quite tolerant in some areas of our life and intolerant in other areas. Of course everyone can learn to be more tolerant, but total tolerance of all things is probably impossible for most people. People have many and varying standards. The point is that when we let the relationship "happen," it usually isn't long before we and our partner discover some of our intolerances. Then we try to make changes in our mate and in our relationship. Conflict usually follows because our mate may not want to change nor have the relationship change in the direction we desire. Without agreed-on ways of handling conflict, unconscious games and strategies may take over, and soon communication is lost.

Marriage and family implies the necessity of management skills. Work, leisure, economics, emotions, interests, sex, children, eating, and the household generally all require effective management in the fully functioning family. We have discussed most of these matters elsewhere in the book but it seems a proper ending to tie them all together under the concept of effective management.

"Surely you can't be serious? Effective management belongs in business, not in my marriage." Yet every married couple, especially if they have children, are running a business. For example, just planning what the family will eat for the next week, buying it, preparing it, and cleaning up afterward requires management and organizational skill, especially if money is in short supply. There are also recurrent personal and family crises that throw off schedules and plans.

In addition to day-to-day management is the planning necessary to achieve long-range goals. Some families seem to move from catastrophe to calamity and back again. Other families seem to move smoothly through life despite the crises that arise periodically. What is the difference? Often it is one of efficient planning and management versus lack of planning and management. Look at the different attitudes toward money of the following two couples:

Jim and Marge went to college with Bill and Sally. They remained close friends after college, as both Jim and Bill got jobs with the same company. Each couple has two children. Marge works periodically and the money she earns is always saved or used to achieve some specific goal such as a trip to Europe or an addition to the house. Sally works most of the time also, but she and Bill don't care much about things such as budgeting. As long as there is enough money to pay the bills, nothing else matters.

"You and Jim are always so lucky. Bill and I have wanted to add an extra master bedroom for ourselves so we could have a retreat away from the children, but we'll never be able to afford it," complains Sally.

"Luck has nothing to do with it. Jim and I have planned to add the bedroom for a number of years. We always budget carefully so our monthly expenses are covered by Jim's salary. That way all of the money I earn less child-care costs goes into savings. The new bedroom represents my last three years of work. I'd hardly call it luck."

Naturally Sally isn't interested in hearing Marge's response. "Luck" is an easier way to explain her friend's new bedroom. Besides, what Marge is telling her is, "Be a better money manager and you, too, can add a new bedroom." This advice will only make her feel guilty and inadequate. "It isn't worth all the trouble to budget money and be tightwads to get a new bedroom," Sally will probably think to herself.

Creative family management in all areas helps to make the family run smoothly and achieve the desired goals. This reduces frustrations and conflicts because there is a feeling of success on the part of family members. Careful planning also helps a family maintain the flexibility necessary to cope with unforeseen emergencies. Such flexibility gives family members a feeling of freedom, a feeling of being able to make choices rather than having choices forced on them by events beyond their control.

The feeling of entrapment that many married persons express occurs in some cases because they do not take the initiative to plan and guide their lives. Rather, they simply react to circumstances. Of course there are times and situations when one can do nothing but react. The poor in particular often have so little control over their lives that they give up planning altogether and live by luck and fate.

Family control and rational planning become more difficult as social institutions multiply and infringe on family responsibilities.

The external stresses on the family have emerged out of necessity. When society begins to develop beyond a primitive level, its members soon find that many tasks are better performed by agencies other than the family. Priests take over the job of interceding with the supernatural; police forces, armies, and fire brigades take over that of protecting the family from physical harm; schools undertake to educate children. And, in the complex modern world, the family often has little voice in what kind of work its members will perform, or where, or for how long; all these matters are decided by impersonal forces of the marketplace or by distant corporations, unions, or government bureaus. (Wernick, 1974, p. 112)

It becomes even more important that planning and foresight and management be an integral part of family life to cope successfully with such outside pressures. The family that actively takes control of its destiny is most often the family that grows and prospers, thereby helping every member toward self-fulfillment.

The Family Will Remain and Diversify

Many try to predict the future of the American family. Their predictions vary from an early death to visualizing new and improved families that will be havens of fulfillment for their members. It is unlikely that families will disappear or that there is any ideal single family structure. All families face problems, both external environmental pressures as well as internal stresses and strains. Older generations will probably always see what seems to them to be family deterioration because their children may

choose different lifestyles from their own. Yet difference in lifestyle and in family structure does not necessarily mean deterioration. Perhaps with increased affluence and education each individual will be able to choose from a wider acceptable variety of lifestyles, thereby increasing the chances that the family will be satisfying and fulfilling to its members.

The family has always been with us and always will be. And it will also change. The family is flexible and changes with societies. This flexibility allows it to survive. It is flexible because humans are flexible and build institutions that meet their purposes at a given time. When we forget the basic flexibility of humans, we then see changes in human institutions as threatening, even when they may in fact be changes that help people meet their needs.

The idea of family has always been a concept over which people have had conflicts. There are many cultures and times change, yet the idea of family has always been one of the central concepts wherever people congregate into a society. Change is an integral part of the concept of family. As Elise Boulding has suggested: "The family has met fire, flood, famine, earthquake, war, economic and political collapse over the centuries by changing its form, its size, its behavior, its location, its environment, its reality. It is the most resilient social form available to humans" (1983, p. 259).

APPENDIX A: CONSUMER PRICE INDEX: GENERAL SUMMARY FOR SELECTED ITEMS

The CPI is not only valuable in helping a purchaser decide what items are good buys in relation to inflation, but it is most interesting to examine just to see how inflation has affected all Americans.

Note that Table A looks at prices from 1967 to 1982.

Table B gives a summary of general groups of items from April of 1982 to April of 1983 followed by a detailed breakdown of the particular items listed within the general item groups.

Source: *Monthly Labor Review*, July 1983, U.S. Department of Labor. Washington, D.C.: Government Printing Office.

TABLE A Consumer Price Index for Urban Wage Earners and Clerical Workers, annual averages and changes, 1967–82

YEAR	ALL ITEMS		FOOD AND BEVERAGES		HOUSING		APPAREL AND UPKEEP		TRANSPORTATION		MEDICAL CARE		ENTERTAINMENT		OTHER GOODS AND SERVICES	
	Index	Percent change	Index	Percent change	Index	Percent change	Index	Percent change	Index	Percent change	Index	Percent change	Index	Percent change	Index	Percent change
1967	100.0	...	100.0	...	100.0	...	100.0	...	100.0	...	100.0	...	100.0	...	100.0	...
1968	104.2	4.2	103.6	3.6	104.0	4.0	105.4	5.4	103.2	3.2	106.1	6.1	105.7	5.7	105.2	5.2
1969	109.8	5.4	108.8	5.0	110.4	6.2	111.5	5.8	107.2	3.9	113.4	6.9	111.0	5.0	110.4	4.9
1970	116.3	5.9	114.7	5.4	118.2	7.1	116.1	4.1	112.7	5.1	120.6	6.3	116.7	5.1	115.8	5.8
1971	121.3	4.3	118.3	3.1	123.4	4.4	119.8	3.3	118.6	5.2	128.4	6.5	122.9	5.3	122.4	4.8
1972	125.3	3.3	123.2	4.1	128.1	3.8	122.3	2.1	119.9	1.1	132.5	3.2	126.5	2.9	127.5	4.2
1973	133.1	6.2	139.5	13.2	133.7	4.4	126.8	3.7	123.8	3.3	137.7	3.9	130.0	2.8	132.5	3.9
1974	147.7	11.0	158.7	13.8	148.8	11.3	136.2	7.4	137.7	11.2	150.5	9.3	139.8	7.5	142.0	7.2
1975	161.2	9.1	172.1	8.4	164.5	10.6	142.3	4.5	150.6	9.4	168.6	12.0	152.2	8.9	153.9	8.4
1976	170.5	5.8	177.4	3.1	174.6	6.1	147.6	3.7	165.5	9.9	184.7	9.5	159.8	5.0	162.7	5.7
1977	181.5	6.5	188.0	8.0	186.5	6.8	154.2	4.5	177.2	7.1	202.4	9.6	167.7	4.9	172.2	5.8
1978	195.3	7.6	206.2	9.7	202.6	8.6	159.5	3.4	185.8	4.9	219.4	8.4	176.2	5.1	183.2	6.4
1979	217.7	11.5	228.7	10.9	227.5	12.3	166.4	4.3	212.8	14.5	240.1	9.4	187.6	6.5	196.3	7.2
1980	247.0	13.5	248.7	8.7	263.2	15.7	177.4	6.6	250.5	17.7	287.2	11.3	203.7	8.5	213.6	8.8
1981	272.3	10.2	267.8	7.7	293.2	11.4	186.6	5.2	281.3	12.3	295.1	10.4	219.0	7.5	233.3	9.2
1982	288.6	6.0	278.5	4.0	314.7	7.3	190.9	2.3	293.1	4.2	326.9	10.8	232.4	6.1	257.0	10.2

TABLE B Consumer Price Index for All Urban Consumers and Revised CPI for Urban Wage Earners and Clerical Workers, U.S. City Average — General Summary and Groups, Subgroups, and Selected Items

GENERAL SUMMARY	ALL URBAN CONSUMERS							URBAN WAGE EARNERS AND CLERICAL WORKERS						
	1982			1983				1982			1983			
	Apr.	Nov.	Dec.	Jan.	Feb.	Mar.	Apr.	Apr.	Nov.	Dec.	Jan.	Feb.	Mar.	Apr.
All Items	284.3	293.6	292.4	293.1	293.2	293.4	295.5	283.7	293.2	292.0	292.1	292.3	293.0	294.9
Food and beverages	276.5	279.1	279.1	280.7	281.6	283.2	284.6	276.8	279.4	279.6	281.1	282.1	283.5	284.9
Housing	309.4	319.0	316.3	317.9	318.5	318.6	320.3	309.2	319.6	316.8	317.0	317.6	319.2	320.2
Apparel and upkeep	191.9	195.4	193.6	191.0	192.0	194.5	195.5	191.2	194.4	192.8	190.0	191.0	194.0	194.8
Transportation	282.9	295.8	294.8	293.0	289.9	287.4	292.3	284.3	297.3	296.3	294.3	291.1	288.6	293.5
Medical care	321.7	342.2	344.3	347.8	351.3	352.3	353.5	320.2	339.8	341.8	345.3	348.9	350.0	351.2
Entertainment	233.9	239.9	240.1	241.5	243.1	244.6	244.6	230.5	236.1	236.5	237.7	239.5	240.8	241.1
Other goods and services	253.8	273.8	276.6	279.9	281.6	281.9	283.2	250.9	270.9	274.0	277.8	279.6	280.0	281.4
Commodities	258.9	267.8	267.7	267.2	266.7	266.7	269.2	259.2	268.2	268.2	268.0	267.8	268.4	270.9
Commodities less food and beverages	247.0	258.2	258.0	256.5	255.2	254.3	257.3	247.2	258.9	258.8	257.8	257.1	257.4	260.3
Nondurables less food and beverages	259.7	271.4	270.0	267.4	265.2	263.4	267.8	261.3	273.3	271.9	269.3	266.9	265.0	269.7
Durables	235.8	246.6	247.3	247.3	247.1	247.4	248.7	234.8	246.2	247.0	247.3	247.8	249.7	251.2
Services	328.4	338.6	335.6	337.9	338.9	339.4	341.2	329.1	339.3	336.2	336.9	337.8	338.5	339.5
Rent, residential	220.1	230.2	230.8	232.2	233.1	233.6	234.5	219.6	229.7	230.2	231.7	232.5	233.1	234.0
Household services less rent of shelter	...	...	100.0	100.9	101.0	101.6	102.0	...	...	...	...	...	...	...
(12/81 = 100)														
Transportation services	290.3	299.9	299.4	300.1	299.9	299.8	300.8	289.2	297.5	296.7	297.1	296.9	296.7	297.2
Medical care services	348.0	371.0	373.4	377.4	381.5	382.2	382.8	345.8	367.7	370.1	374.0	378.2	379.0	379.7
Other services	255.3	269.2	270.0	271.5	272.6	272.9	274.2	253.8	266.8	267.5	269.1	270.2	270.6	272.0
Special Indexes:														
All items less food	282.9	293.6	292.1	292.6	292.6	292.4	294.7	282.5	293.5	292.1	291.9	291.9	292.4	294.4
All items less mortgage interest costs	...	...	100.0	100.2	100.2	100.3	101.0	...	...	...	...	...	...	...
Commodities less food	245.0	256.0	255.8	254.4	253.2	252.4	255.4	245.3	256.7	256.6	255.7	255.0	255.4	258.2
Nondurables less food	255.0	266.1	264.7	262.4	260.5	258.9	263.0	256.6	267.9	266.6	264.2	262.2	260.6	265.0
Nondurables less food and apparel	291.4	306.2	305.2	303.1	299.9	296.5	302.1	292.3	307.5	306.5	304.4	301.1	297.4	303.5
Nondurables	269.3	276.4	275.8	275.2	274.6	274.4	277.3	270.1	277.4	276.8	276.2	275.6	275.3	278.4
Services less rent of shelter (12/82 = 100)	...	...	100.0	100.7	101.0	101.3	101.6	...	...	...	...	...	...	...
Services less medical care	324.0	332.9	329.3	331.4	332.2	332.7	334.5	324.9	334.0	330.4	330.7	331.2	332.0	333.0
Domestically produced farm foods	264.5	265.3	264.8	264.7	266.6	268.4	269.9	266.0	264.4	264.0	265.0	266.0	267.6	269.0
Selected beef cuts	275.1	271.9	270.0	271.2	272.0	272.6	279.4	276.4	273.2	271.2	272.5	273.5	274.0	280.7
Energy[1]	395.7	422.6	419.9	414.5	406.7	399.9	410.0	396.9	423.7	420.8	415.1	406.9	399.8	410.8
Energy commodities[1]	406.6	431.6	425.4	414.9	401.6	388.3	403.2	406.9	431.8	425.6	415.2	401.9	388.7	404.3

| | ALL URBAN CONSUMERS | | | | | | | URBAN WAGE EARNERS AND CLERICAL WORKERS | | | | | | |
| | 1982 | | | 1983 | | | | 1982 | | | 1983 | | | |
GENERAL SUMMARY	Apr.	Nov.	Dec.	Jan.	Feb.	Mar.	Apr.	Apr.	Nov.	Dec.	Jan.	Feb.	Mar.	Apr.
All items less energy	275.7	283.6	282.5	283.8	284.7	285.6	287.0	274.5	282.5	282.2	282.2	283.0	284.4	285.6
All items less food and energy	272.2	281.2	279.9	281.1	282.0	282.6	284.0	270.9	280.2	279.0	279.3	280.2	281.6	282.6
Commodities less food and energy	227.2	236.6	237.1	237.1	237.9	239.1	240.2	226.4	236.2	236.8	237.1	237.9	240.0	241.2
Services less energy	324.5	333.1	329.6	331.8	332.9	333.1	334.8	325.2	333.7	330.1	330.5	331.4	331.9	332.7
Purchasing power of the consumer dollar, 1967 = $1	$0.352	$0.341	$0.342	$0.341	$0.341	$0.341	$0.338	$0.352	$0.341	$0.342	$0.342	$0.342	$0.341	$0.339
FOOD AND BEVERAGES	276.5	279.1	279.1	280.7	281.6	283.2	284.6	276.8	279.4	279.6	281.1	282.1	283.5	284.9
Food	283.9	286.4	286.5	288.1	289.0	290.5	291.9	284.1	286.6	286.7	288.4	289.3	290.7	292.1
Food at home	277.9	278.3	277.8	279.3	280.3	281.9	283.4	277.0	277.4	277.1	278.6	279.7	281.2	282.5
Cereals and bakery products	281.7	285.5	286.3	287.8	288.7	289.8	291.1	280.4	284.1	284.9	286.4	287.4	288.5	289.6
Cereals and cereal products (12/77 = 100)	153.6	153.2	153.4	154.0	154.0	155.0	156.1	154.6	154.1	154.2	154.8	154.7	155.8	156.9
Flour and prepared flour mixes (12/77 = 100)	139.7	139.2	139.5	140.3	139.8	139.4	140.2	140.1	139.5	139.8	140.6	140.1	139.9	140.4
Cereal (12/77 = 100)	165.4	167.2	168.0	168.1	169.2	171.3	173.8	167.4	169.4	170.1	170.3	171.4	173.5	175.9
Rice, pasta, and cornmeal (12/77 = 100)	149.6	146.1	145.3	156.5	145.3	146.0	145.8	150.8	147.3	146.5	147.6	146.3	147.0	146.8
Bakery products (12/77 = 100)	147.5	150.3	150.9	151.7	152.4	152.8	153.3	146.3	149.1	149.6	150.5	151.2	151.6	152.0
White bread	242.8	246.8	248.1	248.9	249.8	252.0	252.1	238.8	242.6	243.9	244.6	245.7	247.8	247.6
Other breads (12/77 = 100)	145.2	147.3	147.6	147.7	148.7	149.0	148.8	147.1	149.4	149.6	149.7	150.6	151.1	150.7
Fresh biscuits, rolls, and muffins (12/77 = 100)	147.6	150.9	151.6	152.6	153.1	152.0	152.5	143.8	146.9	147.6	148.6	149.1	148.0	148.4
Fresh cakes and cupcakes (12/77 = 100)	148.4	150.5	151.5	153.1	154.0	153.8	154.9	146.8	148.8	149.7	151.3	152.2	152.1	153.3
Cookies (12/77 = 100)	150.2	153.6	153.7	153.6	153.7	155.1	156.8	151.2	154.5	154.6	154.6	154.6	156.0	157.6
Crackers, bread, and cracker products (12/77 = 100)	137.3	143.3	144.1	144.9	146.5	146.0	147.2	138.7	144.6	145.5	146.4	147.9	147.3	148.7
Fresh sweetrolls, coffeecake, and donuts (12/77 = 100)	146.8	149.6	150.4	152.3	154.2	154.2	153.7	149.3	152.3	152.9	154.9	156.8	156.9	156.2
Frozen and refrigerated bakery products and fresh pies, tarts, and turnovers (12/77 = 100)	153.4	155.8	155.2	156.8	155.7	156.2	157.1	146.5	148.6	148.4	149.8	149.0	149.4	150.2
Meats, poultry, fish, and eggs	258.3	263.6	261.6	263.0	264.0	264.2	264.2	257.8	263.5	261.5	262.8	263.9	264.0	263.9
Meats, poultry, and fish	264.2	270.8	268.8	270.3	271.7	271.4	271.4	263.6	270.6	268.6	270.0	271.4	271.1	271.0
Meats	263.6	273.6	271.1	272.2	273.2	272.8	273.3	262.8	273.2	270.8	271.8	272.9	272.4	272.9
Beef and veal	274.8	272.0	270.2	271.3	272.2	272.8	279.4	275.3	272.5	270.6	271.8	272.9	273.5	280.0
Ground beef other than canned	266.9	263.0	261.7	262.7	261.8	263.6	267.0	266.9	264.2	262.7	263.7	263.0	264.7	268.0
Chuck roast	285.4	281.7	281.0	281.7	286.9	284.8	291.2	294.1	290.3	289.6	290.4	295.9	293.0	300.2

(Continued on p. 552)

551

GENERAL SUMMARY	URBAN WAGE EARNERS AND CLERICAL WORKERS							ALL URBAN CONSUMERS						
	1983				1982			1983				1982		
	Apr.	Mar.	Feb.	Jan.	Dec.	Nov.	Apr.	Apr.	Mar.	Feb.	Jan.	Dec.	Nov.	Apr.
FOOD AND BEVERAGES—Continued														
Food—Continued														
Meats—Continued														
Round roast	254.0	242.8	245.3	246.6	246.4	244.3	247.9	251.1	239.9	242.6	243.3	243.0	241.4	244.9
Round steak	262.0	257.1	258.0	253.0	251.3	255.1	260.8	263.9	257.9	259.8	255.1	253.5	257.1	262.8
Sirloin steak	276.0	264.5	261.7	254.5	252.7	260.6	272.4	274.8	262.8	260.3	253.1	253.0	259.8	271.1
Other beef and veal (12/77 = 100)	166.8	163.0	162.1	162.1	161.2	162.4	162.1	168.3	164.4	163.5	163.7	162.8	164.1	163.7
Pork	261.7	270.4	272.9	271.4	269.5	273.4	241.0	262.1	271.1	273.6	272.0	270.1	274.2	241.6
Bacon	281.4	293.1	299.5	295.5	296.1	304.0	259.7	276.6	288.7	294.5	290.8	290.8	298.7	255.9
Chops	239.7	244.7	250.3	243.9	240.8	247.0	221.7	241.8	246.4	252.1	245.6	242.4	249.0	223.4
Ham other than canned (12/77 = 100)	113.9	122.4	121.7	126.0	126.4	124.2	102.8	116.7	125.6	125.0	129.2	129.6	127.3	105.4
Sausage	333.1	337.0	334.8	335.0	332.5	338.5	306.3	332.5	336.9	333.9	333.6	332.0	337.7	305.7
Canned ham	277.1	282.2	280.6	279.7	276.9	275.0	348.9	272.0	277.3	276.2	275.2	272.4	270.5	245.6
Other pork (12/77 = 100)	142.8	147.3	149.5	147.1	144.9	148.6	134.5	143.5	148.1	150.4	147.9	145.6	149.6	135.2
Other meats	268.3	269.3	269.0	268.7	269.8	271.5	261.8	268.6	269.7	269.2	269.3	269.7	271.6	262.8
Frankfurters	266.4	270.1	268.6	268.5	268.4	273.8	258.4	267.4	270.8	269.4	269.7	268.9	274.4	259.5
Bologna, liverwurst, and salami (12/77 = 100)	154.3	155.1	154.5	153.9	155.1	156.4	150.3	154.4	155.2	154.5	154.0	155.3	156.6	150.2
Other lunchmeats (12/77 = 100)	137.7	137.0	137.8	137.7	139.8	139.1	131.2	139.7	139.0	139.7	139.9	141.8	141.3	133.2
Lamb and organ meats (12/77 = 100)	140.0	140.9	140.1	140.3	137.5	138.5	145.6	137.0	138.2	137.2	137.4	134.3	135.4	142.6
Poultry	189.0	191.6	191.9	189.4	188.4	190.0	191.5	191.0	193.7	194.0	191.3	190.4	192.0	193.3
Fresh whole chicken	182.3	188.4	188.4	185.0	183.5	187.4	192.0	184.5	190.7	190.6	186.8	185.4	189.3	194.1
Fresh and frozen chicken parts (12/77 = 100)	124.2	125.1	124.6	123.5	123.1	123.5	125.9	125.7	126.6	126.2	125.0	124.8	125.3	127.6
Other poultry (12/77 = 100)	126.6	125.6	127.1	125.7	125.3	124.6	120.8	127.2	126.6	127.7	126.3	126.0	125.4	121.3
Fish and seafood	377.5	378.9	377.5	375.1	368.2	365.3	381.4	379.4	380.1	379.2	376.8	369.6	366.6	382.0
Canned fish and seafood	137.4	137.8	138.5	139.5	138.2	138.4	140.8	137.9	138.3	139.1	140.2	138.9	139.0	141.5
Fresh and frozen fish and seafood (12/77 = 100)	147.7	148.3	147.1	145.0	141.5	139.6	148.0	148.4	148.6	147.6	145.4	141.9	140.0	147.9
Eggs	175.8	175.8	170.0	173.7	173.3	176.2	187.9	174.9	175.0	169.3	172.9	172.5	175.0	186.9
Dairy products	249.4	248.9	249.1	248.9	247.1	246.7	246.8	250.1	249.6	249.7	249.5	247.8	247.4	247.5
Fresh milk and cream (12/77 = 100)	136.1	136.3	136.2	136.2	135.0	134.6	135.3	136.6	136.8	136.7	136.7	135.5	135.1	135.9
Fresh whole milk	222.7	222.6	222.6	222.9	221.1	220.1	221.3	223.5	223.4	223.4	223.7	221.9	220.9	222.2
Other fresh milk and cream (12/77 = 100)	136.1	137.1	136.8	136.3	134.7	134.9	135.7	136.7	137.7	137.3	136.9	135.2	135.4	136.2
Processed dairy products	148.4	147.4	147.7	147.4	146.9	146.9	145.9	148.1	147.2	147.4	147.1	146.6	146.6	145.6
Butter	256.5	256.1	256.2	255.9	254.5	255.1	252.7	253.9	253.5	253.6	253.4	252.1	252.5	250.1
Cheese (12/77 = 100)	146.8	145.8	156.8	145.5	144.9	144.8	144.0	146.5	145.5	145.5	145.2	144.6	144.5	143.7

GENERAL SUMMARY

	ALL URBAN CONSUMERS							URBAN WAGE EARNERS AND CLERICAL WORKERS						
	1982			1983				1982			1983			
	Apr.	Nov.	Dec.	Jan.	Feb.	Mar.	Apr.	Apr.	Nov.	Dec.	Jan.	Feb.	Mar.	Apr.
Ice cream and related products (12/77 = 100)	150.9	152.4	151.8	152.5	153.1	150.7	152.0	150.2	151.5	150.8	151.6	152.2	149.8	151.1
Other dairy products (12/77 = 100)	139.9	140.9	141.7	141.6	141.6	143.9	144.5	140.8	141.5	142.4	142.3	142.3	144.6	145.3
Fruits and vegetables	294.0	276.1	277.6	276.2	278.1	286.9	294.9	290.3	271.3	273.6	272.6	274.5	282.9	291.1
Fresh fruits and vegetables	304.1	268.3	272.3	269.2	272.0	288.6	304.3	298.9	261.0	266.6	264.3	267.1	283.0	298.9
Fresh fruits	306.7	288.9	273.9	268.3	270.5	282.8	291.9	295.5	275.4	262.5	258.9	261.0	272.5	282.2
Apples	287.5	239.4	243.7	244.2	244.0	249.3	299.9	287.8	239.9	243.7	244.8	243.9	249.6	293.0
Bananas	268.5	241.9	242.6	241.3	254.0	257.1	295.1	266.1	241.9	242.0	239.9	250.0	254.6	274.4
Oranges	330.8	399.6	313.0	292.2	286.3	299.1	301.3	300.2	360.4	283.0	267.5	263.1	272.7	274.4
Other fresh fruits (12/77 = 100)	163.4	143.3	144.8	143.1	145.1	154.4	155.8	157.6	137.5	138.7	138.0	139.8	149.0	150.9
Fresh vegetables	301.8	249.1	270.8	270.0	273.4	294.0	316.0	302.0	248.1	270.4	269.2	272.7	292.5	314.0
Potatoes	306.1	240.8	241.3	236.2	240.6	241.1	258.7	300.8	235.9	237.5	231.5	236.5	236.1	253.3
Lettuce	355.2	259.2	334.6	301.3	249.0	247.9	316.0	358.6	259.8	336.0	303.4	250.0	246.6	311.6
Tomatoes	220.5	242.9	272.8	236.8	265.0	352.2	327.5	224.9	249.6	278.4	241.5	269.0	358.1	332.1
Other fresh vegetables (12/77 = 100)	166.3	137.6	142.2	156.0	165.6	175.8	186.9	166.7	137.1	141.5	155.3	165.2	174.9	186.4
Processed fruits and vegetables	285.5	287.3	286.0	286.6	287.4	287.6	287.1	283.3	285.1	283.8	284.3	285.1	285.3	284.8
Processed fruits (12/77 = 100)	148.2	149.7	149.5	150.1	150.8	151.3	150.6	147.7	149.4	149.2	149.8	150.5	151.0	150.2
Frozen fruit and fruit juices (12/77 = 100)	147.1	145.6	143.6	144.7	144.6	145.0	143.9	146.1	144.7	142.6	143.8	143.7	144.1	143.0
Fruit juices other than frozen (12/77 = 100)	151.5	153.4	154.0	154.1	155.3	156.6	155.7	150.4	152.6	153.1	153.1	154.4	155.6	154.6
Canned and dried fruits (12/77 = 100)	145.6	149.1	149.6	150.4	151.0	151.0	150.8	146.2	149.7	150.2	151.1	151.7	151.5	151.4
Processed vegetables (12/77 = 100)	138.6	139.0	138.0	137.9	138.1	137.7	138.0	137.5	137.8	136.8	136.7	136.9	136.6	136.8
Frozen vegetables (12/77 = 100)	144.0	149.0	147.5	149.7	151.2	149.7	150.9	145.3	150.4	148.9	151.2	152.7	151.3	152.5
Cut corn and canned beans except lima (12/77 = 100)	140.5	140.8	140.3	139.5	138.5	138.9	139.6	137.9	144.7	142.6	143.8	136.2	136.4	137.1
Other canned and dried vegetables (12/77 = 100)	135.0	133.0	132.0	131.0	131.1	131.1	130.6	133.5	131.6	130.5	129.6	129.8	129.7	129.2
Other foods at home	331.6	334.3	333.7	337.1	338.2	339.1	339.2	332.6	335.1	334.6	337.9	339.1	339.9	340.0
Sugar and sweets	365.3	370.3	369.2	371.5	370.7	372.8	373.2	365.2	370.1	369.1	371.4	370.6	372.5	373.0
Candy and chewing gum (12/77 = 100)	150.9	149.6	149.5	149.8	149.6	150.3	150.8	150.8	149.5	149.6	149.8	149.6	150.3	150.8
Sugar and artificial sweeteners (12/77 = 100)	159.9	165.2	164.3	167.0	165.9	166.9	168.3	161.1	166.6	165.6	168.5	167.1	168.3	169.7
Other sweets (12/77 = 100)	147.2	152.5	151.7	152.0	152.3	153.4	151.4	145.3	150.2	149.4	149.8	150.2	151.0	149.1

(Continued on p. 554)

GENERAL SUMMARY	ALL URBAN CONSUMERS							URBAN WAGE EARNERS AND CLERICAL WORKERS						
	1982			1983				1982			1983			
	Apr.	Nov.	Dec.	Jan.	Feb.	Mar.	Apr.	Apr.	Nov.	Dec.	Jan.	Feb.	Mar.	Apr.
FOOD AND BEVERAGES—Continued														
Other Foods at Home—Continued														
Sugar and Sweets—Continued														
Fats and oils (12/77 = 100)	260.4	258.6	258.6	259.3	258.0	258.4	258.6	260.4	258.5	258.7	259.3	258.1	258.4	258.4
Margarine	259.6	257.5	256.5	259.4	255.9	255.8	259.6	259.1	256.8	255.4	258.5	255.3	254.5	258.1
Nondairy substitutes and peanut butter (12/77 = 100)	157.3	152.0	151.7	151.6	151.8	151.4	151.5	155.6	150.3	150.2	150.0	150.1	149.7	149.9
Other fats, oils, and salad dressings (12/77 = 100)	129.9	129.8	130.3	130.2	129.8	130.4	129.5	129.5	130.3	130.8	130.7	130.3	131.0	130.1
Nonalcoholic beverages	424.1	426.2	424.3	431.1	432.2	432.7	431.8	426.0	427.9	426.1	432.8	433.9	434.5	433.5
Cola drinks, excluding diet cola	304.9	308.8	307.2	312.9	312.5	314.1	313.1	302.4	306.2	304.8	310.3	310.0	311.5	310.4
Carbonated drinks, including diet cola (12/77 = 100)	143.4	144.8	142.4	145.2	147.4	146.7	146.8	141.5	142.4	140.2	142.8	144.9	144.5	144.5
Roasted coffee	369.6	360.0	361.4	365.0	365.9	363.2	361.4	365.0	354.8	356.2	359.9	360.5	357.9	356.2
Freeze dried and instant coffee	343.4	344.2	346.1	348.2	349.3	349.2	349.5	343.0	343.7	345.6	347.8	349.0	348.8	349.0
Other noncarbonated drinks (12/77 = 100)	138.7	138.8	139.0	141.0	140.6	141.1	140.6	138.9	139.1	139.2	141.3	140.8	141.3	140.9
Other prepared foods	266.6	270.2	270.7	272.6	275.1	276.0	276.9	268.3	271.9	272.4	274.2	276.8	277.5	278.5
Canned and packaged soup (12/77 = 100)	135.7	136.6	136.9	138.1	139.0	140.0	140.9	137.8	138.5	138.9	140.1	141.1	141.9	142.7
Frozen prepared foods (12/77 = 100)	147.2	149.7	149.0	150.6	152.0	153.1	155.0	146.7	149.2	148.5	150.0	151.3	152.2	154.2
Snacks (12/77 = 100)	152.9	153.1	152.7	154.0	157.6	157.9	159.2	155.0	155.2	154.8	156.0	159.6	160.1	161.2
Seasonings, olives, pickles, and relish (12/77 = 100)	153.6	157.1	157.4	159.5	161.1	161.6	159.3	152.7	156.2	156.4	158.5	160.1	160.4	158.3
Other condiments (12/77 = 100)	148.7	151.7	152.6	153.8	154.9	154.9	155.3	150.4	153.4	154.4	155.6	156.8	156.7	157.1
Miscellaneous prepared foods (12/77 = 100)	147.6	150.2	151.0	151.1	151.5	151.7	151.6	147.7	150.3	151.2	151.4	151.7	151.9	151.8
Other canned and packaged prepared foods (12/77 = 100)	143.3	145.0	146.1	146.1	146.4	146.8	147.4	144.6	146.4	147.3	147.3	147.7	148.0	148.7
Food away from home	303.6	311.4	312.6	314.5	315.2	316.5	318.0	306.7	314.6	315.8	317.7	318.4	319.7	321.3
Lunch (12/77 = 100)	147.5	151.6	152.2	153.1	153.3	153.7	154.4	149.1	153.2	153.8	154.8	155.0	155.3	156.1
Dinner (12/77 = 100)	146.3	149.7	150.4	151.3	151.7	152.0	152.5	147.9	151.4	152.1	153.0	153.4	153.7	154.2
Other meals and snacks (12/77 = 100)	148.6	152.7	153.0	154.0	154.5	156.0	157.1	149.3	153.3	153.7	154.6	155.1	156.5	157.7

	ALL URBAN CONSUMERS							URBAN WAGE EARNERS AND CLERICAL WORKERS						
	1982			1983				1982			1983			
GENERAL SUMMARY	Apr.	Nov.	Dec.	Jan.	Feb.	Mar.	Apr.	Apr.	Nov.	Dec.	Jan.	Feb.	Mar.	Apr.
Alcoholic beverages	207.4	210.9	210.9	211.6	213.3	215.1	216.1	209.5	213.0	213.0	213.7	215.6	217.3	218.5
Alcoholic beverages at home (12/77 = 100)	134.6	136.2	136.1	136.5	137.7	139.1	139.7	136.0	137.5	137.4	137.8	139.2	140.6	141.3
Beer and ale	210.5	212.5	212.6	213.3	217.4	219.8	222.5	209.6	211.7	211.7	212.5	216.4	218.6	221.2
Whiskey	147.2	150.7	150.2	150.5	150.9	151.3	151.4	148.0	151.2	150.7	151.2	151.6	151.9	151.9
Wine	236.4	235.9	235.6	235.6	234.7	239.1	236.3	244.4	243.7	243.3	243.0	241.8	246.8	243.9
Other alcoholic beverages (12/77 = 100)	118.2	120.4	120.2	120.6	120.7	121.5	121.5	118.0	120.4	120.1	120.6	120.5	121.2	121.3
Alcoholic beverages away from home (12/77 = 100)	138.4	143.6	144.2	144.8	145.4	145.7	146.5	139.9	144.8	145.3	146.0	146.6	146.9	147.7
HOUSING	309.4	319.0	316.3	317.9	318.5	318.6	320.3	309.2	319.6	316.0	317.0	317.6	319.2	320.3
Shelter (CPI-U)	331.4	340.7	335.9	338.3	339.2	339.3	341.7	332.8	...	...	...	...	...	332.8
Renters' costs	...	...	100.0	100.8	101.2	101.4	101.8	...	...	...	...	...	...	...
Rent, residential	220.1	230.2	230.8	232.2	233.1	233.6	234.5	219.6	...	...	...	...	...	...
Other renters' costs	323.7	337.8	333.0	339.2	340.8	340.6	343.7	322.8	...	...	...	...	...	...
Homeowners' costs[2]	...	...	100.0	100.7	100.9	100.9	101.7	...	...	...	...	...	...	...
Owners' equivalent rent	...	...	100.0	100.7	100.9	100.8	101.7	...	...	...	...	...	...	...
Household insurance	...	...	100.0	100.9	100.9	101.5	102.0	...	...	...	...	...	...	...
Maintenance and repairs	331.6	339.0	337.8	342.9	339.4	339.9	343.6	...	...	...	...	...	...	...
Maintenance and repair services	363.6	373.4	371.4	380.6	373.6	376.7	382.8	...	...	...	...	...	...	...
Maintenance and repair commodities	256.2	257.8	258.5	259.4	259.3	257.7	258.7	...	...	...	...	...	...	...
Shelter (CPI-W)	...	...	...	...	...	...	...	...	343.0	338.0	337.9	338.8	341.1	342.4
Rent, residential	...	...	...	...	...	...	...	...	229.7	230.3	231.7	232.5	233.1	234.0
Other renters' costs	...	...	...	...	...	...	...	...	335.6	330.7	337.3	339.0	339.0	342.3
Lodging while out of town	...	...	...	...	...	...	...	...	349.3	341.4	350.8	353.6	353.1	358.2
Tenants' insurance (12/77 = 100)	...	...	...	...	...	...	...	...	149.1	149.3	151.5	151.5	152.6	153.2
Homeownership	...	...	...	...	...	...	...	...	383.7	376.8	375.9	376.9	379.9	381.2
Home purchase	...	...	...	...	...	...	...	...	290.4	290.9	291.9	293.7	298.9	301.0
Financing, taxes, and insurance	...	...	...	...	...	...	...	...	514.6	495.7	490.2	491.3	491.8	492.2
Property insurance	...	...	...	...	...	...	...	...	409.7	412.1	414.5	417.9	419.2	422.3
Property taxes	...	...	...	...	...	...	...	...	227.5	228.8	230.6	231.4	231.7	232.9
Contracted mortgage interest costs	...	...	...	...	...	...	...	...	663.4	633.5	624.0	625.1	625.7	625.5
Mortgage interest rates	...	...	...	...	...	...	...	...	226.6	215.9	212.0	211.1	207.5	206.0
Maintenance and repairs	...	...	...	...	...	...	...	...	334.9	333.7	337.8	336.2	337.5	339.0
Maintenance and repair services	...	...	...	...	...	...	...	...	374.0	371.7	377.3	374.5	376.6	378.9

(*Continued on p. 556*)

GENERAL SUMMARY	ALL URBAN CONSUMERS							URBAN WAGE EARNERS AND CLERICAL WORKERS						
	Apr.	1982		1983				Apr.	1982		1983			
	1982	Nov.	Dec.	Jan.	Feb.	Mar.	Apr.	1982	Nov.	Dec.	Jan.	Feb.	Mar.	Apr.
HOUSING—Continued														
Shelter—Continued														
Homeownership—Continued														
Maintenance and repair commodities	...	...	...	...	...	...	...		251.6	252.3	253.6	254.5	254.2	253.9
Paint and wallpaper, supplies, tools, and equipment (12/77 = 100)	...	...	...	...	...	...	...		145.9	146.5	148.2	148.0	146.0	145.7
Lumber, awnings, glass, and masonry (12/77 = 100)	...	...	...	...	...	...	...		120.8	121.3	120.5	122.2	124.1	123.4
Plumbing, electrical, heating, and cooling supplies (12/77 = 100)	...	...	...	...	...	...	...		135.3	136.2	137.3	136.6	137.5	137.4
Miscellaneous supplies and equipment (12/77 = 100)	...	...	...	...	...	...	...		141.6	141.2	141.3	142.2	142.4	143.1
Fuel and other utilities	339.2	362.2	364.1	365.4	364.6	363.8	363.6	340.3	363.6	365.5	366.8	365.1	365.2	365.1
Fuels	428.2	461.9	464.0	463.5	461.5	459.7	459.2	427.8	461.7	463.9	463.3	461.2	459.5	459.3
Fuel oil, coal, and bottled gas	641.3	691.3	688.5	671.1	654.0	625.3	610.6	644.0	693.7	690.8	673.4	656.0	627.3	612.8
Fuel oil	666.2	712.8	708.7	689.3	669.7	636.4	618.4	668.4	714.7	710.6	691.2	671.5	637.9	620.4
Other fuels (6/78 = 100)	166.4	189.0	190.4	188.4	187.1	185.9	186.7	167.9	190.3	191.6	189.5	188.1	187.0	187.7
Gas (piped) and electricity	377.8	407.6	410.6	413.5	414.5	418.0	420.5	376.8	406.9	410.0	412.8	413.8	417.5	420.1
Electricity	312.8	318.4	319.6	319.2	320.1	321.2	319.9	311.8	317.3	318.7	318.3	319.4	320.7	319.3
Utility (piped) gas	465.3	543.1	549.6	559.1	560.1	568.3	578.3	463.6	541.6	547.6	556.9	557.6	565.9	576.5
HOUSING														
Fuel and other utilities														
Other utilities and public services	197.7	205.1	206.6	210.1	210.9	211.4	211.7	198.2	205.9	207.3	210.9	211.6	212.2	212.5
Telephone services	160.8	166.6	168.2	171.4	171.7	172.1	171.9	161.0	167.0	168.6	171.7	172.1	172.5	172.4
Local charges (12/77 = 100)	127.9	135.4	137.8	140.6	139.9	140.3	139.9	128.1	135.9	138.1	140.8	140.2	140.6	140.3
Interstate toll calls (12/77 = 100)	119.9	119.7	119.7	121.0	121.8	121.8	121.8	120.2	120.2	120.2	121.5	122.2	122.2	122.3
Intrastate toll calls (12/77 = 100)	108.9	111.1	111.5	114.0	115.9	116.3	116.6	108.7	110.9	111.3	113.9	115.8	116.2	116.6
Water and sewage maintenance	320.7	335.1	335.8	341.6	343.9	345.6	347.5	323.6	338.2	338.9	344.8	347.2	349.0	350.8
Household furnishings and operations	232.6	235.1	235.7	235.8	236.7	237.6	239.9	229.1	231.8	232.3	232.6	233.4	234.6	236.0
Housefurnishings	193.8	195.1	195.3	194.9	195.9	197.1	198.7	191.7	193.0	193.2	193.0	193.8	195.3	196.7
Textile housefurnishings	218.7	222.6	222.0	221.9	228.2	230.3	229.4	221.4	225.8	224.9	224.5	232.2	234.8	233.6
Household linens (12/77 = 100)	135.8	133.8	132.7	131.5	139.0	136.7	134.2	137.0	135.0	134.0	132.6	140.7	137.9	135.3

GENERAL SUMMARY	ALL URBAN CONSUMERS							URBAN WAGE EARNERS AND CLERICAL WORKERS						
	1982			1983				1982			1983			
	Apr.	Nov.	Dec.	Jan.	Feb.	Mar.	Apr.	Apr.	Nov.	Dec.	Jan.	Feb.	Mar.	Apr.
Curtains, drapes, slipcovers, and sewing materials (12/77 = 100)	136.9	144.0	144.4	145.6	145.7	150.9	152.4	139.1	147.5	147.6	148.6	149.5	156.2	157.8
Furniture and bedding	214.7	214.1	215.4	213.9	213.8	215.8	221.6	211.0	210.3	211.6	210.4	210.2	213.2	218.1
Bedroom furniture (12/77 = 100)	142.3	146.2	147.4	146.1	146.6	148.9	152.9	138.9	142.1	143.4	142.6	142.7	146.0	149.4
Sofas (12/77 = 100)	119.3	116.4	118.2	117.3	116.5	118.3	118.9	119.6	117.0	118.8	117.9	117.1	118.9	119.1
Living room chairs and tables (12/77 = 100)	123.2	122.1	122.2	121.6	121.0	122.0	126.2	123.3	122.5	122.5	122.0	121.5	122.6	126.6
Other furniture (12/77 = 100)	142.3	140.1	140.4	139.4	139.8	139.7	144.6	137.9	135.3	135.6	134.6	135.1	136.0	140.2
Appliances including TV and sound equipment	150.6	151.7	151.5	151.9	151.5	151.9	152.3	150.3	151.5	151.4	151.8	151.3	151.7	152.4
Television and sound equipment	108.7	108.1	107.2	107.0	107.1	106.9	107.1	107.7	107.3	106.3	106.1	106.1	105.9	106.2
Television	104.2	102.9	102.6	102.3	101.9	101.2	100.9	103.0	101.7	101.4	101.1	100.5	99.9	99.7
Sound equipment (12/77 = 100)	113.7	113.9	112.4	112.2	112.8	113.1	113.6	112.8	113.1	111.4	111.3	111.8	111.9	112.6
Household appliances	182.1	185.2	186.1	187.6	186.3	187.7	188.5	182.3	185.6	186.7	187.9	186.7	188.0	188.9
Refrigerators and home freezers	184.8	192.7	193.3	193.2	192.2	193.3	193.3	190.6	198.4	199.1	199.2	198.1	198.9	199.2
Laundry equipment	136.4	140.0	141.0	141.5	141.8	142.5	142.7	136.6	140.3	141.4	142.1	142.3	142.9	143.6
Other household appliances (12/77 = 100)	122.9	122.7	123.2	124.7	123.6	124.6	125.4	120.7	120.7	121.5	122.8	121.5	122.7	123.5
Stoves, dishwashers, vacuums, and sewing machines (12/77 = 100)	122.3	120.7	121.5	123.7	122.3	124.2	125.0	119.7	119.2	120.1	121.9	120.2	122.4	123.3
Office machines, small electric appliances and air conditioners (12/77 = 100)	123.5	124.7	125.1	125.8	125.1	125.2	126.1	121.8	122.4	123.0	123.8	122.9	122.9	123.8
Other household equipment (12/77 = 100)	137.8	139.1	139.2	139.1	140.2	140.7	140.4	135.6	137.1	137.1	137.0	137.9	138.6	138.4
Floor and window coverings, infants', laundry, cleaning, and outdoor equipment (12/77 = 100)	140.3	142.6	142.7	141.2	143.3	143.0	143.2	132.9	134.5	134.3	133.2	134.9	135.0	135.3
Clocks, lamps, and decor items (12/77 = 100)	130.2	131.3	131.0	130.8	132.4	133.9	133.3	126.5	126.8	126.6	126.1	127.3	129.2	128.3
Tableware, serving pieces, and nonelectric kitchenware (12/77 = 100)	145.0	144.6	145.1	145.9	145.7	146.4	145.5	140.6	141.0	141.2	141.9	141.8	142.6	142.0
Lawn equipment, power tools, and other hardware (12/77 = 100)	130.8	134.2	134.1	134.1	135.4	135.5	135.9	136.0	139.5	139.2	139.3	140.6	140.9	141.4
Housekeeping supplies	284.9	290.3	292.3	294.0	294.8	295.4	296.9	281.2	287.1	288.8	290.7	291.6	292.2	293.9
Soaps and detergents	280.0	283.5	285.3	288.9	290.1	292.3	294.5	276.3	279.9	281.5	285.0	286.1	288.1	290.4
Other laundry and cleaning products (12/77 = 100)	142.7	147.3	148.0	149.0	149.1	149.5	150.6	141.6	146.2	146.9	147.7	147.9	148.3	149.5
Cleansing and toilet tissue, paper towels and napkins (12/77 = 100)	146.4	148.2	148.6	150.2	150.4	149.3	148.8	146.2	148.1	148.5	150.3	150.5	149.1	148.9

(Continued on p. 558)

GENERAL SUMMARY	ALL URBAN CONSUMERS							URBAN WAGE EARNERS AND CLERICAL WORKERS						
	1982	1982	1982	1983	1983	1983	1983	1982	1982	1982	1983	1983	1983	1983
	Apr.	Nov.	Dec.	Jan.	Feb.	Mar.	Apr.	Apr.	Nov.	Dec.	Jan.	Feb.	Mar.	Apr.
HOUSING—Continued														
Household Furnishings and Operations—Continued														
Housekeeping supplies—Continued														
Stationery, stationery supplies, and gift wrap (12/77 = 100)	131.4	138.3	137.9	138.1	138.6	139.3	139.6	134.6	141.4	141.0	141.1	141.7	142.3	142.7
Miscellaneous household products (12/77 = 100)	147.5	151.6	152.3	153.5	154.3	154.4	154.5	142.4	146.2	146.9	148.3	149.1	149.2	149.2
Lawn and garden supplies (12/77 = 100)	144.7	141.9	145.7	144.3	144.4	145.0	147.2	136.8	134.9	138.5	137.0	137.4	138.5	141.4
Housekeeping services	310.4	314.3	315.0	315.4	315.9	316.4	317.1	309.2	313.7	314.5	315.0	315.6	316.1	316.5
Postage	337.5	337.5	337.5	337.5	337.5	337.5	337.5	337.5	337.5	337.5	337.5	337.5	337.5	337.5
Moving, storage, freight, household laundry, and drycleaning services (12/77 = 100)	152.1	157.7	158.6	159.3	159.8	160.6	160.8	152.2	157.8	158.7	159.5	160.0	160.7	160.8
Appliance and furniture repair (12/77 = 100)	135.6	139.5	140.2	140.4	141.2	141.5	141.7	143.1	137.9	138.5	138.7	139.5	139.8	140.0
APPAREL AND UPKEEP	191.9	195.4	193.6	191.0	192.0	194.5	195.5	191.2	194.4	192.8	190.0	191.0	194.0	194.8
Apparel commodities	181.4	184.3	182.3	179.2	180.2	182.8	183.7	181.3	183.8	181.9	178.7	179.7	182.9	183.5
Apparel commodities less footwear	177.4	180.6	178.4	175.0	176.0	178.9	179.4	177.1	179.8	177.8	174.3	175.3	178.9	179.4
Men's and boys'	183.1	189.0	187.4	184.9	184.4	186.7	187.8	182.9	188.9	187.6	185.2	184.8	187.0	187.9
Men's (12/77 = 100)	115.5	119.3	118.3	116.8	116.2	117.1	117.9	115.7	119.7	118.8	117.4	116.9	117.6	118.3
Suits, sport coats, and jackets (12/77 = 100)	107.6	111.5	108.7	106.5	106.7	109.1	100.3	101.1	104.2	101.7	99.9	100.2	102.1	103.5
Coats and jackets	99.1	103.4	103.2	98.8	98.1	100.0	100.0	100.7	105.4	105.5	100.5	99.9	102.2	102.4
Furnishings and special clothing (12/77 = 100)	138.2	142.4	141.5	142.2	142.6	141.4	142.8	134.5	139.1	137.9	138.7	139.1	137.6	138.6
Shirts (12/77 = 100)	121.3	125.8	126.5	124.5	122.0	121.7	122.0	123.4	128.7	129.2	127.5	125.0	124.4	125.0
Dungarees, jeans, and trousers (12/77 = 100)	109.7	112.6	111.9	111.0	110.5	111.5	112.0	115.1	118.1	117.5	116.5	116.1	117.4	117.7
Boys' (12/77 = 100)	118.3	121.6	120.7	118.9	119.3	123.2	123.5	116.5	119.7	119.0	117.2	117.7	121.4	121.5
Coats, jackets, sweaters, and shirts (12/77 = 100)	111.2	113.7	112.2	108.9	108.1	115.5	115.2	111.5	114.6	113.3	110.4	109.3	116.4	115.7
Furnishings (12/77 = 100)	130.3	132.6	132.4	132.0	132.5	134.0	134.9	126.0	128.5	128.3	128.0	128.4	129.6	130.4
Suits, trousers, sport coats, and jackets (12/77 = 100)	119.0	123.4	122.8	121.5	122.9	124.9	125.5	116.8	120.5	120.0	118.6	120.2	122.3	122.6
Women's and girls'	160.9	162.2	159.6	153.9	155.7	160.0	160.6	163.4	163.8	161.3	155.4	157.2	162.8	163.1

	ALL URBAN CONSUMERS							URBAN WAGE EARNERS AND CLERICAL WORKERS						
	1982			1983				1982			1983			
GENERAL SUMMARY	Apr.	Nov.	Dec.	Jan.	Feb.	Mar.	Apr.	Apr.	Nov.	Dec.	Jan.	Feb.	Mar.	Apr.
Women's (12/77 = 100)	107.1	107.3	105.5	101.8	103.2	106.2	106.5	109.1	108.8	106.8	102.9	104.4	108.4	108.3
Coats and jackets	163.4	169.5	166.3	158.1	160.9	170.1	168.1	172.9	173.2	171.0	161.4	165.5	178.4	177.1
Dresses	166.6	161.4	159.0	152.9	154.9	158.5	161.5	151.1	147.7	144.9	139.8	140.6	144.4	145.7
Separates and sportswear (12/77 = 100)	100.1	100.1	97.1	93.7	94.6	98.5	100.1	101.0	100.9	97.8	94.4	95.3	99.2	101.0
Underwear, nightwear, and hosiery (12/77 = 100)	127.4	130.6	130.8	128.8	130.0	131.0	131.1	127.3	130.2	103.5	128.4	129.7	130.7	130.8
Suits (12/77 = 100)	89.4	87.4	82.8	76.9	79.7	83.7	80.5	111.0	105.8	99.7	91.8	95.6	104.7	99.4
Girls' (12/77 = 100)	106.7	110.4	109.5	105.1	105.1	107.6	108.2	106.9	109.6	109.2	105.0	104.9	108.0	109.2
Coats, jackets, dresses, and suits (12/77 = 100)	98.8	103.9	103.7	95.8	96.5	98.4	97.1	97.6	102.2	102.0	95.2	95.8	97.6	98.5
Separates and sportswear (12/77 = 100)	105.4	106.0	104.1	102.1	101.5	105.6	107.5	107.6	105.1	105.1	102.9	102.0	107.5	109.1
Underwear, nightwear, hosiery, and accessories (12/77 = 100)	122.0	129.3	129.1	125.7	125.8	126.4	127.8	121.0	128.1	128.0	124.9	124.9	125.6	126.9
Infants' and toddlers'	267.0	274.2	273.1	277.1	278.8	280.1	280.4	278.2	285.5	284.2	287.5	289.5	291.0	291.0
Other apparel commodities	210.8	212.7	210.1	211.5	213.4	213.4	214.4	199.5	201.4	199.2	200.1	201.7	201.9	202.5
Sewing materials and notions (12/77 = 100)	118.5	120.0	120.8	120.4	120.5	120.4	121.8	166.9	118.2	118.5	118.5	118.5	118.4	119.4
Jewelry and luggage (12/77 = 100)	143.8	144.9	142.2	143.7	145.4	145.4	145.8	134.5	135.7	133.5	134.4	135.9	136.1	136.2
Footwear	205.6	206.9	205.9	204.8	205.6	206.6	207.5	206.1	206.7	205.8	204.6	205.2	206.1	207.2
Men's (12/77 = 100)	132.3	132.5	132.0	131.4	132.2	133.2	133.9	134.4	134.2	133.7	133.0	133.9	134.8	135.6
Boys' and girls' (12/77 = 100)	130.4	129.3	129.0	130.4	131.2	131.1	130.7	133.6	131.8	131.5	132.9	133.4	133.2	133.4
Women's (12/77 = 100)	125.1	127.6	126.8	124.5	124.6	125.5	126.5	121.1	123.6	122.9	120.4	120.4	121.1	122.0
Apparel services	273.4	282.0	282.8	283.9	285.4	286.7	288.7	271.0	280.3	281.1	282.2	283.6	284.9	287.1
Laundry and drycleaning other than coin operated (12/77 = 100)	163.5	167.9	168.9	169.6	170.3	170.8	171.7	162.0	166.4	167.5	168.1	168.8	169.3	170.3
Other apparel services (12/77 = 100)	142.5	148.1	147.7	148.3	149.1	150.4	152.0	142.7	149.2	148.8	149.4	150.3	151.4	153.1
TRANSPORTATION	282.9	295.8	294.8	293.0	289.9	287.4	292.3	284.3	297.3	296.3	294.3	291.1	288.6	293.5
Private	278.8	291.4	290.4	288.4	285.2	282.7	287.5	281.2	294.1	293.1	290.9	287.6	285.0	289.9
New cars	196.0	199.0	200.1	201.0	201.3	201.2	201.1	195.9	198.7	199.9	200.8	201.0	200.9	200.7
Used cars	285.1	310.5	312.6	311.0	309.1	309.3	312.7	285.2	310.5	312.6	311.1	309.1	309.3	312.7
Gasoline	366.7	388.1	381.3	371.9	359.4	348.6	367.6	367.9	389.5	383.0	373.6	361.2	350.3	369.3
Automobile maintenance and repair	311.9	322.3	323.1	324.4	325.9	326.6	327.4	312.8	323.1	323.8	325.2	326.6	327.4	328.1
Body work (12/77 = 100)	155.0	161.0	161.4	162.2	162.7	163.6	164.7	153.3	159.8	160.2	161.1	161.5	162.5	163.4
Automobile drive train, brake, and miscellaneous mechanical repair (12/77 = 100)	149.5	153.7	154.3	155.4	156.1	156.3	157.3	153.7	157.8	158.3	159.4	160.1	160.3	161.2

(Continued on p. 560)

GENERAL SUMMARY	ALL URBAN CONSUMERS							URBAN WAGE EARNERS AND CLERICAL WORKERS						
	1982			1983				1982			1983			
	Apr.	Nov.	Dec.	Jan.	Feb.	Mar.	Apr.	Apr.	Nov.	Dec.	Jan.	Feb.	Mar.	Apr.
TRANSPORTATION—Continued														
Private—Continued														
Automobile maintenance and repair—Continued														
Maintenance and servicing (12/77 = 100)	144.5	149.3	149.9	150.5	151.1	150.9	151.0	144.0	148.6	149.2	149.9	150.5	150.3	150.4
Power plant repair (12/77 = 100)	149.1	154.4	154.2	154.4	155.4	156.2	156.2	148.6	153.9	153.7	153.9	154.8	155.6	155.7
Other private transportation	255.1	260.7	259.6	259.9	259.7	259.2	258.4	258.2	262.9	261.6	261.5	261.1	260.5	259.3
Other private transportation commodities	214.9	215.1	214.3	215.6	215.0	213.3	212.2	217.3	217.7	216.9	218.0	217.4	215.8	214.7
Motor oil, coolant, and other products (12/77 = 100)	150.7	153.3	153.3	153.9	154.8	154.8	156.1	149.2	152.3	152.3	153.0	153.8	153.8	155.0
Automobile parts and equipment (12/77 = 100)	137.2	137.0	136.5	137.3	136.7	135.5	134.5	139.2	139.0	138.4	139.1	138.5	137.4	136.4
Tires	190.1	190.4	190.0	191.3	190.6	188.1	186.4	193.7	194.0	193.7	194.9	194.1	191.7	190.1
Other parts and equipment (12/77 = 100)	136.2	135.1	133.8	134.3	133.7	133.9	133.4	136.6	135.4	133.9	134.3	133.6	133.8	133.4
Other private transportation services	268.2	275.3	274.2	274.2	274.1	273.9	273.1	276.6	277.5	276.0	275.6	275.2	274.8	273.7
Automobile insurance	270.4	286.9	288.8	292.0	295.6	297.0	299.0	270.2	286.1	288.2	291.3	294.9	296.3	298.2
Automobile finance charges (12/77 = 100)	187.2	178.9	173.8	169.6	165.0	161.9	157.3	186.7	178.1	173.0	168.7	164.0	161.0	156.6
Automobile rental, registration, and other fees (12/77 = 100)	133.3	139.2	139.3	139.8	140.1	141.1	141.4	133.7	140.0	140.1	140.5	140.8	141.9	142.2
State registration	174.2	183.8	183.8	184.6	184.9	186.6	186.6	173.8	183.4	183.4	184.0	184.3	186.3	186.3
Drivers' licenses (12/77 = 100)	123.0	132.8	132.8	132.8	133.5	133.9	133.9	123.0	133.1	133.1	133.1	133.7	134.1	134.1
Vehicle inspection (12/77 = 100)	129.0	128.5	128.5	128.6	128.6	129.2	131.1	130.4	129.8	129.8	129.9	129.9	130.5	132.4
Other vehicle-related fees (12/77 = 100)	149.5	155.0	155.2	155.8	156.2	157.0	157.6	156.4	162.9	163.2	163.9	164.1	165.1	165.4
Public	339.3	356.0	355.6	357.7	355.2	354.5	361.1	333.3	348.2	348.0	349.8	347.7	347.3	353.3
Airline fare	382.7	411.6	408.8	412.3	405.5	402.9	417.2	379.8	408.8	405.9	409.8	401.5	398.9	415.9
Intercity bus fare	367.0	373.8	377.7	381.8	383.8	389.4	394.6	368.7	375.7	379.3	383.3	385.4	392.0	396.9
Intracity mass transit	308.1	316.1	317.7	318.5	319.4	320.1	320.2	307.2	315.7	316.7	317.4	318.3	319.0	319.1
Taxi fare	297.6	300.5	300.8	300.9	301.2	300.8	302.0	307.3	310.1	310.5	310.5	310.8	310.4	311.4
Intercity train fare	332.1	348.3	351.3	351.8	351.8	351.9	352.0	332.1	349.3	351.9	352.3	352.2	352.3	352.5
MEDICAL CARE	327.1	342.2	344.3	347.8	351.3	352.3	353.5	320.2	339.8	341.8	345.3	348.9	350.0	351.2
Medical care commodities	202.4	212.9	213.7	215.3	216.7	218.6	221.2	230.0	213.4	214.0	215.9	217.2	219.0	221.6
Prescription drugs	188.8	201.0	202.8	204.1	205.9	208.7	211.6	189.7	202.1	203.9	205.3	207.1	209.9	212.8
Anti-infective drugs (12/77 = 100)	140.9	150.1	150.9	151.4	153.3	153.8	155.2	142.5	152.3	153.1	153.5	155.5	155.8	157.2

| | ALL URBAN CONSUMERS | | | | | | | URBAN WAGE EARNERS AND CLERICAL WORKERS | | | | | | |
| | 1982 | | | 1983 | | | | 1982 | | | 1983 | | | |
GENERAL SUMMARY	Apr.	Nov.	Dec.	Jan.	Feb.	Mar.	Apr.	Apr.	Nov.	Dec.	Jan.	Feb.	Mar.	Apr.
Tranquilizers and sedatives (12/77 = 100)	152.0	163.5	165.8	166.6	168.2	171.4	174.7	151.8	163.2	165.5	166.4	167.9	171.2	174.5
Circulatories and diuretics (12/77 = 100)	136.7	144.0	144.9	145.9	147.2	151.2	153.4	136.6	143.9	144.8	145.8	147.2	151.0	153.2
Hormones, diabetic drugs, biologicals, and prescription medical supplies (12/77 = 100)	173.3	183.9	185.5	186.6	189.0	192.4	196.1	174.6	185.2	187.0	188.0	190.8	194.2	198.1
Pain and symptom control drugs (12/77 = 100)	153.1	164.0	166.2	167.7	168.6	170.0	171.7	154.6	165.0	168.0	169.5	170.3	171.7	173.4
Supplements, cough and cold preparations, and respiratory agents (12/77 = 100)	144.7	153.4	154.2	155.8	156.4	157.8	159.4	144.8	153.6	154.5	156.2	156.7	158.1	159.7
Nonprescription drugs and medical supplies (12/77 = 100)	143.9	149.9	149.7	151.0	151.6	152.3	153.8	144.6	150.5	150.3	151.8	152.4	153.1	154.6
Eyeglasses (12/77 = 100)	130.1	132.9	133.0	133.9	134.6	134.9	135.1	128.7	131.6	131.8	132.6	133.4	133.7	133.9
Internal and respiratory over-the-counter drugs	231.1	241.9	241.3	244.3	245.1	245.5	248.7	232.5	243.0	242.2	245.7	246.4	246.8	250.2
Nonprescription medical equipment and supplies (12/77 = 100)	138.9	145.2	145.2	145.3	146.1	148.0	149.4	139.7	146.2	146.3	146.3	147.4	149.4	150.6
Medical care services	348.0	371.0	373.4	377.4	381.5	382.2	382.8	345.8	367.7	370.1	374.0	378.2	379.0	379.7
Professional services	297.8	308.3	309.4	312.5	315.4	316.7	318.0	297.9	308.4	309.5	312.7	315.7	316.9	318.4
Physicians' services	322.2	335.3	336.6	341.3	344.8	346.4	348.2	325.2	338.6	339.9	344.6	348.2	349.8	351.8
Dental services	281.1	289.2	290.1	291.6	294.0	294.6	295.7	279.2	287.0	288.0	289.3	291.8	292.3	293.4
Other professional services (12/77 = 100)	142.5	147.2	147.6	149.1	150.5	151.6	151.9	139.4	143.9	144.4	145.7	147.2	148.3	148.5
Other medical care services	408.7	446.8	450.8	455.9	461.3	461.4	461.1	405.4	442.3	446.3	451.3	457.0	457.1	456.9
Hospital and other medical services (12/77 = 100)	169.8	182.6	183.2	185.1	188.6	189.5	190.2	168.3	180.7	181.5	183.4	187.0	187.8	188.4
Hospital room	542.2	586.6	588.5	594.6	604.1	606.2	608.0	535.2	578.7	581.5	587.1	596.7	598.8	600.7
Other hospital and medical care services (12/77 = 100)	166.4	176.0	178.7	180.6	184.5	185.6	186.3	165.5	176.7	177.5	179.4	183.3	184.3	184.9
ENTERTAINMENT	233.9	239.9	240.1	241.5	243.1	244.6	244.6	230.5	236.1	236.5	237.7	239.5	240.8	241.1
Entertainment commodities	238.0	241.4	241.8	242.6	244.5	246.8	246.0	232.0	235.4	236.0	236.7	238.8	240.8	240.5
Reading materials (12/77 = 100)	146.8	153.4	154.3	156.1	156.1	159.3	158.4	146.1	152.7	153.8	155.5	155.5	158.7	157.8
Newspapers	280.1	290.9	294.7	295.7	296.5	299.6	300.2	279.7	290.5	294.8	295.6	296.4	299.8	300.4
Magazines, periodicals, and books (12/77 = 100)	151.6	159.6	159.3	162.6	162.2	167.1	164.8	151.4	159.6	159.2	162.6	162.1	167.3	164.8

(Continued on p. 562)

GENERAL SUMMARY	ALL URBAN CONSUMERS							URBAN WAGE EARNERS AND CLERICAL WORKERS						
	1982			1983				1982			1983			
	Apr.	Nov.	Dec.	Jan.	Feb.	Mar.	Apr.	Apr.	Nov.	Dec.	Jan.	Feb.	Mar.	Apr.
ENTERTAINMENT—Continued														
Entertainment commodities—Continued														
Sporting goods and equipment (12/77 = 100)	132.9	132.1	131.6	131.5	133.4	134.2	133.6	124.7	124.7	124.3	124.4	127.0	127.2	127.5
Sport vehicles (12/77 = 100)	136.1	133.8	133.3	132.9	136.1	137.3	136.3	122.8	122.2	122.0	122.0	126.0	126.4	126.7
Indoor and warm weather sport equipment (12/77 = 100)	120.4	119.9	120.0	120.3	120.5	120.8	121.3	118.6	117.6	117.7	117.0	117.9	118.4	118.9
Bicycles	198.9	198.3	197.1	197.3	196.7	197.8	196.1	200.2	199.5	198.5	198.4	197.7	198.0	197.4
Other sporting goods and equipment (12/77 = 100)	126.3	131.5	130.6	131.4	132.1	131.6	132.0	126.5	131.3	130.0	130.9	131.9	131.5	132.0
Toys, hobbies, and other entertainment (12/77 = 100)	135.4	136.4	136.8	136.8	138.0	138.6	138.5	134.3	135.2	135.6	135.6	136.7	137.3	137.2
Toys, hobbies, and music equipment (12/77 = 100)	134.1	135.5	135.5	135.5	136.9	137.6	137.3	130.7	131.8	132.0	131.9	133.0	133.7	133.4
Photographic supplies and equipment (12/77 = 100)	129.8	129.0	129.7	129.9	131.2	131.6	131.6	131.0	130.1	130.8	131.0	132.3	132.8	132.6
Pet supplies and expenses (12/77 = 100)	141.9	143.4	144.2	144.2	144.9	145.6	145.8	142.7	144.5	145.1	145.1	145.9	146.5	146.9
Entertainment services	228.5	238.2	238.2	240.5	241.6	241.9	243.1	229.2	238.4	238.5	240.8	241.8	242.1	243.3
Fees for participant sports (12/77 = 100)	142.0	149.0	148.9	150.0	150.6	150.9	151.3	143.7	150.1	150.0	151.2	151.7	152.2	152.4
Admissions (12/77 = 100)	132.2	136.9	137.3	139.9	140.9	140.1	141.7	131.2	135.9	136.4	138.8	139.8	139.1	140.7
Other entertainment services (12/77 = 100)	125.2	129.8	129.6	129.8	130.3	131.0	131.6	125.9	130.7	130.6	130.6	131.2	131.8	132.4
OTHER GOODS AND SERVICES	253.8	273.8	276.6	279.9	281.6	281.9	283.2	250.9	270.9	274.0	277.8	279.6	280.0	281.4
Tobacco products	235.1	264.0	272.3	280.3	282.8	283.3	284.9	234.0	263.4	271.9	279.9	282.2	282.7	284.3
Cigarettes	238.0	269.8	279.0	287.6	290.0	290.4	292.0	236.9	268.8	278.0	286.5	288.8	289.3	290.9
Other tobacco products and smoking accessories (12/77 = 100)	139.9	142.8	143.8	145.8	147.8	148.6	149.6	140.1	143.0	143.9	145.8	147.7	148.5	149.5
Personal care	245.9	254.2	254.8	256.1	257.8	257.8	259.1	244.1	252.1	252.5	253.9	255.5	255.8	257.1
Toilet goods and personal care appliances	243.8	253.5	252.2	253.9	256.0	257.1	258.5	244.7	254.1	253.1	254.8	256.8	257.8	259.3
Products for the hair, hairpieces, and wigs (12/77 = 100)	142.9	148.3	146.8	147.1	148.1	148.5	150.9	144.3	147.3	146.2	146.5	147.4	147.8	150.3
Dental and shaving products (12/77 = 100)	149.0	157.2	156.2	157.6	159.3	160.4	160.5	147.6	155.4	154.6	155.9	157.8	158.9	158.9

GENERAL SUMMARY	ALL URBAN CONSUMERS							URBAN WAGE EARNERS AND CLERICAL WORKERS						
	1982			1983				1982			1983			
	Apr.	Nov.	Dec.	Jan.	Feb.	Mar.	Apr.	Apr.	Nov.	Dec.	Jan.	Feb.	Mar.	Apr.
Cosmetics, bath and nail preparations, manicure and eye makeup implements (12/77 = 100)	136.5	141.7	142.2	144.0	145.6	146.0	145.6	137.5	142.3	143.0	144.8	146.4	146.7	146.3
Other toilet goods and small personal care appliances (12/77 = 100)	140.3	144.7	143.2	143.6	144.1	144.9	146.0	143.5	148.4	147.0	147.3	147.7	148.5	149.8
Personal care services	248.7	255.8	258.0	259.0	260.4	259.5	260.7	244.0	250.6	252.4	253.4	254.7	254.3	255.4
Beauty parlor services for women	250.7	258.9	262.1	263.3	264.4	262.4	264.2	244.3	252.1	254.7	255.8	256.8	255.5	257.2
Haircuts and other barber shop services for men (12/77 = 100)	138.8	141.4	141.6	142.0	143.1	143.7	143.8	137.6	140.3	140.4	140.8	141.9	142.6	142.7
Personal and educational expenses	291.9	320.0	320.5	322.1	323.3	323.9	324.9	293.5	321.3	321.7	323.6	325.0	325.7	326.8
Schoolbooks and supplies	263.8	283.1	283.3	288.4	292.0	292.3	292.5	268.0	286.8	287.0	292.4	296.0	296.3	296.5
Personal and educational services	298.7	328.6	329.1	330.2	331.0	331.5	332.7	300.0	329.8	330.3	331.5	332.5	333.2	334.5
Tuition and other school fees	151.4	167.2	167.2	167.3	167.4	167.4	167.6	152.0	167.7	167.7	167.7	167.9	167.9	168.2
College tuition (12/77 = 100)	151.0	166.8	166.8	166.9	167.0	167.0	167.4	151.3	166.9	166.9	167.0	167.1	167.1	167.5
Elementary and high school tuition (12/77 = 100)	152.2	168.7	168.7	168.7	168.8	168.8	168.8	152.9	169.7	169.7	169.7	169.8	169.8	169.8
Personal expenses (12/77 = 100)	160.9	174.1	175.4	178.8	179.6	181.2	183.1	160.5	174.0	175.2	177.9	179.5	181.1	183.1
Special indexes:														
Gasoline, motor oil, coolant, and other products	362.6	383.5	377.0	367.9	355.8	345.2	363.4	363.7	384.8	378.5	369.4	357.3	346.7	365.0
Insurance and finance	. . .	426.2	413.4	. . .	. . .	. . .	. . .	425.9	427.2	414.7	411.1	411.6	411.8	411.6
Utilities and public transportation	305.1	324.1	326.0	329.1	329.4	331.1	333.4	304.0	323.2	325.1	328.1	328.5	330.4	332.6
Housekeeping and home maintenance services	347.5	354.8	354.0	355.3	355.1	356.0	357.3	348.2	355.4	354.4	357.9	356.5	357.9	359.5

(1967 = 100 unless otherwise specified)

[1] Excludes motor oil, coolant, and other products as of January 1983.

[2] See box with "Price Data."

c = corrected.

APPENDIX B: WHEN TO BUY
SELECTED ARTICLES AND FOOD ITEMS

SALE MONTHS	CONSUMER ARTICLES	FOOD ITEMS
January	Linens, baby things, men's and women's clothing, home furnishings, luggage, lingerie, furs, diamonds, cosmetics, and nonprescription drugs	Citrus fruit, cauliflower, potatoes, onions, and turkeys
February	Housewares, hosiery, and fabrics	Citrus fruit, potatoes, greens, celery, snap beans, apples, and canned fruit
March	Hardware, paint, gardening tools, made-to-order slipcovers and drapes, china, glass, women's shoes, and rain gear	Texas carrots, Florida lettuce, oranges, and green peas
April	Paint, wallpaper, building supplies, air conditioners, and tires	Asparagus, artichokes, snap beans, cabbage, carrots, onions, Maine potatoes, and fish items
May	Jewelry, candy, housewares, gardening tools, bed linens and towels, vacation gear, and cleaning supplies	Eggs, Florida corn, and onions
June	Gifts for brides, grads and dads; men's clothing; sporting goods; and small appliances	Apricots, cantaloupes, cherries, and eggs
July	Furniture, bedding, bed linens and towels, and major appliances	Raspberries, blackberries, blueberries, limes, mangoes, peaches, beets, and okra
August	School supplies, summer clothing and equipment, and fall fashions	Corn, peaches, watermelon, cabbage, tomatoes, and seafood
September	Home improvements, sporting goods, china, glassware, major appliances, children's shoes, and auto batteries	Grapes, cucumbers, melons, squash, and lamb
October	Furniture, lamps, outerwear, and furnaces	Apples, cauliflower, grapes, pears, eggplant, and pumpkins
November	Rugs, men's clothing, furnishings, linoleum, liquors, toys, and games	Gourmet foods, avocados, cranberries, persimmons, sweet potatoes, turnips, raisins, and nuts
December	Post-Christmas cards, wrappings, lights, and decorations; toys; games; and housewares	Coconuts, flour, shortening, sugar, spices, and early citrus

Source: Adapted from excerpt from *Consumer Views* 12 (December 1981), © Citicorp 1981.

APPENDIX C:
COUPLES INVENTORY

Personal goal   To look at how sex role behavior influences decision making, autonomy, and intimacy in your relationship with your partner.

Directions   Both partners fill out separate inventories and then compare statements.

1. I am important to our couple because _____

2. What I contribute to your success is _____

3. I feel central to our relationship when _____

4. I feel peripheral to our relationship when _____

5. The ways I show concern for you are _____

6. The ways I encourage your growth are _____

7. The ways I deal with conflict are _____

8. The ways I have fun with you are _____

9. I get angry when you _____

10. I am elated when you _____

11. The way I get space for myself in our relationship is _____

12. The ways I am intimate with you are _____

13. The ways I am jealous of you are _____

14. I have difficulty being assertive when you _____

15. You have difficulty being assertive when I _____

16. The strengths of our relationship are _____
_____

17. The weaknesses of our relationship are _____
_____

18. Our relationship would be more effective if you _____
_____

19. I feel most masculine in our relationship when I _____
_____

20. I feel most feminine in our relationship when I _____
_____

21. I trust you to do/be _____
_____

22. I do not trust you to do/be _____
_____

23. I deal with stress by _____
_____

24. You deal with stress by _____
_____

25. The division of labor in household tasks is decided by _____
_____

26. Our finances are controlled by _____
_____

27. The amount of time we spend with our relatives is determined by _____
_____

28. Our vacation plans are made by _____
_____

29. Our social life is planned by _____
_____

30. Taking stock of our relationship is done by _____
_____

31. I am lonely when _____
_____

32. I need you to _____
_____

Source: Alice G. Sargent, *Beyond Sex Roles*. St. Paul, Minnesota: West, 1977, p. 87.

APPENDIX D: SAMPLE COUNSELOR QUESTIONS FOR COUPLES CONTEMPLATING LIVING TOGETHER

COUNSELOR QUESTIONS	"GOOD" SIGNS AND "CONCERN" SIGNS
1. Could you talk a little bit about how each of you came to the decision to live together?	*Good signs*: Each partner has given considerable thought to the decision, including the advantages and disadvantages of living together. *Concern signs*: One or both partners have given little thought to the advantages and disadvantages of living together.
2. Perhaps each of you could discuss for a minute what you think you will get out of living together?	*Good signs*: Each individual is concerned about learning more about self and partner through intimate daily living. Both wish to obtain further information about each other's commitment to the relationship. *Concern signs*: One or both partners desire to live together for convenience only. They want to live together to show independence from parents or peers.
3. Could each of you discuss what you see as your role and your partner's role in the relationship (for example, responsibilities, expectations)?	*Good signs*: Each individual's expectations of self and partner are compatible with those of partner. *Concern signs*: One or both individuals have given little thought to the roles or expectations of self and/or partner. Individuals disagree in terms of their expectations.
4. Could each of you identify your partner's primary physical and emotional needs and the degree to which you believe that you are able to fulfill them?	*Good signs*: Each individual has a clear understanding of partner's needs and is motivated and able to meet most of them. *Concern signs*: One or both individuals are not fully aware of partner's needs. Individuals are not motivated or able to meet needs of partner.
5. Would each of you identify your primary physical and emotional needs in your relationship with your partner? To what degree have these needs been met in the past? To what extent are these needs likely to be met if the two of you were to live together?	*Good signs*: Each partner clearly understands his or her needs. Most of these needs are presently being met and are likely to continue to be met in a cohabiting relationship. *Concern signs*: One or both partners are not fully aware of their needs. Needs are not being met in the present relationship and/or are not likely to be met if the individuals live together.
6. Could each of you discuss what makes this relationship important to you? What are your feelings toward your partner?	*Good signs*: Partners care deeply for each other and view the relationship as a highly significant one. *Concern signs*: One or both individuals do not care deeply for their partner or do not view the relationship as a highly significant one. Partners have an emotional imbalance, with one partner more involved in the relationship than the other.
7. Could each of you explore briefly your previous dating experiences and what you have learned from them?	*Good signs*: Both individuals have had a rich dating history. Individuals have positive perceptions of self and opposite sex and are aware of what they learned from previous relationships. *Concern signs*: One or both partners have had minimal dating experience. Individuals have negative perceptions of self and/or of the opposite sex and do not seem aware of having learned from their prior relationships.

COUNSELOR QUESTIONS	"GOOD" SIGNS AND "CONCERN" SIGNS
8. Perhaps each of you could talk for a minute about how your family and friends might react to the two of you living together?	*Good signs*: Each individual is aware of the potential repercussions of family and friends should they learn of the cohabiting relationship. Family and friends are supportive of the cohabiting relationship, or couple has considered how they will deal with opposition. *Concern signs*: One or both individuals are not fully aware of possible family and friends' reaction to their living together. Family and friends are not supportive of the cohabiting relationship.
9. Could each of you discuss your ability to openly and honestly share your feelings with your partner?	*Good signs*: Each individual is usually able to express feelings to partner without difficulty. *Concern signs*: One or both individuals have difficulty expressing feelings to partner or do not believe expressing feelings is important.
10. Could each of you discuss your partner's strengths and weaknesses? To what extent would you like to change your partner, relative to their strengths or weaknesses?	*Good signs*: Each individual is usually able to accept feelings of partner. Individuals are able to accept partner's strengths and weaknesses. *Concern signs*: One or both individuals are not able to understand and accept partner. Individuals have difficulty in accepting partner's strengths and weaknesses.
11. How do each of you handle relationship problems when they occur? Can you give some examples of difficult problems you have had and how you have dealt with them?	*Good signs*: Both individuals express feelings openly and are able to understand and accept partner's point of view. Individuals are able to mutually solve problems. *Concern signs*: One or both partners have difficulty expressing feelings openly or in accepting partner's point of view. Couple frequently avoids problems or fails to solve them mutually.

Source: adapted from C. Ridley, D. Peterman, and A. Avery, "Cohabitation: Does It Make For a Better Marriage?" *Family Coordinator* (April 1978):135–36.

APPENDIX E:
MARRIAGE REQUIREMENTS BY STATE*

Marriageable age, by states, for both males and females with and without consent of parents or guardians. But in most states, the court has authority to marry young couples below the ordinary age of consent, where due regard for their morals and welfare so requires. In many states, under special circumstances, blood test and waiting period may be waived.

STATE	WITH CONSENT		WITHOUT CONSENT		BLOOD TEST**		WAIT FOR LICENSE	WAIT AFTER LICENSE
	Men	Women	Men	Women	Required	Other State Accepted		
Alabama(b)	14	14	18	18	Yes	Yes	none	none
Alaska	16	16	18	18	Yes	No	3 days	none
Arizona	16(i)	16	18	18	Yes	Yes	none	none
Arkansas	17	16(j)	18	18	Yes	No	3 days	none
California	18(i)	18	18	18	Yes(n)	Yes	none	none
Colorado	16	16	18	18	Yes(n)	. . .	none	none
Connecticut	16	16(l)	18	18	Yes	Yes	4 days	none
Delaware	18	16(o)	18	18	Yes	Yes	none	24 hrs.(c)
District of Columbia	16	16	18	18	Yes	Yes	3 days	none
Florida	18	18	18	18	Yes	Yes	3 days	none
Georgia	16	16	18	18	Yes	Yes	none(k)	none
Hawaii	16	16	18	18	Yes	Yes	none	none
Idaho	16	16	18	18	Yes(n)	Yes	none(k)	none
Illinois(a)	16	16	18	18	Yes(p)	Yes	none	1 day
Indiana	17(o)	17(o)	18	18	Yes(p)	No	72 hours	none
Iowa	16(o)	16(o)	18	18	Yes	Yes	3 days	none
Kansas	14	12	18	18	Yes	Yes	3 days	none
Kentucky	—(o)	—(o)	18	18	Yes	No	3 days	none
Louisiana(a)	18(o)	16(j)	18	16	Yes	No	none	72 hours
Maine	16(j)	16(j)	18	18	No	No	5 days	none
Maryland	16	16	18	18	none	none	48 hours	none
Massachusetts	—(o)	—(o)	18	18	Yes	Yes	3 days	none
Michigan(a)	18	16	18	18	Yes	No	3 days	none
Minnesota	16(e)	16(e)	18	18	none	. . .	5 days	none
Mississippi	17(q)	15(q)	21	21	Yes	. . .	3 days	none
Missouri(b)	15	15	18	18	none	Yes	3 days	none
Montana	15	15	18	18	Yes(n)	Yes	none	3 days
Nebraska	17	17	18	18	Yes(n)	Yes	2 days	none
Nevada	16	16	18	18	none	none	none	none

*Many states have additional requirements; contact individual state. (a) Special laws applicable to nonresidents. (b) Special laws applicable to those under 21 years; Ala., bond required if male is under 18, female under 18. (c) 24 hours if one or both parties resident of state; 96 hours if both parties are non-residents. (d) None, but both must file affadavit. (e) Parental consent plus court's consent required. (f) None, but a medical certificate is required. (g) Marriage, may not be solemnized within 10 days from date of blood test. (h) If either under 18, 72 hrs. (i) Statute provides for obtaining license with parental or court consent with no state minimum age. (j) Under 16, with parental and court consent. (k) If either under 18, wait 3 full days. (l) If under stated age, court consent required. (m) Va. blood test form must be used. (n) Applicant must also supply a certificate of immunity against German measles (rubella). (o) If under 18, parental and/or court consent required. (p) Statement whether person is carrier of sickle-cell anemia may be required. (q) Both parents' consent required for men age 17, women age 15; one parent's consent required for men 18-20 years, women ages 16-20 years.

****As of 1982

	WITH CONSENT		WITHOUT CONSENT		BLOOD TEST**		WAIT FOR LICENSE	WAIT AFTER LICENSE
STATE	Men	Women	Men	Women	Required	Other State Accepted		
New Hampshire(a)	14(e)	13(e)	18	18	Yes	Yes	5 days	none
New Jersey(a)	—	12	18	18	Yes	Yes	72 hours	none
New Mexico	16	16	18	18	Yes	Yes	none	none
New York	16	14	18	18	Yes(p)	No	none	24 hrs.(g)
North Carolina(a)	16	16	18	18	Yes(p)	Yes	none	none
North Dakota(a)	16	16	18	18	Yes	. . .	none	none
Ohio(a)	18	16	18	18	Yes	Yes	5 days	none
Oklahoma	16	16	18	18	Yes	No	none(f)(h)	none
Oregon	17	17	18	18	Yes	No	3 days	none
Pennsylvania	16	16	18	18	Yes	Yes	3 days	none
Rhode Island(a)(b)	18	16	18	18	Yes(n)	No	none	none
South Carolina	16	14	18	18	none	none	24 hrs.	none
South Dakota	16	16	18	18	Yes	Yes	none	none
Tennessee(b)	16	16	18	18	Yes	Yes	3 days	none
Texas	14	14	18	18	Yes	Yes	none	none
Utah(a)	14	14	18	18	none	Yes	none	none
Vermont(a)	18	16	18	18	Yes	. . .	none	5 days
Virginia(a)	16	16	18	18	Yes	Yes(m)	none	none
Washington	17	17	18	18	(d)	. . .	3 days	none
West Virginia	18	16	18	18	Yes	No	3 days	none
Wisconsin	16	16	18	18	Yes	Yes	5 days	none
Wyoming	16	16	19	19	Yes	Yes	none	none
Puerto Rico	18	16	21	21	(f)	none	none	none
Virgin Islands	16	14	18	18	none	none	8 days	none

APPENDIX F:
DIVORCE REQUIREMENTS BY STATE*

STATE	BREAKDOWN OF MARRIAGE INCOMPATIBILITY	CRUELTY	DESERTION	NON-SUPPORT	ALCOHOL &/OR DRUG ADDICTION	FELONY	IMPOTENCY	INSANITY	LIVING SEPARATE AND APART	OTHER GROUNDS	RESIDENCE TIME	TIME BETWEEN INTERLOCUT'Y AND FINAL DECREES
Alabama	X	X	X	X	X	X	X	X	2 yrs.	A-B-E	6 mos.	none-M
Alaska	X	X	X	...	X	X	X	X		B-C-F	1 yr.	none
Arizona	X	.	.	.	.	.	.	.			90 days	none
Arkansas	...	X	X	X	X	X	X	X	3 yrs.	C-I	3 mos.	none
California[2]	X	.	.	.	.	.	.	X			6 mos.	6 mos.
Colorado[2]	X	.	.	.	.	.	.	.			90 days	none
Connecticut	X	X	X	X	X	X	...	X	18 mos.	B	1 yr.	none
Delaware	X[4]	.	.	.	.	.	.	.	6 mos.		6 mos.	none
District of Columbia	...	.	.	.	.	.	.	.	6 mos.-1 yr.		6 mos.	none
Florida	X	.	.	.	.	.	.	X			6 mos.	none
Georgia	X	X	X	...	X	X	X	X		A-B-F	6 mos.	L
Hawaii	X	.	.	.	.	.	.	.	2 yrs.	K	3 mos.	none
Idaho	X	X	X	X	X	X	...	X	5 yrs.	H	6 wks.	none
Illinois	...	X	X	...	X	X	X	...		I-J	90 days	none
Indiana	X	.	.	.	.	X	X	X			6 mos.	none
Iowa	X	.	.	.	.	.	.	.			1 yr.	none-N
Kansas	X	.	.	.	.	.	.	.		H	60 days	none-M
Kentucky	X	.	.	.	.	.	.	.	1 yr.		180 days	none
Louisiana	...	X	X	X	X	X			1 yr.	C-J-K	12 mos.	none-N
Maine	X	X	X	X	X	...	X	X		H	6 mos.	none
Maryland	...	X	X	.	.	X	X	X	1-3 yrs.	D-I	1 yr.	none
Massachusetts	X[4]	X	X	X	X	X	X	...	6 mos.-1 yr.		1 yr.	6 mos.

Adultery is either grounds for divorce or evidence of irreconcilable differences and a breakdown of the marriage in all states. The plaintiff can invariably remarry in the same state where he or she procured a decree of divorce or annulment. Not so the defendant, who is barred in certain states for some offenses. After a period of time has elapsed even the offender can apply for permission.

(1) Generally 5 yrs. insanity but: permanent insanity in Ut.; incurable insanity in Col.; 1 yr. Wis.; 18 mos. Alas.; 2 yrs. Ga., Ha., Ind., Nev., N.J., Ore., Wash., Wy.; 3 yrs. Ark., Cal., Fla., Md., Minn., Miss., N.C., Tex., W. Va.; 6 yrs. Ida.; Kan.: Incompatability by reason of mental illness or incapacity. (2) Cal., Colo., and Ore., have procedures whereby a couple can obtain a divorce without an attorney and without appearing in court provided certain requirements are met. (3) Other grounds existing only in N.H. are: Joining a religious order disbelieving in marriage, treatment which injures health or endangers reason, wife without the state for 10 years, and wife in state 2 yrs. husband never in state and intends to become a citizen of a foreign country. (4) Provable only by fault grounds, separation for some period, generally a year, proof of marital discord or commitment for mental illness. (A) Pregnancy at marriage. (B) Fraudulent contract. (C) Indignities. (D) Consanguinity. (E) Crime against nature. (F) Mental incapacity at time of marriage. (G) Procurement of out-of-state divorce. (H) Gross neglect of duty. (I) Bigamy. (J) Attempted homicide. (K) Separation by decree in Conn.; after decree: one yr. in La., N.Y., Wis.; 18 mos. in N.H.; 2 yrs. in Ala., Ha., Minn., N.C., Tenn.; 3 yrs. in Ut.; 4 yrs. in N.J., N.D.; 5 yrs. in Md. (L) Determined by court order. (M) 60 days to remarry. (N) One yr. to remarry except Ha. one yr. with minor child; La. 90 days. (O) 6 mos. to remarry. (P) Adultery cases, remarriage in court's discretion. (Q) Plaintiff, 6 mos.; defendant 2 yrs. to remarry. (R) No remarriage if an appeal is pending. (S) Actual domicile in adultery cases. (U) Abuse and neglect of child; physical or mental injury to child. **Enoch Arden Laws.** disappearance and unknown to be alive—Conn., S.C., Va., Vt., 7 yrs. absence; Ala., Ark., N.Y. 5 yrs. (called dissolution); N.H. 2 yrs.

N.B. Grounds not recognized for divorce may be recognized for separation or annulment. Local laws should be consulted.

*As of 1982

STATE	BREAKDOWN OF MARRIAGE INCOMPATIBILITY	CRUELTY	DESERTION	NON-SUPPORT	ALCOHOL &/OR DRUG ADDICTION	FELONY	IMPOTENCY	INSANITY	LIVING SEPARATE AND APART	OTHER GROUNDS	RESIDENCE TIME	TIME BETWEEN INTERLOCUT'Y AND FINAL DECREES
Michigan	X										180 days	none
Minnesota	X									K	180 days	none-O
Mississippi	X	X	X		X	X	X	X		A	6 mos.	none-P
Missouri	X[4]										90 days	none
Montana	X										90 days	none
Nebraska	X										1 yr.	6 mos.
Nevada	X							X	1 yr.		6 wks.	none
New Hampshire[3]	X	X	X	X	X	X	X		2 yrs.	K	1 yr.	none
New Jersey	...	X	X		X	X		X	18 mos.	E-K	1 yr.	none
New Mexico	X	X	X								6 mos.	none
New York	...	X	X			X			1 yr.	K	1 yr.	none
North Carolina	...						X	X	1 yr.	A-E	6 mos.	none
North Dakota	X	X	X	X	X	X	X	X		H-K	12 mos.	none
Ohio	X	X	X		X	X	X	X	2 yrs.	B-G-H-I	6 mos.	none
Oklahoma	X	X	X	X	X	X	X	X		A-B-G-H	6 mos.	none
Oregon[2]	X									B	6 mos.	30 days
Pennsylvania	X	X	X			X	X	X	3 yrs.	C-D-I	6 mos.	none
Rhode Island	X	X	X	X	X	X	X		3 yrs.		1 yr.	3 mos.
South Carolina	...	X	X		X				1 yr.		3 mos.	none
South Dakota	...	X	X	X	X	X					none	none
Tennessee	X	X	X	X	X	X	X			A-H-I-J-K	6 mos.	none
Texas	X	X	X			X		X	3 yrs.		6 mos.	none-O
Utah	...	X	X	X	X	X	X	X		K	3 mos.	3 mos.
Vermont	...	X	X	X		X		X	6 mos.		6 mos.	3 mos.
Virginia	...	X	X			X			6 mos-1 yr.	E	6 mos.	none-P
Washington	X										none	none-R
West Virginia	X	X	X		X	X		X	1 yr.	U	1 yr.	none
Wisconsin	X								1 yr.	K	6 mos.	none-O
Wyoming	X							X	2 yrs.		60 days	none

GLOSSARY

Abortion Induced or spontaneous termination of a pregnancy before the fetus is capable of surviving on its own.

Abstinence One of several premarital sexual values, based on the belief that sexual intercourse between unmarried men and women is wrong.

Adolescence The general social as well as biological changes a child experiences in becoming an adult.

Agape Greek term for spiritual love.

Alienation A feeling of not being a part of a society.

Alternative birth center A special birth center that creates a homelike atmosphere for birth.

Ambivalence Simultaneous liking and disliking of an object or person.

Amniocentesis An important prenatal diagnostic tool. A long hollow needle is inserted through the mother's abdomen and into the amniotic sac, where a sample of the amniotic fluid is drawn off. This fluid contains sloughed-off cells from the fetus that may be examined microscopically for signs of disease or birth defects, enabling early treatment to be instituted. This technique may also determine the baby's gender.

Amniotic fluid The fluid that surrounds and insulates the fetus in the mother's womb.

Anaphrodisiac A drug or medicine that reduces sexual desire.

Androgen The dominant male hormone, which is thought to have an effect on aggression.

Androgynous The quality of having both masculine and feminine personality characteristics.

Aphrodisiac A chemical or other substance used to induce erotic arousal or to relieve impotence or infertility.

Areola The pigmented area surrounding the nipples of the breasts, a significant erogenous zone for about half of the male and female population.

Artificial insemination Induction of semen into the vagina or uterus by artificial means.

Bankruptcy Being financially insolvent, unable to pay one's bills.

Bigamy Being married to two people at the same time.

Binuclear family A family that includes children from two nuclear families; occurs when one or both of the divorced parents remarry.

Birth control Deliberate limitation of the number of children born.

Bisexuality Having sexual relationships with partners of the same and opposite sex.

Budget A plan for balancing expenses with estimated income.

Caesarean section The delivery of a baby by means of a surgical incision through the mother's abdominal and uterine walls. Caesareans are generally performed when the physical condition of the mother or the fetus is such that one or both might not survive the stress of vaginal delivery.

Child snatching The taking of children from the custodial spouse by the noncustodial spouse after a divorce.

Clitoris The small organ situated just under the upper portion of the labia minora of the female genitalia. It is the homologue of the male penis, consists of a shaft and a glans, and becomes erect with sexual arousal. It is also the chief organ for erotic arousal in most women.

Cluster family An artificially contrived family group that meets for companionship, recreation, and other meaningful experiences without the members actually living together.

Cohabitation A man and woman living together in an intimate relationship without being legally married.

Common-law marriage A marriage that becomes legally recognized after the woman and man have lived together for some time as though they were wife and husband. About one third of the states recognize common-law marriage.

Commune A group of people who live together by choice rather than because of blood or legal ties. Also referred to as an intentional community.

Conception Fertilization of the egg by the sperm to start a new human life.

Condom Also known as a "rubber" or "prophylactic," the condom is a thin sheath, usually made of rubber, which is rolled over and down the shaft of the erect penis prior to intercourse. While used primarily as a method of contraception, it also protects against venereal disease.

Congenital defect A condition existing at birth or before, as distinguished from a genetic defect.

Consumer Price Index (CPI) A sample of costs of goods and services collected by the Bureau of Labor Statistics, which are then compared with some arbitrarily set base period (now set at 1967).

Contraception A deliberate action to prevent fertilization of the ovum as a result of copulation.

Contraceptive Any agent used to prevent conception.

Credit buying Purchasing goods by making payments for them over a period of time.

Cunnilingus Oral contact with female genitalia.

D&C (dilatation and curettage) A procedure usually used to induce an abortion during the first twelve weeks of pregnancy. It involves dilating (stretching) the cervix and scraping away the contents of the uterus with a sharp instrument (curette). The operation requires no incision, recovery is usually rapid, and most patients are in the hospital only overnight. (Used as a diagnostic procedure, a D&C is performed to determine the cause of abnormal menstrual bleeding or to determine the cause of bleeding after the menopause.)

Dating Social interaction and activity with a person of the opposite sex.

DES Abbreviation for diethylstilbestrol, known as the morning-after pill. It contains high doses of estrogen and terminates a pregnancy if taken within twenty-four hours of intercourse.

Diaphragm A contraceptive device consisting of a circular piece of thin rubber that is fitted by a physician so that it spans the back of the vagina and covers the cervix. Spermicidal jelly often is used in conjunction with the diaphragm.

Discount interest Interest paid on the full amount initially borrowed even though some of the loan is repaid each month.

Double standard Different standards of appropriate sexual behavior for men than for women; the acceptability for men but not for women of all types of sexual behavior.

Douche Flushing the vagina with water or with a spermicidal agent after intercourse. A relatively unreliable method of contraception.

Dual-career family A marriage in which both spouses pursue their own careers.

Ejaculation The expulsion of semen by the male during orgasm.

Embryo The developing organism from the second to the eighth week of pregnancy, characterized by differentiation of organs and tissues into their human form.

Empty-nest stage Period in a marriage that begins when the last child leaves home and continues until either spouse retires or dies.

Enculturation The process of learning the mores, rules, ways, and manners of a given culture.

Endogamy The inclination or the necessity to marry within a particular group.

Engagement The final courtship stage before marriage; characterized by public knowledge of the coming marriage.

Episiotomy A surgical incision made in the mother's perineum during childbirth in order to prevent tearing of the vaginal tissues.

Eros The physical, sexual side of love; termed "Cupid" by the Romans.

Estrogen Often called the "female hormone," it is active in many important ways, such as directing the differentiation of embryonic tissue into female genitalia, directing the differentiation of prenatal brain tissue that governs various female physiological functions, and directing the development of female secondary sexual characteristics at puberty. It is produced chiefly in the ovaries and adrenal cortex of the female and, to a lesser extent, in the testicles and adrenal cortex of the male.

Exogamy The inclination or the necessity to marry outside a particular group.

Extended family A nuclear or polygamous family and the parental generation. The typical extended family includes the husband, wife, their children, and the parents (or aunts/uncles) of the spouses.

Fallopian tubes The two tubes in the female reproductive system which link the ovaries to the uterus. Eggs released from the ovaries move down these tubes to the uterus.

Family A group of two or more persons who are related by blood, marriage, or adoption (U.S. Census definition). The term usually implies the presence of children, a common residence, and economic cooperation.

Family enrichment programs Groups of three to five families who meet together regularly for mutual care and support and for the development of family potential.

Family life cycle A model designed to explain the behavior patterns of married couples. It divides marriage into various stages according to the number, age, and health of a married couple's children.

Family of orientation The family into which an individual is born or adopted.

Family of procreation The family which one begins by marrying and having one's own children.

Family planning Controlling the number and spacing of children through systematic use of contraceptive methods.

Fellatio Oral contact with male genitalia.

Fetal monitoring Using various instruments to measure the vital signs of the fetus during the birth process.

Fetoscopy Examining the fetus through a small viewing tube inserted into the mother's uterus.

Fetus The name given to the developing human organism from eight weeks after conception until birth.

Gender Attitudes and behavior associated with each of the two sexes.

Genes The subcellular structures within the chromosomes in the cell nucleus that contain the DNA molecules and determine the traits of the differentiating cells of the organism.

Genetic defect An abnormality in the development of the fetus that is inherited through the genes, as distinguished from a congenital defect.

Genitalia The external reproductive organs.

Genotype The underlying genetic trait that, in contrast to the *phenotype*, is not readily observable.

Gonorrhea A venereal disease caused by gonococci. Unlike syphilis, which typically involves the entire body, gonorrhea usually remains localized in the genitalia and is self-limiting, although it may persist and cause serious and permanent damage, including sterility. Symptoms are common in men, but the disease is often asymptomatic in women and difficult to detect.

Gross National Product (G.N.P.) Total value of a nation's annual output of goods and services.

Halo effect The tendency for a first impression to influence subsequent judgments about something.

Hermaphrodite A person who has both male and female organs, or organs that are indeterminant (such as a clitoris that resembles a penis).

Heterogamy The mutual attraction and compatibility of persons with opposite and complementary personality traits—for example, dominance-submission, nurturance-dependence, achievement-vicarious.

Home birth Giving birth at one's home rather than in a hospital.

Homogamy The strongly practical attraction of persons who share similar objective characteristics, such as race, religion, ethnic group, intelligence, education, social class, age, and interests and skills.

Hysterectomy A surgical procedure which removes a woman's uterus. While hysterectomies result in sterility for the woman, they are usually conducted because of a malignancy.

Impotence The inability of a man to experience erection. It may be caused by either physical or psychological factors and is usually temporary.

Incest Copulation between closely blood-tied relatives. The degree of closeness that is considered incestuous depends on social attitudes, but all societies proscribe sexual relations between parents and children and between siblings.

Infanticide The deliberate killing of infants as a measure to control population or for some other socially accepted purpose.

Infertility Inability to produce children.

Inflation A sustained rise in the average of all prices.

Inflationary recession A falling off of business activity at the same time that prices are rising.

Intimacy Experiencing the essence of oneself in intense intellectual, physical, and/or emotional relationships with others.

Intrauterine device Known as the IUD, it is a small object that a physician inserts into a woman's uterus to prevent conception from occurring.

Investment Use of money to earn more money, such as putting it in a business or in stocks.

Jealousy The state of being resentfully suspicious of a loved one's behavior toward a suspected rival.

Labor Changes in a woman's body as it prepares to deliver a child, consisting mainly of muscle contractions and dilation of the cervix.

Laparoscopy A sterilization procedure for females involving the use of a telescope instrument (laparoscope) to locate the Fallopian tubes, which are then cauterized.

Legal separation A legal decree that forbids cohabitation by husband and wife and provides for separate maintenance and support of the wife and children by the husband. A legally separated couple is still bound by the marital contract and may not remarry.

Marriage contract A written agreement between married partners outlining the responsibilities and obligations of each partner.

Masturbation Any voluntary erotic activity that involves self-stimulation.

Menopause The cessation of ovulation, menstruation, and fertility in the woman. It usually occurs between ages forty-five and fifty.

Menstruation The discharge of blood and the unfertilized ovum from the uterus through the vagina; normally occurs every twenty-eight days in women from puberty to menopause.

Mental health A mode of being in which a person is free of mental problems and/or disease.

Middlescence The second adolescence experienced in middle age, usually involving reevaluation of one's life.

Midlife crisis The questioning of one's worth and values, usually beginning sometime in one's forties or early fifties.

Midwife A person, usually a woman, trained to assist in childbirth or, in some countries, to perform delivery.

Miscarriage A spontaneous abortion.

Miscegenation Marriage or interbreeding between members of different races.

Modeling Learning vicariously by observing others' behavior.

Monogamy The state of being married to one person at a time.

Natural childbirth Birth wherein the parents have learned about the birthing process and participate via exercises such as breathing techniques so as to minimize pain.

Naturalism, myth of The belief that two people will naturally get along in marriage if they love each other.

No-fault divorce Divorce proceedings that do not place blame for the divorce on one spouse or the other.

Norm Accepted social rules for behavior.

Nuclear family A group of persons, consisting of a married couple and their children, who live by themselves. The children may be natural or adopted by the couple.

Open marriage A relationship that emphasizes role equality and the freedom for each partner to maximize his or her own potential; may or may not involve extramarital sex.

Oral contraceptive Hormonal materials (in pill form) that suspend ovulation and therefore prevent conception.

Orgasm The climax of excitement in sexual activity.

Ovaries The female sex glands in which the ova (eggs) are formed.

Ovulation The regular monthly process in the fertile woman whereby an ovarian follicle ruptures and releases a mature ovum (egg).

Ovum The female reproductive cell (egg) that when fertilized develops into a new member of the same species.

Paracervical anesthesia Injection of a pain killer, such as novacain, into the cervix to reduce pain during childbirth.

Phenomenology The study of how people subjectively experience their environment.

Philos Greek term for the love found in deep, enduring friendships; a general love of mankind.

Placenta The organ that connects the fetus to the uterus by means of the umbilical cord.

Polyandry A form of marriage in which one woman has more than one husband.

Polygamy Marriage with multiple spouses (as opposed to *monogamy*, with one spouse).

Polygyny A form of marriage in which one man has more than one wife.

Postpartum depression Also known as the blues, it is a feeling of depression, after giving birth, characterized by irritability, crying, loss of appetite, and difficulty in sleeping. Such feelings are thought to be a result of numerous physiological and psychological changes that occur as a result of pregnancy, labor and delivery.

Premature ejaculation The inability to delay ejaculation as long as the male or his partner wishes.

Prenatal Existing or occurring before birth.

Propinquity Nearness in time or place.

Puberty Biological changes a child goes through to become an adult capable of reproduction.

Recession A temporary falling off of business activity.

Reconstituted family A husband and wife, at least one of whom has been married before, and one or more children from previous marriage(s).

Rh factor An element found in the blood of most people that can adversely affect fetal development if the parents differ on the element (Rh negative versus Rh positive).

Rhythm method A birth-control method involving avoidance of sexual intercourse when the egg is in the Fallopian tubes. The "calendar method" and the "temperature method" are used to predict this time. The rhythm method is a relatively unreliable contraceptive technique.

Role Particular type of behavior one is expected to exhibit when occupying a certain place in a group.

Romantic love Love at first sight, based on the ideas that there is only one true love and that love is the most important criterion for marriage.

Rooming-in The practice of placing the newborn in the mother's room after delivery so that the mother (and father) can care for it.

Saline abortion An abortion-inducing procedure in which a salt solution is injected into the amniotic sac to kill the fetus, which is then expelled via uterine contractions.

Self-actualization The process of developing one's cognitive, emotional, social and physical potential.

Semen The secretion of the male reproductive organs that is ejaculated from the penis during orgasm and contains the sperm cells.

Sensitivity training Training in learning to understand and be more aware of one's body, its feelings and functioning.

Serial marriage The process of having a series of marriages, one after the other.

Sex therapy Therapy of any kind designed to help persons overcome sexual problems.

Sexually transmitted disease (STD) Any contagious disease communicated mainly by sexual interaction.

Simple interest Interest paid only on the unpaid balance of a loan.

Socialization The process of a person's learning—from parents, peers, social institutions, and other sources—the skills, knowledge, and roles necessary for competent and socially acceptable behavior in the society.

Spermaticides The chemical substances that destroy or immobilize sperm and are used as contraceptives.

Stepparent The husband or wife of one's parent by a later marriage.

Sterility The permanent inability to reproduce.

Sterilization Any procedure (usually surgical) by which an individual is made incapable of reproduction.

Surrogate mother A woman who becomes pregnant and gives birth to a child for another woman who is incapable of giving birth.

Swinging Agreement by married couples to swap mates sexually.

Syphilis A venereal disease caused by a microorganism called a *spirochete*. Syphilis goes through four stages, each with separate and distinct characteristics, and can involve every part of the body. It is transmitted by contact of mucous membrane or broken skin with an infectious syphilitic lesion.

Testosterone An important component of the male sex hormone androgen. It is responsible for inducing and maintaining the male secondary sexual characteristics.

Transsexualism A compulsion or obsession to become a member of the opposite sex through surgical changes.

Transvestism A sexual deviation characterized by a compulsive desire to wear garments of the opposite sex.

Trial marriage Cohabitation between two people who intend to marry.

Tubal ligation A sterilization procedure for females in which the Fallopian tubes are cut or tied.

Ultrasound Sound waves directed at the fetus that yield a visual picture of the fetus; used to detect potential problems in fetal development.

Umbilical cord A flexible cordlike structure connecting the fetus to the placenta and through which the fetus is fed and waste products are discharged.

Uterus The hollow, pear-shaped organ in females within which the fetus develops; the womb.

Vacuum aspiration An abortion-inducing procedure in which the contents of the uterus are removed by suction.

Vasectomy A sterilization procedure for males involving the surgical cutting of the vas deferens.

Virginity Not having experienced sexual intercourse.

Withdrawal Removing the penis from the vagina before ejaculation. A relatively unreliable method of contraception.

BIBLIOGRAPHY

AB (California) 1960, Berman, Chapter 1308, Statutes of 1978.

Abarbanel, Alice. "Shared Parenting after Separation and Divorce: A Study of Joint Custody." *American Journal of Orthopsychiatry*, April 1979, 320–29.

"Abortion: The Edelin Shock Wave." *Time*, March 3, 1975, 54–55.

Adams, D., Alice Gold, and Anne Burt. "Rise in Female-Initiated Sexual Activity at Ovulation and Its Suppression by Oral Contraceptives." *New England Journal of Medicine*, November 23, 1978, 1145–50.

Adams, Virginia. "Getting at the Heart of Jealous Love." *Psychology Today* 13, no. 2 (May 1980): 38–47.

Addiego, F., et al. "Female Ejaculation?" *Medical Aspects of Human Sexuality*, August 1980, 99–103.

Advertising Age, September 9, 1982.

Albrecht, S. "Correlates of Marital Happiness among the Remarried." *Journal of Marriage and the Family*. November 1979, 857–67.

———. "Reactions and Adjustments to Divorce: Differences in the Experiences of Males and Females." *Family Relations*, January 1980, 59–68.

"All about That Baby." *Newsweek*, August 7, 1978, 66–72.

"The American Family: Future Uncertain." *Time*, December 28, 1970.

American Friends Service Committee. *Who Shall Live?* New York: Hill and Wang, 1970.

American Psychological Association. "Child Abuse Called Epidemic." *Monitor*, January 1976.

American Social Health Association. *Today's V.D. Control Problem: 1978*. New York: American Social Health Association, Committee on the Joint Statement, 1978.

Angier, Natalie. "Dr. Jekyll & Ms. Hyde." *Discover*, November 1982, 28–34.

Apgar, V., and J. Beck. *Is My Baby All Right?* New York: Trident, 1973.

"Auto Loans Push Up U.S. Credit Payments." *Santa Barbara News-Press*, January 12, 1983, C-5.

Bach, G., and R. Deutsch. *Pairing*. New York: Avon, 1970.

———, and P. Wyden. *The Intimate Enemy*. New York: Avon, 1968.

Bachrach, Christine A., and W. D. Mosher. "Voluntary Childlessness in the United States: Estimates from the National Survey of Family Growth." *Journal of Family Issues*, December 1982.

Bader, E., et al. "Do Marriage Preparation Programs Really Help?" Paper presented at the National Council on Family Relations Annual Conference. Milwaukee, Wisconsin, October 1981.

Bagish, H. Personal discussions over the years; student comments about sexual problems came in part from his 1982–1983 students.

Baker, L. G. "In My Opinion: The Sexual Revolution in Perspective." *Family Relations* 32, no. 2 (April 1983): 297–300.

Bandura, A. *Principles of Behavior Modification*. New York: Holt, Rinehart and Winston, 1969.

Bane, Mary Jo. *Here to Stay: American Families in the Twentieth Century*. New York: Basic Books, 1976.

"Bankruptcy—Fresh Start or Free Ride?" *Changing Times*, February 1982, 52–54.

Barclay, A. M. "Bio-psychological Perspectives on Sexual Behavior." In *Sexuality: A Search for Perspective*, edited by D. Grummon and A. Barclay. New York: Van Nostrand Reinhold, 1971, 54–56.

Bardwick, J. "The Sex Hormones, the Central Nervous System, and Effect Variability in Humans." In *Women in Therapy*, edited by V. Bertle and V. Franks. New York: Bruner-Mazel, 1974.

Barnhill, L., G. Rubenstein, and N. Rocklin. "From Generation to Generation: Fathers-to-Be in Transition." *Family Coordinator*, April 1979, 229–35.

Barocas, R., and P. Karoly. "Effects of Physical Appearance on Social Responsiveness." *Psychology Report* 31, 1972, 495–500.

Barrett, C., and H. Noble. "Mother's Anxieties versus the Effects of Long-Distance Move on Children." *Journal of Marriage and the Family* 35 (May 1973): 181–88.

Barrett, Nancy S. "Women in the Job Market: Unemployment and Work Schedules." In R. E. Smith (ed.), *The Subtle Revolution: Women at Work*. Washington, D.C.: The Urban Institute, 1979.

"The Battle over Abortion." *Time*, April 6, 1981, 20.

"Battling a Deadly New Epidemic." *Time*, March 28, 1983, 53.

Becker, G., E. Landes, and R. Michael. "Economics of Marital Instability." Working paper no. 153. Stanford, Calif.: Bureau of Economic Research, 1976.

Bell, R. R. *Marriage and Family Interaction*. Homewood, Ill.: Dorsey, 1975.

Bell, R., and Kathleen Coughey. "Premarital Sexual Experience among College Females, 1958, 1968, and 1978." *Family Relations*, July 1980, 353–57.

Benedek, E., and R. Benedek. "Joint Custody: Solution or Illusion?" *American Journal of Psychiatry*, December 1979, 1540–44.

Berelson, B. *The Population Council Annual Report*. New York: Population Council, 1972.

———, and G. Steiner. *Human Behavior: An Inventory of*

Scientific Findings. New York: Harcourt Brace Jovanovich, 1964.

Berk, R. A., and S. F. Berk. *Labor and Leisure at Home.* Beverly Hills, Calif.: Sage, 1979.

Bernard, J. *The Future of Marriage.* New York: World, 1972.

Bianchi, S., and R. Farley. "Racial Differences in Family Living Arrangements and Economic Well Being: An Analysis of Recent Trends." *Journal of Marriage and the Family,* August 1979, 537–51.

Biddle, B. J. *Role Theory: Expectations, Identities, and Behaviors.* Chicago: Dryden, 1976.

Bienvenu, M. J. "Measurement of Marital Communication." *The Family Coordinator* 19 (January 1970): 26–31.

Blake, Judith. "Is Zero Preferred? American Attitudes toward Childlessness in the 1970s." *Journal of Marriage and the Family,* 41, no. 2 (May 1979): 245–57.

Blood, R. O., and M. C. Blood. "Amicable Divorce." *Alternative Lifestyles* 2, no. 4 (1979): 483–98.

Bohannan, P. *Divorce and After.* Garden City, N.Y.: Doubleday, 1970.

Borland, D. M. "An Alternative Model of the Wheel Theory." *Family Coordinator* 24 (1975): 289–92.

The Boston Women's Health Book Collective. *Our Bodies, Ourselves.* New York: Simon & Schuster, 1973; rev. and exp. ed., 1976.

Boulding, E. "Familia Faber: The Family as Maker of the Future." *Journal of Marriage and the Family,* May 1983, 257–66.

Bower, D. W., and V. A. Christopherson. "University Student Cohabitation: A Regional Comparison of Selected Attitudes and Behavior." *Journal of Marriage and the Family* 39, no. 3 (August 1977), 447–54.

Bowes, W. A., et al. "The Effects of Obstetrical Medication on Fetus and Infant." *Monographs of the Society for Research in Child Development* 35 (1970): 1–55.

Bowman, H. A. *Marriage for Moderns.* New York: McGraw-Hill, 1974.

Brayshaw, A. J. "Middle-aged Marriage: Idealism, Realism and the Search for Meaning." *Marriage and Family Living* 24 (1962): 358–64.

"British Birth Survey 1970." London: William Heinemann Medical Books, 1975.

Broderick, E. "Going Steady: The Beginning of the End." In *Teenage Marriage and Divorce,* edited by S. Farber and R. Wilson. Berkeley, Calif.: Diablo Press, 1967.

Brody, Jane E. "T.V. Violence Cited as Bad Influence." *The New York Times,* December 7, 1975, 20.

———. "Vasectomy Procedure Gains Favor among American Men." *Santa Barbara News-Press,* November 19, 1979, F-20.

Broverman, Inge, et al. "Sex Roles Stereotypes: A Current Appraisal." *Journal of Social Issues* 28 (1972): 59–78.

Bruck, Connie. "Menopause." *Human Behavior,* April 1979, 195–201.

Budd, L. S. "Problems Disclosure and Commitment of Cohabiting and Married Couples." Doctoral dissertation, University of Minnesota, 1976.

Bumpass, L., and A. Sweet. "Differentials in Marital Inst-ability, 1970." *American Society Review,* December 1977, 754–66.

Burchinal, L. "Characteristics of Adolescents from Unbroken, Broken, and Reconstituted Families." *Journal of Marriage and the Family* 26 (January 1964): 44–50.

Burchinal, L., and L. Chancellor. "Survival Rates among Types of Religiously Homogamous and Inter-religious Marriages, Iowa, 1953–1959, Religious Bulletin." Iowa State University: Iowa Agricultural and Home Economics Station, 1962.

Burk, R. J., and T. Weir. "Relationship of Wife's Employment Status to Husband, Wife and Pair Satisfaction and Performance." *Journal of Marriage and the Family* 38 (May 1976): no. 2, 279–87.

Burr, W., and G. Leigh. "Famology: A New Discipline." Presidential address at the annual meeting of the National Council of Family Relations, Washington, D.C., October 13, 1982.

Butler, R. N. "How to Grow Old and Poor in an Affluent Society." Public Interest Report No. 9. *International Journal of Aging and Human Development,* 1973.

Calderone, Mary S. "Love, Sex, Intimacy, and Aging as a Life Style." In *Sex, Love, and Intimacy—Whose Life Styles?,* edited by Mary S. Calderone. New York: SIECUS, 1972.

California Penal Code. Section I, section 1161.5, January 1, 1975.

Campbell, A. *The Sense of Well-Being in America.* New York: McGraw-Hill, 1981.

Canfield, Elizabeth K. "On the Sex Education Frontiers." Talk given at the California Council on Family Relations Annual Conference, Anaheim, Calif., October 18–20, 1979.

Carew, J. "Experience and the Development of Intelligence in Young Children." *Monographs of the Society for Research in Child Development* 45 (1–2, serial no. 183), 1980.

Carlson v. Olson, 256 N.W.2d 249 (1977).

Casler, L. "This Thing Called Love." *Psychology Today,* December 1969.

Cavanagh, J. R. "Rhythm of Sexual Desire in Women." *Medical Aspects of Human Sexuality.* February 1969, 29–39.

CBS Reports. "Boys and Girls Together." Harry Reasoner, February 8, 1980.

Chadwick, B. A., et al. "Marital and Family Role Satisfaction." *Journal of Marriage and the Family* 38 (August 1976): 431–40.

Chafetz, J. *Masculine/Feminine or Human?* Itasca, Ill.: Peacock, 1974.

Cherlin, A. "The Effects of Children on Marital Dissolution." *Demography,* August 1977, 265–72.

———. "Remarriage as an Incomplete Institution." *American Journal of Sociology* 84, no. 3 (1978): 634–50.

Chilman, Catherine S. "Parent Satisfactions, Concerns, and Goals for Their Children." *Family Relations* 29, no. 3 (July 1980a): 339–46.

———. "Social and Psychological Research Concerning Adolescent Childbearing: 1970–1980." *Journal of Marriage and the Family* 42, no. 2 (November 1980b): 793–806.

"Chinese Infanticide Rate Up." *Santa Barbara News-Press.* November 10, 1982, A-2.

Clark, C., et al. "Path-Analytic Model of Postpartum Depression and Somatic Complaints." Paper presented at the American Psychological Association annual convention, Anaheim, California, August 26–30, 1983.

Clark, J. R. *The Importance of Being Imperfect.* New York: McKay, 1961.

Clatworthy, N., and L. Scheid. "A Comparison of Married Couples: Premarital Cohabitants and Non-premarital Cohabitants." Manuscript, Ohio State University, 1977.

Clayton, R., and Janet L. Bakemeier. "Premarital Sex in the Seventies." *Journal of Marriage and the Family*, November 1980, 759–75.

Close, H. "To the Child: On Parenting." *Voices*, Spring 1968.

"College Paying Off for Women." National Center for Education Statistics. *Santa Barbara News-Press*, December 1, 1982.

Coogler, O. S., Ruth Weber, and P. McKenry. "Divorce Mediation: A Means of Facilitating Divorce and Adjustment." *Family Coordinator*, April 1979, 255–59.

Cordell, A. S., et al. "Fathers' Views on Fatherhood with Special Reference to Infancy." *Family Relations* 29 (July 1980): 331–38.

"The Costliest U.S. Cities." U.S. Department of Labor (1981) as reported in *The San Francisco Chronicle*, April 17, 1982.

Cox, F. "Parental Divorce and College Grades." Unpublished paper, Glendale City College, 1960.

———. "Premarital Sex and Religion." Unpublished study, Santa Barbara City College, 1978.

———. *Psychology.* Dubuque, Iowa: Wm. C. Brown, 1973.

Cozby, P. W. "Self-Disclosure: A Literature Review." *Psychological Bulletin* 79 (July 1973): 73–91.

Cromwell, R. E., and V. Thomas. "Developing Resources for Family Potential: A Family Action Model." *The Family Coordinator* 25 (January 1976): 13–20.

Crosby, J. F. "A Critique of Divorce Statistics and Their Interpretation." *Family Relations*, January 1980, 51–58.

———. "The Death of the Family Revisited." *The Humanist*, May–June 1975, 12–14.

Cutler, B. R., and W. G. Dyer. "Initial Adjustment Process in Young Married Couples." *Social Forces* 44 (December 1965): 195–201.

Danzinger, C., and M. Greenwald. *Alternatives: A Look at Unmarried Couples and Communes.* New York: Inst. of Life Insurance, Research Services, 1973.

Darnley, Fred. "Adjustment to Retirement: Integrity or Despair." *The Family Coordinator*, April 1975.

David, H., and Wendy Baldwin. "Childbearing and Child Development: Demographic and Psychosocial Trends." *American Psychologist* 34 (October 1979): 866–71.

DeLamater, J. D., and P. MacCorquodale. *Premarital Sexuality: Attitudes, Relationships, Behavior.* Madison, Wis.: University of Wisconsin Press, 1979.

"Device May Pinpoint Fertile Days." *San Francisco Chronicle*, December 24, 1976.

Dick-Read, G. *Childbirth without Fear.* 4th ed. New York: Harper & Row, 1972.

Dillon, T. F., et al. "Midwifery." *American Journal of Obstetrics and Gynecology* 130, no. 8 (April 15, 1978): 917–26.

Dion, K., E. Berscheid, and E. Walster. "What Is Beautiful Is Good." *Journal of Personality and Social Psychology* 24 (1972): 285–90.

"Divorced Dad Wins $25,000 from Ex-Wife." *Santa Barbara News-Press*, August 8, 1980, A-5.

"Divorced Men in U.S. Remarrying More Often." *Santa Barbara News-Press*, November 5, 1981, A-6.

Dixon, Ruth, and Lenore Weitzman. "Evaluating the Impact of No-Fault Divorce in California." *Family Relations*, July 1980, 297–307.

———. "When Husbands File for Divorce." *Journal of Marriage and the Family*, February 1982, 103–15.

"Doubts about IUDs." *Time*, July 15, 1974, 81.

Duberman, L. *Marriage and Its Alternatives.* New York: Praeger, 1974, 1977.

———. "Step-Kin Relationships." *Journal of Marriage and the Family* 35 (May 1973): 283–92.

Easley, E. B. "Sexual Effect of Female Sterilization." *Medical Aspects of Human Sexuality* 6 (February 1972).

Ebaugh, Helen R. F., and C. A. Haney. "Shifts in Abortion Attitudes: 1972–1978." *Journal of Marriage and the Family* 42, no. 3 (August 1980): 491–500.

Echegaray, M. "Having a Baby without a Doctor: The Rebirth of Midwives." *McCalls* 109 (April 1982): 37–38.

Edwards, J. N., and Janice M. Saunders. "Coming Apart: A Model of the Marital Dissolution Decision." *Journal of Marriage and the Family*, May 1981, 379–89.

"Eighteen-Year-Old Sperm Used in Artificial Insemination." UPI. *Santa Barbara News-Press*, August 12, 1982, E-8.

Elkin, M. "Premarital Counseling for Minors: The Los Angeles Experience." *The Family Coordinator*, October 1977, 429–43.

———. "Drawing Individual and Family Strengths from the Divorce Process." Talk given at the California Council on Family Relations Annual Conference. Santa Barbara, Calif., September 26, 1980.

Elmquist, Marion. "100 Leaders Spend 14% More in 1981." *Advertising Age*, September 9, 1982, 1.

English, Dierdre. "The War against Choice: Inside the Abortion Movement." *Mother Jones*, February/March 1981.

Entwisle, D. R., and S. G. Doering. *The First Birth.* Baltimore, Md.: Johns Hopkins University Press, 1980.

Erikson, E. H. *Childhood and Society.* 2d ed. New York: Norton, 1963.

Etzioni, A. *An Immodest Agenda: Rebuilding America Before the 21st Century.* New York: McGraw-Hill, 1983.

Farber, B. *Family Organization and Interaction.* San Francisco: Chandler, 1964.

Feldberg, R., and J. Kohen. "Family Life in an Anti-Family

Setting: A Critique of Marriage and Divorce." *The Family Coordinator* 25 (April 1976): 151–59.

Ferber, Marianne A. "Labor Market Participation of Young Married Women: Causes and Effects." *Journal of Marriage and the Family* 44, no. 2 (May 1982): 457–75.

"Fewer American Women Reported Using the Pill." *Santa Barbara News-Press*, January 23, 1979.

Fisher, E. "A Guide to Divorce Counseling." *The Family Coordinator* 22 (January 1973): 55–62.

Freidan, Betty. *The Second Stage*. New York: Summit Books, 1981.

———. *The Feminine Mystique*. New York: Dell, 1963.

Friday, N. *My Secret Garden: Women's Sexual Fantasies*. New York: Simon & Schuster, 1974.

Frieze, Irene H., et al. *Women and Sex Roles*. New York: Norton, 1978.

Fromm, E. *The Art of Loving*. New York: Harper & Row, 1956.

Furstenberg, F. "Recycling the Family." *Marriage and Family Review*. New York: Haworth Press, vol. 2, no. 3 (1979).

Gagon, J., and B. Henderson. *Human Sexuality: An Age of Ambiguity*. Boston: Little, Brown, 1975.

Galbraith, J. K. *The Affluent Society*. Boston: Houghton Mifflin, 1958.

Gallup Poll. Reported in *Santa Barbara News-Press*, August 8, 1982, A-7.

Gallup Poll. Reported in *Santa Barbara News-Press*, August 15, 1982, B-2.

Galvin, Kathleen M., and B. J. Brommel. *Family Communication: Cohesion and Change*. Glenview, Ill.: Scott, Foresman, 1982.

Gardner, J. W. *Self-Renewal: The Individual and the Innovative Society*. Rev. ed. New York: Norton, 1981.

Garland, Diana R. "Training Married Couples in Listening Skills: Effects on Behavior, Perceptual Accuracy and Marital Adjustment." *Family Relations*, April 1981, 297–306.

Geller, R. J. "Violence in the Family: A Review of Research in the Seventies." *Journal of Marriage and the Family* 42, no. 4 (November 1980): 873–85.

———, and M. A. Straus. "Violence in American Families." *Journal of Social Issues* 35, no. 2 (1979).

General Mills. "American Families at Work." *The General Mills American Family Report 1980–1981*. Minneapolis, Minn.: General Mills, 1981.

General Mills. "Raising Children in a Changing Society." *The General Mills American Family Report, 1976–1977*. Minneapolis, Minn.: General Mills, 1977.

Gibran, K. *The Prophet*. New York: Knopf, 1923.

Gilbert, S. J. "Self-Disclosure, Intimacy and Communication in Families." *The Family Coordinator* 25 (July 1976): 221–31.

Glenn, N. D., and S. McLanahan. "The Effects of Offspring on the Psychological Well-Being of Older Adults." *Journal of Marriage and the Family* 43 (May 1981): 409–21.

Glenn, N., and Beth Ann Shelton. "Pre-Adult Background Variables and Divorce: A Note of Caution About Overreliance on Explained Variance." *Journal of Marriage and the Family*, May 1983, 405–10.

Glenn, N. D., and C. N. Weaver. "The Marital Happiness of Remarried Divorced Persons." *Journal of Marriage and the Family* 39 (May 1977): 331–37.

———. "A Multivariate Multisurvey Study of Marital Happiness." *Journal of Marriage and the Family* 40 (May 1978): 269–82.

Glick, P. "A Demographer Looks at American Families." *Journal of Marriage and the Family* 37 (February 1975): 15–27.

———. "Divorce and Child Custody and Support." Unpublished paper, 1979a.

———. "Future American Families." In *The Washington COFO Memo*, vol. 2, no. 3. Washington, D.C.: Coalition of Family Organizations, Summer/Fall, 1979b.

———. "The Future Marital Status and Living Arrangements of the Elderly." *The Gerontologist* 19 (1979): 3.

———. "The Life Cycle of the Family." *Marriage and Family Living* 17 (1955): 3–9.

———. "Remarriage: Some Recent Changes and Variations." *Journal of Family Issues* 1, no. 4 (1980): 455–78.

———. "Updating the Life Cycle of the Family." *Journal of Marriage and the Family* 37 (February 1977): 5–13.

Glick, P., and A. Norton. "Marrying, Divorcing, and Living Together in the U.S. Today." *Population Bulletin*, vol. 32, no. 5. Washington, D.C.: Population Reference Bureau, 1979.

———. "Marrying, Divorcing, and Living Together in the United States Today." *Population Bulletin*, vol. 32, no. 5. Washington, D.C.: Population Reference Bureau, 1979.

Glick, P., and G. Spanier. "Married and Unmarried Cohabitation in the United States." *Journal of Marriage and the Family* 42 (February 1980): 19–30.

Goertzel, V., and M. Goertzel. *Cradles of Eminence*. Boston: Little, Brown, 1962.

Goetting, A. "The Normative Integration of the Former Spouse Relationship." *Journal of Divorce* 2 (Summer 1979): 395–414.

Gold, D., and D. Andres. "Developmental Comparisons between 10-Year-Old Children with Employed and Non-Employed Mothers." *Child Development* 49 (1978): 75–84.

Goleman, D. "Special Abilities of the Sexes: Do They Begin in the Brain?" *Psychology Today*, November 1978.

Gordon, H. A., and K. C. Kammeyer. "The Gainful Employment of Women with Small Children." *Journal of Marriage and the Family* 42, no. 2 (May 1980): 327–36.

Gordon, T. *Parental Effectiveness Training*. New York: Peter Wyden, 1970.

Gotwald, W. H., and Gale H. Golden. *Sexuality: The Human Experience*. New York: Macmillan, 1981.

Gross, H. E. "Dual-Career Couples Who Live Apart: Two Types." *Journal of Marriage and the Family* 42, no. 3 (August 1980): 567–76.

Gunter, B. G. "Notes on Divorce Filing as Role Behavior." *Journal of Marriage and the Family*, February 1977, 95–98.

———, and D. T. Johnson. "Divorce Filing as Role Behavior: Effect of No-Fault Law on Divorce Filing Patterns." *Journal of Marriage and the Family*, August 1978, 571–74.

Guttmacher, A. F. *Abortion: A Woman's Guide*. New York: Abelard-Schuman, 1973a.

———. *Birth Control and Love.* New York: Macmillan, 1969.

———. *Birth Control, Pregnancy, Birth and Family Planning: A Guide for Expectant Parents in the 1970s.* New York: Viking, 1973b.

Hanna, S. L., and P. K. Knaub. "Cohabitation before Marriage: Its Relationship to Family Strengths." *Alternative Lifestyles* 4 (1981): 507–22.

Hannan, M. T., and Nancy B. Tuma. "Income and Marital Events: Evidence from an Income-Maintenance Experiment." *American Journal of Sociology* 82 (May 1977): 1186–1211.

Hansen, G. L. "Reactions to Hypothetical Jealousy Producing Events." *Family Relations*, October 1982, 513–18.

Hardin, G. "Abortion and Human Dignity." Lecture at the University of California, Berkeley, April 29, 1964.

Harlap, S., and P. Shiono. "Alcohol, Smoking, and Incidence of Spontaneous Abortions in First and Second Trimester." *The Lancet*. July 26, 1980, 173–76.

Hart, T. M. "Legalized Abortion in Japan." *California Medicine* 107 (October 1967): 334–37.

Hartman, W. E., and Marilyn A. Fithian. *Treatment of Sexual Dysfunction.* Long Beach, Calif.: Center for Marital and Sexual Studies, 1972.

———. Basic lecture series, Institute for Advanced Study in Human Sexuality. San Francisco, Calif., October 1979.

Hatcher, R. A., et al. *Contraceptive Technology 1980–1981.* New York: Irvington, 1980.

Hatfield, Elaine, and G. W. Walster. *A New Look at Love.* Reading, Mass.: Addison-Wesley, 1978.

Havighurst, R. J., B. L. Neugarten, and S. S. Tobin. "Disengagement and Patterns of Aging." In *Middle Age and Aging: A Reader in Social Psychology*, edited by B. L. Neugarten. Chicago: University of Chicago Press, 1968.

Hawkins, J., and K. Johnson. "Perceptions of Behavioral Conformity, Imputation of Census, and Marital Status." *Journal of Marriage and the Family* 31 (August 1969): 507–11.

Haynes, J. M. *Divorce Mediation.* New York: Springer, 1981.

Hechinger, Grace. "Happy Mother's Day: April Fool." *Newsweek*, May 1981.

Hecht, Annabel. "DES: The Drug with Unexpected Legacies." *FDA Consumer*, May 1979, 14–17.

Heiman, Julia R. "Women's Sexual Arousal—The Physiology of Erotica." *Psychology Today*, April 1975, 91–94.

Helfer, R., and C. Kempe, eds. *The Battered Child.* Chicago: University of Chicago Press, 1974.

Hetherington, E. M. "Divorce: A Child's Perspective." *American Psychologist*, October 1979, 851–65.

Hetherington, E. M., et al. "Divorced Fathers." *Psychology Today*, April 1977, 42–46.

Hetherington, M. M. "The Aftermath of Divorce." In *Mother-Child, Father-Child Relations*, edited by J. H. Stevens, Jr., and M. Matthews. Washington, D.C.: National Association for the Education of Young Children, 1978.

Hicks, M., and M. Platt. "Marital Happiness and Stability: A Review of the Research in the Sixties." *Journal of Marriage and the Family* 32 (November 1970): 553–74.

Hill, C., Z. Rubin, and L. Peplau. "Breakups before Marriage: The End of 103 Affairs." *Journal of Social Issues* 32 (1976): 147–68.

Hill, Elizabeth A., and Lorraine T. Dorfman. "Reaction of Housewives to the Retirement of Their Husbands." *Family Relations*, April 1982, 195–200.

Hill, W. F. *Hill Interaction Matrix Scoring Manual.* Los Angeles: University of Southern California, Youth Studies Center, 1961.

Hiltz, S. Roxanne. "Helping Widows: Group Discussions as Therapeutic Technique." *The Family Coordinator*, July 1975, 331–36.

Hite, Shere. *The Hite Report: A Nationwide Study of Female Sexuality.* New York: Macmillan, 1976.

———. *The Hite Report on Male Sexuality.* New York: Knopf, 1981.

Hobbins, J. C., ed. *Diagnostic Ultrasound in Obstetrics.* New York: Church and Liningstone, 1979.

Hoffman, L. W. "Effects of Maternal Employment on the Child—A Review of the Research." *Developmental Psychology* 10 (1974): 204–28.

Hoffman, S., and J. Holmes. "Husbands, Wives, and Divorce." In *Five Thousand Families*, edited by G. Duncan and J. Morgan. Ann Arbor: Institute for Social Research, University of Michigan, 1976.

Hoffman, W., and J. D. Manis. "Influences of Children on Marital Interaction and Parental Satisfactions and Dissatisfactions." In *Child Influences and Family Interaction: A Life-Span Perspective*, edited by R. M. Lerner and G. B. Spanier. New York: Academic Press, 1978.

"Home Tests for Pregnancy." *Newsweek*, September 3, 1979, 69.

Honeycutt, J. M., C. Wilson, and C. Parker. "Effects of Sex and Degrees of Happiness on Perceived Styles of Communicating in and out of the Marital Relationship." *Journal of Marriage and the Family*, May 1982, 395–406.

Honig, Alice S. "What We Need to Know to Help the Teenage Parent." *Family Coordinator*, April 1978, 113–19.

Hornung, C. A., and B. Claire McCullough. "Status Relationships in Dual-Employment Marriages: Consequences for Psychological Well-Being." *Journal of Marriage and the Family* 43, no. 1 (February 1981): 125–41.

Houseknecht, Sharon. "Childlessness and Marital Adjustment." *Journal of Marriage and the Family*, May 1979, 259–65.

———, and Anne S. Macke. "Combining Marriage and Career: The Marital Adjustment of Professional Women." *Journal of Marriage and the Family* 43, no. 3 (August 1981): 651–61.

"How Long till Equality." *Time*, July 12, 1982, 20.

Howe, Louise K. *Pink Collar Workers.* New York: Putnam, 1977.

Hunt, M. *The Natural History of Love.* New York: Knopf, 1959.

———. "Sexual Behavior in the 1970s; Part II: Premarital Sex." *Playboy*, November 1973, 74–75.

Hunt, R., and E. Rydman. *Creative Marriage.* Boston: Holbrook, 1976.

Hupka, R. B. "Societal and Individual Roles in the Expression of Jealousy." In *Sexual Jealousy*, chaired by H. Sigall.

Symposium presented at the meeting of the American Psychological Association, San Francisco, August 1977.

Huston, T., and G. Levinger. "Interpersonal Attraction and Relationships." *Annual Review of Psychology, 1978.* Palo Alto, Calif.: Annual Reviews, 1978.

"In Search of Sexual Desire." *Time,* April 4, 1983, 80.

Insel, P. M., and W. T. Roth. *Health in a Changing Society.* Palo Alto, Calif.: Mayfield, 1976.

"IUD Debate." *Time,* May 26, 1980, 60.

Ivey, M., and J. Bardwick. "Her Body, the Battleground." *Psychology Today,* February 1972, 50–54.

Jacques, J., and Karen Chason. "Cohabitation: Its Impact on Marital Success." *The Family Coordinator,* January 1979, 35–39.

Johns Hopkins University study prepared for Population Information Program at the Hopkins Hygiene and Public Health School as reported in the *Santa Barbara News-Press,* January 23, 1979.

Johnson, Carolyn K., and Sharon Price-Bonham. "Women and Retirement: A Study and Implications." *Family Relations,* July 1980, 381–85.

Johnson, M. P. "Commitment: A Conceptual Structure and Empirical Application." *Sociological Quarterly* 14 (1973): 395–406.

Jones, E. E., and C. Wortman. *Ingratiation: An Attributional Approach.* Morristown, N.J.: General Learning, 1973.

Jones, H. B., and H. C. Jones. *Sensual Drugs.* New York: Cambridge University Press, 1977.

Jorgensen, S. R., and Janis C. Gaudy. "Self-Disclosure and Satisfaction in Marriage: The Relation Examined." *Family Relations,* July 1980, 281–87.

Jourard, S. M. *Personal Adjustment.* New York: Macmillan, 1963.

"Just How the Sexes Differ." *Newsweek,* May 18, 1981, 72–83.

Kahn, H., and A. Wiener. "The Future Meanings of Work: Some 'Surprise-Free' Observations." In *The Future of Work,* edited by F. Best. Englewood Cliffs, N.J.: Prentice-Hall (Spectrum), 1973.

Kanter, R., et al. "Coupling, Parenting, and the Presence of Others: Intimate Relationships in Communal Households." *The Family Coordinator* 24 (October 1975): 433–52.

Kapecky, G. "Unmarried—But Living Together." *The Ladies Home Journal,* July 1972, 66.

Kaplan, H. S. *Disorders of Sexual Desire.* New York: Brunner-Mazel, 1979.

Kargman, M. W. "Stepchild Support and Obligations of Stepparents." *Family Relations,* April 1983, 231–38.

Katchadourian, H. A., and D. T. Lunde. *Fundamentals of Human Sexuality.* New York: Holt, 1972.

Keller, D. E. "Women's Attitudes Regarding Penis Size." *Medical Aspects of Human Sexuality,* January 1976, 178–79.

Kerckhoff, A. "More of the Same." *Contemporary Psychology* 22 (1977): 189–90.

———, and K. E. Davis. "Value Consensus and Need Complementarity in Mate Selection." *American Social Review* 27 (1962): 295–303.

Kerckhoff, R. "Marriage and Middle Age." *The Family Coordinator,* January 1976, 5–11.

Kerr, Carmen. *Sex for Women Who Want to Have Fun and Loving Relationships with Equals.* New York: Grove Press, 1977.

Kieffer, C. M. "Consensual Cohabitation: A Descriptive Study of the Relationships and the Sociocultural Characteristics of Eighty Couples in Settings of Two Florida Universities." Master's thesis, Florida State University, 1972.

———. "New Depths in Intimacy." In *Marriage and Alternatives: Exploring Intimate Relationships,* edited by R. Libby and R. Whitehurst. Glenview, Ill.: Scott, Foresman, 1977, 267–93.

Kinsey, A., et al. *Sexual Behavior in the Human Female.* Philadelphia: Saunders, 1953.

———. *Sexual Behavior in the Human Male.* Philadelphia: Saunders, 1948.

Kirschner, B., and L. Wallum. In *Contemporary Families and Alternative Lifestyles,* edited by E. Macklin and R. Rubin. Beverly Hills, Calif.: Sage, 1983.

Klaus, M., et al. "Maternal Attachment." *New England Journal of Medicine* 286 (March 2, 1972): 460–63.

Kline, J., et al. "Drinking during Pregnancy and Spontaneous Abortion." *The Lancet,* July 26, 1980, 176–80.

Knox, D., and K. Wilson. "Dating Behavior of University Students." *Family Relations,* April 1981, 255–58.

Kogan, B. A. *Human Sexual Expression.* New York: Harcourt Brace Jovanovich, 1973.

Kolodny, R. C. Masters and Johnson Institute Seminar on Human Sexuality. Los Angeles, December 6–7, 1982.

Kolodny, R. C., et al. "Depression of Plasma Testosterone Levels after Chronic Intensive Marijuana Use." *New England Journal of Medicine* 290 (April 18, 1974): 872–74.

Kosteic, J., and G. Preti. "Birth Control Through Saliva Changes." *Science Digest,* December 1982, 91.

———. "New Oral Test for Fertility." *Science Digest,* December 1982, 91.

Krantzler, M. *Creative Divorce.* New York: Evans, 1973.

Lacon, Tincy. "Single Again." *The Single Parent.* Parents Without Partners, 1976.

Ladas, Alice K., J. D. Perry, and B. Whipple. *The G Spot and Other Recent Discoveries about Human Sexuality.* New York: Holt, Rinehart & Winston, 1982.

LaManna, M. A., and A. Riedmann. *Marriages and Families.* Belmont, Calif.: Wadsworth, 1981.

Landis, P. H. *Making the Most of Marriage.* 5th ed. Englewood Cliffs, N.J.: Prentice-Hall, 1970.

LaRossa, R., and M. M. LaRossa. *Transition to Parenthood.* Beverly Hills, Calif.: Sage, 1981.

Lasswell, Marcia E. "Looking Ahead in Aging: Love after Fifty." In *Love, Marriage, Family,* edited by M. Lasswell and T. Lasswell. Glenview, Ill.: Scott, Foresman, 1973.

———, and N. Lobsenz. *Styles of Loving.* Garden City, N.Y.: Doubleday, 1980.

Latham v. *Latham,* 274 Ore. 421, 541 P.2d 144 (1976).

Laws, J. L. "A Feminist Review of Marital Adjustment Literature: The Rape of the Locke." *Journal of Marriage and the Family* 33 (August 1971): 483–516.

Lear, H. "Vasectomy—A Note of Concern." In *Vasectomy: Follow-up of 1000 Cases, Simon Population Trust–Sterilization Project.* Cambridge, Eng.: Simon Population Trust, 1969.

Leboyer, F. *Birth without Violence.* New York: Knopf, 1975.

Lederer, W. J., and D. D. Jackson. *The Mirages of Marriage.* New York: Norton, 1968.

Leiblum, S., and L. Pervin, eds. *Principles and Practice of Sex Therapy.* New York: Guilford Press, 1980.

LeMasters, E. E., and J. DeFrain. *Parents in Contemporary America.* Homewood, Ill.: Dorsey Press, 1983.

Leo, J. "Cleansing the Mother Tongue." *Time*, December 27, 1982, 78.

LeShan, E. J. *The Wonderful Crisis of Middle Age.* New York: David McKay, 1973.

Leslie, G. "Personal Values, Professional Idealogies and Family Specialists: A New Look." *The Family Coordinator*, April 1979, 157–62.

Lessard, S. "Aborting a Fetus: The Legal Right, the Personal Choice." *The Washington Monthly* 4 (August 1972): 29–37.

Levinger, G. "Marital Cohesiveness and Dissolution: An Integrative Review." *Journal of Marriage and the Family* 27 (January 1965): 19–28.

———, and O. C. Moles, eds. *Divorce and Separation: Context, Causes and Consequences.* New York: Basic Books, 1979.

———, D. Senn, and B. Jorgensen. "Progress toward Permanence in Courtship: A Test of the Kerckhoff-Davis Hypotheses." *Sociometry*, 1970, 427–43.

Lewis, R. A., and G. B. Spanier. "Theorizing about the Quality and Stability of Marriage." In *Contemporary Theories about the Family*, vol. 1, edited by W. R. Burr. New York: Free Press, 1979, 268–294.

Lewis, R., G. Spanier, V. Storm, and C. Lettecka. "Commitment in Married and Unmarried Cohabitation." Paper presented at the annual meeting of the American Sociological Association, San Francisco, 1975.

Libby, R. W. "Creative Singlehood as a Sexual Lifestyle: Beyond Marriage as a Rite of Passage." In *Marriage and Alternatives: Exploring Intimate Relationships*, edited by R. Libby and R. Whitehurst. Glenview, Ill.: Scott, Foresman, 1977.

Liebert, R. M., J. M. Neale, and E. S. Davidson. *The Early Window: Effects of Television on Children and Youth.* Elmsford, N.Y.: Pergamon Press, 1973.

———, and R. W. Poulas. "Television and Personality Development: The Socializing Effects of an Entertainment Medium." In *Child Personality and Psychopathology: Current Topics*, vol. 2, edited by A. Davis. New York: Wiley, 1975.

Lindemann, Barbara. "The Sex Role Revolution." In *American Marriage: A Changing Scene?* by F. Cox. Dubuque, Iowa: Wm. C. Brown Company, 1976, 175–88.

Linton, R. *The Study of Man.* New York: Appleton, 1936.

Locksley, Anne. "On the Effects of Wives' Employment on

Marital Adjustment and Companionship." *Journal of Marriage and the Family* 42, no. 2 (May 1980): 337–46.

Long, T. "Interviews with 300 Latchkey Children: Results and Implications for Service." Paper presented at the American Psychological Association Annual Convention, Anaheim, California, August 26, 1983.

Lopata, Helena Z. *Women as Widows.* New York: Elsevier, 1979.

Lowenthal, M. F., M. Thurnher, and D. Chiriboga. *Four Stages of Life: A Comparative Study of Women and Men Facing Transitions.* San Francisco: Jossey-Bass, 1975.

Lyness, J. L., M. Lepetz, and K. Davis. "Living Together: An Alternative to Marriage." *Journal of Marriage and the Family* 34 (May 1972): 305–11.

Maccoby, Eleanor E., and Carol N. Jacklin. *The Psychology of Sex Differences.* Palo Alto, Calif.: Stanford University Press, 1974.

MacDonald, R. H. "Surrogate Motherhood: New Fertility Frontier or Shades of 1984?" Paper presented at annual conference of the National Council on Family Relations, Washington, D.C., 1982.

Mace, D., and V. Mace. "Counter-Epilogue." In *Marriage and Alternatives: Exploring Intimate Relationships*, edited by R. Libby and R. Whitehurst. Glenview, Ill.: Scott, Foresman, 1977, 390–406.

———. *We Can Have Better Marriages.* Nashville: Abingdon, 1974.

Macklin, Eleanor. "Nonmarital Cohabitation." *Marriage and Family Review*, March/April 1978a, 1–12.

———. "Nonmarital Heterosexual Cohabitation: An Overview." In *Contemporary Families and Alternative Lifestyles*, edited by E. Macklin and R. Rubin. Beverly Hills, Calif.: Sage, 1983.

———. "Review of Research on Nonmarital Cohabitation in the United States." In *Exploring Intimate Lifestyles*, edited by B. I. Murstein. New York: Springer, 1978b.

MacLeod, J. S. "How to Hold a Wife: A Bridegroom's Guide." *The Village Voice*, February 11, 1971.

Magrab, Phyllis R. "For the Sake of the Children: A Review of the Psychological Effects of Divorce." *Journal of Divorce* 1 (1978): 1424–32.

Maher, C. "No-Fault Divorce—No Rush to End Marriage." *Los Angeles Times*, January 16, 1979.

Malatesta, et al. "Acute Alcohol Ingestion and Female Orgasm." To be published in *Journal of Sex Research*. Research referred to by R. C. Kolodny at Masters and Johnson Institute Seminar on Human Sexuality, Los Angeles, December 6–7, 1982.

Maloney, E. R. *Human Sexuality.* New York: McGraw-Hill, 1982, 128–29.

"Man Wins Office Sex Suit." *Time*, August 2, 1982, 19.

"Many Women Still See Job Prejudice." Gallup Poll. Reported in the *Santa Barbara News-Press*. August 15, 1982, B-2.

Marotz-Baden, Ramona, et al. "Family Form or Family Process? Reconsidering the Deficit Family Model Approach." *The Family Coordinator*, January 1979, 5–14.

Marvin v. Marvin, 18 Cal.3d 660, 134 California Reporter 815, 557 P.2d 106 (1976).

———. *Family Law Reporter* 5 (1979): 3109.

———. *Family Law Reporter* 7 (1981): 2661.

Maslow, A. H. *The Farther Reaches of Human Nature*. New York: Viking, 1971.

———. *Motivation and Personality*. 2d ed. New York: Harper & Row, 1970.

———. *Toward a Psychology of Being*. 2d ed. Princeton, N.J.: Van Nostrand, 1968.

Masters, W. H., and V. E. Johnson. *Human Sexual Inadequacy*. Boston: Little, Brown, 1970.

———. *Human Sexual Response*. Boston: Little, Brown, 1966.

———. *Masters and Johnson Institute Seminar on Human Sexuality*. Los Angeles, Calif., December 6–7, 1982.

———. "Sex and the Aging Process." *Journal of American Geriatrics Society*, September 1981, 385–90.

Masters, W. H., et al., eds. *Ethical Issues in Sex Therapy and Research*, vol. 11. Boston: Little, Brown, 1980.

Matějček, Z., Z. Dytrych, and V. Schüller. "The Prague Study of Children Born from Unwanted Pregnancies." *International Journal of Mental Health* 7 (1979): 63–74.

Maugh, T. H. "Marijuana: New Support for Immune and Preproductive Hazards." *Science* 190 (1975): 865–67.

May, K. A. "Factors Contributing to First-Time Fathers' Readiness for Fatherhood: An Exploratory Study." *Family Relations* 31, no. 3 (July 1982): 353–62.

———. "Management of Detachment and Involvement in Pregnancy by First-Time Expectant Fathers." Doctoral dissertation, University of California, San Francisco, 1979.

May, R. *Love and Will*. New York: Norton, 1970.

McCarthy, J. "A Comparison of the Probability of the Dissolution of First and Second Marriages." *Demography* 15, no. 3 (1978): 345–59.

McCary, J. L., and S. P. McCary. *Human Sexuality*. Belmont, Calif.: Wadsworth, 1982.

McGuiness, Diane, and K. Pribram. "The Origins of Sensory Bias in the Development of Gender Differences in Perception and Cognition." In *Cognitive Growth and Development: Essays in Honor of Herbert C. Birch*, edited by Morton Bortner. New York: Brunner-Mazel, 1979.

McKean, K. "Closing in on the Herpes Virus." *Discover*, October 1981, 75–78.

McMorrow, F. *Middlescence: The Dangerous Years*. New York: Strawberry Hill, 1974.

Mead, Margaret. "Jealousy: Primitive and Civilized." In *Woman's Coming of Age*, edited by S. D. Schmalhausen and V. E. Calverton. New York: Morrow, 1948, 1968.

Mendelson, J. H. "Marijuana and Sex." *Medical Aspects of Human Sexuality*, November 1976, 23–24.

Miller, B. C., and D. L. Sollie. "Normal Stresses during the Transition to Parenthood." *Family Relations* 29 (October 1980): 459–65.

Miller, H. L., and P. S. Siegel. *Loving: A Psychological Approach*. New York: Wiley, 1972.

Miller, M., and W. Revinbark. "Sexual Differences in Phys-

ical Attractiveness as a Determinant of Heterosexual Liking." *Psychology Report* 27 (1970): 701–2.

Miller, R. L. *Personal Finance Today*. St. Paul, Minn.: West, 1979, 1983.

Miller, R. L. *Economic Issues for Consumers*. St. Paul, Minn.: West, 1975.

Miller, S., et al. "Recent Progress in Understanding and Facilitating Marital Communication." *The Family Coordinator* 24 (April 1975): 143–52.

Monahan, T. P. "National Divorce Legislation: The Problem and Some Suggestions." *The Family Coordinator* 22 (July 1973): 353–58.

Money, F., and R. Athanasiou. "Eve First, or Adam?" *Contemporary Psychology* 18 (December 1973): 593–99.

Money, J., and A. A. Ehrhardt. *Man and Woman, Boy and Girl: The Differentiation and Dimorphism of Gender Identity From Conception to Maturity*. Baltimore: Johns Hopkins University Press, 1972.

Montagu, A. *Touching: The Human Significance of Skin*. New York: Harper & Row, 1972.

Montague, M. F. A. *Prenatal Influences*. Springfield, Ill.: Charles C Thomas, 1962.

Montgomery, Barbara M. "The Form and Function of Quality Communication in Marriage." *Family Relations*, January 1981, 21–30.

Monthly Labor Review. "Family Budgets: Retired Couple's Budgets, Final Report, Autumn, 1981." Washington, D.C.: U.S. Government Printing Office, November 1982, 37–38.

Moore, Kristin A., and Sandra L. Hofferth. "Effects of Women's Employment on Marriage: Formation, Stability and Roles." In *Marriage and Family Review*, vol. 2, no. 2. New York: Haworth Press, Summer 1979.

Morris, D. *Intimate Behavior*. New York: Random House, 1971.

Morris, J. *Conundrum*. New York: Harcourt Brace Jovanovich, 1974.

Mosher, W. D. "Fertility and Family Planning in the 1970s: The National Survey of Family Growth." *Family Planning Perspectives*, November/December 1982: 314–20.

———. "Reproductive Impairments among Currently Married Couples: United States, 1976." *Advance Data*. U.S. National Center for Health Statistics, H.E.W., no. 55, January 24, 1980.

"Most Women View Ideal Lifestyle as Being a Wife and Worker." Gallup Poll. Reported in the *Santa Barbara News-Press*. August 8, 1982, A-7.

Mott, F. L., and Sylvia Moore. "The Causes of Marital Disruption among Young American Women: An Interdisciplinary Perspective." *Journal of Marriage and the Family*, May 1979, 355–65.

Murdock, G. "Sexual Behavior: What Is Acceptable?" *Journal of Social Hygiene* 36 (1950): 1–31.

Murstein, B. I. *Love, Sex, and Marriage through the Ages*. New York: Springer, 1974.

———. "Mate Selection in the 1970s." *Journal of Marriage and the Family*, November 1980, 777–92.

Myricks, Noel. "The Law and Alternative Lifestyles." In

Contemporary Families and Alternate Lifestyles, edited by E. D. Macklin and R. H. Rubin, Beverly Hills, Calif.: Sage, 1983.

———. " 'Palimony': The Impact of Marvin v. Marvin." *The Family Coordinator*, April 1980, 210–15.

Nass, G. D., R. W. Libby, and M. P. Fisher. *Sexual Choices.* Monterey, Calif.: Wadsworth Health Sciences Division, 1981.

National Federation of Independent Business Research and Education Foundation. Poster based on statistics from Keith Bush, "Retail Prices in Moscow and Four Western Countries in March 1982." San Mateo, Calif., 1982.

National Institute of Health. *Cesarean Childbirth*. Consensus Development Conference Summary, vol. 3, no. 6. Washington, D.C.: U.S. Government Printing Office.

National Institute of Mental Health. "Admission Rates to Outpatient Psychiatric Services per 100,000 Population Eighteen Years and Over by Marital Status." Washington, D.C.: U.S. Government Printing Office, 1973.

Neubardt, S. "Observations of a Practicing Gynecologist." In *Sexuality: A Search for Perspective*, edited by D. Grummon and A. Barclay. New York: Van Nostrand Reinhold, 1971, 2–17.

Neugarten, Bernice L., and Karol K. Weinstein. "The Changing American Grandparent." *Journal of Marriage and the Family* 26 (May 1973).

"The New Morality." *Time*, November 21, 1977, 111.

"The New Scarlet Letter." *Time*, August 2, 1982, 62–66.

New York Times, The. December 12, 1974.

"No Difference Seen in Childbirth Methods." AP *Santa Barbara News-Press*, April 15, 1980, A-5.

Norton, A. J. "Changes in American Living Arrangements." Paper presented at the annual meeting of the American Psychological Association, Washington, D.C., August 1982.

———. Letter to author, June 20, 1983.

"Not So Merry Widowers." *Time*, August 10, 1981, 45.

"Number of Working Women Rises 95% in Twenty Years." U.S. Department of Labor. Reported in *Santa Barbara News-Press*, November 15, 1982, A-12.

Nye, F. I. "Emerging and Declining Family Roles." *Journal of Marriage and the Family* 36 (1974): 238–44.

———, and L. Hoffman, eds. *The Employed Mother in America.* Chicago: Rand McNally, 1974.

Oakley, M. A. "Test Tube Babies," *Family Law Quarterly.* Winter, 1979, 385–400.

O'Neill, N., and G. O'Neill. *Open Marriage.* New York: Avon, 1972.

Oppenheimer, V. K. "Divorce, Remarriage and Wives' Labor Force Participation." Paper presented at the annual meeting of the American Sociological Society, Chicago, 1977.

Orlinsky, D. E. "Love Relationships in the Life Cycle: A Developmental Interpersonal Perspective." In *Love Today: A New Exploration*, edited by H. A. Otto. New York: Dell, 1972, 135–50.

"Other 'Firsts' in the ERA Decade." *People*, July 5, 1982, 40.

Otto, H. "Marriage and Family Enrichment Programs: Report and Analysis." *The Family Coordinator* 24 (April 1975): 137–42.

Packard, V. *The Hidden Persuaders.* New York: Pocket Books, 1958.

Paige, K. "Women Learn to Sing the Menstrual Blues." *Psychology Today*, September 1973.

Pantelakis, S., et al. "Influence of Induced and Spontaneous Abortions on the Outcome of Subsequent Pregnancies." *American Journal of Obstetrics and Gynecology*, July 15, 1973, 799–805.

Parke, R. D. *Fathers.* Boston: Harvard University Press, 1981.

Peel, J., and M. Potts. *Textbook of Contraceptive Practice.* Cambridge, Eng.: Cambridge University Press, 1970.

Peplau, L. A., Z. Rubin, and C. T. Hill. "Sexual Intimacy in Dating Relationships." *Journal of Social Issues*, vol. 33, no. 2 (1977): 86–109.

Peterman, D. J., et al. "A Comparison of Cohabiting and Noncohabiting Students." *Journal of Marriage and the Family* 36 (May 1974): 344–55.

Peterson, E. "The Impact of Maternal Employment on the Mother-Daughter Relationship." *Marriage and Family Living* 23 (1961): 355–61.

Pfeiffer, V. I., and G. Davis. "Sexual Behavior in Middle Age." In *Normal Aging II.* E. Palmor (ed.). Durham, N.C.: Duke University Press, 1974.

Piatrow, P., W. Rinehart, and J. Schmidt. "IUDs—Update on Safety, Effectiveness, and Research." *Population Reports*, ser. B, no. 3 (May 1979).

Pierce, C., and J. Sanfaco. "Man/Woman Dynamics: Some Typical Communication Patterns." In *Beyond Sex Roles*, edited by A. Sargent. St. Paul, Minn.: West, 1977.

"Pills Taken Off Market." *Santa Barbara News-Press*, March 1976.

Pleck, J. H., and M. Rustad. "Husbands' and Wives' Time in Family Work and Paid Work in the 1975–1976 Study of Time Use." Working paper. Wellesley, Mass.: Wellesley College Center for Research on Women, 1980.

"The Plight of America's Two Million Widowers." *U.S. News & World Report*, April 1974, 59–60.

Popenoe, P. *Family Life.* Washington, D.C.: George Washington University Medical Center, 1974.

Porter, K. L., and B. Demeuth. "The Impact of Marital Adjustment on Pregnancy Acceptance." *Maternal-Child Nursing* 8, no. 2 (1979): 103–13.

"Pregnant Women and Smoking." *Forum*. February 1980, 9–10.

Prescott, J. W. "Developmental Neuropsychophysics." In *Brain Function and Malnutrition: Neuropsychological Methods of Assessment*, edited by J. W. Prescott, et al. New York: Wiley, 1975.

———. "Early Somatosensory Deprivation as an Ontogenetic Process in the Abnormal Development of the Brain and Behavior." *Medical Primatology* 21 (1970): 102–6.

———. "Phylogenetic and Ontogenetic Aspects of Human Affectional Development." In *Selected Proceedings of the*

1976 International Congress of Sexology, edited by R. Gemme and C. C. Wheeler. New York: Plenum, 1976.

President's Council of Economic Advisors. "Economic Report of the President." Washington, D.C.: U.S. Government Printing Office, 1982.

Press, A. "Divorce American Style." *Newsweek*, January 10, 1983, 42–43.

Price-Bonham, Sharon, et al. "Divorce: A Frequent 'Alternative' in the 1970s." In *Contemporary Families and Alternative Lifestyles*, edited by E. D. Macklin and R. H. Rubin. Beverly Hills, Calif.: Sage, 1983, 125–46.

Proulx, Cynthia. "Sex as Athletics in the Singles Complex." *Saturday Review*, May 1973.

"Public Remains Closely Divided over High Court's Abortion Ruling." *Santa Barbara News-Press*, July 31, 1983, A-9.

Putney, S. *The Conquest of Society*. Belmont, Calif.: Wadsworth, 1972.

Queen, S. A., and R. W. Habenstein. *The Family in Various Cultures*. Philadelphia: Lippincott, 1974.

Rallings, E. M., and F. I. Nye. "Wife-Mother Employment, Family and Society." In *Contemporary Theories about the Family*, vol. 1, edited by W. R. Burr et al. New York: Free Press, 1979, 203–6.

Ramey, J. Presentation to Groves Conference on Marriage and the Family, Mount Pocono, Pennsylvania, 1981.

Rank, M. R. "Determinants of Conjugal Influence in Wives' Employment Decision Making." *Journal of Marriage and the Family* 44, no. 3 (August 1982): 591–604.

Rapaport, R., and R. Rapaport. "Men, Women and Equity." *The Family Coordinator* 24 (October 1975): 421–32.

"The Redbook Report on Sexual Relationships." *Redbook*, October 1980, 73–80.

Reiss, I. L. "Essay." In *Marriage: For and Against*, edited by H. Hart et al. New York: Hart, 1972, 234–51.

———. "The Family in the 80's." Talk given at the National Council of Family Relations Winter Board Meeting, San Diego, February 29, 1980.

———. *Family Systems in America*. 3d ed. Hinsdale, Ill.: Dryden Press, 1980.

———. "Toward a Sociology of the Heterosexual Love Relationship." *Marriage and Family Living*, May 1960.

Risman, B. J., et al. "Living Together in College: Implications for Courtship." *Journal of Marriage and the Family* 43, no. 1 (1981): 77–83.

Rheinstein, M. *Marriage Stability, Divorce and the Law*. Chicago: University of Chicago Press, 1972.

Riley, L. E., and E. A. Spreitzer. "A Model for the Analysis of Lifetime Marriage Patterns." *Journal of Marriage and the Family* 36 (February 1974): 64–71.

Robinson, I. E., and D. Jedlicka. "Change in Sexual Attitudes and Behavior of College Students from 1965 to 1980: A Research Note." *Journal of Marriage and the Family* 44, no. 1 (February 1982): 237–40.

Robinson, J. P. *How Americans Use Time: A Social Psychological Analysis of Everyday Behavior*. New York: Praeger, 1977.

Roehner, J. "Fatherhood in Pregnancy and Birth." *Journal of Nurse-Midwifery* 21 (1976): 13–18.

Rogers, C. *Becoming Partners: Marriage and Its Alternatives*. New York: Delacorte Press, 1972.

———. "Communication: Its Blocking and Facilitation." Paper read at Centennial Conference on Communications, Northwestern University, October 11, 1951.

Rollin, B. "Motherhood: Who Needs It?" *Look*, September 22, 1970.

Rollins, B. C., and K. L. Cannon. "Marital Satisfaction over the Family Life Cycle: A Reevaluation." *Journal of Marriage and the Family* 36 (May 1974): 271–83.

Roncek, D., R. Bell, and H. Chaldin. "Female-headed Families: An Ecological Model of Residential Concentration in a Small City." *Journal of Marriage and the Family*, February 1980, 157–69.

Rosen, L. R. "Enjoying Sex during Pregnancy." *Sexology Today*, March 1980, 50–53.

Rosenthal, R., and L. Jacobson. *Pygmalion in the Classroom*. New York: Holt, 1968.

Rossi, A. "A Biosocial Perspective on Parenting." *Daedalus*, Spring 1977, 1–31.

———. "The Biosocial Side of Parenthood." *Human Nature*, June 1978, 72–79.

———. "Why Seek Equality between the Sexes: An Immodest Proposal." *Daedalus*, Spring 1964.

Rubin, E., et al. "Prolonged Ethanol Consumption Increases Testosterone Metabolism." *Science* 191 (1976): 563–64.

Rubin, Lillian B. *Worlds of Pain: Life in the Working Class Family*. New York: Basic Books, 1976.

Rubin, Z. *Liking and Loving*. New York: Holt, 1973.

———. "Seeking a Cure for Loneliness." *Psychology Today*, October 1979, 82–90.

———, and G. Levinger. "Disclosing Oneself to a Stranger: Reciprocity and Its Limits." *Journal of Experimental Psychology* 11 (1975): 233–60.

———. "Naturalistic Studies of Self-Disclosure." *Personality, Sociology, and Psychology Bulletin* 2 (1976): 260–63.

———. "Theory and Data Badly Mated: A Critic of Murstein's SVR and Lewis's PDF Models of Mate Selection." *Journal of Marriage and the Family* 36, no. 2 (1974): 226–31.

Rubinstein, E. A. "Research Conclusions of the 1982 NIMH Report and Their Policy Implications." *American Psychologist*, July 1983, 820–25.

Ruman, Marilyn, and Marcia Lamm. "Divorce Mediation: A Team Approach to Marital Dissolution." *Trial*, March 1983, 80–86.

Russ-Eft, Darlene, Marlene Sprenger, and Anne Beever. "Antecedents of Adolescent Parenthood and Consequences at Age Thirty." *The Family Coordinator*, April 1979, 173–79.

Russell, B. "Our Sexual Ethics." In *Why I Am Not a Christian*. New York: Simon & Schuster, 1957, 171–72.

Rutlege, A. L. *Premarital Counseling*. Cambridge, Mass.: Schenkman, 1966.

Sabalis, R. F., and G. W. Ayers. "Emotional Aspects of

Divorce and Their Effects on the Legal Process." *The Family Coordinator*, October 1977, 391–94.

Sanderson, J. "Her New Life Begins on a Jarring Note." *Santa Barbara News-Press*, December 19, 1982, D-13.

Saxton, L. *The Individual, Marriage and the Family*. Belmont, Calif.: Wadsworth, 1977.

San Francisco Chronical. U.S. Dept. of Labor (1981). April 17, 1982.

Santa Barbara News-Press. March 20, 1977, B-4.

Santa Barbara News-Press. August 8, 1980.

Santa Barbara News-Press. National Center for Educational Statistics. December 1, 1982.

S.B. (California) 252, Chapter 2, Article 1, Sec. 4100.

S.B. (California) 1479, Deukmejian, Chapter 1308, Statutes of 1978.

Schachter, S. "The Interaction of Cognitive and Psychological Determinants in Emotional State." In *Advances in Experimental Social Psychology*, vol. 1, edited by Leonard Berkowitz. New York: Academic Press, 1964.

Scharf, Kathleen F. "Teenage Pregnancy. Why the Epidemic?" *Working Papers for a New Society*. Center for the Study of Public Policy Inc., March/April 1979.

Schauble, P., and C. Hill. "A Laboratory Approach to Treatment in Marriage Counseling: Training in Communication Skills." *The Family Coordinator* 25 (July 1976): 277–84.

Schorr, D. "Go Get Some Milk and Cookies and Watch the Murders on Television." *The Washingtonian*, October 1981.

Schultz, D. A., and S. F. Rodgers. *Marriage, the Family and Personal Fulfillment*. Englewood Cliffs, N.J.: Prentice-Hall, 1975.

Schulz, D. *Human Sexuality*. Englewood Cliffs, N.J.: Prentice-Hall, 1979.

Schwartz, M. F., J. Money, and Karenlee Robinson. "Biosocial Perspectives on the Development of the Proceptive, Acceptive and Conceptive Phases of Eroticism." *Journal of Sex and Marital Therapy* 7, no. 4 (Winter 1981): 243–55.

Scoresby, A. L. *The Marriage Dialogue*. Reading, Mass.: Addison-Wesley, 1977.

Scott, J. *Early Experience and the Organization of Behavior*. Belmont, Calif.: Brooks/Cole, 1968.

Seal, K. "A Decade of No-Fault Divorce: What it Has Meant Financially for Women in California." *Family Advocate* 1 (Spring 1979): 10–15.

Seelbach, W. C., and C. J. Hansen. "Satisfaction with Family Relations among the Elderly." *Family Relations*, January 1980, 91.

Seligman, C., N. Paschall, and G. Takata. "Effects of Physical Attractiveness on Attribution of Responsibility." *Canadian Journal of Behavioral Science* 6 (1974): 290–96.

Shanas, Ethel. "Older People and Their Families: The New Pioneers." *Journal of Marriage and the Family*, February 1980, 9–15.

Shaywitz, M., D. Cohen, and B. Shaywitz. "Behavior and Learning Difficulties in Children of Normal Intelligence Born to Alcoholic Mothers." *Journal of Pediatrics* 96, no. 6 (1980): 978–82.

Sheehy, Gail. *Passages: Predictable Crises of Adult Life*. New York: Bantam Books, 1977.

Sheresky, N., and M. Mannes. *Uncoupling: The Art of Coming Apart*. New York: Viking, 1972.

Sherfey, M. J. *The Nature and Evaluation of Female Sexuality*. New York: Random House, 1972.

Shettles, L. B. "Predetermining Children's Sex." *Medical Aspects of Human Sexuality* 5 (June 6, 1972): 178–85.

Shostrom, E. L. "Group Therapy: Let the Buyer Beware." *Psychology Today*, May 1969.

Sidel, Ruth. *Families of Fengsheng*. Baltimore, Md.: Penguin, 1974.

Sigall, H., and E. Aronson. "Liking for an Evaluator as a Function of Her Physical Attractiveness and the Nature of the Evaluations." *Journal of Experimental Social Psychology* 5 (1969): 93–100.

Silverman, Phyllis. "The Widow as a Care Giver in a Program of Preventative Intervention with Other Widows." *Mental Hygiene* 54 (1970).

Singer, Dorothy. "A Time to Reexamine the Role of Television in Our Lives." *American Psychologist*, July 1983, 815–16.

Singer, J., and I. Singer. "Types of Female Orgasm." *Journal of Sex Research* 8, no. 4 (November 1972): 255–67.

Singer, J. L., and D. G. Singer. *Television, Imagination and Aggression: A Study of Preschoolers*. Hillsdale, N.J.: Erlbaum, 1981.

———, and L. R. Sherrod. "Prosocial Programs in the Context of Children's Total Pattern of TV Viewing." Paper presented at the biennial meeting of the Society for Research in Child Development, San Francisco, March 1979.

Skinner, D. A. "Dual-Career Family Stress and Coping: A Literature Review." *Family Relations* 29, no. 4 (October 1980): 473–81.

Skolnick, A., and J. Skolnick. *Family in Transition*. 3d ed. Boston: Little, Brown, 1980.

Smith, D. C., R. Prentice, D. J. Thompson, and W. L. Herrman. "Association of Erogenous Estrogen and Endometrial Carcinoma." *New England Journal of Medicine* 293, no. 23 (December 4, 1975): 1164–67.

Smith, M. J. "The Social Consequences of Single Parenthood: A Longitudinal Perspective." *The Family Coordinator*, January 1980, 75–81.

Smith, R. E., ed. *The Subtle Revolution: Women at Work*. Washington, D.C.: Urban Institute, 1979.

"Smoking and the Fetus." *Human Nature*, May 1978, 13.

Spanier, G., et al. "Marital Adjustment over the Family Life Cycle: The Issue of Curvilinearity." *Journal of Marriage and the Family*, May 1975, 263–75.

Spanier, G. B., and P. C. Glick. "Marital Instability in the United States: Some Correlates and Recent Changes." *Family Relations*, July 1981, 329–38.

Spock, B. "What about Our Children?" In *Family Strengths: Positive Models for Family Life*, edited by Nick Stinnett et al. Lincoln, Neb.: University of Nebraska Press, 1980.

Stambul, H., and H. Kelly. "Conflict in the Development of Close Relationships." In *Social Exchange in Developing Relationships*, edited by R. Burgess and T. Huston. New York: Academic Press, 1978.

Starr, R. H. "Child Abuse." *American Psychologist*, October 1979, 872–78.

Stein, P. *Single Life*. New York: St. Martin's Press, 1981.

Steiner, G. "Family Stability and Income Guarantees." In *The Washington COFO Memo*, vol. 2, no. 4. Washington, D.C.: Coalition of Family Organizations, Winter 1979.

Steinmetz, Suzanne K. *The Cycle of Violence: Assertive, Aggressive, and Abusive Family Interaction*. New York: Praeger, 1977a.

———. "The Use of Force for Resolving Family Conflict: The Training Ground for Abuse." *The Family Coordinator*, January 1977b.

———, and M. Straus. *Violence in the Family*. New York: Harper & Row, 1974.

"A Steno Who Said 'No'!" *Newsweek*, April 30, 1979.

Stetson, D., and G. Wright. "The Effects of Laws on Divorce in American States." *Journal of Marriage and the Family* 37 (August 1975): 537–47.

Stinnett, N. "In Search of Strong Families." In *Building Family Strengths*, edited by N. Stinnett, B. Chesser, and J. Defrain. Lincoln, Neb.: University of Nebraska Press, 1979, 23–30.

Stone, J. J., and J. Church. *Childhood and Adolescence*. New York: Random House, 1973.

Straus, M. A. "Husbands & Wives as Victims and Aggressors in Marital Violence." Paper presented at the annual meeting of the American Association for the Advancement of Science. San Francisco, January 1980.

———. "Leveling, Civility, and Violence in the Family." *Journal of Marriage and the Family* 36 (1974): 13–29.

———. "Measuring Intrafamily Conflict and Violence: The Conflict Tactics (CT) Scales." *Journal of Marriage and the Family* 41, no. 1 (1979): 75–88.

———, R. J. Geller, and S. K. Steinmetz. *Behind Closed Doors: Violence in the American Family*. New York: Doubleday, 1980.

Streib, G. F. "Older Families and Their Troubles: Familial and Social Responses." *The Family Coordinator* 21 (January 1972).

Suelzle, M. "Women in Labor." *Trans-action* 8 (November–December 1970): 50–58.

Sugimoto, E. *A Daughter of the Samurai*. Garden City, N.Y.: Doubleday, 1935.

Sunbeam Music Corp. "Do You Love Me?" From *Fiddler on the Roof*. New York, N.Y.: Sunbeam Music Corporation, 1964.

"Superkids? A Sperm Bank for Nobelists." *Time*, March 10, 1980, 49.

"Surrogate Mother Fighting to Keep Unborn Child." *Santa Barbara News-Press*, March 22, 1981, A-3.

Tavris, C. *The Longest War: Understanding Sex Differences*. New York: Harcourt Brace Jovanovich, 1978.

"Testing Fetuses." *Time*, March 24, 1980, 48.

Tillich, P. *Dynamics of Faith*. New York: Harper & Row, 1957.

Todres, R. "Runaway Wives: An Increasing North American Phenomenon." *The Family Coordinator*, January 1978, 17–21.

Tognoli, J. "Male Friendship and Intimacy across the Life Span." *Family Relations* 29 (1980): 273–79.

"Toxic Shock Illness Cases Rise." *The Houston Post*, August 29, 1980.

Turnbull, S. K., and J. M. Turnbull. "To Dream the Impossible Dream: An Agenda for Discussion with Stepparents." *Family Relations*, April 1983, 227–30.

"Turning Back a Tide of Personal Bankruptcy." *Business Week*, June 14, 1982, 32.

Udry, J. R. "Marital Alternatives and Marital Disruption." *Journal of Marriage and the Family*, November 1981, 889–97.

———. *The Social Context of Marriage*. 3d ed. Philadelphia: Lippincott, 1974.

Ullian, D. Z. "The Development of Conceptions of Masculinity and Femininity." In *Exploring Sex Differences*, edited by B. Lloyd and J. Archer. London: Academic Press, 1976.

United Press International. "Marijuana, Impotency Linked." *Houston Post*, March 2, 1971.

United Press International in *Santa Barbara News-Press*, August 12, 1982, E-8.

Updike, J. In "The New Baby Boom." *Time*, February 22, 1982, 52.

U.S. Bureau of the Census. "Fertility of American Women: June, 1979." *Current Population Reports*, ser. P-20, no. 358. Washington, D.C.: U.S. Government Printing Office, 1980.

U.S. Bureau of the Census. "Household and Family Characteristics: March, 1981." *Current Population Reports*, ser. P-20, no. 371. Washington, D.C.: U.S. Government Printing Office, May 1982a.

U.S. Bureau of the Census. "Household and Family Characteristics: March, 1982." *Current Population Reports*, ser. P-20, no. 381. Washington, D.C.: U.S. Government Printing Office, 1983.

U.S. Bureau of the Census. "Marital Status and Living Arrangements: March, 1981." *Current Population Reports*, ser. P-20, no. 372. Washington, D.C.: U.S. Government Printing Office, 1982.

U.S. Bureau of the Census. "Marital Status and Living Arrangements: March, 1982." *Current Population Reports*, ser. P-20, no. 380. Washington, D.C.: U.S. Government Printing Office, 1983.

U.S. Bureau of the Census as reported in *Santa Barbara News-Press*, November 5, 1981.

U.S. Bureau of the Census. "Money Income and Poverty Status of Families and Persons in the United States: 1980." (Advanced Data from the March 1981 Current Population Survey), *Current Population Reports*, ser. P-60, no. 127. Washington, D.C.: U.S. Government Printing Office, 1981.

U.S. Bureau of the Census. "Population Profile of the United States, 1976." *Current Population Reports*, ser. P-20, no. 307. Washington, D.C.: U.S. Government Printing Office, 1977.

U.S. Bureau of the Census. Unpublished Current Population Survey data, June 1975.

U.S. Department of Health, Education, and Welfare, Public Health Services, Center for Disease Control. *Morbidity and Mortality Weekly Report*, vol. 13, no. 54, 1966, and vol. 22, no. 53, Washington, D.C.: U.S. Government Printing Office, 1975.

U.S. Department of Health and Human Services. "Contraceptive Efficacy among Married Women Aged 15–44 Years." DHHS pub. no. (PHS) 80-1981. Hyattsville, Md.: U.S. National Center for Health Statistics, May 1980.

U.S. Department of Health and Human Services. "Trends in Contraceptive Practice: United States, 1965–1976." DHHS pub. no. (PHS) 82-1986. Hyattsville, Md.: U.S. National Center for Health Statistics, February 1982.

U.S. Department of Labor, Bureau of Labor Statistics News. *Monthly Labor Review.* Washington, D.C.: U.S. Government Printing Office, July 1982.

U.S. Department of Labor, Bureau of Labor Statistics. "Occupational Profile of the Female Labor Force, 1977." Washington, D.C.: U.S. Government Printing Office, 1977.

U.S. Department of Labor, Bureau of Labor Statistics. "Unemployment Rates by Sex and Age, Seasonally Adjusted." *Monthly Labor Review.* Washington, D.C.: U.S. Government Printing Office, March 1983.

U.S. Department of Labor, Bureau of Labor Statistics. Unpublished tabulations from the Current Population Survey, 1978.

U.S. Department of Labor, Employment and Training Administration. *Employment and Training Report of the President.* Washington, D.C.: U.S. Government Printing Office, 1978.

U.S. National Center for Health Statistics. "Advance Report: Final Divorce Statistics, 1976." *Monthly Vital Statistics Report*, vol. 27, no. 5, supplement, Washington, D.C.: U.S. Government Printing Office, 1977.

U.S. National Center for Health Statistics. "Advance Report of Final Natality Statistics, 1980." *Monthly Vital Statistics Report*, vol. 31, no. 8, supp. DHHS pub. no. (PHS) 83-1120. Hyattsville, Md.: U.S. Public Health Service, November 1982.

U.S. National Center for Health Statistics. "Divorce and Divorce Rates: United States." *Vital and Health Statistics*, ser. 21, no. 29, Washington, D.C.: U.S. Government Printing Office, 1976.

U.S. National Center for Health Statistics. "Final Natality Statistics, 1977." *Monthly Vital Statistics Report* 27, no. 12 (supplement). Washington, D.C.: U.S. Government Printing Office, 1979.

U.S. National Center for Health Statistics. "Provisional Statistics: Births, Marriages, Divorces, and Deaths for 1978." *Monthly Vital Statistics Report*, vol. 27, Washington, D.C.: U.S. Government Printing Office, 1979.

U.S. National Center for Health Statistics. *Vital Statistics of the United States.* Special Reports 37, Washington, D.C.: U.S. Government Printing Office, 1975.

U.S. Office of Human Development. Administration on Aging. Publication no. (OHD) 77-2006, Washington, D.C.: U.S. Government Printing Office, 1976.

U.S. Public Health Services Center for Disease Control. *Morbidity and Mortality Weekly Report*, vol. 13, no. 54, 1966 and vol. 22, no. 53. Washington, D.C.: U.S. Government Printing Office, 1975.

Van Caspel, Venita. *Money Dynamics for the 1980s.* Reston, Va.: Reston Publishing, 1980.

Verbrugge, Lois. "Marital Status and Health." *Journal of Marriage and the Family*, May 1979, 267–85.

Vickery, Clair. "Women's Economic Contribution to the Family." In *The Subtle Revolution: Women at Work*, edited by R. E. Smith. Washington, D.C.: Urban Institute, 1979.

Vincent, C. E. "Familia Spongia: The Adaptive Function." *Journal of Marriage and the Family* 28 (1966): 29–36.

———. *Sexual and Mental Health.* New York: McGraw-Hill, 1973.

Vines, N. R. "Adult Unfolding and Marital Conflict." *Journal of Marital and Family Therapy* 5, no. 1 (1979): 5–14.

Wakin, E. "Living as a Widow: Only the Name's the Same." *U.S. Catholic*, July 1975.

Waldron, H., and D. K. Routh. "The Effect of the First Child on the Marital Relationship." *Journal of Marriage and the Family* 42, no. 4 (November 1981): 785–88.

Walker, Kathryn E., and Margaret E. Woods. *Time Use: A Measure of Household Production of Family Goods and Services.* American Home Economic Association, 1976.

Waller, W. *The Old Love and the New: Divorce and Readjustment.* Carbondale, Ill.: Southern Illinois University Press, 1967.

Wallerstein, J. "Children and Parents 18 Months after Parental Separation: Factors Related to Differential Outcome." Paper presented at the National Institute of Mental Health Conference on Divorce, Washington, D.C., February 1978.

———, and Joan Kelley. "California's Children of Divorce." *Psychology Today*, January 1980, 67–76.

Walster, E., and E. Berscheid. "Adrenaline Makes the Heart Grow Fonder." *Psychology Today*, June 1971, 46–50, 62.

The Washington Post, October 11, 1982, A-1, A-13.

Waters, H. F. "The Hite Report on Male Sexuality." *Newsweek*, June 15, 1981, 104.

Watson, R. E. "Premarital Cohabitation v. Traditional Courtship: Their Effects on Subsequent Marital Adjustment." *Family Relations*, January 1983, 139–47.

Wedeck, H. *Love Potions through the Ages.* New York, 1962.

Weinberg, R. "Early Childhood Education and Intervention." *American Psychologist*, October 1979, 912–16.

Weiss, R. *Marital Separation.* New York: Basic Books, 1975.

Weitzman, Lenore J. *The Marriage Contract.* New York: Free Press, 1981.

———. "Sex-Role Socialization." In *Women: A Feminist Perspective*, edited by J. Freeman. Palo Alto, Calif.: Mayfield, 1975, 105–44.

Welch, C. E., and Sharon Price-Bonham. "A Decade of No-Fault Revisited: California, Georgia and Washington." *Journal of Marriage and the Family*, May 1983, 411–18.

Wernick, R., and Editors of Time-Life Books. *The Family.* New York: Little, Brown, 1974.

West's Annotated California Codes: Civil Code, sections 4000 to 5099. St. Paul, Minn.: West, 1983.

Whelan, E. M. "Human Sex Ratio as a Function of the Timing of Insemination within the Menstrual Cycle: A Review." *Social Biology* 21 (1974): 379–84.

White House Conference on Families: Final Report. Washington, D.C.: U.S. Government Printing Office, 1981.

Whitehurst, R. N. "Sex Role Equality and Changing Meanings of Cohabitation." Paper presented at the annual meeting of the North Central Sociological Association, Windsor, Canada, May 1974.

Williams, R. "Alimony: The Short Goodbye." *Psychology Today*, July 1977, 71.

Willscher, M. K. "Reversing Vasectomy." *Medical Aspects of Human Sexuality*, August 1980, 6.

Wilson, E. O. *On Human Nature.* Boston: Harvard University Press, 1978.

Wilson, G., and D. B. Abrams. "Effects of Alcohol on Sexual Arousal in Male Alcoholics." *Journal of Abnormal Psychology* 87, no. 6 (December 1978): 609–16.

Wilson, G. D., and R. J. Lang. "Sex Differences in Fantasy Patterns." *Personality and Individual Differences* 2 (1981): 343–46.

Wilson, G., and D. M. Lawson. "Expectancies, Alcohol and Sexual Arousal in Women." *Journal of Abnormal Psychology* 87, no. 3 (June 1978): 358–67.

Wilson, K. L., et al. "Stepfathers and Stepchildren: An Exploratory Analysis from Two National Surveys." *Journal of Marriage and the Family* 37 (August 1975): 526–36.

Winch, R. F. *The Modern Family.* New York: Holt, 1971.

Wolfe, Linda. "The Sexual Profile of That Cosmopolitan Girl." *Cosmopolitan*, September 1980.

Wolfers, J. "Psychological Aspects of Vasectomy." *British Medical Journal* 4 (October 31, 1970): 297, 300.

World Almanac and Book of Facts, 1983. New York: Newspaper Enterprise Association, 1983.

Yang, C. K. Sociology of family course given at the University of Hawaii, Summer 1970.

Yankelovich, D., et al. *Raising Children in a Changing American Society.* Minneapolis: General Mills, 1977.

Young, W. C. "The Mammalian Ovary." In *Sex and Internal Secretions*, 3d ed., edited by W. C. Young. Baltimore, Md.: Williams & Wilkins, 1961.

Zablocki, B. *The Joyful Community: An Account of the Bruderhof, A Communist Movement Now in Its Third Generation.* Baltimore, Md.: Penguin, 1971.

Ziel, H. K., and W. D. Finkle. "Increased Risk of Endometrial Carcinoma among Users of Conjugated Estrogens." *New England Journal of Medicine* 293, no. 93 (December 11, 1975): 1167–70.

Zilbergeld, B., and M. Evans. "The Inadequacy of Masters and Johnson." *Psychology Today*, August 1980, 29–43.

Zube, Margaret. "Changing Behavior and Outlook of Aging Men and Women: Implications for Marriage in the Middle and Later Years." *Family Relations*, January 1982, 147–56.

AUTHOR INDEX

SUBJECT INDEX